A CONSTRUCTIVE CHRIS[...]
FOR THE PLURALISTIC W[...]

SPIRIT AND SALVATION

Veli-Matti Kärkkäinen

WILLIAM B. EERDMANS PUBLISHING COMPANY

GRAND RAPIDS, MICHIGAN

Published 2016 by
Wm. B. Eerdmans Publishing Co.
2140 Oak Industrial Drive N.E., Grand Rapids, Michigan 49505

Printed in the United States of America

22 21 20 19 18 17 16   7 6 5 4 3 2 1

Library of Congress Cataloging-in-Publication Data

Names: Kärkkäinen, Veli-Matti, author.
Title: Spirit and salvation / Veli-Matti Kärkkäinen.
Description: Grand Rapids, Michigan : William B. Eerdmans Publishing Company, [2016] |
    Series: A constructive christian theology for the pluralistic world ; volume 4 |
    Includes bibliographical references and index.
Identifiers: LCCN 2015045613 | ISBN 9780802868565 (pbk. : alk. paper)
Subjects: LCSH: Holy Spirit. | Salvation — Christianity.
Classification: LCC BT121.3 .K374 2016 | DDC 231/.3 — dc23
LC record available at http://lccn.loc.gov/2015045613

www.eerdmans.com

This book is dedication to my beloved Doktorvater,
Prof. Dr. Tuomo Mannermaa,
Professor of Ecumenics (University of Helsinki),
who passed away in the same month this manuscript was finished.

A world-renowned Luther expert and ecumenist, he not only taught me theology but also modeled a wonderful spirit of respect and honor. Although my own constructive work lacks all the depth and wit of my teacher, I also know that any little merit it may have is directly indebted to my mentor.

Contents

PART II: SALVATION

Abbreviations

A&D   *Angels and Demons: Perspectives and Practice in Diverse Religious Traditions.* Edited by Peter G. Riddell and Beverly Smith Riddell. Nottingham: Apollos, 2007

ANF   *The Ante-Nicene Fathers: Translations of the Writings of the Fathers down to* A.D. *325.* Edited by Alexander Roberts and James Donaldson et al. 9 vols. Edinburgh, 1885-1897. Public domain; available at www.ccel.org

Aquinas, *ST*   *The Summa Theologica of St. Thomas Aquinas.* 2nd and rev. ed. 1920. Literally translated by Fathers of the English Dominican Province. Online Edition Copyright © 2008 by Kevin Knight; http://www.newadvent.org/summa/

BC   *The Book of Concord: The Confessions of the Evangelical Lutheran Church.* Translated by Theodore G. Tappert. Philadelphia: Fortress, 1959

BDB   Brown, F., S. R. Driver, and C. A. Briggs. *A Hebrew and English Lexicon of the Old Testament.* London: Oxford University Press, 1907

Calvin, *Institutes*   John Calvin. *Institutes of the Christian Religion.* Translated by Henry Beveridge. Available at www.ccel.org

C&C   *Chaos and Complexity: Scientific Perspectives on Divine Action.* Edited by Robert John Russell, Nancey Murphy, and Arthur R. Peacocke. Vatican City and Berkeley, Calif.: Vatican Observatory and Center for Theology and the Natural Sciences, 1995

CD	Karl Barth. *Church Dogmatics.* Edited by Geoffrey William Bromiley and Thomas Forsyth Torrance. Translated by G. W. Bromiley. 14 vols. Edinburgh: T. & T. Clark, 1956-1975. Online edition by Alexander Street Press, 1975
DEHF	*Divine Emptiness and Historical Fullness: A Buddhist-Jewish-Christian Conversation with Masao Abe.* Edited by Christopher Ives. Valley Forge, Pa.: Trinity, 1995
E&E	*Evolution and Emergence: Systems, Organisms, Persons.* Edited by Nancey Murphy and William R. Stoeger. Oxford: Oxford University Press, 2007
EJ	*Encyclopedia Judaica.* Edited by Michael Berenbaum and Fred Skolnik. 2nd ed. 17 vols. Detroit: Macmillan Reference, USA, 2007. Available at http://www.bjeindy.org/resources/library/encyclopediajudaica/
ER	*Encyclopedia of Religion.* Edited by Lindsay Jones. 2nd ed. 15 vols. Detroit: Macmillan Reference USA/Gale, Cengage Learning, 2005
GDT	*Global Dictionary of Theology.* Edited by Veli-Matti Kärkkäinen and William Dyrness. Assistant editors, Simon Chan and Juan Martinez. Downers Grove, Ill.: InterVarsity, 2008
GLC	*God, Life, and the Cosmos: Christian and Islamic Perspectives.* Edited by Ted Peters, Muzaffar Iqbal, and Syed Nomanul Haq. Surrey, U.K.: Ashgate, 2002
HDT	*Heidelberg Disputation.* In *Luther's Works,* vol. 31. American ed. (Libronix Digital Library). Edited by Jaroslav Pelikan and Helmut T. Lehman. Minneapolis: Fortress, 2002
HRC	*Handbook of Religious Conversion.* Edited by H. Newton Malony and Samuel Southard. Birmingham, Ala.: Religious Education Press, 1992
IRDSW	*Interdisciplinary and Religio-Cultural Discourses on a Spirit-Filled World: Loosing the Spirits.* Edited by Veli-Matti Kärkkäinen, Kirsteen Kim, and Amos Yong. New York: Palgrave Macmillan, 2013
IRM	*International Review of Mission*
JBC	*Jesus beyond Christianity: The Classic Texts.* Edited by Gregory A. Barker and Stephen E. Gregg. Oxford: Oxford University Press, 2010
JDDJ	*Joint Declaration on the Doctrine of Justification*

JWF	*Jesus in the World's Faiths: Leading Thinkers from Five Religions Reflect on His Meaning.* Edited by Gregory A. Barker. Maryknoll, N.Y.: Orbis, 2008
LW	*Luther's Works.* American ed. (Libronix Digital Library). Edited by Jaroslav Pelikan and Helmut T. Lehman. 55 vols. Minneapolis: Fortress, 2002
NP	*Neuroscience and the Person: Scientific Perspectives on Divine Action.* Edited by Robert John Russell, Nancey Murphy, Theo C. Meyering, and Michael A. Arbib. Vatican City and Berkeley, Calif.: Vatican Observatory and Center for Theology and the Natural Sciences, 1999
NPNF[1]	*A Select Library of the Nicene and Post-Nicene Fathers of the Christian Church.* Edited by Philip Schaff. 1st ser. 14 vols. Edinburgh, 1886. Public domain; available at www .ccel.org
NPNF[2]	*A Select Library of the Nicene and Post-Nicene Fathers of the Christian Church.* Edited by Philip Schaff and Henry Wace. 2nd ser. 14 vols. Edinburgh, 1890. Public domain; available at www.ccel.org
OHRS	*The Oxford Handbook of Religion and Science.* Edited by Philip Clayton. Associate editor, Zachary Simpson. Oxford: Oxford University Press, 2006
Pannenberg, *ST*	Wolfhart Pannenberg. *Systematic Theology.* Translated by Geoffrey W. Bromiley. 3 vols. Grand Rapids: Eerdmans, 1991, 1994, 1998
Pannenberg, *TA*	Wolfhart Pannenberg. *Anthropology in Theological Perspective.* Translated by Matthew J. O'Connell. Philadelphia: Westminster, 1985
Pelikan, *CT*	Jaroslav Pelikan. *The Christian Tradition: A History of the Development of Doctrine.* Vol. 1, *The Emergence of the Catholic Tradition (100-600).* Vol. 2, *The Spirit of Eastern Christendom (600-1700).* Vol. 3, *The Growth of Medieval Theology (600-1300).* Vol. 4, *Reformation of Church and Dogma (1300-1700).* Chicago: University of Chicago Press, 1971, 1974, 1978, 1984
PL	Patrologia latina [= Patrologiae cursus completus: Series latina]. Edited by J.-P. Migne. 217 vols. Paris, 1844-1864
QCLN	*Quantum Cosmology and the Laws of Nature: Scientific Perspectives on Divine Action.* Edited by Robert John

	Russell, Nancey Murphy, and C. J. Isham. Vatican City: Vatican Observatory Publications, 1993
RCP	*Repentance: A Comparative Perspective.* Edited by Amitai Etzioni and David E. Carney. Lanham, Md.: Rowman and Littlefield, 1997
SBE	*Sacred Books of the East.* Translated by Max Müller. 50 vols. Oxford: Oxford University Press, 1879-1910. Also available at www.sacred-texts.com
Schleiermacher, *CF*	Friedrich Schleiermacher. *The Christian Faith.* Edited by H. R. Mackintosh and J. S. Stewart. London and New York: T. & T. Clark, 1999
SPDA	*Scientific Perspectives on Divine Action: Twenty Years of Challenge and Progress.* Edited by Robert John Russell, Nancey Murphy, and William R. Stoeger, S.J. Vatican City and Berkeley, Calif.: Vatican Observatory and Center for Theology and the Natural Sciences, 2008
TDNT	*Theological Dictionary of the New Testament.* Edited by Gerhard Kittel and Gerhard Friedrich. Translated by Geoffrey W. Bromiley. 10 vols. Grand Rapids: Eerdmans, 1964-1976
Tillich, *ST*	Paul Tillich. *Systematic Theology.* 3 vols. Chicago: University Press of Chicago, 1951, 1957, 1963
USW	*Understanding Spiritual Warfare: Four Views.* Edited by James K. Beilby and Paul Rhodes Eddy. Downers Grove, Ill.: InterVarsity, 2012
UW	*The Unseen World: Christian Reflections on Angels, Demons, and the Heavenly Realm.* Edited by Anthony N. S. Lane. Carlisle, U.K.: Paternoster, 1996
WA	Weimarer Ausgabe (the Weimar edition of Luther's works)
WJW	*The Works of John Wesley.* Grand Rapids: Baker, 2002
WJWBE	*The Works of John Wesley.* Bicentennial ed. Nashville: Abingdon, 2005

Unless otherwise indicated, all citations from patristic writers come from the standard series listed above.

Josephus's writings are from the Sacred Texts Web site: http://www.sacred-texts.com/jud/josephus/index.htm.

Unless otherwise indicated, contemporary Roman Catholic documents, documents of Vatican II, papal encyclicals, and similar works are quoted from the official Vatican Web site: www.vatican.va. This includes also dialogue documents with Lutherans, Reformed, Anglicans, Methodists, and Pentecostals.

Contemporary World Council of Churches documents are quoted from their official Web site: http://www.oikoumene.org/, unless otherwise indicated.

The sources used for postbiblical Jewish literature are as follows:

Midrashic commentary literature is from *Midrash Rabbah*. Translated and edited by H. Freedman and Maurice Simon. 10 vols. 3rd imprint. London: Soncino Press, 1961 (1939). Available at https://archive.org/details/RabbaGenesis.

Talmud references are from *The Babylonian Talmud*. Translated and edited by I. Epstein. 35 vols. London: Soncino Press, 1952. Available at http://www.come-and-hear.com/tcontents.html.

Mishnah texts are from eMishnah.com (2008) at http://www.emishnah.com/Yoma.html.

Zohar references are from *The Zohar*. Translated by Harry Sperling, Maurice Simon, and Paul P. Levertoff. 2nd ed. 5 vols. London and New York: Soncino Press, 1984.

All others, unless otherwise noted, are from http://www.earlyjewish writings.com/ (e.g., Philo of Alexandria).

The Qur'anic references, unless otherwise indicated, are from *The Holy Qur'ān: A New English Translation of Its Meanings* © 2008 Royal Aal al-Bayt Institute for Islamic Thought, Amman, Jordan. This version of the Qur'ān is also available online at http://altafsir.com.

Hadith texts are from the Hadith Collection Web site: http://www.hadithcollection.com/ (2009-).

Buddhist texts, unless otherwise indicated, are from "Tipitaka: The Pali Canon." Edited by John T. Bullitt. *Access to Insight,* May 10, 2011. Available at http://www.accesstoinsight.org/tipitaka/index.html.

Bhagavad-Gita texts are from the translation by Ramanand Prasad. EAWC Anthology, 1988. Available at http://eawc.evansville.edu/anthology/gita.htm.

All other Hindu texts, unless otherwise indicated, are from the Sacred Texts Web site: http://www.sacred-texts.com/hin/index.htm.

Preface

This book is one of the five volumes in the series titled CONSTRUCTIVE CHRISTIAN THEOLOGY FOR THE PLURALISTIC WORLD. The goal of the series is to present a dynamic constructive Christian theology for the pluralistic world shaped by cultural, ethnic, sociopolitical, economic, and religious diversity. While robustly Christian in its convictions, building on the deep and wide tradition of biblical, historical, philosophical, and contemporary systematic traditions, this project seeks to engage our present cultural and religious diversity in a way Christian theology has not done in the past. Although part of a larger series, each volume can still stand on its own feet, so to speak, and can be read as an individual work. The introductory chapter gives a brief orientation to the method chosen.

We have already published three volumes, namely, *Christ and Reconciliation* (2013), *Trinity and Revelation* (2014), and *Creation and Humanity* (2015), and one more is yet to come: *Church and Hope*. The ultimate goal of the series is to provide a fresh and innovative vision of Christian doctrine and theology in a way that, roughly speaking, follows the outline, if not the order, of classical theology. Along with traditional topics, theological argumentation in this series also engages a number of topics, perspectives, and issues that systematic theologies are missing, such as race, environment, ethnicity, inclusivity, violence, and colonialism. A consistent engagement with religious and interfaith studies is another distinctive feature of this series.

As with so many other books, I owe greater gratitude than I am able to express to my Fuller Theological Seminary editor Susan Carlson Wood, with whom I have had an opportunity to work on more than twelve books. She has the unique capacity to help revise my second-language speaker's English into American prose. I also want to sincerely thank my research assistant and doctoral student at Fuller, Dan Brockway, whose diligent and insightful search for sources helped me widen the conversation. In addition, I give warm thanks to another doctoral student of mine, Jongseock Shin, who checked the accuracy of each and every bibliographic reference — not a small task!

Introduction: In Search of a New Methodological Vision for Constructive Theology

While gratefully building on the deep and wide theological reflection in Christian tradition and in the diversity of contemporary approaches, the current project also continues sympathetic critique and corrective work concerning the grave limitations and omissions in earlier works. Particularly alarming in all systematic theological presentations (unless they are intentionally "contextual," in which case they do not attempt a comprehensive doctrinal task) is the limitation of conversation partners and writings consulted to white Euro-American males — to whose company I also belong! To rectify this serious weakness, the current project not only seeks a robust and consistent dialogue with the best of historical materials but also includes as equal dialogue partners theologians from across the current diversity of genders, races, geographical and social locations, and agendas such as liberationism and postcolonialism. A related — and if possible, even more striking — failure in Christian theology across the theological disciplines is the lack of engagement with other living faith traditions. Indeed, even constructive theology in the beginning of the third millennium is still done as if doctrines and teachings of other faiths did not even exist. Although a great number of specialized interfaith and comparative theological studies are emerging, they are just that — *specialized* — and make no attempt to provide a comprehensive Christian vision for the sake of the pluralistic world. Finally, this project is also convinced of the need to broaden the dialogue to include a wide and deep interdisciplinary environment. This means that, where relevant, insights and findings from various types of natural sciences as well as behavioral and sociocultural fields will be integrated into the systematic reflection.

Against my initial intuitions, rather than developing this new methodological vision in an abstract and formal methodological discussion, which usually ends up being just that — *abstract* and *formal,* neither interesting nor useful — the current project deals with method along with the material presentation. Whereas the more comprehensive and detailed methodological vision was laid out in the lengthy introduction to the first volume, *Christ and Reconciliation,* each subsequent volume continues and sharpens methodological orientations as it goes. Hence, let it suffice to summarize in a brief outline the methodological vision presented and defended in the first volume.[1] The vision for doing constructive theology in a religiously pluralistic and culturally diverse "post-" world — postmodern, postfoundationalist, poststructuralist, postcolonial, postmetaphysical, postpropositional, postliberal, postconservative, postsecular, post-Christian — can be sketched like this:

> Systematic/constructive theology is an integrative discipline that continuously searches for a coherent, balanced understanding of Christian truth and faith in light of Christian tradition (biblical and historical) and in the context of the historical and contemporary thought, cultures, and living faiths. It aims at a coherent, inclusive, dialogical, and hospitable vision.

As the ultimate goal of constructive theology is not a "system," the nomenclature "systematic" is most unfortunate! Rather, it seeks for a coherent and balanced understanding. In terms of the theory of truth, it follows the suit of coherence theory. One current way of speaking of coherence is to compare it to a web or a net(work), which underwrites postfoundationalist rather than foundationalist epistemology. That metaphor is fitting as it speaks of the attempt to relate every statement to other relevant statements and ultimately to the "whole." The way this current project conceives coherence has not only to do with intratextual coherence but also with the fit of theological statements with reality.

Integrative discipline means that, to practice constructive theology well, one has to utilize the results, insights, and materials of all other theological disciplines (including their contemporary diversity), cultural studies, religious studies, and natural (and other relevant) sciences. This means that the constructive theologian asks many questions — say, in relation to inclusivity, violence, care for the environment, and natural sciences — that the Bible

---

1. Since that discussion contains detailed bibliographic references, I will not repeat them here.

and much of church history are silent about. At the end of the constructive task, however, the constructive theologian should make sure the proposal is in keeping with biblical revelation and, hopefully, with the best of tradition and contemporary theology.

If the principle of coherence in the search for the truth of Christian doctrinal claims is taken seriously, it also means that by its very nature, constructive theology should seek to engage not only theological resources but also cultural, religious, sociopolitical, and other resources. Two tasks emerge from this orientation: first, the challenge of cultural and social diversity, and second, the engagement of religions and their own claims for meaning and truth. Constructive theology should make every effort to seek an inclusive vision in a "post-" world with preference for locality, particularity, and difference over "globality," universality, and sameness, as well as within the Christian church that has become a truly "world church" with the majority of believers in the Global South, who are young persons, women, and the poor. Inclusivity allows for diverse, at times even contradictory and opposing, voices and testimonies to be part of the dialogue. That said, the constructive theologian in search of inclusivity is not blind to her or his own limitations. As a middle-aged European white male — despite my long and varied global experience — I am not only "perspectival" in a particular way, but I also carry with me limitations and prejudices, similarly to a young African female theologian or a veteran Asian male theologian; those limitations in each case are just materially rather different. All our explanations are humble and modest, and hence viable for dialogue and conversation.

Is this, then, an exercise in "contextual" theology? No, if this term means that there are theologies that are not contextual ("mainline" theologies done by Euro-American males) and others that are contextual, namely, that of women and other liberationists, postcolonialists, and theologians from the Global South. Another reason for rejecting the nomenclature "contextual" for this project is that that the presentation of Christian doctrine done solely by traditional and current Euro-American men would merely be "enriched" or "ornamented" — in the second movement — by insights from other theologians and theological agendas such as liberationist. While that would give some hearing for nontraditional voices, those would still be made optional and "elective." In contrast to these common misconceptions, the current project is based on the conviction that all theologies are contextual since all theologies emerge out of and are shaped by the context. They are just differently contextual. Of course, more space is devoted to theologies created by men than by women, by Euro-Americans than by Africans/Asians/Latin Americans, and by "mainstream" theologians than by "contextual" theologians (as the terms are rightly understood), for the simple reason that the former provide much of the literature and sources to be found. Indeed, all contemporary theological movements and agendas have their roots in the long and variegated Christian tradition.

The term "dialogical" in a more specific sense here means an intentional and intense engagement of other living faith traditions. As a result, systematic argumentation and discussion must be informed and challenged by theology of religions, which in a more general sense reflects on the relation of the Christian faith to other religions, and more importantly, by comparative theology, whose purpose is to look at specific, focused issues among religions. An important methodological guide in the comparative approach is to look for topics and themes pertinent to each tradition even when the comparison is done from a particular, in this case Christian, perspective.

Theology that is robustly inclusivistic in its orientation, welcoming testimonies, insights, and interpretations from different traditions and contexts — hence, authentically inviting and dialogical — honors the otherness of the Other. It calls for deep learning about the Religious Other. It also makes space for an honest, genuine, authentic sharing of one's convictions. In pursuing the question of truth as revealed by the triune God, constructive theology also seeks to persuade and convince with the power of dialogical, humble, and respectful argumentation. Theology, then, becomes an act of hospitality, giving and receiving gifts. That some leading postmodern thinkers (Derrida, Levinas) are deeply suspicious of the possibility of "gift" is no reason to not seek such giving. While only God gives perfect gifts, theologians in search of God's wisdom and love may also exchange gifts of inclusivity, belonging, mutual learning, and enrichment — in other words, be sharers of hospitality.

The current volume focuses on two interrelated themes: pneumatology, the doctrine and spirituality of the Holy Spirit, and soteriology, the doctrine of salvation. Following the trinitarian approach that undergirds the whole multivolume project, we attempt a new and fresh vision of the Spirit and salvation. At the beginning of each part, a detailed note orients the reader to the order and topics to be discussed.

I. SPIRIT

1. Introduction: In Search of a Plural, Holistic Pneumatology

How to Speak of the Spirit in the Contemporary World — or Whether to Speak at All!

Although the secular West has lost touch with religious and pneumatological sensibilities, in the long history of religions — and even in human history at large — spirit-talk has been familiar and intimate. Usually the Spirit is first experienced and lived out and only subsequently reflected on conceptually. Unlike modern theology, particularly the university-based European theology that often looks at experience with suspicion, a constructive holistic pneumatology should not eschew the experiences of men and women but rather incorporate them in theological reflection.[1] Although it is true that to "begin with experience may sound subjective, arbitrary and fortuitous," it does not have to be so. To have an experience of the Spirit may also be a gateway to having communion with the triune God. As Moltmann puts it, "[b]y experience of the Spirit I mean an awareness of God in, with and beneath the experience of life, which gives us assurance of God's fellowship, friendship and love."[2] This kind of deep and robust experience is not unknown in the contemporary world. Just think of the experience of many Africans, whether Christian or not: "The most vital aspect of the African experience of the Spirit is implied

---

1. For a theological analysis of experience, see Moltmann, *Spirit of Life*, chap. 1. For the now-classic discussion of "experience" from a hermeneutical and philosophical perspective, see Gadamer, *Truth and Method*, pp. 335-54 particularly.
2. Moltmann, *Spirit of Life*, p. 17.

in their knowledge of God as Source-Being, which implies his immanence as well as his control and maintenance of the universe."[3]

What the Asian American (Malaysian Chinese) Pentecostal theologian Amos Yong names the "cosmology of personal agency" has a long and lasting legacy in human history and is by no means a matter only of a bygone era. In such cosmology, beyond the physical causes are spirits, even divine spirits. In contrast to this spirit sensitivity, most people in the post-Enlightenment West live under "natural cosmologies"[4] that are essentially monist (materialist). There are of course variations to this dual theme, such as the continuing attempts toward "reenchantment without supernaturalism," to cite the title of a book by process philosopher David Ray Griffin.[5] Yet a "foundational" difference exists between these two kinds of experiences of the Spirit's presence or absence. Whereas for many people the Spirit experience is the most intimate and familiar part of life, for others it is virtually unknown and abstract.

The acknowledgment of this divide is the starting point for the constructive pneumatological proposal of the Reformed German Michael Welker and his *God the Spirit* (ET 1994). The problem of "the modern consciousness of the distance of God"[6] has to do with the total alienation from God of most modern (Western) people. In contrast, Welker observes, among Pentecostals/charismatics and some other Christians there is a vivid, almost childlike enthusiasm about God's presence here and now. Whereas for Pentecostals and charismatics God seems to be near, for many Christians the talk about the Spirit of God makes no sense. The secular common sense intuits God's Spirit as "ghost" (pp. 1-13).

Theological tradition must bear some blame for this. Welker blames theology for modernity's captivity to three forms of Western thought, none of which allows for the "reality of the Spirit." The first is "old European metaphysics," which assumes one universal system of reference established by religion. In this scheme, the Spirit is conceived as ubiquitous, a totalizing universal force or structure. Second is "dialogical personalism," which builds on an I-Thou encounter (of Martin Buber and his followers, including Barth). In this the Spirit is that which creates and sustains divine-human (and human-human)

---

3. Idowu, "The Spirit of God," p. 12.

4. Yong, "On Binding, and Loosing," pp. 4-5.

5. Griffin, *Reenchantment without Supernaturalism.* For an assessment of these attempts, see McGrath, *The Re-enchantment of Nature;* Yong, "Discerning the Spirit(s)," pp. 315-29.

6. The title for chap. 1 in Welker, *God the Spirit.* Page references to this work have been placed in the next few paragraphs.

relationship. In the third form, "social moralism," the Kantian dream of religion as the source of progress is in the forefront; in it the human participates in God's work in the world. The first version does not allow for specific, "charismatic" or otherwise extraordinary works of the Spirit. Although the second form is not without biblical support, in that the Spirit is the "Go-Between," it also limits the Spirit's role to the personal, social, and pious spheres. While the last form is not without its merits, it also may at its worst reduce the Spirit to a principle of moral and common human good (pp. 40-49).

As a corrective to these reductionist and limited pneumatological gateways, Welker "seeks first to articulate the broad spectrum of experiences of God's Spirit, searches and quests for the Spirit, and skepticism toward the Spirit that define the contemporary world" (p. ix). Instead of abstract and numinous accounts of the Spirit, "pneumatologies of the beyond," which associate the Spirit with strange and obscure actions and experiences removed from real life, Welker seeks to speak of the Spirit and experiences of the Spirit in specific, concrete, earthly terms; this is "realistic" pneumatology (pp. 46-49; see also pp. 338-39). Instead of highlighting the few biblical passages that depict the Spirit as an incomprehensible, numinous power, he advises us to major in the majority of references that speak about the Spirit in concrete, understandable terms (pp. 50-51 especially). That paradigm funds a "pluralistic" (see pp. 21-27) approach that is in keeping with the diversity and complexity of the contemporary world and the celebration of plurality in various postmodern visions (pp. xii, 28-40). Commensurate with his pluralistic approach, Welker criticizes traditional approaches in which the Spirit's function is merely to create union and unity. Instead, he argues, the Spirit also champions diversity and plurality: "The action of God's Spirit is pluralistic for the sake of God's righteousness, for the sake of God's mercy, and for the sake of the full testimony to God's plenitude and glory" (p. 25). Pentecost is a grand example of this kind of diversity in that, "[t]hrough the pouring out of the Spirit, God effects a world-encompassing, multilingual, polyindividual testimony to Godself" (p. 235). Plurality in itself cannot be celebrated without reservation, because there is also a form of "individually disintegrative pluralism." What is worth advocating is "the life-enhancing, invigorating pluralism of the Spirit" (pp. 25-27).

My pneumatological proposal in this volume reflects some of the key themes Welker presents. Yet it is also radically different in that its vision of a proper pneumatological paradigm goes way beyond what the German Reformed theologian envisioned. I propose that a definite shift from a "unitive" to a "plural" paradigm of pneumatology is needed. That will challenge, critique, and correct all systematic/constructive proposals set forth so far.[7] Particularly unique in my proposal is the relating of the Spirit of God to other spirits and powers, including the spirits of other religions — themes that are totally lacking in all previous systematic pneumatologies.

From a "Unitive" to a "Plural" Paradigm of Pneumatology

In the introduction to his acclaimed pneumatological volume *The Spirit of Life* (ET 1992), Moltmann laments that "a new paradigm in pneumatology has not yet emerged."[8] While his own proposal breaks new ground on more than one count, particularly in its vision of a "holistic pneumatology,"[9] the process of paradigm change is still to be completed. I would like to suggest a shift from what I call a "unitive" paradigm in which only one Spirit (of God) is considered, while the rest of the spiritual realities are being dismissed, to a "plural" paradigm. The latter accounts for the Spirit of God in a highly pluralistic cosmology with many spirits, powers, and spiritual realities.[10] In the plural cosmology, the Spirit of God is also related to the (great and smaller) spirits of other religions. Why is this shift needed? Because of cultural and religious

7. The missiologist Kirsteen Kim's *The Holy Spirit in the World*, it seems to me, intuits something similar, although she approaches the doctrine of the Spirit from the perspective of her own discipline and hence casts it in a different mode from mine. Similarly, the systematic theologian Amos Yong's many contributions to pneumatology, particularly in religion-science and theology of religions/comparative theology topics, point in the same direction; even he, however, has not yet offered any kind of comprehensive systematic/constructive theological account of the Spirit in the new paradigm. My recent editorial collaboration with Kirsteen Kim and Amos Yong in the production of the 2013 collection of essays, *Interdisciplinary and Religio-Cultural Discourses on a Spirit-Filled World: Loosing the Spirits*, provided yet another opportunity to clarify and sharpen my own methodological approach to the Spirit. Consider also the important emerging discussion of a program that has many intentions in common with what is called here plural cosmologies: *Polydoxy: Theology of Multiplicity and Relation*. Also noteworthy are attempts by some native people to create plural cosmologies, e.g., Emily Cousins, "Mountains Made Alive."

8. Moltmann, *Spirit of Life*, p. 1.

9. The English translation of the subtitle, *A Universal Affirmation*, is neither accurate nor very helpful. The German original, *Eine ganzheitliche Pneumatologie*, means "holistic pneumatology," and that is the nomenclature also used in the preface (p. xiii); it could also be translated as "all-encompassing" or "comprehensive." Moltmann also labels his pneumatology "holistic" elsewhere in the book; see p. xiii.

10. Kirsteen Kim speaks of the same distinction using the terms "one-spirit" and "many-spirit" pneumatologies and cosmologies ("The Potential of Pneumatology," p. 338).

plurality, the rise of postmodern philosophies, as well as transformations in scientific paradigms, among other reasons.

Even when critiquing traditional and contemporary pneumatologies for their limitations and reductionism, this proposal is also deeply indebted to them. It seems like many aspects of the paradigm change already loom on the horizon; they just need to be identified and theologically defined. Indeed, there are exciting and exhilarating developments under way that point to the *transformation* of Christian pneumatology. This promise lies in the robust and intentional desire to widen and make more inclusive the theological understanding of the ministry of the Spirit. In that wider and more inclusive outlook (which will be carefully noted and documented in the ensuing discussion) — while not leaving behind traditional topics such as the Trinity, Scripture, and salvation — the Spirit is also connected with topics such as creation, humanity, and eschatology, as well as political, social, environmental, and other "public" issues. This is a great corrective to tradition.

Although one must resist the temptation to describe the pneumatological tradition in terms that are too uniform and homogenous — for the simple reason that there are already in the history of pneumatology dramatic differences, divergences, and surprises — it is also the case that by and large pneumatology was too often bound within certain theological, ecclesiastical, and cultural strictures. Those strictures were more often than not European (later, European American), male-driven, ecclesiastical-sacramental, and individualistically oriented "spiritualist" orientations. In the past the doctrine of the Spirit was mainly — but not exclusively — connected with topics such as the doctrine of salvation, the inspiration of Scripture, some issues of ecclesiology, and individual piety. In the doctrine of salvation, the Spirit represented the "subjective" side of the reception of salvation, whereas Christology formed the objective basis. In the doctrine of Scripture, the Spirit played a crucial role in both inspiration and illumination of the Word of God. In various Christian traditions, from mysticism to pietism to classical liberalism and beyond, the Spirit's work was seen mainly in relation to animating and refreshing one's inner spiritual life. While ecclesiology was usually built on christological foundations, the Spirit was invoked to animate and energize already existing structures. In other words, the role of the Spirit in traditional theology was quite reserved and limited. It is this reductionism that has been challenged in many ways by contemporary pneumatologies. All of that is to be commended.

On the other side, it seems to me that by and large Christian pneumatologies, even with these necessary and important improvements, are still imprisoned in the paradigm of "unitive" pneumatology. Other spirits, powers, and energies are not seen as worthy of academic discussion and inclusion in respectable pneumatological presentations. Particularly striking is the lack of relating the *Christian* understanding of the Spirit(s) to the understandings of other living faith traditions. A recent personal experience of that kind of "bound" pneumatology may illustrate this malaise. An anonymous reviewer of one of my recent manuscripts affirmed the careful and detailed historical and systematic study of the development of Christian doctrine of the Spirit but then complained harshly that, first, global and contextual views do not merit inclusion in that prestigious theological collection and, second, even more importantly, the discussion of non-Christian, "pagan," interpretations of the spirit in African folk religions, Islam, and various Hindu and Buddhist movements must be deleted. Against the intentions of the reviewer, I took the critique as an affirmation of my project: the review in itself not only exposed the limitations of pneumatologies but also pointed to the need for a revision. Happily, the publisher happened to take my side!

Why has the unitive paradigm persisted so? Among other things, its persistence has to do with the still continuing hegemony of the Enlightenment epistemology according to which everything *non*natural in religiosity should be dismissed — an idea that hardly sounds "natural" to most Christians, or even most people of the world! This omission of "supernatural" powers and spirits stands in marked contrast to the beginnings of the Christian tradition when, in keeping with the worldview of the ancients, the world was filled with spiritual powers. Just consider the cosmology of the New Testament — whether Jesus' own ministry or the worldview of the Apocalypse — and you get the picture. Christian tradition until the time of the Enlightenment — and in some quarters beyond that — continued to take for granted plural cosmologies and pneumatologies. Rightly, the historian of dogma Jaroslav Pelikan notes,

> Christian apocalypticism reflected a supernaturalistic view of the world, which Christian believers shared with other religious men of antiquity. . . . Traffic was heavy on the highway between heaven and earth. God and spirits thickly populated the upper air, where they stood in readiness to intervene at any moment in the affairs of mortals. And demonic powers, emerging from the lower world or resident in remote corners of the earth, were a constant menace to human welfare. All nature was alive — alive with supernatural forces.[11]

11. Pelikan, *CT* 1:1.

Of course, there is no returning to the outdated premodern worldview (as Walter Wink has reminded us for decades). That said, however, the radical changes in philosophy, science, and globalization have also helped us see the deeply reductionist and forced nature of the Enlightenment epistemological strictures. The rediscovery of the plural paradigm of considering the Spirit/spirits/powers in Christian pneumatology does not have to mean a return to a lost idyllic mind-set of pre-Enlightenment times. Rather, it means a robust and courageous re-turn to a more complex, plural, and multilayered account of reality in the midst of which the Spirit of the almighty God is at work in innumerable ways. One does not have to subscribe to any particular tribe of postmodernism to acknowledge the need for plurality. Whereas modernity celebrated unity, oneness, and homogeneity, postmodernity embraces "the growing fascination with 'the other.' The tendency to celebrate the different and suspect the same, to prefer *heteron* over *tauton*, *aliter* over *idem*, the alien over the identical, may be one of the defining peculiarities" of our age.[12] In this kind of pluralist milieu, religious sensibilities, including pneumatological sensibilities, may have a better place to flourish. Whereas in the past "scientific modernity and traditional religion" were formative forces, nowadays — even with the diminishing of organized religion in the Global North — "experientialism" is on the rise and a part of the global religious resurgence,[13] claims Harvey Cox. This is happening not only in Christianity but also in some other religions.[14]

A number of sources and constituencies may assist the plural pneumatological paradigm. This project has found the following ones to be promising, as well as invitations to deeper scrutiny:

- A diverse group of studies and approaches highlighting the importance of "intimations of transcendence"[15]
- Postmodern sensibilities in the Global North
- The current attempts to transform and make more inclusive the dominant scientific paradigm, particularly with regard to the conception of cosmology[16]
- Theologies from the Global South[17]

12. Shults, "Theological Responses to Postmodernities," p. 1.
13. Cox, *Fire from Heaven*, pp. 299-301.
14. See, e.g., Nasr, ed., *Islamic Spirituality*.
15. See Wiebe, *God and Other Spirits*.
16. For a highly constructive proposal, see Yong, "A Spirit-Filled Creation?"
17. I have been helped among others by Kalu, "*Sankofa*," pp. 135-52; Onyinah, "Deliv-

- Emerging global Pentecostal/charismatic theologies[18]
- Some native (First Nation) spiritualities

With these desiderata and sources in mind, let us sharpen and deepen the methodological approach by looking at yet another issue touched on but often not widely discussed in pneumatological treatises, namely, the relationship between the divine Spirit and human spirit. The way that relationship is negotiated has everything to do with the goal of constructing a plural and *holistic* account of the Spirit.

The Mutual Dynamic of the Divine and Human Spirit

As was often the case, Barth was instrumental in bringing to light a wide-ranging theological issue when, in his 1929 essay "The Holy Spirit and Christian Life," he vehemently subjected to criticism any liberal equation between the divine Spirit and human spirit.[19] Notwithstanding the highly problematic nature of his own proposal — which, not surprisingly, went to the other extreme by radically separating the two — the way Barth highlighted the importance of the issue is useful for constructive theology. According to Barth, the divine and human spirits have to be kept separate because there is no continuity between the Creator and creation. Furthermore, this separation is accentuated by the fact that not only is the human "spirit" different from the divine Spirit because of creatureliness but it is also at variance with God. In other words, there is an antithesis between the divine (revelation) and human (experience).[20]

Behind Barth's criticism is of course the nineteenth-century (and earlier) liberal and idealist equation of the spirit of God with the human spirit, as exemplified in the NT giant F. C. Baur's conception of the spirit as "Christian consciousness."[21] Other liberal luminaries such as A. Ritschl and F. D. E.

---

erance as a Way of Confronting Witchcraft," pp. 181-202; for a wider source, see K. Kim, *Holy Spirit in the World.*

18. See my introduction to *The Spirit in the World:* "Pentecostalism and Pentecostal Theology in the Third Millennium," pp. xiii-xviii.

19. For the theological urgency of clarifying the issue, see Lai and So, "Zhang Chunyi's Chinese Buddhist-Christian Pneumatology," pp. 70-71.

20. Barth, "The Holy Spirit and Christian Life."

21. Baur, *Paul the Apostle of Jesus Christ,* vol. 2, pt. 3, chap. 1 (p. 123).

Schleiermacher represented the same view.[22] Similarly, the Chinese Christian-turned-Buddhist Zhang Chunyi developed a materially similar kind of view, drawing also from his newly rediscovered Buddhist sources in which the Holy Spirit is identified with "Buddha nature" (of which, more below in chap. 5). By identifying the Buddha nature and the Holy Spirit, the door was opened for identifying the Holy Spirit with the human spirit because each person born into this world already possesses the Buddha nature (and hence also the Holy Spirit).[23]

This immanentist pneumatology is of course at odds with the biblical view of the Spirit and is theologically thin because of a lack of surplus; the divine Spirit does not "add" anything significant to the human spirit. In this respect, the small but highly sensational book by Hermann Gunkel, another nineteenth-century biblical scholar, *The Influence of the Holy Spirit,* which sought to exposit as carefully as possible "the popular view of the apostolic age and the teaching of the apostle Paul" (in the words of his subtitle), provided a robust counterargument to liberal pneumatology (although Gunkel himself continued to be thoroughly liberal in his mind-set).[24] Gunkel proposed that rather than a moral-ethical humanist spirit, the OT account of the Spirit is known for its mighty charismatic manifestations and "effects."[25] Both in the OT and in many parts of the NT, particularly in the book of Acts, "the spirit is associated not with what is humanly comprehensible, with a discernible purpose, but with the inexplicable and overpowering effects it exercises over

22. For Schleiermacher's view of the Spirit, see Kärkkäinen, ed., *Holy Spirit and Salvation,* pp. 241-46.

23. Lai and So, "Zhang Chunyi's Chinese Buddhist-Christian Pneumatology," pp. 64-66 particularly. (Zhang even goes further and identifies the Holy Spirit, the human spirit, and evil spirits [pp. 67-68].) Somewhat erroneously, Pan-Chiu Lai argues that the identification of the divine and human spirits is not necessarily a deviation from mainline Christian tradition, as it was also a thought of some of the Fathers (e.g., Origen, *On First Principles* 4.1.36) or Reformers such as Ulrich Zwingli, who was open to the idea of some people being saved apart from the knowledge of Christ. This is, however, a category mistake and hardly can be sustained by textual analysis. See Lai, *Towards a Trinitarian Theology of Religions,* pp. 126-27.

24. An ironic indication of the deep influence of modernism and liberalism on Gunkel's own view of the Spirit, though, is that he adopted the cessationist downplaying of the miraculous view of his own times. Just see Gunkel, *Influence of the Holy Spirit,* pp. 37-38. One cannot help but think of the contemporary christological genius Albert Schweitzer and his personal view of Christ as the diametrical opposite of his newly constructed *biblical* idea of an eschatological figure who expected a transcendent divine intervention!

25. The original German title *(Die Wirkungen des Heiligen Geistes)* uses the term "effects of the Holy Spirit" rather than the more general English translation "influence."

its witnesses,"[26] as is most strikingly evident in the phenomenon of glosso-lalia.[27] Gunkel also rediscovered two other highly significant insights that subsequently have helped reorient the study of pneumatology: the close link between Jewish pneumatology and the (early) Christian view of the Spirit (against those detractors who used to dub the Judaism of the "intertestamental period" void of the Spirit),[28] as well as the diversity of NT pneumatologies (in defeat of one unified view of the Spirit). Although the way Gunkel himself formulated these three formative insights — the importance of the effects of the Spirit, the nature of Jewish pneumatology, and the diversity of NT pneumatologies (particularly when it comes to the alleged radical difference between Lukan charismatically oriented emphasis and Paul's soteriological emphasis)[29] — is in need of refining and correction, his groundbreaking contribution to pneumatology is worth rediscovering.

For our current discussion, most meaningful is Gunkel's radical reorientation and rediscovery of the charismatic and extraordinary workings of the Spirit, which helped challenge the modernist liberal consensus. As important as that rediscovery was, it also ironically helped wedge a radical divide between the immanentist, "natural" workings of the divine Spirit and its nature-transcending effects. The NT pneumatologist Jack Levison, who takes Gunkel as the main protagonist in his *Filled with the Spirit* (2009), defines succinctly the main question brought about by the German scholar: "If the spirit is to be associated exclusively with the supernatural and mysterious, what then is to be made of the spirit of life, the spirit that gives breath?"[30] Gunkel's resolution briefly is this: while in the OT the divine spirit is shared with humans (Gen. 2:7) to the point that the two, the divine and human, may be virtually equated, in the NT theology it takes a *donum superadditum* to have the Spirit (save Jesus, who was inspired from his birth).[31] Only in Jesus' life, therefore, is there the "anomalous confluence of the spirit as creative life-giver

---

26. As paraphrased by Levison, *Filled with the Spirit*, p. 5.

27. Gunkel, *Influence of the Holy Spirit*, p. 30.

28. For a critique of that position, see Levison, *Filled with the Spirit*, p. 220; part 2 is devoted to the investigation of Second Temple Jewish literature. See also, Levison, *The Spirit in First-Century Judaism*, p. 238.

29. The Lukan and Pauline juxtaposing is also represented by twentieth-century biblical pneumatologists such as Eduard Schweizer, "The Spirit of Power: The Uniformity and Diversity of the Concept of the Holy Spirit in the New Testament" (1952). For a detailed scrutiny of leading NT pneumatologies in this respect, see Menzies, *Development of Early Christian Pneumatology*, pp. 18-47.

30. Levison, *Filled with the Spirit*, p. 7.

31. Gunkel, *Influence of the Holy Spirit*, p. 16.

and the spirit as the cause of divine effects in human beings."[32] This distinction between divine and human spirit became a stated theme, a separation, in the twentieth-century mainstream pneumatology, as is evident in luminaries G. W. H. Lampe and others.[33]

Levison's main goal as a biblical scholar is to take to task this "artificial, anachronistic, and decidedly unnecessary division that serves only to obscure the relationship that exists in Israelite literature between God's initial gift of the spirit and a subsequent endowment of the spirit." In his mind, in the Jewish literature "[t]he two, the so-called life principle and the spirit of God . . . were understood to be one and the same."[34] Things, however, changed in the NT and particularly in subsequent Christian theology. Whereas in the Jewish literature the "natural" and "supernatural" are considered to be the same, in the latter the "supernatural" is clearly distinguished from the natural works of the Spirit. So convinced is Levison of the lack of distinction in Israelite literature between the Holy Spirit and the spirit of life that he chooses to put "spirit" in lowercase.

What to think of Levison's argument? Is the radical juxtaposing between the OT and the NT/early Christian views of the Spirit justified? Without downplaying the significance of Levison's corrective and proposal for constructive theology — particularly early Christian theology's deep indebtedness to Jewish pneumatology and the diversity of various NT traditions of the Spirit — it also is hardly satisfactory as such. It is fairly easy to see that not all OT references to the spirit of God support Levison's desire to identify the divine Spirit with the human; "there is a strand where the Spirit of God is more naturally understood as a *donum superadditum* of special empowering, including most obviously Judg. 3.10; 6.34; 14.6, 19; 15.14; 1 Sam. 10.6, 10; 11.6; 16.13, 1 Chron. 12.18" and others.[35] Neither is it true that the NT and early Christian pneumatology's insistence on the *donum superadditum,* the salvific "gift" and "charismatic endowment" of the Spirit, necessarily has to lead to an artificial separation between the Spirit's work and identity. Rather, as leading contemporary systematic pneumatologists (the Orthodox J. Zizioulas, the Roman Catholic K. Rahner, the Lutheran W. Pannenberg, the Reformed J. Moltmann, the Baptist/evangelical C. Pinnock, the Pentecostal A. Yong, among others) argue, in the work of the one and the same divine Spirit there are various facets. Surely, the diversity of the biblical testimonies to the Spirit

32. Levison, *Filled with the Spirit,* p. 8.

33. For a detailed discussion of Lampe, G. Gerlemann, A. Berholet, and others, see Levison, *Filled with the Spirit,* pp. 8-11.

34. Levison, *Filled with the Spirit,* p. 12.

35. Turner, "Levison's *Filled with the Spirit,*" pp. 195-96.

depicts the same Spirit in various roles, works, and tasks. Even the fact that in the NT, particularly in Pauline teaching, human life prior to the reception of the salvific gift is viewed as devoid of the Spirit, is not a statement against the spirit of life but rather a reminder about the need to put one's faith in Christ. Why can't a plural pneumatology speak of the salvific work of the Spirit in terms of the "excessive"?[36]

In sum: all proposals briefly engaged in this section, namely, classical liberalism's immanentist conflation of the divine and human spirit, Barth's total separation between the human spirit and the divine Spirit, as well as Levison's rejection of *donum superadditum,* are in need of correction. The first one hardly calls for a sustained engagement: a mere reference to the biblical testimonies (notwithstanding exegetical disputes) suffices to show its modernist redundancy. Barth's radical juxtaposing of the divine Spirit and human spirit (or divine revelation and human experience thereof) is to be rejected and corrected. Tillich rightly saw this in his profound correlation of the divine and human spirits, a thematic issue for his theology at large.[37] He spoke of "spiritual presence," the Holy Spirit universally present as a dimension of life, gaining fullest expression in humanity. Although his own extreme view must be corrected — that is, the idea that to know the Holy Spirit one *must* know the human spirit, which, of course, makes the divine Spirit a prisoner to the human spirit[38] — his critique of Barth is spot-on.[39]

Moltmann's panentheistically oriented dynamic mutual conditioning of the divine Spirit and the human spirit helps further clarify and deepen the relationship between the two.[40] He rightly insists on a mutual correlation. A dynamic balance "is to be found in God's *immanence* in human experience, and in the *transcendence* of human beings in God. Because God's Spirit is present in human beings, the human spirit is self-transcendently aligned towards God. Anyone who stylizes revelation and experience into alternatives ends up with revelations that cannot be experienced, and experiences with-

---

36. Similarly argued in Macchia, "The Spirit of Life and the Spirit of Immortality," p. 71 particularly.

37. Tillich, *ST* 3:111-38.

38. See Tillich, *ST* 3:22, 114, particularly.

39. See Tillich, *ST* 3:111-12 for the profound idea of *ecstasy,* that is, the human spirit "going out" *(ek-stasis)* of itself "in" to the divine Spirit, without ceasing to be the human spirit.

40. In Kärkkäinen, *Trinity and Revelation,* chap. 10, a novel proposal of "classical panentheism" is presented and defended. While not to be identified with Moltmann's panentheism, it shares important common features with it as well as with a number of other, similar kinds of moderate panentheism in various strands of current theology.

out revelation."[41] The Spirit of God is not so external to human experience that it cannot be experienced (contra Barth), nor is the Spirit of God so much identified with the human spirit that its otherness is denied (contra liberalism). This dynamic correlation of the divine and human points in the same direction as Tillich's profound idea of *ecstasy,* that is, the human spirit's "going out" *(ek-stasis)* of itself "in" to the divine Spirit, without ceasing to be the human spirit.[42]

The ultimate goal of dynamic constructive theology of the Spirit is a truly *"holistic doctrine of the Holy Spirit":* "It must be holistic in at least two ways. On the one hand, it must comprehend human beings in their total being, soul and body, consciousness and the unconscious, person and sociality, society and social institutions. On the other hand it must also embrace the wholeness of the community of creation, which is shared by human beings, the earth, and all other created beings and things."[43] Levison's incapacity to hold together the deep continuity between the Spirit of God as she is at work in creation, providence, historical occurrences, and ordinary human experiences on the one hand, and on the other, as a special gift of salvation, celebration of sacraments, Pentecostal experiences of charismatic endowment, and spiritual discernment, follows a dualistic paradigm of a sort. The plural paradigm overcomes it. Two programmatic citations from Pannenberg suffice to summarize the holistic, unitive-plural paradigm aimed at in this project:

> God's Spirit is not only active in human redemption as he teaches us to know the eternal Son of the Father in Jesus of Nazareth and moves our hearts to praise of God by faith, love, and hope. The Spirit is at work already in creation as God's breath, the origin of all movement and all life, and only against this background of his activity as the Creator of all life can we rightly understand on the one hand his work in the ecstatics of human conscious life, and on the other hand his role in the bringing forth of the new life in the resurrection of the dead.[44]

> [T]he same Holy Spirit of God who is given to believers in a wholly specific way, namely, so as to dwell in them (Rom. 5:5; 1 Cor. 3:16), is none other

---

41. Moltmann, *Spirit of Life,* p. 7, emphasis in original. Similarly, Barth's dichotomist view is rejected by Hendry, *Holy Spirit in Christian Theology,* pp. 96-117.

42. Tillich, *ST* 3:111-12; see also, Lai and So, "Zhang Chunyi's Chinese Buddhist-Christian Pneumatology," pp. 73-74.

43. Moltmann, *Spirit of Life,* p. 37.

44. Pannenberg, *ST* 3:1.

than the Creator of all life in the whole range of natural occurrence and also in the new creation of the resurrection of the dead. . . . The work of the Spirit of God in his church and in believers serves the consummating of his work in the world of creation. For the special mode of the presence of the divine Spirit in the gospel and by its proclamation, which shines out from the liturgical life of the church and *fills* believers, so that Paul can say of them that the Spirit "dwells" in them, is a pledge of the promise that the life which derives everywhere from the creative work of the Spirit will finally triumph over death, which is the price paid for the autonomy of creatures in their exorbitant clinging to their existence, in spite of its finitude, and over against its divine origin.[45]

With this methodological vision of a plural, holistic pneumatology as a guide, let us delve into the details of a contemporary pneumatology in the first part of the volume, to be followed by the discussion of salvation (for which an orientation is provided in the beginning of part 2).

Before that, a short note on the language used of the Spirit is in order: Should we use masculine or feminine — or perhaps neuter — pronouns? While all theologians agree that the categories of human experiences do not apply to the divine, it is also clear that the only way to speak of God is to employ concepts and metaphors taken from our own life. Otherwise, why would we speak of God as Father and Son?

While the Spirit's "gender" is less intuitively decided than that of the two other trinitarian members, theological tradition has normally used the masculine referent. This project at times uses masculine and at other times uses feminine pronouns to balance and correct one-sided male-dominant language.[46] (For the theological reasons, see the detailed discussion in chap. 14 of *Trinity and Revelation*.) In some religions such as Hinduism, it is not uncommon to speak of the feminine aspects of God. Just recall the importance of *shakti* traditions. Also, in some Christian spiritual movements both paternal and maternal aspects of the Spirit have been highlighted without any thematic theological reflection. In the Spirit movements in Korea in the beginning of the twentieth century, both paternal and maternal aspects existed side by side.[47] Materially

---

45. Pannenberg, *ST* 3:1-2, 11-12, emphasis in original.

46. See further, Murray, "Holy Spirit as Mother," pp. 312-20; Samartha, "Holy Spirit and People of Other Faiths," p. 254; K. Kim, *Holy Spirit in the World*, p. 21.

47. J.-G. Kim, "Korea's Total Evangelization Movement," pp. 45-73; S.-H. Kim and Y.-S. Kim, "Church Growth through Early Dawn Prayer Meetings," pp. 97-98.

similar is the pan–South Asian concept of yin and yang, which helped conceive the role of the Holy Spirit in terms of both masculinity and femininity.[48]

An Orientation to Part 1

The structure of part 1, pneumatology "proper," follows the underlying insight in which the work of the Spirit is being envisioned in mutually related concentric circles, as it were, beginning from the most comprehensive and "universal" sphere:

- The Spirit in Creation (chap. 3)
- The Spirit in the Cosmos (chap. 4)
- The Spirit among Religions (chap. 5)
- The Spirit in Society (chap. 6)

Part 2 will then zoom in on the Spirit in personal and communal salvation. The order of discussion is intentionally from the larger to the private, from the Spirit's work as the principle of life, bringing forth and sustaining all creaturely existence, to the Spirit's relation to other cosmic spirits and powers, including those of other religions, to the "public ministry" of the Spirit in culture, history, politics, economy, and arts — finally to the specific salvific tasks in the lives of Christians and Christian communities. The orientation to part 2 further clarifies the theological significance of the order of discussion.

Before anything else, chapter 2 will establish the deity of the Spirit along with the Father and Son. For a plural pneumatology that seeks to relate the Spirit of the Jewish-Christian Bible to other spirits in the created reality, including those of other religions, it is of utmost importance to clarify and defend the Christian confession of her deity. Christian confession of the deity of the Spirit belongs of course to the domain of the doctrine of the Trinity. Building on the full-scale discussion of the trinitarian doctrine attempted in *Trinity and Revelation* (part 2), the chapter will take a careful look at the theological significance of the slow historical process that culminated in the confession of the deity of the Spirit. The ecumenical significance of the *filioque* clause, the issue of how to define the procession of the Spirit in Trinity, is also part of the chapter and deepens the proposal outlined in chapter 11 of *Trinity and Revelation*.

---

48. K. Kim, *Holy Spirit in the World*, pp. 112-17.

Building on the constructive trinitarian theology of creation attempted in *Creation and Humanity*[49] in dialogue with natural sciences and four living faiths (Judaism, Islam, Buddhism, and Hinduism), chapter 3 will deepen the role of the Spirit in the bringing into existence and sustaining of creation. An important part of the discussion is the relating of the Spirit to the sciences' understanding of what makes the cosmos and life come into being. The chapter also takes a brief look at the biblical Spirit of Life in relation to theologies of creation in two other Abrahamic faiths and cosmologies of origins in Asiatic faiths.

One of the most distinctive features of the current project is the long chapter 4 with its focus on spirits, powers, and spiritual realities in Christian imagination and that of other religions. A "spirit-filled cosmos" is proposed and defended, particularly against the rampant denial of that in the contemporary naturalistically based scientific paradigm. Taking account of the rich biblical-historical traditions of angelology and demonology as well as those of the contemporary Global South (Africa, Asia, Latin America) and worldwide Pentecostal/charismatic movements, we will attempt to elucidate a theology of resisting and redeeming powers (W. Wink), including exorcism.

The focus of chapter 5 is the pneumatologies of four living faiths (Judaism, Islam, Buddhism, and Hinduism) and their relationship to the Christian view of the Spirit(s). A careful construal of the account of the Spirit/spirits is attempted for each faith tradition, based on the formative scriptural and theological sources (OT and rabbinic Judaism; Qur'an and Hadith; and so forth), and thereafter correlated with Christian pneumatology.

The last chapter in this part (6) focuses on the role of the Spirit in society and culture. Under the nomenclature "the public spirit" (an idea borrowed from Welker), the pneumatological aspects of sectors such as history, economy, politics, and the arts will be investigated. That discussion will not come to an end until the last chapter of part 2, which seeks to relate the Spirit's work in salvation to communal, societal, and cultural dimensions.

---

49. Part 1. On a detailed trinitarian construal, see chap. 3 therein.

2. The Spirit of the Triune God

The Slow Progress of the Doctrine of the Spirit: A Theological Reflection

The task of this chapter is straightforward and focused. It seeks to construct and clarify the Christian understanding of the deity of the Spirit of God in the context of the trinitarian faith. With the proliferation and diversity in contemporary ecumenical and global theologies, I believe it is possible to outline the commonly shared, defining convictions among those who continue affirming the essence of classical trinitarian doctrine. Only Unitarians of various sorts and those pluralists and others who opt for a modalistic view of the Christian doctrine of God may find this definition too restrictive.

After the introductory chapter, which argued for a robust shift from a unitive to a plural paradigm of pneumatology, it may come as a surprise that such a move does not have to mean a thinner doctrinal formulation of the deity of the Spirit and Trinity. Indeed, it does not. On the contrary, those who seek to relate the Spirit of God to the spirit(s) of other religions and spirits/powers/forces in the cosmos and society recognize the need to think clearly and accurately about the distinctive nature of a Christian trinitarian confession of the Spirit.

The discussion must necessarily proceed historically for the simple reason that only against the historical developments can the meaning and significance of the doctrinal understanding of the deity of the Spirit be appreciated. In this respect, the patristic and creedal contours stand in the forefront. (In the rest of the discussion, the later pneumatological developments, particularly those of the twentieth century, will be carefully and thoroughly engaged.) That said, it goes without saying that no attempt is made to provide any kind of comprehensive historical study of pneumatology;[1] for the sake of systematic and constructive argumentation, it suffices to highlight those developments and controversies considered the most critical for our current understanding.

The Theological Significance of the Spiritual Experience

As is well known, the development of pneumatological doctrine progressed even more slowly and painstakingly than did the doctrinal understanding of Christ and Trinity.[2] In the early centuries it was not uncommon to see confusion between the "Spirit" and "Word" (Son),[3] as evident, for example, in the famous apologist Justin Martyr's claim that "[i]t is wrong, therefore, to understand the Spirit and the power of God as anything else than the Word, who is also the first-born of God."[4] No less a giant than Origen advocated the strange idea of the derivation of the Spirit from the Logos. From the premise that the Holy Spirit is created, it follows, according to this great theologian, that we "must necessarily assume that the Holy Spirit was made through the Logos, the Logos accordingly being older than he."[5]

Understandings of the origins and "derivation" of the Spirit similarly stayed somewhat vague, often conceived in emanationist terms.[6] Similarly, the relationship between Son and Spirit remained somewhat ambiguous for

---

1. An excellent source is the three-volume work of Burgess, *The Holy Spirit: Ancient Christian Traditions; The Holy Spirit: Eastern Christian Traditions; The Holy Spirit: Medieval Roman Catholic and Reformation Traditions.* A detailed historical account with original textual evidence is also provided in Kärkkäinen, ed., *Holy Spirit and Salvation.*

2. The Fathers also linked the slow progress with the progressive nature of revelation in the Bible: "The Old Testament proclaimed the Father openly, and the Son more obscurely. The New manifested the Son, and suggested the Deity of the Spirit." Gregory of Nazianzus, *On the Holy Spirit* 26.

3. The second-century writing 2 *Clement* is a case in point: the proper distinction between Son and Spirit is confused in sayings such as the following, which speaks of those who abuse the flesh: "Such a one then shall not partake of the spirit, which is Christ." 2 *Clement* 14; similarly, also *The Shepherd of Hermas, Similitude* 9.1. For such examples in Justin Martyr, see Kelly, *Early Christian Creeds,* p. 148.

4. Justin Martyr, *First Apology* 33. Astonishing examples of equating the Spirit and Son with each other can also be found in Tertullian's writings targeted against modalism, *Against Praxeas* 7, 8.

5. Origen, *Commentary on John* 2.6.

6. E.g., Athenagoras of Athens, *A Plea for the Christians* 10, speaks of the Spirit as "an effluence of God, flowing from Him, and returning back again like a beam of the sun."

centuries.[7] Regarding the emerging linking of the Spirit to Trinity, both Theophilus of Antioch and Irenaeus defined the threeness in terms of God, Word, and Wisdom.[8] Theophilus equated the Spirit with the Word, while Irenaeus equated it with Wisdom![9] Because of the lack of a confession of the full deity of the Spirit, at times the Spirit was ranked as the "third" member in the Divine Society.[10]

These examples suffice to show the slow progress of the doctrine of the Spirit. Constructive theology, however, should inquire into material and theological reasons behind the slow development. Perhaps it is far more than just a historical curiosity and may yield some theological insights as well. One of these reasons has to do with the primacy and importance of the *spiritual experience:* "Long before the Spirit was a theme of doctrine, He was a fact in the experience of the community."[11] The Spirit indeed is usually the first "contact point" between human beings and God.[12] Theologically, the order of knowledge proceeds from the Spirit, through the Christ, to God.[13] The Indian ecumenist Stanley J. Samartha captures well this point: "To most Christians the Holy Spirit is associated not so much with doctrine as with life. It is in the unwrapping of the gift of God in Jesus Christ that the Spirit becomes alive in the hearts and minds of Christians. The Spirit inwardly nourishes the new life in Christ and guides the community of believers in their acts of witness and service in the world. The Spirit makes the koinonia in Christ real to the believers."[14]

---

7. Behind that is the lack of clarity in the NT: "The NT statements do not clarify the interrelations of the three but they clearly emphasize the fact that they are interrelated." Pannenberg, *ST* 1:269. A related factor is the apparent parallelism in the Old Testament between Word *(dabar)* and Spirit. O'Collins, *The Tripersonal God*, pp. 23-34, 91.

8. Theophilus of Antioch, *Theophilus to Autolycus* 2.15; Irenaeus, *Against Heresies* 4.20.3.

9. For the early history of the doctrine of the Spirit, see further, Kärkkäinen, *Pneumatology*, pp. 37-46 especially.

10. Justin Martyr, *First Apology* 13.

11. Schweizer, *"Pneuma,"* 6:396.

12. "If Father points to ultimate reality and Son supplies the clue to the divine mystery, Spirit epitomizes the nearness of the power and presence of God." Pinnock, *Flame of Love*, p. 9.

13. Basil (*On the Holy Spirit* 18.47) puts it well: "Thus the way of the knowledge of God lies from One Spirit through the One Son to the One Father, and conversely the natural Goodness and the inherent Holiness and the royal Dignity extend from the Father through the Only-begotten to the Spirit." To honor this "economic" approach to the knowledge of God, the trinitarian theology must take its beginning point in the economy of salvation rather than in abstract speculation into the mystery of God. For informed discussion, see Grenz, *Rediscovering the Triune God*, pp. 24-32; Pannenberg, *ST* 1:292-98.

14. Samartha, "Holy Spirit and People of Other Faiths," p. 250. See also, the insightful remarks by the Roman Catholic Elizabeth A. Dreyer, "An Advent of the Spirit," p. 123.

What Welker names "early, unclear experiences of the Spirit's power,"[15] referring to the first OT references to the Spirit, may also be applied to the spiritual experiences in early Christianity. That the Spirit of God was manifest and at work in the world and in the church particularly was robustly affirmed. That the doctrine of the Spirit was not yet formulated is a separate fact and should not lead the contemporary observer into the misconception that therefore the role of the Spirit was undervalued. A number of examples demonstrate the conviction of the Spirit's important role in Christian life and the church even if its exact form and meaning were yet to be decided. Just think of the linking of the Spirit to the inspiration of Scripture,[16] forgiveness of sin,[17] theological anthropology (another whole area that was still in the making),[18] and a number of ecclesiological topics such as preaching and the establishment of Christian communities,[19] the sacraments,[20] leadership (including the episcopacy),[21] and church life in general.[22] Furthermore, the unity[23] and holiness[24] of the church were tightly linked to the Spirit. As in the NT, there was also a deep link between the experience of the Spirit and eschatological consummation, not only among the enthusiasts but also among the "mainline" Fathers.[25] Throughout the early history, there is also the vivid, enthusiastic, and at times ecstatic charismatic experience of the Spirit.[26] As in the NT (Acts 19:2), the possession of

15. Borrowed from Welker, *God the Spirit*, the title of chap. 2.

16. Walter, *First Epistle to the Corinthians*, p. 45; see also, p. 8.

17. Augustine, *Sermons* 21.28.

18. See Tatian, "The Theory of the Soul's Immortality," in *Address to the Greeks* 13, 15.

19. Clement, *First Epistle to the Corinthians*, chap. 42.

20. Tertullian's *On Baptism* is also a great pneumatological treatise.

21. For Hippolytus, the presbyter in Rome and Irenaeus's pupil, the Holy Spirit guaranteed the faithful transmission of Christian tradition in the service of which the episcopal office also functioned. *The Refutation of All Heresies* 1, preface. Not surprisingly, the episcopal ordination was seen as a charismatic event: Hippolytus, *The Apostolic Tradition* 2; 3.1-6, in *The Apostolic Tradition of Hippolytus*, pp. 33-34.

22. For the classic statement of Irenaeus concerning the pneumatological foundation of the church, see *Against Heresies* 3.24.1.

23. Cyprian, *Treatise on the Unity of the Church* 9.

24. Ignatius, *Epistle to the Philadelphians* 7.

25. Basil, *On the Holy Spirit* 16.40.

26. Speaking in tongues was well in use in the third century, as evident in Irenaeus, *Against Heresies* 5.6.1. For other accounts of various charismatic experiences and listing of gifts in the church, see Tertullian, *A Treatise on the Soul* 9; Origen, *On First Principles* 2.7.3. The anonymous early writing (related to Tertullianus) *The Passion of the Holy Martyrs Perpetua and Felicitas* is a collection of charismatic, ecstatic experiences and visions. For a number of other examples and textual evidence, see Kärkkäinen, ed., *Holy Spirit and Salvation*, chaps. 1-5.

the Spirit was routinely taken as the mark of Christian faith and holiness.[27] At times an appeal to continuing charismatic gifting was required for authentication of church leadership.[28] This litany alone tells us there was an emerging and growing intuition of the profound influence of the Holy Spirit in the divine economy despite the lack of clearly defined and formulated doctrinal canons.

Practical needs related to liturgy and Christian life also guided the doctrinal formulation (hand in hand with biblical reading). The habit of mentioning the Spirit alongside the Father and Son in doxologies, prayers, and baptismal liturgies,[29] as well as the belief that Christ's salvific benefits were conveyed to men and women by the Spirit, seemed to require the full divine status of the third member of the Trinity.[30] This is the essence of the ancient rule *lex orandi lex credendi* (the law of prayer [is or becomes] the law of believing).[31]

In sum: notwithstanding the deep and wide spiritual experience and the emerging consciousness of the need to affirm the equality of the Spirit in the Trinity based on soteriological, liturgical, and other "practical" reasons, what or who the Spirit is was often only dimly grasped in early theology. In addition, a material reason why the Spirit's role remained more obscure and vague for a long time has to do with the particular nature of the Spirit in biblical and traditional understanding.

The Elusive Nature of the Spirit

Both in biblical traditions and in people's general mind-set, the Spirit is more subtle and less concrete a phenomenon than Son and Father. It is far easier to find metaphors and symbols for Father and Son that have an everyday counterpart. Related to the elusive nature and "shyness" of the Spirit is also

27. See, e.g., *The Shepherd of Hermas* 2.11.

28. Tertullian, *Against Marcion* 5.8; *Against Celsus* 1.2 (about discovering doctrinal truths); Pseudo-Macarius, *The Fifty Spiritual Homilies* 19.1; 23.2, in *"The Fifty Spiritual Homilies"* and *"The Great Letter,"* pp. 146, 156, respectively.

29. For Saint Basil's defense of the formula: "Glory to the Father with the Son together with the Holy Spirit," see *On the Holy Spirit* 19.48.

30. A case in point is Origen, for whom it was impossible to think of regeneration or deification (the Eastern Church's designation for salvation) apart from the full cooperation of the Father, Son, and Spirit, and who pushed the doctrinal reflections toward the idea of the full equality of the three. *On First Principles* 1.3.5. For a classic statement of the coworking in deification of the Spirit and Son, see Irenaeus, *Against Heresies* 4.20.5. For the remarkable litany of the Spirit's works in salvation and deification, see Basil, *On the Holy Spirit* 15.36.

31. See further, Congar, *I Believe in the Holy Spirit*, 1:65-166; 3:19-214.

the biblical perception that the Holy Spirit never draws attention to herself but rather turns our attention to the Son and through the Son to the Father. On that basis, tradition at times speaks of the Spirit as the "Third Unknown." Furthermore, the naming of the Spirit as the "bond" of love between the Father and Son might have contributed to the lack of articulating the personal nature of the Spirit. While certainly this idea has both a biblical basis and theological validity, in the hands of less incisive theologians it may also turn into a nonpersonal conception of the Spirit. "Love" or "bond" doesn't have to be as "personal" as Father and Son.

Yet another factor in the slow progress in doctrine certainly has to do with ecclesial concerns. From the second-century Montanists all the way through Reformation "enthusiasts" to modern-day Pentecostals, groups have claimed the authority of the Spirit over human leaders of the church — or as it was often perceived, over the written Word of God — and were encountered with hostility and suspicion. Thus, a need was felt to control the Spirit. The Montanists were excommunicated,[32] Andreas von Karlstadt and other *Schwärmer* (enthusiasts) were accused by Luther of devouring the Holy Spirit, "feathers and all,"[33] and early Pentecostals at Azusa Street (Los Angeles) were ridiculed and ostracized beyond measure even in news media.[34]

The Eastern Orthodox Church persistently reminds us of still another reason for the slow progress in doctrinal understanding of the Spirit. It has to do with the *filioque* clause, which may have subordinated the Spirit under the Son and thus made theological reflection on the Spirit less urgent. Nevertheless, the deity of the Spirit was finally established both among the Greek- and Latin-speaking theologians. To that topic we turn next.

The Eventual Consolidation of the Deity of the Spirit

As in the formulation of christological and trinitarian doctrines, much of the energy behind the development of pneumatological doctrine came from the threat and challenge of heretical views. Against modalistic teachers, Tertullian established the distinction among Father, Son, and Spirit on the inner relations of the trinitarian members. On the basis of the Paraclete passages in

---

32. For a brief, reliable source, see Tabbernee, "'Will the Real Paraclete Please Speak Forth!'" pp. 97-118.

33. For comments, see Zahl, "Rethinking 'Enthusiasm,'" p. 341.

34. For reports, see Robeck, *Azusa Street Mission and Revival*, chap. 2 particularly.

John 14, Tertullian suggested that the Son distinguished both the Father and the Spirit from himself.[35] Similarly, Origen affirmed that Jesus' referring to the Father and the Paraclete as distinct from himself implies the existence of three persons and one shared substance or entity.[36] While distinguished from each other, the trinitarian persons also share unity, which later creedal tradition referred to as *homoousios* (consubstantial). Tertullian surmised that the Johannine Jesus' saying "I and the Father are one" means that Father and Son are of "one substance,"[37] and this denotes an identity of substance rather than numerical unity.[38] By extension, the Son and Spirit are of the same substance with the Father.[39] Thus, we can speak of God's one "substance" and three distinct yet undivided "persons."[40] Technically this is what the Western Church's semicanonized way of expressing its faith in the Trinity says *(una substantia, tres personae)*. Materially, this formulation leads to the full establishment of the deity of the Spirit. Among the Greek Fathers, Origen finally came to this idea — after much vacillation — when he affirmed that "nothing in the Trinity can be called greater or less, since the fountain of divinity alone contains all things by His word and reason, and by the Spirit of His mouth sanctifies all things."[41]

The fourth-century Greek-speaking Alexandrian theologians were fighting against heretical views of the Spirit on several fronts, including against the *Tropicii* (Tropici), a group that was not willing to give the same divine status to the Spirit as to the Son. Like the Arian heresy in Christology, the Tropici's view rejected the full equality of the Spirit vis-à-vis other trinitarian members.[42] Athanasius's *Letters to Serapion on the Holy Spirit* insisted on the indivisibility of the Trinity as a proof of the equal status of the Spirit.[43] Gregory

35. Tertullian, *Against Praxeas* 9, quoting John 14:28 and 14:16.

36. Origen, *Homilies on Numbers* 12.1, referenced in Pannenberg, *ST* 1:272 n. 48.

37. Tertullian, *Against Praxeas* 2.

38. Tertullian, *Against Praxeas* 25.

39. Tertullian, *Against Praxeas* 3.

40. Tertullian, *Against Praxeas* 2.

41. Origen, *On First Principles* 1.3.7. While this statement is in keeping with the later orthodox tradition, ironically the background to this statement can be found in Origen's speculation about the different spheres of operation of the trinitarian persons: the Father's in creation, the Son's in salvation, and the Spirit's in inanimate creation; this idea was supposed to guard the unity of the Trinity. Neither idea — different spheres of operation or defense of unity on this basis — can hardly be sustained in light of creedal traditions.

42. Athanasius, *Letters to Serapion* 1.21, in Anatolios, *Athanasius*, pp. 220-21.

43. Athanasius, *Letters to Serapion* 1.20, in Anatolios, *Athanasius*, p. 219. A strong defense of the unity of the Trinity and the Spirit's role therein can also be found in Gregory of Nyssa's *On "Not Three Gods."*

of Nazianzus's *On the Holy Spirit* vehemently rejected all heretical notions of the created nature of the Spirit: if there ever was a time when the Father was not — meaning he was not eternal because there was a beginning — then the Son would not be eternal either, nor by derivation the Spirit.[44] Basil the Great's *On the Holy Spirit* was the main tool in rejecting another major pneumatological heresy: that perpetrated by the *Pneumatomachoi*, the "fighters of the Spirit" who undermined the Nicean orthodoxy and thus echoed Arian misgivings about the Son's equality with the Father. The reference to the Spirit's preexistence was one of the tactics to oppose the "pneumatological Arianism."[45] Basil's brother Gregory of Nyssa penned *On the Holy Trinity of the Godhead of the Holy Spirit to Eustathius* and *On the Holy Spirit against the Followers of Macedonius*, in which he defended the Cappadocian conviction of the equality of the Spirit. With Arian and Eunomian tendencies, Macedonius compromised the Spirit's divinity and full equality with the Father. Against those heresies, Gregory argued that the Holy Spirit is "essentially holy," as are the Father and the Son. Like the other two members of the Trinity, the Spirit is characterized by divine attributes "of imperishability, of unvariableness, of everlastingness, of justice, of wisdom, of rectitude, of sovereignty, of goodness, of power, of capacity to give all good things, and above them all life itself."[46] Everywhere, the Greek Fathers affirmed boldly the equality of the Spirit with the Son.[47] Undoubtedly one of the chief motives behind the vigorous and persistent opposition to all forms of heretical pneumatological views was not only the Fathers' conviction that intellectual and doctrinal clarity was at stake; these defenders of orthodox faith took those who denied the full deity of the Spirit as "transgressors."[48]

In the Latin-speaking church, Saint Augustine's clarification of trinitarian and pneumatological contours helped further consolidate the deity of the

44. Gregory of Nazianzus, *On the Holy Spirit* 4.

45. See Basil, *On the Holy Spirit* 19.49.

46. Gregory of Nyssa, *On the Holy Spirit against the Followers of Macedonius; NPNF*[2] 5:323.

47. Athanasius insisted that the Spirit is in Christ as the Son is in the Father (Athanasius, *Letters to Serapion* 1.20, in Anatolios, *Athanasius,* p. 219). Similarly, Cyril of Jerusalem urged Christians to regard the Spirit in the same way as the Father and Son (*Catechetical Lectures* 4.16). For a helpful discussion, see Kelly, *Early Christian Doctrines,* pp. 258-63, and Letham, *The Holy Trinity,* pp. 149-53. Important contributions to emerging pneumatological doctrine came also from Gregory of Nazianzus, who in his *Orations* (esp. 29, 30, and 31) discusses widely the deity of the Spirit and the Spirit in relation to Father and Son. For a helpful discussion, see Letham, pp. 159-64.

48. Basil, *On the Holy Spirit* 11.27.

Spirit. Although all trinitarian members are holy, what makes the third person unique is that the "Holy Spirit is a certain unutterable communion of the Father and the Son."[49] In other words, "He is the Spirit of the Father and Son, as the substantial and consubstantial love of both."[50] While acknowledging that any of the members of the Trinity could be called love, on the basis of biblical passages such as 1 John 4:7-19 and Romans 5:5, Augustine came to the conclusion that the Spirit particularly can be called Love, the bond of love uniting Father and Son, and derivatively, uniting the triune God and human beings.[51] The New Testament statements such as "God is Spirit" (John 4:24) and "The Lord is the Spirit, and where the Spirit of the Lord is, there is freedom" (2 Cor. 3:17) helped the bishop to clarify the twofold reference of the term "Spirit": on the one hand, it speaks of God's nature as "invisible and incomprehensible," and on the other hand, as the Gift of God given to the believer, in other words, as the name of the third person of the Trinity.[52] More daring than the Cappadocians, Augustine felt comfortable in calling the Holy Spirit "Very God, Equal with the Father and the Son."[53] The bishop's summary statement, claiming to be based on wide Christian tradition, leaves no doubt about the deity and full equality of the Spirit in Trinity: "the Father, and the Son, and the Holy Spirit intimate a divine unity of one and the same substance in an indivisible equality. . . . [T]he Holy Spirit is neither the Father nor the Son, but only the Spirit of the Father and of the Son, Himself also co-equal with the Father and the Son, and pertaining to the unity of the Trinity."[54]

The authoritative formulation of the Spirit was finally ratified in the ecumenical creeds. Whereas the Fathers at Nicea were irreducibly brief in their confession — "And [we believe] in the Holy Ghost"[55] — in the Creed of Constantinople I (381) the consubstantiality of the Spirit was officially confirmed: "And [we believe] in the Holy Ghost, the Lord and Giver-of-Life, who proceedeth from the Father, who with the Father and the Son together is wor-

---

49. Augustine, *On the Trinity* 5.11.12.

50. Augustine, *Tractates on John* 105.

51. Augustine, *On the Trinity* 15.17.31. While Augustine's way of supporting the designation of the Spirit as love is somewhat complex here, the main point is clear: that as love the Spirit is what unites Father and Son. See also, e.g., *On the Trinity* 15.17.27.

52. Hilary of Poitiers, *On the Trinity* 2.31-32.

53. Augustine, *On the Trinity,* the preamble to chap. 6 in book 1, p. 22 (1.6.13); see also, e.g., 1.2.4.

54. Augustine, *On the Trinity* 1.4.7; for another classic, similar kind of statement, see Augustine, *Letter 169 to Bishop Evodius; NPNF*[2] 1:540.

55. *NPNF*[2] 14:3.

shipped and glorified, who spake by the prophets." Although far from any kind of systematic statement, the Constantinopolitan elaboration of aspects of pneumatological doctrine and the Spirit's tasks is worth noting.[56] First, the equal status of the Spirit was officially confirmed in that the Holy Spirit is to be "worshiped and glorified together with the Father and the Son."[57] Related to this is the mention of the proceeding of the Spirit from the Father, reminding us of the trinitarian structure of the creed and confession of faith in the Spirit. Second, naming the Spirit the "Giver-of-Life" makes an integral connection with the doctrine of salvation. (Unlike the twentieth-century theologians, the drafters of the creed most probably did not intentionally link the life-giving Spirit with creation.) Third, the soteriological connection is brought home also in the nomenclature "Holy" Ghost, in other words, the Spirit's sanctifying work in the life of the believers.

Fourth, in keeping with later theological developments, the connection between the inspiration of prophetic Scripture and the Holy Spirit was established at Chalcedon (echoing NT statements such as 2 Tim. 3:16 and 2 Pet. 1:20-21). Fifth, considering more broadly the wider context of the third article of the creed, we note that the Spirit is linked closely with the church and liturgy. The ecclesiological connection is further enhanced by the statement about belief in the one, holy, apostolic, and catholic church and the communion of saints immediately following belief in the Spirit. It might also be significant that this same article, after the Spirit and the church, also mentions belief in the forgiveness of sins. Soteriological and ecclesiological themes are interrelated in that, according to the earliest faith of Christians, salvation and forgiveness can only be had in the church. Furthermore, there is not only the ecclesiological but also the eschatological context for the confession of the Spirit. The article ends with a statement about the resurrection of the body and eternal life. While later theology by and large missed the integral connection between eschatology and pneumatology, in the biblical testimonies the link is established with the expectation and fulfillment of the pouring out of the Spirit as the launching of the final days (Joel 2 and Acts 2).

56. I was inspired by Thorsen, *Explorations in Christian Theology,* chap. 19.
57. *NPNF*[2] 14:163.

The Trinitarian Personhood of the Spirit

The Spirit in the Trinitarian Communion

The distinctively *Christian* understanding of the divine Spirit is trinitarian in its experience and form.[58] Unlike much of theological tradition, which took the unity as a self-evident point of departure, contemporary constructive theology begins with the threeness — Father, Son, and Spirit, as they appear in the NT narrative — and then clarifies the way the unity may be affirmed.[59] In the following the Spirit's role in the Trinity will be further clarified. For a full-scale discussion and constructive proposal of the trinitarian doctrine, the reader should go to chapter 11 of *Trinity and Revelation*.

An essential component in the slow progress of the establishment of the Spirit's deity had to do with the ambiguity about her personhood. In the biblical testimonies, both impersonal (such as wind, fire, water) and personally driven (such as Paraclete or Teacher) metaphors can be found;[60] the former category is much more dominant. Because the NT does not offer much hermeneutical help in settling the issue, the question of the personhood of the Spirit has been deeply intertwined with the shifting paradigms of how to best understand "person[hood]" in the given cultural context. Unlike in the past, the key to establishing personhood in contemporary culture and theology has to do with relationality and community.[61] Whereas in tradition, *persona* was conceived in individualistic terms — so much so that even mid-twentieth-century theologians such as Barth and Rahner were looking for alternative terms for "person" in order to avoid the absurd implications of individualism applied to God — in contemporary culture personhood is another way of saying belonging, relationality, communion, community.[62] This is one of the most important insights of the contemporary trinitarian renaissance, which

---

58. The significance of the remarkable shift from the OT's uncompromising monotheism to trinitarian monotheism "was spawned by the theological puzzle posed by the early church's confession of the lordship of Jesus and the experience of the indwelling Holy Spirit, both of which developments emerged within the context of the nonnegotiable commitment to the one God of the Old Testament that the early believers inherited from Israel." Grenz, *Rediscovering the Triune God*, p. 7.

59. See Moltmann, *Trinity and the Kingdom*, pp. 19, 64.

60. See J. Y. Lee, *Trinity in Asian Perspective*, p. 95.

61. "Being a person in this respect means existing-in-relationship." Moltmann, *Trinity and the Kingdom*, p. 172. For the details and historical developments, see Kärkkäinen, *The Trinity*, pp. 59-64.

62. So also, Moltmann, *Spirit of Life*, pp. 10-11. The German Catholic Heribert Mühlen's

also opens new venues for considering the trinitarian communal personhood of the Spirit. Its historical roots go all the way back to the Eastern Fathers.[63] "At the heart of God, the Cappadocians saw an interpersonal communion or *koinonia,* with communion as the function of all three divine persons and not simply of the Holy Spirit. For this interpersonal model of the Trinity, God's inner being is relational, with each of the three persons totally related to the other two in 'reciprocal delight' — to borrow an Athanasian expression."[64]

Defining the divine essence in terms of relations allows both for the reciprocal, mutually dependent understanding of relations between Father, Son, and Spirit and also for an account of the God-world relationship based on mutuality rather than distance. In this understanding, "constitutive for each person of the Trinity are the other two persons and the relation to them. The world, in turn, does not arise as a self-unfolding of the divine subject who makes the world but as God's free bringing forth of a world that differs from God out of the overflow of God's love. It is the product of the mutual activity of the Father, Son, and Spirit."[65] Against common suspicions, this is not to reduce trinitarian members into "relations" but rather is a way of reminding us of the commonsense truth that essential to personhood is relationality.

The turn to a relational understanding of personhood has helped the re-discovery of communion theology, whose roots go back to the NT witness that where the Spirit is, there is the principle of *koinonia.* That idea is also widely attested in patristic theology.[66] The main thesis of the widely acclaimed *Being as Communion* (1985) by the Orthodox John Zizioulas is simple and profound: rather than "one substance," the "Holy Trinity is a *primordial* ontological concept and not a notion which is added to the divine substance."[67] This means that communion, relationality, is an ontological, primary statement about God. The Bible expresses it with the statement that God is love (1 John 4:8).[68]

Echoing Zizioulas, some leading feminist theologians have reminded us

---

idiosyncratic way of naming the relational communion is I-THOU-WE: see Mühlen, *Der Heilige Geist als Person;* for an engagement, see Vondey, *Heribert Mühlen.*

63. Gregory of Nazianzus said it well: "When I say God, I mean Father, Son, and Holy Spirit." In other words, the only way to think of God is to think of one God as existing as Father, Son, and Spirit. *Oration on the Theophany, or Birthday of Christ* 38.8.

64. O'Collins, *The Tripersonal God,* pp. 131-32.

65. Grenz, *Reason for Hope,* p. 60.

66. See Grenz, *Social God,* pp. 3-14.

67. Cf. "In the Beginning Is Communion," chapter title in Boff, *Trinity and Society,* p. 9.

68. Zizioulas, *Being as Communion,* pp. 17, 46; Zizioulas, "Teaching of the 2nd Ecumenical Council on the Holy Spirit," p. 37; Zizioulas, "Human Capacity," p. 410.

that if communion and relationality are ontologically primary about God, that means "God, too, lives from and for another: God the Father gives birth to the Son, breathes forth the Spirit, elects the creature from before all time. . . . God's rule is accomplished by saving and healing love."[69] Materially similar themes can be found among some theologians from the Global South such as the Roman Catholic Charles Nyamiti of Tanzania, who builds his ancestral-driven Christology and pneumatology on the deep "African sense of participation."[70] The late Canadian Baptist Clark Pinnock grasped deeply and put in perspective the profound theological implications of a robust relational communion theology of the divine Spirit with the focus on the "liveliness of the Trinity and the identity of the Spirit within a loving relationality":

> Let us consider the Spirit as One who bonds the loving fellowship that God is and creates access to the Father through the Son (Eph 2:18). The Spirit reaches out to creatures, catches them up and brings them home to the love of God. . . . Spirit is the ecstasy that implements God's abundance and triggers the overflow of divine self-giving. . . . The universe in its entirety is the field of its operations . . . [a]nd the Spirit is present everywhere, directing the universe toward its goal, bringing to completion first the creational and then the redemptive purposes of God.[71]

The Spirit's role in the Trinity is not only integrally related to the Father from whom she derives but also to the Son. This brings us to "Spirit Christology," a dominant theme in the NT, particularly in the Synoptic Gospels. Although the detailed historical-systematic discussion of Spirit Christology, including a contemporary constructive proposal, belongs to the christological volume (*Christ and Reconciliation,* chap. 8), the importance of the theme to pneumatology calls for focused remarks.

"Spirit Christology" — Christological Pneumatology

Trinitarian pneumatology implies and necessitates an account of the mutual relationship between the Spirit and Christ. The integral, mutually conditioned relationality between the two is evident everywhere in the Gospels and is also

---

69. LaCugna, *God for Us,* p. 383; see Baker-Fletcher, *Dancing with God.*
70. Nyamiti, *African Tradition,* p. 62.
71. Pinnock, *Flame of Love,* pp. 21, 50; see also, p. 60.

assumed in the rest of the NT. Jesus' birth (Matt. 1:18-25; Luke 1:35) and its announcement[72] (Luke 1:35, 67); his baptism[73] (Matt. 3:16; Mark 1:10; Luke 3:22; John 1:33); his testing in the wilderness (Matt. 4:1; Mark 1:12; Luke 4:1); his anointing (Luke 4:18-21); his ministry with healings, exorcisms, and other miracles (Matt. 12:28; Luke 4:18; 11:20); the eschatological ministry of Jesus as the Baptizer in the Spirit (Matt. 3:11) — these are all attributed to the Spirit. Importantly, Jesus was also raised to new life by the power of the Spirit (Rom. 1:4), so much so that he "became a life-giving spirit" (1 Cor. 15:45).

Although not yet made a theological theme, the Spirit Messiah ("the Anointed") is of course present in various OT traditions. Particularly in the prophetic literature, the messianic figure appears as anointed and empowered by the Spirit of God (Isa. 11:1-8; 42:1-4). Rightly then, Moltmann reminds us that "Jesus' history as the Christ does not begin with Jesus himself. It begins with the *ruach*/the Holy Spirit."[74] In that sense it can also be said that the workings of the Spirit precede those of the Son.[75] Therefore, with justification, tradition can speak not only of the sending of the Spirit by the Son but also of the sending of the Son by the Spirit: "[T]he Spirit was upon Christ; and . . . as He sent the Spirit, so the Spirit sent the Son of God."[76] As the Son of God, Jesus Christ is "a Spirit-creation."[77] Another way of naming this template is to speak of "pneumatological Christology" and — correspondingly — a "christological pneumatology."[78]

For constructive theology, it is critical to recall that while in the NT[79] —

72. See also, Hilary of Poitiers, *On the Trinity* 2.26-27.

73. The coming of the Spirit at Jesus' baptism was an occasion for a number of profound pneumatological accounts in later theology, as evident, e.g., in Cyril of Jerusalem, *Catechetical Lectures* 3.11-14; Ambrose, *Of the Holy Spirit* 3.1.1-6; Bede, *Commentary on the Acts of the Apostles*, pp. 102-3 (on Acts 10:38a).

74. Moltmann, *Way of Jesus Christ*, p. 73. The Benedictine Kilian McDonnell, in "The Determinative Doctrine of the Holy Spirit," p. 154, rightly emphasizes that a robust Spirit Christology can only be maintained if "the Spirit belongs to Jesus constitutively and not merely in a second moment."

75. Moltmann, *Spirit of Life*, pp. xi, 60. On the "messianic expectations of the Spirit" in the OT, see pp. 51-57.

76. Ambrose, *On the Holy Spirit* 3.1.1.

77. Kasper, *Jesus the Christ*, p. 251; see also, Nissiotis, "Pneumatological Christology as a Presupposition of Ecclesiology," p. 236.

78. Moltmann, *Way of Jesus Christ*, pp. 73-74.

79. To be more precise, following Moltmann (*Spirit of Life*, p. 58), whereas the Synoptic Gospels present a thoroughgoing Spirit Christology, Paul and John, having this as a premise, put forth *"a christological doctrine of the Spirit"* (emphasis in original). Importantly, the oldest christological formula spoke of Jesus in terms of the dynamic of "after the flesh" and "after the Spirit" (1 Tim. 3:16; 1 Pet. 3:18). This template was soon adopted by the earliest theologians,

and among the Fathers, particularly in the East[80] — christological explanations and categories were pneumatologically oriented,[81] soon thereafter the Logos (Word) paradigm became dominant, at times almost exclusively.[82] The Chalcedonian incarnational Christology of course represents the culmination of that process: therein the presence and influence of God in Jesus the man was explained as the function of the eternal Logos. That said, a contemporary reader must be reminded that, unlike in recent times, early theological tradition did not see Spirit and Logos Christologies as alternatives but rather as complementary; that is, reference to the Spirit was another legitimate way of explaining the unique presence of God and the coming together of the divine and human natures in one person.[83] A wonderful example here is Tertullian, a great architect of Logos and two-nature Christology (or "two-substance" Christology, as he preferred to call it) who also advocated a robust Spirit Christology.[84]

Not surprisingly, a number of approaches to Spirit Christology have emerged in contemporary theology, particularly during the past few decades, with differing agendas and points of view. A fairly common approach both among the exegetes (such as J. D. G. Dunn) and the systematicians (such as P. Newman and G. Lampe) is not only to set up with each other the Spirit and Logos approaches but also to assume that the classic trinitarian canons, particularly concerning the doctrines of the incarnation and the deity of Christ, cannot be maintained with the shift to Spirit Christologies. In *Christ and Reconciliation* (chap. 8), I have provided a critique and an alternative constructive proposal siding with a number of contemporary theologians who refuse to go with an either/or model and rather work toward a complementary, though

---

including Ignatius (*To the Ephesians* 7), and documents such as 2 *Clement* (9.5); Kelly, *Early Christian Doctrines*, p. 138; see pp. 142-49 for many other early examples from Cyprian, Hippolytus, and others.

80. Athanasius, *Letters to Serapion* 1.19-20, in Anatolios, *Athanasius*, pp. 217-18; Gregory of Nazianzus, *Oration* 41; *On Pentecost* 14; Gregory of Nyssa, *On the Holy Spirit*. See also, Maximus the Confessor, *Commentary on the Our Father* 1-2 (Berthold trans., pp. 103-4).

81. Rosato, "Spirit Christology," p. 424. For a useful scrutiny of biblical and patristic Spirit Christologies, see Balthasar, *The Spirit of Truth*, pp. 48-51 and pp. 37-39, respectively.

82. There was of course an important apologetic reason for the rise of the Logos explanation: unlike the OT/Jewish tradition in which an important way of explaining the presence and efficacy of God made reference to the Spirit (just think of Gen. 1:2), in much of Greek-Hellenistic culture that was virtually unknown. The concept of the Logos, however, was well known and well received. See further, Pinnock, *Flame of Love*, p. 91.

83. See Moltmann, *Way of Jesus Christ*, p. 74; Haight, "Case for Spirit Christology," pp. 276-77.

84. See Tertullian, *Against Praxeas* 5 and 6.

distinct, understanding of the Logos and Spirit templates. For the purposes of this discussion, it suffices that we be warned not to "diminish the importance of the Spirit for Christology. Logos Christology is not the whole story; indeed, if we exaggerate it we may eclipse the mission of the Spirit and effect its subordination to that of the Son."[85] This note takes us to the critical issue of the *filioque* — a deep, dividing issue that up to the present has hindered a common ecumenical confession of the role of the Spirit in the Trinity.

The Filioque *Question: Is the Derivation of the Spirit Still a Dividing Issue?*

Whereas the original form of the Nicene-Constantinopolitan Creed (381) ruled that the Holy Spirit "proceeds from the Father," soon the Latin theologians added the dual procession of the Spirit from both the Son and the Father. Notwithstanding the continuing historical debates about the history of this ecumenically one-sided addition,[86] it is clear that in the first major breach of the Christian church in 1054, the *filioque* clause played a major role along with political, ecclesiastical, and cultural issues. Why was *filioque* ("and from the Son") added? The NT is ambiguous about the procession of the Spirit. On the one hand, according to John, Jesus is said to send the Spirit (John 16:7).[87] On the other hand, the Spirit is said to be sent by the Father in response to Jesus' prayer (14:16) and in his name (14:26). Because a fuller and more detailed discussion of the meaning of the *filioque* clause can be found in the context of the doctrine of the Trinity (chap. 11 of *Trinity and Revelation*),[88] let us briefly deepen our understanding of the issue from a pneumatological (rather than a general trinitarian) point of view.

Until recently it was a commonplace to claim that because of his Neoplatonic leanings, Augustine's one-sided emphasis on the unity of the divine essence hindered him from accounting for distinctions.[89] This made Western

85. Pinnock, *Flame of Love*, p. 91.

86. The standard view is that this addition was first accepted by the Council of Toledo in 589 and ratified by the 809 Aachen Synod. It was incorporated in later creeds such as that of the Fourth Lateran Council in 1215 and the Council of Lyons in 1274.

87. According to John 15:26, Jesus will send the Spirit (called *Parakletos* here), who proceeds from the Father.

88. See also, the more extensive discussion and constructive proposal in my "Is the Spirit Still the Dividing Line?" pp. 125-42.

89. "It is impossible to do contemporary Trinitarian theology and not have a judgment on Augustine." M. R. Barnes, "Rereading Augustine's Theology of the Trinity," p. 145.

and Eastern approaches to the Trinity diametrically opposed to each other.[90] This view, however, might lack needed nuances and may even be somewhat misleading.[91]

In light of recent research we know that, on the one hand, even for the leading Eastern theologians, a balanced view of the threeness was far from commonplace and that, on the other hand, threeness was not a foreign idea to Augustine (notwithstanding his poor knowledge of Greek [theology]).[92] Augustine affirmed both the consubstantiality and the distinctions of the Son and Spirit[93] and understood relations as eternal.[94] Pannenberg, who otherwise is somewhat critical of the Augustinian legacy, has shown convincingly that "Augustine took over the relational definition of the Trinitarian distinctions which the Cappadocians, following Athanasius, had developed. He made the point that the distinctions of the persons are conditioned by their mutual relations."[95] He also conceived the Spirit as communion (of the Father and the Son), their shared love, and a gift.[96] In book 8 of *De Trinitate*, he develops Trinity with the help of the idea of interpersonal love in terms of filiation and paternity. The Father is Lover, the Son the Beloved, and the Spirit the mutual Love that connects the two. The Eastern idea of *perichoresis*, mutual interpenetration, can hardly be called a stranger to Augustine's views.[97]

Well known are Augustine's reflections on the Spirit in the Trinity. He

90. Prestige, *God in Patristic Thought*, p. 237; Margerie, *Christian Trinity*, pp. 110-21. This alleged state of affairs has made some speak of even the "theological crisis of the West." Gunton, "Augustine, the Trinity," pp. 33-58. Gunton further argues that Augustine did not correctly understand the tradition, certainly not the teaching of the Cappadocians, and ended up viewing the divine substance "behind" relations. For the Cappadocians, so this critic says, on the contrary, relations are "ontological," whereas for the bishop of Hippo they are only "logical." Gunton, *Promise of Trinitarian Theology*, pp. 38-43 especially.

91. The most vocal critic of the alleged Neoplatonic influence on Augustine is M. R. Barnes, "Rereading Augustine's Theology of the Trinity," pp. 145-76. A careful, cautious interpretation, quite critical of the old consensus, is offered in Studer, *Trinity and Incarnation*, pp. 167-85.

92. Cary, "Historical Perspectives on Trinitarian Doctrine," p. 9.

93. E.g., Augustine, *Letters* 169 (*NPNF*[2] 1:540): "The Son is not the Father, the Father is not the Son, and neither the Father nor the Son is the Holy Spirit. . . . [T]hese are equal and co-eternal, and absolutely of one nature . . . an inseparable trinity."

94. Pannenberg, *ST* 1:284.

95. Pannenberg, *ST* 1:284, with reference to Augustine, *On the Trinity* 8.1.

96. Augustine, *On the Trinity* 5.11.12; 15.27.50 (communion); 15.17.27 (love); 5.12.13; 5.15.16 (gift).

97. See particularly Augustine, *On the Trinity* 6.10.12.

conceives of the Spirit as communion (of the Father and the Son),[98] their shared love,[99] and a gift.[100] What about the Spirit's procession in this context? Augustine argues that the Spirit proceeds "originally" from the Father and also in common from both the Father and Son, as something given by the Father.[101] It is clear that even when the Son is included in the act of procession of the Spirit, it is not from two sources but rather from a single source in order to protect the divine unity.[102]

That said, it is historically undisputed that in the post-Augustinian traditions the unity took the upper hand. In the later tradition, the Augustinian idea of the Spirit as shared love more often than not led to nonpersonal accounts of the Spirit.[103] It is also possible that the *filioque* was seen to strengthen the rejection of Arianism, as the mentioning of the Son alongside the Father as the origin of the Spirit could be interpreted as a way of defending consubstantiality.[104] Finally, as the link between the Trinity and salvation history began to weaken, the trinitarian doctrine became more abstract and speculative. These developments contributed to the marginalization of the Spirit in theology and the Christian life.[105]

Historical debates aside, what is at stake with the *filioque?* According to the Christian East, it is highly problematic because *filioque* was a one-sided addition without ecumenical consultation;[106] because it compromises the monarchy of the Father as the source of divinity (a key trinitarian conviction in the Christian East, in contrast with the West);[107] and because it seems to

---

98. Augustine, *On the Trinity* 5.11.12; 15.27.50. See further, Ratzinger, "The Holy Spirit as *Communio,*" pp. 324-27.

99. Augustine, *On the Trinity* 15.17.27; Augustine, *Tractates (Homilies) on the Gospel of St. John* 105.7.3.

100. Augustine, *On the Trinity* 5.12.13; 5.15.16.

101. Augustine, *On the Trinity* 15.26.47. Against common suspicions, Augustine then defends the idea of the Father as the sole source of the deity, a key Eastern point of insistence. See also, Augustine, *On the Trinity* 4.20.29.

102. Augustine, *On the Trinity* 5.14.

103. Hilberath, "Pneumatologie," pp. 446-47.

104. Oddly enough, Richard Haugh surmises that the addition happened just by way of transposition without any conscious theological reason. Haugh, *Photius and the Carolingians,* pp. 160-61.

105. See Grenz, *Rediscovering the Triune God,* p. 8. See also, Gunton, *Promise of Trinitarian Theology,* p. 39.

106. "Can a clause deriving from one theological tradition simply be inserted in a creed deriving from another theological tradition without council?" Stylianopoulos and Heim, eds., *Spirit of Truth,* p. 32.

107. It is an established view in the East that the Father is the "source" (*arche*) of the divinity. In defense, see, e.g., Ware, *The Orthodox Church,* pp. 210-14.

subordinate the Spirit to Jesus, which in turn may lead to an anemic pneumatology in the doctrine of the church, doctrine of salvation, and so forth.[108]

Notwithstanding the overly passionate and at times historically biased critique by the Eastern tradition, its main target should not be dismissed.[109] At the same time, it can be argued that while ecumenically it is not permissible to alter a commonly agreed, binding church pronouncement without the other party's consent, that does not necessarily make it heretical. It is highly ironic that notwithstanding its extremely high regard for scriptural authority, the Eastern Church is not willing to grant the importance of the lack of clarity about the derivation of the Spirit in the NT. That observation alone should help avoid the charge of heresy. While there are those few contemporary theologians who support the *filioque* for one reason or another,[110] there is a wide consensus among Western theologians, both Roman Catholic and Protestant, about the need to delete the addition and thus return to the original form of the creed[111] or search for an alternative formulation, such as that the

108. Vladimir Lossky has most dramatically articulated the charge of "Christomonism" against Western theology. According to him, Christianity in the West is seen as unilaterally referring to Christ, the Spirit being an addition to the church, to its ministries and sacraments. Lossky, "The Procession of the Holy Spirit." See also, Nissiotis, "Main Ecclesiological Problem of the Second Vatican Council." All three objections — that it was a unilateral act, that it subordinates the Son to the Spirit, and that it compromises the Father's monarchy — were already presented by the most vocal critic in history, the ninth-century patriarch of Constantinople Photius, in his *On the Mystagogy of the Holy Spirit*, pp. 51-52, 71-72 especially.

109. For an important Orthodox statement, see Needham, "Filioque Clause," pp. 142-62.

110. Well known is the defense of *filioque* by Karl Barth, who feared that dismissing it would mean ignoring the biblical insistence on the Spirit being the Spirit of the Son (*CD* I/1, p. 480). Gerald Bray defends the addition with reference to the doctrine of salvation. In his opinion, the Eastern doctrine of *theosis* with its focus on pneumatology severs the relationship between Son (atonement) and Spirit. Bray, "The *Filioque* Clause," pp. 142-43. While I disagree with Bray, I also commend his relating the question of the *filioque* to the Spirit, which is indeed at the heart of Eastern theology. For this, see further, the comment by Theodore Stylianopoulos ("Biblical Background of the Article on the Holy Spirit," p. 171): "At stake was not an abstract question but the truth of Christian salvation." For this quotation, I am indebted to Letham, *The Holy Trinity*, p. 203.

111. For a helpful discussion, see Vischer, *Spirit of God, Spirit of Christ*. For Roman Catholic support of the removal of the *filioque* clause, see Congar, *I Believe in the Holy Spirit*, 3:72-75. In addition to Moltmann and Pannenberg, to be discussed in what follows, a strong defender of the Eastern view has been the Reformed theologian Thomas F. Torrance, who was instrumental in the Reformed-Orthodox dialogue. For the dialogue, see T. Torrance, ed., *Theological Dialogue between Orthodox and Reformed Churches*, 2:219-32. For his own views in this respect, see T. Torrance, *Trinitarian Perspectives*, pp. 110-43. For these references to Torrance, I am indebted to Letham, *The Holy Trinity*, p. 218 n. 66.

Spirit proceeds "from the Father through the Son."[112] Moltmann has for years appealed for the removal of the addition and has suggested a more conciliar way of putting it, namely, that the Spirit proceeds "from the Father of the Son." He wants to emphasize the biblical idea of the reciprocity of Spirit and Son.[113] The alternative to *filioque,* "from the Father through the Son," would also be acceptable to the Christian East. It would defend the monarchy of the Father (and in that sense, some kind of subordination of the Son to the Father, an idea not foreign to the East) and still be ambiguous enough.[114]

The removal of the *filioque* clause does not have to make theologians blind to seeing the benefits behind the idea. The *filioque* may highlight relationality and communality, the Spirit being the shared love between Father and Son (and by extension, between the triune God and the world). Furthermore, on this side of Pentecost, it reminds us of the importance of resurrection and ascension: the risen Christ in Spirit is the presence of Christ. "In this work of transcending and applying the historical event of Jesus Christ to our personal lives, we must think of the Spirit as proceeding from Jesus Christ."[115] Appreciating these benefits, however, need not lead to refusing to delete the clause (or amending it in a way acceptable to the East). In the same vein, the liabilities of the Western tradition's pneumatology mentioned above — the thin pneumatology of much of traditional Western theology of the church and salvation — do not go away with the mere fixing of the creedal clause.

Having now established the deity of the Holy Spirit in the context of the Christian doctrine of the Trinity, it is time to begin the work of relating the Spirit to the works of the triune God in the world, as well as claims about the Spirit(s) in the cosmos and among other faith traditions. The first task is to look at the work of the divine Spirit in the world God has created, the role of the Spirit in creation.

---

112. Bobrinskoy, *Mystery of the Trinity,* pp. 302-3.

113. Moltmann, *Trinity and the Kingdom,* pp. 178-79, 185-87.

114. Bobrinskoy, *Mystery of the Trinity,* pp. 302-3. I am indebted to Letham, *The Holy Trinity,* p. 217 n. 64. For incisive comments, see also, O'Collins, *The Tripersonal God,* p. 139.

115. Peters, *God as Trinity,* p. 66.

3. The Spirit in Creation

Creation as the Gift of Divine Hospitality: A Trinitarian Account of Creation

In his exposition of the creation narrative in Genesis (1:2), Luther paints this most delightful and poetic trinitarian picture of the Spirit at work in creation: "The Father creates heaven and earth out of nothing through the Son . . . the Word. Over these the Holy Spirit broods. As a hen broods her eggs, keeping them warm in order to hatch her chicks, and, as it were, to bring them to life through heat, so Scripture says that the Holy Spirit brooded, as it were, on the waters to bring to life those substances which were to be quickened and adorned. For it is the office of the Holy Spirit to make alive."[1]

While Christian tradition has always attributed the creation to the God of the Bible, it has not always been successful in establishing a distinctively *trinitarian* account of creation.[2] Even luminaries such as Thomas Aquinas seemed to conceive creation predominantly as the work of the one God as the "first cause."[3] Thomas's approach in this respect is inferior to that of Luther or many of the Fathers. To the Cappadocian Saint Basil, the great ancient pneumatologist, we owe this classical rule: "And in the creation bethink thee

---

1. Luther, *Lectures on Genesis* 1-5; in *LW* 1:9; for comments, see Prenter, *Spiritus Creator,* p. 192.

2. For an important discussion, see Anne Hunt, *Trinity,* chap. 5: "Trinity and Creation, Ecology and Evolution."

3. Aquinas, *ST* 1.44.1.

first, I pray thee, of the original cause of all things that are made, the Father; of the creative cause, the Son; of the perfecting cause, the Spirit; so that the ministering spirits subsist by the will of the Father, are brought into being by the operation of the Son, and perfected by the presence of the Spirit."[4]

But why create the world? if we may ask. Isn't the eternal trinitarian life in itself the most profound blessedness and fecundity? Behind the trinitarian account of creation is a robust theology of gift, divine hospitality. Ultimately, there is no other "reason" for the creation than the infinite goodness and love of God. Even more: not only is the triune God lavishing upon us the gift of creation. God also donates God's own being, the Ultimate Gift — or, as tradition also puts it, the "uncreated grace." In Luther this trinitarian theology of divine self-donation comes to a remarkable clarity and beauty:

> These are the three persons and one God, who has given himself to us all wholly and completely, with all that he is and has. The Father gives himself to us, with heaven and earth and all the creatures, in order that they may serve us and benefit us. But this gift has become obscured and useless through Adam's fall. Therefore the Son himself subsequently gave himself and bestowed all his works, sufferings, wisdom, and righteousness, and reconciled us to the Father, in order that restored to life and righteousness, we might also know and have the Father and his gifts. But because this grace would benefit no one if it remained so profoundly hidden and could not come to us, the Holy Spirit comes and gives himself to us also, wholly and completely.[5]

In this divine giving, bringing into existence the cosmos, the triune God works jointly. Creation is the united work of Father, Son, and Spirit.[6] This is to follow the ancient rule of the indivisibility of the works of the Trinity *ad extra.*[7]

---

4. Basil, *On the Holy Spirit* 16.38.

5. *LW* 37:366; WA 26:505-6; an important discussion of the hospitality of God can be found in Newlands and Smith, *Hospitable God.*

6. For promising efforts to cast a trinitarian doctrine of creation in the scientific context, see K. H. Reich, "Doctrine of the Trinity," pp. 383-405; Polkinghorne, "Universe in a Trinitarian Perspective"; Bozack, "The Thermodynamical Triple Point," pp. 39-41.

7. Although formulated by Augustine and often called "Augustine's rule," it is by no means his invention. It is rather the common doctrine of Christian tradition; see, e.g., Athanasius, *Letters to Serapion* 1.28; *Four Discourses against the Arians* 2.18, 41; 3.12, 15; Gregory of Nyssa, *On "Not Three Gods"* 5; Augustine, *Letter* 174.17; *On the Trinity* 1.7; 2.3, 9; 5.15; Aquinas, *ST* 1.32.1; 1.45.6.

In the trinitarian logic, the Son/Logos represents the agency and distinction of creation from God, whereas the Spirit — the "Go-Between"[8] — is the life principle and bond of unity between God and creation, as well as among the creatures[9] (as discussed in chap. 3 of *Creation and Humanity*). Because it is a trinitarian act, it allows for an authentic personal interaction between the triune God and the world, affirming both intimate connection and real distinction. Furthermore, trinitarian theology safeguards the divine freedom and makes the coming into existence of the created reality the function of the divine love and goodness.[10] At the same time, it honors the God-given limited freedom of creation as distinct but not separate from the Creator: "If the world is too closely tied to the being of God, its own proper reality is endangered, for it is too easily swallowed up into the being of God, and so deprived of its own proper existence."[11]

Even when the trinitarian logic has been followed, too often the theologies of creation have not been attentive to the distinct role of the Spirit; rather, Father and Son have been in the forefront.[12] That said, the desire to highlight the Spirit's role in bringing about and sustaining life has nothing to do with setting up a "competition" among the trinitarian members — as if to say that the Spirit can do more than the Son! Rather, it is to acknowledge the distinctive contribution of the Spirit in the joint trinitarian work of God.[13]

Beginning from the mid–twentieth century, the Spirit's role in the Trinity in general and her cosmic, life-giving power in particular have been rediscovered in theology. The following section will investigate the implications of that profound development in order to prepare us for a deeper, constructive reflection on the pneumatological-trinitarian theology of creation. That dis-

---

8. "As a believer in the Creator Spirit, I would say that deep within the fabric of the universe, the Spirit is present as the Go-Between who confronts each isolated spontaneous particle with the beckoning reality of the larger whole and so compels it to relate to others in a particular way; and that it is he who at every stage lures the inert organisms forward by giving an inner awareness and recognition of the unattained." J. V. Taylor, *The Go-Between God*, p. 31.

9. For the classic statement about the need to affirm relationality by Albert Einstein himself, see Einstein, *Autobiographical Notes*, p. 31; for important discussion, see Vondey, "Holy Spirit and the Physical Universe," pp. 30-31.

10. For comments, see Gunton, *The Triune Creator*, pp. 53-56.

11. Gunton, *The Triune Creator*, p. 66. Barth's way of highlighting both the correspondence and dissimilarities between the uncreated and created realities, between the inner-trinitarian fellowship and the fellowship of God and the creatures, is an important principle (see *CD* III/1, p. 50).

12. Similarly Yong, *The Spirit of Creation*, p. 23.

13. So also, Rogers, *After the Spirit*, p. 60.

cussion will lead us into an engagement of contemporary natural sciences for a better understanding of the origin and continuation of the life of the cosmos. Particularly important a topic in current religion-science dialogue is the condition and nature of divine acts. To a contemporary trinitarian theology of creation also belongs the urgent task of ecology and flourishing of nature, for which pneumatology contains profound resources.

The Theological Rediscovery of Cosmic Pneumatologies

Parallel to what happened in Christology in terms of the replacement of the cosmic vision of Christ's agency in creation and reconciliation (Col. 1:15-17; Heb. 1:3-4)[14] by the reductionist and pietist personalist Savior figure, the Spirit's role as the omnipresent agency of bringing and sustaining all life (Gen. 1:2; Ps. 104:29-30) was often lost in tradition. The gradual rediscovery of this lost cosmic pneumatology is one of the most exciting developments in recent theologies.[15] It allows us to highlight the Spirit's capacity in bringing about life in the trinitarian act of creation. As the eco-feminist Elizabeth Johnson reminds us, "Of all the activities that theology attributes to the Spirit, the most significant is this: the Spirit is the creative origin of all life. In the words of the Nicene Creed, the Spirit is *vivificantem,* vivifier or life-giver. This designation refers to creation not just at the beginning of time but continuously: the Spirit is the unceasing, dynamic flow of divine power that sustains the universe, bringing forth life."[16] While not a new or novel idea in theology — just recall the rich metaphors employed in the medieval mystical traditions of Hildegard of Bingen's "greening" of the Spirit or Saint Bernard of Clairvaux's "living water"[17] or Thomas Aquinas's hymn of creation[18] — what makes the current rediscovery of the Spirit's creative agency significant is that thereby the whole ministry, role, and work of the Spirit is put in a robust cosmic, evolutionary, and scientific context.[19]

As recently as in 1982, we could still hear complaints about the omission

---

14. See chap. 4 in *Creation and Humanity.*

15. Moltmann, *God in Creation,* p. xiv; for the "Cosmic Spirit," see pp. 98-103.

16. Johnson, *Women, Earth, and Creator Spirit,* p. 42; see also, Pinnock, *Flame of Love,* pp. 49-50.

17. See Dreyer, "An Advent of the Spirit," pp. 123-62.

18. In Donahoe, *Early Christian Hymns,* pp. 155-59.

19. An accessible and highly insightful account is by the Australian Roman Catholic Denis Edwards, *Ecology at the Heart of Faith,* chap. 3 particularly.

in mainline pneumatologies of cosmic dimensions. In his acclaimed state-of-current-pneumatology essay "The Determinative Doctrine of the Holy Spirit," the American Benedictine Kilian McDonnell lamented that both in "Protestantism and Catholicism, the doctrine of the Holy Spirit, or pneumatology, has to do mostly with private, not public experience," and that therefore pneumatology has lost connection with the rest of the world and life. Hence, he proposed, in contemporary theology a definite turn is needed "from a theology of the Word to a theology of the world."[20]

Not surprisingly, the Benedictine theologian finds much to commend in Tillich's life- and world-affirming theology in general and in his pneumatology in particular.[21] Importantly, Tillich's account of "life and its ambiguities" reflected the evolutionary worldview in which reality is seen in terms of "the metaphor of 'dimension,' together with correlative concepts such as 'realm' and 'grade.'" These all relate to a "multidimensional unity of life."[22] Furthermore, in contrast to theological tradition, Tillich also considered the "theology of the inorganic," not only organic life.[23] When speaking of "the basic functions of life," he considered the categories of self-identity, self-alteration, and "self-integration," culminating in "self-creation" and "self-transcendence," all dynamic conceptions in which the Spirit is at work.[24] The rest of Tillich's pneumatology contains a profound analysis of the forms of "the Spiritual Presence" in human spirit,[25] religion, culture, and morality — and interspersed is the discussion of the meaning of spiritual presence in the "new being" (Christ) and "new community" (church).

That said, Tillich's conception of the Spirit's role in the world also suffers from limitations that must be corrected on the way toward a fully trinitarian-pneumatological account. Tillich's placement of his discussion "The Spirit of Life" in the third volume of his systematics shares two interrelated problems. First, it makes the Spirit's work derivative from and

20. K. McDonnell, "The Determinative Doctrine of the Holy Spirit," p. 142. Thus the title of his recently released landmark work, *The Other Hand of God: The Holy Spirit as the Universal Touch and Goal.*

21. K. McDonnell, "The Determinative Doctrine of the Holy Spirit," p. 155.

22. Tillich, *ST* 3:14-15; this first chapter at the beginning of his pneumatology is titled "Life and Its Ambiguities."

23. Tillich, *ST* 3:18.

24. Introduced in *ST* 3:30-31 and subsequently discussed one at a time.

25. Tillich's way of relating the divine and human spirits in a mutual manner is dramatically different from the robust juxtaposing in Barth's pneumatology as presented in Karl Barth and Heinrich Barth, "Der Heilige Geist und das christliche Leben," pp. 39-105. For Moltmann's harsh criticism of Barth, see Moltmann, *Spirit of Life,* pp. 6-7.

dependent on that of the Son[26] and Father. Second, it thus moves the Spirit from the first to the second moment. These concerns are ironically reflected in Tillich's conception of the divine Spirit as the "answer" to the questions related to the ambiguities of life.[27] On the contrary, the Spirit is as much a "question" (challenge) to culture and sciences as an answer. Related, Tillich's modalistic orientation with a thin trinitarian conception assigns to the Spirit a secondary role. Nevertheless, Tillich's achievements are noteworthy in the rediscovery of a new pneumatology.

Around the same time, the Lutheran Tillich's contemporary, the Dutch Reformed theologian Hendrikus Berkhof, attempted a powerful revision of his own tradition's pneumatology in light of the heritage of classical liberalism and the new challenges of the twentieth-century context. In his 1964 work *The Doctrine of the Holy Spirit*, Berkhof envisioned the Spirit as the "vitality" of God, "God's inspiring breath by which he grants life in creation and re-creation."[28] With reference to a number of key OT passages from Genesis 1:2 to Job 33:4, he said that "[w]e understand that the same God in action, the same *ruach* working in the deeds of salvation, is also the secret of the entire created world. . . . God's Spirit creates and sustains the life of nature." Rightly he observed that "[t]his relation between the Spirit and creation is much neglected in Christian thinking."[29] Behind Berkhof's emerging creation pneumatology is the correct understanding that "'Spirit' means that God is a vital God, who grants vitality to his creation," and therefore the Spirit can be defined as "God's inspiring breath by which he grants life in creation and re-creation."[30] Unfortunately, as with Tillich (and even more radically), Berkhof's pneumatology suffers from a deep modalistic orientation.

Among contemporary theologians, Pannenberg has spoken robustly of the need to overcome the reductionist tendencies in the Christian conception of the Spirit and forge an integral link with the whole of creation.[31] This is also the way to secure the principle of continuity among the many works of the Spirit:

26. Surprisingly, Tillich (*ST* 2:180) makes the subordinationist tendency a theological theme: "that the Christ is not the Christ without the church makes the doctrines of the Spirit and of the Kingdom of God integral parts of the christological work."

27. Tillich, *ST* 3:4.

28. H. Berkhof, *Doctrine of the Holy Spirit*, p. 14.

29. H. Berkhof, *Doctrine of the Holy Spirit*, pp. 95-96.

30. H. Berkhof, *Doctrine of the Holy Spirit*, p. 14.

31. Pannenberg, "Doctrine of the Spirit," pp. 11-12. For a similar metaphorical correspondence between spirit and field, see also, T. Torrance, *Christian Doctrine of God*, p. 83.

God's Spirit is not only active in human redemption as he teaches us to know the eternal Son of the Father in Jesus of Nazareth and moves our hearts to praise of God by faith, love, and hope. The Spirit is at work already in creation as God's breath, the origin of all movement and all life, and only against this background of his activity as the Creator of all life can we rightly understand on the one hand his work in the ecstatics of human conscious life, and on the other hand his role in the bringing forth of the new life in the resurrection of the dead.[32]

The German Lutheran theologian Pannenberg's Reformed colleague Moltmann, with his highly acclaimed book *The Spirit of Life* — with the original German subtitle *Eine ganzheitliche Pneumatologie* ("a holistic pneumatology")[33] — reflects the same desire for an all-encompassing, life-affirming account of the work of the Spirit. For that to happen, the meaning of the word "Spirit" needs revision, Moltmann surmises. He not only affirms enthusiastically the evolutionary framework but also anticipates important current insights according to which it is reductionist to consider "spirit" as "mind" or "reason" (let alone "ghost"), and rather imagines "spirit" as the principle of life and as "unity of life power."[34]

Whereas Berkhof's and Tillich's attempts to rediscover the creational role of the Spirit suffered from the lack of a fully trinitarian account, Pannenberg's and Moltmann's robustly trinitarian pneumatologies come to aid here. As long as there is the "tendency to view the Holy Spirit solely as *the Spirit of redemption*," notes Moltmann, the Spirit's main task will be to give "men and women the assurance of the eternal blessedness of their souls." But then this "redemptive Spirit is cut off both from bodily life and from the life of nature." The irony is that Christians "then seek and experience in the Spirit of Christ a power that is different from the divine energy of life, which according to the Old Testament ideas interpenetrates all the living." Behind this "continuing Platonization of Christianity" is not only a general trinitarian anemia but also a continuing affirmation of the subordinationist *filioque* clause:

> This has meant that the Holy Spirit has come to be understood solely as "the Spirit of Christ," and not at the same time as "the Spirit of the Father."

---

32. Pannenberg, *ST* 3:1.

33. The English translation of the subtitle of Moltmann's *Spirit of Life,* namely, *A Universal Affirmation,* is neither accurate nor very helpful. The German original means "holistic pneumatology," and that is the nomenclature also used in the preface (p. xiii); it could also be translated as "all-encompassing" or "comprehensive."

34. Tillich, *ST* 3:21-24 particularly.

As *the Spirit of Christ* it is *the redemptive Spirit.* But the work of creation too is ascribed to the Father, so *the Spirit of the Father* is also *the Spirit of creation.* If redemption is placed in radical discontinuity to creation, then "the Spirit of Christ" has no longer anything to do with Yahweh's *ruach.*[35]

The possibility of perceiving God in all things and all things in God is grounded theologically on the understanding of the Spirit of God as the power of creation and the wellspring of life (Job 33:4; Ps. 104:29ff.). Every experience of a creation of the Spirit is hence also an experience of the Spirit itself, Moltmann argues.[36] He rightly notes that a turn to a robust creational pneumatology pushes theology toward panentheism, as it attempts to "discover God *in* all the beings he has created and to find his life-giving Spirit *in* the community of creation that they share."[37] In light of the fact that "God's *ruach* is the life force immanent in all the living, in body, sexuality, ecology, and politics,"[38] we can speak of "immanent transcendence."[39] Berkhof puts it even more dramatically: "So intimate is the Spirit to man's life that we sometimes feel ourselves on the brink of pantheism."[40]

This remarkable rediscovery in mainline Euro-American theology of cosmic and creational pneumatology, coupled with a panentheistic way of conceiving the God-world relationship, receives a lot of support from eco-feminists (such as Elizabeth Johnson and Sallie McFague), science-religion advocates, and theologians of the First Nations, as well as in accounts of the Spirit among theologians in the Global South.[41] An important contribution of feminist theologians involves highlighting the importance of metaphors and "models" of God (McFague, J. Soskice, and Johnson, among others).[42] These thinkers rightly remind us that the literalist, patriarchal, male-dominated language of God easily leads to dualistic, hierarchical, and oppressive accounts of the God-world relationship. Those concepts and models of God major on

---

35. Moltmann, *Spirit of Life,* pp. 8-9, emphasis in original.

36. Moltmann, *Spirit of Life,* p. 35.

37. Moltmann, *God in Creation,* p. xi, emphasis in original; similarly Johnson, *Women, Earth, and Creator Spirit,* p. 42.

38. Moltmann, *Spirit of Life,* pp. 225-56.

39. Moltmann, *Spirit of Life,* p. 35.

40. H. Berkhof, *Doctrine of the Holy Spirit,* p. 95.

41. For specific textual testimonies and editorial explanations, including rich bibliographies, see my *Spirit and Salvation,* chaps. 14-17.

42. A useful discussion particularly with regard to creation, including theology-science dialogue, is McFague, "Models of God," pp. 249-71.

power images such as king and ruler. Hence, the biblically based images such as "God as potter who creates the cosmos by molding it, God as speaker who with a word brings the world to be out of nothing,"[43] or "God the creator as mother who gives birth to the universe"[44] are needed to critique and balance theological language.

On the basis of these leads and the best intuitions of tradition, a new constructive proposal dubbed "classical panentheism" was constructed and defended in my *Trinity and Revelation* (chap. 10 particularly). That model seeks to steer a radical middle road between transcendence-driven classical theistic ways of conceiving the God-world relationship and deeply immanentist-driven contemporary panentheisms of process thought and some less radical feminist, postcolonial, and other approaches. A dynamic, pneumatologically loaded trinitarian theology funds the project of classical panentheism. With these insights in mind, let us attempt a constructive account of a creational pneumatology, first exploiting theological resources and then, in the subsequent main section, drawing also from natural sciences and philosophy of science.

Toward a Creational Pneumatology

The Cosmic Divine Breath of Life

Among the many "attributes" of the infinite creator God, none surpasses the importance of the description of the "living God," God as the source of life. Indeed, the God who "'has life in Himself' . . . (John 5:26)" is "livingness" in the inner-trinitarian divine life, not only in relation to creation.[45] To be God is to be Life. In other words, while we think of God's existence "as an active presence in the reality of the world . . . [we] must think of it as an existence transcending the world and worldly things" in order for us to be able to affirm God as "eternal and thus high above the perishability of created things."[46] This is what the crucial biblical description of God as "spirit" (John 4:24) means; God's "spirituality" is a statement not about separation from the world but rather about God infinitely transcending (and thus also embracing) the limitations and features of the created "flesh."

43. McFague, "Models of God," p. 250.
44. McFague, "Models of God," p. 249.
45. Wynne, "The Livingness of God," p. 192.
46. Pannenberg, *ST* 1:357.

Early theology had a hard time in affirming the idea of God's Spirit as the spirit of life. Following Hellenistic philosophy, theology conceived the divine spirit as "will" or "reason" in order to avoid the absurd idea of associating God with anything material — with absurd notions of divisibility, composition, extensions, and locality — because of the mistaken interpretation of the incomparability of God as incorporeal. The nonphysical affirmation, however, seemed necessary in light of the Stoic understanding according to which even the divine *pneuma* was a very fine substance, stuff.[47] With that danger lurking, the turn to defining "spirit" in terms of reason and will seemed both necessary and a useful tactic. To define (divine) Spirit as rationality — which by the time of modernity became "mind" in Descartes — is not as much wrong as it is reductionist. What I mean is this: the conception of the Spirit as reason (or will) misses the mainline biblical, particularly OT, teaching according to which *ruach* is a life-embracing principle of life. Not only reason or will but also the bodily, the earthly, the "animal" — everything created and living — owes its existence to the divine Spirit.

Only with a return to a holistic and comprehensive biblical account of the *ruach Yahweh* as the life principle, not detached from but rather energizing and supporting all life of the cosmos, including the physical/material, could theology correct the pneumatological deficit.[48] That turn also helps rediscover the ancient conviction that "[t]here is a cosmic range to the operations of the Spirit, the Lord and giver of life. . . . Spirit is the ecstasy that implements God's abundance and triggers the overflow of divine self-giving. . . . The universe in its entirety is the field of its operations."[49] According to the biblical testimony, *ruach Elohim* "was moving over the face of the waters" (Gen. 1:2),[50] "breathing in" life (2:7) into creatures.

---

47. Pannenberg, *ST* 1:372-73.

48. See the important discussion in Moltmann, *Spirit of Life,* p. 40.

49. Pinnock, *Flame of Love,* pp. 49-50.

50. Even a quick look at biblical commentaries tells us how widely the meaning of the expression "Spirit of God" has been debated. Briefly put: Is it a reference to a rushing wind sent by God or to "God's Spirit"? Not only is the rendering "the wind of God" unknown in the canon and hence highly inconceivable, but also, more importantly, from the Christian theological perspective, the understanding of the reference to the third person of the Trinity (notwithstanding the absence of this rendering in the original Jewish canon) hardly needs justification. For an important statement in support, see Jenson, "Aspects of a Doctrine of Creation," p. 22; for an important discussion with a leading exegete in support of this interpretation, see Montague, "Fire in the Word," pp. 37-40. It is significant that already Luther in his *Lectures on Genesis* (*LW* 1:8) defends the "Spirit of God" over against the interpretation as "wind."

> By the word of the LORD the heavens were made,
>   and all their host by the breath [*ruach*] of his mouth. (Ps. 33:6)[51]

This very same divine energy also sustains all life in the cosmos. All creation is "en-spirited by God"[52] and needs the divine breath for its continuance and activity:

> When you [Yahweh] send forth your Spirit [*ruach*], they are created;
>   and you renew the face of the ground. (Ps. 104:30 NRSV)

Similarly, when Yahweh "take[s] away their breath [*ruach*], they die / and return to the dust" (v. 29).[53] Moltmann's summary comment is on target: in biblical traditions, "all divine activity is pneumatic in its efficacy."[54] In the Christian East, both in tradition and in contemporary theology, the linking of the Spirit with creation has been a rule and custom. The Russian-born Sergius Bulgakov puts it succinctly:

> In the Divine life, the Holy Spirit realizes the fullness adequate to this life and plumbs the depths of God by a unique eternal act. In creaturely being, the Holy Spirit is the force of being and the giver of life, but, according to the very concept of creation, this being and this life exist only as becoming, that is, not in fullness but only in the striving toward fullness. . . . This natural grace of the Holy Spirit, which constitutes the very foundation of the being of creation, exists in the very *flesh* of the world, in the matter of the world.[55]

---

51. Passages such as this (Ps. 33:6) alone would repudiate Gerhard von Rad's odd claim that the cosmological, creative notion of the Spirit is unknown to the OT; *Genesis*, pp. 49-50. For a careful repudiation of von Rad's thesis, see Hubbard, "The Spirit and Creation," pp. 71-90. In support of the cosmological interpretation is also the widespread ancient rabbinic interpretation to that effect; see Ochs, "Genesis 1–2," p. 9; I am indebted to Yong, *The Spirit of Creation*, p. 155.

52. McDaniel, "Where Is the Holy Spirit Anyway?" p. 171.

53. For profound comments see Calvin, *Commentary on Psalms 93–119*, in *Calvin's Commentaries: Psalms 93–119*, vol. 4, on 104:29. Available at http://www.ccel.org.

54. Moltmann, *God in Creation*, p. 9; see further, pp. 9-13, for an exposition of the role of the Spirit in creation, including the connection to the Nicene (Constantinopolitan) Creed's reference to the Holy Spirit as the Giver of Life, usually connected only with the "new life" in Christ.

55. Bulgakov, *The Comforter*, p. 220, emphasis in original.

To do justice to the infinite nature of the cosmic breath of life, constructive theology ought to search for diverse metaphors, symbols, and other elusive conceptual devices.[56] Metaphors — fittingly called means of "misnaming"[57] in that they allow us "an intuitive perception of the similarity of the dissimilars"[58] — not only help us say "more" than mere propositions, they also facilitate participatory knowledge as a remedy to the one-sided possessive, technocratic hegemony of the post-Enlightenment world. At the same time, metaphors also help us appreciate the relational, mutually dependent, and symbiotic nature of all created processes.[59] Seeking to capture some of the rich potential of creational pneumatology, Moltmann suggests the following kinds of metaphors, which also relate to scientific explanations:[60]

- The formative metaphors: the Spirit as energy, as space, and as gestalt
- The movement metaphors: the Spirit as tempest, as fire, and as love
- The mystical metaphors: the Spirit as source of light, as water, and as fertility

Theological imagination from the Global South has added many more important metaphors. The Korean-born theologian J. Y. Lee speaks of "[c]loth as a metaphor of the Spirit [that] protects and sustains all things on earth. Unlike the shield, a masculine metaphor of protection, it is closely associated with a feminine image in Asia. Women weave cloth and use it for the protection and decoration of the body." Drawing from the rich Confucian traditions, Lee continues: "The Spirit as *ch'i* also weaves through the entire cosmos and gives life. The Spirit is a weaver and a protector of all things on earth, for cloth is the symbol of her presence." He also employs metaphors of mother, both human and animal, and "kettle," related to cooking, and concludes: "In fact, the Spirit as *ch'i* is the vitality of the material principle, and the nourishment of soul is, in fact, the nourishment of the body."[61]

Before deepening and widening the investigation into the creative works

56. Moltmann, *God in Creation*, p. 2. The use of metaphors is not limited to theology; even science needs them and uses them liberally. Just think of expressions such as "big bang," "big bounce," "big crunch," and others. Soskice, *Metaphor and Religious Language*, p. 99; Happel, "Metaphors and Time Asymmetry."

57. See Polanyi and Prosch, *Meaning*, p. 75.

58. Aristotle, *Poetics*, chap. 22.

59. For important comments, see Moltmann, *Experiences in Theology*, p. 162.

60. Moltmann, *Spirit of Life*, chap. 12.

61. J. Y. Lee, *Trinity in Asian Perspective*, p. 104.

of the Spirit, we need another reminder of the trinitarian contours. Two important caveats must be added. First, the biblical teaching of God-as-Spirit has to do with the fact that "[l]ying behind God's relationship to the world as the giver of life is a prior internal divine relationship, an eternal relationship within the triune God," namely, that "as the Father has life in himself, so he has granted the Son also to have life in himself" (John 5:26).[62] There are both a trinitarian note here and the reminder of the importance of the immanent Trinity as the basis of all our reflections on the works and actions of God in the world. Second, from the trinitarian perspective, it must be added that God is not *only pneuma*. He is also a personal reality — more precisely a threefold personal reality. The divine Spirit exists in "personal centers," in the Father, the Son, and the Holy Spirit. In all of his creation, God the Father is working through his Word and through his life-giving Spirit.[63] As long as constructive theology minds the (immanent) divine nature of the Spirit of God, in the eternal communion of the three, and therefore also the Spirit's personal nature, pneumatological imagination has the freedom to experiment with various ways to highlight the energy, vitality, and dynamic of the divine breath of life in the created reality.

The "Earthly" and Embodied Nature of the Creator Spirit

Above we discussed tradition's misguided (although well-meant) attempt to defend God's unbounded and infinite nature/essence by avoiding its linking with "spirit" (to combat the physical connotations of that era's understanding of *pneuma*). Another way tradition sought to defend the uniqueness of the divinity — including the Spirit — was by emphasizing transcendence in fear that too close a linking with the "earth" might compromise the absolute divine freedom. Both of these tactics led to the separation of the divine Spirit from the earthly, fleshly, created. An unfortunate implication was that spirit(uality) was elevated above the physical, and at times the two were even put in opposition.[64] In the witty expression of the American religious scholar Eugene F. Rogers Jr., "The Spirit, who in classical Christian discourse 'pours out on all flesh,' had, in modern discourse, floated free of bodies altogether."[65] As a result, "the Spirit has grown dull because [it is] unembodied."[66] The removal of the spirit from

62. Grenz, *Theology for the Community of God*, p. 83.
63. See Berkson, *Fields of Force*.
64. See Rivera, *Touch of Transcendence*, p. 7.
65. Rogers, *After the Spirit*, p. 1.
66. Rogers, *After the Spirit*, p. 3.

the "earthly," however, is misguided. The most profound theological statement against divorcing the divine Spirit from creation and the physical is the incarnation, an event of embodiment. Consider the statement by Moltmann: "If we wish to understand the Old Testament idea of the spirit, we must forget the word 'spirit,' which belongs to Western culture. Unlike in Greek, Latin, and contemporary Western languages in which spirit is taken as an antithesis to bodily and material, in the OT, the basic term (Yahweh's) *ruach* means strong wind or tempest. Its theological meaning is the principle of life."[67]

Interestingly, this same point was made already in the nineteenth century by Johann Christoph Blumhardt, from whom Barth, Moltmann, and other twentieth-century luminaries drew. Speaking of "the redemption of the body," Blumhardt states, "*The Spirit must embody itself. It must enter into our earthly life; it must happen that deity be born in flesh so that it can overcome this earthly world. God is active Spirit only when he gets something of our material underfoot; before that, he is mere idea. The Spirit would govern life.*"[68] This is what Rogers means by saying "the Spirit befriends matter."[69] Similarly, leading eco-pneumatologist M. I. Wallace wishes to "retrieve a central but neglected Christian theme — the idea of God as carnal Spirit who imbues all things — as the linchpin for forging a green spirituality responsive to the environmental needs of our time." He says: "I believe that hope for a renewed earth is best founded on belief in God as Earth Spirit, the compassionate, all-encompassing divine force within the biosphere who inhabits earth community and continually works to maintain the integrity of all forms of life."[70] This is because "spirit" in the biblical understanding is not something opposed to "earthly" or "bodily," but rather is the divine life-energy.[71] The classical doctrine of the divine omnipresence also teaches us that God exists in everything. God is never really distant from creation, but neither can God be equated with the creaturely. The distinction lies in this: God *is* being, but all created things only *have* being. Creatures have their being by virtue of participation in God's being.[72] Consider what Irenaeus said: "For no part of Creation is left void of Him: He has filled all things everywhere, remaining present with His own Father."[73]

67. Moltmann, *Spirit of Life*, p. 40.
68. In Eller, ed., *Thy Kingdom Come*, p. 18, emphasis in original.
69. Rogers, *After the Spirit*, p. 55.
70. M. Wallace, *Fragments of the Spirit*, p. 6.
71. Moltmann, *Spirit of Life*, pp. 225-26; see also, p. 40.
72. A. M. Clifford, "Creation," p. 218.
73. Irenaeus, *Against Heresies* 8.1.

The biblical metaphors of the Spirit taken from nature are meaningful and justified. Just consider these: the "animating breath," "the healing wind," "the living water," and "cleansing fire."[74] To speak of the "earthen spirit"[75] is not to undermine the divine uniqueness of the Spirit but rather to speak of the divine infinity in which finite and infinite are both transcended and embraced simultaneously.[76] In other words, grounding creation in God is not to subsume the divine life in the immanent but rather to give meaning and "ground" to creation itself.[77] In the words of the postcolonialist M. Rivera: "God is irreducibly Other, always beyond our grasp. But not beyond our touch."[78] Useful in this respect is the feminist Kathryn Tanner's distinction between "contrastive" and "noncontrastive" accounts of divine transcendence. Whereas the former contrasts transcendence and immanence inversely, meaning that the more focus on one, the less focus on the other, the latter "suggests an extreme of divine involvement with the world — a divine involvement in the form of a productive agency extending to everything that is in equally direct manner." In other words, the "noncontrastive" approach saves God from becoming one being among others and rather supports divine transcendence simultaneously with robust presence and activity everywhere.[79] "The God who is transcendent in relation to the world, and the God who is immanent in that world are one and the same God."[80] A merely immanentist account of God makes God sympathetic but powerless; a merely transcendent account, on the other hand, distances God from earthly realities. Even in deepest immanence, God is *infinitely* present and beyond![81]

An important benefit from affirming the panentheistic immanence of the transcendent Creator Spirit in the world relates to one of the most urgent tasks for contemporary theology: the preservation of the earth.[82] While all

74. M. Wallace, *Fragments of the Spirit*, p. 8; for other nature metaphors from the Bible, see M. Wallace, *Finding God in the Singing River*, pp. 6-9.

75. For this term I am indebted to M. Wallace, "Christian Animism," pp. 203-6. Wallace and some other contemporary theologians also speak of "Christian animism" to underline the earthly nature of the Spirit. See M. Wallace, *Green Christianity*, pp. 1-10; Abram, *Becoming Animal*.

76. For a detailed discussion of "relational transcendence," see chap. 5 in Rivera, *Touch of Transcendence*.

77. Cf. Rivera, *Touch of Transcendence*, p. 2.

78. Rivera, *Touch of Transcendence*, p. 2.

79. K. Tanner, *God and Creation*, chap. 2; see also, Rivera, *Touch of Transcendence*.

80. Moltmann, *God in Creation*, p. 15.

81. Cf. Cone, *Black Theology of Liberation*, p. 76.

82. As stated by the International Conference on Environmental Pollution and Remedi-

religious traditions have their role to play in the conservation of nature (a topic studied in chap. 14 of *Creation and Humanity*), let us focus here on Christian pneumatological potential.

"Green Pneumatology" and the Flourishing of Nature

Although Christian tradition's track record of keeping the earth is mixed at best — indeed, no better or worse than that of other faith traditions, let alone secular ideologies such as atheistic communism — deeply embedded in our spiritual tradition is the link between the Holy Spirit and the flourishing of nature. Just recall the numerous nature metaphors related to the Spirit in biblical traditions[83] and the above-mentioned nature-affirming visions in medieval mystical traditions — and beyond. Similarly, many contemporary nature metaphors such as J. Y. Lee's "cloth" or "weaver" invoke images of care[84] and supplement masculine God-language with female images of the Spirit, which are often more sensitive to the beauty and fragility of nature.[85]

In green pneumatological imaginations, the Holy Spirit has been depicted in terms of the "Wounded Spirit."[86] M. Wallace reminds us, "[i]f Spirit and earth mutually indwell each other, then God as Spirit is vulnerable to loss and destruction insofar as the earth is abused and despoiled."[87] While the theological depths of the metaphor of the Wounded Spirit should be harvested, it also has to be put in perspective. Some eco-theologians' talk about the vulnerability of the Spirit of God due to eco-catastrophe in terms of deicide, the "death of god,"[88] should be rejected. Behind this rhetoric is a naive and mistaken reductionist conception of the omnipotent, omniscient, and transcendent (Spirit of) God as prisoner to a tiny, insignificant planet that is among billions of other planets in one galaxy of a universe of (at least) ten

---

ation: "Environmental pollution is considered to be our world's most dangerous and constant threat" (http://icepr2013.international-aset.com/index.html) (7/14/2013).

83. On the beauty of the earth described through the sensibilities of the Spirit's presence on the Day of Pentecost, see Fatula, *Holy Spirit*, pp. 33-34.

84. J. Y. Lee, *Trinity in Asian Perspective*, p. 104; for other metaphors, see K. Kim, *Holy Spirit in the World*, p. 181.

85. Boff, *Holy Trinity*, p. 92; Comblin, *Holy Spirit and Liberation*, p. 49; Müller-Fahrenholz, *God's Spirit*, p. 24. For biblical and historical background, see S. Harvey, "Feminine Imagery for the Divine."

86. M. Wallace, "The Green Face of God," pp. 450-53.

87. M. Wallace, "The Green Face of God," p. 451.

88. M. Wallace, "The Green Face of God," p. 452.

billion other galaxies! The "eco"-wounds of the Spirit may be real, but they are far from fatal.

The task of a properly conceived green pneumatology is to help us imagine metaphors of flourishing, thriving, blossoming, and greening. A counterpart to that task is to cultivate our sensibilities toward the endangerment of nature and its diverse species. Both aspects help cultivate pneumatological sensibilities in the service of nature care.

The final task in this short outline of a cosmic, earthly, green pneumatology is to link the act of creation to its final culmination in the eschatological renewal of the heavens and the earth, the coming of the righteous rule of the triune God. Again, a robustly trinitarian account is needed even when the Spirit's distinctive tasks will be highlighted.

Spirit, Resurrection, and Eschatology: On the Way to the Final Consummation

The divine Spirit is not only the source and agency of creation and sustenance. The Spirit's mission is also to complete the divine economy. According to the ancient trinitarian *taxis,* the Spirit's role is that of the perfecter: "In the operation and the indwelling of the Spirit, the creation of the Father through the Son, and the reconciliation of the world with God through Christ, arrive at their goal. . . . All the works of God end in the presence of the Spirit."[89] In the words of the quantum physicist–priest J. Polkinghorne, "the sanctifying work of the Spirit is a continuing activity that awaits its final completion in the creation of the community of the redeemed, a consummation that will be manifested fully only at the eschaton."[90] The Creator Spirit is also the power of the eschatological renewal and consummation, the new creation (2 Cor. 5:17).[91] Already in the OT, particularly in Second Isaiah, the promise of "new creation" becomes a key theological theme. When Yahweh, the Creator, is "doing a new thing" (43:19), nothing less than a cosmic renewal will happen ("Every valley shall be lifted up, / and every mountain and hill be made low; / the uneven ground shall become level, / and the rough places a plain"; 40:4), and the "Glory of the LORD shall

---

89. Moltmann, *God in Creation,* p. 96; see also, Polkinghorne, "Hidden Spirit and the Cosmos," p. 171.

90. Polkinghorne, "Hidden Spirit and the Cosmos," p. 171.

91. Grenz, *Theology for the Community of God,* p. 379. See also, Oladipo, *Development of the Doctrine of the Holy Spirit,* p. 100.

be revealed" (40:5). Creation and *continuing* creation are linked together. Similarly, creation and redemption are integrally linked — but neither one is subsumed under the other; they are both presented as integral moments of one divine economy.[92]

The task of constructive theology is to help shift tradition's one-sided interest in "protological creation," the past, to "eschatological creation," the future. On the basis of Christ's resurrection, theology looks forward to the final redemption of not only spiritual but also bodily life.[93] It is highly significant that the resurrection of Christ is an eschatological act brought about by the power of the Father's Spirit (Rom. 1:4; 8:11; 1 Cor. 15:45).[94] Moltmann summarizes masterfully the relation of original creation to the resurrection, to the outpouring of the Spirit at Pentecost, all the way to the eschatological consummation:

> According to the New Testament testimonies, the outpouring of the Spirit and the experience of the energies of the Holy Spirit in the community of Christ belongs to the eschatological experience of salvation. The gift of the Spirit is the guarantee or "earnest" — the advance payment — of glory (II Cor. 1.22: 5.5; Eph. 1.14). The powers of the Spirit are the powers of the new creation. They therefore possess men and women, soul and body. They are the powers of the resurrection of the dead which proceed from the risen Christ and are testified to the world through the church, which is charismatically wakened to eternal life.... The power of the Spirit is the creative power of God, which justifies sinners and gives life to the dead. The gift of the Holy Spirit is therefore eternal life.[95]

Irenaeus's "evolutionary" view could have helped theology to find a better balance between the focus on the "innocence of the Paradise" and awaited perfection in the new creation. His theology conceived even the human person as the image of God in the process of continuing development and maturity.[96] Unlike the modernist naive optimism of linear develop-

92. R. J. Clifford ("The Hebrew Scriptures," p. 517) notes that the theme of new creation is linked with that of the exodus, the event that brought Israel into existence in the first place. For this reference, I am indebted to A. M. Clifford, "Creation," p. 203.

93. Moltmann, *God in Creation*, pp. 65-69. In expositing this theme, Moltmann references key pneumatological texts in Rom. 8:11; Joel 2:28; and Rom. 8:19-26.

94. See further, G. Thomas, "Resurrection to New Life," pp. 255-76.

95. Moltmann, *God in Creation*, p. 95.

96. Irenaeus, *Against Heresies* 4.38, section titled "Why Man Was Not Made Perfect

ment, however, Irenaeus understood clearly that the process of redemption and perfection "involves a faction, a breaking up,"[97] and is far from a smooth path.

The main Christian symbol of eschatology, namely, the kingdom of God, should not be reduced to merely individual hope or even the future hope of the whole people of God. Christian hope of the eschatological consummation includes the whole of God's creation, "the integration of the real history of human beings with the nature of the earth."[98] This holistic and "earthly" eschatological vision is masterfully expressed by the American Anabaptist theologian Thomas A. Finger: "Since the new creation arrives through God's Spirit, and since it reshapes the physical world, every theological locus is informed by the Spirit's transformation of matter-energy."[99] Christ's resurrection through the life-giving Spirit is already a foretaste of the "transformation of matter-energy" in new creation, "a transformation of the present nature *beyond* what emergence refers to."[100] The pneumatologically loaded eschatological openness of creation points to final consummation in which matter and physicality — no more than time — are not so much "deleted" as they are transformed, made transcendent, so to speak.[101]

Having briefly developed some key themes in the cosmic-creational pneumatology, we turn now to the urgent task of engaging the theological doctrine of the Spirit with contemporary natural sciences.

The Divine Spirit and the Natural Sciences

Setting the Context for Spirit-Science Engagement

A detailed investigation of the mutual relationship between Christian theology and the natural sciences, with the focus on the doctrine of creation and contemporary physical sciences' account of the origins of the cosmos and workings of natural processes, forms the core of *Creation and Humanity* (part 1). An integrally related task of that study is the investigation into the

---

from the Beginning." For an important discussion, see R. E. Brown, "On the Necessary Imperfection," pp. 17-25.

97. Farrow, "St. Irenaeus of Lyons," p. 348, cited in Gunton, *The Triune Creator*, p. 56.
98. Moltmann, *God in Creation*, p. xi.
99. Finger, *A Contemporary Anabaptist Theology*, p. 563.
100. R. Russell, *Cosmology*, p. 37, emphasis in original.
101. R. Russell, *Cosmology*, pp. 37-38.

relationship between theological anthropology (a trinitarian doctrine of the image of God) and contemporary sciences' (paleoanthropology, evolutionary biology) and philosophy of mind's account of the evolution of humanity and the nature of human nature (part 2). Building on the trinitarian theology of creation attempted therein (chap. 3), the current chapter seeks to deepen the analysis of a pneumatological conception of creation.

Since the main principles of the most current scientific account of the origins and workings of the cosmos are well known, thanks to a growing number of accessible publications by leading scientists, let it suffice to summarize them most briefly. In the standard big bang theory, currently the basis of all scientific cosmological speculations even among those who advocate revised versions, the cosmos came into being about 13.7 billion years ago from a singularity of zero size and infinite density (usually marked as $t = 0$ in which t denotes time) and has since expanded to its current form. This is supported by the relativity theory (both specific and general) and quantum physics, and it has received remarkable experimental confirmation of its basic intuitions (such as the Hubble discovery in the 1920s, which tells us that galaxies are receding from us, implying that the cosmos is "expanding," and the microwave background radiation discovery in the 1960s, which is believed to be an echo from the original big bang).

The big bang theory simply looks back in time to the point when expansion began and to the "beginning point." Because of extremely complicated questions, particularly regarding the "inflation period" immediately following the big bang (the so-called Planck time, 10^{-43} seconds, the shortest measure of time) to which no known scientific laws apply, revisions of the standard model are under way. Most well known is the Hartle/Hawkins quantum model, in which there is no "beginning" in time, although the cosmos is finite with regard to origins. In addition, more radical forms of quantum cosmologies are emerging all the time (including various types of "bouncing" or "oscillating" models in which big bounces, rather than one single big bang, succeed each other endlessly, as well as "multiverse" proposals, that is, ours is only one among many, perhaps infinitely many, universes). Theologically speaking, however, none of these poses a serious problem because the most foundational theistic belief (including other Abrahamic faiths) has to do with the contingency of the cosmos on the Creator. The world is neither self-originating nor self-sustaining. How the "logistics" might be best understood — the domain of sciences — is neither a threat nor an alternative to creation theology, but rather, a necessary dialogue partner.

Regarding the evolution of humanity, current evolutionary sciences assume that about 5-7 million years ago a definite deviation of initial human development started when that lineage separated from the closest counterpart(s). Through a long and complex hominid lineage, about 100,000-40,000 years ago a definite, perhaps "revolutionary" development happened, leading up to contemporary *Homo sapiens,* with unprecedented skills in the use of tools and other distinguishing marks. As a result, unique intellectual, emotional, social, and religious capacities characterize humanity among other animals. From the scientific-philosophical point of view, the capacity for self-transcendence marks the defining boundary line from other species. Theologically, the distinction is named the image of God.

Now, what does the Spirit — and trinitarian pneumatology — have to say to this scientific picture? The leading religion-science expert P. Clayton sets the context wonderfully:

> Suppose for a moment that, as theists believe, an eternal divine Spirit really did create this cosmos. Suppose that it was God's intent to produce beings capable of knowing God and working in harmony with the Spirit. Suppose, further, that it was also God's intent that they should do so not as machines but as *imago Dei* — creatures made in the image of God, agents who are freely responding to the divine lure. . . . [P]hilosophers refer to [this view] collectively as *personalist theism.*[102]

The Spirit and (Force) Fields: A Metaphorical Correlation

The return to the biblical account of the *ruach Yahweh* as the life principle, not detached from but rather energizing and supporting all life of the cosmos, has helped theology build a bridge with the scientific account of evolution and life.[103] Indeed, much has happened in the twentieth century in terms of radical shifts in the scientific paradigm itself that, while challenging to theology, also offer new ways to consider the role of the Spirit in the cosmos. Wolfgang Vondey observes: "Post-Newtonian physics speaks of the physical universe in terms of such concepts as energy, radiation, magnetism, waves, and field theories. Recent theological investigations speak of the Holy Spirit in surprisingly similar terms, among them the notions of energy, radiation, space, force, field, and light."[104]

---

102. Clayton, "The Spirit in Evolution and in Nature," p. 187, emphasis in original.
103. See the important discussion in Moltmann, *Spirit of Life,* p. 40.
104. Vondey, "Holy Spirit and the Physical Universe," p. 4; see also, his "Holy Spirit and

Pannenberg was one of the first theologians to correlate the theological concept of the Spirit and the notion in physics of force field(s). He famously argued that the biblical notion of "God as spirit" might have consonance with the current scientific view of life as the function of "spirit/energy/movement,"[105] expressed with the concept of (force) field.[106] "The presence of God's Spirit in his creation can be described as a field of creative presence, a comprehensive field of force that releases event after event into finite existence."[107] Pannenberg is of course quick to admit that "[a]t a first glance this biblical view of life is hard to reconcile with modern opinions. For modern biology, life is a function of the living cell or of the living creature as a self-sustaining (above all self-nourishing) and reproducing system, not the effect of a transcendent force that gives life."[108] That said, he notes rightly that the concept of force (or energy or field) is used in physics to describe movement and change. Although Faraday's nineteenth-century field theory has been revised dramatically in the wake of relativity theories and quantum physics, Pannenberg believes that from a theological viewpoint the basic idea regarding "bodies themselves as forms of forces that for their part are no longer qualities of bodies but independent realities that are 'givens' for bodily phenomena," in other words, "force fields,"[109] may still be useful when metaphorically conceived. While contemporary physics sees no need to resort to any divine Spirit to explain the fields, for theologians it may provide an opening. Particularly important in this respect is the metaphysical origin of the field concept in Greek philosophy: therein *pneuma* was considered to be a very fine stuff that permeated all the cosmos and held everything together in the cosmos.[110]

The theological justification for establishing the metaphorical correlation is not dependent on dialogical reasons alone (that is, in order to facilitate

---

Time." Vondey offers a highly insightful and necessary contrast between the Newtonian and Einsteinian worldviews and their implications for pneumatology.

105. Pannenberg utilizes the insight of Pierre Teilhard de Chardin that energy is always the physical manifestation of a spiritual reality; Pannenberg, "Spirit and Energy," pp. 82-84.

106. Pannenberg, "God as Spirit — and Natural Science."

107. Pannenberg, *ST* 1:194. The well-known critique of the physicist-priest Polkinghorne of some aspects of Pannenberg's use of "field" by M. Faraday (which, of course, has been quite radically revised since) does not materially invalidate his theological approach. Polkinghorne, "Wolfhart Pannenberg's Engagement with the Natural Sciences." For a similar critique but also a highly creative constructive proposal, see Morales, "Vector Fields as the Empirical Correlate of the Spirit(s)."

108. Pannenberg, *ST* 2:77.

109. Pannenberg, *ST* 2:80.

110. Pannenberg, *ST* 2:81.

a closer connection between religion and science). Theology also has its own material reasons for considering the divine Spirit as "field" in that, as explained above, the Spirit is conceived as the all-pervasive cosmic principle of life.[111] Notwithstanding the necessary critique targeted against Pannenberg's use of the outdated nineteenth-century field concept,[112] the basic intuition is spot-on. By calling the Spirit "field," we are of course using a metaphor or analogy; this metaphor's justification has to be assessed for its general appropriateness, rather than on whether it exactly fits all aspects of the scientific explanation. It seems to me that the metaphorical correlation of the divine Spirit in terms of field(s) goes well with what Tillich hinted at with his evolutionary-driven dynamic account of the Spirit of Life and that Moltmann similarly makes a whole-scale pneumatological program.

Linking the Spirit to life force, Moltmann also redefines the classic theological concept of the communion or fellowship of the Spirit in a way that encompasses the whole "community of creation," from the most elementary particles to atoms to molecules to cells to living organisms to animals to human beings to communities of humanity. In this "fellowship as process," all human communities are embedded in the ecosystems of the natural communities, and live from the exchange of energy with them.[113] While deeply immanentist — following some well-known biblical intuitions (Ps. 139) — the conception of the dynamic work of the Spirit as divine presence (field) also bespeaks the divine transcendence: "On the one side the Spirit is the principle of the creative presence of the transcendent God with his creatures; on the other side he is the medium of the participation of the creatures in the divine life, and therefore in life as such."[114]

---

111. Pannenberg, *ST* 2:83.

112. The typical concerns among scientists and theologians have to do with the wisdom of using the pre-Einsteinian and prequantum theory of Faraday rather than any of the contemporary ones; the failure to identify which of the many existing field theories Pannenberg invokes; and most importantly, the ambiguity about whether he uses them analogically or as a way of (virtual) identification of field and Spirit of God (as it seems at least in his pneumatologically driven theology of angels). For these and others, see Polkinghorne, "Wolfhart Pannenberg's Engagement with the Natural Sciences," pp. 151-58; Polkinghorne, "Fields and Theology," p. 796; Barr, "Theology after Newton," pp. 31-33. A highly insightful discussion is in Worthing, *God, Creation, and Contemporary Physics*, pp. 117-24. Instead of the modern field concept, Erwin T. Morales has chosen the contemporary theory of vector fields as the connecting point with pneumatology: "Vector Fields as the Empirical Correlate of the Spirit(s)."

113. Moltmann, *Spirit of Life*, pp. 225-26.

114. Pannenberg, *ST* 2:32.

The Spirit of Novelty and Constant Emergence

The divine Breath not only gives birth to life and sustains it, the Spirit is also the continuing source of novelty and emergence. Because of the presence in creatures of the transcendent God through his Spirit, creatures are open to dimensions that transcend their lives. What the current scientific account calls "emergence" is theologically depicted as the work of the Holy Spirit as the agent of novelty and new forms of life.[115] (For a brief discussion of emergence, see chap. 4 below; a more detailed treatment of emergence occurs in chap. 6 of *Creation and Humanity*.)

In other words, the divine Spirit is the principle not only of creatures' openness to the future but also of self-transcendence: "When we say that the creation's Creator indwells both every individual creature and the community of creation, we mean that the presence of the infinite in the finite imbues every finite thing, and the community of all finite things, with self-transcendence."[116] That comes to the fore in growth and development, and in the continuous desire to reach out beyond the limits of finite existence. This means that the "seeds" of new potentialities and processes are already planted by the Creator in the created order. This is finely expressed by the late Romanian Orthodox theologian Dumitru Staniloae:

> In fact, if the rational fabric of the world must have a subject who thinks it, a subject who is truly the one who knows and is master of the created world, this subject in communion is able to effect, even through created consciousness, the gathering together and transformation of matter into spirit. The creator Spirit who is the origin of the rationality of nature given material form and of the conscious subjects connected to it, is also their goal, a goal in which human subjects find their full unity in conjunction with that nature through which they communicate and which has itself been raised to a condition completely overwhelmed by spirit. . . . The divine Spirit is able not only to produce modifications much greater than these upon the energy from which the forms of the world are made but also to produce this energy itself as an effect of his own spiritual energy, imprinting on it potentially the forms that will become actual in their own time.[117]

---

115. Staniloae, *Experience of God,* 2:60.

116. Moltmann, *God in Creation,* p. 101.

117. Staniloae, *Experience of God,* 2:6. Several other theologians have highlighted the

Historically we can discern here a correlation with the way Christian Aristotelianism used the concept of "information," which literally means to "in-form" (existing matter).[118] This is not to ignore the marked difference between the medieval and current scientific worldviews because of radically changed scientific and philosophical understandings, but rather to point to an important thematic connection. The most important difference has to do with the fact that whereas in Aristotelianism energy is something independent from matter, in the contemporary relativistic understanding of reality, mass (matter) and energy are intertwined to the point of being exchangeable (as matter can be seen as a manifestation of energy).

The great gain of the current understanding is the close link between energy and information. Pannenberg puts it succinctly: "Information now came to denote the unusual or improbable nature of an event that is being caused, or has been caused, by energy." Hence, the concept of novelty is linked with probability rather than predetermined outcomes and can be linked also to the openness to the future, of which the Spirit is the source.[119] This conviction is supported by the robust accent on the Spirit's omnipresence, as the result of which "the whole creation is a fabric woven and shot through by the efficacies of the Spirit. Through his Spirit God is also present in the very structures of matter. Creation contains neither spirit-less matter nor non-material spirit; there is only *informed* matter."[120]

Pannenberg summarizes these insights and puts them in a trinitarian framework: "The defining of information in terms of probability theory enables modern theology to view information as a measure of the creaturely new that through the Spirit proceeds with each new event from the creative power of God. As a measure of the creative workings of the divine Spirit, the concept of information is subject to the Logos. The differing information content of events constitutes their uniqueness by which they are an expression of the creative activity of the Logos."[121] Indeed, the order and novelty are a

---

importance of self-transcendence, particularly the following three Catholic theologians (Austrian, German, and Australian, respectively): Rahner, *Foundations*, pp. 178-203; Kasper, *The God of Jesus Christ*, p. 227; D. Edwards, *Ecology at the Heart of Faith*, p. 37.

118. While Aquinas (*ST* 1.45.2) distinguished sharply this formation from the original divine act of creation that brought into existence both matter and form, we no longer have to do so as categorically.

119. Pannenberg, *ST* 2:111-12 (p. 111). Pannenberg reports Weizsäcker as the originator of the link between information and energy (n. 285).

120. Moltmann, *God in Creation*, p. 212, emphasis in original.

121. Pannenberg, *ST* 2:112. Curiously, with the exception of Pannenberg, even trinitarian

joint work of the Son, the Logos, and the Spirit. In the process of evolution, beginning from the Spirit's "moving" above the primeval chaos, there is always a highly complex mix of chance and telos, determinism and freedom, resulting in ever-new forms and potentialities while also maintaining the intricate order and constancy.[122] "The long and unfinished development known as evolution testifies to just how much novelty, just how much surprise, the universe is capable of spawning out of pre-given order or chaos. In every instance the living Spirit empowers, lures, prods, dances on ahead."[123]

So far we have talked about the work and presence of the creative Spirit in the cosmos in general terms, as life principle, agency of novelty, and emergence. Can we move from here to talk about more specific divine acts in light of contemporary scientific worldviews?

The Spirit's Continuing Creation and Divine Acts in the World

One of the greatest challenges to contemporary (philosophical) theology is how to continue affirming the conditions and possibility of divine acts. The dilemma can be simply put: on the one hand, there is no way for Christian theism, any more than other Abrahamic traditions, to get around the belief in continuing divine acts in history (including salvation history). Just a glance at the scriptures of Christianity, Judaism, and Islam makes this clear. On the other hand, modern science considers the universe a closed physical system following its regular and law-like processes.[124] Even for scientifically informed theists, the positing of a God who "intervenes" in the regularities of the closed world smacks of intervention — an awkward act of "fixing" what went wrong.[125] The evolutionary theory with its focus on chance has further helped make divine acts obsolete. In other words, in a world of sciences char-

---

theology has failed to offer sustained reflections on the relationship between Logos and Spirit in creation; some insights are also offered by O'Murchu, *In the Beginning*, pp. 43-47.

122. Clayton, "The Spirit in Evolution and in Nature," pp. 187-96.

123. Johnson, *Women, Earth, and Creator Spirit*, p. 44.

124. That statement, however, has to be qualified since even in science the laws of nature are not iron-clad strictures but are rather approximations of how natural processes seem to function. Theologically we have to say that, while contingent (because even laws are created), the laws do not mean absolute determinism nor lack of chance. See further, Ward, *God, Faith, and the New Millennium*, p. 98; for a detailed discussion (including corollary topics such as causality), see chaps. 6 and 7 in my *Creation and Humanity*.

125. Clayton, "Impossible Possibility," p. 249.

acterized by determinism and causal closure (that is, all events have ultimately only physical causes), any nonnatural divine act or "intervention" appears highly problematic.[126]

Modern theology, thus, was left at an impasse: one either dismissed the sciences and affirmed continuing divine action (conservatives) or one made divine actions merely a subjective interpretation (liberals), thereby avoiding the conflict with the sciences but at the same time losing any meaningful account of divine acts. Fortunately, the recent "Divine Action" project (sponsored by the Center for Theology and Natural Sciences, Berkeley, California, and the Vatican Observatory, Vatican City)[127] has developed a promising new tactic to find a way out of the dilemma. This proposal is known under the cumbersome nomenclature Non-Interventionist Objective Divine Action (NIODA).[128] Briefly put, it argues for real, continuing, and ubiquitous divine acts in the world, including also special acts such as responses to prayer, but in a noninterventionist manner.[129] In other words, this new paradigm believes itself able to speak of divine acts without the dangers of intervention.

The NIODA project is made possible by the shift from the iron-clad determinism of the Newtonian worldview with its causal closure to quantum physics, which envisions orderly, but to some extent indeterminate, processes of the world at various levels (according to the main Copenhagen interpretation of Heisenberg). Probability is thus the mode of explanation and is not due to lack of knowledge but rather to the nature of reality. The establishment of divine action with the help of quantum theory emphasizes "God's operational presence in the most basic processes of nature known to us,"[130] that is, in the subatomic, whose effects are also proliferated to the larger processes and events. Here an analogical-metaphorical use of the scientific concept of force field is appropriate: "The presence of God's Spirit in his creation can be described as a field of creative presence, a comprehensive field of force that releases event after event into finite existence."[131] Furthermore, the benefits

---

126. See further, Peacocke, *Theology for a Scientific Age*, pp. 139-41.

127. The landmark project here is *Scientific Perspectives on Divine Action (SPDA)*. The 2008 *SPDA* provides an assessment of the twenty-year-long interdisciplinary work, and contains six major volumes of publications.

128. See *SPDA*; an up-to-date summary, analysis, and assessment is provided by R. Russell, "Challenges and Progress," pp. 3-56; Clayton, "Toward a Theory of Divine Action," pp. 85-110.

129. For a basic definition, see R. Russell, *Cosmology*, p. 112.

130. Gregersen, "Special Divine Action," p. 194.

131. Pannenberg, *Introduction to Systematic Theology*, p. 49.

of chaos theories are also utilized by many NIODA advocates. Although deterministic, physical processes are so complex and multifaceted that at their best only probabilistic explanations can be had. Related to these resources is the combination of both bottom-up and top-down/whole-part explanations, the use of emergence theory, as well as supervenience (that is, once emerged, new levels of processes cannot be reduced to the lower ones). Quantum theory also seems to acknowledge the importance of consciousness (at least for "measurement" and observation). A detailed investigation of all these matters with meticulous documentation can be found in *Creation and Humanity*, particularly chapters 6 and 7. This project builds on the NIODA scheme, even though some of its features had to be theologically corrected and fine-tuned.

The NIODA paradigm is in need of linking with a robust trinitarian-pneumatological account in which the omnipresent and omnipotent God through his Spirit permeates every inch of the cosmos. This is to avoid the God-of-the-gaps fallacy and an external way of viewing divine action. Contemporary theology finds great resources for this even in Christian tradition. As Gregory of Nyssa put it: "For all things depend on Him who is, nor can there be anything which has not its being in Him who is. . . . [A]ll things are in Him, and He in all things. . . . He Who holds together Nature in existence is transfused in *us;* while at that other time He was transfused throughout *our nature*."[132] Astonishingly, Gregory's thinking is so thoroughly participatory and holistic that even heaven for him does not represent merely something transcendent but rather "pervades all creation and . . . does not exist separated from being."[133] That this idea is not a commodity of one theological tradition (in this case, the Eastern Church) nor considered strange even in classical theism (let alone in forms of contemporary panentheism) can be easily seen with quotations from thinkers as different as Thomas and Luther, respectively: "God is in all things; not, indeed, as part of their essence . . . [but] as an agent is present to that upon which it works. For an agent must be joined to that wherein it acts immediately and touch it by its power."[134] God "himself must be present in every single creature in its innermost and outermost being, on all sides, through and through, below and above, before and behind, so that nothing can be more truly present and within all creatures than God himself with his power."[135]

132. Gregory of Nyssa, *The Great Catechism* 25, emphasis in original; available at http://www.ccel.org/ccel/schaff/npnf205.xi.ii.xxvii.html (03/21/2014).

133. Gregory of Nyssa, "On What It Means to Call Oneself a Christian," p. 87; I am indebted to Zimmermann, *Incarnational Humanism*, p. 235.

134. Aquinas, *ST* 1.1.8.

135. Luther, WA 23:133; *LW* 37:58.

In light of these theological and scientific considerations, we can summarize the main thrust of a trinitarian theology of continuing creation (providence) and divine action: "The trinitarian God works in and through the process of the universe, through laws and boundary conditions, through regularities and chance, through chaotic systems and the capacity for self-organization."[136] Consequently, theologically we must hold on to the widest and most diverse possible account of divine action in the world, rather than getting stuck in debates about whether there is only one preferred way of explaining it, say, either quantum or chaos indeterminacy. Furthermore, very importantly, we should not seek to reveal the "'causal joint' between divine action and created causality" simply because we can't[137] — or else we could read God's mind! Rather, the theologian's task is to remove the obstacles in the way of a coherent, ubiquitous, and robust account of continuous divine acts, both "general" and "special." Here the insight of the late British theologian Colin Gunton is highly significant. Whatever problems may relate to the interpretation of the Spirit of God in terms of force field, he argues, it has great value for the question of how to understand God's action: the idea of the Spirit's work "as interacting fields of force rather than billiard-ball-like entities bumping into one another, is of extreme importance in showing that the world is open to God's continuing interaction with it."[138] This means that

> the creator's love — his energy at work through the mediating action of the Son and the Spirit — not only made the universe, consisting of diverse and interacting fields of force organized in different ways, but also shows itself in the day to day upholding and directing of what has been made.... It is important to stress that according to such a conception no distinction in principle is to be drawn between the ordinary and the extraordinary. God's action, as energy giving rise to energy variously organized, may be conceived to shape the day to day life of the world, even sometimes miraculously — in anticipation of its eschatological destiny — without violating

136. D. Edwards, "Discovery of Chaos," p. 170.

137. D. Edwards, "Discovery of Chaos," pp. 172-73. Herein is the limited value of the (in many ways highly problematic) categorical separation of "horizontal" (secondary, creaturely) and "vertical" (primary, divine) causation in Schleiermacher: whereas in the former, no reference to God should be made, in the latter, everything should be attributed to God, rather than particular acts. This is of course a radically revised version of Thomas's distinction between primary (God's direct actions) and secondary (God's action via created agents) causation. See Tracy, "Particular Providence and the God of the Gaps," pp. 296-98, including long n. 14.

138. Gunton, *The Triune Creator,* p. 175.

that which is "natural," because what is natural is that which enables the creation to achieve its promised destiny.[139]

Although I would speak less of energy and more of information, Gunton's profound trinitarian statement makes the point.

Only a robust trinitarian panentheism (classical panentheism), as advocated in this project, funds a dynamic, multifaceted divine action, providence, and causality. To be the Creator is far more than being the world's cause. While causality should not be eliminated from the theological thesaurus,[140] the main focus is to be placed on the living, dynamic, creative presence of the Creator in the world:

> If the Creator is himself present in his creation by virtue of the Spirit, then his relationship to creation must rather be viewed as an intricate web of unilateral, reciprocal and many-sided relationships. In this network of relationships, "making," "preserving," "maintaining" and "perfecting" are certainly the great *one-sided* relationships; but "indwelling," "sympathizing," "participating," "accompanying," "enduring," "delighting" and "glorifying" are relationships of *mutuality* which describe a cosmic community of living between God and all his created beings.[141]

The last task in this chapter relates to the role of the Spirit(s) of creation in other faith traditions. As emphasized, the plural pneumatological paradigm cannot be content with a monolithic account of the spirit(s).

Spirit(s) and Creation in Other Faith Traditions

For the purposes of a plural pneumatology paradigm, it is essential to widen the scope of theological investigation not only in the natural sciences but also in cosmologies of other faith traditions. That, however, has to be attempted in a way that does not subsume a different "theological" structure of the religious other under one's own theology but rather seeks to discern genuine differences as much as similarities. In that complex task, it is useful to make a distinction between Abrahamic traditions and Asiatic traditions. The task of this short

139. Gunton, *The Triune Creator*, p. 176.
140. Contra Moltmann, *God in Creation*, p. 14.
141. Moltmann, *God in Creation*, p. 14, emphasis in original.

section is limited for two reasons. First, a detailed investigation into the "doctrines of creation" in four living faiths (Islam, Judaism, Hinduism, Buddhism) is to be found in *Creation and Humanity* (chap. 5), including the creation of humanity (chap. 14). Second, the pneumatologies of other traditions are more fully investigated below in chapter 5.

Before going into the details of any specific faith tradition, let us reflect on whether a distinctively *trinitarian* pneumatology of creation even in principle can be linked with other faith traditions, none of which have such a trinitarian "foundation." This project builds on the intuition that even if trinitarian parallels could not be found in other traditions (for a detailed discussion, see chap. 15 in *Trinity and Revelation*), comparative theology should continue the painstaking dialogical investigation concerning the "ultimate" notion of the deity (and/or spirit). It is just that the comparative theologian should be very careful in not too hastily claiming similarities between the concepts of the Spirit(s) among radically differing faith traditions. Let me illustrate this with a simple case study: as much as there might be some correlations between the Christian doctrine of God (the Holy Spirit) and the Mahayana Buddhist concept of sunyata ("emptiness"), those alleged correlations only relate to generic Judeo-Christian ideas of conceiving of God as "spirit(ual)" and have absolutely nothing to do with creedal confession of the Holy Spirit as trinitarian "person."[142]

Between the three Abrahamic and Asiatic faith traditions a foundational difference exists in the overall understanding of the origins of the cosmos. Whereas the former uncompromisingly confess God (Yahweh, triune God, Allah) as the Creator and thus *materially* affirm the idea behind *ex nihilo* (for details, see chaps. 3 and 6 in *Creation and Humanity*), neither Asiatic faith has a doctrine of creation understood in the sense of Abrahamic theisms. While Hinduism's diverse cosmologies, based on Vedic traditions, Bhagavad-Gita (the "Bible" of the common folks), and numerous Puranas (inspired spiritual literature), link the origins of the cosmos to deities, they are totally opposed to any notions of *ex nihilo*. An infinite cyclical view is the major cosmological vision in various Hindu traditions. When it comes to Buddhism, particularly the original Theravada, even the deities are removed from the origination. The defining concept of "dependent origination"[143] (or "causal interdependence")

142. Another issue is that I myself am much less convinced than some of my comparative theology colleagues that even generic correlations can be found between sunyata and the Christian concept of (Spirit of) God; my argument can be found in chap. 15 of *Creation and Humanity*.

143. See *Paticca-samuppada-vibhanga Sutta: Analysis of Dependent Co-arising*, of

rejects any "first cause." Even the main Mahayana traditions (which entertain belief in myriads of deities of various sorts) by and large refrain from making the origination of the cosmos a matter of divinity. *Lotus Sutra*, the "catechism" of the Mahayana tradition, states categorically that the cosmos was "not derived from an intelligent cause" nor has it any purpose.[144] Rather, the cosmos is everlasting and without beginning.[145]

That said of Asiatic traditions, including even Theravada Buddhism, nothing would be more mistaken than to establish a parallel with contemporary atheistic scientific naturalism, which considers the coming into existence and workings of nature as self-explanatory. Both Hinduism and Buddhism (except for a few isolated marginal nontheistic traditions) are deeply idealist in the philosophical and theological sense, meaning that ultimately all reality derives from the spiritual. Contemporary scientific naturalism, on the contrary, is materialistically monist; that is, all that is derives from the physical (however the "physical" may be understood in current quantum worldview).[146] In Hinduism, Brahman (not to be confused with Brahma, one of the main classic deities), "spirit," is the origin of everything. On this basis, the leading Hindu (Vedanta) teacher of the twentieth century, Sri Aurobindo, spoke freely of "the manifestation of God in matter" and said the reason evolution can happen is that "Life is already involved in Matter and Mind in Life because Matter is a form of veiled Life, Life a form of veiled consciousness."[147] He was well informed in science-religion dialogue, and one of his aims was to defeat scientific naturalism's refusal to consider "nonnatural" (spiritual) factors.[148] As a result, totally unlike in the Global North, in India spirituality and science are intimately related.[149]

Going back to Abrahamic traditions, which uncompromisingly make the origin of the cosmos a divine work, let us ask if anything more specific can be said of the role of pneumatology. As is obvious, with Judaism, Christian tradition shares the important creational and cosmic pneumatology of the OT.

Samyutta Nikaya 12.2, for the famous analysis of Gautama (or Gotama) concerning the idea of "Dependent Origination."

144. *Lotus Sutra* 5.80.

145. *Lotus Sutra* 13.19.

146. For a detailed investigation into the relation of Christian theology and four living faith traditions with various forms of naturalisms, scientific and other, see chap. 2 in *Creation and Humanity*.

147. Aurobindo (Ghose), *The Life Divine*, bks. 1, 4, 5, respectively.

148. As exposited by Ward, *Religion and Creation*, p. 94.

149. See Witsz, "Vedānta, Nature, and Science," pp. 30-39.

Hence, there is significant agreement about the role of the *ruach Yahweh* as the principle of life. Beyond that, of course, the paths diverge, as Judaism categorically rejects the notions of a trinitarian understanding of the Spirit. When it comes to Islam, although some of the approximately twenty references to the Spirit (of God) in the Qur'an link the Spirit with the creation of humanity (Q 15:29; 21:91; 32:9; 38:72; 66:12), there is no kind of direct link with anything resembling the cosmic role of the Spirit in Christian tradition.

The investigation into the theological meaning of the cosmic Spirit continues in the next chapter as we turn our attention from creation and providence to spiritual "powers," a topic rich in Christian tradition as well as in the four other living faiths. Although in the area of creation fewer parallel teachings can be found among these faith traditions, with regard to angels, demons, and other powers, a richer reservoir awaits.

4. The Cosmic Spirit and Powers

Radical Shifts in the Interpretation of Spirits and Powers in Theological Tradition

From the Center to the Margins

It is often said — somewhat inaccurately — that whereas in the biblical canon angelology flourishes, in the creedal tradition there is nothing on the topic. It is more accurate to say that whereas the creedal tradition pre-supposes the existence of heavenly beings ("of all things both seen and unseen"), early creeds of the undivided church do not detail the content of the belief.[1] That the spiritual realities and beings were taken fully seriously but that their nature and functions were yet to be theologically developed is manifested in the early testimony of Origen: "Regarding the devil and his angels, and the opposing influences, the teaching of the Church has laid down that these beings exist indeed; but what they are, or how they exist, it has not been explained with sufficient clearness."[2] It looks like there were no such debates that occasioned controversies. Another reason for the reservation among the Fathers was that belief in angels was not unique to Jews and Christians but was, rather, common at the time, ranging from

---

1. See Slesinski, "Bulgakov's Angelology," pp. 184-85. At the 1215 Lateran Council, in opposition to the Albigensians, a more detailed creedal explanation was offered. See N. Tanner, ed. and trans., *Decrees of the Ecumenical Council,* 1:230.

2. Origen, *De principiis,* preface, 6; see also, bk. 3.

Egyptian mythology and Mesopotamian and Iranian religions to those of the Greeks and Romans.[3]

As is well known, the worldview of the ancients not only was open to notions of supernatural forces, but it took them as something thoroughly "natural." The world was filled with spirits, spiritual powers, "spiritual warfare," and similar experiences and intuitions. Just consider the cosmology of the New Testament, whether Jesus' own ministry or the worldview of the Apocalypse, and you get the picture.[4] Rightly the historian of dogma Jaroslav Pelikan notes,

> Christian apocalypticism reflected a supernaturalistic view of the world, which Christian believers shared with other religious men of antiquity.... Traffic was heavy on the highway between heaven and earth. God and spirits thickly populated the upper air, where they stood in readiness to intervene at any moment in the affairs of mortals. And demonic powers, emerging from the lower world or resident in remote corners of the earth, were a constant menace to human welfare. All nature was alive — alive with supernatural forces.[5]

Building on the rich biblical reservoir, Christian tradition, beginning from the Fathers,[6] developed a rich and creative angelology, which culminated in the highly speculative presentations in medieval theology,[7] the most well known of which is the nine-layer cosmic vision in *The Celestial Hierarchy* of Pseudo-Dionysius the Areopagite.[8] Although less speculative, even medieval masters such as Aquinas devoted huge intellectual efforts to a detailed scrutiny of angelology.[9] That said, by and large Christian tradition has followed Calvin's "rule of modesty and sobriety"[10] when it comes to speaking of angels.

In contrast with tradition, modern thinkers rejected or seriously marginalized belief in spiritual beings — whether based on Descartes's method of

---

3. Slesinski, "Bulgakov's Angelology," p. 187.

4. For a meticulous investigation, see Bolt, "Jesus, the Daimons and the Dead," chap. 5.

5. Pelikan, *CT* 1:132; the citation is from Case, *Origins of Christian Supernaturalism*, p. 1.

6. For Augustine, see *City of God*, chaps. 8–9; 11–12.

7. Keck, *Angels and Angelology*.

8. *The Celestial Hierarchy* can be found in Dionysius the Areopagite, *Works*, 2:1-66.

9. Aquinas, *ST* 1.50-64 and 106-14. An accessible discussion of angels in Augustine, Pseudo-Dionysius, Aquinas, the Reformers, and Milton can be found in Noll, "Thinking about Angels," pp. 2-13.

10. Calvin, *Institutes* 1.14.4.

doubt[11] or D. F. Strauss's causal closure (that is, ultimately everything can be explained in terms of physical factors)[12] or Hobbes's dismissal of metaphysics ("doctrine of devils")[13] — and rejected everything that did not cohere with "natural religion." Even John Locke's seasoned openness to a generic notion of "intelligent creatures above us" because of "chasms or gaps" in the physical world has little in common with the traditional doctrine of angels. At the end of Schleiermacher's doctrine of creation, his discussion of angels — in keeping with his methodology — argues that while there is no principled reason why such beings could not exist, they are irrelevant to "religious feelings" and thus there is no need to try to settle the issue.[14] Not surprisingly, for the majority of scholars of the twentieth century, "an ontology of angels, fallen or unfallen, is hardly credible."[15] Ironically — and often against their will — Protestant missionaries who went out to the mission lands also tended to proliferate "secular" impulses that included a thin view of angels,[16] at times even virtual rejection of them.[17]

However, folk psychology still resists the overly critical scholarly opinion: according to a 2008 Pew Survey, a large majority of American adults (79 percent) believe in miracles, and almost as many (68 percent) believe that angels and demons are active in the world.[18] Massive scholarly evidence reveals a universal and ubiquitous belief in angels, demons, and spirit possession across the history of humanity and religious traditions.[19] It is highly ironic for theologians — many of whom dismiss the reality of the spiritual powers altogether — that a growing number of equally if not more naturalistically oriented social

11. Descartes, *Meditations on the First Philosophy, Meditation* III, 3.43.

12. For D. F. Strauss, see Pannenberg, *ST* 2:106.

13. Hobbes, *Leviathan* (1651) (1909 ed.), pt. 4, chap. 45.

14. Schleiermacher, *CF* §42 epithet, p. 156.

15. O'Connor, *God and Inscrutable Evil*, p. 114. So also, Küng, *On Being a Christian*, p. 369. Classically the rejection of miracles and spirits was formulated by Bultmann, *New Testament and Mythology*, p. 4.

16. Imasogie, *Guidelines for Christian Theology in Africa*, pp. 51-53.

17. See Wink, *Unmasking the Powers*, p. 1. In a programmatic essay, "The Flaw of the Excluded Middle," the late missiologist Paul Hiebert used the term "excluded middle" to identify the typical modern Christian attitude in the Global North that cannot grasp angels, spirits, and similar phenomena between God and humans/nature.

18. Pew Research Center, "Summary of Key Findings," pp. 11-12.

19. Goodman, *How about Demons?* Reiterer, Nicklas, and Schöpflin, eds., *Angels;* Keener, "Spirit Possession as a Cross-Cultural Experience"; Keener, *Miracles,* appendices A and B, contain a massive amount of evidence of spirit-possession phenomena. For this and the following two footnotes I am indebted to Eddy and Beilby, "Introduction," pp. 17-20.

scientists, psychologists, psychiatrists, and anthropologists are willing to at least leave open the question of the ontological status of the spirits,[20] with some few even willing to affirm spirits.[21] In postmodern times, it is also well known that a resurgence of interest in angels and spiritual experiences in the general population, including its literature and entertainment,[22] as well as in some quarters of the secular academy,[23] has taken place.[24]

The Resurgence of Interest in Spiritual Powers in Twentieth-Century Theology

To the great surprise of many, beginning in the middle of the twentieth century an interest in angels, demonic forces, and spiritual beings resurfaced in theology. Even more astonishingly, it began to flourish in mainstream Euro-American theology. Well known is P. Tillich's linking of demonic forces with the depth psychology of C. G. Jung. Too bad Tillich did not develop the theme beyond repeated references in the first volume of his *Systematic Theology*.[25] The biggest contribution, also well known, came from Barth.

Barth's overly long methodological preface to angelology[26] rightly calls for a middle way between the "far too interesting mythology of the ancients" and the demythologization of the modern (p. 369). Opposing both natural theology and philosophical speculation, he advises sticking with biblical teaching alone (p. 372), albeit not blindly and without reflection (p. 373). Divinatory imagination and poetic speech are needed for a topic that transcends historical

---

20. Goodman, *How about Demons?* pp. 123-26; Goldberg, *Speaking with the Devil*, p. xii; so also, Dwyer, *Divine and the Demonic*.

21. Betty, "The Growing Evidence"; R. Gallagher, "Case of Demonic Possession."

22. See Summers-Minette, "Not Just Halos and Horns"; Partridge, "Satanism and the Heavy-Metal Subculture."

23. For the (in)famous *Course on Miracles* (originally published in 1975 by Helen Schuchman, a research psychologist at Columbia University, New York), the official mouthpiece of the "channeling literature" and its metaphysical monistic worldview, see Bradby, "Coping with the Non-Existent." "Channeling" simply refers to a person's being a channel of information from sources other than normal consciousness. This belief, however, does not typically lead to the affirmation of the existence of evil powers and demons, but to its rejection. It is widely believed that channeling (rather than mere personal experiences) forms the backdrop for the rise of various New Age movements in the second half of the twentieth century.

24. For the hugely successful and highly acclaimed HBO TV miniseries *Angels in America*, see http://www.hbo.com/movies/angels-in-america/index.html (3/20/2014).

25. See, e.g., Tillich, *ST* 1:134, 139-40, 216-17, 222-27.

26. Found in Barth, *CD* III/3. Page numbers in the text refer to this volume.

contours (p. 374). For Barth, angels are God's ambassadors. This is to secure the functional rather than ontological nature of biblical angelology. Indeed, Barth opines, the Bible does not speak much about the nature of angels, only about their work (p. 410). Angels are in the service of God (pp. 451-52). As such, they are "ministering spirits" (Heb. 1:14; *CD* III/3, p. 452), representatives of heaven, and witnesses to the divine activity. Locating angels in "heaven" — which for Barth is not God's dwelling but rather earth's spiritual and incomprehensible counterpart[27] — relates to his idea of heaven as the starting point for God's movement toward the creatures (pp. 432-33).[28]

In contrast to earlier theology, Barth emphatically rejects the theological tradition that posits demons as fallen angels, deriding it as "one of the bad dreams of the older dogmatics" (p. 251). Instead, he relates the demonic to the semimagical elusive concept of *das Nichtige* ("Nothing"), a domain of utmost "opposition and resistance" against which "God asserts Himself and exerts His positive will."[29] Rather than merely privation (Augustine), ultimately evil is "inimical to the will of the Creator and therefore to the nature of His good creature . . . opposition and resistance to God's world-dominion . . . an alien factor" (*CD* III/3, p. 289).

In the aftermath of Barth, a different type of reenvisioning of powers started on both sides of the Atlantic focusing on the influence of powers, dominance, and oppression in sociopolitical structures and ideologies. This could happen in more than one way. While traditionally the powers have been conceived as more or less spiritual realities,[30] in this new approach they could also be imagined as spiritual and, at the same time, created social realities.[31] This was the approach of the little but significant book by the Dutch Reformed theologian Hendrikus Berkhof, *Christ and the Powers.* Speaking of powers as structures undergirding all human and societal life, he envisions them as providing cohesion and preserving from disintegration: these structures can

27. Barth, *Dogmatics in Outline,* p. 61.

28. Similarly Welker: "The doctrine of angels illumines . . . God's particular personality, and the particular ways God takes up contact with what is creaturely, as well as the particular problems of taking up that contact" ("Angels in the Biblical Traditions," p. 368).

29. Barth, *CD* III/2, pp. 327, 351. Ironically, Barth devotes quite a bit of space to considering the "Nothing"; see *CD* III/3, pp. 289-368.

30. A sophisticated defense is that of Arnold, *Ephesians.*

31. Regarding some earlier writers whose both-and interpretation is less consistent and elusive, see Caird, *Principalities and Powers;* Ellul, *Ethics of Freedom.* Be that as it may, particularly Ellul (with a number of other writings) is an important influence behind Wink's reconstruction of powers.

be social units such as family or tribe, religious or other ideological beliefs, etc.[32] The American Mennonite theologian John H. Yoder, who translated Berkhof's book, developed the idea in his *Politics of Jesus* by further analyzing the structures into religious, intellectual, moral, and political categories.[33] The late Canadian Baptist theologian Stanley J. Grenz's "structures of existence" concept continues this interpretation; he envisioned them as "those larger, suprahuman aspects or dimensions of reality which form the inescapable context for human life and which therefore condition individual and corporate human existence."[34]

Following this both-and hermeneutics of powers, Grenz underlines that although the structures have no independent reality apart from humankind, they also transcend humanity and lie beyond human control. As such they are "quasi-independent" and "quasi-personal."[35] Here comes the link to the biblical, particularly the Pauline, way of speaking of principalities and powers. This means that between the structures of existence and the biblical talk about angels and spirits there is no total identification.[36] Because originally the structures were meant to facilitate human life, they were created good by God. However, they can be abused and manipulated for evil — and they often are. As structures of cohesion, "by holding the world together, they hold it away from God, not close to Him."[37] Now, as a result, "[through] the diabolical misuse of structures, evil realities bring humans into structural bondage," including slavery to powers and demand for uncompromising loyalty. The structures become a channel for evil, though still under the Lordship of Christ.[38] Ultimately part of God's creation and Christ's reconciliation, "the structures will one day conform to the reign of God."[39] On the basis of Pauline teaching in the first chapter of Colossians and related passages, Berkhof summarizes this vision:

---

32. H. Berkhof, *Christ and the Powers*, pp. 30-35; similarly, also Cobble, *Church and the Powers*, p. 5.

33. J. H. Yoder, *The Politics of Jesus*, p. 145.

34. Grenz, *Theology for the Community of God*, p. 228.

35. Grenz, *Theology for the Community of God*, p. 230. In keeping with tradition, Grenz understands angels and demons as personal.

36. H. Berkhof, *Christ and the Powers*, pp. 23-26; Grenz, *Theology for the Community of God*, p. 231.

37. H. Berkhof, *Christ and the Powers*, p. 30; so also, Grenz, *Theology for the Community of God*, p. 233.

38. Grenz, *Theology for the Community of God*, pp. 233-35 (p. 233).

39. Grenz, *Theology for the Community of God*, p. 235.

God reconciles the Powers — and not only men — with Himself through Christ's death. This thought is strange to us; we usually think of reconciliation as an act relating only to persons. Here Paul uses it in a broader sense, as meaning a restoration of proper relationships. In this sense the Powers as well are objects of God's plan of redemption. By virtue of this purpose they will no longer lie between man and God as barrier, but can and shall return to their original functions, as instruments of God's fellowship with His creation.[40]

Because of this eschatological vision, Christians can anticipate that Christ's continuing cosmic rule breaks into the realm of the structures of existence.[41]

A related, alternative interpretation of powers merely as immanent structures, though really influencing affairs of society and human life, comes from the late American NT scholar Walter J. Wink, whose trilogy on the powers has become a contemporary classic;[42] many have followed in some way or another his proposal.[43] For Wink, the powers are "the spiritualities of institutions, the 'within' of corporate structures and the inner essence of outer organizations of power." The outer aspect consists of "political systems, appointed officials, the 'chair' of an organization, laws," whereas the "invisible pole, an inner spirit or driving force . . . animates, legitimates, and regulates its physical manifestation in the world."[44] Although dismissing as outdated the concepts of "angels," "principalities and powers," as well as "Satan" after the worldview of the ancients — which is also "accidentally" that of the biblical writers[45] — in a radical difference from Bultmann's demythologization program, Wink takes the powers as "real" (albeit not in the traditional sense). They are social, cultural, political, financial, global powers. What do we do with the powers

---

40. H. Berkhof, *Christ and the Powers*, p. 41.

41. Grenz, *Theology for the Community of God*, p. 235.

42. For a summary statement and refinement of the program of powers, see Wink, *The Powers That Be*. For highly useful recent engagements of Wink's program, see Gingerich and Grimsrud, *Transforming the Powers*; Seiple and Weidmann, eds., *Enigmas and Powers*.

43. Many have followed Wink in reducing the powers from their traditional "spiritual" (metaphysical, ontological) status and making them immanent forces: see Horsley, *Jesus and the Powers*. Pagels, *The Origins of Satan*, is a strictly sociological interpretation of the demonic.

44. Wink, *Naming the Powers*, p. 5.

45. Wink, *Unmasking the Powers*, pp. 172-73. In contrast to the "traditional" worldview of the ancients with their robust belief in spirits and the "materialist" view of the moderns with their total rebuttal of them all, Wink (*The Powers That Be*, pp. 19-22) proposes an "integral" worldview that, while critical of the "supernatural" interpretation, still takes the powers as real (albeit as immanent).

according to Wink? They must be "redeemed" because they were good originally, then became evil.[46] The key to redeeming powers is in the Jesus kind of lifestyle: nonviolent, peaceful, and free. That is set against the "domination system of the powers" of the world.[47] With traditional theology, Wink believes in the final reconciliation of the powers, but in contrast with tradition, he envisions reconciliation pantheistically in terms of the "sublimation of evil into the godhead."[48] In sum: Wink's unique contribution is that on the one hand, with the modernists (and "liberal" theology), he rejects the time-bound metaphysical conception of powers by making them by and large immanent.[49] But in contrast to the modernists, he considers those powers not only real but also such that their influence goes robustly beyond the physical and visible.[50]

The leading Pentecostal constructive theologian Amos Yong has taken up the earlier powers proposals and reconstructed them in a highly creative and insightful manner in the wider context of plural pneumatology, "spirit-filled cosmos"[51] (on which more below). Pneumatology is also the gateway to considering angels in Pannenberg. In a highly creative move, Pannenberg puts pneumatological resources in dialogue with theological tradition and current scientific field-theories in constructing a new account of angels and powers. As far as we consider "the Divine Spirit as a field that in its creative working manifests itself in time and space," he surmises that an analogy can be found in viewing biblical and patristic ideas of angels as "spiritual entities and powers that work in both nature and history either at the command of God or in demonic autonomy against God."[52] Rather than personal in the traditional sense, these powers are forces and influences. Indeed, Pannenberg concludes:

> Fundamentally the angels of the biblical traditions are natural forces that from another angle might be the object of scientific descriptions. If we

46. Wink, *Engaging the Powers*, pp. 65-85.

47. Wink, *Engaging the Powers*; see p. 44 for the chart contrasting the two systems.

48. Wink, *Unmasking the Powers*, p. 39. Deeply indebted also to process theism, Wink's approach finds a lot of resistance there; see further, Griffin, "Why Demonic Power Exists," pp. 223-39.

49. It seems to me Yong's interpretation of Wink as the advocate of both spiritual and "earthly" interpretations of powers is somewhat confusing and lacks nuance in that respect (Yong, *In the Days of Caesar*, p. 148). One should rather stick with Wink's own terminology and speak of "inner" (which still are immanent) and "outer" aspects of the powers.

50. Similarly to Tillich, Wink (*Unmasking the Powers*, pp. 25-26) is drawn to Jung's psychological archetypes, which transcend individual human beings.

51. Yong, *The Spirit of Creation*, pp. 173-225; see also, his *In the Days of Caesar*, pp. 121-65.

52. Pannenberg, *ST* 2:102.

define forces like wind or fire or stars as angels of God, then we are relating them to God their Creator and to the human experience of being affected by them as servants of God or as demonic powers that oppose his will. Why should not natural forces in the forms in which we now know them be viewed as God's servants and messengers, i.e., as angels?[53]

Before engaging critically these contemporary Christian interpretations of powers and attempting a constructive proposal, let us inquire into the experiences and theological meaning of the powers in other faith traditions.

Spirits and Powers among Living Faith Traditions

Angels and Demons in Abrahamic Traditions

Although belief in angels, demons, and spiritual beings among secular Jews (a majority of whom reside in the United States) is mixed, over half of them no longer affirm the traditional belief;[54] among religious Jews that belief is still high, and spiritual powers have a definite place in the scriptural tradition.[55] As is well known, the OT term *malak* (messenger) can be used of both divine and human agents; only the context determines the meaning. A special category is the "angel of Yahweh" (Gen. 19; Exod. 14:19; among others), at times identifiable with God himself. Well known also is the fact that postexilic Judaism creatively adopted features of Persian (Iranian) and Zoroastrian[56] angelology; however, this does not justify viewing Jewish theology of powers as by and large the function of Persian tradition. Somewhat like Christian tradition in which medieval theology brought about the most sophisticated angelology, in the Jewish Kabbalah the most creative reflection on spiritual beings emerged.[57]

---

53. Pannenberg, *ST* 2:106-7.

54. Pew Research Center, "Summary of Key Findings," pp. 11-12.

55. The importance of spirits, good and evil, is also well known in the Qumranic literature, an important influence also to the NT; see Lichtenbarger, "Spirits and Demons." Among the main Jewish movements in the NT times, only the Sadducees refused to believe in spirits (Mark 12:18; Acts 23:8).

56. To give an example: the demon Asmodeus in the book of Tobit derives from the name of the Zoroastrian god of anger, Aeshmadaeva. For other examples, see Piras, "Angels," p. 345.

57. Interestingly, Kabbalah teachers were drawn to the fight between Jacob and the angel of the Lord in Gen. 32 as the starting point of angelic speculation. Understandably, the book of Ezekiel also inspired thinking of spiritual beings (Piras, "Angels," p. 345).

The appearance of demons, the evil spiritual beings, in the OT is infrequent, particularly in the postexilic period — although throughout the canon there are less pronounced and more elusive themes of cosmic conflict and chaos (Job 3:8; 7:12; 9:13; 38:8-11; Pss. 29:3-4; 74:13-14; 89:9-10; Isa. 27:1; 51:9-11).[58] Differently from Asiatic and other pagan traditions, the role of both good and evil angels is always subordinated to Yahweh, and thus dualism is avoided. Even the role of Satan, which gradually evolves over history, is that of a subordinate — in some cases, even Yahweh's servant (as in Job).[59]

This clear and uncompromising distinction between God and other spiritual beings carried over to Christian tradition and became even more marked in patristic theology. Building on Jewish angelology, the Fathers worked at "limiting the mythological and poetic developments of Judaic and Gnostic angelology and emphasized the role of angels as intermediaries in the action of salvation and their role as servants." Even when angelic beings were invoked and adored (as ruled in the Council of Laodicea in 336), their role as intermediary and subordinate to the triune God was emphasized in patristic theology.[60]

Of the three Abrahamic faiths,[61] it is in Islam that angels and spiritual beings play the most significant role, whether in scriptural tradition or in (folk) piety.[62] Belief in angels is one of the key tenets of Islamic belief, and their denial is regarded as a rejection of the Word of God.[63] Their importance is also highlighted in that, unlike Jewish-Christian tradition, there is a well-known scriptural teaching about angels' creation prior to that of humans and about Allah's consultation with them before creating humans (Q 38:71-72).[64] Somewhat similarly to the OT, the Qur'an provides various kinds of artistic portraits of angels (such as having hands and two, three, or four wings; Q 35:1; 6:93) and speaks of their ministering in various kinds of tasks of service and messaging, including intercession (Q 53:25). A further similarity is an allusion

---

58. For a detailed study, see G. Boyd, *God at War*, pp. 73-113. For a rich bibliographic resource, see the introduction to Eddy and Beilby, eds., *Understanding Spiritual Warfare*, pp. 13-15.

59. Stephens, "Demons," pp. 2277-78.

60. Piras, "Angels," p. 346.

61. Still a useful resource is Jung, *Fallen Angels*.

62. Highly useful and accessible accounts of Islamic angelology are Riddell, "How Allah Communicates"; Bannister, "Angels in Islamic Oral Tradition"; Musk, "Angels and Demons in Folk Islam."

63. Piras, "Angels," p. 347.

64. MacDonald, "Creation of Man and Angels."

to the hierarchy of angels, Gabriel being the most prominent, and Michael second. The most important angelic task is that of Gabriel as the messenger from whom Muhammad receives the divine revelation. No wonder that highly sophisticated angelologies were constructed by leading Islamic philosophers and theologians. In Avicenna's vision there emerges a large variety of intermediate spiritual beings ("ten cherubic intelligences"). Philosophers such as Suhrawardi incorporated in their highly sophisticated speculations influences from Neoplatonism, Zoroastrianism, and so forth.

A special class of heavenly beings, the *jinn* — hugely important in folk Islam — are mentioned often in the Qur'an. They are made of fire (as opposed to humans, who are made of clay). "Jinns have a social organization and family life, and interact variously with humans, including through romantic love and intermarriage. They can be contacted through various forms of magic, and may respond favorably, but can also be easily offended and will react accordingly. At times they behave playfully, teasing and tricking humans."[65] They are endowed with freedom of the will, and there is ambiguity about whether they are evil or good. In folk religion, they are frequently invoked for magical and miraculous purposes. Spiritual healers often address the *jinn* as part of their rituals.[66]

Spiritual Beings and Powers in Asiatic Faiths

The role and nature of angelic beings and powers in Asiatic faith traditions are more complex than in monotheistic traditions.[67] In Hinduism, the contours and definitions are quite elusive. It is often particularly difficult to make a clear distinction between deities and nondivine spiritual beings, which in monotheistic faiths is categorical.[68] In contrast to Abrahamic traditions, even the main deities (such as Vishnu) get entangled in numerous ways in the lives and

65. Stephens, "Demons," p. 2280.

66. Newby, "Angels"; "Jinn."

67. I don't see it as useful — and certainly not as necessary — to limit the investigation of the topic of angels and powers to the monotheistic faiths (or traditions with strong monotheistic leanings such as Zoroastrianism), as argued by Piras, "Angels," p. 343.

68. The main reason is that in Hinduism the same vital force *(prana)* undergirds all forms of existence from the inanimate to the (most) divine; see Gnanakan, "The Manthiravadi," p. 141. The classic proposal that angels and titans (of Greek mythology), as well as *devas* and *asuras,* were more or less identical has not won much support. See Coomaraswamy, "Angel and Titan."

workings of what Western terminology would name less-than-divine beings. Furthermore, not all demons are evil as in Abrahamic traditions.[69] The belief in reincarnation blurs any absolute distinction between human and "super-human" (angelic, demonic) beings. To make the issue more complicated, even *devas* (the godlike or divine beings) are subject to reincarnation; but also, it is not impossible for humans in some cases to be reincarnated as *devas*. Because of the complex, multimillennial history of religious and cultural beliefs, it is no wonder that there is a rich diversity of beliefs and traditions and rituals related to either invoking good spirits or trying to cast away evil spirits. "In the Vedas and epics, suprahuman beings are mentioned whose exact nature, and their differences from everyday humans, are often unclear. *Rakshasas*, *pisacas*, and *vetalas* are demon-like beings that haunt graveyards, threaten the living, and feed on human flesh; some are ghosts, others are suprahuman. *Pitrs* are ancestral spirits."[70]

Like the relation of Judaism to Christianity, Hinduism provides Buddhism basic scriptural and religious traditions even when those traditions were critiqued and at times significantly revised, as particularly in the Theravada tradition. This applies to the heritage of spiritual powers as well. Buddhist traditions have wide and rich demonological traditions with many local colors.[71] Somewhat similar to the temptations of Jesus on the eve of his public ministry, in early Buddhist tradition Mara, the arch-devil, along with his three daughters, Rati (Desire), Raga (Pleasure), and Tanha (Restlessness), sought to dissuade Gautama from achieving enlightenment.[72] Although the Theravada

69. Stephens, "Demons," p. 2275. This paragraph is also indebted to Witzel, "Vedas and Upanisads," pp. 71-73. A highly nuanced discussion of the "sura" (virtuous) versus "asura" (evil) dichotomy in Hindu cosmology concerning the complexity of determining which are good and which are evil is Gabriel, "The Sura-Asura Theme in Hinduism"; see also, appendix B (pp. 274-77) for a highly useful listing with explanations of deities and spiritual beings. Highly useful reference works include Bhattacharyya, *Indian Demonology*; Sutherland, *Disguises of the Demon*. *Yaksa* is an ambiguous (almost) pan-Asian term referring to (originally) benevolent spirits that also have a dark side.

70. Stephens, "Demons," p. 2276. For the Buddhist notion of the "spirits," a wide and elusive concept, see Law, *Buddhist Conception of Spirits*.

71. For a fine presentation of some of those, see Yong, *Pneumatology and the Christian-Buddhist Dialogue*, chap. 9. I am not quite sure what to think of the claim that "[t]here is no concept of radical evil in Buddhism." Even a cursory look at some ancient demonologies might persuade one of the contrary. See Southwold, "Buddhism and Evil," p. 138.

72. For scriptural references and introductory discussion, see Guruge, "The Buddha's Encounters with Mara the Tempter," particularly section 2. The standard discussion is W. Boyd, *Satan and Mara*; for a more accessible discussion, see Wikramagamage, "Mara as Evil in Buddhism," pp. 109-15.

tradition soon (against its initial intentions, one may argue) began to develop quite sophisticated visions of spiritual beings, that development was even more massive in the various Mahayana traditions and their extremely rich folk piety. Mahayana was also deeply influenced by local cultures, particularly in China, Japan, Tibet, and beyond.[73]

This brief discussion of "other spirits" in four living faiths reveals that there is a remarkable consistency concerning the place of spiritual beings across different traditions, both monotheistic, polytheistic, and "non"-theistic (Theravada). Similarly, belief in spiritual beings seems not to be limited to any cultural or geographical location or to any specific racial group. It is also clear that the basic structure and orientation of the religion, whether strictly monotheistic or not, determines the place of the powers vis-à-vis the Ultimate Reality. In Abrahamic faiths, they are strictly put under the lordship of God. Furthermore, it seems that a division into evil and good forces is a basic human religious intuition even when the boundary line may be variously (or at times ambiguously) drawn. Finally, it is clear that all major faith traditions assume the belief in the influence of the spirits on the affairs of the humans and the world. It is curious that what is now considered the normative opinion in post-Enlightenment academia in the West — that spirits are but an archaic, outdated, and mistaken imaginary fantasy — is historically a new and novel view.

A Note on the Form and Logic of Argumentation

Having now surveyed and analyzed the main turns in the interpretations of angels, demons, and powers in Christian tradition up to the end of the twentieth century, and having taken a brief look at the theme in four living faiths, we will devote the rest of the chapter to a constructive proposal in three interrelated stages. First, in the following section, a preliminary constructive proposal concerning the nature and role of angels, demons, and powers will be attempted in critical dialogue with the views studied.

While in the first section the focus is more on what traditional theology calls angelology (proper), in the third section ("Encountering Evil Powers and the Demonic: A Theological Proposal") the focus shifts more toward demonology — although, at the same time, keeping in mind that neither biblically nor theologically is it advisable to treat that distinction in too stark of terms (even

73. For a useful summary, see *Encyclopædia Britannica Online*, s.v. "angel and demon."

though the distinction needs to be made both thematically and heuristically, notwithstanding some loud voices to the contrary among theologians).

In between these two sections, the middle one ("Toward a Theology of the Spirit-Filled Cosmos") is a proposal addressing the need to construct a cosmology in keeping with a plural pneumatology. That effort feeds into both the previous and the following sections' discussions, although for the sake of pedagogical clarity it is placed between them.

Angels and Powers in a Constructive Theological Perspective: A Tentative Proposal

The Reformed American theologian Amy Plantinga Pauw succinctly sets the tone for a contemporary consideration of angels, spirits, and powers: "I propose the practice of Baroque musical ornamentation as an analogy to the place of reflection on angels and demons in Christian theology. It is not the main melody, but functions to enhance the main theological themes — God, creation, Christ, salvation, eschatology, and so on."[74] Indeed, talk about powers is deeply related to the internal coherence of theism. While any talk about spiritual beings among most theologians seems to be impossible particularly vis-à-vis the current scientific worldview, that fear in itself is ironic at best for one wishing to continue affirming theism. Indeed, "it seems a bit odd to profess belief in God while sneering at belief in other spiritual powers."[75]

Biblical testimonies to angels and spiritual powers abound — with the curious exception that there is nothing about angels or other spiritual beings in the creation narratives of Genesis 1–2.[76] That observation, however, does not diminish the importance of considering spiritual beings as created beings in light of later biblical testimonies (particularly those of the NT). The importance of affirming their created nature is to place them under the Creator. Furthermore, in contrast from the (then) contemporary Hellenistic philosophies and religions in which "spirit" was linked with eternity and immutability as opposed to "flesh" and the "earthly," Judeo-Christian tradition adds yet another category in the stratified nature of reality, namely, "created spirit."[77]

In the NT, spiritual realities are often treated in a manner that sug-

---

74. Pauw, "Where Theologians Fear to Tread," p. 39.
75. Pauw, "Where Theologians Fear to Tread," p. 41.
76. Noble, "The Spirit World," pp. 192-94.
77. Noble, "The Spirit World," p. 193.

gests a nonpersonal nature. Just think of expressions such as seven spirits or lampstands, torches, stars, and so forth (Rev. 1:4-20). The mention of four winds (Rev. 7:1; cf. Heb. 1:7) is a reference to cosmic forces, including heavenly "hosts," stars (Isa. 40:26). Importantly, the NT also uses nomenclature such as "principalities," "powers," and "thrones" (Rom. 8:38-39; 1 Cor. 15:24; Eph. 1:21; 1 Pet. 3:22).[78] From a pneumatological point of view, what is really significant is the naming of heavenly, angelic forces as "spirits" *(pneumata)* (Heb. 1:14; 12:9; Rev. 1:4; etc.), including "ministering" spirits (Heb. 1:14). What is clear is that all these powers are both created in Christ (Col. 1:16)[79] and subjected under the Lordship of Christ (2:15). Barth was thus mistaken in denying that the Scripture says something about the nature of angels, particularly that they are created, subjected under Christ's Lordship, are ministering spirits, and so on.[80] His opinion is also mistaken for the obvious fact that any description of function assumes some knowledge of the agent.

Departing from Christian tradition, Barth also failed to affirm the fallen nature of some angels.[81] Barth's insistence that demons, having "no common root" with angelic creatures, are a mythological personification of nothingness, "that element of contradiction and opposition which exists on the left hand of God and is thus subject to His world-dominion,"[82] is mere speculation without traditional or theological basis. Even worse, Barth speculatively locates them in "a sphere of contradiction and opposition which as such can only be overthrown and hasten to destruction."[83] On the contrary, according to the biblical testimonies, the powers are fallen (1 Pet. 3:22; most probably also Gen. 6:1-4),[84]

78. For details, see Arnold, *Powers of Darkness;* Gatumu, *Pauline Concept of Supernatural Powers.*

79. Similarly in *1 Clement* 59.3.

80. Indeed, with regard to the depiction of "ministering spirits," Barth had to admit that it comes close to defining angels (*CD* III/3, p. 452). See further, Pannenberg, *ST* 2:103.

81. Materially similar, though unrelated, to my knowledge, is the innovative thesis by Wesley Carr that "powers" in the NT (at least in Ephesians and Colossians) have nothing to do with the demonic; they are merely angelic powers, and the demonic/cosmic interpretation is a matter of second-century and later Christian tradition. Carr, *Angels and Principalities.* This view is hardly convincing, and even Wink debunks it as exegetically totally mistaken in *Naming the Powers,* p. 6.

82. Barth, *CD* III/3, p. 523.

83. Barth, *CD* III/3, p. 522.

84. Affirmed at the Fourth Lateran Council of 1215 (canon 1): "The devil and the other demons were indeed created by God good by nature but they became bad through themselves" (as opposed to human beings, who "sinned at the suggestion of the devil"), in *Internet Medieval Sourcebook,* http://www.fordham.edu/halsall/basis/lateran4.asp (8/7/2013).

an idea that led to the belief in the fall of angels in Jewish apocalyptic (echoed in 1 Pet. 3:19).[85] Although one may not wish to affirm the whole mythical-speculative tradition of the angelic fall after Jewish-Christian tradition, there are no grounds for categorically excluding the demonic spirits from the rest of the spiritual beings, that is, angels. At the same time, the biblical account gives precious few details, if any, of how the powers fell.[86] That said, although fallen, the powers will be redeemed, as Berkhof, Yoder, Grenz, Wink, and others have rightly argued (Col. 1:15-20; Eph. 1:20-21).[87]

The relation of the "spirits" to the Absolute Spirit is a complicated matter in light of biblical testimonies. Unlike with any other creatures, there is at times a virtual identification of God with angels (Gen. 18:2; 21:17-21; 31:11-13; Exod. 3; Judg. 13:21-23; and so forth). This identification was the reason for Barth's mistaken notion that therefore the angels do not have independent being;[88] but that cannot be, because creaturely existence by definition means independence from the Creator.[89]

What about the origin of angelic beings? As said, even the creation narratives do not discuss that topic. In keeping with evolutionary theory and the idea of emergence (on which more details in the last main section of the chapter), this project argues that spiritual beings can be envisioned as emergent realities that evolve gradually as part of God's long-term creative process. That said, we have to leave open several questions: on the basis of biblical revelation, we do not know "when" (timewise) angelic beings emerged; tradition's assumption that they are "older" than humans seems to be well taken. How their emergence relates to the evolvement of the physical/material is similarly an unresolved issue in theology. For disembodied beings, as angels are con-

---

85. An important early statement is in Tertullian, *Apology*, chap. 22. For an extended treatment of the fall of angels, building on the exegetical tradition of the Fathers and later Christian tradition, see J. Edwards, *Works*, vol. 2, chap. 11 (particularly pp. 608-11), at http://www.ccel.org. By and large unknown, Edwards's contribution to modern angelology is significant; for details, see McClymond and McDermott, *Theology of Jonathan Edwards*, chap. 18. A brief discussion is in Pauw, "Where Theologians Fear to Tread," pp. 44-51.

86. Rightly noted by Calvin, *Institutes* 1.14.16. We also have to remember that there is no teaching about the angelic fall in Gen. 1–3 (no more than in Rom. 5), although Christian tradition so speculated. For details, see chap. 15 in Kärkkäinen, *Creation and Humanity*.

87. So also, Yong, *In the Days of Caesar*, pp. 149-51. In this regard, Ellul's reluctance to consider them God's creations in the first place and also redeemable must be rejected; see Ellul, *The Subversion of Christianity*, p. 179; Ellul, *Ethics of Freedom*, p. 159.

88. Barth, *CD* III/3, p. 480. Therefore, Barth surmises, angels cannot disobey because they do not have a will to do so (p. 480).

89. Rightly noted by Pannenberg, *ST* 2:104.

ceived in Christian tradition, to speak of emergence out of the physical does not seem warranted,[90] particularly because even the physical in theistic belief derives ultimately from the spirit(ual). Nor do we know if the evolutionary process of spiritual beings continues or not. And so forth.

What about the personal nature of angels?[91] In contrast from the current theological majority view but in concurrence with Christian tradition, I wish to affirm their personal nature in some real sense. There are two grounds for this. First is the uncontested biblical teaching. Christian tradition had good biblical reasons for conceiving of angels and demons as spiritual agents with intelligence and will (1 Kings 22:19-21; Dan. 10:5-21; Matt. 4:3-11; Mark 5:6-13).[92] Even those theologians who disagree with their having personality do not contest that the Bible clearly seems to assume it. Even Pannenberg, who contests their personhood, has to admit that "[t]he forces that are in the service of God's lordship over creation may obviously become autonomous centers of powers."[93] Any talk about "autonomous centers of powers," however, implies a fairly definite form of personhood! The other reason for affirming some type of personality for angels is related to the emergence argument: as in humans, who have gradually emerged into self-conscious beings with personality, there is no reason in principle to deny that possibility for other beings in the cosmos. That said, in keeping with a plural pneumatology, constructive theology can easily imagine various types of angelic beings from "personal" to ecclesial (Rev. 2–3), to institutional/corporeal (such as the principalities and powers), to terrestrial (as in Judg. 13:20; Heb. 1:7; Rev. 7:1-2; 16:5), all the way to celestial spirits and forces (Job 38:7; Isa. 40:26; Luke 2:13; Heb. 12:22; Rev. 5:11).[94] While one should not be dogmatic about issues as elusive as angelology, it is useful to say at least that constructive theology in search of a plural pneumatology can envision various classes of spiritual beings in keeping with the rich and diverse biblical witnesses and traditional theology.

What about the demonic powers? If evil at large is but the privation of good and thus not an ontological reality (but rather its destruction and perversion, as Augustine and much of Christian tradition has taught), it seems reasonable to think that notions of demons' personal nature must be much more reserved than with regard to angels. This is not to deny their objec-

---

90. Contra Yong, *Spirit of Creation*, p. 213.

91. Pannenberg (*ST* 2:106) calls this the "greatest difficulty besetting the traditional doctrine of angels."

92. See further, Yong, *The Spirit of Creation*, p. 214.

93. Pannenberg, *ST* 2:105.

94. For details, see Yong, *The Spirit of Creation*, pp. 214-16.

tive nature as an emergent reality but rather to argue that even then they are parasitic.[95] Like good angels, evil demonic beings can be envisioned under many categories, from the archetypal primeval chaos, to destructive powers, to "domination systems" (social, historical, political, economic, religious, and so on), to regional and geographic entities, and even "anticelestially as fallen angels."[96]

On the question of the personhood of powers, what concerns me even in such a nuanced pneumatological account as Pannenberg's is its deeply "de-mythologizing" tendency. Claiming that natural forces such as wind or fire or stars can be considered "angels" (messengers) of God is not necessarily problematic. What is problematic is the claim that this is the most we can say about powers' nature and identity.

What about the debate concerning the powers' spiritual or immanen-tist nature? Wink has of course done a great service in exposing the mod-ernist reductionism in its denial of powers. His desire to tackle the biblical text in light of Christian tradition and the post-Enlightenment world is to be acknowledged. What bothers me most is Wink's totally nonmetaphysical interpretation of powers. Whatever one thinks of the status of metaphysics in contemporary theology and philosophy, denying all metaphysical implications of the Christian idea of powers is unacceptable to me. I also wonder why one should juxtapose the traditional (and contemporary) "literal" understanding — despite its many problematic applications and experiences — with the cur-rent understanding related to powers. Couldn't a plural cosmology have them both? Unlike Wink, this project's positing of a plural pneumatology clearly points to the dual interpretation. It seems to best do justice to the diversity of the NT materials and also to the theological intuitions of the church. Not only in Paul but also in the Lukan corpus we see the dual reference to the nature of the powers (recall that Luke's writings comprise about as much text as all the authentic Pauline letters). In Lukan interpretation the angels/powers are both spiritual (Luke 9:1; Acts 1:7; 8:19; 26:18) and sociopolitical (Luke 12:11; 20:20; 22:25; Acts 9:14; 26:10, 12).[97]

What is the theological meaning of the Bible's connecting angels with heaven, God's dwelling place (Ps. 33:6)? While heaven may be related to the divine incomprehensibility and inaccessibility to the human mind,[98] it seems

---

95. For careful similar reflections, see Yong, *In the Days of Caesar,* pp. 162-63.
96. For details, see Yong, *The Spirit of Creation,* pp. 218-19.
97. Yong, *In the Days of Caesar,* p. 149.
98. Barth, *CD* III/3, p. 3.

to me that its theological meaning, as Moltmann rightly highlights, has to do with openness to the future and new opportunities.[99] On this basis, Pannenberg makes the brilliant observation that to the extent powers and spirits are creatures, "the field forces and their activities that direct the course of nature have a temporal structure that is oriented to the future," and that as soon as "they close themselves against the future of God, the kingdom of his possibilities, and thus become closed systems," they are the God-opposing powers and forces the Bible speaks of. Could that be a way to explain the NT conviction that the whole world is under the control of evil forces (John 12:31; 14:30; 16:11; Eph 2:2)?[100] In contrast to these fallen forces, in the work of the Spirit, the future of God and the dawning of God's righteous rule embodied in the ministry of the Son are already present.[101]

The reference to eschatological consummation and the angels' role as witnesses to the future, however, should not be understood as making them merely abstract, "heavenly" beings with no effects on life here on earth. Pannenberg's way of connecting them with the workings of the natural world contains a kernel of truth. Even more robustly, Rahner linked them with this world. However, Rahner goes too far in making angels virtually merely immanent forces — and doing so, he acknowledges that this understanding is in conflict with traditional understandings that make them spirits and present at creation.[102] But why should we go either with (Barth's) mainly heavenly or with (Rahner's) mainly earthly interpretation? Couldn't a plural pneumatology have them both?

The topic of encountering the demonic powers will be taken up at the end of this chapter, once the need to construct a theology of the spirit-filled world vis-à-vis the scientific worldview is considered carefully.

99. Moltmann, *God in Creation*, pp. 159-63 particularly. A highly insightful essay is Deane-Drummond, "Jürgen Moltmann on Heaven."

100. Pannenberg, *ST* 2:108.

101. See Pannenberg, *ST* 2:109.

102. Rahner, "On Angels," 19:252-74. Another curious and novel feature is Rahner's speculation that angels might be "eschatological beings" who come into being later in the evolutionary process. He defines them as "regional subjectivities," that is, as modes of transcendental consciousness that are not linked to the cosmos through the kinds of bodies that humans have, but, analogous to the human soul-body form of life, they have a special connectedness to certain regions of cosmic reality. For details, see M. R. Barnes, "Demythologization in the Theology of Karl Rahner."

Toward a Theology of the Spirit-Filled Cosmos

The discussion has indicated so far that a plural pneumatology developed in this project cannot be content with the reductionism of much of contemporary theology in virtually denying the reality of spiritual powers. In critique of that standard unitive pneumatology that reigns in the theological academy of the Global North, this project boldly suggests a theology of a spirit-filled cosmos. The most serious challenge, calling for careful theological and philosophical consideration, relates to contemporary natural sciences and their underlying naturalism. This project claims that taking the natural sciences seriously does not necessarily lead to the denial of spiritual powers in the cosmos. Importantly, the theist is compelled to conclude that the positing of "little spirits" in the cosmos is no more challenging or "unnatural" than that of the "Big Spirit" (God). Theism's internal coherence, as mentioned above, hinders us from rejecting spiritual beings with appeal to dogmatic naturalistic reasons.

On top of scientific and theological considerations, strong appeal to the theological envisioning of spiritual powers comes from the two segments of world Christianity that, combined, constitute the majority of the Christian church, namely, the Pentecostal/charismatic phenomenon and the Christianity of the Global South. Constructive theology can bypass these "majority" views only to its detriment; at least these testimonies should be carefully considered even when theology's critical task cannot be left behind.

Spirits and Scientific Naturalism

There is no denying that between the general worldview of post-Enlightenment Christian theology and the biblical-patristic ethos (stretching all the way to the advent of modernity) there is a radical difference regarding the discernment and acknowledgment of spirits and spiritual realities.[103] Even among those moderns who continue affirming belief in the "Great Spirit" (God), belief in lesser spirits has been in steady decline. However, while this trend is strong among Christian theologians, it is much less so among scholars of other faith traditions.

The difficulty with and refusal to acknowledge other spirits have everything to do with the rise to prominence — first among the scientists and philosophers and soon thereafter among theologians and scholars of religions

103. See Wiebe, *God and Other Spirits.*

— of various forms of naturalism. A multifaceted and complex concept in contemporary philosophy/theology, naturalism can be, roughly speaking, divided into three subcategories. First, there is "scientism," or what I have named "antisupernaturalist" or antitheistic naturalism, which categorically rejects any notions of metaphysical transcendence. This is the mainstream view among scientists who care to delve into philosophical reflections. Second, there is what I have called — for lack of a better term — "'religion-friendly' [non] theistic naturalism," which, unlike the former, does not reject religion per se, although at the end of the day it declines to acknowledge the reality of the divine in any theistic sense. Instead, it makes either creativity or the process of emergence ("creation") or something else the ultimate. (Confusingly, many advocates of this view such as Wesley J. Wildman prefer to call it theistic naturalism, which for me is a contradiction in terms, as there is no *theos* in this view.) Third, there is theistic naturalism proper, as represented most brilliantly by the late biochemist-priest Arthur C. Peacocke. In that view, belief in God on a theistic worldview is robustly affirmed, although (as in Peacocke's case) no divine "intervention" such as miracles is allowed.[104] Although the third option, namely, theism proper, is fully affirmed in the present project, its deep internal inconsistency — namely, the acceptance of theism after Abrahamic faith traditions but the rejection of any "supernatural" actions of God in the world God has created — should be corrected; behind it lies a mistaken notion of what divine action is, including an outdated modernist concept of the category of the miraculous.[105] Without repeating the long and detailed discussion appearing elsewhere (chaps. 2 and 7 in *Creation and Humanity*), I reiterate the main point for this discussion: not only do the anti- or nontheistic forms of naturalism rule out any meaningful notion of theistic spirits/spiritual beings/spiritual powers, but also theistic naturalism (particularly among many believing religion-science advocates) seems to have a very hard time in accounting for them. Briefly put: a spirit-filled cosmos with powers seems soon to be an extinct species of worldviews. But is that a necessary conclusion? Before attempting a response, let us ask: Why is this topic worth discussing in a constructive theology? What is theologically at stake here? The answer is that

---

104. For a detailed analysis and assessment of forms of naturalism and their significance for theology (including theology-science dialogue), see chap. 2 in *Creation and Humanity*. While I of course affirm Peacocke's theism, I also critique the deep inconsistency of that position, namely, the acceptance of theism following Abrahamic faith traditions but the rejection of any "supernatural" actions of God in the world God has created; see chap. 7 in Kärkkäinen, *Trinity and Revelation*.

105. For a detailed discussion, see chap. 7 in *Creation and Humanity*.

a number of issues, having to do with both theology's internal coherence (see the next section) and theology's relation to the sciences and secular worldview, are at stake. Let us begin from the latter, keeping in mind the remarks on forms of naturalism briefly stated above.

Although the spirit-defeating scientism along with nontheistic naturalism and ontological/metaphysical physicalism reigns behind all work in the natural sciences (as well as in many behavioral-social sciences), there are also indications of a wide reconsideration under way with regard to ontology. Among the questions reflected upon are, what is "matter" in general, and of what "stuff" is the cosmos (and life as we know it) made of? While this reconsideration has little or nothing to do with religions and gods in general (and hence has little if any apologetic value), its significance for the continuing quest for a more comprehensive cosmology from a theistic perspective should not be dismissed. To begin with, theologians and philosophers should remind the scientists that the default position in which one moves from methodological physicalism (that is, natural processes are to be studied as strictly from an empirical point of view as possible, without positing any kind of supernatural causes) to ontological physicalism (that is, all that there is, is the physical) is unwarranted. In other words, attempting to establish a metaphysical claim on the basis of scientific observation is a category mistake: science, to be science, cannot go beyond its limits (although scientists, often even in the name of science, break this law all the time!). This is not to try to disprove — in principle — the possibility of naturalist materialism as the (most) correct answer to the ultimate question; it is rather to raise the needed critical question as to how far scientism can be taken as the default position.

More to the point of this discussion, it seems to many that in general current science is moving away from what "physical" used to mean even in the near past. Just mind these well-known facts that any scientific work currently assumes as the basis: even for the hard-core materialist, "matter" is but energy and field (waves?); according to the theory of relativity, mass is nothing but a form of energy (in relation to the speed of light); in quantum mechanics, viewing subatomic entities as particles is complementary to regarding them as probability waves; and so forth.[106] The point is that "the twentieth century, which began with what could be regarded as an empirical demonstration of the materialistic atomistic vision of Democritus, saw a progressive 'dematerialization' of physics. . . . Modern physics, then, has something quite different in view regarding the structure of the universe than the ordinary parlance used

---

106. See further, Sikkema, "Physicist's Reformed Critique," p. 22.

by the 'nonreductive physicalist.'"[107] Indeed, how vastly different contemporary materialism is through the lens of force fields, quantum theory, and string theory.[108] Ironically, as is well known, "matter" is not a well-defined scientific concept (whereas "mass" and "energy" are well-defined concepts).[109]

Consider also the existence of consciousness and the mental — including morality and religiosity. Although undoubtedly these are materially conditioned processes, to claim that that is all they are leads to the paradoxical conclusion that then the "matter" we speak of has little or nothing in common with our current scientific understanding! We need to find new ways of negotiating and envisioning what "physical/material" and "nonphysical/nonmaterial" may mean.[110] Here comes the importance of the necessary theistic presupposition of the Spirit (God, divine Spirit) as the ultimate source of everything. Rightly the (formerly) Oxford theologian-philosopher Keith Ward reminds us of how radically different idealism as a metaphysical position is from physicalism/materialism of contemporary naturalism in its claim that "the material world . . . exists as an environment created by a primordial mind in which finite minds can exist in mutual self-expression and interaction. . . . It totally reverses the modern myth that minds are by-products of a purely material evolutionary process, completely determined by physical events in their bodies and brains."[111]

In this light, it seems to me premature for theology to jump on that kind of scientism-cum-physicalism bandwagon that in principle rules out spirits of all sizes, so to speak. Hence, I feel sympathy for the philosopher-theologian Philip Clayton's preference for a "monism" that is not physicalist in itself, although it takes physicality most seriously. He argues that we should not assume that the "entities postulated by physics complete the inventory of what exists," while insisting that "[r]eality is ultimately composed of one basic kind of stuff."[112] That kind of monism can be used in support of a plural pneumatology and stratified cosmology. It would allow for a more holistic and diversified ontology of created reality characterized, or qualified, by various modal aspects. Thereby it would not try to say the last word on the topic that in light of current scientific knowledge is still open-ended (and might remain so for a long time!).

107. Sikkema, "Physicist's Reformed Critique," p. 25.

108. Ward, *More Than Matter*, chap. 2.

109. Stoeger, "Mind-Brain Problem," pp. 133-35; see also, Heller, "Adventures of the Concept."

110. Stoeger, "Mind-Brain Problem," p. 132.

111. Ward, *More Than Matter*, p. 57.

112. Clayton, *Mind and Emergence*.

At the same time, this kind of approach to reality would also fund a more robust multidimensional and pluralist approach in the sciences: "[R]ecognizing the physical as one aspect among others will help develop a more fully orbed philosophy of science, recognizing the importance of the different methodologies of inquiry that rightfully play roles in the other scientific disciplines, rather than focusing on what some regard as the highly problematic ontology of the entities of mechanics due to their lying so far beyond imagination."[113] Even such a staunch physicalist (and atheist) as the American philosopher Jaegwon Kim is honest enough to admit that "Physicalism is not the whole truth, but it is the truth near enough."[114] (While that may sound like a lame concession, for longtime readers of Kim's evolving views, it is a huge step!)

If physicalism is not the final answer, why could we not envision what Amos Yong names "emergentist and evolutionary cosmology" with many spirits? It would be done in dialogue with philosophy and science of emergence and the best of religious and theological traditions. Emergence most foundationally means "that new and unpredictable phenomena are naturally produced by interactions in nature; that these new structures, organisms, and ideas are not reducible to the subsystems on which they depend; and that the newly evolved realities in turn exercise a causal influence on the parts out of which they arose."[115] This understanding would defeat the principle of "physical closure" that seeks to explain everything in the world in terms of physical processes and entities.[116] Emergence allows a plural theory of causation with bottom-up and top-down/whole-part causation. Indeed, careful study of nature reveals various types of causalities at work, "from classical Newtonian causality, to gravity, to the influence of quantum fields, to the 'holistic constraints' or integrated systems — and on to the pervasive role of mental causes in human life."[117] Noteworthy in this regard are also quantum theory's entanglement causality (in which particles or events vastly distant from each other "mysteriously" co-vary) and its acknowledgment of the influence of intentionality (if not otherwise, then at least in "measurement" and observation).[118] In this kind of cosmos, not only is there "weak" emergence, which,

---

113. Sikkema, "Physicist's Reformed Critique," p. 26.

114. J. Kim, *Physicalism, or Something Near Enough*, p. 6.

115. Clayton, *Mind and Emergence*, p. vi; for the history, see chap. 1.

116. See Clayton, *Mind and Emergence*, pp. 4-7. For an important discussion, see N. Murphy, "Reductionism," pp. 19-39.

117. Clayton, "Impossible Possibility," pp. 254-55.

118. See P. C. W. Davies, *Other Worlds*, pp. 132-33. See also, Stapp, *Mind, Matter, and Quantum Mechanics*. I am indebted to Clayton's essay.

while proposing new levels and patterns, still maintains in principle the physical closure (or something close to that), but also "strong" emergence, which, as defined above, speaks of the capacity of new patterns and processes to exert causal influence.[119] While the theologian in search of a plural account of cosmology should not naively believe that even the strong form of emergence necessarily leads to the acknowledgment of transcendent beings, strong emergence supports the defeat of causal closure and allows the presence of spirits.[120] Particularly the emergence of consciousness (which not only allows for self-transcendence and intelligence but also the grasping of transcendentals, the good, the beautiful, and the true) strongly speaks for the spiritual nature of the cosmos.[121] Coupled with strong theological reasons, particularly the belief among all theists in the Great Spirit as the origin of everything in the cosmos, a spirit-filled cosmos may be a viable option and such that while it deviates radically from *ideological* scientism, it might not have to be in conflict with what the findings of current *scientific* cosmology (including evolutionary sciences) have so far revealed about origins and evolvement.

"God and Other Spirits": The Question of Theism's Internal Consistency

The most important *systematic*-theological reason for the continuing affirmation of a spirit-filled world has to do with the internal consistency of theism in general and that of Abrahamic faith traditions in particular.[122] As mentioned, the affirmation of the Great Spirit (God) with the simultaneous rejection of small spirits (all other spiritual realities) is logically and intellectually simply unfounded.[123] Here we are speaking of ultimate metaphysical ramifications of our worldview. Let me illustrate this with an example from current discussions in theological anthropology. Among theistic scientists, particularly neuroscientists and philosophers of mind, an influential account of the nature of human nature is physicalist, that is, ultimately everything regarding the human person can be said to derive from the material/physical realities.[124]

---

119. See also, Clayton, "Conceptual Foundations of Emergence Theory."

120. For a highly nuanced and insightful discussion, see Gregersen, "Emergence."

121. See also, Yong, *The Spirit of Creation*, pp. 211-13.

122. As finely put in Braaten, *That All May Believe*, pp. 109-10.

123. Pauw, "Where Theologians Fear to Tread," p. 41; so also, Murphree, "Can Theism Survive without the Devil?" p. 231.

124. Theistic materialists critically qualify their position by (often) naming it "non-reductive" physicalism, that is, although everything in the world derives from the physical, hav-

When probed, that view is of course only penultimate because all theists — not only in Abrahamic but also in Hindu and Buddhist traditions — claim that ultimately everything has its origin (and end) in the spiritual reality.[125] "God is spirit" (John 4:24) is the Christian scriptural way of saying it. In that light, one's view of the nature of human nature — or more widely, of the nature of nature at large — does not really matter when it comes to the dividing line between theism and nontheism. Even the theistic ontological materialists believe in the spiritual reality as the ultimate.

Intuitively, rather than as a result of critical reflection, from the first Christian centuries until the advent of modernity, the spirit-filled cosmos was taken for granted. A definitive patristic account of reality discerned "seven spirits": God, Jesus, Holy Spirit, Satan, holy and fallen angels, as well as the survival of the human soul (spirit) at death.[126] Two critical qualifications here put the traditional view in a proper perspective: on the one hand, not everything traditional is worth repeating if it clearly can be shown to be either false or in need of radical revision. Many of the beliefs of traditional Christianity (as well as those of other living faiths) may be time-bound, outdated opinions. On the other hand, it is the task of *critical* scholarship to sort out which beliefs are more than that, in the sense that, even if formulated in an outdated way, their material core still should be maintained. It simply is unfounded to claim that should we affirm the belief in spiritual beings, then we must stick with all aspects of the outdated biblical cosmology, including a "flat earth" and creation in six days.[127] What we have to do is to determine in light of our best current knowledge how to best express

---

ing emerged, it cannot be reduced back to merely physical processes; for a detailed discussion, see chap. 12 in *Creation and Humanity*. Therein I defend a view that I call "multidimensional monism," which, in agreement with nonreductive physicalism, affirms the deeply materialistic constitution of all human processes, including the mental, but in contrast with physicalism, does not endorse ontological materialism. Rather, it advocates a penultimate "neutral monism" that affirms the simultaneous mutual conditioning of the mental-physical — on the analogy of the superposition principle of quantum physics in which two states, so to speak, can be in place at the same time — (or even simultaneous mutual conditioning of many dimensions, not only mental and physical, but something we can hardly name yet) — and ultimate idealist monism (Spirit, God).

125. "[B]ehind and beyond the physical universe, there is a realm of purely spiritual beings, in whose affairs we have become implicated." Mascall, *The Christian Universe*, p. 110, quoted in Wiebe, *God and Other Spirits*, p. 3.

126. Origen, *De principiis*, preface; for other examples, see Wiebe, *God and Other Spirits*, pp. 1-2.

127. This mistaken notion is present in Munro, "Are Demons Real?" p. 38; for a critique, see G. Boyd, "The Ground-Level Deliverance Model," p. 141.

the deepest intuitions of the case. While it is no longer feasible to conceive the emergence of the cosmos and life on earth as a sudden appearance of ready-made forms but rather as a result of about 14 billion years of slow evolution, the deepest theological intuitions behind the time-bound and outdated cosmology are absolutely indispensable to all Abrahamic theistic traditions: rather than self-originating or self-sustaining, the cosmos is the work of the Creator and depends for its life on continuing divine action. No new discoveries in natural sciences — even in new forms of quantum cosmology that even seem to make obsolete or at least unnecessary the idea of a beginning in time — can replace the foundational theistic principle of contingency.[128]

In a parallel way, I propose that for a credible theistic Christian theology the deepest intuitions of the spirit-filled plural cosmology should be affirmed and maintained against the flood of naturalist-materialist scientism that rules among scientists and philosophers (of science). At the same time, constructive theology should sort out the form in which the conception of the spirit-filled cosmos is expressed in the beginning of the third millennium, in light of natural sciences and religious plurality. That is, of course, the task of constructive theology.

In that task, constructive theology should also mind much more robustly than it has so far the virtual universality of belief in spirits and spiritual powers throughout global Christianity, as well as among followers of other religious traditions. To that discussion we move next. Along with Christian tradition, the robust affirmation of a spirit-filled cosmos prevails everywhere in global Christianity and among Pentecostals/charismatics. Those testimonies and experiences must be incorporated into our theological reasoning.

Spiritual Experiences in Global Christianity and among Pentecostals/Charismatics

Among Pentecostal/charismatic Christians, belief in spiritual beings is taken for granted and engagement with them is a daily experience. The belief in spiritual beings includes the existence of angels and demons, and their influence on the world and human affairs.[129] While equally affirmed by Pentecos-

---

128. For details, see chap. 6 in *Creation and Humanity.*
129. Kay, "Pentecostals and Angels"; Dyer, "Angels and Pentecostals"; for a succinct discussion and basic sources, see also, Yong, *The Spirit of Creation,* pp. 175-78. For a recent doctrinal definition by a Pentecostal theologian, see Baker, "Created Spirit Beings," pp. 179-94.

tals in the Global North, interest in and enthusiasm over spiritual beings are more dynamic and pervasive in the Global South.[130] Part of the engagement of evil spirits is the widespread practice of exorcism.[131] What the late Ghanaian theologian Ogbu Kalu says of African Pentecostals applies to the rest of them: in encountering evil spirits and forces, they "apply fasting, prayer retreats, researches on the dominant spirit possessing the gates of the communities, and prayer actions,"[132] among other activities.

But why should constructive theology be interested in Pentecostals' and charismatics' testimonies and experiences of the spiritual realities? One reason is that Pentecostal/charismatic Christianity's influence in world Christianity is manifold and broad. Pentecostals and charismatics not only constitute over a quarter of all Christians but their number is also rapidly growing. Their influence is in no way limited to their own communities because, unlike any other major movements in Christian history, Pentecostalism is thoroughly an ecumenical movement. Just consider this fact: within the Roman Catholic Church, which comprises half of all Christians, the size of the charismatic renewal movement is larger than the membership of any individual Protestant or Anglican global community! Hence, Pentecostal influences proliferate widely and deeply within the largest Christian church — and beyond. Furthermore, unlike most mainline Protestants, the members of the Pentecostal/charismatic communities not only spread their message in their neighborhoods but also have launched massive evangelization campaigns all over the globe. Only the Catholic Church's continuing missionary activity forms a (nearly) comparable force in world Christianity to that of Pentecostals/charismatics.

Being wide open to the reality of spiritual beings is of course not limited to Pentecostals/charismatics; it is a defining feature of Christianity in Asia, Africa, and Latin America.[133] In many locations of the Global South — in radical contrast with the post-Enlightenment Global North — "Myriads of spirits are reported . . . but they defy description almost as much as they defy the scientist's test tubes in the laboratory."[134] Just consider the rich spirit-traditions of many Asian lands: "The cult of the spirits and cosmic forces as the Bons (Tibet), Devas (South-Asia), Nats (Burma), Phis (Thailand, Laos, Cambodia),

---

130. Ma, *When the Spirit Meets the Spirits,* chap. 4 particularly; Anderson, *Zion and Pentecost,* chap. 6; Heredero, *Dead Rescue the Living.*

131. Kalu, *"Sankofa,"* pp. 135-52; Onyinah, "Deliverance as a Way of Confronting Witchcraft," pp. 181-202.

132. Kalu, *African Pentecostalism,* p. 218.

133. See Lak, preface to *Doing Theology with the Spirit's Movement in Asia,* p. vi.

134. Mbiti, *African Religions and Philosophy,* p. 77.

the ancestral spirits (in the Confucian cultures of China, Korea, Vietnam, the Kalash in Pakistan) and the Kami (Japan) are an essential element of the spirituality of primal religions."[135] The Confucian concept of chi aptly illustrates the cosmic dimension of the Spirit of God, animating and vitalizing all life, including the material body.[136] Similarly, to cite the description of the grand old man of African theologies, John Mbiti:

> The universe [in Africa] is composed of visible and invisible parts. It is commonly believed that, besides God and human beings, there are other beings who populate the universe. These are the spirits. There are many types of spirits. God is their Creator, just as he is the Creator of all things. The spirits have a status between God and men, and are not identical with either. But people often speak about them in human terms, or treat them as though they had human characteristics such as thinking, speaking, intelligence and the possession of power which they can use as they will. Because the spirits are created by God, they are subordinate to him and dependent on him, and some of them may be used by God to do certain things.[137]

For Africans, the world of the spirits is as real as the visible world, perhaps even more real.[138] Life and world are believed to be governed by God, the ancestors, and (other) spirits. Among the spirits, the ancestors, living closer to the living community, are a central feature of all African religiosity. Unlike in the Global North, in the South religion permeates all of life.[139]

What in contemporary parlance would be called supernatural is rampant among the Christians in the Global South and is in keeping with the wider context of their respective cultural and religious climates.[140] Local theologians

135. "The Spirit at Work in Asia Today," p. 23; J. Y. Lee, *Trinity in Asian Perspective*, pp. 95-98. See also, Yun, *Holy Spirit and Ch'i*.

136. J. Y. Lee, *Trinity in Asian Perspective*, pp. 95-96.

137. Mbiti, *Introduction to African Religion*, p. 70; see also, Asamoah-Gyadu, "Spirit and Spirits in African Religious Traditions."

138. Adeyemo, "Unapproachable God," pp. 130-31; for the diversity of African notions of the spirits, see appendix A (pp. 271-73) in *A&D*.

139. Mbiti, *African Religions and Philosophy*, p. 2; Ferdinando, "Spiritual Realm in Traditional African Religion," pp. 22-23.

140. For an important comparative investigation, see Ferdinando, "Screwtape Revisited." See also, Kapolyo, *Human Condition*; Mbiti, *Concepts of God in Africa*. For a sample of representative texts with comments from pneumatologies of the Global South, see Kärkkäinen, ed., *Holy Spirit and Salvation*, chaps. 15 (Africa); 16 (Asia); and 17 (Latin America).

are prone to remark that this development is hardly surprising in light of the "secularizing" tendencies of much of theology imported from the Global North.[141] The reality of the spirit world also poses a threat that makes life vulnerable. For Christians it also makes spiritual warfare an essential part of spirituality, including witchcraft.[142] Again, unlike in the Global North, where faith may often be mainly a matter of cultural alignment, rational believing, or pietistic cultivation, among those Christians in the Global South who live surrounded by the powers, the power of the Holy Spirit is invoked as the resource and shield.[143] Here lies a reason for the rapid "Pentecostalization" of Africa and the rapid advancement of Pentecostal/charismatic spiritualities in other global contexts.[144]

But, again, what has this to do with constructive theology? Isn't this more a matter of sociology and anthropology of religion? Hardly so — although even in the beginning of the third millennium much of systematic/doctrinal theology is still done as if these two extremely wide and influential developments, namely, the explosive growth of Pentecostal/charismatic Christianity and the shift from the North to the Global South of Christianity, had no effect whatsoever! Just consider the numerical shift: already now two-thirds of Christians can be found in the Global South. By 2050, only about one-fifth of the world's three billion Christians will be non-Hispanic whites.[145] What is happening was aptly called by the late Ghanaian theologian Kwame Bediako "the renewal of a non-Western religion." As a result, "the centers of the church's universality [are] no longer in Geneva, Rome, Athens, Paris, London, New York, but Kinshasa, Buenos Aires, Addis Ababa and Manila."[146] The critical question for theologians in the elite academia of the Global North — most of them training scholars and ministers for churches with declining membership and rampant passivity of participation — is whether they are willing to allow the expressions of the majority of Christians to play any role in theologizing. Even

141. Imasogie, *Guidelines for Christian Theology in Africa,* p. 81.

142. Onyinah, "Akan Witchcraft and the Concept of Exorcism."

143. Imasogie, *Guidelines for Christian Theology in Africa,* p. 81. For the importance of distinctively African theology for that context, see Muzorewa, *Origins and Development of African Theology,* p. 84. There is wide interest in anthropology, sociology, and religious studies in the resurgence of witchcraft: Geschiere, *The Modernity of Witchcraft;* Meyer, *Translating the Devil.*

144. See Anderson, "Demons and Deliverance in African Pentecostalism," pp. 42-62; N. G. Wright, "Charismatic Interpretations of the Demonic."

145. See Parratt, "Introduction," p. 1. The dramatic shift has been definitively analyzed in Jenkins, *The Next Christendom.*

146. Quoted in Bediako, *Christianity in Africa,* p. 154.

more importantly: whether after much critique of early missionary generations for not allowing indigenous churches to do self-theologizing, the contributions of an emerging theological academy from Pentecostals/charismatics and the Global South will be taken seriously. While that would not of course mean a return to a noncritical pre-Enlightenment mentality, it would urge a critical assessment among Western theologians of such naturalistic presuppositions that are not necessarily essential to the current developments in the sciences or philosophy.[147] (It is ironic that the same theological academia in the North that at its best considers the testimonies of the Global South and Pentecostal/charismatic Christians as interesting field-study data, and at worst as superstition, is surprisingly open to all kinds of fancy and weird forms of pantheism, spiritualism, and even magic among neopagan and similar scholars, as long as they are not followers of the Abrahamic faith traditions — as a glance at the American Academy of Religion's annual meeting program clearly shows!)

That said, personal experiences — even when they seem to be universally held throughout ages and across cultural, racial, and gender borders — look like highly dubious data for theology. Indeed, the theologian must exercise critical judgment. Neither Schleiermacher's making religion merely a function of the hermeneutics of human religious experiences nor the methodological demand of some students-of-religion scholars that religious experience should be the main source of data "upon which theorizing about the ontological claims in religion properly depends"[148] can be adopted as the basis for solid theology. No amount of study of religious experiences can negotiate the question of the truth of theological statements.

Nevertheless, it is against both the tradition of Christian theology — the way it emerged as second-order reflection on (first-order) religious experiences — and common sense to neglect in theologizing the importance of universal, consistent, and persistent human experience. Even when the "universal" human experience is subjected to critical scrutiny, it may be a window into ontologically significant religious/theological insights. Furthermore, one has to remember that a limited human mind has no direct access to "God's truth"; the access is always anthropologically — and thus experientially — mediated. Here again, we come to the importance of holding on to the postfoundationalist epistemological approach in which "[i]nterpreted experience engenders

---

147. See González, *Mañana*, p. 49. So also, my *Pneumatology*, p. 147: "In our contemporary world, theology has the burden of showing its culture sensitivity. Theology can no longer be the privilege of one people group. Instead, it must be context specific as it addresses God and God's world in specific situations and in response to varying needs and challenges."

148. Wiebe, *God and Other Spirits*, p. v.

and nourishes all beliefs, and a network of beliefs informs the interpretation of experience."[149] The least critical scholarship can do is thus to incorporate the growing number and diversity of continuing experiences of and belief in spiritual powers among the majority of Christians into the matrix of theological argumentation and put them in sympathetic and critical dialogue with other "sources of theology," including Christian tradition, contemporary theology, philosophy, sciences, cultural studies, and so forth. That work has hardly begun.

The consideration of this issue, namely, the role of spiritual experiences (in this case, of spiritual beings and powers), will continue as we focus on the theological conditions and meaning of the demonic in the spirit-filled cosmos, an even more challenging topic to contemporary theology.

Encountering Evil Powers and the Demonic: A Theological Proposal

Engaging and Resisting the Demonic Powers

One of the topics that the allegedly *critical* (Western) theological scholarship does not dare touch is the demonic — as universally experienced and believed in across all cultures and religious traditions as it is. One wonders how that intentional omission aligns with a truly critical mind-set. William James's warning about the closed-mindedness of his psychology colleagues applies no less to contemporary theologians: "The refusal of modern 'enlightenment' to treat 'possession' as a hypothesis to be spoken of as even a possibility, in spite of the massive human tradition based on concrete experience in its favor, has always seemed to me a curious example of the power of fashion in things scientific. That the demon-theory . . . will have its innings again is to my mind absolutely certain. One has to be 'scientific' indeed to be blind and ignorant enough to suspect no such possibility."[150]

To ignore a topic is not to explain it away. As the sociologist of religion Peter Berger noted decades ago, the incapacity of the modern mind to discern angels and demons still leaves totally open the question of whether they really exist or not.[151] Demons hardly disappear by virtue of theologians' silence.

149. Shults, *The Post Foundationalist Task of Theology*, p. 44.

150. James, "Report on Mrs. Piper's Hodgson-Control," p. 118, cited in Eddy and Beilby, "Introduction," p. 18.

151. Berger, *A Rumor of Angels*, p. 52.

As much energy as Barth devoted to scrutinizing the biblical theology of angels, he saw the topic of the demonic and powers so inconsequential to theology that he offered only a "quick, sharp glance" at it.[152] Tillich's attention to the demonic in pneumatology as part of "life and its ambiguities"[153] stays at such a generic level that its implications for theology and Christian life can safely be left out of the discussion.[154] It is ironic that even the most current constructive theologies are simply silent about the whole topic! That is particularly striking with Moltmann, who speaks so much of the importance of developing a holistic pneumatology, an account of the Spirit freed from pietistic, ecclesiastical, and cultural strictures. Even when talking about the destructive forces in the world that threaten the work of the Spirit of Life, he is completely silent about evil spirits or demons — or even angels! Even his extended treatment of suffering, ecological disasters, and sociopolitical injustices does not inspire any thinking on spirits and powers.[155] (To Moltmann's credit, however, he includes a section on exorcism in his Christology.) With all their criticism of injustice, suffering, and evil in the world, neither feminist and other female pneumatologists nor postcolonialists or other liberationists offer much in this regard either. Even the criteria for the discernment of the spirit(s) are by and large missing in contemporary pneumatologies.[156]

The situation is totally different for the Gospel authors. The Gospels describe vividly the acts of demons or evil spirits as they afflict humans. In keeping with the strict Judeo-Christian distinction between God and the creatures, these demonic forces are subjected under and obey Jesus. Ironically, at times the demons proclaim Jesus' power before witnesses by obeying his adjurations (Matt. 8:32; Mark 5:13; Luke 8:33; see also Luke 4:41) or through explicit verbal declarations (Matt. 8:29; Mark 1:23-25, 34; Luke 4:41). Pauline

152. Barth, *CD* III/3, p. 519.

153. Tillich, *ST* 3:102-6. As is well known, Tillich also speaks of the demonic in terms of archetypes of depth psychology and in reference to an awareness of the suprahuman power of the demonic in literature in the first volume of *Systematic Theology*.

154. His earlier context speaking of the demonic in relation to the theology of history might have opened new venues for the theology of powers, but he never developed it much further. See Tillich, *The Interpretation of History*, pp. 77-96; see also, his treatment of economics, particularly capitalism, in relation to the demonic, in Tillich, "Kingdom of God and History," particularly pp. 131-32.

155. One reviewer of *The Spirit of Life*, who obviously had studied the work in much detail, reports that Moltmann lets it suffice to refer to evil spirits in passing in a couple of footnotes! Stibbe, "'A British Appraisal,'" p. 13.

156. As noted, concerning Moltmann's *Spirit of Life*, by S. Chan, "'An Asian Review,'" p. 39.

traditions similarly are no strangers to the demonic (1 Cor. 10:20-21; 1 Tim. 4:1). As a way of summary of the NT, we see that

> Jesus and the Gospel writers present Satan as Jesus's declared personal adversary (*Mark* 3:23; *Luke* 11:18-21), paralleling the representation of Satan as Yahweh's adversary in Jewish apocrypha and further confirming Jesus's divinity. The rivalry between Jesus and Satan is developed in Saint Paul's *Epistles* and the *Book of Revelation;* the latter provides dramatically explicit visualizations of the divine Christ and the demonic hordes arrayed against him. *Luke, John, Paul,* and *Revelation* (e.g. chapter 12) consolidate the portrait of Satan as the leader of numerous evil angels who fell from Heaven because of their rebellion — not against Yahweh but against Christ (*Luke* 10:18; *Eph.* 2:1-2; 6:11-13; 2 *Cor.* 6:14-16; *Col.* 2:15).[157]

Wink's *Powers* trilogy is of course a delightful exception to the silence about the evil powers and demonic among mainstream theologians. As useful as his analysis is in highlighting the role of powers in society (economy, politics, law, and so forth), his totally immanentist scheme has little connection to the current discussion of the demonic in light of theological tradition. While appreciative of Wink's achievements, the American open theist advocate G. Boyd attempts to correct Wink's nontranscendent orientation and offer instead a robust "warfare theodicy" that would allow for the dual interpretation of evil powers. Boyd's basic contention is that not only in the biblical world but also in ancient cultures at large, as well as in the global cultures outside the hegemony of the (European-originated) Enlightenment, the dominant worldview "centers on the conviction that the good and evil, fortunate or unfortunate, aspects of life are to be interpreted largely as the result of good and evil, friendly or hostile, spirits warring against each other and against us," without at the same time denying "that evil is also a reality of the human heart and of human society."[158] Dismissing as too thin an explanation the idea of evil as privation, Boyd insists that "God's good creation has in fact been seized by hostile, evil, cosmic forces that are seeking to destroy God's beneficent

---

157. Stephens, "Demons," p. 2279. Standard massive reference works include the following by J. Russell, *The Devil: Perceptions of Evil from Antiquity to Primitive Christianity; Satan: The Early Christian Tradition; Lucifer: The Devil in the Middle Ages;* and *Mephistopheles: The Devil in the Modern World.*

158. G. Boyd, *God at War;* this monograph is a meticulous study of the OT and NT concerning themes related to spiritual "warfare" between the powers and Yahweh/Jesus Christ. For a succinct summary, see chap. 1 in G. Boyd, *Satan and the Problem of Evil.*

plan for the cosmos."[159] In this battle, Satan, allied with his spiritual powers, represents *the* enemy of God. Yet not all evil in the world can be attributed to Satan (although ultimately, Boyd argues, "no explanation that ignores his activity is adequate").[160] Some of the evils are due to bad human choices (and yet others to "natural" evil).

No wonder Boyd not only prefers the ancient *Christus Victor* model as the main model of salvation but even considers it the "biblical" model.[161] At the heart of *Christus Victor* is the cosmic battle between God and resisting powers, conquered by Christ. Along with the Son, Father and Spirit also participate in the cosmic battle.[162] Fearing that the traditional view of evil depicted as part of the divine plan leads to resignation rather than revolt, Boyd wishes to encourage Christians to participate in the "good fight" against the evil forces.[163] Therefore, he believes that prayer can make a real difference as it participates — on God's side — in the continuing battle between God and God's enemies.

Boyd's warfare theodicy's benefit is twofold with regard to this project. First, it succeeds in highlighting a more comprehensive account of the demonic when compared to that of Wink. Second — in material agreement with Wink, albeit focusing more on traditional spiritual exercises — Boyd's model also urges Christians to do something about the demonic and its powers. That said, it is also beset with problems, two of which merit comment in this context.[164] First, notwithstanding the wide attestation in the Bible of "warfare" (power-laden) images, by no stretch of imagination can it be said that this set of images is *the* dominant one.[165] On the contrary, the God-world relationship is depicted under many different and complementary metaphors, images, or models, among which "warfare" is one. Therefore, second, it is far from certain that one specific metaphor of salvation, in this case *Christus Victor,* should be made the dominant one, much less the only one (*Christ and Reconciliation,* chap. 3, develops a trinitarian theology of reconciliation utilizing various metaphors).

159. G. Boyd, *God at War,* p. 19.

160. G. Boyd, *Satan and the Problem of Evil,* p. 18.

161. G. Boyd, *God at War,* chap. 9.

162. G. Boyd, *Satan and the Problem of Evil,* p. 18.

163. G. Boyd, *God at War,* pp. 21-22.

164. In chap. 8 of *Creation and Humanity,* I engage and critique Gregory Boyd's "warfare theodicy" in relation to natural evil.

165. A balanced scrutiny of "powers" in the biblical canon is Parsons, "Binding the Strong Man."

While Wink's pacifist, "Jesus-style" resistance is not likely to raise moral concerns, the rhetoric behind Boyd's — and certainly the NT traditions' — urge to resist and oppose evil powers and the demonic easily raises a moral concern among contemporary scholars, particularly with those who have totally demythologized the demonic. Those moral concerns resonate so strongly among some that they recommend that "we should abandon the idea of evil" as it makes us believe in incredible spiritual monsters and makes us demonize other people.[166] Perhaps we should move with Nietzsche "beyond good and evil." For the majority of people not willing to abandon the concept of evil, a moral objection may arise whenever Christians — or followers of other faith traditions, for that matter — are urged to stand against the evil forces and powers for the fear that it may result in strengthening violence, self-righteousness, and exclusion. Nahi Alon and Haim Omer expressed this concern in no uncertain terms: "The *demonic view* is a way of experiencing an evolving attitude that begins with doubt, thrives with suspicion, ends with certainty, and aims at decisive militant action. When it seeps into a relationship, a highly negative view of the other evolves, which in turn may lead to symmetrical counter accusations. Thus a vicious cycle arises in which both sides become more and more entrenched in their negative positions."[167]

Part of this moral concern is the widely spread — and even among the scholars, highly uncritical — blaming of religions for violence, particularly of Abrahamic faiths[168] (a topic discussed in detail in chap. 13 of *Trinity and Revelation*).[169] Particularly pertinent here is the blame put not only on the OT description of Yahweh as "the man of war" but also on the seemingly violent and warfare-driven sayings of Jesus (Matt. 10:34) and in Paul (Eph. 6:12), behind which lie Jewish apocalyptic eschatology's exclusivism and militant attitudes and fear of judgment. Without being able to tackle that broad and complicated scholarly discussion with widely differing opinions,[170] I simply refer to a dominant scholarly conclusion: Jesus and the early church radically revised

---

166. Cole, *The Myth of Evil*, p. 23, cited in Eddy and Beilby, "Introduction," p. 3. This paragraph is indebted to that source (pp. 2-13) with regard to some other references as well.

167. Alon and Omer, *The Psychology of Demonization*, p. 1, emphasis in original.

168. For a rebuttal of the myth of violence, see Albertz, "Monotheism and Violence," pp. 373-87.

169. Furthermore, chap. 12 of *Christ and Reconciliation* discusses violence in relation to Jesus' suffering and death on the cross, and chap. 16 of *Creation and Humanity* discusses violence, particularly among religious traditions, in relation to human flourishing.

170. Basic sources and views are succinctly presented in Eddy and Beilby, "Introduction," pp. 8-12.

and reidentified the "enemy" by shifting it from humans (Romans and other Gentiles) to cosmic, spiritual forces, ultimately Satan.[171] If that interpretation is true, then it means that Christian discourse of spiritual warfare and encountering the evil has nothing to do with militancy, holy war, or exclusion. It has nothing to do with fighting other human beings but rather with resisting evil powers. Related is the fact that rather than searching for the "speck" in other faith traditions one should focus on the "log" in our own eyes (Matt. 7:3). "[T]he struggle between the Holy Spirit and the spirits of this world, between God and idols, between truth and distortions of truth, is going on *within* every religious community in history. Christians should avoid the temptation of transforming it into a struggle *between* Christianity and other religions in the world."[172]

Furthermore, rather than arrogance and pride, all Christian service should be characterized "by humility of spirit, trust in the liberating power of God, and the giving of one's own life for the sake of others on earth."[173] Hence, Christians who are really fighting against men and women are functioning in direct violation of the NT teaching (Eph. 6:12). Any attempt to identify "spiritual warfare" with "holy war" is totally unacceptable, as it is violence and inhospitality.[174]

Christians should also mind that — in contrast to some well-meant contemporary missions rhetoric — the NT does not contain military metaphors in its descriptions of the evangelistic and missionary task of the church. The NT reminds the church time after time of the Great Commission, including teaching and baptizing the nations, but never utilizes military terminology.[175] Other religious traditions similarly should analyze the liabilities and resources in their own traditions to combat violent and militant tendencies.

What about exorcism and "spiritual warfare," that is, casting out evil spirits and dealing with demonic influences through prayers and spiritual rites, activities widely present not only in the biblical canon but also in Christian

---

171. N. T. Wright, *Jesus and the Victory of God*, pp. 450-51; Middleton, *Radical Martyrdom and Cosmic Conflict*, p. 134; for a highly useful essay, see Eddy, "Remembering Jesus' Self-Understanding," especially pp. 249-53.

172. Samartha, "Holy Spirit and People of Other Faiths," p. 260, emphasis in original.

173. Eddy and Beilby, "Introduction," pp. 11-12.

174. See Eddy and Beilby, "Introduction," pp. 6-7. It is encouraging to find out that in a recent Ph.D. study on the opinions of members of six American churches in which language of spiritual warfare is common, no correlation was found between that and any militant, violent, or oppressive attitudes. Durst, "Fighting the Good Fight," p. 243.

175. Love, "Muslims and Military Metaphors," p. 67; see also, Beaton, "New Testament Metaphors and the Christian Mission," pp. 60-64.

history and currently among many quarters of global Christianity and among Pentecostals/charismatics?

Whether Exorcism and "Spiritual Warfare" Belong to the Engagement of Powers

Against the prejudices of many Western scholars, not only demons and evil spirits but also the rituals and techniques of exorcism were widely common in the ancient world, and are common also throughout contemporary living traditions, whether in Buddhism,[176] Hinduism,[177] Islam,[178] or elsewhere. Furthermore, no one contests that the narrative of the NT presents a portrait of Jesus as an itinerant healer and exorcist.[179] Ironically, it is the recent third quest of the historical Jesus that finally has taken seriously and as integral to the person and ministry of Jesus the theme of the "mighty deeds." Whereas the pre-Enlightenment theology took the miraculous acts as proof of the divinity of Jesus of Nazareth, the Enlightenment epistemology of the original quest bluntly rejected their factual and historical nature.[180] Neither one of these approaches is valid.

176. For rich documentation, see Yong, *Pneumatology and the Christian-Buddhist Dialogue,* pp. 208-17, with rich documentation from various locations.

177. Opler, "Spirit Possession in a Rural Area of Northern India," pp. 553-66.

178. Exorcism is so widespread in folk Islam and in many other contexts that one can easily find up-to-date primers even on the Internet such as the "Simple Guide on Islamic Exorcism," http://islamicexorcism.wordpress.com/2009/11/04/simple-guide-for-islamic-exorcism/ (3/19/14).

179. Twelftree, *Jesus the Exorcist.* The miracle tradition of the NT belongs to the earliest strata and thus cannot be eliminated without serious violence to the literary integrity of the Gospels. Particularly Mark, believed to be the earliest Gospel, builds his narrative almost totally on the miracle tradition. See Dunn, *Jesus and the Spirit,* p. 70, for a summary statement. See also, Kasper, *Jesus the Christ,* p. 89; for the listing of the most important arguments in defense of the historical validity of most Gospel miracles stories, see pp. 90-91. With regard to exorcisms, a class of miracles highly suspect in the modernist mind-set, Dunn (p. 44) goes so far as to say that Jesus' ministry as exorcist "belongs to the base-rock historicity of the Gospels" and that even Strauss, the critic, took exorcisms as something historically fairly probable.

180. N. T. Wright, *Jesus and the Victory of God,* p. 188: "Few serious historians now deny that Jesus, and for that matter many other people, performed cures and did other startling things for which there was no obvious natural explanation." See also, p. 194. Walter Kasper (*The God of Jesus Christ,* p. 91) agrees. (Wright is a biblical scholar and Kasper a systematician.) Miracles are of course not limited to Christian sources. The existence of miracles in rabbinic and Hellenistic sources is well documented. For a brief discussion, see Kasper, *Jesus the Christ,* p. 90.

N. T. Wright importantly notes that the miraculous acts are an integral part of the story and ministry of Jesus, and there "is no dividing line, enabling us to bracket off" them from the rest of his ministry, teaching, pronouncing forgiveness, and reaching out to the outcasts and others.[181] Against the prejudice of the Enlightenment mind-set, even exorcisms belonged integrally to Jesus' ministry. The same *exousia* (authority, power) present in his words (Mark 1:22) was present in the expulsion of demons (v. 27). These unclean spirits recognized Jesus for the person he was, "the Holy One of God" (v. 24). The theological meaning of exorcisms and healings can be discerned in the wider context of Jesus' ministry and person. Unlike much well-meaning apologetics, either traditional or contemporary, in the Gospels the mighty deeds are not a means of "proving" the deity of Jesus but rather — as in the OT prophets and charismatic leaders — an indication of the power of God at work. Thereby the mighty deeds also indicate God's approval of the ministry of Jesus. Rather than a product of *Beelzebub,* the mighty deeds are the function of the Spirit of God (Mark 3:20-30). This is the meaning of the favorite NT terms *terata* and *semeia,* "signs." They point to God's power at work for salvation and deliverance vis-à-vis contestation to the contrary, in arguments that the miracles had their origin in the opposing evil forces. Jesus' acts of deliverance pointed to the coming of the kingdom of God: "But if it is by the Spirit of God that I cast out demons, then the kingdom of God has come upon you" (Matt. 12:28). Healings and deliverances also helped restore excluded people to the covenant community.[182]

Particularly in the book of Acts, the practice of exorcism and casting out devils continued along with healings and other miraculous acts as an integral part of the church's regular activity of prayer, liturgy, sacraments, and missionary outreach (5:16; 8:7; 13:6-12). In Philippi, a slave girl was delivered from under the evil powers (16:18). Even a few mass exorcisms are recounted, such as the one in Ephesus as a response to the failed exorcism of the sons of Sceva. Burning of books related to the practice of magic was the public renunciation of the evil (19:19).[183] Arbitrarily determining narratives of healings, exorcisms, and other mighty deeds to be historically false fables while taking the teaching and pronouncing of forgiveness by Jesus and the early church as authentic is hardly a "neutral" scholarly judgment. Behind it is a deeply skewed

181. So also, N. T. Wright, *Jesus and the Victory of God,* pp. 189, 193.

182. See Wenham, "Christ's Healing Ministry," pp. 115-26; N. T. Wright, *Jesus and the Victory of God,* pp. 192-93; also p. 189.

183. For the difference between the settings of these two exorcism events, one nonliturgical, the other one sacred, see Witherington, *The Acts of the Apostles,* p. 582.

modernist epistemology that has a hard time exercising self-criticism against its own unsaid presuppositions.

Against the predictions of Western theologians,[184] as mentioned, Christians in the Global South, even after the coming of modernity, continue encountering the demonic in various forms. They also believe that the gospel has much to do with the engagement of the demonic. No wonder, in that context, that the importance of the *Christus Victor* model comes to the fore (although, as mentioned, it cannot be taken as *the* model of reconciliation). The Nigerian Paul Omieka Ebhomielen has investigated the application of the *Christus Victor* framework to the demonic in Africa and concluded that there is great potential application of God's power and victory over the forces of evil, including over its effects such as fear and insecurity, as well as the idea of cosmic redemption along with personal and social redemption.[185] He also argues that the cross, when viewed through the lens of *Christus Victor*, makes more sense to Africans. Behind the innocent sacrifice is the conflict or struggle between God and evil rather than the Anselmian view of satisfaction: "In Christ, the divine love struggled with evil in order that the divine will might be realized."[186] For many Africans, the world is a "battleground," a key idea in Aulen's depiction of the earliest model of atonement.[187] No wonder that in the deliverance sessions of many churches in the Global South as well as some charismatic churches elsewhere it is typical to hear people shout victory in the name of Jesus and the Lord's authority over all powers and principalities, including physical, mental, and spiritual.[188]

According to the Pentecostal theologian Amos Yong, who is deeply engaged in religion-science and interfaith dialogue, the resistance to demonic forces may take many forms, including "prayer, fasting, the charisms, spiritual warfare in its various guises, as well as through the methods of exorcism deployed by Jesus himself." Then he elaborates in an important manner:

> If the traditional rite of exorcism was designed to expel evil and destructive spiritual realities from the lives of people, then contemporary rites expose and unmask the privative and perverted nothingness of demonic realities. Exorcisms thus can function at various levels:

184. See, e.g., Parrinder, *Witchcraft*, pp. 202-3.
185. Ebhomielen, "Gustaf Aulen's *Christus Victor* View," pp. 276-82.
186. Ebhomielen, "Gustaf Aulen's *Christus Victor* View," p. 283.
187. Ebhomielen, "Gustaf Aulen's *Christus Victor* View," p. 289.
188. For a careful account, see Onyinah, "Deliverance as a Way of Confronting Witchcraft."

- Personally, resulting in healing of fractured self-identities (e.g., in terms of Jungian theory);
- Socially, resulting in reconciliation between people (i.e., in terms of the enactment of spiritual warfare against greed);
- Politically, resulting in shalom that includes justice (namely, in terms of undermining territorial spirits).[189]

At the same time, theology's task is to subject the habits of exorcisms and spiritual warfare to critical analysis. This critical task in my mind relates particularly to a fairly new phenomenon under nomenclatures such as "power encounter," "territorial spirits," "spiritual strongholds," "spiritual mapping," and the like. In some Pentecostal/charismatic circles[190] and Global South communities, these kinds of applications of the ancient deliverance motif have received increasing attention.[191] In (semi)popular literature advocating this hermeneutic, it is common to identify spiritual warfare at various levels: "ground level," dealing with influences of the evil in individuals; "occult level," defeating false ideologies such as Satanism, New Age, or Masonry; and "strategic level," fighting "high ranking principalities and powers as . . . demonic entities [which] are assigned to geographical territories and social networks . . . also referred to as territorial spirits."[192] Among these advocates, the theme of spiritual warfare is made central in preaching, teaching, missionary strategizing, and the general ethos of Christian life.

Unfortunately, solid critical scholarly literature produced by the ad-

189. Yong, *The Spirit of Creation,* p. 223; for more details, see Yong, *In the Days of Caesar,* chap. 8.

190. Somewhat ironically, this phenomenon is quite marginal in (classical) Pentecostalism, the movement that began in the beginning of the twentieth century and is now represented by established Pentecostal denominations such as Assemblies of God, the International Foursquare Gospel, the Church of God in Christ, and various types of apostolic churches. Even among the so-called charismatic movement at large — that is, renewal communities influenced by Pentecostal spirituality that decided to stay within the established churches (such as Catholic Charismatic Renewal) — the phenomenon is not typical. On the contrary, the "spiritual warfare" model has gained prominence among some newer charismatic communities, the so-called Third Wave Pentecostal-type independent communities that are not part of the first two, more established categories. Particularly from the classical Pentecostal side, theologically founded critique has been directed toward the abuses and extremes of the warfare model.

191. For basic ideas by the most noted international advocate, see Wagner and Greenwood, "The Strategic-Level Deliverance Model"; for a scholarly presentation and assessment, see Scotland, "The Charismatic Devil."

192. Wagner and Greenwood, "The Strategic-Level Deliverance Model," p. 179.

vocates of this kind of "spiritual warfare" is missing, and therefore it is very difficult to offer a fair and comprehensive theological assessment.[193] The question to those who are not willing to exercise self-critical judgment either in biblical hermeneutics or with regard to charismatic phenomena is this: Why would these charismatics wish to apply contemporary critical methods of investigation in medicine, law, sociology, and say, agriculture, but not in religion and theology? Because of lack of critical scholarship, there tends to be a deep black-and-white mentality in the rhetoric, if not in the theologizing, of the spiritual warfare advocates: "us" and "them," "Christians" and "non-Christians," and so forth. Part of that liability is an unnuanced listing of "enemies" to be tackled — in some cases even "Eastern religions" per se are named as Satanism and similar practices under the "occult-level" warfare.[194] Related is the spiritualizing tendency: behind abortion, homosexuality, certain spiritual practices, and similar problems, various types of "spirits" are identified and fought.

Apart from the lack of support from biblical sources and tradition, this spiritualizing also begins to cut legs out from under a careful and thoughtful ethical-moral consideration. It may also hinder people in need from receiving practical support and help, such as women facing the issue of abortion.[195] Also not unknown are the practices among some Pentecostals/charismatics to demonize not only what they see as satanic or occultic but — particularly in the political rhetoric — those who otherwise oppose that particular group's economic, political, or social agenda.[196] Finally, there is the highly problematic tendency not only to ritualize and overly systematize the spiritual battle with all kinds of "spiritual mapping" techniques but also to make the main practice

193. What is troubling about the advocacy literature, some of which claims to be academic in nature, is not only the lack of (self-)critical judgment but also uncritical demand to resist typical scholarly critique, particularly in biblical hermeneutics. Albeit leaning toward caricature — and certainly lacking charity — worthwhile is the critique of the hermeneutics in Wink and Hardin, "Response to C. Peter Wagner and Rebecca Greenwood."

194. Wagner and Greenwood ("The Strategic-Level Deliverance Model," p. 179) include under the "occult-level" warfare, along with Satanism, also Eastern religions. This page has a subtitle: "Occult-Level Warfare." Not infrequently among some Pentecostals/charismatics, the Muslims are identified as enemies; Yong, *In the Days of Caesar*, p. 132. Although it is true that there was a polemical edge in the early church's relation to religions, particularly in the book of Acts, there is very little, if any, direct demonization; for thoughtful reflections, see Yong, pp. 153-54.

195. So also, G. Boyd, "Response to C. Peter Wagner and Rebecca Greenwood," pp. 210-15.

196. For examples and sources, see Yong, *In the Days of Caesar*, pp. 131-34.

something that does not have unambiguous biblical support.[197] This concern relates particularly to the program of "territorial spirits," which are resisted and fought through various kinds of spiritual practices. While the church endorses beliefs and practices that also go beyond the Bible (but not against it), it is theologically highly suspicious — particularly when it comes from the intentionally biblicist and fundamentalist movement — to construct a whole spiritual program without biblical (and Christian tradition's) support. Mere practical reasons, often referred to, hardly justify that choice.[198]

Going back to the wider question of the legitimacy and necessity of a proper use of exorcisms and deliverance, constructive theology should be able to affirm both that legitimate need and the need to critique the theological and practical liabilities and extremes of the recent "spiritual warfare" model. The need for this dynamic balance also relates to the topic of the next chapter — the discernment of the Spirit of God among the spirits and truth claims of other religious traditions.

197. G. Boyd wonders whether there might be even counterexamples to territorial warfare in the Bible, such as Dan. 10:20, in that the angel did not invite Daniel to join in his battle against the "prince of Persia" ("Response to C. Peter Wagner and Rebecca Greenwood," p. 210).

198. So also, G. Boyd, "Response to C. Peter Wagner and Rebecca Greenwood," p. 211.

5. Discerning the Holy Spirit among Religions

For Orientation: The Theological Significance of the Spirit(s) among Religions

As the Indian theologian Joseph Pathrapankal states, "Spirit *(pneuma)* is the basic datum of religious experience in all religions. . . . Spirit is also one of the fundamental concepts in the history of philosophy." Even more, the Spirit is "the foundational reality which makes possible for the humans to exercise their religious sense and elevate their self to the realm of the divine."[1] No wonder, then, that part of the cosmic orientation of all traditional and most contemporary cultures in the Global South has to do with the deep and wide sense of spirits and spiritualities in religions. Hence, the importance of the theme of the discernment of the Spirit and spirits in the religiously plural world. Particularly challenging is that task in highly syncretistic contexts where several robust religious affiliations coexist. Take Japan as an example: as highly industrialized and economically developed as it is, its syncretistic religiosity has not waned at all. Shinto and Buddhism, which have historically mixed with each other, are highly tolerant concerning each other and other faiths. There is also a highly syncretistic folk religiosity with many local colors. The total number of people claimed by Shinto and Buddhism in Japan is twice the number of the whole population![2]

Another Indian theologian, Stanley J. Samartha, notes that in re-

1. Pathrapankal, "Editorial," p. 299.
2. See Fukuda, *Developing a Contextualized Church*, p. 59.

cent years the question of the discernment of the spirits has "somewhat aggressively thrust itself on the theological consciousness of the church."[3] Ironically, however, "[i]n many theology textbooks, even those devoted particularly to the work of the Holy Spirit, one looks in vain for a careful, sympathetic, and extended treatment of the work of the Spirit in relation to the life and thought of people of other faiths, cultures, and ideologies."[4] This is true particularly in the Global North.[5] Asian Christian theologians have been the first ones to "enter into [this] almost uncharted territory which is liberally strewn with anti-heretic mines"[6] and seek for pneumatological resources in engaging other faiths. The Korean American Koo D. Yun has discerned some interesting connections between the key Confucian/Chinese concept of chi and the Holy Spirit;[7] the comparative work of another Asian American (Malaysian Chinese), Amos Yong, between the Mahayana Buddhist notion of sunyata and the Christian concept of the Holy Spirit belongs to the same genre;[8] similarly, the Japanese theologian Naoki Inoue has highlighted both similarities and differences between the Shinto and Buddhist pantheistic traditions of his homeland and some panentheistic Christian pneumatologies.[9] And so forth.

The inclusion of the topic of interfaith encounter in the discussion of pneumatology thus requires no justification in this pluralistic world of ours. But how to proceed is a matter of some methodological reflection. Unlike the theology-of-religions discourse, which usually treats "religions" as if they were more or less a uniform concept, the task of comparative theology is to tend to particularities and details. Hence, each particular encounter — say, between Christians and Muslims or between Christians and Buddhists — has to be framed and conducted as much as possible according to the unique features of the parties involved, including attention to the differences within each tradition (including Christianity). For pneumatology, mindfulness of

---

3. Samartha, *Between Two Cultures*, p. 187.

4. Samartha, *Courage for Dialogue*, p. 76; for a programmatic statement of the role of Spirit, see pp. 10-14.

5. For the ecumenical significance of a pneumatological approach to religions, see the comment by the former WCC General Secretary Konrad Raiser, "The Holy Spirit in Modern Ecumenical Thought," p. 384.

6. Samartha, "Holy Spirit and People of Other Faiths," p. 251.

7. Yun, *Holy Spirit and Ch'i*. What is remarkable is that it seems like chi is a "universal concept" among cultures and religions, whether it is called this or not; see Emeghara, "Igbo Concept of Chi," pp. 399-405.

8. Yong, *Pneumatology and the Christian-Buddhist Dialogue*.

9. Inoue, "Spirit and Spirits in Pantheistic Shintoism."

the differences between encounters is particularly significant. Whereas within the Abrahamic traditions the task is to delineate the subtle divergences as much as the commonalities (because of the commonly shared scriptural-historical "foundations"), in the encounter with Asiatic traditions the first major task is to inquire whether talk about the divine Spirit even makes sense. To make things even more complicated, Buddhist and Hindu traditions have marked differences. Whereas no one would doubt the centrality of the generic concept of Spirit (Brahman/*atman*) in Vedic Hinduism and most Hindu movements, in the oldest and original Theravada tradition the concept of *the* divine Spirit is highly questionable. Somewhat similarly to Hinduism, the Mahayana, on the other hand, has a rich repertoire of spirits (plural) but the question about the "One Spirit" — a crucial theme for all Abrahamic faiths — is highly complex.

In this chapter, first, the two cousin Abrahamic faiths will be engaged with regard to their main teachings about the divine Spirit and their relation to Christian claims about the Spirit. Second, Hinduism and Buddhism will be investigated from the pneumatological perspective. The final section of the chapter seeks to draw lessons from the pneumatological interfaith investigation and suggest some theological guidelines that also help us in the remainder of the book's topics.

Ruach in Jewish Traditions

Spirit in Rabbinic Judaism

Because — unlike with any other faith tradition — Christians share with Jews the major part of the sacred Scriptures, no separate study of the OT pneumatologies is attempted here. Although that choice subjects the investigation to the potential Christian bias of "baptizing" the Jewish Bible into a Christian theological framework, I believe it is possible to avoid that trap by highlighting, where relevant, the differing interpretations (which have to do primarily with the sharp difference in the doctrine of God with emphasis either on unity or unity-in-trinity). At all times, the Christian interpreter must remember the Nicene-Constantinopolitan creedal statement that we believe in the Holy Spirit "who spoke through the prophets." That the Spirit spoke through "*the prophets of Israel,* seems to broaden the pneumatological basis to include the Jews." Indeed, the authoritative ecumenical study of the creed states: "Christians and Jews might be able to come nearer to each other by studying their respective expectations of God's final kingdom and by seeking ways of common services to humankind in this perspective."[10]

Although references to the "spirit" abound in the OT (including about 100 occurrences of the "Spirit of God" alone),[11] in the vast rabbinic literature[12] the interest in the *Shekinah,* the divine immanence of Yahweh, usually overshadows the discussion of the *ruach.*[13] An obvious reason for focusing less on the "Holy Spirit" in postbiblical Jewish theology seems to be apologetic, that is, the avoidance of making too close a connection with the NT and emerging Christian theology of the Spirit.[14] Recently it has been suggested that the rabbis, mainly for political reasons, might have intentionally undermined the importance of prophecy and the Holy Spirit in order to establish the religious norms and their own authority in the society, in other words, for the stability of the religious establishment.[15] Be that as it may, we have to take into consideration also the well-known fact that according to the rabbinic sources, *Ruah ha-Kodesh* has left Israel. Again, that question is complicated and debated (in both Jewish and Christian scholarship); yet it is part of the core rabbinic tradition. That, however, never meant that interest in the Spirit was therefore lost — or

10. *One God, One Lord, One Spirit,* pp. 102-3, emphasis in original; see also, Samartha, "Holy Spirit and People of Other Faiths," pp. 255-56.

11. The expression "Holy Spirit" per se occurs only three times in the OT: Ps. 51:11; Isa. 63:10, 11. See further, Averbeck, "Breath, Wind, Spirit," p. 25.

12. The somewhat ambiguous term "rabbinic literature" can be understood in a wider sense that denotes basically all rabbinic works after the second century c.e., including all major types of works such as commentaries, or in a more technical sense focusing on midrashic and Talmudic works (in themselves a massive body of literature including also oral works). I am using the term in the former sense. A highly useful primer is Neusner, *Introduction to Rabbinic Literature.* For a brief discussion of Christian theologians, see my *Trinity and Revelation,* chap. 8.

13. Whereas in the whole massive Talmudic and midrashic literature there are about 80 passages concerning the Holy Spirit, one finds over 100 "major references" to and discussions of *Shekinah.* Gertel, "Holy Spirit in the Zohar," p. 92. The rabbinic literature's lack of interest in pneumatology can be seen in that still the only major authoritative monograph is Abelson, *Immanence of God in Rabbinical Literature.* The importance of *Shekinah* comes to the fore even in that work, as more space is devoted to that concept than to the Holy Spirit.

14. Cf. Abelson (*Immanence of God in Rabbinical Literature,* p. 379), who considers this motif a "moot point." On the contrary, the Christian NT scholar W. D. Davies has famously argued that in some important early rabbinic works such as the *Mekilta* of Rabbi Ishmael, a pervasive importance of "the Spirit" can be discerned, but much of that grows (perhaps largely unconsciously) from anti-Christian polemic. W. D. Davies, "Reflections on the Spirit in the Mekilta."

15. S. A. Cohen, *Three Crowns,* chap. 3; Danan, "Divine Voice in Scripture," pp. 34-35.

even that Israel would have been done with the divine Spirit in the first place. Consider this observation: "Even as *Ruah ha-Kodesh* is said to have departed from Israel in her role of inspiring the prophets, in her personified form she continues to speak as part of the ongoing Midrashic dialogue with the Sages."[16]

Before deepening the investigation into the features of rabbinic pneumatologies, an important question about their roots and major influences calls for a brief reflection. That has also much to do with the NT and early Christian pneumatologies. In the Qumran literature, chronologically closest to the biblical texts, "Spirit and spirits — including both angels and demons — are a frequent concern . . . which also introduces the formulation '*Ruah Kodesh*' (without the definite article and sometimes with possessives 'his' or 'your') to refer to the holy spirit of God or even of human beings."[17] This means that with the exception of using the designation "Holy Spirit" more often, the Qumranic usage, roughly speaking, parallels that of the OT. At the same time, the diverse roles of the Holy Spirit — from enlightenment, to the guidance of the righteous, to the forgiveness of sins, to prophecy and inspiration — are also an important bridge to the NT pneumatology.[18] In another early body of literature, the apocryphal and pseudepigraphic writings, many of the references to the Holy Spirit seem to be of Christian origin and linked with trinitarian connotations;[19] that is another indication of the cross-fertilization of Jewish and Christian theologies.

Based on the scriptural teachings, the rabbinic literature considers *Ruah ha-Kodesh,* "holy spirit" or "spirit of holiness," to be the divinely given power of prophecy and leadership. At the same time, the rabbis also "introduce a new application of the term by personifying it as a metonym for God, in ways which draw on Biblical and Hellenistic concepts of the hypostatization of Wisdom as Torah. This personified *Ruah ha-Kodesh* is importantly linked with the *Shekinah,* the present immanence of Yahweh."[20] Behind the semipersonified

---

16. Danan, "Divine Voice in Scripture," p. vii. There is also the interesting alternative view according to which the Holy Spirit left individuals but not the community at large, as argued in Urbach, *The Sages,* p. 577. I am not competent to assess which view best represents the vast textual evidence.

17. Danan, "Divine Voice in Scripture," p. 77. The standard source is Sekki, *Meaning of Ruah at Qumran.*

18. See Danan, "Divine Voice in Scripture," pp. 77-80.

19. See, e.g., Charlesworth, ed., "Hellenistic Synagogal Prayers," pp. 686-88. That rabbinic tradition does not consider highly (at times, not at all) apocryphal and pseudepigraphic literature does not diminish its meaning as an early testimony.

20. Danan, "Divine Voice in Scripture"; I am deeply indebted to that work with regard

conception of the Holy Spirit may also be the similar conception of the *hokmah* in Proverbs.[21] Generally speaking, the rabbinic literature focuses on these two aspects of the *Ruah ha-Kodesh*: the source of inspiration/revelation and the (semi)personified nature.[22]

Something else can be said about rabbinic views of the Spirit in light of the most current research, which also includes important contributions from some Christian scholars. John R. Levison has not only helped reorient Christian pneumatology (as discussed in the introductory chapter above), but he has also revealed significant evidence of the dynamism and vitality of Second Temple Judaism. Based on scrutiny of the vast array of pseudepigrapha, Qumran scrolls, and Hellenistic Jewish writings, he summarizes: "The era that gave birth to Judaism was, then, an era of spiritual dynamism, during which pinpricks in Israel's scriptures burst into life. It was an era when more, not less, attention was accorded the holy spirit within, when the fiery inebriation of ecstasy took hold, when authors legitimated their modes of scriptural interpretation by appealing to the presence of the spirit within, when an entire community could be filled with the spirit."[23]

As with other religious traditions, pneumatology in Judaism has undergone significant revisions and transformations, particularly when it comes to mystical and charismatic movements. Let us focus next on the medieval testimonies from the Kabbalah, when the rabbinic "mainline" teaching encountered and was influenced by deep mystical visions.

The Mystical Visions and Experiences of the Spirit in Kabbalah

As the Jewish theologian Elliot B. Gertel notes, "[t]he Zoharic literature, compiled in the late thirteenth century, represents a culmination of Kabbalistic

---

to many details of rabbinic theology of the Spirit. I have also gleaned from Unterman, Kreisel, and Horwitz, "Ru'ah Ha-Kodesh," pp. 506-9.

21. Abelson, *Immanence of God in Rabbinical Literature*, pp. 199-201; Danan, "Divine Voice in Scripture," pp. 26-27. For a sensitive (to Jewish intuitions) essay by a Christian exegete, see Longman, "Spirit and Wisdom," pp. 95-110. In the leading Hellenistic-Jewish philosopher Philo, the connection between wisdom, Logos, and *Shekinah* became an important theme. Unterman, Kreisel, and Horwitz, "Ru'ah Ha-Kodesh," pp. 507-8.

22. For a highly detailed analysis, see chap. 3 in Danan, "Divine Voice in Scripture."

23. Levison, *Filled with the Spirit*, p. 221; part 2 is devoted to the investigation of Second Temple Jewish literature. See also, Levison's monograph *The Spirit in First-Century Judaism*, p. 238.

readings and re-readings of ancient Jewish texts on that theme, as well as a response to Christian and Gnostic concepts of Holy Spirit."[24] Highly mystical and charismatic, this Kabbalah literature born in the Middle Ages puts more emphasis on spiritual experience. That is not to say that rabbinic literature in itself was void of that,[25] but in Kabbalah it comes to the fore. "The mystic's ideal is communion with God. His soul reaches out in loving yearning to embrace God. And he knows that he has found God, because he has felt the thrill of His answering love."[26]

Similar to rabbinic literature, in *Zohar* the Holy Spirit is identified with the *Shekinah*, the highest of divine emanations *(s'firot)*.[27] It accompanies the people of God and represents the powerful divine immanence in the world.[28] In a profound manner, this association is manifest in Queen Esther's clothing herself "with Malcut," the royal apparel — the divine *Shekinah!*[29] As in later Christian tradition, in rabbinic teaching *Shekinah* and Holy Spirit convey revelation from God,[30] including guidance in practical matters (such as Moses in the census)[31] and future events.[32] Whereas *Zohar* testifies to the agency of the Holy Spirit behind David's composition of songs (67a), the Talmud (*Pesahim* 117a) attributes it to *Shekinah*. The Zoharic tradition assumes that in the absence of the name of the author, we can consider the Holy Spirit the author of the psalm![33]

Importantly, David is depicted as the man who earnestly yearned for the experience of the Spirit: "True, it was the Holy Spirit that spoke through him, but had not David yearned continually for the Holy Spirit, it would not have rested upon him. It is always thus: the Holy Spirit will not descend upon a man unless he, from below, moves it to come."[34] Gertel adds this important observa-

---

24. Gertel, "Holy Spirit in the Zohar," p. 80.

25. Indeed, the above-mentioned authoritative source on rabbinic pneumatology claims that even in rabbinic literature the mystical ideal is strongly presented. Not all Jewish interpreters, however, affirm that claim without many qualifications. See Danan, "Divine Voice in Scripture," p. 23.

26. Abelson, *Immanence of God in Rabbinical Literature*, p. 5.

27. For the key concept of "divine emanations" *(s'firot)*, including *Malchut (Shekinah)*, see Halamish, *Introduction to the Kabbalah*, chap. 9.

28. See Gertel, "Holy Spirit in the Zohar," p. 81.

29. As reported in Ginzberg, *Legends of the Jews*, 1:329.

30. *Leviticus Rabbah* 1:5.

31. *Leviticus Rabbah* 4:6. For the Spirit's guidance in Moses' killing of the Egyptian (Exod. 2:12), see *Zohar* 2:13b.

32. See *Genesis Rabbah* on Gen. 48:2-12.

33. Gertel, "Holy Spirit in the Zohar," p. 82.

34. *Zohar* 2:140a. Behind David's yearning might also be the implication of the peniten-

tion: "Through the prodding of the Holy Spirit, David's songs impart mysteries of the *s'frot*, such as unification of the *Shekinah* with the other *s'frots*."[35] Other key biblical figures such as Elisha, who wished to have a double portion of his master's spirit — that is, the ability to perform twice as many miracles as Elijah — are connected with the power of the Spirit.[36] Moses is offered a highly powerful and glorious experience in which "God brought forth a holy spirit from the depths of a sapphire stone in which it was hidden, and crowned it with crowns, and illumined it with two hundred and forty-eight lights, and stationed it before Him and gave over unto its charge the whole of His own House-hold, with one hundred and seventy-three keys." This is followed by other mystical appearances.[37]

Something curious about the pneumatology of *Zohar* is not the existence of evil spirits or "non-holy spirit"[38] but that it "posits secondary 'holy spirits,' that derive from the *Shekinah* and other emanation-related holy spirits." To those belong each soul's possession of "the twenty-two letters of the alphabet" as they "pass through *Malchut*, or the *Shechinah*, the 'Mother of the spirits.'"[39] Even angels can be called holy spirits.[40]

Contemporary Jewish Pneumatologies

In light of the richness and diversity of traditions, it comes as no surprise that, like other topics in contemporary Jewish theology, pneumatology has been conceived in more than one way. From a Christian perspective, it is interesting to note the influence of Greek-Hellenistic and later modernist philosophies on the conception of the Spirit in Judaism as well. The magisterial work *Religion of Reason out of the Sources of Judaism* by Hermann Cohen (d. 1918), one of the most famous Jewish philosophers and theologians in modern times, took

---

tial Ps. 51 concerning the departure of the Spirit and traditional teaching (Babylonian Talmud *Yoma* 22b; *Sanhedrin* 107a) that after the affair with Bathsheba, the *Shekinah* had left him; see also, Cage, *The Holy Spirit*, p. 37. Noteworthy also is the teaching that the Holy Spirit departed from Abraham because of Lot's worship of idols (*Zohar* 1:85a).

35. Gertel, "Holy Spirit in the Zohar," p. 82; he refers further to *Zohar* 1:179a.

36. *Zohar* 1:181b.

37. *Zohar* 2:53b.

38. As Gertel names it ("Holy Spirit in the Zohar," pp. 87-88).

39. Gertel, "Holy Spirit in the Zohar," p. 88, on the basis of *Zohar* 2:73b-74a; other passages also speak of "holy spirits," in the plural, such as 2:150a.

40. *Zohar* 2:173.

not only the Enlightenment but particularly Kant's philosophy as the guiding framework for outlining doctrines. The chapter "The Holy Spirit" (note the title!) follows strictly an ethical-moral Kantian direction and fittingly begins with the question: "What is human morality?"[41] It is striking that this ethical-anthropological orientation leads to an idea according to which "in Jewish monotheism the holy spirit is not so much related to God as to man, so that it is not thought of as a specific characteristic of God."[42] For Cohen, the only "religious" meaning of the Holy Spirit is to act as the agent of holiness.

The presentation of the theme of the spirit in the work of the leading Jewish rabbi and theologian of the last generation, Samuel S. Cohon's *Jewish Theology* (1971), is no different from a typical Christian doctrine of the Spirit during the first half of the twentieth century (except for its quite polemic antitrinitarian approach). The theme of the Spirit plays a marginal role in his other work, *A Historical and Systematic Interpretation of Judaism and Its Foundations* (similarly to his rabbinic forebears, *Shekinah* plays a much more visible role). The focus is on anthropological tasks of the Spirit with no mention of her cosmic role in creation or public role in the society. Echoing Philo's way of defining God in philosophical terms, as a pure immaterial intellect,[43] Cohon argues for a purely "spiritual nature" of God that cannot be in any way related to the material, including the "material deity" of Christian trinitarianism (because of Christ's incarnation). Indeed, he acknowledges that "this conception of God appears subtle and abstract," but that "it does not strip Him of reality."[44] Surprisingly, the only major discussion of *ruach* (fewer than 4 pages in a monograph of almost 500 pages!) is under the heading "Biblical Psychology." While rightly reminding the reader that "flesh" *(basar)* in the OT denotes the whole human being, not only the physical, and that the soul-body dualism should not be taken in terms of moral dualism of good and evil, he sticks with standard Western philosophical dualism of "immaterial element" (soul) and body. Even when Cohon in passing mentions the *ruach* moving above the primeval chaos (Gen. 1:2), he misses all cosmic-creational implications and only uses it as an illustration of the close connection between the spiritual and material in the human being.[45] In keeping with much of Jewish theology — and contrasting with traditional Christian pneumatology — the Spirit is not

---

41. H. Cohen, *Religion of Reason*, p. 100.
42. H. Cohen, *Religion of Reason*, p. 101.
43. Levison, *The Spirit in First-Century Judaism*, p. 238.
44. Cohon, *Jewish Theology*, pp. 236-37 (p. 237).
45. Cohon, *Jewish Theology*, pp. 348-49.

even mentioned in relation to salvation. All in all, Cohon's theological *summa* is no anomaly among leading Jewish dogmatics.

Even the more recent work by Louis Jacobs, *A Jewish Theology*, which seeks to revise and update earlier theological presentations, has an equally marginal discussion of pneumatology. "Holy Spirit" is mentioned briefly in relation to scriptural inspiration[46] and Messiah.[47] The remaining few references are linked with humanity, either at the personal or the communal level.[48] The otherwise enlightening discussion of creation (chap. 7) is void of pneumatological references, even when referring to Genesis 1:2 (and *ruach* appears only once in the whole book).

A markedly different approach is the pneumatology of the contemporary American rabbi Rachel Timoner. Her 2011 title *Breath of Life* bears much resemblance to current Christian pneumatologies of Moltmann and some eco-feminists such as Elizabeth Johnson. Timoner shares the interesting personal experience that, having announced the book's subtitle during the writing process, *God as Spirit in Judaism,* she was often asked what exactly it means to consider "God as Spirit" (in contrast to the more generic idea of God's spiritual nature as opposed to any notions of materiality). American Jews in particular tend to connect the idea of God as Spirit with the third person of the Christian Trinity.[49] Unlike her distinguished contemporary predecessors, Timoner links *ruach* first and foremost with "life-giving breath, a simple wind, and the spirit that animates creation."[50] Highly insightful is the rabbi's rephrasing of the first verses of Genesis in light of the current big bang theory: "In the beginning of God's creation there was *tohu vavohu,* a chaotic soup of energy. There was thick and opaque darkness over the endless depths of the vacuum of nothing. Then *ruach Elohim merachefet al pnei hamayim* — then the spirit of God vibrated over the soup. And God said, 'Let there be light.' And matter and radiation separated, and there was light."[51]

The Christian reader is struck by one of the most delightful pictures of the divine Spirit at work in creation, namely, the midrashic picture of God fluttering like a nesting dove over her fledgling chicks[52] — a metaphor also known to Luther!

---

46. Jacobs, *A Jewish Theology*, p. 199.
47. Jacobs, *A Jewish Theology*, p. 296.
48. For the communal, see Jacobs, *A Jewish Theology*, p. 63.
49. Timoner, *Breath of Life*, p. xvi.
50. Timoner, *Breath of Life*, p. xviii.
51. Timoner, *Breath of Life*, p. 8.
52. Timoner, *Breath of Life*, p. 5.

This contemporary rabbi also corrects her counterparts by linking *ruach* not only to creation — or interpretation and inspiration, the favorite rabbinic themes — but also to redemption in a most holistic manner.[53] In keeping with Christian pneumatologists, Rabbi Timoner also discusses topics such as "embodied spirit"[54] and deep interconnection and relationality between the physical and mental/spiritual, personal and communal,[55] human and the rest of creation, and so forth.

The Spirit of Yahweh and the Holy Spirit

Although the systematician should always mind the exegete's recurrent warning that it is not justified "simply to assume that the '*ruah* of God/Yahweh' in the OT is the same as the Holy Spirit in the NT,"[56] that fear should also not paralyze the theologian (as seems to be the case with many OT scholars) from establishing the deep connection between the Spirit of Yahweh and the divine Spirit of the NT. To fail to establish the identity between the two would lead to the absurd conclusion of the lack of identity between Yahweh and the Father of Jesus Christ. That said, to cultivate the attitude of hospitality, the Christian theologian should also hasten to remind the Jewish counterpart of the different *interpretations* of the nature of the commonly confessed Spirit. Even when both confess God as Spirit, that does not lead to an agreement about its theological implications. The doctrine of the Trinity is of course the dividing line — and yet, it is a vastly different dividing line from that of the dialogue between, say, Hindu Brahman/*atman* and the third person of the Trinity.

Between the Jewish and Christian theologies, talk about the Spirit has to do with how to conceive of the Spirit of the one God in relation to the divine hypostatizations. Even when that discussion is not likely to lead to unanimity, the conversation partners speak of the one and same God, the Spirit. In this context, without delving again into the details from the discussion above on

53. The first major part of Timoner, *Breath of Life*, is devoted to the topic of the Spirit in creation. Another important, similar discussion draws from Artson, "Vibrating over the Face of the Deep," pp. 40-47.

54. Timoner, *Breath of Life*, pp. 17-19.

55. For a highly insightful reading of OT pneumatology from a communal-cosmic perspective, see the essay by the Indian theologian Kalluveettil, "Towards the New Age of the Spirit."

56. For a careful repudiation of von Rad's thesis, see Longman, "Spirit and Wisdom," p. 95.

the divinity of the Holy Spirit in Christian tradition (chap. 2), let it suffice to recall those remarks: the anticipatory significance of the existence of the semipersonified agents along with Yahweh in the OT (Word, Name, Glory, Wisdom); to those could also be added the identification in the *Zohar* (based on the midrashic tradition) of the creative Spirit of Genesis 1:2 with the Messiah who was created during the first days of creation,[57] notwithstanding its marginal role in Jewish theology. Those references are not meant to convince the Jewish counterpart of the validity of the trinitarian confession of faith, to which also belongs the dual nature of the divine Spirit as God and as the third person of the Trinity.[58] Their significance, rather, is to make more meaningful and understandable the rise of the trinitarian conception of God (and thus, trinitarian pneumatology) for the emerging Christian sect that grew from the Jewish monotheistic soil.

Alongside the continuing deep differences in the doctrine of God[59] — which have focused far more on the role of Jesus the Christ (discussed extensively in *Christ and Reconciliation,* chaps. 10 and 15) — Christians and Jews should appreciate the great cross-fertilization between the two traditions when it comes to pneumatology. Christian pneumatology owes everything to the Jewish scriptural traditions of the Spirit of God.[60] On the other hand, as discussed above, with the rise of Christian interpretations, rabbinic Judaism also had to clarify its own theology of *ruach.* While an intentional dialogue about the Spirit has hardly begun even in the beginning of the third millennium (and even the christological exchange had to wait until the nineteenth century), we can see some common developments between the two sister traditions. Both Jewish and Christian scholars have, for example, established the

---

57. *Zohar* 1:240a; Gertel ("Holy Spirit in the Zohar") identifies *Genesis Rabbah* 82:4 as the midrashic reference.

58. The Christian theologian Michael Lodahl rightly stresses that whether the term used in ancient Jewish texts for God's immanence was *ruach, pneuma,* or *Shekhinah,* it signifies a way "of referring to God's presence and activity, rather than to a being or beings hypostatically distinct from God." Lodahl, *Shekhinah/Spirit,* p. 57.

59. A somewhat polemical, although generally speaking highly useful, source from the Jewish perspective, is Gertel, "'Holy Ghost' and Judaism," pp. 34-55. Part of the polemics, she considers "Holy Spirit" almost exclusively a Christian trinitarian designation and hence minimizes its role in rabbinic writings.

60. For an important discussion, see M. R. Barnes, "Beginning and End of Early Christian Pneumatology." Barnes establishes not only the grounding of Christian pneumatology in Jewish traditions during the first two centuries of key developments but also the replacement (by Tertullian, Origen, and others) of some biblical Jewish orientations by Greek Hellenistic influences.

affinity between the then-contemporary movements of Zoharic spirituality and Franciscan mysticism.[61] Also highly interesting is the claim by Arthur Green that the feminization of *Shekinah* in the *Zohar* may have to do with a "Jewish response to the great popular revival of Marian piety in the twelfth century Western church."[62] Mystical-charismatic spirituality often provides fertile soil for boundary crossing.

Contemporary Christian pneumatology is deeply indebted to the OT theologies of the Spirit. The dramatic reorientations in contemporary Christian pneumatologies that have dramatically widened the sphere and ministry of the Holy Spirit to encompass cosmic, creational, and other public domains can be attributed by and large to the rediscovery of the key OT perspectives of the *ruach Yahweh* as the cosmic principle of life. That move corrected and revised the deeply reductionist pneumatologies of the past (stemming both from Hellenistic and from modernist sources). At the same time, some of the most recent constructive Jewish pneumatologies have learned from Christian advances — either directly or indirectly.

Among the few emerging attempts among Christian theologians to address the interfaith challenge between the two Abrahamic sister faiths through the lens of pneumatology, one stands out, namely, Michael E. Lodahl's *Shekinah/Spirit: Divine Presence in Jewish and Christian Religion* (1992). It is a process theistic–driven "conversation" between the two traditions.[63] Although process theism demands that Lodahl minimize the importance of the trinitarian doctrine to Christian pneumatology, making such a marginalization a key asset of the dialogue does not sound like a promising tactic to me. There are other ways to combat a Christian theological triumphalism that regretfully has laid the groundwork for previous anti-Semitism.[64] My critique of Lodahl is not meant to suggest that Christian trinitarian pneumatology could not reconsider its "foundations" — deriving as it does from Jewish sources! — but that a distinctively *Christian* approach to dialogue that depends on minimizing its most distinctive doctrine (in this case, based on resources not convincing to most theologians outside the process family) does not advance a broad-based interfaith exchange. Somewhat similar doubts arise for me about attempts to diminish or make too abstract the concept of the church/synagogue with appeal to pneumatological resources (the church as the "spiritual" body) in

---

61. Baer, *History of the Jews in Christian Spain*, 1:270-71.

62. Green, "*Shekinah*, the Virgin Mary, and the Song of Songs"; I am indebted to Gertel, "Holy Spirit in the Zohar," p. 93.

63. For orientation to the main ideas, see Lodahl, *Shekinah/Spirit*, pp. 4-7.

64. Lodahl, *Shekinah/Spirit*, pp. 67-73, 107-10.

order to overcome the deep ecclesiological divide between these two peoples of God.[65]

The other Abrahamic faith's conception of the Spirit bears significantly less similarity to Christian pneumatology. Yet it too draws from many of the same wells. To that discussion we turn next.

Ruh in the Qur'an and Islamic Spiritualities

The Spirit in the Qur'an

Among a number of widely debated and complex questions concerning Islamic pneumatology, few observations are undisputed in contemporary (Islamic and Christian) scholarship. First, whatever creative revisions the Prophet and particularly later theological tradition introduced, the Muslim teaching about and spirituality relating to the Spirit are deeply indebted to older Abrahamic traditions. That affinity of course relates to language as well: the basic term *ruh* is of course a Hebrew cognate and, roughly speaking, shares the same meaning: breath, wind, or air. Second, unlike its usage in Judeo-Christian Scriptures, in the Qur'an the noun never appears in the plural, nor does it have the meaning of "soul" (for which the other main term, *nafs*, is used).[66] Third, as in other scriptures, there is a definite development already within the Qur'anic depictions of the spirit having to do with the Prophet's changing life circumstances; those "contextual" changes shed much light on the theological meaning as well. The development is even more dramatic in theological history. Finally, although the "coincidence between *ruh al-kudus* ['Holy Spirit'] and Christian doctrine of the Holy Ghost cannot be accidental,"[67] neither should we fail to acknowledge the deep underlying differences among these two theologies.

What is now regarded as the classic standard study was written by the Jesuit Islamist Thomas O'Shaughnessy in 1953: *The Development of the Meaning of Spirit in the Koran.* The twenty Qur'anic references to *ruh* can be divided

---

65. An attempt to revise *pneumatologically* the Lutheran Robert Jenson's Christian theology of Israel as the people of God (with which I am generally in material agreement) by a Pentecostal theologian is M. Chan, "Reflecting on Roots."

66. Shellabear, "Meaning of the Word 'Spirit,'" pp. 356-57. Mylrea and 'Abdul-Masih's *Holy Spirit in the Qur'an and the Bible* contains a great deal of valuable material, but its uncritical Christian apologetics makes it a skewed scholarly source.

67. Macdonald, "Development of Spirit in Islam: I," p. 28.

into four "sense-groups," which also roughly correspond to the typical chronological scheme of the passages.[68] The first stage relates to the sayings about the angels and the spirit. On Muhammad's Night of Ordainment, "The angels and the Spirit descend in it by the leave of their Lord with every command" (Q 97:4). Two similar passages speak of the spirit as (semi)personal and of angels "ascending" (70:4) and "standing arrayed" (78:38).[69] In the Jewish Bible, a striking parallel is the narrative of the spirit sent by Yahweh delivering an intentionally deceitful message from Yahweh in the presence of kings and the prophet Micaiah (1 Kings 22:19-21). In the NT, the Spirit (of God, as God) of course acts as person on a number of occasions (furthermore, in one such passage, the term designating angels is "spirits," Heb. 1:14). In some early Christian writings such as those of Saint Ephrem, most probably known to the Prophet, the narrative of spirit and angels acting together is virtually identical to the passages above,[70] indicating the use of these writings.

The second sense-group is about the sharing of Allah's spirit with humans. Herein the Qur'an makes a definite shift from a (semi)personal agent to an impersonal breath: it is said of Allah that he "breathed of My Spirit in" Adam. The nonpersonal nature of spirit fits well this second phase of the Prophet's ministry in Mecca when the unity and omnipotence of Allah are in need of confirmation. An important theological observation is that the breathing in relates only to Adam (Q 15:29; 32:8; 38:72)[71] and Jesus (Q 4:171; 19:17; 21:91; 66:12). For the Judeo-Christian reader of the Qur'an, the breathing of God's spirit into Adam of course reminds one of Genesis 2:7, in which Yahweh "breathed into his nostrils the breath of life." Interestingly, the linking in the Qur'an of Adam and Jesus[72] has parallels in Paul's theology (Rom. 5:12-21; 1 Cor. 15:22, 45); this idea was picked up widely by early Christian theology, particularly the Syrian tradition, some of which the Prophet might

---

68. O'Shaughnessy, *Development of the Meaning of Spirit*, pp. 67-68, contains the finalized sense-group listing, and pp. 13-15 the chronological list. The importance of chronology in the Qur'anic study is highly significant not only for historical-critical reasons but also for theological reasons, particularly in light of the principle of "abrogation," that is, the later revelation surpasses the former and becomes *the* orthodox position.

69. In yet another passage, Q 16:2, the spirit, associated with angels, is also definite but being passively "sent down."

70. Saint Ephrem, "Eighty Rhythms upon the Faith against the Disputers," *Rhythm* 5:1, 2, pp. 120-21; for further parallels with Judeo-Christian traditions, see O'Shaughnessy, *Development of the Meaning of Spirit*, pp. 16-23.

71. So also, e.g., *Sahih Muslim*, book 1, "Faith," ##373, 378.

72. Consider this important statement in Q 3:59: "Truly, the likeness of Jesus in God's sight, is as Adam's likeness. He created him of dust, then said He to him, 'Be,' and he was."

133

have known at least to some extent.[73] Importantly, the Qur'anic depiction of the spirit in this context is some kind of material/physical force. A similar idea can be found in earlier Hebrew Scriptures as well as in the Greek-Hellenistic, particularly Stoic, philosophies. However, "[t]he concept of spirit as immaterial being was to be rediscovered in a later development of Islamic thought under the influence of Christianity and Greek philosophy and is read into the Koran only by the later commentators."[74] Hence, the NT teaching that "God is spirit" (John 4:24) is ambiguous to Islamic ears at best and heretical at the worst. The difficulty with speaking of Allah as spirit is heightened by the idea of angelic beings as "spirits" (lowercase), which of course are created, whereas Allah is uncreated.[75]

It is curious that in the Qur'an not only is Jesus highly regarded — indeed, the next highest prophet to Muhammad[76] — but also his mother's role is prominent (just consider the long nineteenth chapter, *Surat Maryam*). The passages in which spirit and Jesus are linked have to do with Mary and the virginal conception, a result of Allah's sending his Spirit (19:17; so also 21:91; 66:12).

The most remarkable passage about Jesus in the Qur'an is 4:171: "O People of the Scripture, do not go to extremes in your religion, and do not say about God except the truth: the Messiah, Jesus the son of Mary, was only the Messenger of God, and His Word which He cast to Mary, and a spirit from Him."[77] A number of theological points are to be noted here. First, although the Jews are also the "People of the Book," by this late period of Muhammad's life (4:171 is now routinely dated to the Medina period, the last years of the Prophet's preaching), the link with Christian faith, albeit also much more polemical than earlier, is considered integral. Second, as a word of warning: the Christian reader should not overexegete the title "Messiah" — any more than "Prophet" — because as highly regarded nomenclatures as they are, in Islam they have nothing to do with deity (even Muhammad himself, the last "seal of the Prophets," is of course not divine). Third, the Christian theologian has to

---

73. See O'Shaughnessy, *Development of the Meaning of Spirit*, pp. 27-33.

74. O'Shaughnessy, *Development of the Meaning of Spirit*, p. 30. An example is the statement of the spirit in al-Ghazali, *Alchemy of Happiness*, chap. 1, p. 3: "Although he is not from everlasting, yet he lives forever; and though his body is mean and earthly, yet his spirit is lofty and divine." See also, comments by Macdonald, "Development of Spirit in Islam: I," p. 154.

75. See further, Gorder, *No God but God*, p. 119; Macdonald, "Development of Spirit in Islam: I," pp. 40-41.

76. For a detailed discussion, see chap. 10 in Kärkkäinen, *Christ and Reconciliation*.

77. For useful discussions among some major Muslim theologians, see Steenbrink, "Jesus and the Holy Spirit"; Hakim, "The Spirit and the Son of the Spirit."

be careful also in interpreting the title Allah's "word," which has nothing to do with the theology of the divine Logos; indeed, as even the immediate context indicates, the Prophet means the word that was spoken by Allah to Mary's ear that caused the birth of Jesus in her pure womb (also implied in 66:12).[78]

All that said, what then is the meaning of the Qur'anic saying that Jesus is a spirit from Allah?[79] How much of that can be linked either to the Hebrew Bible's idea of *ruach Yahweh* as a creative principle or even semipersonified agent (similar to *dabar* or *kabod,* "word" and "glory" of Yahweh) or to the NT idea of the creative Spirit? With regard to the latter question, the same sura gives a clear answer, as it continues immediately: "So believe in God and His messengers, and do not say, 'Three.' Refrain, it is better for you. Verily, God is but One God. Glory be to Him, that He should have a son! To Him belongs all that is in the heavens and in the earth. God suffices as a Guardian" (4:171). Any linking of Jesus' lofty titles with divinity — and by implication with the Spirit — is categorically ruled out.[80] Neither is it right to make too tight a connection with the OT semipersonified notion of the spirit because of the fear of *shirk,* that is, "associating" anything created with God.

The third sense-group of *ruh* sayings in the Qur'an is the least understood, as these sayings link the spirit with the *amr*: "And they will question you concerning the Spirit. Say: 'The Spirit is of the command [*amr*] of my Lord. And of knowledge you have not been given except a little'" (17:85;[81] also 16:2; 40:15; 42:52). The context of the saying seems to be confrontational, as the Prophet is asked a question by an unidentified opponent (a Meccan adversary?). Not only is the exact meaning of *amr* disputed — "command" or "affair" or even a "thing"[82] — but also the rest of the sura, concerning the meaning

---

78. The creative command *kun* (be) is used in many instances when speaking of the "creation" of Jesus (as in 19:35). The only other contexts where it is used are in relation to creation (as in 36:82) and with regard to the final resurrection. If the Christian theologian seeks to find Islamic parallels with the biblical idea of the divine word (the OT *Dabar Yahweh* and the NT *Logos*) — as in Ps. 33:6 and John's prologue — then it is the Qur'an as the divine "word" that has some parallels. More on that in chap. 10 of *Christ and Reconciliation* and chap. 8 of *Trinity and Revelation.*

79. In *Hadith Qudsi* #36, "The Authority of Anas," Jesus is called "Allah's word and spirit."

80. So also, *Sahih Bukhari,* book 55, "Prophets," #644.

81. The questioners are Jews in the Hadith commentary on this verse in *Sahih Bukhari,* book 93, "Oneness, Uniqueness of Allah," #554; *Sahih Bukhari,* book 92, "Holding Fast to the Qur'an and Sunnah," #400.

82. For an extended discussion, see O'Shaughnessy, *Development of the Meaning of Spirit,* pp. 33-40.

of the expression "little knowledge," is disputed. Is that a warning about not claiming too much knowledge of the spirit? There was a lengthy dispute among the classical commentators about that.[83] Al-Ghazali's oft-quoted maxim is illustrative: "Whoever says that the *ruh* is created is a heretic; whoever says that it is eternal is an unbeliever."[84]

The final sense-group relates to the important theme of "Holy Spirit," or to put it more faithfully Qur'anic, the "Spirit of Holiness." These occurrences emerge at the end of the Prophet's ministry, as he also becomes better informed on Christian faith and the role of Jesus. Importantly, three times the spirit of holiness is linked with Jesus in terms of Allah "strengthening" or "confirming" him (2:87, 253; 5:110); also, some other faithful ones are strengthened with a spirit from Allah (58:22). Furthermore, the Qur'an is linked with the spirit of holiness sent down (16:102).[85] Also significant, the noun "holiness" appears in the Qur'an only in relation to *ruh,* which adds to the importance of the expression "the spirit of holiness." What is remarkable also is that, in another sura, the angel Gabriel is treated as identical to the "Holy Spirit"; just comparing 16:102 with 2:97 makes this clear — and it is a scholarly conviction that the latter sura, being later chronologically, overrules the former.[86]

This somewhat detailed scrutiny of Qur'anic pneumatology confirms that important shifts have taken place from a semipersonified picture of spirit as agent, to a totally nonpersonal (perhaps even in some sense physical) creative influence, to its use in connection with Allah doing his "business" in the world, and finally to the spirit of holiness. If the Gabriel passage is theologically dominant, then it is another definite deviation from any kind of divine account that would parallel the Christian trinitarian conception.[87]

83. See further, Macdonald, "Development of Spirit in Islam: I," pp. 30-31.

84. Quoted in Macdonald, "Development of Spirit in Islam: I," p. 39; for a detailed discussion of al-Ghazali's pneumatology, see Macdonald, "Development of Spirit in Islam: II," pp. 154-58.

85. We should refrain from reading this sura in terms of the Judeo-Christian view of the inspiration of Scripture not because Islam doesn't have a theology of divine authority of the Qur'an — it does, even more strongly than probably any other faith — but because in Islam the reception of the divine word comes "directly from heaven" through the intermediacy of the angel (Gabriel); the prophet's only task is to "recite" the text. There is no development, deepening, or other tasks left for the Spirit as in Christian doctrine.

86. In Hadith literature, both the identification and separation of (Holy) Spirit and Gabriel continues: see *Sunan Abu-Dawud,* book 41, "General Behavior," #4997; and *Sahih Muslim,* book 31, "The Merits of the Companions," #6081, respectively (available at http://www .searchtruth.com/book_display.php).

87. Although it certainly is true that in the NT, the Spirit (of revelation) seems to act

Mystical and Charismatic Experiences of the Spirit in Sufism

Although rich and wide philosophical-theological clarification and debate about the Spirit (including its relation to Gabriel and to the human spirit) have continued in Islamic tradition, grassroots-level enthusiasm of the spiritual experience — as it has in Christian tradition — has flourished in a dynamic manner. Experiences that contemporary theology would call mystical and charismatic are a common feature among masses of folk Islam, particularly in movements drawing from the rich spirituality of Sufism.[88] The rapid and steady growth of Sufism and related spiritualist movements is explained partly by the fact that, generally speaking, the "Muslim East has no preliminary prejudice against spirit manifestations as exists with us" in the West.[89] No wonder that throughout the years "power encounter" and miraculous acts have been enthusiastically acknowledged and claimed to lie behind many conversions.[90] As in Christian enthusiastic movements, its doctrinal orthodoxy has been constantly at stake.

Particularly important is Sufism's virtual identification of the Spirit of Holiness/Holy Spirit with God himself; hence, the great thirteenth-century Persian poet Farid ad-Din Attar could call Allah "the Universal Spirit."[91] As often happens in folk spirituality, the founder's role is elevated; in Sufism this elevation led almost to a divinization of Muhammad, which was an abomination to the Prophet himself![92] This is related to the widespread custom (even outside of Sufism) to build preaching and spirituality around the Beautiful Names of Allah; the name "Spirit of Holiness" was often added to them. So amorphous are many Sufi movements in their doctrinal beliefs[93] that it is not uncommon even today, let alone earlier, to find prayer beads (perhaps precur-

---

like an intermediary (1 Cor. 2:10; Eph. 1:17), making that a parallel with the Islamic idea of Gabriel does not make much sense to me; see O'Shaughnessy, *Development of the Meaning of Spirit*, pp. 47-48; for further details about "Gabriel the Spirit," see pp. 51-57.

88. An up-to-date self-description of contemporary Sufism with ample resources can be found on the official Web site of the International Association of Sufism at http://ias.org/sufism/introduction-to-sufism/ (3/21/2014).

89. Macdonald, "Development of Spirit in Islam: II," p. 166.

90. See Malek, "Islam Encountering Spiritual Power."

91. Cited in Macdonald, "Development of Spirit in Islam: II," p. 163. That this development was not limited to Sufism is evident also in the theology of Ibn al-Arabi, who along with al-Ghazali is certainly the greatest Sufi intellectual; for details, see pp. 163-65.

92. Kritzeck, "Holy Spirit in Islam," p. 109.

93. That said, we have to recall that perhaps the greatest intellectual mind of all Islam, al-Ghazali, was also Sufi (or at least deeply and widely influenced by its mystical spirituality).

sors to the Christian rosary) that include God the "Father," God "the Word," and God "the Spirit" — without of course in any way endorsing Christian trinitarian faith![94]

All in all, Sufi mysticism focuses on love and spiritual unity as well as on spiritual experiences. It is said of Husayn ibn Mansur Al-Hallajah, a famous ninth-century Sufi mystic, that he "was so full of the Holy Spirit that he could no longer distinguish himself from God" — which of course was too much for the establishment, leading to his crucifixion in 922.[95] Sufis from of old have also been enthusiastic missionaries, and scholars agree that, for example, they have been key in the spreading of Islam to the African continent.[96]

Discerning Differences and Searching for Commonalities

As with Jewish and Christian traditions, the Islamic theology of the Spirit has undergone significant shifts. As mentioned above, this includes the shift from a semipersonified agency to a nonpersonal influence to the linking of the Spirit with various works of Allah in the world, and finally to the focus on holiness. There is also the important mystical and charismatic experience of the Spirit represented most profoundly but not exclusively by various Sufi movements. At the grassroots level, that forms a major element even in contemporary Islamic spirituality.[97]

The Christian analyst of Islamic pneumatology easily finds many common points, and those should be appreciated. They include the close relationship of *ruh* to Jesus, including the virginal conception, its relationship to the Word of God, the ministry of strengthening the faithful, and so forth. At the same time, as already implied, one must be careful not to interpret common theological terms such as "spirit" and "word" without taking into consideration the underlying deep theological differences such as the unity versus the triunity of God, and seeing Jesus as a human prophet versus through the lens of "two-nature" Christology. It is neither hospitable nor useful to ignore differences[98] or to relegate them to mere "systematic-doctrinal" obstacles that can be

94. See Kritzeck, "Holy Spirit in Islam," p. 106.

95. Kritzeck, "Holy Spirit in Islam," p. 110.

96. See Kritzeck and Lewis, eds., *Islam in Africa*, particularly pp. 87-109.

97. See Woodberry, "Sufism."

98. As when some African Independent Churches claim that the prophethood of Muhammad has been inspired by the Holy Spirit; Olujide and Olujide, *Quran Testifies*, pp. 44-52. I am indebted to Yong, *The Spirit Poured Out on All Flesh*, p. 265.

overruled by "practice"[99] — unless differences are used as a way of starting and facilitating mutual conversations.[100] A deeply felt classic difference of opinion between the Christian and Muslim theologies has to do with the relationship of the Holy Spirit to the Prophet. That theme deserves deeper and wider scrutiny.

The debate has to do with how to translate and interpret the identity of the Johannine metaphor of the Holy Spirit, Paraclete. While not universally held among the Muslims, there is a long and wide tradition of identifying the Paraclete with Muhammad. Particularly in folk Islam, that is a dogmatic opinion. The dispute goes back to the interpretation of Qur'an 61:6 and its connection to John 15:26-27 and 16:7:

> And when Jesus son of Mary said, "O Children of Israel I am indeed God's messenger to you, confirming what is before me of the Torah and bringing good tidings of a messenger who will come after me, whose name is Ahmad." Yet when he brought them, they said, "This is manifest sorcery!" (Q 61:6)

> "Nevertheless I tell you the truth: it is to your advantage that I go away, for if I do not go away, the Counselor will not come to you; but if I go, I will send him to you." (John 16:7)

Now the *parakletos* ("Counselor") of John 16:7[101] is equated with *Ahmad* of Qur'an 61:1 (in many English renderings, the "Praised One"). In Islamic tradition a version of Muhammad's name is Ahmad.[102] Furthermore, there is

---

99. As in Jørgensen, "'Word of God' and 'Spirit of God.'" Except for this "practical" conclusion that I cannot theologically live with, the essay is highly useful and instructive.

100. Nor should we pay too much attention to the historical fact that on the way to the full acknowledgment of the Spirit's divinity, the at times semipersonal and elusive conception of the Spirit bore more resemblance to the Islamic (and Jewish conception) than a fully developed trinitarian view. In every religious tradition, development in ideas and beliefs takes time. Interestingly, the Pentecostal Amos Yong wonders if correlations can be found in the economic Oneness Pentecostal theology of the Spirit, which, unlike trinitarian Pentecostalism (to which Yong himself belongs), wants to stay only at the economic level and refuses to acknowledge the binding power of the Nicene and later doctrinal formulations. Yong, *The Spirit Poured Out on All Flesh*, p. 264.

101. A similar statement is found in Ibn Ishaq's biography of the Prophet Muhammad, in which John 15:23 is cited, apparently from a Syriac source. Guillaume, *The Life of Muhammad*, pp. 104-7.

102. Schacht, "Ahmad," p. 267; W. Watt, "His Name Is Ahmad," pp. 110-17; Guthrie and Bishop, "The Paraclete, Almunhamanna and Ahmad," pp. 251-56.

a statement in Ibn Ishäq's biography of the Prophet Muhammad, in which John 15:23-26 is cited from a Syriac source that identifies the *parakletos* with *munah-hemanā*, Syriac for Muhammad.[103] Those Muslim interpreters who make this identification may accuse Christians of changing the supposed original Greek word *periklytos* ("Praised one") to *parakletos* ("Comforter").[104]

There are, however, a number of problems with this identification, the most obvious one being that there is absolutely no textual evidence for it in Greek manuscripts of the NT. Furthermore, it is doubtful if Muhammad himself would have endorsed this interpretation.[105] These and other reasons convincingly show the falsity of the identity of the *Paracletos* with the Islamic Prophet. Kenneth Cragg summarizes the wide scholarly consensus about the Qur'an 6:61 exegesis:

> What is certainly clear is that it cannot be related to the sayings of Jesus in the Gospels about the Paraclete. Those sayings in no way relate to a purely prophetic spokesman whose coming, six centuries after, would in no sense be relevant to Jesus' disciples in their immediate first-century situation. His promise was to them and to their posterity in unbroken sequence. It did not, in its Gospel context, relate to a generation fifteen generations on, and after a silent hiatus of non-fulfilment.[106]

However, one related theme may find commonality between Islamic and Christian spiritualities, and it has to do with "remembering." The main task of the Johannine Paraclete is "to bring to your remembrance all that I [Jesus] have said to you" (John 14:26). The theme of remembering is crucial to Islamic tradition. Indeed, the Qur'an itself is named *Al-Dhikr*, the "Reminder." Hence, the central exhortation and promise: "So remember Me, I will remember you; and be thankful to Me, and be not ungrateful towards Me" (Q 2:152). Whereas

---

103. "But when the Comforter *(munahhemanä)* has come whom God will send to you from the Lord's presence, and the spirit of truth which will have gone forth from the Lord's presence, he shall bear witness of me and you also, because you have been with me from the beginning." Cited from Wheeler, "Arab Prophets of the Qur'an and Bible," p. 34. Ibn Ishäq adds that *munahhemanā* is Syriac for Muhammad, and that in Greek it is *baraqlītus*, both of the terms being used by Jesus as references to the coming of the Prophet Muhammad. Guillaume, *The Life of Muhammad*, p. 104.

104. Spencer, *Islam and the Gospel of God*, p. 8; Wheeler, "Arab Prophets of the Qur'an and Bible," pp. 33-34 particularly.

105. Cf. the Islamic scholar Ess, "Islam and the Other Religions," pp. 99-100.

106. Cragg, *Jesus and the Muslim*, p. 266.

in Islamic tradition the main way of practicing remembering is the recital and study of the Qur'an, in Christian spirituality it also entails the liturgical celebration of the memory of Jesus Christ in the Eucharist (1 Cor. 11:23-26).[107]

As mentioned, the principle of hospitality seeks to discern both genuine differences and potential areas of convergence. It allows honoring the otherness of the Other while at the same time seeking for continuing mutual dialogue and deepening of understanding. With this principle in view, the Roman Catholic Islamist James Kritzeck's words are of great promise regarding the continuing exchange of pneumatological insights among the three Abrahamic traditions: "In the honest and serious search for and with the 'Holy Spirit' lies one of Islam's most appealing and endearing aspects. It may prove to be the most significant one of all to be considered if the Sons of Abraham are ever to be one in faith, in hope, and in love, praising forever the glory of the Father, the victory of the Son, and the comfort, the gifts, and . . . 'the delicious taste' of the Holy Spirit."[108]

Atman and the Holy Spirit:
Pneumatology in Hindu-Christian Perspective

Atman *Is Brahman*

What can be said without reservation is that Christian and Hindu traditions are united in the common belief in the Spirit[ual] as the ultimate reality. The veteran Indian theologian-ecumenist M. M. Thomas puts it well: "In the major religious tradition of India, Hinduism, all thinking about God and the world starts with *Brahman,* the Universal Spirit which is the ultimate reality. The creative process is conceived as the unfolding of the Spirit. The Spirit is one without a second; and all creation is the manifestation of the Spirit."[109] What is much more challenging is defining more precisely how to best express in Hindu terms what Christian faith simply and briefly states in saying "God is Spirit" (John 4:24). It is not that Hindu traditions are not deeply imbued with the presence of spirit(s) and spiritual realities; indeed, "[i]n religion where there is no clear and definite notion of a personal god [as in Hinduism], the

---

107. For highly insightful discussion, see Cragg, *Jesus and the Muslim,* pp. 260-62, 269, 272-74.

108. Kritzeck, "Holy Spirit in Islam," p. 111.

109. M. M. Thomas, "The Holy Spirit and the Spirituality for Political Struggles," p. 216.

powers and elements of nature with their massive and irresistible impact have influenced the human mind in raising its religious and divine consciousness" and brought about a rich tradition of beliefs, rites, and rituals having to do with the spiritual.[110] Nor does Hindu philosophy lack words that could be translated "spirit" — there are many, such as *atman, antaryamin,* and *shakti.* The difficulty lies in finding not only their true meaning but also their role and relation to the divine. Whereas in the previous chapter the focus was on the spirits (plural) of the cosmos, here the question deals with the role of the spirits (or their counterparts) and their relation to the divine Spirit, and even more foundationally, whether there is a divine Spirit in Hinduism, and what kind the divine Spirit might be.

Any inquiry into the "pneumatology" of Hinduism must begin with the most foundational statement in Vedic Upanishadic texts: "that Self [At-man] is indeed Brahman."[111] Variously translated as "the Supreme" or similar, "Brahman is the one ultimate reality in Hinduism,"[112] notwithstanding the presence of three *(trimurti)* or many deities, even a pantheon of them, as its manifestations (for details, see *Trinity and Revelation,* chap. 15). As the ultimate reality, Brahman is beyond all qualities, definitions, limits — to use the Western philosophical terminology, it is absolutely infinite.[113] Brahman consists of all things,[114] and, "without undergoing any modification, passes, by entering into its effects (the elements), into the condition of the individual soul,"[115] and therefore the divine can be discerned within each person and in everything. Brahman is *the* Grand Spirit of that religion.

If Brahman is the ultimate reality, then, *atman* is the ultimate about everything else. Whereas everything else in the world changes, *atman* does not. Whereas in Christian (and Abrahamic) traditions only God — in his trinitarian life — is eternal, and creation is not, in Hinduism everything, including *atman,* is coeternal with Brahman;[116] Hindu philosophy does not know anything like the doctrine of creation after Abrahamic traditions.[117]

---

110. John, "Complementary Dimensions," p. 327.

111. Brihadaranyaka Upanishad 2.5.2; p. 113.

112. Sharma, *Classical Hindu Thought,* p. 1.

113. See further, Sharma, *Classical Hindu Thought,* pp. 49-51.

114. Brihadaranyaka Upanishad 4.4.5 (*SBE* 15:176): "That Self is indeed Brahman, consisting of knowledge, mind, life, sight, hearing, earth, water, wind, ether, light and no light, desire and no desire, anger and no anger, right or wrong, and all things."

115. Sankara, *Vedanta Sutras* 2.3.17; *SBE* 38:30.

116. For details, see Dwivedi, "Classical India," p. 45.

117. See, e.g., Satapatha Brahmana 10.5.3.1; *SBE* 43:374-75. This is not to say that in the

Even though *atman* is routinely translated as "soul," in no way is that individually driven Western concept a good way to communicate the meaning of the Sanskrit word *ātman* (for "soul," a better term is *jiva*).[118] It is best left untranslated, but if it must have an English rendering, "spirit," carefully considered, might be the best. What is wrong, however, is to make it merely an "inner" spirit vis-à-vis the "Ultimate Spirit" (Brahman), as is customary in Western writings. While of course *atman* in one sense denotes the "inner spirit," it is not so subjectively understood, but rather is a reality as an interpenetration or integral union with Brahman. Just consider this famous statement from Brihadaranyaka Upanishad: "He (Brahman or the Self) entered thither, to the very tips of the finger-nails, as a razor might be fitted in a razor-case, or as fire in a fire-place. He cannot be seen, for, in part only, when breathing, he is breath by name; when speaking, speech by name; when seeing, eye by name; when hearing, ear by name; when thinking, mind by name. All these are but the names of his acts."[119]

That *atman* is far more than just an "inner spirit" of humanity comes to the fore in the idea that even for *devas* (deities, divine beings), to know "I am Brahman" means that Brahman "himself is [or becomes] their Self [Atman]."[120] Furthermore, corresponding to the five Brahman "realities," in the *atman* five strata (such as space or air or fire) can be discerned. Each stratum is the inner core of the one preceding it, ultimately leading to the innermost core, *ananda,* the "bliss," where the identity of *atman* with Brahman is discerned.[121]

Before delving deeper into the potential correlations between *atman* and Christian pneumatology, let us relate it more carefully to Brahman. This relating also takes us into deep and fierce debates among Vedanta traditions. While, as said, all Vedanta schools affirm the unity between Brahman and *atman,* deep disagreements concern the ways to define the unity. Using Christian terminology, this is the debate about the relationship between God and the

---

vast Upanishadic literature one couldn't find statements that, taken alone, would not seem to imply the idea of "creation" (e.g., Brihadaranyaka Upanishad 1.2.1; *SBE* 15:74; Taittiriyaka Upanishad 2.7.1; *SBE* 15:59). These statements, however, must be understood within the unitive system of Hindu thought.

118. For the Hindu anthropology and concept of "soul," see chap. 14 in *Creation and Humanity.*

119. Brihadaranyaka Upanishad 1.4.7; *SBE* 15:87.

120. Brihadaranyaka Upanishad 1.4.10; *SBE* 15:88. For details with many more textual examples, see Klostermaier, *Survey of Hinduism,* pp. 198-201 particularly.

121. Khandogya Upanishad 6.8; *SBE* 1:99-101; for explanations, see Klostermaier, *Survey of Hinduism,* p. 198.

world.[122] With oversimplification, the big picture (with innumerable internal variations) is this: under the leadership of the ninth-century Sankara, a radical monism was worked out *(advaita)*; under the twelfth-century Ramanuja, the monism was qualified to make room for some distinction between God and the world *(visistadvaita)*; in the thirteenth-century theology of Madhva, a (qualified) duality was presented as a robust challenger. For our purposes, the debate between Sankara and Ramanuja is crucial.[123]

According to Sankara, all commonsense subject-object separation should be discarded because it is a result of *adhyāsa*, "superimposition."[124] This means that the phenomenal world is not the "real" (or truest, as it were) existence. Of course the phenomenal world exists, but it is "appearance" in the sense that it is not the ultimate.[125] Although there is a kind of dualism in Sankara, namely, between the "real" and "appearance," that distinction does not posit the kind of categorical dualism present in much of Western thought between spirit and matter: "God, ultimately reality, permeates all material manifestations, and hence . . . there is no fundamental antagonism between matter and spirit, world and God." At all times, Hindu vision seeks to expe-

---

122. As Sara Grant (*Towards an Alternative Theology,* p. 35) points out, "In India as in Greece, the ultimate question must always be that of the relation between the supreme unchanging Reality and the world of coming-to-be and passing away, the eternal Self and what appears as non-Self" (the study compares Aquinas and Sankara). For a highly useful discussion, see Klostermaier, *Survey of Hinduism,* chap. 13.

123. The spirituality of the common people in India, guided by Gita and expressing itself in some form of *bhakti* devotion and spirituality with endless (often local) customs and colors (to which usually also belong local deities), is not as monistic as *advaita* and so is much closer to Ramanuja's qualified view. The term "inconceivable identity-in-difference" is routinely used to describe this qualified monism. According to this interpretation, everything is simultaneously one with and different from the Supreme Being, Lord (who comes with various names; common folk in India follow either the god Shiva [Shaivites] or Vishnu [Vaishnavites], the latter of which is best known through its *avatara* cult, particularly of Krishna).

124. Klostermaier, *Survey of Hinduism,* p. 373. Moving beyond typical categorical thinking, Sankara famously claims that "the relation of Ruler and ruled does not exist" apart from the "phenomenal world." Sankara, *Vedanta-Sutras* 2.1.14, p. 330. A related fallacy is *avidya*, "nescience," which is incapable of distinguishing between relative and absolute being; see Sankara, *Vedanta-Sutras* 2.1.27; *SBE* 34:352.

125. "The world of appearances is real though not self-subsistent." Ward, *Religion and Revelation,* p. 146. Well-known illustrations of Sankara include mistaking a rope for a snake (*Vedanta-Sutras* 1.3.18, p. 189) and elephants seen in dreams for real ones (1.2.12, p. 123). Sankara's modern interpreter Swami Vivekananda goes quite far as he says that "[t]his universe does not exist at all; it is an illusion. The whole of this universe . . . [is] all dreams." Vivekananda, "Steps of Hindu Philosophic Thought," in *Complete Works,* vol. 1, n.p. For a balancing and correcting statement of Sankara's view, see Lipner, *Hindus,* p. 14.

rience "the harmony of dualities."[126] Grasping the principle of oneness, as in illumination, is the key to salvation (and freedom from the samsara).[127] The many complex details aside, it seems to me that Sankara's whole project is to help men and women come to the liberating knowledge in which all distinctions are overcome, as truly *atman* is Brahman. If this is not pantheism, what then is?[128] We also must keep in mind the fact that Brahman is not something other than all things, but rather, it "is the same as that Self, that Immortal, that Brahman, that All."[129]

Ramanuja's *visistadvaita* offers a massive critique and an alternative proposal to Sankara's strict monism. That Ramanuja seeks to challenge the unqualified monism of his famed predecessor is of course not to introduce dualism in any (Western) sense, but rather to offer a more sophisticated — *qualified* — account of *advaita*. He posits distinction but not any kind of dualistic separation between God and world — ultimately, that distinction relates to distinction within Brahman (because of the identity between Brahman and *atman*). Ramanuja famously intuits the world as the body of God. Often his way of speaking of the world as the body being animated by the divine spirit, being dependent on it, and being guided by Brahman, sounds strikingly similar to some contemporary Christian, deeply panentheistic conceptions.[130] An important related idea is what Christian and Western philosophical tradition calls "infinity" — the concept that "God contains all finite realities, both good and evil, but also transcends them. God is with and without form . . . changing and changeless, is with and without existence in a changing world, is both father and mother of all beings, is incomprehensible and yet reveals himself, is separate from all beings yet united with all beings."[131]

Even this overly brief description reveals that Ramanuja's qualified monism at face value (at least) seems closer to the need of Abrahamic faiths to distinguish between God and the world. His theology also seems to allow at least some kind of personal deity (although hardly in the sense of that of the

---

126. Menon, "Hinduism and Science."

127. Sankara, *Vedanta-Sutras* 1.1.1, pp. 13-14 (p. 14). Sankara's emphasis on true knowledge hence makes highly suspect the popular claim that he is a mystic to whom a deep experience per se would be the key to salvation. For an informed discussion, see Thatamanil, *Immanent Divine*, pp. 60-62 and passim.

128. Contra Ward, *Images of Eternity*, pp. 18-19.

129. Brihadaranyaka Upanishad 2.5.1; the following verses repeat that idea over and over again.

130. Ramanuja, *Vedanta-Sutras* 2.2; *SBE* 48:261-62.

131. Carman, *Majesty and Meekness*, p. 146.

Abrahamic faiths). For Sankara the ultimate reality is of course impersonal and pantheistically conceived.[132]

In Search of Parallels between Hindu and Christian Concepts of the Divine Spirit(s)

In light of the deep spirituality of Indian cultures and religions, it comes as no surprise that Indian Christian theologians have shown remarkable interest in the Holy Spirit through the lens of Indian spiritualities.[133] Two kinds of tactics have been tried in this search for potential correlations between the two "pneumatologies." One is to focus on the concept of "spirit" per se, and the other one is to place the Spirit in the trinitarian context and see if any links can be found.[134] Let us take a look at each of them briefly and then offer a wider theological assessment.

Atman, Shakti, and Agni

The alleged connecting point between the concept of *shakti* and God's Spirit is the extraordinary power and energy of *shakti*. In Hinduism, that power is not limited to the workings of humans but also relates to some deities, particularly Durga and Kali, the prominent female deities.[135] These goddesses are believed to be executors of both destructive and constructive work with the help of the energy of *shakti*. Even more important with regard to parallels with the Holy Spirit is the belief in *shakti* as the energy of creation; at times it is called the "Universal Creator."[136] Although *shakti* traditions, including its most

132. Sankara's highly contested (by other Hindu movements) solution to the obvious challenge, namely, how to posit the "Supreme Being" or "Self" without any notion of knowledge and will — thus notions of "personality" — is the divide between the *nirguna* and *saguna Brahman*. Whereas the former is without any qualities and thus beyond human grasping, the latter has qualities and is thus known. Ultimately, however, Sankara intuits the Brahman as neither "being" nor "nonbeing." For textual examples, see Thatamanil, *Immanent Divine*, p. 77.

133. See R. Boyd, *Introduction to Indian Christian Theology*, pp. 241-43; Wilfred, "Towards a Better Understanding of Asian Theology."

134. Highly useful investigations are P. V. Joseph, *Indian Interpretation of the Holy Spirit*; K. Kim, *Mission in the Spirit*; for a synopsis, see her "Holy Spirit in Mission in India."

135. For the meaning and significance of the feminine in *shakti*, see Eck, *Encountering God*, pp. 136-43.

136. Kumar, "An Indian Appreciation," p. 29. The Christian theologian should not take

important writing — Devi Bhagavata Purana, with its elaborate narrations and glories of various aspects of the feminine energy — are not authoritative to all Hindus (as they are to most Shiva followers), *shakti* is widely embraced by Hinduism.[137] Because of the multiformity of Hindu traditions regarding the spirit, their use by Christians can also vary, some of whom seek to be orthodox, others placing emphasis on contextualization at any cost.[138] An example is P. Chenchiah, a Christian convert from Hinduism and member of the "Rethinking Group" (established in the 1930s).[139] Having left behind Chalcedonian Christology, he considers *shakti* the "Yoga of the Spirit"[140] that comes "from outside" for renewal and reinvigoration. The Holy Spirit is "the new cosmic energy," rightly understood, "the human energy that is sought to be harnessed to the Christian task."[141] Ultimately, "the Holy Spirit transcends all historical limitations and surpasses all geographical boundaries and becomes the Paramapurusha and Anthryamin, the universal dweller in the hearts of men."[142] When speaking of the Spirit as new cosmic energy, he uses the term *mahasakti,* the "great power."[143]

Some Indian Christian theologians have linked *shakti,* the divine energy, with Spirit Christology. A tendency is to identify the risen Christ with the Spirit. Although Spirit Christology does not have to compete with the Chalcedonian "two-nature" Christology — and during the early centuries they were considered complementary — like some leading contemporary Western theologians (such as J. D. G. Dunn) who identify and finally subsume the risen Christ under the living Spirit,[144] the South Indian V. Chakkarai claimed

---

the terms "creator" and "creation" in the context of Hinduism as implying any kind of creation *ex nihilo* along the lines of Abrahamic faiths. Rather, they mean "coming into existence" or "emergence." For Hindu views of "creation," see chap. 5 in *Creation and Humanity.*

137. For a detailed explanation and samples of texts, see Daniélou, *Myths and Gods of India,* chap. 20.

138. For its use by Upadhyaya, see R. Boyd, *Introduction to Indian Christian Theology,* p. 76.

139. For details, see R. Boyd, *Introduction to Indian Christian Theology,* chap. 8.

140. R. Boyd, *Introduction to Indian Christian Theology,* p. 155. Other Indian Christians have also appealed to yoga. Through Saiva Siddantic Yoga, A. S. Appasamy claimed to have had the experience of receiving the Holy Spirit and gaining a clearer vision of Christ. Later he practiced Advaita Vedantic Yoga and recommended it for use by Christians, though without accepting the Vedantic philosophy as a whole. See his *Use of Yoga in Prayer,* pp. 10-13, 17.

141. Cited in Kumar, "An Indian Appreciation," p. 30.

142. As paraphrased by Kumar, "An Indian Appreciation," p. 30.

143. R. Boyd, *Introduction to Indian Christian Theology,* p. 156.

144. For details of Spirit Christology, see chap. 8 in *Christ and Reconciliation.*

that "[t]he Holy Spirit is Jesus Christ Himself, taking His abode within us."[145] Indeed, he goes further and states that while "Jesus Christ is the Incarnation or Avatār of God . . . the Holy Spirit in human experience is the Incarnation of Jesus, Christ."[146] A creative theologian, Chakkarai also calls the Holy Spirit the *antarātman,* the "Inner Spirit," or *antaryāmin,* the "Indweller," which he then identifies with Christ.[147]

In addition to *atman* and *shakti,* other Hindu concepts have been invoked as candidates for correlation. One has to do with fire, which is also linked with many core religious symbols such as light, candles, incense, sacrifices, and so forth. Fire is a common metaphor for the Spirit in Judeo-Christian Scriptures. In the Vedic religion, one of the main earlier deities, Agni, is the god of fire.[148] The very first hymn of the Vedas (Rig Veda) sings praises to Agni in a way that a perceptive Christian may quite easily find in it common themes with the Holy Spirit: "I magnify Agni, the purohita, the divine ministrant of the sacrifice, the Hotri priest, the greatest bestower of treasures."[149] The word *purohita,* spoken of the deity, refers to his most distinctive task, namely, the priestly work.[150] As priest, he represents both heaven and earth. Another important task of Agni is that of purifier, including cleansing from sins.[151] Agni is also the giver of wisdom and the source of illumination.[152] Hence, the "sapient-minded Priest"[153] is linked with Truth. No wonder Agni is believed to be the main inspirer of the Vedic sacred scripture; indeed, "Agni is the mouth of God, and speech . . . is considered to be fire."[154] Importantly, Agni is also depicted as "'God in human beings,' 'the immortal in mortal,' 'the divine guest.'"[155] Hence, the confident prayer of intimacy and union at the end

---

145. Cited in R. Boyd, *Introduction to Indian Christian Theology,* p. 173.

146. Cited in R. Boyd, *Introduction to Indian Christian Theology,* p. 174.

147. R. Boyd, *Introduction to Indian Christian Theology,* p. 174.

148. Of the approximately 1,000 hymns devoted to deities in Rig Veda, the oldest part of the Vedic scripture, about one-fifth deal with Agni alone; the very first and last hymns also happen to be devoted to Agni. See, e.g., Rig Veda 1.1.1, 12, 13, 26, 27, etc. There are also joint hymns such as 1.1.19 to Agni and Maruts. This section is deeply indebted to John, "Complementary Dimensions," pp. 329-32, although I also develop it a bit differently than she does.

149. Rig Veda 1.1.1, following the translation from Sanskrit in John, "Complementary Dimensions," p. 329.

150. See Eck, *Encountering God,* p. 128.

151. Rig Veda 4.2.4; see also, the prayer in 1.97.

152. See, e.g., Rig Veda 1.105.14.

153. Rig Veda 1.1.5; see also, 1.1.6.

154. John, "Complementary Dimensions," p. 337.

155. A. A. McDonnell, *Hymns of the Rig Veda,* pp. 10-11, cited in John, "Complementary

of the first hymn: "Be to us easy of approach, even as a father to his son: Agni, be with us for our weal."[156] The glorious assets and benefits of Agni, the god of fire, are summed up in the very last hymn of the same Rig Veda (10.159), the main thrust of which is harmony and unity among all, including humans and divine beings:

1   THOU, mighty Agni, gatherest up all that is precious for thy friend.
    Bring us all treasures as thou art enkindled in libation's place.
2   Assemble, speak together: let your minds be all of one accord,
    As ancient Gods unanimous sit down to their appointed share.
3   The place is common, common the assembly, common the mind, so
    be their thought united.
    A common purpose do I lay before you, and worship with your gen-
    eral oblation.
4   One and the same be your resolve, and be your minds of one accord.
    United be the thoughts of all that all may happily agree.

Christian theology should appreciate the surprisingly rich and deep in-
terconnections between Agni and the Holy Spirit. The shared fire symbolism,
with a number of related implications such as offerings, praise, and purification, is in itself instructive. Other commonalities can be found, including the
task of creating unity and harmony. Differences are also obvious, and comparative theology should mind them: whereas in Hindu tradition Agni is one of
the deities in the pantheon of gods (and, except for the highly elitist Brahmin
caste, largely unknown to the masses), in Christian theology the Holy Spirit
is divine — indeed, God — and as such also agent of a number of other tasks,
including creation. Nevertheless, the parallelism between Agni and the Holy
Spirit contains surprisingly many common themes related to the functions
of each.

Trimurti, Saccidananda, *and "Advaitic Trinitarianism"*

Christian theologians, both from outside and within India, have acknowledged some parallels between the deeply triune pattern of aspects of Hindu

---

Dimensions," p. 330. For Agni's role as the presence in human houses and families, see Rig
Veda 1.27.7-8.

156. Rig Veda 1.1.9.

and Christian theology and spirituality.[157] It is interesting that while a search focused particularly on the "trinity" of classical deities — Brahma, Vishnu, and Shiva (the Trimurti) — began as early as the sixteenth century,[158] Hindu cult has been slow to pay much attention to threeness.[159] The reason Christians should be interested in this pursuit is that although the mere existence of three deities would hardly be more than coincidence, the fact that they are manifestations of the one and same Brahman may be significant.[160] The theological commonality between the generic idea of Trimurti and Trinity, however, may not be hugely promising. As the great Indian neo-Hindu-turned-Christian-Catholic Brahmabandhab Upadhyay argued, the reason Trimurti is not the same as the Trinity is that the former is only a phenomenal aspect of the divine. That is dramatically different from the Christian confession. In the cyclical worldview of Hinduism, at the cosmic dissolution, the Trimurti dissolves and is no more; by contrast, the Christian Trinity is God's own inner identity, eternal and unchanging.[161] Furthermore, this "father of Indian theology" surmises that in Hinduism, Brahma, Vishnu, and Shiva are but material, imperfect, and even sinful, drastically unlike Father, Son, and Spirit — pure, spiritual, and holy.[162] For these and related reasons (and supported by insightful critique from the Hindu side),[163] the Trimurti never provided anything significant either to the doctrine of the Trinity or particularly to Christian pneumatology. That conclusion, however, is not the whole story; some other avenues are worth trying.

157. A useful reflection by a highly knowledgeable Christian layperson, a physicist by training, is J. Joseph, "Trinitarian Experience of a Christian and Advaitic Experience of a Hindu." For a wider survey of triadic patterns in religions, see Parrinder, "Triads"; for a detailed comparison with the Christian doctrine of the Trinity, see chap. 15 in *Trinity and Revelation*.

158. As early as the sixteenth century, the Jesuit Thomas Stephens attempted to identify parallels between Christian and Hindu trinities. Many other Catholic missionaries followed suit, including such luminaries as the seventeenth-century Roberto de Nobili. On the Protestant side, Bartolomeo Ziegenbalg made the first major effort at comparison. Clooney, "Trinity and Hinduism."

159. Most well known is the hymn of Kālisāda, known to Westerners through Emerson's poem "Brahma" (Basham, *The Wonder That Was India*, p. 310).

160. Radhakrishnan, ed., *The Principal Upanisads*, p. 815, cited in Sharma, *Classical Hindu Thought*, p. 73. One reason certainly is the waning of interest in Brahma worship; see Sharma, pp. 79-81.

161. *Writings of Brahmabandhab Upadhyay,* 1:79; I am indebted to Clooney, "Trinity and Hinduism," p. 312.

162. *Writings of Brahmabandhab Upadhyay,* 2:287b.

163. See the critique by Ram Moham Roy, the founder of the strictly monotheistic neo-Hindu reform movement Brāhma Sāmaj, in Clooney, "Trinity and Hinduism," p. 316.

A more promising bridge can be found in the ancient concept of *saccidananda* ("being," "wisdom," "bliss"), which goes beyond the generic idea of three-deities-linked-with-each-other and probes more deeply into the nature of the divine. The opening lines of the most widely used handbook of *advaita* Vedanta, *Vedantasara of Sadananda,* opens with these words: "I take refuge in the Self, the Indivisible, the Existence-Knowledge-Bliss Absolute, beyond the reach of words and thought, and the Substratum of all, for the attainment of my cherished desire."[164] The term "self" here is *paramatman,* and "Existence-Knowledge-Bliss" is *sat-cit-ananda.* Relate this to another statement in the same manual: "Reality is Brahman which is without a second and is Existence, Consciousness, and Bliss,"[165] in which "reality" refers to *atman.* So, here in two brief but theologically pregnant statements, Brahman is identified with *atman* and *sat-cit-ananda,* as well as the ultimate "bliss." Accordingly, Indian Christians have seen parallels in the concept of *ananda* with the Holy Spirit, the bringer of joy and blessedness (Gal. 5:22; Rom. 14:17; 1 Thess. 1:6; and so forth).[166]

The noted Hindu reformer Keshub Chunder Sen of the nineteenth century picked up this connection and envisioned in his "That Marvellous Mystery — the Trinity" a triangle: Brahma is on top as *cat* (Being), and "Divinity coming down to humanity is the Son; Divinity carrying up humanity to heaven is the Holy Ghost."[167] Deeply knowledgeable of the inner logic of Christian classical trinitarian canons, he further expounds: "Whether alone or manifest in the Son, or quickening humanity as the Holy Spirit, it is the same God, the same identical Deity, whose unity continues indivisible amid multiplicity of manifestations."[168] Here the *theological* connections between the threeness of the Brahman as manifested in *saccidananda* and three-in-unity of the Christian God run deep. Other Hindu theologians, particularly the French Catholic priest and monk Jules Monchanin, better known as Swami

---

164. *Vedantasara of Sadananda* 1 (p. 1), trans. and ed. Nihilananda. Another classical passage is Taittiria Upanishad 2.1; *SBE* 15:54; for comments, see Hiriyanna, *Essentials of Indian Philosophy,* p. 22.

165. *Vedantasara of Sadananda,* p. 33 (pp. 20-21).

166. See May, "The Trinity and Saccidananda," p. 92. On the basis of the revelation of Christ through yoga, A. J. Appasamy tried to reinterpret the doctrines of the Trinity and the Logos. He experienced God as light, Spirit as Sakti, and Christ as a spiritual body or a Suksma Sarira, which reflects God — the Eternal Divine Son and the Divine Birth of the Eternal Son. He had the conviction that the Holy Spirit is working through yoga not only among Christians but also among Hindus. Appasamy, *An Indian Interpretation of Christianity,* pp. 4-8.

167. Sen, *Keshub Chunder Sen,* p. 228, cited in Clooney, "Trinity and Hinduism," p. 316.

168. Sen, *Keshub Chunder Sen,* p. 228, cited in Clooney, "Trinity and Hinduism," p. 316.

Paramarubyananda, the cofounder (with Henri Le Saux, commonly known as Swami Abhishiktananda) of the famed ashram dedicated to the Trinity, have continued this promising work.[169]

It says volumes of the great potential of this metaphor that both Christian and Hindu teachers have developed it, although understandably not all Hindus in a way that follows Christian orthodoxy. Take, for example, the legendary American-based late Hindu yogi Yogananda. In his vision,

> "The Father *(Sat)* is God as the Creator existing beyond creation (Cosmic Consciousness). The Son *(Tat)* is God's omnipresent intelligence existing in creation (Christ Consciousness . . .). The Holy Ghost *(Aum)* is the vibratory power of God that objectifies and becomes creation." But these are provisional, since "at the time of cosmic dissolution, the Trinity and all other relativities of creation resolve into the Absolute Spirit."[170]

While that Hindu interpretation cannot be reconciled with Christianity, as a *Hindu* interpretation it deserves attention.

How should we assess these attempts? The Christian Hinduologist Francis Clooney observes of the attempts:

> That the record is mixed should not surprise us. We know that the rich, deep Christian tradition of trinitarian theology, so nuanced and difficult, did not come together easily or suddenly in the earliest Church; rather, it took centuries to put together right insights into the three persons of God. . . . [Similarly] it was very hard indeed to explain in India the fine points of trinitarian thought. . . . However we might imagine the reality of the Trinity in India, it would be unreasonable to expect a neatly parallel language in Hinduism, such as could be easily adopted to Christian uses.[171]

In line with that, I would offer this tentative conclusion. On the one hand, these attempts at correlation are as much justified and necessary as Christian tradition's millennia-long conversation with and borrowing from Western non-Christian sources, particularly from philosophy. On the other hand, their value is heuristic and suggestive and not too many hopes should be placed on

169. See Le Saux, *Saccidananda*.

170. From Clooney, "Trinity and Hinduism," p. 318, citing Yogananda, *The Second Coming of Christ*, p. 1594.

171. Clooney, "Trinity and Hinduism," pp. 320-21; for other critical notes about the incompatibility, see May, "The Trinity and Saccidananda," pp. 95-97.

their capacity to overcome deep and meaningful differences among not only religious traditions but also, in this case, the worldview differences, including notions of time and history.

What distinguishes Raimundo Panikkar's attempt to find parallels between Hindu and Christian spiritualities — by far the most sophisticated and ambitious in nature — is not only its theological depth but also the desire to place it in a wider context of the religious diversity at large. That effort deserves a closer look. The son of a Spanish Catholic mother and an Indian Hindu father, the late (d. 2010) Roman Catholic polymath placed himself at the confluence of the four rivers: Hindu, Christian, Buddhist, and Secular.[172] In his small yet highly significant book *The Trinity and the Religious Experience of Man* (1973), Panikkar claims that all religions reflect a trinitarian substructure, although, of course, it is named differently in various traditions. His choice term is the neologism "cosmotheandrism," in which "the divine, the human and the earthly . . . are the three irreducible dimensions which constitute the real."[173] Briefly put, there is an intimate interaction of God, humankind, and the cosmos. For Christians, this is expressed in the doctrine of the Trinity, which, while distinctively Christian, is not exclusively so.[174] Pannikkar's "advaitic Trinitarianism"[175] is wary of all dualisms, and he argues that there "are not two realities: God and man (or the world). . . . Reality itself is theandric; it is our way of looking that causes reality to appear to us sometimes under one aspect and sometimes under another."[176] Applied to the ancient problem of unity and diversity in the trinitarian God, the advaitic principle implies that Father and Son are not two, but they are not one either; it is the Spirit who unites and distinguishes them.[177]

What would a cosmotheandric vision of the Trinity and Spirit look like? Father is "Nothing," the Absolute without name;[178] indeed, there is no "Father" in himself; the "being of the Father" is "the Son" (based on his reading of John

172. Panikkar, *Unknown Christ of Hinduism*, p. 30.

173. Panikkar, *The Cosmotheandric Experience*, p. ix; see also, Ahlstrand, *Fundamental Openness*, p. 134.

174. See Panikkar, *The Trinity*, p. viii. Trinity is the "junction where the authentic spiritual dimensions of all religions meet" (p. 42).

175. Cousins, "Panikkar's Advaitic Trinitarianism"; for the term "advaitic," see especially p. 120. For a fine exposition and engagement, see Adiprasetya, *An Imaginative Glimpse*, pp. 12-38 and chap. 3.

176. Panikkar, *The Trinity*, p. 75.

177. Panikkar, *The Trinity*, p. 62.

178. Panikkar, *The Trinity*, p. 46.

14:6).[179] In the *kenosis*, the Father gives himself totally to the Son. Thus the Son is "God."[180] Panikkar believes this interpretation finds parallels in the Buddhist (Mahayana) concept of sunyata ("emptiness"), as well as in the nonduality of advaitic Hinduism.[181] The Spirit is "immanence," to use the ancient metaphor: the Father is the source of the river, the Son the river that flows from the source, and the Spirit is the ocean in which the river ends.[182] From the Hindu perspective, the Spirit can be described as the "Divine *Sakti* penetrating everything and manifesting God, disclosing him in his immanence and being present in all his manifestations."[183]

Panikkar's main contribution in my understanding is the elevation of the doctrine of the Trinity to a central place not only in Christian theology but also particularly in comparative theology. This is a healthy, badly needed corrective, as many leading theologians of religions bluntly dismiss the topic (such as J. Hick).[184] With his bold move, Panikkar has offered a major critique of typical pluralisms. The implications of his trinitarian doctrine, especially the insistence on diversity-in-unity, are another major asset. In addition, the fact that he has been able not only to "contextualize" the doctrine but also to relate it to his own Asian context and religiosity is an admirable achievement. Its challenges are many and obvious; in this context we do not have to tackle them in detail;[185] suffice it to say this much: neither the idea of the Father as "nothing" (or even: "no-thing") nor the shifting of the Son into the primacy of the Father has biblical or creedal basis. Although the generic idea of the Spirit as immanence and energy matches the Judeo-Christian teaching, the lack of a *trinitarian* conception of the Spirit as the Holy Spirit does not meet *Christian* criteria. Therefore, it is justifiable to ask the question that indeed Panikkar asks of himself: "Why do I persist, then, in still speaking of the Trinity when, on the one hand, the idea that I give of it goes beyond the traditional idea by Christianity?"[186] While generic

179. Panikkar, *The Trinity*, p. 47.

180. Panikkar, *The Trinity*, pp. 45-47.

181. "God is total Silence. This is affirmed by all the world religions. One is led towards the Absolute and in the end one finds nothing, because there *is* nothing, not even Being." Panikkar, *The Trinity*, p. 52; for comments, see Ramachandra, *Recovery of Mission*, p. 91.

182. Panikkar, *The Trinity*, p. 63.

183. Panikkar, *Unknown Christ of Hinduism*, p. 57.

184. See further, chap. 14 in *Trinity and Revelation*.

185. For a more extensive engagement, see Kärkkäinen, *Trinity and Religious Pluralism*, chap. 8. In *Christ and Reconciliation*, chap. 9, I have engaged Panikkar's pluralistic Christology.

186. Panikkar, *The Trinity*, p. 43.

reference to "tradition" suffices for Panikkar, I am much less enthused by a pneumatology based on a trinitarian view that only phenomenologically matches that of classical Christianity.[187]

The Nontheistic Hindu Spirit(s) and the Divine Holy Spirit: A Theological Assessment

These few examples[188] suffice to illustrate the richness of Indian Christian theology's long search for a proper understanding of the Spirit of God in Hindu soil. The theological assessment must begin with the most obvious question, finely formulated by the Sri Lankan Jesuit Aloysius Pieris. He notes that anyone who argues for the presence of the Spirit of God at work in the religions of Asia must confront the challenge of Asia's nontheistic spirituality: "if the Spirit of God is operative in them, then isn't nontheism also a manifestation of the Spirit?"[189] Or to put it another way: "When Christians speak of God as Spirit, we do not speak of 'one third' of God, but of the full presence of God."[190] Against this backdrop, Pieris's clarification of the conditions for the discernment of the divine Spirit from a Christian perspective is placed in a proper perspective: "Christian theism, taken minimally, is a recognition of One Personal Divine Absolute who is also the Creator-Redeemer of all, and as such is also a belief shared by Islam, but absent in almost all the major religious traditions. . . . It is this minimal definition of theism that we invoke as the practical criterion for determining the character of these other belief systems."

He goes on to list the most obvious examples of the nontheistic nature of major Asian religions, including Brahman-*atman* of Vedantic Hinduism with a nonpersonal Absolute, and (Theravada) Buddhism's denial of the Divine Absolute in the first place. Even nirvana, a candidate for Buddhist ultimacy, "is regarded as 'liberation as such,' and not as an Absolute Reality that liberates." Furthermore, the many gods of Asian religions are not ultimately "members of a polytheistic pantheon" but are, strictly speaking, "forces of nature." Their

187. See the serious reservations expressed by Ahlstrand, *Fundamental Openness*, pp. 152-56 especially.

188. This survey was not of course comprehensive. For example, I did not engage Samartha's identification of the Holy Spirit with *advaita* (as the spirit of unity) simply because it does not make much sense to me and seems to be a category mistake; see Samartha, *Courage for Dialogue*, p. 83; see also, his *Living Faiths and Ultimate Goals*, p. xvii.

189. Pieris, "Holy Spirit and Asia's Religiousness," p. 126.

190. Eck, *Encountering God*, p. 119.

study belongs more to cosmology than theology.[191] Finally, this Jesuit observes that although they are, strictly speaking, nontheistic, Asian traditions such as Buddhism and Hinduism are *"profoundly religious,"* which leads to the ironic conclusion of a "religious atheism"! Thus, the implication for our discussion: "Should the Spirit of God who has been poured upon 'all flesh' . . . be acknowledged also as the Spirit of this 'non-theistic religiousness'; that is to say, the Spirit of the 'No-God' systems of beliefs and practices in vogue among the vast masses of Asia?"[192]

On top of nontheism, he sees the nonpersonal nature of the Absolute in Hinduism as another related major challenge. (It cannot be brushed away with a mere remark about the problems related to the notion of "person" in Christian theology.) From the perspective of Abrahamic traditions, one can hardly think of an authentic "experience of God that does not lead to interpersonal dialogue" or "an authentic spirituality in which God is not a 'thou.'"[193] All of this, however, goes directly against the Hindu pursuit. Swami Abhishiktananda puts it well: "In the eyes of the Vedāntin the proclamation of God's transcendence by Jews or Muslims is invalidated by the very fact that they dare to formulate it. To prostrate oneself before God is doubtless a very noble thing; yet in the very act of prostrating, is not the believer asserting himself over against God?"[194] The thrust of this argument cannot be set aside by the (justified in itself) observation that Abrahamic theologians certainly have been found guilty at times of relying too much on the power to define the divine and even asserting themselves over God; those are misinterpretations of true theism. Nor is this argument invalidated by the Vedantin insistence on experience rather than knowledge *(jnana)* as the final authority to negotiate the nature of the Ultimate (expressed in sayings such as "Reason may discuss, but experience *knows*").[195]

Advaitic traditions in particular insist on the mystical experience rather than knowledge or consciousness as the means to "know" God:[196] "It is thus not a matter of a subject knowingly apprehending an object, but an intentional grasping of total Reality through the experience of absorption into pure

---

191. Pieris, "Holy Spirit and Asia's Religiousness," p. 127.

192. Pieris, "Holy Spirit and Asia's Religiousness," p. 128.

193. Panikkar, *The Trinity,* p. 29.

194. Le Saux, *Saccidananda,* p. 44.

195. Le Saux, *Saccidananda,* pp. 44-46 (p. 46).

196. See the highly advaitic-driven statement in Panikkar, *Myth, Faith, and Hermeneutics,* pp. 304-5.

consciousness."[197] Panikkar's advaitic trinitarian pneumatology faithfully reflects this as it envisions the experience of an impersonal Reality as something "which in some way 'inhales' us into himself." This is the Spirit, "God of the Upanishads" that "does not speak; he is not Word. He 'inspires.'"[198] The pitting of experience against knowledge, however, is hardly justified. Experience and knowledge are deeply intertwined and mutually conditioned.

It is somewhat ironic that those Christian theologians who are eager to establish similarity between Brahman and the triune God/Holy Spirit as the Ultimate either dismiss the question of the nonpersonal nature of the former or downplay it. That, however, is a sign not of Christian hospitality but rather of either ignorance on the Christian side concerning the teachings of Hindu advaitism or lack of respect for the otherness of the Other. Briefly put: all Hindu traditions (with the possible exception of popular folk pietism) consider attaching any notion of "personality" to the Absolute as restriction. "A 'Personal Absolute' is a contradiction in terms."[199] To Panikkar's credit, he follows the advaitic logic to its end much more faithfully than most of his Christian counterparts when he admits that in his Hindu-Christian vision, the "immanent" God, Spirit, cannot be person.[200]

Furthermore, whereas in Abrahamic faiths the "'experience of liberation' and the 'experience of God who liberates'" are inseparable aspects of the same phenomenon, in Asian traditions salvation ultimately is *detachment*. Even when uniting with the Ultimate, an eternal union — such as union with the triune God in Christian vision — is not the goal, but rather a dissolution into the ocean of nothingness. There is "a deep seated desire not for union with God as a supremely intelligent and compassionate being, but for unity, even absorption into, the Infinite as a strictly impersonal principle of existence and activity."[201] Therefore, for Christian pneumatology to follow the advaitic path to its end is nothing less than "a striking illustration of the triumph of monism over orthodox Christian theism."[202] A corollary implication is that all distinctions between the human and divine spirit are erased.[203]

If so, how to proceed then — unless one is content with a lack of di-

197. Satyavrata, "Holy Spirit and Advaitic Hindu Spirituality," p. 37.

198. Panikkar, *The Trinity*, pp. 27-29.

199. Pieris, "Holy Spirit and Asia's Religiousness," p. 131.

200. Panikkar, *The Trinity*, pp. 31, 63, and so forth.

201. Bracken, *The Divine Matrix*, p. 137.

202. Satyavrata, "Holy Spirit and Advaitic Hindu Spirituality," p. 40.

203. On the implications of this for the doctrine of creation and theological anthropology, as well as soteriology, see Satyavrata, "Holy Spirit and Advaitic Hindu Spirituality," p. 40.

alogical engagement and with the theological status quo? Pieris, whose insightful critique of the uncritical oblivion to the nontheistic and nonpersonal nature of Asian traditions I just endorsed, surprisingly argues that it is not theism but a "praxis" — "non-idolatrous (that is greedless) . . . spirituality of the beatitudes" — that should be the basis of interreligious dialogue. Because "[h]appiness or the joy of living is one of the fruits of the Spirit (Gal. 5:22)," that and other spirit-cultivated virtues should be the focus.[204] Although I fully endorse Pieris's call for a virtuous, greedless spirituality that resists the idol of Mammon, I cannot accept his marginalization of the theological basis. That said, I would be the last theologian to dismiss the promise of and the need for a patient and painstaking comparative engagement. Dialogical comparison just has to be crystal clear about the potential conflicts and differences between traditions and the potential commonalities. In that endeavor, some trinitarian guidelines may be of help. To those we turn after first considering Buddhist "pneumatology."

Sunyata, Sambhogakaya, and the Holy Spirit: Pneumatology in Buddhist-Christian Perspective

The Quest for the Ultimate Reality

The search for correlates between the Christian Holy Spirit and conceptions of the Spirit in Buddhist traditions is an utterly complicated quest.[205] Possibly even more nontheistic than most Hindu movements, the Buddhist schools not only do not acknowledge a Creator[206] but also do not acknowledge a "beginning" (they espouse the idea of "co-dependent Origination").[207] Also undisputed, neither Brahman nor Gautama himself has anything like the status

204. Pieris, "Holy Spirit and Asia's Religiousness," p. 135.

205. In this context I pass the continuing debate about whether Buddhism, particularly Theravada, can be regarded as a religion. Technical discussions aside, it seems to me that failing to include Buddhist tradition in an interfaith engagement would be a fatal error, if not for other reasons, then because it is followed by hundreds of millions of adherents and — minimally put — functions similarly to religions.

206. Neither does Buddhism "accept the notion of a transcendent ruler of the universe or of a savior outside one's self." Abe, "Kenotic God and Dynamic Sunyata," p. 53.

207. For a detailed discussion, see chap. 5 in *Creation and Humanity*. Concerning the idea of a "Creator or Supreme God," the Buddhist Minoru Nambara goes so far as to say that "this was disregarded from the outset as nonsense, as a mere shadow." "Ultimate Reality," pp. 119-20.

of the Ultimate. The former was rejected as Buddhism separated itself from the parent religion, Hinduism, and the founder's role, notwithstanding great differences among various Buddhist denominations, never became divine in any theistic tradition's sense.[208] That said, three qualifications have to be added. First, Theravada's alleged "atheism" is not only a misnomer but also has nothing in common with modern Western atheism. Gautama never rejected belief in deities and gods but rather considered them irrelevant — and more often than not distracting — to the pursuit of one's enlightenment, which ultimately is one's own business. Second, what is explained above is not to deny the highly "animistic"[209] phenomenology of Buddhism as it is practiced and believed all over the world among the faithful — surprisingly, including most Theravadins. Spirits and spirituality are alive and well therein. Third, the rejection of Creator and creation has very little in common with contemporary scientific naturalism, which posits the material/physical as the origin of all that is.[210] Along with all other major faith traditions, Buddhism is idealist in its ontology (or to be more minimalist: it definitely is not materialist) and is of course deeply metaphysically loaded with the belief in life "beyond death."

As in Hinduism, the quest for potential commonalities between the Christian theology of the Holy Spirit and a Buddhist notion of the "Spirit" has everything to do with whether there is and what might be the Ultimate Reality. Recall that in this chapter, the discussion focuses on relating the theistic divine Holy Spirit of the Christian tradition to the "Ultimate" Spirit of religions (complementary to the previous chapter, which emphasized the many

208. Whereas the Theravada takes him as a "wonderful man" *(acchariya manussa)* by virtue of the enlightenment, mainline Mahayana considers the historical Buddha one of the many faces of the cosmic, eternal buddhahood; only in the Pure Land form of Mahayana does there emerge the Savior figure of Amida Buddha, but even then the difference from the Christian God/divine Christ is categorical. Perhaps the closest parallel to the theistic God is *Lotus Sutra*'s theology of the eternal Buddha, important in Japanese Nichiren Buddhism, in addition to Pure Land. Furthermore, the concept of Ādi Buddha, "the Original Buddha," narrated in *Kālacakra Tantra*, among others, approximates and might have been influenced by theistic traditions. See further, Baier, "Ultimate Reality in Buddhism and Christianity," p. 103.

209. I am well aware of the caution by scholars, particularly scholars of religion and anthropology, toward continuing to use the term "animism." While other concepts such as "folk religion" adequately convey much of the meaning, probably no other term so appropriately highlights the importance of the spirits/spiritual at the core (Lat. *anima*).

210. Ironically, Buddhism does not even make a distinction between "spirit" and matter after most other religious traditions, let alone sciences; see Rahula, *What the Buddha Taught*, p. 21. It also means that Buddhism is not ready to reduce self/soul/mind to the physical as with contemporary scientific reductionism; see Burns, "'Soul-Less' Christianity," p. 94.

spirits). Several candidates have been proposed for consideration as the Ultimate Reality, ranging from sunyata ("emptiness"), to Tathâgata ("suchness"), to Dharmakaya, to nirvana/*nibbana*.[211] (A detailed discussion of each in relation to the question of God in Christian tradition can be found in chap. 15 of *Trinity and Revelation*.)

Of these (and possible other candidates), it seems to me that for the current pneumatological discussion the most pregnant concepts are sunyata and Dharmakaya; these two have also been the focus of interest of those Christian theologians who have been looking for pneumatological (and trinitarian) commonalities. But before pursuing these concepts more deeply, let us ask this obvious question: Are there any terms that simply terminologically refer to the domain of the spirit/soul — now that Brahman has been left behind and, as is well known, the term "soul," when spoken of anthropologically, is considered to be no-self *(anattā)?* Indeed, there is the ancient Buddhist tradition of naming "suchness" as "soul" (in current translations, also "mind"). The authoritative second-century Mahayana manual for teaching monks, *The Awakening of Faith*, seeks to clarify the principles of ultimate reality, addressing the question, What is Mahayana?

> It is the soul of all sentient beings *(sarvasattva)*, that constitutes all things in the world, phenomenal and supra-phenomenal. . . . Because the soul in itself, involving the quintessence of the Mahâyâna, is suchness *(bhûtatathatâ)*, but it becomes [in its relative or transitory aspect, through the law of causation] birth-and-death *(samsâra)* in which are revealed the quintessence, the attributes, and the activity of the Mahâyâna. The Mahâyâna has a triple significance. The first is the greatness of quintessence. Because the quintessence of the Mahâyâna as suchness exists in all things, remains unchanged in the pure as well as in the defiled, is always one and the same *(samatâ)*, neither increases nor decreases, and is void of distinction. The second is the greatness of attributes. . . . The third is the greatness of activity, for it [i.e., Mahayana] produces all kinds of good work in the world, phenomenal and supra-phenomenal.[212]

While it is impossible to say with any certitude whether what is meant here is something like Hindu *atman*, it is clear that "soul"/"suchness" here

---

211. Although mentioned separately here, these concepts related to the Ultimate Reality are also deeply intertwined.

212. Asvaghosa, *Awakening of Faith* II, pp. 53-54.

"signifies that which constitutes the ultimate foundation of existence, one great whole in which all forms of individuation are obliterated, in a word, the Absolute."[213] I wish this theme would have been pursued in greater detail, particularly with Christian scholars, with regard to its dialogical value. At the moment, we have to leave it here with hopes for further elucidation.

Sunyata and Trikaya

Routinely translated as "(absolute) emptiness," *sunyata* is "entirely unobjectifiable, unconceptualizable, and unattainable by reason or will."[214] According to the classic formulation of the *Heart Sutra (Prajnaparamita-sutra)*, "Form is Emptiness, Emptiness is form . . . in Emptyness [*sic*] there is no form, no feeling, no recognition, no volitions, no consciousness; no eye, no ear, no nose, no tongue, no body, no mind . . . no ignorance and no extinction of ignorance . . . no aging and death and no extinction of aging and death; likewise there is no Suffering, Origin, Cessation or Path, no wisdom-knowledge, no attainment and non-attainment." Astonishingly, this sutra, one of the shortest of all, although profoundly important (it is recited by many monks on a daily basis), even says that "all dharmas are Emptyness."[215] Hence, it makes sense what Masao Abe (Tokyo School of Japan) says: "Sunyata is not self-affirmative, but *thoroughly* self-negative. . . . [E]mptiness not only empties everything else but also empties itself."[216] If that sounds predominantly negative to Christian ears, Abe notes that at its core, "in Sunyata, regardless of the distinction between self and other, humans and nature, humans and the divine, everything without exception is realized *as it is* in its *suchness* (in Sanskrit, *tathata*, which may also be rendered as 'is-ness')."[217]

How would sunyata and divine *Pneuma* relate to each other in a Chris-

---

213. The editor's explanatory note in Asvaghosa, *Awakening of Faith* III.1.B, p. 62. This explanation is confirmed in the text itself, e.g., in III.B, p. 64: "Bodhisattvas of the Dharmakâya, having recognised that subjectivity and the transcending of subjectivity have no reality of their own [i.e., are relative], have become emancipated from the intermediate form of particularization."

214. Abe, "Kenotic God and Dynamic Sunyata," p. 50. For an insightful and careful attempt by a Christian systematician to clarify the meaning of *sunyata* to the Western and Christian mind-set, see Ott, "The Convergence."

215. *Heart Sutra* (no translator given, n.p.; available at http://www.sacred-texts.com/bud/tib/hrt.htm).

216. Abe, "Kenotic God and Dynamic Sunyata," p. 51.

217. Abe, "Kenotic God and Dynamic Sunyata," p. 52.

tian perspective? Not many details are provided by theologians, although in numerous discussions of sunyata, some reference is made or implied to its counterpart role as either the Ultimate Reality at large or in relation to the Holy Spirit in particular. Indicative of this lack of specification, even the two current massive explorations into Buddhist pneumatology by a Christian theologian, the Pentecostal Amos Yong, assume at the general level some commonality but fail to specify it. Indeed, Yong — rightly so, in my opinion — mentions at the outset that "[i]n the Buddhist case *shunyata* functions in a non-theistic context," and therefore he finds it useful to relate it to pneumatological anthropology and the discussion of creation at large.[218] I get nervous, however, when concepts such as dynamism and relationality are related to sunyata in terms of alleged commonalities. While I of course know that the concept does not mean "nothing" in the Western sense, its original meaning hardly means to denote those values — perhaps not even parallels to mental causation and emergence (in a scientific sense).[219]

All in all, it seems to me highly dubious to try to relate that foundational Mahayana concept to anything resembling not only personality but also divinity in the Abrahamic faiths' robust theistic sense. One has to stretch concepts beyond credibility — and one wonders, what might be the Buddhist response? Would a Buddhist really take it as a sign of hospitality?

Perhaps a more meaningful connecting point can be discovered in the concepts related to the "three bodies" *(trikaya)* doctrine of the Mahayana. Let us first locate the term in relation to the all-important concept of Dharmakaya. As mentioned, the concepts relating to the search for the Ultimate Reality in Buddhist traditions overlap and also mutually inform and condition each other. In this light, it makes sense that, against the common misunderstanding, neither "suchness" nor Dharmakaya is nothing (in the absolute Western sense). *The Awakening of Faith* asserts that "suchness or Dharmakâya in its self-nature *(svabhâva)* is not a nothing *(çûnyatâ)* but envelops in full immeasurable merits *(guna)* which make up its true nature."[220] While both "suchness" and Dharmakaya function in some sense similarly to the theistic notion of God, it is also evident that in any way equating that with the Christian trinitarian view of God as the communion of three persons is hardly a justified move. However, the term "Dharmakaya" may serve as a bridge to the key Mahayana concept of trikaya.[221]

218. Yong, *Pneumatology and the Christian-Buddhist Dialogue,* p. 59; a similar tactic is followed in his *Cosmic Breath.*

219. Cf. Yong, *Pneumatology and the Christian-Buddhist Dialogue,* chap. 3.

220. Asvaghosa, *Awakening of Faith* III.2.A, p. 108.

221. See further, Habito, "On Dharmakaya as Ultimate Reality."

At the time of the emergence of the Mahayana tradition, the original Theravada concept of *arahant* (the person who has achieved enlightenment) was revised into Boddhisattva, the Enlightened One who for the sake of others postpones stepping into nirvana.[222] To reconcile the traditional teaching of the Buddha having entered the bliss and this new idea of the Boddhisattva, the idea of the trikaya (lit. "three bodies") emerged.[223] Trikaya has been named with some justification the "Buddhist Trinity."[224] Briefly put, it is something like this: the "three bodies" are three interrelated ways to access the manifestation and knowledge of Buddha. The *nirmāṇa-kāya* is the "historical body" of Buddha in this life, particularly as Gautama, who was enlightened. *Sambhoga-kāya*, "heavenly body," also called "blissful body," refers to some kind of transcendent Buddhas who guide the Boddhisattvas, men and women who have been enlightened but for the sake of others wish to postpone entering nirvana. These heavenly bodies may also appear in historical forms, if need be. These include Amida Buddha, the Buddha of the Infinite Light, and Avalokitesvara of Pure Land Buddhism, among others. The *dharma-kaya* is the most ultimate form of the "three bodies," that is, "doctrine," and could be translated in various ways, such as "essential body" or "cosmic body." As a type of ultimate cosmic principle, the essence of reality, it also is beyond dualistic pairs such as immanence and transcendence. An important later tradition of trikaya teaches that the three bodies are not only present in Buddhas and Boddhisattvas but also in all humans. Understandably, rich diversity characterizes the various trikaya traditions; the diversity is intensified in deeply syncretistic contexts such as Japanese[225] and Chinese[226] Buddhism.

222. Simultaneously the huge *Jataka* literature continued emerging and widening with hundreds of legends of Gautama's previous lives. For this process and the deification of Buddha, see Dayal, *Bodhisattva Doctrine in Buddhist Sanskrit Literature*, pp. 19-29.

223. For a highly informative and useful account of the history of the development of various trikaya traditions in Mahayana, see Habito, "Trikaya Doctrine in Buddhism"; see also, Schmidt-Leukel, "Buddha and Christ as Mediators," pp. 157-59.

224. Franck, "A Buddhist Trinity." In *The Rhythm of Being*, published just before his death in 2010, Panikkar returned once again to the theme of the Trinity among religions, including the Buddhist doctrine of trikaya. The book contains his 1989 Gifford Lectures. Understandably, not all Buddhists have been happy about the Christian use of trikaya. As early as the seventeenth century, the Chinese Buddhist Ouyi Zhixu compared the Christian idea of the preexistence and incarnation of Jesus with the Buddhist teaching of trikaya and found it a poor plagiarization of Buddhist beliefs. Zhixu (no title provided), in *Jesus beyond Christianity*, pp. 229-30.

225. For current Japanese theologians of trikaya, see further, Fritsch-Oppermann, "Trikaya and Trinity."

226. China offers yet another feature of the diversity: although the trikaya has been well

Now, the application of trikaya to the Christian doctrine of the Trinity usually goes this way: whereas Dharmakaya may have some parallels with Father, and Nirmanakaya with Jesus the Christ, the Incarnated One, the Holy Spirit is associated with Sambhogakaya, the "Middleman," to use a neologism in this respect. As with the Holy Spirit, Sambhogakaya is associated with empowerment, bliss, and peace (recall that it is most often named "the body of bliss"). In some real sense, both the Holy Spirit and Sambhogakaya also function as the link between the Ultimate and the human/creaturely. "Both the Holy Spirit and the Sarbhogakaya [sic] represent an inflow of the omnipresent reality that empowers the believer on a new plane."[227] Although the correlations between the Holy Spirit and Sambhogakaya are "abstract structural parallels," beset with foundational divergences, the dialogical value of the trikaya doctrine is noteworthy.[228] J. C. Cleary puts the comparison in a proper theological perspective: "Both concepts are related to states of transfiguration, but the analogy between them cannot be pressed very far. The Holy Spirit concept is left vague, and in many trinitarian formulations plays scarcely any role. The Sambhogakaya concept, on the other hand, is associated with the bodhisattva career, which is central to Mahayana Buddhism."[229]

A Theological Assessment and an Agenda for the Future

How similar to the concept of the Holy Spirit — the divine Spirit, God as Spirit — is either Sambhogakaya or sunyata? Without repeating the serious problems deriving from the nontheism of both Hinduism and Buddhism (and even intensified in the latter) discussed in the previous main section, let us try to deepen that analysis. The Buddhist tradition at-large begins from the premise that neither "Being nor God, but Sunyata" is ultimate.[230] Nor does

---

known in China, popular devotion usually centered on different groups of three, especially Amitabha Buddha, Sakyamuni Buddha (Gautama), and Bhaisajya Buddha (Buddha of Healing). Habito, "Trikaya Doctrine in Buddhism," p. 52.

227. Cleary, "Trikaya and Trinity," p. 65; notwithstanding inaccuracies in the exposition of Christian pneumatology, that essay is a most useful nontechnical comparative primer for Christians. See also, Yong, "From Azusa Street to the Bo Tree and Back," pp. 223-25.

228. So also, Cleary, "Trikaya and Trinity," p. 66.

229. Cleary, "Trikaya and Trinity," p. 72.

230. Abe, "Kenotic God and Dynamic Sunyata," p. 50. For a useful study of Abe's view, see Sabatino, "No-God." On Abe's dialogue with Christian theologians, see C. Jones, "Emptiness, Kenōsis, History, and Dialogue."

Buddhism "accept the notion of a transcendent ruler of the universe or of a savior outside one's self."[231] I can't help but agree with K. Ward that "the whole Buddhist world-view and discipline leads away from theism."[232] Hans Küng rightly observes that sunyata and Dharmakaya (as well as nirvana) have "brought about a twilight of the gods or idols," as they have replaced the Hindu gods and Brahman as the ultimate explanation; "they have not put any other gods — not even the Buddha — in their place."[233]

Masao Abe draws the conclusion that, as shocking as it is, it is also familiar to those who know Buddhist logic. Referring to the divine *kenosis* of Christian faith, he interprets: "God's self-emptying must be understood not as partial but as total to the extent that God's infinite unrelatedness has no priority over relatedness with the other and that God's self-emptying is dynamically identical with God's abiding and infinite fullness."[234] From this follow two important corollaries: that "God . . . [is] Each and Every thing," and that in this "completely kenotic God, personality and impersonality are paradoxically identical."[235] If this is not something like pantheism on the one hand and nonpersonalism on the other, then I do not know what it is; furthermore, any meaningful notion of divine transcendence is thrown out.[236] Importantly, the process theologian Marjorie Suchocki remarks in response to Abe that Trinity is the way to affirm both otherness and diversity on the one hand and unity on the other hand. Hence, pantheism is not an option, although the divine and human are integrally related. Furthermore, in Christian tradition, the inner-trinitarian relations are not interpreted according to the principle of radical self-emptying. "To the strong contrary, the coinherence signified by

231. Abe, "Kenotic God and Dynamic Sunyata," p. 53.

232. Ward, *Religion and Revelation*, p. 166.

233. Küng, "God's Self-Renunciation and Buddhist Self-Emptiness," p. 221. That is true, but I respectfully differ from Küng's assessment in his further argumentation that whereas it seems to be true that "Nirvana, Emptiness, and Dharmakaya appear in this sense as parallel terms for the Ultimate Reality," I doubt whether "[their] function is analogous to that of the term 'God,'" and therefore also doubt that "what Christians call 'God' is present, under very different names, in Buddhism, insofar as Buddhists do not refuse, on principle, to admit any positive statements" (p. 221).

234. Abe, "Kenotic God and Dynamic Sunyata," p. 38.

235. Abe, "Kenotic God and Dynamic Sunyata," pp. 40-41.

236. As the Buddhist Nambara ("Ultimate Reality," p. 129) categorically states: "In Buddhism there is no transcendence: The absolute that encompasses everything and dissolves everything in itself is sometimes called nothing, sometimes everything, and sometimes suchness *(tathatā)* — such as being is — because there is neither nothing nor being."

perichoretic union is one that requires the irreducible otherness within the trinitarian structure."[237]

Recall that the main reason why Buddhism from its inception rejected the Brahman as the ultimate reality was Gautama's enlightening vision of *pratitya-samutpada* ("dependent co-origination"), which also makes the permanent "soul" meaningless *(anattan)*. There is nothing "outside" the world, so to speak. "Even the ultimate does not exist by itself," Abe reminds us.[238] Hence, it seems to me that rather than attempting an artificial and failing correlation between the two traditions, Christian theology would do well to honor the deepest intuitions of the counterpart: first, unlike any *monotheistic* tradition, Buddhism is happy with a plurality of answers to "one question" without suppressing the diversity; second, unlike any *theistic* tradition, Buddhism, even in its major Mahayana forms, makes every effort to resist the tendency to rely on gods and hence on any kind of theistic Spirit (even if their existence and role in the world thereby need not be denied after modern Western antitheistic ideology); and third, therefore, Buddhism and Christianity represent deeply and radically different paths. Wouldn't that kind of tentative conclusion serve an authentic, hospitable dialogue better than a forced, one-sided (!) *"con*-sensus"?

Because of these difficulties, following the path of the Jesuit A. Pieris, some Buddhists and Christians are wondering if social action, ethical behavior, or liturgical practices could provide the platform for shared belief in the Holy Spirit. To the Tibetan Thich Nhat Hanh, "mindfulness is very much like the Holy Spirit. Both are agents of healing. When you have mindfulness, you have love and understanding, you see more deeply, you can heal the wounds in your own mind. . . . Mindfulness helps us touch nirvana, and the Holy Spirit offers us a door to the Trinity."[239] The Christian Amos Yong believes that "provisionally, at least, the Holy Spirit could be discerned to be present and active even in Buddhist rituals opposing world's forces of destruction insofar as the biblical fruits of the Spirit, for example, could be detected."[240] Many other such examples could be found on both sides.

I have a two-part response. The first is the affirmation of the need for and importance of shifting the attention from the quest for the Ultimate Spirit/ Reality to ethics and praxis, including spirituality (inclusively understood).

237. Suchocki, "Sunyata, Trinity, and Community," p. 145; see also, the critique of Abe by Pannenberg, "God's Love and the Kenosis of the Son," pp. 246-47.

238. Abe, "Beyond Buddhism and Christianity," p. 232.

239. Hanh, *Living Buddha, Living Christ,* pp. 14, 20.

240. Yong, *Does the Wind Blow the Middle Way?* p. 266.

Prayer, spirituality, meditation, and liturgy might establish an important common platform for the consideration of pneumatological topics.[241] There is also an important place for other kinds of common pneumatological pursuits in which the spirit spoken of means creative energy or creativity or relationality or something similar (in any case, these kinds of themes can be commonly affirmed). A. Yong's enthusiasm over the possibility of finding common themes between the two anthropologies, including current neuroscientific insights, may point to something important. He has argued with some success that pneumatological lenses may provide a shared avenue for that consideration.[242] Similarly, there are promising avenues in Christian theology of creation and Buddhist philosophy of codependent origination in relation to the Spirit of God and sunyata.[243]

The key is to mutually define the contours of the discussion. This is the second part of my response. My disagreement comes when the claim is issued (such as that of Pieris) that this "practical" approach should replace the theological/doctrinal/philosophical investigation. What concerns me is that the theological contours of these exchanges are not clarified adequately, particularly on the question of the theistic versus nontheistic notion of Ultimate Reality and its implications for the doctrine of the Spirit/spirit(s). A religiously pluralistic world calls for such a fine-tuned conceptual analysis.

There is also a place for exchanges where — similar to the Hindu context — Christian theology is willing to listen to and learn from a Buddhist interpretation of the Christian pneumatology. Although those attempts are not likely to persuade many Christians to revise their pneumatological canons — nor are they meant to do that in most cases — they may also lead into a deeper understanding of the Judeo-Christian view of the Spirit. A fruitful example is the reading of the book of Acts — often named among Christian readers as "The Acts of the Holy Spirit" — from a Buddhist perspective by the Japanese Soho Machida, with a focus on "recognizing some of the similarities between the *function* of the Holy Spirit and Buddhist truth or Dharma."[244] In the true spirit of comparative theology, Machida correctly observes the differences, particularly when it comes to the Buddha nature and the Holy Spirit: "The former . . . gives an impression of something static and self-contained, whereas the latter is an entity that moves back and forth between the Absolute and

---

241. As highlighted by Knitter, *Without Buddha I Could Not Be a Christian*, pp. 20-23.

242. Yong, "Christian and Buddhist Perspectives," pp. 143-65; Yong, *Pneumatology and the Christian-Buddhist Dialogue*, chaps. 2, 3, 4; Yong, *The Cosmic Breath*, chaps. 7, 8 particularly.

243. Yong, *The Cosmic Breath*.

244. Machida, "Holy Spirit through a Buddhist Lens," p. 87, emphasis added.

humans."[245] Furthermore, he notes that belief in doctrines does not play much of a role among the Japanese and that whatever is believed about the Ultimate Reality, it certainly majors in the nonpersonal and transcendent.[246] What the Buddhists may learn from the Christian spirituality of the Holy Spirit has to do with the immediacy of faith: "The idea of the Holy Spirit qua Dharma can help Buddhists break this invisible barrier and bring back immediacy to their two-sided faith. By directly entering one's heart, the Holy Spirit eliminates the gap between the savior and the saved."[247]

Two twentieth-century Chinese Buddhists, Liu Zitong and Zhang Chunyi, also deserve special attention in this respect. Liu Zitong built on the ancient Mahayana tradition when stating that the "Holy Spirit is originally without coming or going," and therefore, similar to the Buddha nature, "this means all sentient beings are originally Buddhas."[248] In other words, according to this Buddhist-Christian pneumatology, sayings that seem to imply the coming of the Holy Spirit (John 7:39) belong to the "dharma-gate of life and death," but not to the ultimate gate of "True Suchness." "In reality, all sentient beings can become Buddhas because the Holy Spirit, neither leaving nor coming, originally and always lives in their hearts."[249] The Christian Buddhist colleague Chunyi agrees with his contemporary, although during his Christian years he had stuck with another view.[250] That Christian theology teaches otherwise — namely, making a distinction between the "spirit of life" given to all creatures and the soteriological gift of the Spirit as the function of the new birth — is rejected by both of these Buddhists and attributed to the lack of knowledge of higher Buddhist wisdom by early Christian teachers.[251] They also equate the divine and human spirit and, gleaning from Buddhist (and Hindu) cosmology, do not see any kind of ontological difference between evil and divine spirit(s); it is rather a matter of function and orientation.[252]

---

245. Machida, "Holy Spirit through a Buddhist Lens," p. 89.

246. Machida, "Holy Spirit through a Buddhist Lens," pp. 89-91.

247. Machida, "Holy Spirit through a Buddhist Lens," p. 92.

248. Cited from the Chinese original in Lai and So, "Zhang Chunyi's Chinese Buddhist-Christian Pneumatology," p. 61.

249. Lai and So, "Zhang Chunyi's Chinese Buddhist-Christian Pneumatology," pp. 61-62.

250. Lai and So, "Zhang Chunyi's Chinese Buddhist-Christian Pneumatology," pp. 62-65.

251. Lai and So, "Zhang Chunyi's Chinese Buddhist-Christian Pneumatology," p. 62.

252. Lai and So, "Zhang Chunyi's Chinese Buddhist-Christian Pneumatology," pp. 65, 67-68.

What to think of these explorations? It is clear that the proposals represent important divergences from the mainline Christian tradition and, therefore, will remain marginal to most Christians. That said, we should acknowledge the efforts by the Buddhist dialogue partners.

Having investigated the potential parallels to the Holy Spirit in other faith traditions, we now, in the final section of the chapter, seek to develop some guidelines for how the discernment of the Spirit(s) among religions may happen from the perspective of Christian tradition. Rather than an abstract treatment, as is the habit in the theology of religions, the detailed comparative theological exercise conducted here provides a platform for a more specific approach.

Trinitarian Guidelines for the Discernment of the Spirit(s)

The Turn to Pneumatology and Its Liabilities

In light of the urgency of relating the Christian doctrine of God to the intuitions of the divine in other living faiths, it comes as no surprise that in recent decades Christian theologians have toyed with various tactics to find common ground.[253] As long as Christian theology built on a more or less exclusivist base, the point of departure for theology-of-religions discourse was the finality of Christ as the only way to God. A turn to theo-centrism seemed to give more space for opening up to other religions: while Christ is one way to the Father, he is not the only one. God is bigger than any single religion. Soon, theologians from across the ecumenical spectrum enthusiastically initiated a turn to the "Spirit." The turn to pneumatology seemed to promise a lot. After all, doesn't the Spirit speak for universality while Christ speaks for particularity? This project argues that none of these turns in themselves suffice, and they each lead to an impasse of various sorts; what is needed is a robust trinitarian-pneumatological approach.

To clarify and defend that thesis, let us first consider the reasons and rationale for the turn to the Spirit and then provide a trinitarian critique and proposal. In that context, a theology of the discernment of the Spirit(s) also

---

253. For details, see Kärkkäinen, "'How to Speak of the Spirit among Religions': Trinitarian Prolegomena"; "'How to Speak of the Spirit among Religions': Trinitarian 'Rules'"; chap. 14 in *Trinity and Revelation*. A useful and up-to-date discussion is also that of Yong, *Pneumatology and the Christian-Buddhist Dialogue*, pp. 8-21.

calls for clarification. At all times, the discussion of the Holy Spirit among the spirits of other religions that was conducted above is kept in mind.

An indication of the wide appeal of the pneumatological approach to religious plurality and interfaith encounters is the contribution made by theologians from the youngest Christian family, namely, Pentecostals/charismatics.[254] The book of the Asian American (Chinese Malaysian) Amos Yong, *Beyond the Impasse: Towards a Pneumatological Theology of Religions,* sets forth three "axioms" for the development of a pneumatological theology of religions. First, God is universally present and active in the world through the Spirit. Second, God's Spirit is the life-breath of the *imago Dei* in every human being and the presupposition of all human relationships and communities. And third, the religions of the world, like all else that exists, are providentially sustained by the Spirit of God for divine purposes.[255] Building on these widely embraced principles, in his book *The Spirit Poured Out on All Flesh: Pentecostalism and the Possibility of Global Theology,* Yong argues that

> a pneumatologically driven theology is more conducive to engaging [interfaith issues] . . . in our time than previous approaches. . . . [R]eligions are neither accidents of history nor encroachments on divine providence but are, in various ways, instruments of the Holy Spirit working out the divine purposes in the world and that the unevangelized, if saved at all, are saved through the work of Christ by the Spirit (even if mediated through the religious beliefs and practices available to them).[256]

For him, a pneumatological theology of religions is an "effort to understand both the immensely differentiated experiences of faith and the multifaceted phenomena of religious traditions and systems that is informed by experiences of the Spirit in the light of Scripture, and vice versa."[257]

Similar turns to the Spirit could be documented from across the ecumenical spectrum. The question emerges, why turn to pneumatology?[258] Among the reasons given, first is the alleged openness of pneumatology vis-

---

254. Pinnock, "Evangelism and Other Living Faiths," pp. 208-18; Pinnock, *Flame of Love,* chap. 6; Richie, *Speaking by the Spirit;* C. Clarke, "Wide Reach of the Spirit."

255. Yong, *Beyond the Impasse.*

256. Yong, *The Spirit Poured Out on All Flesh,* pp. 235-36; see also, his *Hospitality and the Other.*

257. Yong, *Discerning the Spirit(s),* p. 24.

258. For important discussions, see Dupuis, *Toward a Christian Theology,* pp. 185-203; D'Costa, "Holy Spirit and the World Religions," pp. 279-311.

à-vis the particularity of the christologically oriented approach.[259] Classical Christology's idea of the unique incarnation of Jesus Christ has been found particularly restrictive in this regard.[260] In that sense, the turn to pneumatology parallels the shift from Christocentrism to theo-centrism among the "first-generation pluralists."[261] It has also been argued that whereas the christological approach focuses on "whether or not they were or are salvific, a pneumatological theology of religions asks whether or not and how, if so, the religions are divinely providential instruments designed for various purposes."[262] As a way of response: I cannot see why pneumatology per se would speak of the role of religions any more than, say, patrology or Christology; indeed, that question, as any great theological topic, is deeply trinitarian. All members of the Trinity work together in works "outside" God. Perhaps what is meant by those who highlight the pneumatological importance of religions is that the turn to the Spirit makes mandatory the task of the discernment of the spirits. Although, even there, trinitarian contours are of course necessary, it is the domain of the Spirit to guide the church in the work of the discernment.[263]

Yet another reason advanced in support of the turn to the Spirit has to do with Spirit Christology. As mentioned above, some Indian theologians — following the lead of some exegetes (Dunn) and systematicians (Lampe) — have basically identified the risen Christ with the Spirit and thus claimed to be able to get around the particularity of Christ. This move, however, is not justified either exegetically or systematically. Christ and Spirit are mutually conditioned (as the Augustinian rule of the indivisibility of the works of the Trinity in the world says) but should also be distinguished (or else, we lose the doctrine of the Trinity — which, indeed, these modalistically oriented scholars are willing to do!). The second problem is — employing the Irenaean idea of Word and Spirit as "two hands" of God — that this "heterodox solution seems to either

---

259. See further, Knitter, "A New Pentecost?" pp. 32-41; Samartha, "Holy Spirit and People of Other Faiths," p. 258; O'Leary, "Emptiness and Dogma," p. 172.

260. Of all the recent proposals to negotiate the uniqueness of Christ, the strangest is the reference to the possibility of reincarnation of non-Christians who never had a chance to respond to Christ: Jathanna, *Decisiveness of the Christ Event.*

261. "First-generation pluralists" is my term for the pluralism represented by Hick, Knitter, Samartha, and others who endorse the idea of a "rough parity" of religions and reject real differences. For a detailed exposition and critical assessment, see chap. 14 of *Trinity and Revelation*; concerning christological issues particularly, see chap. 9 in *Christ and Reconciliation*; D'Costa, *Meeting of Religions*, pp. 1-40.

262. Yong, "Holy Spirit and the World Religions," p. 191.

263. See Yong, "Holy Spirit and the World Religions," pp. 191-92.

amputate one hand so Christ's distinctness evaporates (a binitarian solution), or make one hand do the job of two, so that Christ is controlled by the Spirit (a form of modalism)."[264]

These criticisms of the one-sided pneumatological turn suffice to convince us that for all its benefits, the appeal to the Spirit alone cannot redeem the promise of a solid Christian engagement of other religions. The pneumatological approach has to be anchored firmly in a trinitarian framework. Before attempting an outline of such a program, let us focus on a crucial issue mentioned a number of times but not yet discussed: *the discernment* of the Spirit(s). Let us frame that discussion in this manner: in a truly trinitarian framework, the discernment of the Spirit(s) happens in an integral christological environment.

The Christological Criteriology of the Discernment of the Spirit(s)

Rather than the abstract task of the discernment of the spirits at large, the OT most often connects discernment with the encounters with false prophets.[265] Interestingly, the postbiblical church's theological tradition has focused on the issues of spirituality and morality in its work of and teaching about discernment.[266] The NT's contribution is that the "discernment of spirits" is named as one of the gifts of the Holy Spirit (1 Cor. 12:10).[267] Although its importance is properly highlighted, the NT does not offer many details as to how the task should be conducted and what its parameters should be (apart from its christological contours). Because the NT does not discuss other religions, understandably no direct guidelines can be found concerning the discernment of the spirits outside the church.

Theologically speaking, the task of spiritual discernment encompasses the domains of both the church and the world. In addition to criteria for discerning evil/demonic spirits, discernment also has much to do with the

---

264. D'Costa, "Holy Spirit and the World Religions," p. 283.

265. For well-known biblical narratives of discernment of spirits, see Levison, "A Stubborn Missionary."

266. Joseph Lienhard offers a good survey of the interpretation of the term in the patristic era; see his "On 'Discernments of Spirits.'" A useful and accessible brief overview of biblical, historical, and contemporary global perspectives can be found in Yong, "Discernment."

267. For a fine biblical study, including both the OT and NT, see Schweizer, "On Distinguishing between Spirits"; see also, Martin, "Discernment of Spirits, Gift of."

capacity and resources to identify the work of God's Spirit or the divine Spirit vis-à-vis other spirits (the spirits of other religious traditions, whether good or evil). For the sake of this discussion, let us mind the simple fact that if Christian mission is *missio Dei*, then "mission amounts to participating in the mission of God carried out by the Spirit," which of course demands that we be able at least tentatively to recognize the Spirit of God.[268] Indeed, this was in the minds of ecumenists preparing for the 1991 WCC Canberra Assembly, which focused on the Holy Spirit. It was no longer merely about "*whether or not the Spirit is at work among people of other faiths*" but rather about "how to *discern* the presence and work of the Spirit."[269] This question became particularly important in relation to the claims of the presence of God's Spirit among other faith traditions, a conviction affirmed tentatively but not fully clarified.[270]

Although many kinds of criteria have been set forth, there is wide agreement that there are "no simple phenomenological criteria by which we can test the presence of the Holy Spirit."[271] Ultimately, it is a theological and spiritual process of judgment and assessment. There is wide agreement among Christians of various persuasions that Christology is the most important source of criteriology. This is clearly taught in the NT, for example, in the Johannine tradition: "Every spirit which does not confess Jesus is not of God" (1 John 4:3).[272] Similarly, according to Paul, "no one can say 'Jesus is Lord' except by the Holy Spirit" (1 Cor. 12:3). Indeed, it can be said that Jesus Christ is "the face of the Spirit";[273] looking at the Spirit is to look at Jesus Christ. As the missionary bishop Lesslie Newbigin used to say, "the Holy Spirit does not lead past, or beyond, or away from Jesus."[274] The highlighting of the christological criterion is not meant to downplay the importance of other criteria but rather to put them in proper perspective; generally speaking, the christological contours are

268. Dunn, *The Christ and the Spirit,* 2:72.

269. Samartha, "Holy Spirit and People of Other Faiths," p. 259, emphasis in original.

270. "We see the nurturing power of the Holy Spirit working within, inspiring human beings in their universal longing for, and seeking after, truth, peace and justice" (Rom. 8:18-27). "Love, joy, peace, patience, kindness, goodness, faithfulness, gentleness, self-control," wherever they are found, are the fruit of the Spirit (Gal. 5:22-23; cf. Rom. 14:17). "Religious Plurality and Christian Self-Understanding," #32 (CWME San Antonio 1989); http://www.wcc-coe.org/wcc/what/interreligious/cd45-02.html (3/28/2014).

271. Hiebert, "Discerning the Work of God," p. 151.

272. Yong, "Holy Spirit and the World Religions," p. 193; so also, K. Kim, *Holy Spirit in the World,* p. 167.

273. Bevans, "God Inside Out," p. 104.

274. Newbigin, *The Light Has Come,* pp. 216-17.

most important in interfaith encounters.[275] The appeal to ethical and liberative praxis, along with Christ, is also important.[276]

As soon as the discernment happens outside one's own "household of faith," which it does continuously in the religiously plural world, this dilemma arises: "If we discern the Spirit using Christian (e.g., biblical) criteria, we end up either 'christianizing' the other insofar as we find the Spirit to be present, or 'demonizing' the other insofar as we find the Spirit absent."[277] These dangers should be kept in mind, but they should lead neither to the uncritical affirmation of the Spirit's work everywhere nor to the idea of the incommensurability of Christian pneumatology with other traditions; the latter conclusion would mean leaving behind the dialogue.[278] On the one hand, the Christian is bound to use his or her criteria to discern the Spirit(s) in other religions; on the other hand, the spirit of hospitality requires that he or she be open to the criteria drawn from the tradition of the Other.[279] Furthermore, the discernment has to happen in the spirit of hospitality and mutual honor, as well as self-repentance whenever we are convicted by the same Spirit that we are acting against the values of the kingdom of Christ.

We have to keep in mind at all times that our task is discernment, not controlling the Spirit of God.[280] Indeed: "To ask whether or how the Holy Spirit is at work in the world is to remind the church that the Spirit is not under our control and that it may even challenge us to repent and reform."[281] Finally, we have to remember that "[w]e cannot of course provide ready-made answers for these questions. For one thing, divine activity defies and transcends human understanding."[282] The discernment of *God*'s Spirit demands wide horizons and by definition is filled with freedom and unpredictability.[283] Even at its

275. The typical ones beyond the christological and ethical include love, unity, right use of charisms, and so forth. See, e.g., K. Kim, *Holy Spirit in the World*, pp. 168-69. Although necessary for other purposes, too generic for these specific purposes are also Hans Küng's criteria in "What Is True Religion?" pp. 231-50.

276. Yong, "Holy Spirit and the World Religions," p. 199. Cf. Simmer-Brown, "Suffering and Social Justice."

277. Yong, "Holy Spirit and the World Religions," p. 192.

278. Similarly, Yong, "Holy Spirit and the World Religions," p. 192.

279. See further, Yong, *Discerning the Spirit(s)*, pp. 140-43; on Muslim discernment, see Michel, "Criteria for Discerning the Movement of Holy Spirit in Islam."

280. Samartha, "Holy Spirit and People of Other Faiths," pp. 259-60.

281. Bergen, "Holy Spirit in the World," p. 84.

282. Ukpong, "Pluralism and the Problem of the Discernment of Spirits," p. 416; see also, K. Kim, "How Will We Know When the Holy Spirit Comes?" pp. 94-95.

283. K. Kim, *Holy Spirit in the World*, p. 167.

best, human discernment is always that, *human,* and thus provisional.[284] A fine example of this is the long-term and still unresolved debate about the spirit(s) at the WCC Canberra Assembly, occasioned particularly when the Korean Christian shamanist Hyun Kyung Chung controversially invoked the spirits of her ancestors.[285] A work in progress, discernment is not only provisional but also communal and deeply ecumenical in nature; ultimately, it calls for engagement beyond faith traditions.

Trinitarian Guidelines and the Spirit's Invitation to Relational Engagement with Religions

In support of an openness to other religions, well-meaning — but, I fear, somewhat mistaken — references are routinely made by Protestant theologians to the Eastern Orthodox tradition's alleged pneumatological openness. Oft-cited is the Lebanese metropolitan Khodr's call to "transcend the notion of 'salvation history' *(Heilsgeschichte)* in order to recover the meaning of the *oikonomia.*" The reason such transcending is necessary, according to the metropolitan, is that at the heart of the economy of Christ "is the fact that it makes us participate in the life of God. It must involve reference to eternity and the work of the Holy Spirit."[286] Even taken by itself, let alone when placed in the deeply trinitarian framework of Eastern theology and spirituality, any kind of pluralistic proposal claiming Orthodox tradition (that is, pneumatological without integral christological-trinitarian criteria) has little support.[287] What Eastern Orthodox tradition is strongly advancing is a robust trinitarian approach to religions. Having constructed a trinitarian theology of interfaith encounter in *Trinity and Revelation* (chap. 14) and critiqued the failure of the Enlightenment-based pluralisms to deliver on the promises of openness and hospitality, I will limit my final remarks on the Spirit's role in this trinitarian-

284. K. Kim, *Holy Spirit in the World,* p. 167.

285. For discussion and documentation, see K. Kim, "Spirit and 'Spirits' at the Canberra Assembly"; see also, H. K. Chung, "'Han-pu-ri.'"

286. Khodr, "Christianity in a Pluralistic World," p. 136.

287. For a typical (mis)reading, see Samartha, "Holy Spirit and People of Other Faiths," p. 251. Although Konstantine himself is Eastern Orthodox, his proposal (along with senior religious scholar Ninian Smart) for a "universal theology" is unsatisfactory against both the criteria of his own tradition and general trinitarian theology at large. *Christian Systematic Theology in a World Context* ends up outlining a "trinitarian" doctrine on a mixture of religious traditions. For an exposition and critique, see my *Trinity and Religious Pluralism,* chap. 14.

driven approach. I will advance three broad principles, all of which are also deeply intertwined.

The first is the trinitarian presence of the Spirit in the world. Following the ancient rule of the indivisibility of the works of the Trinity *ad extra,* all forms of the Spirit's presence, whether as the life principle or as the (soteriological) "gift" or as the inspiration behind religious and ethical insights, are related to the Father and Son. The Spirit does not have her separate offshore office, as it were, but rather works from the Father's house. The late senior Roman Catholic theologian of religions, Jacques Dupuis, nicely corrects three typical errors in this respect. The first error puts Christ and God in opposition, as if one could choose *either* a "theo-centric" *or* a "christocentric" option. The second error suggests either "regno-centrism" (the idea of the kingdom of God at the center) or "soterio-centrism" (salvation, rather than a Savior, at the center) at the expense of Christology. The third error is to champion that kind of pneumatological approach that tends to diminish the role of Jesus Christ as more limited than that of the Spirit. The freedom of the Spirit cannot be set in opposition to the person and ministry of Jesus Christ, any more than that of the Son to the Father.[288]

The second principle states that, therefore, the Spirit and Christ form one divine economy. In the New Testament, the Son and Spirit presuppose each other. The Spirit is Christ's Spirit and Christ is the Spirit's Christ, so to speak. A trinitarian Spirit Christology "show[s] the influence of the Holy Spirit throughout the earthly life of Jesus, from his conception through the power of the Spirit (see Luke 1:35) to his resurrection at the hand of God by the power of the same Spirit (see Rom. 8:11)."[289] Wherever the Spirit inspires the knowledge of God, whether in the sphere of the church or outside of it, salvation brought about by the Spirit is referred to the saving work of Christ — his incarnation, death, and resurrection. As Dupuis says, there are not "two distinct channels [that of the Son and the Spirit] through which God's saving presence reaches out to people in distinct economies of salvation,"[290] but one. Making the relationship between the Christ and the Spirit mutually presupposing in no way denies the universal, cosmic sphere of the ministry of the Spirit. Rather, it addresses the issue of recognizing which Spirit, whose Spirit. Speaking of the universal presence of the Spirit integrally related to the particularity of Jesus and his cross helps us qualify and critique the mantra

---

288. Dupuis, *Toward a Christian Theology,* pp. 193-95.
289. Dupuis, *Toward a Christian Theology,* p. 206. So also, Pannenberg, *ST* 3:16-17.
290. Dupuis, *Toward a Christian Theology,* p. 196.

according to which the Spirit represents universality and the Son, particularity. This is correct to a point, but not as an absolute rule. Consider biblical passages such as the prologue to the Gospel of John, which paints a picture of the Word in no less universal terms.[291] If Christology is depicted in both particular and universal terms, what can be said about the Spirit in this respect? The Spirit not only speaks of universality but also speaks of particularity; any talk about the Spirit in a trinitarian context is always specific even if universal in its scope. Otherwise, we lose all basis to distinguish *whose Spirit.*

According to the third principle, Christians should heed "the Holy Spirit's invitation to relational engagement"[292] among religions, to use the delightful phrase of yet another Roman Catholic theologian, Gavin D'Costa. The Christian is entitled to witness to the triune God's saving will and, at the same time, must be prepared to learn from the Other. "The other is always interesting in their difference and may be the possible face of God, or the face of violence, greed, and death. Furthermore, the other may teach Christians to know and worship their own trinitarian God more truthfully and richly."[293] In the words of the postcolonial feminist Mayra Rivera, herein lies the "possibility of transformation . . . in the encounter with the transcendence in the flesh of the Other, and yet how can we meet the other as Other — as transcendent to us — if we are not ourselves transformed?"[294] Only trinitarian theology provides this kind of "context for a critical, reverent, and open engagement with otherness, without any predictable outcome,"[295] and it makes possible, to follow another postcolonialist feminist, Luce Irigaray, "touching which respects the other."[296] Hence, the profound statement of the Jewish philosopher Levinas can also be fully affirmed from a Christian perspective: "through my relation to the Other, I am in touch with God."[297] Other religions are important for the Christian church in that they help the church penetrate more deeply into the divine mystery. This is the essence of what D'Costa calls the Spirit's call to "relational engagement." The acknowledgment of the gifts of God in other religions by virtue of the presence of the Spirit — as well as the critical discernment of these gifts by the power of the same Spirit — means a real trinitarian basis to Christianity's openness toward other religions. Writes D'Costa: "if the Spirit

---

291. See further, Dupuis, *Toward a Christian Theology*, pp. 188-89.
292. Section title in D'Costa, *Meeting of Religions*, p. 109.
293. D'Costa, *Meeting of Religions*, p. 9.
294. Rivera, *Touch of Transcendence*, p. 118.
295. D'Costa, *Meeting of Religions*, p. 9.
296. Irigaray, *I Love to You*, p. 124.
297. Levinas, *Difficult Freedom*, p. 17.

is at work in the religions, then the gifts of the Spirit need to be discovered, fostered, and received into the church. If the church fails to be receptive, it may be unwittingly practicing cultural and religious idolatry."[298] That is of course the task of the discernment of spirits.

Having discussed the Holy Spirit's role and work in creation, among cosmic spirits, and in religions, we take up the last main topic of part 1: to relate the divine Spirit to issues of public interest, from history to politics to arts to entertainment. That is the focus of the next chapter.

298. D'Costa, *Meeting of Religions*, p. 115.

6. The Public Spirit and Solidarity of Others

The Spirit as the "Public Person"

The Widening of the Pneumatological Horizon

Traditionally pneumatology has mainly focused on the spirituality and inner life of the faithful, particularly in the communication of the salvific benefits wrought by Christ to the believer. The Spirit's communal dimensions have been by and large limited to the church, even if generic remarks about the Spirit's work in creation are made. Salvation history rather than universal history has been seen as the arena of the Spirit. With good reasons, then, a number of leading contemporary theologians such as the Catholic McDonnell and Protestants Moltmann and Pannenberg have lamented this privatization tendency (as discussed above in chap. 3).

Over against this limitation, we have also registered throughout the discussion significant suggestions to widen the sphere of the Spirit to include creation (chap. 3), the cosmos (chap. 4), and religions (chap. 5). Yet another critical step in the move from a unitive to a plural paradigm has to do with the continuing rediscovery of the role of the Spirit and spirits in history, politics, economics, as well as arts and entertainment.[1] Other significant, similar efforts have to do with relating the Spirit with ethics and virtues, care of the environment, gender

---

1. On history, see P. Oden, "Chaos or Completion"; on politics, S. C. H. Kim, "Spirits of the Political"; on economics, Wariboko, "Spirits and Economics"; and on the arts and entertainment, Johnston, "Art and the Spiritual."

equality, work, and politics, including sociopolitical liberation and equality.[2] Some postcolonialists have joined the effort, claiming that "it will be necessary to understand immigration history, racism, hybridity, and hyphenated reality to get a glimpse of how a new pneumatology can emerge and address the issues of domination and imperialism in our context."[3] Promisingly, even the youngest theological tradition, Pentecostalism, has picked up the importance of linking the empowerment and gifting of the Spirit with sociopolitical and other public realities in Latin American contexts and beyond.[4] According to the Pentecostal Yong, "such engagement shows an emerging awareness that salvation is not only an otherworldly anticipation but also a this-worldly experience, manifest in the material, economic, social, and political dimensions of human existence."[5] Not for nothing does the German Reformed pneumatologist Michael Welker discern in the emergence of liberation theologies and other similar movements a sure sign of the Spirit's new work in the world.[6] The late Roman Catholic trinitarian theologian and feminist Catherine Mowry LaCugna summarizes succinctly the many arenas of the Spirit's work in the world and in our lives:

> The Spirit is involved in every operation of God in the economy. The Spirit hovered over the waters at creation; the Spirit spoke through the prophets. Jesus was conceived, anointed, led, accompanied, inspired by the Spirit. Only in the Spirit can we confess Jesus as Lord; the Spirit makes us holy and enables our praise of God. The Spirit gathers together what has been sundered — races, nations, persons. The Spirit is God's power active in creation, history, personality. The Spirit who animates the praise of God incorporates persons into the deepest regions of divine life. We must continually remind ourselves that this divine life is bestowed and active in history and human personality, not locked up in itself.[7]

2. On ethics and virtue, see Lewis, "A Pneumatological Approach to Virtue Ethics." As for care of the environment, I construct a pneumatologically loaded theology of the flourishing of nature in my *Creation and Humanity*, chap. 8. For a more radical, semipantheist proposal, see M. Wallace, "Christian Animism." On gender equality, see Johnson, *She Who Is*; Prichard, *Sensing the Spirit*; on work, Volf, *Work in the Spirit*; and on politics, Müller-Fahrenholz, *God's Spirit*; Comblin, *Holy Spirit and Liberation*.

3. G. Kim, *The Holy Spirit, Chi, and the Other*, p. 2.

4. In Latin America, see Villafañe, *The Liberating Spirit*; for elsewhere, see Wilkinson and Studebaker, eds., *A Liberating Spirit*; Yong, *In the Days of Caesar*.

5. Yong, *The Spirit Poured Out on All Flesh*, pp. 38-39.

6. Welker, *God the Spirit*, pp. 16-17; similarly, Cormie, "Movements of the Spirit in History," p. 253.

7. LaCugna, *God for Us*, p. 362.

In this wide and inclusive theological horizon, the Spirit of God who is not content only to work in Christian spheres, but is active also in political, religious, intellectual, and secular environments,[8] can be named the "Public Person."[9] Indeed, the "universe in its entirety is the field of its [the Spirit's] operations," and therefore we can discern the Spirit "directing the universe toward its goal."[10]

The Rediscovery of the Spirit in History

These attempts to widen the sphere of pneumatology were importantly prepared by the earlier generation of theologians. Even before that, there was the groundbreaking work of the philosopher Hegel, to whom the purpose of history itself was "to bring the idea of Spirit into consciousness, moving from an implicit, unconscious instinct to a more fully realized, fully aware embrace of freedom."[11] Notwithstanding Hegel's nonpersonal and modalistic (despite his idiosyncratic "doctrine of the Trinity") way of conceiving the Spirit, its universal and history-laden orientation has influenced significantly some leading twentieth-century pneumatologists. Just consider Tillich's life- and culture-affirming theology in general and his pneumatology in particular.[12] His profound discussion of "life in Spirit" (third volume of *Systematic Theology*) expands and widens the Spirit's horizon from the inorganic to the organic to the personal to the ecclesiastical to all dimensions of society — arts, culture, and politics.[13] In all this, Tillich considers the meaning of "the spiritual presence" in the human spirit, religion, culture, and morality, not to ignore Christology and the church! Another contemporary, the Dutch Reformed theologian Hendrikus Berkhof, attempted a powerful revision of his own tradition in light of

8. Welker, *God the Spirit,* p. 308.

9. Such pneumatology can also be seen as a subset of "public theology." See S. C. H. Kim, "Spirits of the Political."

10. Pinnock, *Flame of Love,* p. 50; similarly, J. Y. Lee, *An Emerging Theology in World Perspective,* p. 13: "The Holy Spirit is ever present throughout history"; see also, C.-S. Song, *Third Eye Theology,* p. 13.

11. P. Oden, "Chaos or Completion," p. 71; the easiest access to Hegel's basic ideas in this respect is section 3 in his *Reason in History:* "The Idea of History and Its Realization," pp. 20-49. On Pannenberg's theological use and re-visioning of Hegelian ideas, see Oden, pp. 74-77 and passim.

12. K. McDonnell, "The Determinative Doctrine of the Holy Spirit," p. 155.

13. Tillich, *ST* 3:14-15; this first chapter, at the beginning of his pneumatology, is titled "Life, Its Ambiguities, and the Quest for Unambiguous Life."

the heritage of classical liberalism and the challenges of the twentieth-century context, envisioning the Spirit as the all-present "vitality" of God. These and other mid-twentieth-century theologians were following in the footsteps of the nineteenth-century Dutch neo-Calvinist statesman and theologian Abraham Kuyper and his forebears.

One of the greatest contributions of Kuyper was the further development of the Reformed idea of "common grace," which he conceived pneumatologically. Making a distinction between the "inner" and "outer" facets of common grace — which "impacts the whole of our human life" — Kuyper describes its comprehensive domain:

> One common grace aims at the *interior*, another at the *exterior* part of our existence. The former is operative wherever civic virtue, a sense of domesticity, natural love, the practice of human virtue, the improvement of the public conscience, integrity, mutual loyalty among people, and a feeling for piety leaven life. The latter is in evidence when human power over nature increases, when invention upon invention enriches life, when international communication is improved, the arts flourish, the sciences increase our understanding, the conveniences and joys of life multiply, all expressions of life become more vital and radiant, forms become more refined, and the general image of life becomes more winsome. . . . It is because the Spirit endowed natural man with great faculties that Aristotle could gain such a tremendously broad knowledge, Caesar could conquer and rule so many lands, the ancient Greeks could devise such lasting architecture, Shakespeare could write such enduring plays as *Macbeth* and *Hamlet,* Beethoven could compose his *Fifth Symphony,* Einstein could formulate the theory of relativity. These are the gifts of the Holy Spirit.[14]

Not only are the interior and exterior dimensions of common grace integrally united, so are also common and "special grace," because all of them "find a higher unity in Christ," and because in all of that "the Father [works] together with the Son and the Holy Spirit." Indeed, the special grace presupposes the common grace, and vice versa.[15] Lamenting the theological tradition's limitation of the work of the Holy Spirit to merely the "spiritual" realm, Kuyper notes: "From the whole Scripture teaching we therefore conclude that the Holy Spirit has a work in connection with mechanical arts and official

---

14. Kuyper, "Common Grace," p. 181, emphasis in original.
15. Kuyper, "Common Grace," pp. 170, 184-85.

functions — in every special talent whereby some men excel in such art or office. This teaching is not simply that such gifts and talents are not of man but from God like all other blessings, but that they are not the work of the Father, nor of the Son, but of the Holy Spirit."[16]

In light of these historical and contemporary rediscoveries, it is clear now that the limiting of the Spirit's ministry to *salvation* history alone is not feasible. Two theological considerations support that conviction. First, salvation history is an integral part of universal history. Key events of salvation history — from the exodus to the conquest to the exiles' return to the Promised Land to the birth of the Messiah to the cross and resurrection and ascension, as well as the founding of the church at Pentecost — all happen in "secular" history. Second, the God of the Bible is the Creator and hence also Consummator of the whole of the cosmos. Hence, the final coming of God's kingdom means the purification, judgment, and renewal of all that exists. In all of that, the Spirit works together with Father and Son. Not for nothing did the Catholic Rahner make the profound statement that "The world is drawn to its spiritual fulfillment by the Spirit of God, who directs the whole history of the world in all its length and breadth towards its proper goal."[17] Similarly, the Reformed Berkhof reminds us that insofar as "we know God in his mighty acts in history, we can recognize his actions also in his work in creation and preservation. We understand that the same God in action, the same *ruach* working in the deeds of salvation, is also the secret of the entire created world."[18] In this light Berkhof makes this important summary statement: "The work of the Spirit in our modern so-called secularized world reminds us of the fact that our exalted Lord is not only the Head of his church but also primarily the Head of the world."[19]

The widening of the sphere of the Spirit, however, introduces a further challenge, namely, the need to discern the spirits, as the work of the Spirit in history and the world is often ambiguous. Although ambiguity applies also to the Spirit's work within the church, it is still more intense outside.[20] Considering the task of discernment, we should pay attention to the fact that "the

---

16. Kuyper, *Work of the Holy Spirit*, p. 39; see also, pp. 43-45 (available also at www.ccel.org).

17. Rahner, "The One Christ and the Universality of Salvation," p. 203; see also, Rahner, *Foundations*, p. 139: "[T]he whole history of creation is already borne by God's self-communication in this very creation."

18. H. Berkhof, *Doctrine of the Holy Spirit*, p. 95.

19. H. Berkhof, *Doctrine of the Holy Spirit*, p. 104.

20. Cf. H. Berkhof, *Doctrine of the Holy Spirit*, p. 104.

Spirit's work of humanizing men and their social structures is a parable. . . . It is a signpost toward the glorification of the universe, the conformity of mankind with its Head."[21] To the nature of the parable belong ambiguity, tentativeness, and the need for hermeneutical guidelines. Hermeneutics do not always agree with each other. The discernment of the Spirit in history and world events is always contested, and the results are provisional. Certainly there are moments when, with much justification, we may perceive the Spirit at work: "Whenever in history we encounter driving forces that build up love, that conciliate where differences live together in harmony, there we discern the ineffable presence of the Holy Spirit's action."[22] Those moments, however, occur only every now and then. Most of the time, it is much more blurry. The Catholic feminist Elizabeth Johnson describes well the ambiguity: "The complexities of the experience of Spirit therefore, are cogiven in and through the world's history: negative, positive, and ambiguous; orderly and chaotic; solitary and communal; successful and disastrous; personal and political; dark and luminous; ordinary and extraordinary; cosmic, social, and individual."[23] The ambiguity also bears a positive aspect as it brings the church and world together in a dialectic of mutual learning and correction: "The church needs the instruction of the Spirit in world history in order to understand the cosmic consequences of her preaching. And the world needs the church to give meaning to its development, lest mankind's emancipation end in boredom and futility."[24]

Beyond the general affirmation of the presence of the Spirit in history, can we say anything more specific? What would this Spirit have to do with economics, arts, entertainment, and other areas that have been almost exclusively ignored in pneumatological theologies?

The Spirit in Arts and Entertainment

This section asks, "How are we to understand the spiritual significance of art given our pneumatologically infused culture"[25] and the widening horizon of the doctrine of the Spirit? Several recent polls indicate that one-fifth of Amer-

21. H. Berkhof, *Doctrine of the Holy Spirit*, p. 104.
22. Boff, *Trinity and Society*, p. 94.
23. Johnson, *She Who Is*, p. 124.
24. H. Berkhof, *Doctrine of the Holy Spirit*, p. 104. Cf. Moltmann (*Spirit of Life*, p. 143): "The hidden presence in world history of the divine justice in God's Spirit 'destabilizes,' so to speak, human systems of injustice, and sees to it that they cannot last."
25. Johnston, "Art and the Spiritual," p. 85.

icans, soon to be more, take art as the main gateway to spirituality;[26] similar findings from the U.K. strengthen that impression.[27] This means that not only is there a general link between art and spirituality, an intuition going far and deep in Christian tradition; there is also a specific linkage between the search for the Spirit in the current world and artistic experiences. The theologian is prompted to raise the question of what kind of spirituality this is. What is its relation to the Spirit of God? Or to other spirits?

A significant shift is happening in the study of pneumatology, as reflection on art's spiritual — and derivatively, theological — meaning is conducted not only through the lens of the artistic products but also through the *experience* of art.[28] At the same time, the concept of "art" is becoming inclusive, encompassing also the various forms of *popular* arts and entertainment. In light of their massive influence on culture and human lives, it is of utmost importance to continue probing into their theological meaning.[29]

In the experience of art, widely understood, the theologian may discern the elevation of the human person from immanence toward transcendence, as finely put in George Steiner's *Real Presences*: "All good art and literature begin in immanence. But they do not stop there. Which is to say, very plainly, that it is the enterprise and privilege of the aesthetic to quicken into lit presence the continuum between temporality and eternity, between matter and spirit, between man and 'the other.'"[30] On that basis, it can be said that creativity is "metaphysical" and "theological" in its very nature.[31]

Not only are theologians rediscovering and opening up to the more inclusive pneumatological appreciation of the arts, but some of them are also placing the consideration of the arts' spiritual and theological meaning in the context of religious plurality. This is aided by important cultural shifts, particularly the ethos of the current neo–Romantic age and some postmodern sensibilities. A leading American art-and-theology expert, Robert Johnston, argues

26. For details, see Barna, *Revolution;* similarly, the sociologist of religion Wuthnow, *All in Sync*, p. xiv.

27. Hay, *Something There*, p. 23.

28. The programmatic essay here is Johnston, "Art and the Spiritual." My discussion owes to his.

29. See Johnston, *Reel Spirituality.* For the emerging theological reflection on popular arts, particularly film and cinema, see resources of the Reel Spirituality initiative of the Brehm Center (Fuller Theological Seminary, Pasadena, Calif.) at http://www.brehmcenter .com/initiatives/reelspirituality/. On the role and meaning of the Spirit and spirits in relation to (American) horror movies, see Staggs, "*Pneumakinesis* and Stephen King."

30. Steiner, *Real Presences*, p. 227, cited in Johnston, "Art and the Spiritual," p. 89.

31. Steiner, *Real Presences*, pp. 215, 216.

rightly in my mind that, as a result, in the beginning of the third millennium, "the aesthetic has been given permission to again be understood in the context of the Spirit's encounter with humanity. Along with our engagement with other religions, the arts are forcing a broader understanding of Spirit, not to mention the spirits, and spirituality. In the process, they are providing perhaps the most significant opportunities and challenges on the horizon today for those seeking to understand Christian pneumatology more comprehensively."[32]

Johnston correctly notes that shifting the traditional trinitarian starting point from the Word (Christ) to the Spirit may help us in the discernment of the theological value of art in other faith traditions.[33] Oscillating between the two starting points is justified, as it does not have to violate the integrity and mutually conditioned work of the trinitarian members; this tactic is rather about where to begin the theological discernment.

The widening of the pneumatological horizon is not only about loosing the Spirit from the strict contours of pietistic and ecclesiastical spheres to encompass the whole of history. It is also about how we understand the nature of the Spirit as the Public Person. To that analysis and its implications we now turn.

The Solidarity of Others

By and large, modern Western culture, and thus also theology, has tended to identify the Spirit with individualistic and self-referential notions of personhood. With roots in the Aristotelian[34] and Hegelian[35] notions of self-referentiality, the spirit of Western culture and philosophy — currently also spread all over the world because of Western cultural hegemony — is charac-

32. Johnston, "Art and the Spiritual," p. 93.

33. Johnston, "Art and the Spiritual," p. 93.

34. Aristotle, *Metaphysics* 12.1072b: "Now thinking in itself is concerned with that which is in itself best, and thinking in the highest sense with that which is in the highest sense best. And thought thinks itself through participation in the object of thought; for it becomes an object of thought by the act of apprehension and thinking, so that thought and the object of thought are the same, because that which is receptive of the object of thought, i.e. essence, is thought." The English term "thought" is the Greek *nous,* which is also routinely translated as "spirit/Spirit." Available at http://www.perseus.tufts.edu/hopper/text?doc=Perseus%3Atext %3A1999.01.0052%3Abook%3D12%3Asection%3D1072b.

35. Note that Hegel's *Philosophy of Mind* (p. 315) ends with the direct citation from Aristotle cited in the previous footnote and that the German word translated "Mind" is of course "Spirit" *(Geist).*

terized by individualism, self-certainty, self-possession, self-production, and domination of other people and nature.[36] Fittingly, a term for this attitude has been coined: "egology."[37] The Korean theologian Bo-Myung Seo rightly sees links between this self-referentiality, Western modernity's turn to subjectivity, the establishment of "self/I" as a means of setting up one's own subjectivity over against the other(s), and the resulting all-pervasive forces of colonialism.[38] Behind the colonialist power play is an underlying anthropology of "the other as non-person";[39] that is, colonialism does not honor the otherness of the Other but rather imposes an identity on the Other. It thus denies the opportunity for the Other to be a person (or community of persons). These and other modernist tendencies are another way of affirming one's self over against each other and exercising power over the other.

This modernist paradigm must be unmasked and radically revised. In contrast to self-referentiality, the biblical Spirit of God refuses to succumb to solipsism, self-worship, and self-affirmation but rather cultivates communion and mutuality, and points to Christ and through Christ to the Father.[40] The Spirit rather cultivates the solidarity of others. What are the theological and social implications of this statement?

The Dialectic of Differentiation and Interdependence

The Korean American Anselm K. Min correctly diagnoses a main challenge of our pluralistic world:

> The globalization of the world brings together different groups into common space and produces a twofold dialectic, the dialectic of *differentiation*, in which we are made increasingly aware of differences in nationality, culture, religion, ethnicity, gender, class, language; and the dialectic of

---

36. Welker, *God the Spirit*, pp. 282-84, particularly; on p. 295 Welker in a summary way calls this notion of spirit "the cult of this [Aristotelian-Hegelian-modernist] spirit."

37. Levinas, *Totality and Infinity*, p. 44.

38. Seo, *Critique of Western Theological Anthropology*.

39. For commentary on such developments in the conquest of America, see Todorov, *Conquest of America*.

40. Welker, *God the Spirit*, pp. 312-14 (p. 312). Here Welker utilizes Niklas Luhmann's concept of "domain of resonance": human beings acquire the features of personhood only by being formed in diverse webs of relationships, whether in relation to parents or friends or other significant persons. Luhmann, *Ecological Communication*, pp. 15-21.

interdependence in which we are compelled to find a way of living together despite our differences. The central challenge of the globalizing world is how to manage and transform this twofold, antithetical dialectic of simultaneous differentiation and interdependence into a solidarity of others, the mutual solidarity of those who are different.[41]

Although there are several resources in Christian tradition that help overcome the tension of this dialectic, particularly the *kenosis* of Christ — his self-sacrificial love and self-offering — for the sake of this discussion the key can be found in the biblical account of how the Spirit relates to the Father and the Son. In the Bible, the Spirit does not call attention to herself. She empowers and bears witness to another one — Jesus Christ — and through him to the Father. Min argues, "The Holy Spirit is self-effacing, selfless God whose selfhood or personhood seems to lie precisely in transcending herself to empower others likewise to transcend themselves in communion with others."[42] As a result, we can discern the Spirit "exercising an influence that reaches into diverse contexts and . . . enabling people from diverse contexts to strengthen each other and to serve each other, promoting what is best for each other." The same Spirit "places people in the community of conscious solidarity, the community of responsibility and love of persons who can accept their own finitude and perishability."[43] As a result, "[i]nasmuch as human beings are taken into this communion, their isolation as weak, consumeristically corrupted individualities, intoxicated by the mass media and without public resonance, is dissolved both for them and through them."[44] This work of the Spirit leads to what can be appropriately named the "anthropology of the Other" as opposed to anthropology of "the other as nonperson," mentioned above.

Another way of naming this affirmative attitude comes from the Jewish philosopher Emmanuel Levinas: "philosophy of the Other." It seeks to create space for and affirm the "infinite" otherness of the Other. With the term "infinity," Levinas seeks to confront the modernist desire to reduce and eliminate the absolute otherness of the Other (within the "totality") and underline its boundless nature.[45] The Other can thus not be known or made an object. Ultimately, only "face-to-face" encounter can facilitate an encounter in which

---

41. Min, *Solidarity of Others*, p. 1, emphasis in original.
42. Min, *Solidarity of Others*, p. 118.
43. Welker, *God the Spirit*, pp. 280, 282.
44. Welker, *God the Spirit*, p. 308.
45. Levinas, *Totality and Infinity*, pp. 51, 68; see Levinas, "Trace of the Other," p. 346.

true "presence" happens.[46] For Levinas, the absolute honoring of the Other is not merely a nice mental gesture; it is philosophy as "first ethics." "Truly 'facing' the Other puts me in question and obliges me."[47] Building critically on the work of Levinas and others, the late Russian literary critic Mikhail Bakhtin sought to replace the "monologic solipsism" and subjectivism of Western modernity[48] with the "dialogical principle"[49] in order to honor the otherness. Bakhtin rightly saw the importance of the Other in the Christian tradition, particularly in Christ's teaching where we find an "infinitely deepened I-for-myself — not a cold I-for-myself, but one of boundless kindness toward the other; an I-for-myself that renders full justice to the other as such."[50]

The Holy Spirit as the spirit of *koinonia,* the eternal bond of love, is the source of this kind of anthropology of the Other. In the fellowship of the Spirit the antagonism of individualism and collectivism is resolved for the sake of unity-in-diversity/diversity-in-unity. In the fellowship of the Spirit is also found a medicine against "a nihilist play of sheer alterity," a liability of Levinas and other postmodernists (particularly of Derrida)[51] who are responding to another extreme, namely, "totality and its ontology of war."[52] However, it is not "the absolutization of difference but its sublation into the solidarity of the different precisely for the sake of justice and liberation" that is needed in our pluralistic world.[53] Trinity testifies to the irreducible difference as well as the complete sharing, perichoretic mutuality of the Three. "The Holy Spirit brings

46. "The face is a living presence; it is expression. . . . The face speaks." Levinas, *Totality and Infinity,* p. 66; see also, pp. 50-51; for "face's" resistance to being objectified, see pp. 194, 197.

47. Levinas, *Totality and Infinity,* p. 207. For useful reflections on Levinas's implications for theological anthropology, see Seo, *Critique of Western Theological Anthropology,* chap. 6. The Latin American Enrique Dussel's *Philosophy of Liberation* similarly utilizes resources from Levinas to construct an anthropology of the Other.

48. Recall his oft-quoted statement that "I" has no "alibi in existence." Bakhtin, *Toward a Philosophy of the Act,* p. 41. For finding this source, I am indebted to Seo, *Critique of Western Theological Anthropology,* p. 96.

49. See the useful study by Todorov, *Mikhail Bakhtin.*

50. Bakhtin, "Author and Hero," p. 56, cited in Seo, *Critique of Western Theological Anthropology,* p. 96.

51. Derrida's motto ("the wholly other is every other") celebrates alterity — indeed, infinite alterity — to the point that not only every other human person but also God remains the other. For a highly insightful theological critique of Derrida's position, see Min, *Solidarity of Others,* chap. 2.

52. Min, *Solidarity of Others,* p. 7; see chap. 1 for the discussion "Levinas and the Liberation of the Other."

53. Min, *Solidarity of Others,* p. 47; see chap. 4, "From Difference to the Solidarity of Others."

about this communion and solidarity by unifying the divided, reconciling the alienated, and incorporating them into the body of the Son."[54]

The solidarity of others can never be affirmed merely as a generic principle. It should have specific, concrete ways of manifestation. A continuing challenge in this regard is the relationship between men and women.

The Dialectic of Gender: Difference and Fellowship

The proper context to consider the dialectic of gender difference is community — community understood in the most inclusive sense, including also the relation of women and men to the community of nature.[55] The communal perspective places in the widest possible horizon the *imago Dei* — the main anthropological concept that informs our understanding of both men and women as well as their communities. The image of God consists of men and women in their wholeness, in their full, gender-specific community with one another.[56] God is not known in the "inner chamber of the heart," or at a solitary place, but in the true community of women and men. As a result, the experience of God and God's Spirit is "the social experience of the self and the personal experience of sociality."[57] Clearly, the modernist conception of self-referentiality and self-affirmation against the other is pointing in a different direction from the community and belonging wrought by the Spirit of God. God the Spirit represents values radically different from the spirit(s) of modernity and self-referentiality. On the Day of Pentecost, when the eschatological Spirit was poured out on all flesh in anticipation of a new community of men and women in the new creation, both men and women, young and old, free and slaves, were recipients of God's empowering spiritual power.[58] Moltmann puts it succinctly:

> According to the promise in Joel 2:28-30 "It shall come to pass in the last days, says the Lord, that I will pour out my spirit on all flesh; and your sons and your daughters shall prophesy" (cf. Acts 2:17ff.). The eschatological

54. Min, *Solidarity of Others*, p. 83; see also, chap. 6, "Solidarity of Others in the Movement of the Holy Spirit."

55. For a fuller discussion of gender equality, particularly in the context of the doctrine of the Trinity, see chap. 13 in *Trinity and Revelation*.

56. For the discussion of male-female distinction in relation to *imago Dei*, see chap. 11 in *Creation and Humanity*.

57. Moltmann, *Spirit of Life*, p. 94.

58. Demarest, *Sex and Spirit*, pp. 38-39.

hope for the experience of the Spirit is shared by women and men equally. Men and women will "prophesy" and proclaim the gospel. According to the prophecy in Joel 2, through the shared experience of the Spirit the privileges of men compared with women, of the old compared with the young, and of masters compared with "men servants and maidservants" will be abolished. In the kingdom of the Spirit, everyone will experience his and her own endowment and all will experience the new fellowship together.[59]

To that fellowship also belongs the rest of creation. It is not divorced from but rather deeply ingrained in the fellowship of nature and in solidarity with it. Feminist and other female theologians have reminded us for several decades that the broken solidarity between men and women results in violation of the environment. The leading Catholic feminist Elizabeth Johnson's *Women, Earth, and Creator Spirit* rightly argues that "[t]he exploitation of the earth, which has reached crisis proportion in our day, is intimately linked to the marginalization of women, and . . . both of these predicaments are intrinsically related to forgetting the Creator Spirit who pervades the world in the dance of life."[60] Instead of the power-laden hierarchic dualism that too often is accompanied by abuse of nature, the other sex, and one's own body, the fellowship of the Spirit builds community, belonging, and mutuality. That is the way toward a new wholeness, a new community of equals.[61]

Pneumatologies developed mainly by (Euro-American, mostly aging) men are in dire need of being complemented by fresh theologies of the Spirit. An important aspect of pneumatologies created by women theologians of various stripes is their sensitivity to the aesthetic. Along with the liberationist impulse, several female theologians' way of speaking of the Spirit includes the qualities of beauty, intimacy, and shared love, as in the Roman Catholic Mary Ann Fatula's account:

> We ourselves know this Spirit, just as we intuitively know the air we breathe and without which we cannot live, for the Spirit lives with us and *is* deep within us (John 14:17). Though we may not always realize it, we experience the Holy Spirit's closeness when we are near our loved ones and our life feels good and sweet to us. We feel the Spirit's joy, too, as we savor the perfumes of springtime, when nature all around us bursts into

59. Moltmann, *Spirit of Life*, pp. 239-41.
60. Johnson, *Women, Earth, and Creator Spirit*, p. 2.
61. Johnson, *Women, Earth, and Creator Spirit*, p. 25.

bloom. Even hard times bring us the Holy Spirit's fragrance, for all that the Spirit touches is anointed with joy. . . . Nothing created — not even the greatest ecstasy nor the most exquisite tenderness — can describe this happiness which the Holy Spirit *is* at the heart of the Trinity. . . . The Holy Spirit of love . . . dwells in us as our inseparable and intimate friend, our beloved "Paraclete" and counselor, our advocate and helper, our comfort and consoler.[62]

Cultivating aesthetic sensitivities in pneumatology is not another way of making one gender (typically female) a "weaker" sex and thus marginalizing or patronizing the theology of Spirit. It is rather an attempt to enrich, balance, and make more inclusive the talk about the Spirit in relation to many dimensions of creaturely and human life. The turn to the aesthetic helps make both men and women wiser and more sensitive to the promptings of the Spirit. It also fosters intimacy rather than distance, mutual care rather than selfish withdrawal. Tradition's occasional habit of naming the Spirit of God in maternal and feminine terms is a welcome means for correcting one-sidedly masculine discourse.[63] According to the biblical promises, the role of the Spirit involves activities more usually associated with maternity and femininity in general: inspiring, helping, supporting, enveloping, bringing to birth. Of all the trinitarian persons, the Holy Spirit is most often related to intimacy. Men and women can learn together the grammar of equality and complementarity when searching for diverse pneumatological metaphors.

So far in this chapter we have talked about the Spirit of God in her public role, whether in history and its various areas or in relation to the question of encountering the Other, which brings to light the dialectic of differentiation and interdependence at various levels. We now widen that point of view to consider the role of other spirits and powers. How are they related to the public arena?

Powers, Spirit(s), and Liberation

Speaking of the presence and power of the Holy Spirit in the society and culture opens up the question of whether opposing spirits and powers are also

---

62. Fatula, *Holy Spirit,* pp. 2, 5, 22, emphasis in original.

63. For remarkable female metaphors of the Spirit, see Catherine of Siena, *The Dialogue* 141, p. 292; for other related Spirit-metaphors by Catherine, see *The Letters of St. Catherine of Siena,* vol. 1, 52, p. 161; *The Prayers of Catherine of Siena,* prayer 18, p. 158.

at work. This does not seem to concern most theologians. Most "mainline" theologians simply refrain from touching on the issue — even those such as Moltmann and liberationists of various sorts who otherwise speak of injustice, discrimination, racial divisions, and economic struggles. On the other hand, Pentecostals/charismatics and others who speak of powers and spirits in more traditional ways usually do it unrelated to structural and social sins.

Walter Wink's program of "powers" is a marvelous exception in contemporary theology and points to the third way. As discussed above (chap. 4), Wink argues that the powers are "the spiritualities of institutions, the 'within' of corporate structures and the inner essence of outer organizations of power." The outer aspect consists of "political systems, appointed officials, the 'chair' of an organization, laws."[64] Although Wink definitely rejects the identification of these powers with the traditional notion of the demonic, the "principalities and powers," as well as "Satan," for him the powers are nevertheless "real." They are social, cultural, political, financial, global powers. And they must be "redeemed": originally the powers were good but they became evil. The key to redeeming powers is in the Jesus kind of lifestyle: nonviolent, peaceful, and free. That is set against the "domination system of the powers" of the world.[65]

I see much in common with Wink in the American Roman Catholic pneumatologist Bradford Hinze's reading of Jesus' approach to societal evil:

> Throughout Jesus' mission and ministry one can find forms of talking back to destructive social power systems associated with patterns of exclusion and disrespect for marginalized groups. Jesus' parables and aphorisms provide idioms of resistance to power regimes: the first shall be last, and the last first, it is not what goes into your mouth that makes you unclean, but what comes out of it. The parables of the rich man and Dives and the Good Samaritan disparage those who are not responsive to those suffering from poverty and the brutality of everyday life, and commend those, even the unexpected outsiders, who dare to get involved. Jesus' beatitudes offer another form of talking back by portraying an upside-down world, a challenge to dominative powers, where the poor and the meek are blessed, and the rich and arrogant are cursed. Jesus imagines a new way of being into life by talking back.[66]

64. Wink, *Naming the Powers*, p. 5.
65. Wink, *Engaging the Powers*; see p. 44 for the chart contrasting the two systems.
66. Hinze, "Talking Back, Acting Up," p. 156.

Hinze has listened carefully to the laments[67] of contemporary people who suffer under the destructive powers causing unemployment, prejudice, violence, lack of health care, lack of access to education and housing, and so forth. While undoubtedly there are various personal reasons behind these social problems, the problems cannot all be blamed on individuals.[68] Like Wink and liberationists, Hinze is convinced that these structural sins and powers call for human cooperation in tackling them. For him, faith-based community organizing is the "most effective way to wrestle with destructive powers . . . by forming communities that are ecumenical, interfaith, and intercultural to challenge them."[69] Christians and congregations who participate in faith-based community organizing "understand the life-giving powers at work in their relational networks in terms of the work of the Spirit of God, not only among Christians, but also in the wider public realm. The agency of the Spirit is recognized in the communicative practices that create the conditions for people to share their deepest aspirations and their laments and form bonds of affection, solidarity, and collective action." Christians discern the "good spirits of religiously affiliated partners and civic-minded, nonreligious, collaborators, but this same Spirit can be detected in business leaders and government officials who change policies and practices when challenged."[70]

That said, Hinze argues that ultimately, however, there cannot be a "'dualism of the Spirit' versus the demonic in the public arena." Rather, what is needed is the cultivation of a "spiritual tolerance for ambiguity in the ongoing struggle where there is far more fluidity and dynamism at work in the public arena."[71] If I correctly interpret his thought, it seems to me that while Christians are bound to discern the work and existence of evil spirits and structures, for the sake of the common good that should not hinder their working toward better solutions and liberation. This is not to refrain from "talking back and acting up" against oppressive structures, but neither does it mean demonizing professions such as business or structures such as markets in themselves. Reform is always possible and a hoped-for solution.

---

67. See Hinze, "Ecclesial Impasse."

68. Hinze, "Talking Back, Acting Up," p. 157; he presents a taxonomy of powers in contemporary society like this (p. 164): (1) social oppression, (2) economic injustice, (3) racism, (4) sexism and heterosexism, (5) consumerism and materialism, (6) isolating individualism, (7) religious extremism and radical secularism, and (8) fatalism, apathy, and nihilism.

69. Hinze, "Talking Back, Acting Up," p. 158. For the philosophy and activities, see Warren and Wood, *Faith-Based Community Organizing*.

70. Hinze, "Talking Back, Acting Up," p. 162.

71. Hinze, "Talking Back, Acting Up," p. 162.

Wink's and Hinze's analyses of and calls for resisting and reforming evil social powers and spirits at work in various institutions, ideologies, and structures are necessary and laudable. For the sake of the common good, constructive theology can only support that move. However, for the sake of this particular discussion, namely, the investigation of a plural (rather than unitive) pneumatological paradigm, the immanentist (nontranscendent) nature of these analyses should also be noted. In this context, we can do that briefly as we build on and refer the reader to the more detailed discussion above in chapter 4. Apart from Wink and Hinze, the same reticence — which we have registered several times in this discussion — among theologians to speak of spirits and powers (either good or evil) in the contemporary world and the cosmos is manifest in relation to society, including culture, politics, economics, and entertainment.

We are prompted to ask whether contemporary theology's silence about the "societal" spirits might be more understandable in light of the fact that by and large the NT and early Christian tradition related the demonic to the personal rather than the societal. Even if that were true — and it is true only with qualifications (even the biblical idea of exorcism "may also have held social connotations for early Christian audiences who associated the rule of Satan with Roman imperialism")[72] — I fear the main reason for the omission in current theology is an uncritical accommodation to the modernist epistemology. With all the sophistication of his approach, I see the modernist reductionism at work even in Wink's strategy of "redeeming powers." With all its many merits, it stops short of affirming any kind of transcendent dimension to powers. The same is probably the case with Hinze (although his emerging proposal awaits further clarification). As mentioned, whatever one thinks of the status of metaphysics in contemporary theology and philosophy, denying all metaphysical implications of the Christian idea of powers seems unnecessary and unacceptable. On the other hand, one does not have to go as far as the American open theist Boyd, who one-sidedly seems to support the view of traditional Christianity that "the good and evil, fortunate or unfortunate, aspects of life are to be interpreted largely as the result of good and evil, friendly or hostile, spirits warring against each other and against us,"[73] and that, therefore, we are at all times in a warfare zone, so to speak. A radical

---

72. Sorensen, *Possession and Exorcism*, p. 166, cited in Hinze, "Talking Back, Acting Up," p. 156. See also the important studies linking the early church's demonology with wider political implications: Horsley, *Jesus and the Powers*; Myers, *Binding the Strong Man*.

73. G. Boyd, *God at War*, p. 13. For a succinct summary of his argumentation, see chap. 1 in G. Boyd, *Satan and the Problem of Evil*.

middle road is available in which, following Wink and Hinze, concerted efforts can be made to analyze and tackle — in collaboration with all people of good will, whether other Christians or people of other faiths or followers of no faith — the devastating effects of societal powers and structures. At the same time, contra Wink and others, there is a need to be open to a plural understanding of powers and spirits linked to greater realities than merely human-made ones. Not only "the social discernment of spirits"[74] but also wider *spiritual* discernment is called for.

An important part of the spiritual discernment work in the public arena has to do with the other extreme in the global church, namely, overenthusiastic attribution to spirits and powers of many aspects of societal processes and events. A representative example from the current African scene illustrates and makes the point. Speaking of "spirits-infested commodities," based on a common belief in many societies that commodities coming from the marketplace are loaded with spiritual forces or powers that may in turn lead to recycling of these commodities into the marketplace from the spiritual realm filled with spirits,[75] the Nigerian American Pentecostal ethicist Nimi Wariboko astutely observes:

> There is a market for spirits. Right from antiquity through to the present, spirits have been traded and exchanged hands based on transfer of consideration. Spirits are also noted to bring handsome profits, commodities, and cargoes to their owners or controllers. There is always trading on (perceived) exclusive access to spirits. To this day, gaining knowledge and powers in spiritual matters requires that one go through a certain established priesthood program after paying a fee. Spirits are "put up" for show through manipulation of objects and persons considered possessed by ghosts and spirits. And religious specialists continue to offer the services of their spirits in the marketplace for profits and access to power.[76]

Although similar connections between manipulating a "market" and (evil) forces are known in biblical history (in Acts 8 Simon offers to buy the power of the Holy Spirit from the apostle Peter) and later church history (the medieval Catholic Church mixed alms and salvation)[77] — and indeed, even in

74. Hinze, "Talking Back, Acting Up," pp. 162-63.
75. As reported, e.g., by Meyer, "Commodities and the Power of Prayer," p. 151; see also, Wariboko, "Spirits and Economics," pp. 145-47.
76. Wariboko, "Spirits and Economics," p. 146.
77. Ekelund et al., *Sacred Trust.*

other faiths, for example, Islam[78] — that does not make it either desirable or justified. Religious manipulation in relation to money is just that, *manipulation,* and should be rejected. Similarly, a spiritually based quest for prosperity, even when not manipulated, should be subjected to severe criticism.[79]

What about other faith traditions and their capacity to discern spirits and powers in the society with a view to restoration and liberation? Without being able to tackle in any detail this complicated question, we refer the reader to the main insights from the discussion in *Creation and Humanity:* there (chap. 16) we investigate the liberative resources for human flourishing at the personal and societal, including global, levels, not only in Christianity but also in four other living faiths. When it comes to the Abrahamic faiths, it is indisputable that, at least in theory, they all share the same God-centered and "earth-driven" vision for human flourishing at all levels. God's justice and holiness set the standard for Jewish, Christian, and Islamic pursuit of justice, equality, and fairness. History matters as it unfolds toward the final resolution in which God will be "all in all," to use Christian parlance. With somewhat differing nuances, all three sister faiths envision the eschatological fulfillment in terms of community of men and women in the renewed cosmos (less so in Islam but still present).

In the Asiatic faiths, it is indisputable that "[t]he religious struggle within this framework of metaphysical unity and mystic vision is to find room for a purposive cosmic and historical movement which has ultimate spiritual significance."[80] Particularly in the Hindu traditions with their ahistorical view of reality, their understanding of this world as "appearance," in the sense that "beyond" it is the truly abiding form of existence and the pursuit of one's own liberation from the karmic cycle of personal existence, clearly points in another direction than the lasting value of work toward betterment of this world. In that respect, various Buddhist traditions do not significantly differ from the mother faith, although in Theravada a this-worldly ethical orientation comes to the fore. That pursuit, however, is not for the sake of the "common good" so much as it is a way for personal "salvation," release from existence as *dukkha* (suffering). Even the Mahayana tradition's compassionate waiting for the achievement of enlightenment of others by the enlightened ones ultimately has personal liberation as the goal and provides little motivation for investing

78. This phenomenon is of course not limited to Christianity; for its Islamic manifestations, see Peel, *Religious Encounter and the Making of the Yoruba.*

79. See, e.g., Wiegele, *Investing in Miracles.*

80. M. M. Thomas, "The Holy Spirit and the Spirituality for Political Struggles," p. 216.

in this fleeting world. The same general orientation of Asiatic religions also characterizes the attitudes toward the flourishing of nature, differently from what is usually assumed in popular opinion — which considers Buddhism and Hinduism nature-friendly as opposed to Abrahamic faiths' dismissive point of view (as discussed in detail in chap. 8 in *Creation and Humanity*).

Having now outlined and discussed in some detail the form and content of the new emerging pneumatology based on a "plural" rather than a "unitive" paradigm, we focus on the question of salvation and the Spirit's role therein. The introduction of the holistic and plural paradigm will significantly help revise and reorient traditional talk about the "order of salvation" *(ordo salutis)*. As with all other topics, the Christian vision of salvation will also be put in a sympathetic and critical dialogue with the "salvific" intuitions of other faith traditions.

II. SALVATION

7. From *Ordo Salutis* to a Salutary Communion

Traditional Accounts of Soteriology and the Need for Revision

Prior to the Reformation there was very little interest in outlining the temporal or logical sequence of the process of salvation, even in the great medieval *summae*.[1] Yet Protestant orthodoxy[2] in particular developed highly sophisticated presentations of "steps" in the reception and experience of salvation wrought by the Holy Spirit. Some biblical passages, especially Romans 8:29-30, were often invoked as establishing a precedent. A typical definition is this: "The ordo salutis describes the process by which the work of salvation, wrought in Christ, is subjectively realized in the hearts and lives of sinners. It aims at describing in their logical order, and also in their interrelations, the various movements of the Holy Spirit in the application of the work of redemption."[3]

Understandably the order of topics varies among traditions. Whereas for Lutherans, justification through faith comes first (as evident in the detailed discussion in the Formula of Concord), for the Reformed, the starting point is the prior "elective" work of God. Hence, following Christ's work finished at the cross, the *ordo* was discussed under rubrics such as "the application

---

1. See Henzel, "Perseverance within an Ordo Salutis." A healthy warning against the tendency to systematize soteriology comes from none other than a Reformed theologian, Berkouwer, *Faith and Justification*, p. 25.

2. For the discussion of Lutheran *ordo* in light of current concerns, see Forde, "Christian Life," pp. 395-469. For an analysis of the soteriology of the Reformed theologian T. Beza (the ablest successor of Calvin), see Muller, *Christ and the Decree*, pp. 79-96.

3. L. Berkhof, *Systematic Theology*, pp. 415-16.

of salvation by the grace of the Holy Spirit," and included topics of election, calling, faith, justification, regeneration, union, sanctification/renewal, and glorification. Understandably for the Arminians, because of their unique understanding of election and predestination, the order is somewhat different: outward call, faith/election, repentance, regeneration, justification, perseverance, and glorification. In response to the Reformation, the Catholic Church's Council of Trent began from water baptism and divine-human cooperation in the preparation of the sinner for justification.[4]

These kinds of differences are understandable in differing spiritualities and theological orientations of Christian churches. "Protestants have tended to think through the categories of justification and sanctification. The Roman Catholic tradition has often seen salvation through the lens of transformation and renewal. Eastern Orthodox traditions have emphasized participation and deification."[5] While embracing the Protestant type of understanding of salvation, Anabaptists also focus on discipleship and "practical Christianity," and Pentecostals on empowerment and healing.[6]

Contemporary international and ecumenical theology — except for the conservative Reformed theologies and traditions under their influence[7] — shows little interest in this kind of analytic exercise; theologies from the Global South impose a virtual moratorium on the topic itself. The Lutheran Pannenberg's soteriological discussion, while detailed and long (within the doctrine of the church in the third part of his systematics), hardly mentions the term and refuses to follow any certain order.

Moltmann's creative revision of soteriological discussion in his pneumatology points out correctly that the analytic steps "are not stages in the experience of the Spirit . . . [but rather] different aspects of the one single gift of the Holy Spirit."[8] Moltmann begins with the consideration of "the Spirit of life" and highlights the importance of the Spirit to all of life, including bodily life (chap. 4). The next stage is the "liberation of life," where he speaks of social and political freedom (chap. 5). The "justification of life" speaks not only of the individual's justification but also of justice for the oppressed and other victims, including the structures of societies (chap. 6). The "rebirth to life" relates to "new creation" both at the individual and cosmic levels and hence radically

---

4. For details, see Kärkkäinen, *"Ordo salutis,"* pp. 622-23.

5. Lints, "Soteriology," p. 260.

6. For the centrality of soteriology as a controlling principle for theology, see Braaten, *Principles of Lutheran Theology,* p. 63.

7. See the conservative Calvinist Baptist Erickson, *Christian Theology,* pp. 907-84.

8. Moltmann, *Spirit of Life,* p. 82; references in parenthesis are to this work.

expands the notion of "regeneration" (chap. 7). Similarly, the "sanctification of life" calls for holiness in the personal life as well as the need to honor the sanctity of all life (chap. 8). In contrast to usual discussions, Moltmann also includes the "charismatic powers of life," including speaking in tongues and healing, in his *ordo salutis* (chap. 9). He finishes by developing a theology of mystical union that would achieve a balance between action and meditation (chap. 10). While the current project develops the theology of salvation independently from either Moltmann or others, inspiration from his groundbreaking life-affirming and "earth-centered" approach should be acknowledged.

In Search of a Holistic, Communal, and Cosmic Trinitarian Soteriology

The Plurality of Soteriological Metaphors

The beginning point of both the doctrine of reconciliation (atonement) and the doctrine of soteriology is that the *idea* of salvation — like that of "sin"[9] — is depicted with a number of metaphors in the biblical testimonies. It refers to the gracious act of the triune God in rescuing, renewing, and completing the destiny of humanity and the whole of creation.[10] The biblical vision of reconciliation and salvation is multicolored and employs a variety of metaphors. It is deeply embedded in the OT and Jewish world, although, as the ensuing discussion will reveal, Christian tradition develops the insights drastically differently because of its trinitarian christocentric "foundation."[11] A number of metaphors drawn from Torah and contemporary cult and culture, including the Greco-Roman environment, were available to the first Christians, such as "the language of Jewish law *(justify)* and holy rite *(sanctify),* of medical healing and military rescue *(heal* and *save),* of kingship and its ties *(adopt, wed),* of life processes *(born* and *reborn),* of commercial exchange *(redeem* and *reconcile)."*[12] Unlike the Reformation-driven guilt-, judgment-, and penitence-oriented accounts of justification that dominated the soteriologies of the Christian West, in the theology of the first millennium — and through-

---

9. For details, see chap. 14 in my *Creation and Humanity.*

10. See J. Watt, ed., *Salvation in the New Testament;* C. Wright, *Salvation Belongs to Our God.*

11. For an important warning against ignoring the Jewish background in soteriology, see McClendon, *Doctrine,* p. 108.

12. McClendon, *Doctrine,* pp. 106-7, emphases in original. For a detailed study of soteriological metaphors, see chap. 11 of my *Christ and Reconciliation.*

out history in the Eastern tradition — sin and guilt were not in the forefront but rather in the redemptive and reconciliatory work of Christ.

Salvation and a Trinitarian "Objective Pneumatology"

Traditional ways of approaching the topic of soteriology are not only somewhat polemical and highly abstract, but there is also too clear-cut a distinction, if not a separation, between Christology and soteriology, the person and work of Christ. In correction, the current project argues that the "unifying centre can only be the person of the mediator, 'who became for us God's wisdom, righteousness, sanctification and redemption' (1 Cor. 1:30)."[13] A related issue is the separation between the work of Christ (as objective) and the work of the Spirit (as subjective). To correct that liability, we have to keep in mind the importance of a robust "Spirit Christology,"[14] present everywhere in the NT. Christology and pneumatology are mutually conditioned and "dependent" on each other. Christ is both the giver and the recipient of the Spirit. The Spirit not only "delivers" the benefits wrought by Christ in his reconciling work but also is the eschatological Spirit of new resurrected life. The Catholic theologian W. Kasper puts it succinctly: "participation in the Holy Spirit mediated by Jesus Christ in the life of God" is Christian salvation.[15] Hence, a truly trinitarian account of soteriology is needed.

It is not the case that the Western Church's *ordo salutis* would not have considered the importance of the Spirit. Recall that it is located under pneumatology! However, the Spirit's role has been made secondary to that of the Son, as it has had to do merely with the "subjective" reception of the "objective" work wrought by Christ. This is, however, "soteriological subordinationism." While in no way diminishing the work of the Son, the Spirit's work cannot only be considered "subjective" as in traditional presentations of the *ordo salutis*. It was through the Spirit that the Father raised Jesus from the dead (Rom. 1:4), the act that led to our justification (Rom. 4:25). Christ's cross requires the Spirit's resurrection, and vice versa. In a qualified sense of the word, the Spirit's work is thus as "objective" as that of Christ,[16] albeit differently: Christ's coming, ministry, self-surrender to the point of death on the cross, resurrection, and

13. Kasper, *Jesus the Christ*, p. 253.

14. For a detailed discussion and constructive proposal, see chap. 8 in *Christ and Reconciliation*.

15. Kasper, *Jesus the Christ*, p. 254.

16. For details, see Thompson, *Holy Spirit in the Theology of Karl Barth*.

current "teaching" ministry through the Paraclete all require the "objective" work of the Spirit. Even more: this objective pneumatology "also involves the Spirit's mission to indwell the creation by first indwelling the Son. The embrace of the Spirit thus takes ambiguous creaturely life into the circle of love and justice enjoyed within God as Father, Son, and Spirit."[17] Only thus can we come to the place in which the mutually conditioning work of the Spirit and Christ is understood in an inclusive way as both justifying God in his faithfulness to creation and making it possible for the creatures to truly participate in the life divine through and in the Spirit.

Several contemporary Protestant theologians have acknowledged this pneumatological lacuna and have worked toward rectifying it. Pannenberg places talk about soteriology under the telling heading "The Basic Saving Works of the Spirit in Individual Christians" in his discussion of pneumatology and ecclesiology.[18] Moltmann's revisionist pneumatology, as tentatively presented above, similarly argues robustly that the beginning point of soteriology is the holistic, ever-present, cosmic, and earthly Spirit of God. There is no place for dualism between earthly/spiritual, sacred/secular, individual/communal, and so forth.[19]

Moltmann joins hands with different types of liberation theologies for whom salvation can never be "spiritual" in a way that leaves behind the material, social, political — the "mundane."[20] It is not about leaving behind spirituality but rather about living out a "spirituality of liberation," to cite an important book title by Jon Sobrino, which, as the subtitle puts it, leads "toward political holiness."[21] For such renewed, healed, and empowered life to flourish, the Spirit's role as "the charismatic powers of life" should be rediscovered.[22] To charismatic effects belong freedom from bondage under the powers, and healing, whether physical or mental. Similarly, empowerment and gifting are the workings of the charismatic energies. Here again, much help can be gained from the pneumatologies of the Global South, as discussed in part 1. Protestant soteriologies should also give a fair hearing to the Eastern Orthodox tradition's robust talk about divine-human *synergy* in salvation. It is not Pelagianism,[23]

17. Macchia, *Justified in the Spirit*, p. 133.
18. The heading is on p. 135 of Pannenberg, *ST*, vol. 3.
19. Moltmann, *Spirit of Life*, p. 84.
20. See Comblin, *Holy Spirit and Liberation*, pp. 94-95, 99-100.
21. Sobrino, *Spirituality of Liberation*, p. 49.
22. Title of chap. 9 in Moltmann, *Spirit of Life*.
23. I am indebted to Fredrik Cleve, "Samtalen mellan Finlands och Rysslands kyrka," p. 84.

but insists on a different kind of anthropology and a legitimate divine-human *synergy*. All cooperation is graced.

The personal and cosmic ramifications of salvation should not be juxtaposed. Rather, they belong integrally together. Pannenberg's radical relocating of soteriology in the context of ecclesiology points to the deeply communal nature of Christian vision. Indeed, not only is he linking *ordo salutis* tightly with the doctrine of the church, he is placing the discussion right in the middle of it.[24] This reordering does not of course imply that the church is the source of salvation; only the triune God is. (The complex relationship between the personal possession of faith and its ecclesial mediation is discussed in detail in the introduction to ecclesiology.)[25]

To the communal and cosmic dimensions, the integrally eschatological, future-driven aspect should be added. Rightly, Pannenberg speaks of the "Spirit as an eschatological gift that aims at the eschatological consummation of salvation."[26] The reference to the final eschatological consummation must also be related to origins, creation. The Spirit "at work in creation as God's mighty breath" is the same Spirit who raised Jesus from the dead, the same Spirit of God given to believers in a wholly special way, namely, to dwell in them (Rom. 5:5; 1 Cor. 3:16). This means that "[t]he work of the Spirit of God in his church and in believers serves the consummating of his work in the world of creation," even when there is "the special mode of the presence of the divine Spirit in the gospel and by its proclamation, which shines out from the liturgical life of the church and fills believers, so that Paul can say of them that the Spirit 'dwells' on them, [and] is a pledge of the promise" of life eternal.[27] Particularly in the Christian West, the link between the work of the Spirit in salvation and creation should be rediscovered.[28]

With these important current insights in mind, I take a lesson from and modify the proposal of the Reformed thinker F. LeRon Shults by renaming *ordo salutis* "salutary communion." Building on the wider context in Romans 8 with the *locus classicus* of verses 29-30, including the whole salvation history, the importance of community, and even cosmic dimensions, we may say that "Paul is not so much interested in identifying the effective mechanical causes of an *ordo salutis* that moves an individual from one predetermined state to

---

24. In Pannenberg, *ST,* vol. 3, *ordo salutis* topics are located in two major ecclesiological discussions, namely, chap. 12, §3, and chap. 13, part II, §§1-4.

25. A similar orientation can also be found in Horton, *The Christian Faith,* p. 561.

26. Pannenberg, *ST* 3:xiii; so also, pp. 6-7, 12.

27. Pannenberg, *ST* 3:2-3.

28. See further, Pannenberg, *ST* 3:2-3, 17.

another, as he is in depicting the *salutary ordering* of person in community, which is the manifestation of the in-breaking reality of the redemptive reign of the Spirit of Christ among the people of God."[29] Rather than abstract speculation into salvific mysteries, "[s]alvation embraces all persons and the whole person," including liberation from all oppressive structures and powers, as liberation theologians have correctly insisted.[30] In that light, salvation can be called a "revolution," to follow the American Baptist James McClendon Jr. The dawning divine rule is "pointing us beyond history and its limits to glimpse God breaking into human life with a new order, a fulfillment, that transforms everyday life."[31] Another American constructive theologian, the Anabaptist Thomas N. Finger, with his placement of soteriology, beginning from "The Personal Dimension" to "The Communal Dimension," under the general heading "The Coming of the New Creation," speaks the same language.[32]

An Orientation to Part 2

Recall that in the beginning of part 1, the vision of a holistic trinitarian Christian account of the work of the Spirit was set up as the task for this volume. Therein, the interrelated "spheres" of the divine Spirit's workings were investigated at the following interrelated levels:

- the Spirit in the triune divine life (chap. 2)
- the Spirit in the cosmos as Creator Spirit (chap. 3)
- the Spirit and spiritual powers (chap. 4)
- the Spirit among religions (chap. 5)
- the Spirit in history, culture, and society (chap. 6)

And now, in part 2, the focus will be on the Spirit in the personal and communal life of believers (chaps. 7–14).

The next chapter (chap. 8) will pick up the investigation of chapter 5 and focus on liberative and salvific visions in four other living faiths — a topic routinely and systemically ignored by all Christian *ordo salutis* discussions. Although, similar to part 1 (and the rest of the five-volume project), interfaith

---

29. Shults and Sandage, *Faces of Forgiveness,* p. 156, emphasis in original.

30. Gutiérrez, *A Theology of Liberation,* p. 97, cited in Shults and Sandage, *Faces of Forgiveness,* p. 156; so also, Cone, *God of the Oppressed,* p. 210.

31. McClendon, *Doctrine,* p. 105.

32. Finger, *A Contemporary Anabaptist Theology,* part 2.

exercises appear throughout the development of Christian theology, an initial outlining of Jewish, Muslim, Buddhist, and Hindu "soteriologies" will be presented before the detailed treatment of Christian views. This brief discussion presupposes the fairly detailed discussion of their pneumatologies in part 1. Of course, I do the presentation of other faith traditions as an outsider — but I also do it as an interested student who wishes to understand their best and formative ideas as well as possible.

In the traditional *ordo salutis*, the topics investigated in chapter 9, titled "The Divine Favor and Invitation for Eternal Fellowship," include the doctrine of election and calling. The goal of the chapter is to help get us beyond the centuries-long impasse in the understanding of how the loving and gracious God initiates the process of salvation and seeks a personal relationship with men and women. After careful study of the historical debates, a robustly trinitarian theology of election will be provided that steers a radical middle course between the Scylla of Pelagianism and the Charybdis of extreme Augustinian Calvinism. This constructive proposal is also put in dialogue with views of freedom, election, and calling in other faith traditions.

The topics of conversion, repentance, and forgiveness of sins will be radically recast in chapter 10, "(Re-)Turning to God — and to the Neighbor," as they are investigated not only in light of the rich discussions in Christian tradition but also in light of sociopolitical issues (conversion), cultural diversity (repentance), and the wide interdisciplinary study in psychology and other behavioral sciences (forgiveness). Similarly, each topic engages Jewish, Muslim, Buddhist, and Hindu teachings.

The longest chapter of part 2 is 11, "One with God: Rightwising, Renewal, and Integrity of Life," whose themes include justification, sanctification, and deification. The chapter seeks to provide a new and fresh ecumenical proposal in order to help Christian churches move beyond the soteriological impasse. It suggests that it is possible for Eastern Orthodox, Roman Catholic, and Anglican-Protestant churches (including Methodist, Anabaptist, and Pentecostal) to embrace a wide convergence concerning how, in union with the triune God, men and women are "pronounced" and made righteous/deified, in order to grow into the likeness of the same God.

To correct the astonishing lacuna in all presentations of *ordo salutis*, both traditional and contemporary, chapter 12, titled "Healing, Restoration, and Empowerment," breaks new ground in systematic-constructive theology by developing a theology of healing, restoration, and human flourishing, as well as an ecumenical theology of "Spirit baptism" with a view to empowerment, energizing, and gifting for life, service, and ministry. Because healing is a common theme among religions, our discussion of it will engage insights and challenges from other faith traditions as well.

Another standard feature of soteriologies is their individualistic slant. To combat and correct that, chapter 13 picks up the discussion from the last chapter of part 1 (chap. 6) with a focus on the Spirit's role in history and society and expands the horizons of the salvific vision to encompass the themes of "reconciliation, liberation, and peacebuilding," to quote the chapter title. It deals with reconciliatory implications of the Christian gospel at communal, societal, and (inter)national levels, and so also points toward discussions in ecclesiology focused on the church's mission in the world.

The short "Epilogue: The Faithfulness of God and the End of Human Yearning" (chap. 14) develops the last themes in soteriologies, namely, perseverance of saints and their glorification. At the same time, the chapter seeks to build a link between soteriology and eschatology with an emphasis (again!) on a holistic vision in which personal, communal, and cosmic renewal in God's new creation is the ultimate goal.

8. Visions of "Salvation" and Liberation among Religions

Introduction: The Topic of "Salvation" in Interfaith Context

Two caveats are needed to put this chapter in perspective. The first has to do with the topic itself: salvation.[1] How justified is it to apply the Christian notion of salvation to other religions, particularly Asiatic religions? Even among Abrahamic faiths, the question of salvation is utterly complex.[2] It seems to me, however, that not only is it appropriate to use that term, but the term is also necessary to ensure that dialogue is not stalled among religions. As long as careful discernment of differences among religions is kept in mind, it is legitimate to consider the ultimate goals of religions using a concept particular to one religion, in this case to Christianity. In other words, comparative theology should not seek to minimize or soften differences when they are truly perceived, but neither should it fail to seek potential commonalities.[3]

Although it would be absurd to expect to paint a meaningful picture of the soteriology of four different religions in one short chapter — even one religion requires more space! — it is possible to sketch a "vision," a perspective, an outline of key convictions. That is what this chapter is all about; before each later chapter engages in more detail relevant to elements of soteriology in other religions, it is useful to consider the big picture of salvation in Jewish, Islamic,

---

1. Coward, *Sin and Salvation*, p. 3.
2. See Cragg, "God and Salvation (an Islamic Study)," p. 156; so also the convert to Islam, Muhammad Asad, "The Spirit in Islam," p. 53.
3. So also, Coward, *Sin and Salvation*, p. 4.

Buddhist, and Hindu traditions. While the investigation of hamartiology (the doctrine of sin) and Christology (the person and work of the Savior) would of course be needed to outline a vision of liberation, that work is not done in this volume; the reader is referred to relevant sections in other volumes in this series.

Any interfaith conversation brings to the fore the question of the conditions for understanding between two different horizons and perspectives. The German hermeneutical philosopher H.-G. Gadamer has reminded us that all true "understanding is ultimately self-understanding."[4] Rather than external, understanding is an "internal" process that also shapes us. Knowledge in the humanities in particular is a process not between "subject" and "object" but rather between two "subjects" whose horizons of (self-)understanding cohere and mutually influence each other. In relation to interfaith dialogue, this means that, on the one hand, I as a Christian should not — and cannot — imagine putting aside my convictions, and that, on the other hand, those very convictions are in the process of being reshaped, sometimes even radically altered.[5] "In understanding we are drawn into an event of truth and arrive, as it were, too late, if we want to know what we are supposed to believe."[6]

Unlike the rest of our discussion, this orientation does not attempt any engagement with Christian tradition. Again, to honor the integrity and "big picture" of the soteriological/liberative goals of each tradition, their respective doctrines and emphases are set forth as accurately and as sympathetically as an outsider ever is able to do.

Salvation as Redemption and Submission in Abrahamic Faiths

Somewhat counterintuitively, the Semitic faiths do not share a unified conception of human misery. The traditional Christian doctrine of original sin (however that is formulated) is not shared by Jewish and Islamic traditions. They understand sin in terms of "incurring the 'punishments' or disadvantages of ignorance of God, lack of self-control, and short-sighted restriction of moral concern." These two Abrahamic traditions insist on human freedom to choose

---

4. Gadamer, *Truth and Method*, p. 251. For reminding me of Gadamer's importance to interfaith conversation, I wish to acknowledge Sutton, "Salvation after Nagarjuna," pp. 2-16.

5. See Sutton, "Salvation after Nagarjuna," pp. 4-5.

6. Gadamer, *Truth and Method*, p. 484; for understanding as an event, see also, pp. xxii, 157, 478.

and responsibility for the choice.[7] Notwithstanding these important differences from Christian theology, it is also important to underline the significant common basis. All three Abrahamic faiths place humanity before God, and in that light assess what is wrong with us. Though somewhat differently, they all consider the "origin" of sinfulness in the deviation of humanity from the Creator. Hence, not surprisingly, all three scriptural traditions share the common narrative of the Fall and its consequences, even when their interpretations differ from each other quite dramatically. Jewish and Muslim interpretations share more in common than Christian ones do with the other two. Because sin is ultimately deviation from God, it takes God to fix the problem, notwithstanding graced human response and collaboration.

Redemption and Sin in Jewish Theology

Instead of original sin, the Jewish (rabbinic) tradition speaks of two tendencies or urges in every human being, namely, *yetzer ha tov* and *yetzer ha ra'*, "for good" and "for evil." While the "inclination" to evil in itself is not evil but rather a necessary impulse of life, what matters is which of the two inclinations is the guiding force in life. Hence, the main term for repentance from evil is *teshuvav*, literally "turning" (to God).[8] This is not to undermine the seriousness of the sinful tendency, which is "not an isolated act, but a state of consciousness, so that one sin leads to others." Indeed, it is the goal of the Yahwist account to highlight the wide diffusion of moral evil (Gen. 4; 6:5-12; 8:21; 9:20-27; 11:1-9).[9] Yet no type of "original sin" is affirmed.[10]

Rather than "salvation," Jewish theology speaks typically of "redemption"; a key idea in the term has to do with deliverance.[11] Consider how often the term "redeemer" (and "to redeem") appears in the most common Jewish

---

7. Ward, *Religion and Human Nature*, p. 175.

8. Jacobs, *A Jewish Theology*, p. 243. See further, Kepnes, "'Turn Us to You and We Shall Return.'"

9. Cohon, *Essays in Jewish Theology*, p. 225; see also, Jacobs, *A Jewish Theology*, pp. 246-47.

10. *2 Baruch* (54:15, 19; 19:3; 48:42-43; 59:2) teaches that even after Adam's sin, which brought about death, each new generation has to choose their own path. For details, see chap. 15 in *Creation and Humanity*.

11. Coward, *Sin and Salvation*, p. 5. The term appears about 130 times in the OT and is derived from two roots, *pdh*, used originally in commercial law, and *g'l*, stemming originally from family law. Leslie et al., "Redemption," p. 151.

daily prayer, the Amidah.[12] While not limited to national deliverance, the idea is present in most Jewish traditions even beyond Zionism.[13] Similar to creation, which is the work of the past, present, and future, redemption covers all tenses.[14]

What about faith and belief? According to Israel Abrahams, in the Jewish "Bible there are no articles of faith or dogmas in the Christian or Islamic sense of the terms." Rather than invitation to believe (in an intellectual sense), the biblical call is for faithfulness, which can be used of both God and the human person. The reason for the absence of catechism (in the Christian sense) is the emphasis on conduct and ethics. That is not to deny the presence of theological reflection and doctrines in later Judaism. Those came, however, largely because of apologetic need and external pressure. The Shema (Deut. 6:4) is of course the basis and foundation of Jewish faith. Monotheism is more than a belief; it is the central thrust of Jewish (and Islamic) faith tradition.[15]

What unites Jewish and Christian soteriologies is that salvation comes through the Messiah. Ironically, however, it is in the vastly different interpretation of the meaning of the Messiah where the deepest differences among the two traditions come to the fore. The objection to the Christian Messiah was classically formulated by Martin Buber: the Messiah could not possibly have come because "[w]e know more deeply, more truly, that world history has not been turned upside down to its very foundations — that the world is not yet redeemed. We *sense* its unredeemedness."[16] Obviously, behind the Jewish no to the Christian claim for the arrival of the Messiah is a different concept of salvation. Rightly or wrongly, Jewish theology considers the Christian version of redemption "happening in the spiritual sphere, and in what is invisible."[17] Furthermore, different from the Christian messianic hopes, Jewish theology discerns the coming of Messiah as the fulfillment of all hopes for redemption, whereas Christian tradition — slowly and painfully, as the NT eschatology shows — came to understand the coming of

---

12. English translation can be found, e.g., in http://www.chabad.org/library/article_cdo/aid/867674/jewish/Translation.htm (7/20/2014); for comments, see Coward, *Sin and Salvation*, pp. 5-6.

13. For details, see Leslie et al., "Redemption," pp. 152, 155.

14. For details, see Neusner, *The Way of Torah*, p. 14; Coward, *Sin and Salvation*, p. 6.

15. Abrahams, Haberman, and Manekin, "Belief," pp. 290-91 (p. 290).

16. Buber, *Der Jude und Sein Judentum*, p. 562, emphasis in original, cited in Moltmann, *Way of Jesus Christ*, p. 29. See also, Kogan, *Opening the Covenant*, pp. 90-95.

17. Scholem, "Zum Verständnis der messianischen Idee," p. 7, cited in Moltmann, *Way of Jesus Christ*, p. 29.

Messiah in two stages.[18] But even then, the role of the Messiah in Judaism is to serve as the *agent* of reconciliation rather than the one who reconciles; only Yahweh can do that.[19]

Although the sacrificial system is part of the Jewish tradition, the Christian idea of vicarious atonement, on which the salvation of the world is based, is not part of Jewish theology because "the problem of sin had already been dealt with in the Torah."[20] In addition to the lack of a doctrine of original sin and the Fall after the Christian interpretation that necessitates divine atonement through the death of Messiah, the main reason for this is that the transcendent goal of salvation in the afterlife is not at all as central as in Christianity.[21] Particularly in Talmudic traditions, "[t]he sages know nothing of a miraculous redemption of the soul by external means. There is no failing in man, whether collectively or as an individual, which requires special divine intervention and which cannot be remedied, with the guidance of the Torah, by man himself."[22] (Only in mystical Kabbalah are the "inner" aspects of redemption prominent.)[23] Following the Torah and its commandments, as the chosen people, and thus testifying to God's unity and holiness, is the way of "salvation" in Judaism.[24] Importantly, "[t]he prophets emphasized that what the Torah required from people was not just religious observance but also moral behavior — indeed that both morality and religion form a unity in the teaching of the Pentateuch as they do in the nature of God."[25] The "new obedience" required of the people of God is not based on sacrifice but on the covenant. Covenant will give true knowledge of God, as God's will "would be engraved in the very heart of the people. . . . Thus shall the knowledge of God become the common possession of all Israel and through Israel all the nations of the world."[26]

What about contemporary Jewish theology? Notwithstanding great diversity, this much can be said: "In modern Jewish thought redemption has been viewed as referring to the eventual triumph of good over evil, to the striv-

---

18. See further, Moltmann, *Way of Jesus Christ*, pp. 30, 16-18.

19. Lyden, "Atonement in Judaism and Christianity," pp. 50-54.

20. Kogan, *Opening the Covenant*, p. 116.

21. For supporting authoritative statements, see Urbach, *The Sages*, p. 679; see also, the whole chapter on redemption (pp. 649-92).

22. Leslie et al., "Redemption," p. 152.

23. See Leslie et al., "Redemption," p. 153.

24. Kogan, *Opening the Covenant*, pp. 11-13.

25. Coward, *Sin and Salvation*, p. 7.

26. Epste, *Judaism*, p. 61, cited in Coward, *Sin and Salvation*, p. 8.

ing of individuals to self-fulfillment, to the achievement of social reforms, and also in terms of the reestablishment of a sovereign Jewish state."[27] Importantly, even some leading Orthodox thinkers such as Joseph B. Soloveichik, for whom redemption is linked with faith and *mitzvot* (commandments), include in the concept "the idea that the human capability of renewal and self-transformation manifests itself especially in times of human distress"; the human person's control over himself or herself is a sign of redemption.[28]

What about the youngest Abrahamic tradition and its salvific vision?

Submission and Ignorance in Islam

Islam's understanding of the human condition is closer to that of Judaism than to that of Christianity. While acknowledging the beauty of humanity as the creation of God, it does not endorse a perfect state in Paradise along the lines of (older) Christian tradition. Furthermore, while taking a very realistic account of the current state of humanity, no trace of original sin or "total depravity"[29] is endorsed. Qur'an 95:4-6 is representative: "Verily We created man in the best of forms. Then, We reduced him to the lowest of the low, except those who believe and perform righteous deeds, for they shall have an unfailing reward."[30] Whatever weaknesses the Fall brought about — there are no fewer than three accounts of Adam and Eve in the Qur'an (20:115-27; 7:10-25; 2:30-38)[31] — the idea of the lostness of humanity because of sin is missing (without denying the otherwise negative results of disobedience). The closest parallel to the idea of "lostness" is the ignorance of the right way and unwillingness to submit to Allah, acts that are conscious choices.[32]

Because Muslims categorically reject the doctrine of original sin and the radical sinfulness of all, they do not envision redemption in the way Christian tradition does, namely, as a divine gift.[33] There is absolutely no doctrine of

27. Leslie at al., "Redemption," pp. 154-55 (p. 154).

28. Leslie et al., "Redemption," p. 155.

29. See Iqbal, *Reconstruction of Religious Thought in Islam*, p. 85.

30. In a number of places the Qur'an also speaks of weaknesses, frailties, and liabilities of humanity: Q 4:28; 10:12; 14:34; 16:4; 17:11; 33:72; 70:19; 96:6; 103:2; etc. For details, see Scudder, "The Qur'an's Evaluation of Human Nature," p. 75.

31. For details, see *Creation and Humanity*, chap. 15.

32. See Siddiqui, "Being Human in Islam," p. 21.

33. See Zebiri, *Muslims and Christians Face to Face*, pp. 216-17; Moser, "Cataclysmic Fall or a Fumbling Slip?" pp. 231-38.

atonement in Islam after the Christian teaching. Indeed, as does Judaism — and if possible, even more vehemently — Islam rejects the Christian idea of salvation stemming from divine sacrifice. Muslim theology has a hard time intuiting why the justice and fairness of God would ever require a sacrifice and shedding of blood. Allah is of course sovereignly free to forgive (or not to forgive) apart from any such requirements. And on the basis of Qur'anic teaching, it may be legitimate to infer that no one else can "pay" for the sins of others, not even Allah.[34] No need to add that in Islam there is hardly anything like what Christianity names "redemption" or "regeneration."[35]

This is not to deny the presence of grace and mercy in Islam. Even a cursory look at the Qur'an shows the prevalence of the idea of Allah as merciful.[36] Consider this important sura: "[W]ere it not for Allah's grace upon you and His mercy, not one of you would have ever been pure, but Allah purifies whom He pleases" (24:21). That mercy, however, does not translate in Islam into an idea of "justification by faith." Everything is about submitting to the will of Allah, particularly by observing the Five Pillars (shahadah, salat,[37] sawm, zakat, hajj). Access to Paradise will be granted as a "reward for what they used to do" (56:24). "Allah has prepared . . . forgiveness and a mighty reward" for those who "submit" and "obey"; obedience includes almsgiving and fasting (33:35).[38] Where the mercy of Allah comes to the fore is in the completion beyond the balancing act of good and bad as evidenced in this statement (6.160): "Whoever brings a good deed, he shall have ten like it, and whoever brings an evil deed, he shall be recompensed only with the like of it, and they shall not be dealt with unjustly."[39] While one's efforts and good deeds certainly are required in getting access to Paradise, God's mercy is necessary as a surplus. It is in this respect that the numerous references to the merciful nature of Allah — indeed, in the first line of each sura of the Qur'an[40] — have to be interpreted. According to the Islamic tradition (Hadith), this principle applied even to the Prophet himself.[41]

In sum: "salvation" in Islam means simply submission to Allah. But the

---

34. Q 6:164; see also, 2:233.

35. Robson, "Aspects of the Qur'anic Doctrine of Salvation," p. 217.

36. See further, Cragg, "God and Salvation (an Islamic Study)," pp. 155-66.

37. On the importance of prayer, see al-Ghazali, *Inner Dimensions of Islamic Worship*, p. 19.

38. For many more such references, see Anees, "Salvation and Suicide," pp. 275-76.

39. Similarly, e.g., 64:17. See also, Martindale, "A Muslim-Christian Dialogue," pp. 69-71.

40. The only exception is sura 9.

41. Anees, "Salvation and Suicide," p. 276.

fact that salvation ultimately depends on whether or not one wishes to submit does not mean that therefore believing is marginalized.[42] One cannot submit if one persists in ignorance of the revealed will of God.[43] Belief goes hand in hand with repentance (Q 3:16-17; 19:60) and "the works of righteousness," that is, good deeds (4:57).[44] While submission to Allah is a personal matter, in Islam it is also integrally linked with the *ummah* (community) and confession of faith.[45] In its widest sense the "total submission of human will to the will of God" is expressed in three forms:

1. Through *islam,* which determines the institutionalized way of worshiping God.
2. Through *iman,* which is faith in God, his angels, his prophets, his books — all the revealed books of God — and the last day, that is, the day of resurrection.
3. Through *ahsan,* which refers to good actions, or righteous living, and which the Prophet interpreted as worshiping God "as though you see him, for if you do not see him he nonetheless sees you." So to be a true *muslim* (that is, to be in "submission") to God, whether you are a Christian, a Jew, a Hindu, a Buddhist, or whatever, is always to live in the presence of God.[46]

Although the technical term "salvation" *(najāt)* occurs only once in the Qur'an (40:41), the verbal from which it derives is fairly common, particularly denoting deliverance from dangers of various kinds.[47] Another common word is *furqan,* which appears frequently in the Qur'an (2:53; 2:185; 3:4; 8:29; 8:42; 21:48; 25:1). Its basic meaning (beyond salvation) is "distinction" or "criterion" (between right and wrong).[48] Yet another important soteriological term is *falah* (success). The main point is not only that success may happen both in

---

42. The six mandatory tenets are the unity of God, divine predestination, angels, Qur'an, prophets, and last day. For details, see Muhammad, *A Compendium of Muslim Theology,* pp. 3-15.

43. See Coward, *Sin and Salvation,* p. 63.

44. Q 4:57; similarly 4:122.

45. For details, see Dharmaraj, "Sin and Salvation," p. 54; Greear, "*Theosis* and Muslim Evangelism," pp. 139-41.

46. Ayoub, "Trinity Day Lectures," p. 8.

47. Robson, "Aspects of the Qur'anic Doctrine of Salvation," p. 205. See further, Nickel, "Islam and Salvation," pp. 4-5; Crollius, "Salvation in the Qur'an," pp. 125-39.

48. "Furqan, al-," in *The Oxford Dictionary of Islam.*

this life and in the life to come, but that ultimately the human person is faced either with a positive outcome, success, or a negative one, failure.[49]

While deliverance from sin does not have to be excluded from the Islamic vision of salvation, it is fair to say that deliverance from eternal punishment, often depicted as "fire"[50] of hell, seems to be at the forefront.[51] Indeed, "'[s]alvation' in the *Quran* is not the bestowal of a new creation, nor an act of power and victory over sin and death; rather, it is primarily an escape from judgment and entry into paradise."[52]

What about "assurance of salvation"? Although Qur'anic promises to those who believe and do good deeds seem assuring, there are also warnings throughout not to fall away.[53] Although one may lose salvation, every believer can also trust Allah's "guidance" (an almost technical term in the Qur'an referring to the divine help for believers, as in 4:51; 6:157; 17:84; 28:49; 67:22; and so forth).[54] Ultimately, Allah is absolutely sovereign in his dealings with humanity, and therefore the Christian (Calvinistic) idea of the "perseverance of the saints" is foreign to Islam.

Like other faith traditions' mystical movements — and unlike the "text-book" official teaching — Sufism focuses on personal devotion and repentance. As argued in part 1, Sufi mysticism has an amazingly wide appeal among the ordinary faithful, probably influencing deeply more than half of all Muslims. In their spirituality the idea of union with God — theologically a most scandalous idea in light of normal Muslim teaching — comes to the forefront:

> The Sufi doctrine of a direct and personal experience with God passed by the claim of the orthodox theologians that they were the guardians of the truth, in exclusive possession of the science of theology and law. *But they could not stem the tide of Sufism, for it seemed to fill a great need in the soul of many Muslims.* Finally the great Muslim theologian, Al Ghazzali, managed to combine orthodoxy and Sufism into one system of thought, in which he retained all the tenets of orthodoxy and at the same time made Sufi thought respectable.[55]

49. Denny, "Salvation in the Qur'an," p. 206; Coward, *Sin and Salvation*, p. 60.

50. See, e.g., Q 2:24, 39, 80-81, 119, 126, 167, 174-75, 201, 217, 221, 257, 266, 275.

51. Robson, "Aspects of the Qur'anic Doctrine of Salvation," pp. 205-6.

52. Greear, "*Theosis* and Muslim Evangelism," p. 130; similarly, R. Miller, "Muslim Doctrine of Salvation," p. 145.

53. Q 6:82; see also, 4:13. Robson, "Aspects of the Qur'anic Doctrine of Salvation," p. 213.

54. For details, see Robson, "Aspects of the Qur'anic Doctrine of Salvation," pp. 215-26.

55. R. Miller, "Muslim Doctrine of Salvation," p. 188, emphasis in original, cited in

No wonder some interesting parallels have been discerned between the Christian doctrine of *theosis* and the Sufi pursuit of union with God.[56]

We have outlined briefly the ways of redemption and submission in two Abrahamic faiths, and it is time to delve into visions of liberation in two Asiatic traditions. We will begin with Hinduism and then focus on Buddhism.

The Human Condition in Asiatic Traditions: Diagnosis and Solution

The Christian philosopher-theologian Stephen T. Davis has offered an interesting comparison between "karma" and "grace," archetypes of a sort of two religious orientations. He does that by abstracting from religions such as Hinduism and Buddhism on the one hand and Christianity and Judaism on the other hand.[57] While different in many ways, these two systems of salvation — Asiatic and Abrahamic — share some foundational similarities, including the view that the deepest human need is spiritual, that moral right and wrong are in some sense "objective" realities, and that justice is a transcendent reality beyond this world.[58] The differences, however, are great and many, argues Davis. The karmic religions reject the idea of a personal God and rather assume an impersonal absolute "reality." The karmic view is based on a strict cause-and-effect formula. It envisions "salvation"[59] as a release from the karmic cycle as one progresses in the path of "enlightenment." Basically, karma attributes the human predicament to lack of awareness or insight. In contrast, Davis continues, grace religions assume a personal God in whose image human beings have been created and to whom they are responsible. The initiative of salvation comes from God, apart from one's own merits. Only God is able to resolve the main human dilemma: sin stemming from the Fall.[60]

How reliable is this juxtaposition of these two religious family traditions? Although, as explained in the introduction to this chapter, no attempt is made

---

Greear, "*Theosis* and Muslim Evangelism," p. 162. A highly useful and accessible presentation of all things Sufi by Dr. Alan Godlas of the University of Georgia titled "Sufism — Sufis — Sufi Orders" is at http://islam.uga.edu/Sufism.html (7/29/2014).

56. Nasr, "Prayer of the Heart in Hesychasm and Sufism," pp. 195-203.

57. Cf. Bloom, *Shinran's Gospel of Pure Grace*.

58. S. T. Davis, "Karma or Grace," pp. 237-38.

59. Of course, the notion of "salvation" itself is a grace-based concept, owing to Christianity, Judaism, and perhaps Islam.

60. Even though my exposition is based on S. T. Davis, "Karma or Grace," pp. 238-42, I have also expanded it.

to provide dialogue here, tentatively one can say that, on the one hand, there certainly are foundational differences of orientations between Abrahamic and Asiatic faiths but that, on the other hand, the borderlines are elusive and at times cross each other. Consider Alfred Bloom's striking book title discussing Pure Land tradition, *Shinran's Gospel of Pure Grace,* and Hinduologist Bradley J. Malkovsky's *The Role of Divine Grace in the Soteriology of Śaṃkarācārya.* On the Abrahamic side, think of the centrality of ethical pursuit and "works" in the soteriology of both Judaism and Islam. And so forth.

The only meaningful way to proceed in the investigation is to pursue with patience the painstaking path of comparative theological exercises. A more detailed look at representative faith traditions' key scriptural teachings and formulated doctrines, one by one, may provide raw materials for careful dialogue. Let us begin with the Hindu visions of liberation.

Ignorance, "Superimposition," and Moksa: *Release in Hindu Vision(s)*

Any attempt to give a generic description of Hindu views of liberation must acknowledge the virtual impossibility of that task for well-known reasons such as that the whole nomenclature "Hinduism" is a modern umbrella concept coined in the West, that it has virtually no binding doctrinal or creedal basis,[61] and that there is such an unbelievable diversity of views, local beliefs and rites, and so forth. With these caveats clearly in mind, we first must consider the human condition. It is clear that no concept of sin, let alone a Fall, after Abrahamic tradition can be found in any Hindu movements. That said, there is a deep intuition that something is wrong with us!

The standard for what is right and true among all Hindu movements is *dharma,* the "duty," the correct way of life, including all activities and spheres of life. "Sin,"[62] as its opposite, is *adharma.*[63] The ultimate beginning point for the investigation of human misery in Hinduism — as in Buddhism — however, is not the analysis of wrong deeds, behavior, or attitudes. *Adharma* belongs to the wider context in Hindu philosophy of human "bondage" to *avidya,* "ignorance" (called by Shaivists *anava,* "congenital ignorance concerning the ultimate"). Ignorance makes one cling to *māyā,* "fiction," and thus subject

---

61. Probably the only "required" tenet of faith has to do with the transmigration of souls. Coward, *Sin and Salvation,* p. 89.

62. Similarly to Buddhism, Hinduism has worked out lists of sins to avoid, Bhagavad-Gita 16.2; see also, Klostermaier, *Survey of Hinduism,* pp. 168-72.

63. See Khan, *Concept of Dharma in Valmiki Ramayana,* p. 34.

to effects of karma, leading to rebirths over and over again. Only with the removal of this "ignorance" can the soul's essential nature as pure spirit be restored.[64] This is the general principle that applies to most Hindu traditions. What is distinctive in the *advaita* version involves the concept of "superimposition" *(adhyâsa)*: the human predicament stems "from this wrong knowledge" (nescience) that is not able "to distinguish the two entities (object and subject) and their respective attributes, although they are absolutely distinct, but to superimpose upon each the characteristic nature and the attributes of the other, and thus, coupling the Real and the Unreal."[65] As a result of this superimposition (that is, assigning the attributes of the self to the object, and vice versa), humans envision themselves as finite, vulnerable, and decaying (thus not identical with the changeless, eternal Brahman) and — even worse — attribute finite characteristics to the Absolute.[66] The Christian reader, however, must be reminded that there is absolutely no sudden "fall" either in the life of humanity at large or in every human person's life; "rather, ignorance is the root cause of the very process of beginningless transmigration and so is a congenital inheritance carrying with it accumulated results generated by innumerable actions performed over countless lifetimes"[67] in the samsaric cycle of rebirths. Furthermore, unlike in theistic forms of Hinduism, in *advaita* there is "[n]o God to be afraid of."[68] Here is a profound difference between the diagnoses of nontheistic Hinduisms (as well as Theravada Buddhism) and those of Abrahamic traditions.[69]

What about grace in Hindu doctrine? Something similar to "grace" can be found in theistic Hinduism and, indeed, is a steady part of the *bhakti* tradition, particularly in the Bhagavad Gita.[70] Consider this oft-quoted verse (18.58): "When your mind becomes fixed on Me, you shall overcome all difficulties by My grace."[71] Regarding the pursuit of salvation, theistic forms of Hinduism such as Vaishnavism (whose most famous philosopher is the qual-

---

64. See further, Klostermaier, *Survey of Hinduism,* chap. 13.

65. Sankara, *Commentary on Vedanta Sutras,* part I, 1.1.1; *SBE* 34:4. On ignorance, see *Brahma-Sutra-Bhasya* I.iv.3, p. 249.

66. I am helped here by Thatamanil, *Immanent Divine,* chap. 2 (although I do not agree with all of his interpretations of Sankara; see chap. 15 in *Creation and Humanity*).

67. Thatamanil, *Immanent Divine,* p. 36.

68. Vivekananda, "Is Vedanta the Future Religion?" in *Complete Works,* vol. 8 (n.p.).

69. In *Creation and Humanity* (chap. 15) I discuss widely the well-known problems (and internal self-contradictions) of Sankara's analysis.

70. See further, Painadath, "Integrated Spirituality of the Bhagavad Gita," pp. 305-24.

71. Similarly 18.62.

ified *advaita* Ramanuja) emphasize *bhakti,* devotion to a personal god (which may often be locally determined).[72] Sri Sarvepalli Radhakrishnan reminds us that notwithstanding many differences in doctrine, all Vaishnava schools "agreed in rejecting the conception of māyā, in regarding God as personal, and the soul as possessed of inalienable individuality, finding its true being not in an absorption in the Supreme but in fellowship with him."[73] Differently from *advaita,* Bhagavad Gita clearly assumes a relationship to a personal God. According to Paulos M. Gregorios, the Gita teaches that the personal God is above the impersonal Brahman, whereas in the Upanishads and in the Vedanta system, especially in Sankara, the personal God is only a permissible form in which to conceive an ultimate reality that in fact is purely without any attributes at all.[74] Gregorios supports his thesis with the well-known passage from the Gita: "Setting aside all noble deeds, just surrender completely to the will of God (with firm faith and loving contemplation). I shall liberate you from all sins (or bonds of karma). Do not grieve."[75] In Sankara, however, the human person's own initiative and commitment to the pursuit of liberative knowledge are the key.[76] For Sankara's advaitic vision, "the nature of liberation is a state of oneness with Brahman."[77]

In sum, although the concept of grace and divine benevolence is not completely foreign to Hindu traditions, the clear emphasis is on human striving and quest. The key is the enlightenment insight into the true nature of reality.[78] Indeed, the quest for final liberation might be the most distinctive feature of all Hindu paths of salvation.[79] Rather than "salvation," the common term *moksa,* "liberation," is used in Hinduism. It is safe to say that, by and large, Hindu movements "aim at the practical end of salvation. The systems mean by release (moksa) the recovery by the soul of its natural integrity, from which sin and error drive it." Because ignorance is the main problem, an in-

---

72. For challenges in Ramanuja's concept of grace, see Carman, *Majesty and Meekness,* pp. 94-96.

73. Radhakrishnan, *Indian Philosophy,* 2:661-62; for the importance of *bhakti* to Ramanuja, see also, pp. 703-5.

74. Gregorios, *Religion and Dialogue,* p. 68.

75. Bhagavad Gita 18.66. One can also refer to passages such as 11:44 and 18:56.

76. It is highly noteworthy that according to Karingadayil (*From Darkness to Light,* p. 188), so far very little investigation has been conducted into Sankara's view of grace. The only main study is Malkovsky, *The Role of Divine Grace in the Soteriology of Śaṃkarācārya.*

77. Radhakrishnan, *Indian Philosophy,* 2:639.

78. See, e.g., Isa Upanishad 5.9.

79. See further, Organ, *Hindu Quest for the Perfection of Man,* p. 5.

sight or "realization" is needed for release.[80] The ultimate goal of all sacred scriptures — whose divine authority, particularly that of the Vedas, is strongly affirmed[81] — is to help gain this liberative insight. In Hinduism, *mukti* can be experienced either in this life or in the life to come. In an emancipated person after death, all desire has come to an end.[82] The still-living liberated person (called *jivan-mukti*) can be called a "saint," using wider religious language.[83]

By now it is evident that there are differing diagnoses of the human condition among various Hindu movements. Hence, the tradition provides various types of paths with distinctive emphases. While not exhaustive in any way, a typical textbook presentation knows three *margas*: one focused on devotion *(bhakti)*, one on knowledge *(jnana)*, and one on effort (or work, *karma)*.[84] For the common folks following theistic Vaishnavism in its wide denominational and geographic diversity (as well as other less-known theistic interpretations), the devotional *bhakti-marga* is the way of salvation.[85] The teaching of the Gita is the guide here: "But, to those who worship Me as the personal God, renouncing all actions to Me; setting Me as their supreme goal, and meditating on Me with single minded devotion; I swiftly become their savior, from the world that is the ocean of death and transmigration, whose thoughts are set on Me, O Arjuna. Therefore, focus your mind on Me alone and let your intellect dwell upon Me through meditation and contemplation. Thereafter you shall certainly come to Me" (12.6-8).

In the Bhagavad Gita, the devotion is often focused on Krishna, the most important *avatara* of Vishnu (discussed in chap. 10 of *Christ and Reconciliation*).[86] Although based on the Gita, the way of devotion and love of God

80. Radhakrishnan, *Indian Philosophy*, 2:27. For a lucid discussion, see also, Sivaraman, "The Meaning of *Moksha*," pp. 2-11.

81. For a detailed discussion, see chap. 8 in *Trinity and Revelation*.

82. Dasgupta, *History of Indian Philosophy*, 2:245. On *moksa* during one's lifetime, see Sankara, *Brahma Sutra* 4.1.15, 19.

83. For a detailed discussion, see Dasgupta, *History of Indian Philosophy*, 2:245-72. For a shorter, accessible account, see S. Gupta, "Jivanmukti," pp. 4925-26. While not affirmed by all Hindu traditions (as evident in the important *Yoga Vasistha* epic), it is still the typical view.

84. For a reliable, accessible account, see Klostermaier, *Survey of Hinduism*, chap. 9 *(karma)*, chap. 12 *(jnana)*, and chap. 15 *(bhakti)*. The rest of part 2 of the book includes details on each of those.

85. Majumdar, *Bhakti Renaissance*, p. 159. As practical tools for devotion, Gita (2.23, 39) suggests yoga techniques. The ancient yoga-guide widely used in *bhakti* devotion is Patanjali's *Yoga Sutras*, written about 200 C.E.

86. For a useful discussion (in dialogue with Christology), see Largen, *Baby Krishna, Infant Christ*.

is not unknown in Vedic scriptures either. Recall that the very first hymn of Rig Veda, the oldest scripture, speaks of the devotion to and intimacy with the Lord. While in general *the notion of bhakti* is hardly mentioned, some of the Upanishads clearly teach it (Katha Upanishad, Mundaka Upanishad, and Vetasvatara Upanishad particularly). "It is an affective participation of the soul in the divine nature, a most intense devotion to God, by which one tries to unite oneself with the supreme."[87] Although the strict *advaita* of Sankara prefers other paths,[88] in the qualified *advaita* of Ramanuja, Vishnu devotion *bhakti* is an important part.[89] It is rightly said that Ramanuja helped to save (folk) Hinduism from "philosophers-only religion" and to connect it with the rich and variegated Vishnu and Shiva theistic spiritualities.[90]

On the contemporary scene, *bhakti* devotion is widely known in the West through the work of Swami Bhaktivedanta (d. 1977) and his International Society for Krishna Consciousness.[91] According to him, Krishna created all humans from his own nature, and his "grace is there waiting, but it is the duty of the devotee to remove the obstacles to Krishna's grace so that Krishna consciousness will result. One must surrender and engage in devotional service" helped by detailed practical exercises.[92]

If *bhakti* is for common folks, on the other end of the spectrum, among the most philosophically minded thinkers, particularly within the strict *advaita* of Sankara, *jnana-bhakti* is the way to pursue release from superimposition and ignorance. Indeed, "One can never think of Advaita without leaving a note on the concept of knowledge. It is a system built upon the foundation of knowledge, both of God and of the self as sources of enlightenment. The path of knowledge is the best Advaitic approach to the realization of God. The end and goal of all morality is jñāna or realization."[93] This kind of liberative knowledge that discerns the absolute unity is based on the scriptures

87. Karingadayil, *From Darkness to Light,* pp. 158-59; for a great discussion, see Majumdar, *Bhakti Renaissance.*

88. Note, however, that Sankara's extensive writings are not void of devotional materials, as is evident particularly in the magnificent book of *Sivanandalahari* (available at http://www.shaivam.org/english/sen_shivaananda.htm [6/25/2014]).

89. For a highly useful discussion, see Narayanan, "Karma, Bhaktiyoga and Grace," pp. 57-94.

90. See Coward, *Sin and Salvation,* p. 111.

91. For teachings and activities, see the society's Web site: http://iskcon.org/ (7/03/2014).

92. Coward, *Sin and Salvation,* pp. 114-15.

93. Karingadayil, *From Darkness to Light,* p. 164. For formative statements of Sankara, see his *Crest Jewel of Wisdom,* verse 419; available at http://www.sacred-texts.com/hin/cjw/cjw05.htm; so also, e.g., Sankara, *Brahmasutrabasya* 1.i.4; Sankara, *Atmabodha,* p. 302.

(Upanishads)[94] but can be had only when that indirect insight becomes (as in enlightenment) direct and immediate.[95]

In modern advaitic Hinduism as represented by teachers such as Swami Vivekananda (d. 1902), the importance of the "personal experience" of enlightenment insight is even more stressed, in contrast to mere knowledge of it on the basis of scripture. This also illustrates the turn to the subject and subjective experiences in modern times.[96] It is clear that whereas *bhakti-marga* as a universal way of salvation (according to the Gita) is available to all, *jnana-marga* is only for some few.[97] The attainment of liberation is a long process: while sin and evil (in the Abrahamic traditions' sense) are not the main obstacle, those who pursue liberation also seek to overcome selfish, evil, and negative attitudes and acts.[98] Nevertheless, the Upanishads are optimistic about final perfection at the end of the spiritual path that leads to enlightenment.[99] Particularly important in its pursuit is continuous meditation (on which advaitic Vedanta has much to say and teach).[100] The knowledge path culminates in renunciation, which at its core means the "denial of anything real outside of or additional to the infinite reality of God"; ultimately, renunciation means to "bid good-bye" not only to the body but even to one's own ego. Only Brahman remains.[101]

The third path, *karma-marga,* holds a most fundamental position in Indian religious thought and is not necessarily an alternative to the other two. It is closely related to the notion of transmigration. "Karma marga is considered as the best way suited for people who are particularly drawn by social service, alleviation of human suffering and organizational activity, and whose constant compulsion for work is directed towards the divine."[102] Karma is also connected with liberation because liberation consists in the complete freedom from karma and from all its consequences.[103] The Upanishads, espe-

---

94. Of the importance of the scriptures for the attainment of salvation, see Karingadayil, *From Darkness to Light,* pp. 167-71.

95. Karingadayil, *From Darkness to Light,* pp. 164-65; see Mundaka Upanishad 3.2.3; also 3.1.9; 3.2.1. See also the important narrative in Chandogya Upanishad 7.25.2.

96. See Coward, *Sin and Salvation,* pp. 107-8.

97. See Karingadayil, *From Darkness to Light,* pp. 164-65.

98. On purification as a result of liberative pursuit, see Maitri Upanishad 4.4; Brihadaranyaka Upanishad 5.14.8.

99. See further, Coward, *Sin and Salvation,* pp. 99-100.

100. See Karingadayil, *From Darkness to Light,* pp. 171-84.

101. Karingadayil, *From Darkness to Light,* pp. 184-88 (esp. pp. 184, 187).

102. Karingadayil, *From Darkness to Light,* p. 154.

103. See Bhagavad Gita 4.16 for the well-known questions of what is karma and a-karma.

cially Brihadaranyaka and Chandogya, speak of the greatness of *karma-marga*. *Karma-marga* emphasizes that a person, by his or her very nature, is divine, and can attain liberation by the person's own moral forces and good deeds.[104]

The complementary nature of the *trimarga* is indicated by the importance the Gita places on it. The most famous passage in this regard is the teaching of Lord Krishna to Arjuna on proper duty. The key is the right motivation: the duty has to be done without any consideration of the gain to oneself.[105] In the twentieth century, the most well-known advocate of this path has been Mahatma Gandhi. Incidentally, he called the Gita his "spiritual dictionary."[106]

Even Sankara, with his total focus on knowledge, never rejected the importance of the works path; he just took it as subservient to a higher way.[107] Having now discussed some important Hindu movements' diagnoses of and proposed solutions to the human condition, we finish the chapter by highlighting Buddhist analyses and visions.

Dukkha *and Enlightenment: Buddhist Visions of Liberation*

While dealing elsewhere (*Trinity and Revelation,* chap. 15) with the complicated issue of whether Buddhism is a "religion" at all, and if it is, whether it is theistic, let me remind the Christian reader that any inquiry into the human condition in Buddhism should be prefaced by the wider framework in which all Buddhist traditions work out their own distinctive visions of liberation. The foundational presuppositions include the rejection of the idea of permanence and the self-existence of anything, including "self"[108] (or even of gods), and the doctrine of "dependent co-origination."[109]

As is well known — but too often not well understood! — the basic Buddhist diagnosis of the human condition is based on the idea of *dukkha*. Rather than rendering it as "suffering" (or "pain" or "stress"), it is best to leave the term without English translation to avoid misunderstanding. It is intentionally an

104. Karingadayil, *From Darkness to Light,* p. 155.

105. Bhagavad Gita 2.47-48. For Ramanuja's comments on this passage, see *The Gitabhasya of Ramanuja,* p. 55.

106. See Coward, *Sin and Salvation,* p. 117. For Gandhi's comments on the Gita passage (2.47), see Gandhi, *The Bhagavad Gita according to Gandhi,* p. 14.

107. Karingadayil, *From Darkness to Light,* pp. 155-56.

108. The doctrine of dependent co-origination is investigated in detail in chap. 5 of *Creation and Humanity.*

109. The concept of no-self is discussed in detail in chap. 14 of *Creation and Humanity.*

ambiguous word. With all their differences, all Buddhist schools consider *duk-kha* to be the main challenge in life and, consequently, extinction of *dukkha* to be the main goal, the *summa* of everything in Buddhism and its scriptures.[110] Suffering is inescapable as long as one is in the circle of life and death, samsara. To be more precise, it is the craving that is the real root and cause (the second "Noble Truth").[111] Behind the (misplaced) craving, according to the Buddha, is ignorance. The logic of the emergence and continuation of suffering rooted in craving due to ignorance[112] is indebted to the law of *kamma*.[113] As in Hinduism, though, we have to be warned against imagining any kind of idea of "fall." "Whereas Augustine understood such bondage through the lens of Genesis as an ontologically substantial fallen state, Buddhists have viewed it as a continual, momentary process of construction by habits of thought and reaction so profoundly habitual that they seem ineluctable."[114]

Inquiring into the way of "salvation" in Buddhism is appropriate in light of Gautama's own focus on liberation rather than on abstract, meaningless speculations.[115] That said, the Christian reader is reminded that in no Buddhist movement is Gautama a deity after Christian tradition, and therefore a "Savior has no place in the Buddhist worldview. An individual must control and be responsible for his or her own destiny."[116] The person is one's own refuge, and no one else, not even Buddha, can save one from the law of *kamma*.[117] In other words, Buddhism, particularly in its original "orthodox" version, is "an atheistic and humanistic system that locates human beings at the center of their existence and believes that humankind can overcome the problem of human suffering by their own endeavors. It also implies the denial of . . . [a] Savior who delivers humankind from suffering."[118] Although many movements of Mahayana acknowledge the concept of grace and (divine) assistance in search of liberation, ultimately liberation is dependent on one's own effort. Buddha taught his disci-

110. Chandngarm, *Arriyasatsee*, pp. 9-14.

111. Like the notion of *dukkha*, the term *tanha* ("craving" or "desire") used by Buddha is a multifaceted concept. The classic passage of the fire-like power of craving is *Adittapariyaya Sutta: The Fire Sermon*, of Samyutta Nikaya 35.28; also famous is *Tanha Sutta: Craving*, of Samyutta Nikaya 4.199.

112. See Eckel, "Beginningless Ignorance," pp. 49-72.

113. See further, Dammapitaka, *Dictionary of Buddhism*, p. 60.

114. Makransky, "Buddhist Analogues of Sin and Grace," p. 4.

115. See Sutton, "Salvation after Nagarjuna," p. 17.

116. Boonyakiat, "A Christian Theology of Suffering," p. 114.

117. *Dhammapada* 12.4; *SBE* 10 (in some other versions, 12.160); similarly 20.4 (*SBE* 20:276).

118. Boonyakiat, "A Christian Theology of Suffering," p. 115.

ples: "Monks, be islands unto yourselves, be your own refuge, having no other; let the Dhamma be an island and a refuge to you, having no other."[119] Gautama's role is that of a mentor or guide,[120] similar to that of *dhamma*.[121] Hence, not "faith" but confidence in the Teacher's instructions is needed.[122]

"Enlightenment" — or insight — is the favored soteriological term. Following the teachings of Buddha as expressed in the "Noble Eightfold Path,"[123] as well as emulating his experience, moves one toward the goal of "direct, embodied knowledge of the unconditioned, Nirvana."[124] This simply means defeating the power of *dukkha*. Buddha's foundational distinction between the "conditioned" and "unconditioned" existence means a distinction between the *dukkha* existence, under the power of craving, leading to samsaric rebirth over and over again, and the release from under *kamma*.[125]

What I have so far explained about the human condition and human effort to pursue the liberative insight is shared by all Buddhist traditions. As in Hinduism, there are denominational differences. The basic distinction for our purposes is between Theravada[126] and the later Mahayana families. These later movements have adopted a more theistically oriented cosmology and have highlighted the importance of notions of grace and mercy. Mahayana has also developed a growing tradition of spiritual exercises in pursuit of liberative insight.[127] In Mahayana, the Boddhisattva — different from the Theravada Arahat — is willing to postpone his or her own entrance into the *nibbana* to help others reach the goal.[128] Even that, however, is not the function of a "savior" but rather the function of a "good neighbor," even when the Boddhisattva may grant his own merit to help the other.[129]

---

119. *Attadiipaa Sutta: An Island to Oneself,* of Samyutta Nikaya 22.43.

120. *Ganakamoggallana Sutta: The Discourse to Ganaka-Moggallana,* of Majjhima Nikaya 107; see also, *Vatthupama Sutta: The Simile of the Cloth,* of Majjhima Nikaya 7.

121. For the close relationship between Gautama and *dhamma*, see Samyutta Nikaya 22.87.

122. See Rahula, *What the Buddha Taught,* p. 8.

123. For "The Middle Way" or the Noble Eightfold Path, see Rahula, *What the Buddha Taught,* chap. 5.

124. Makransky, "Buddhist Analogues of Sin and Grace," p. 5.

125. Makransky, "Buddhist Analogues of Sin and Grace," pp. 7-8.

126. For an overview, see Carter, "The Path Is Not My Way."

127. See Largen, *What Christians Can Learn from Buddhism,* pp. 108-29.

128. For the path of liberation in Zen Buddhism, the main Japanese movement also highly popular in the West, see Unno, "When Broken Tiles Become Gold."

129. For differences between Mahayana and Theravada in this respect, see J. R. Davis, *Poles Apart,* pp. 98-104.

The most distinctive vision of liberation can be found in the Mahayana Pure Land tradition developed by Shinran (1173-1263), which, as is well known, entertains some ideas materially close to Christian soteriology.[130] It can be illustrated with the ancient Indian distinction between two kinds of determinative metaphors of salvation. The "monkey path," depicted by a baby monkey clinging tightly to the back of the mother on a dangerous walk, signifies self-power; whereas the "cat path," illustrated by the kitten being held by the mother at the nape of its neck, speaks of Other-power. The Pure Land (known also as Shin Buddhism), which is predominantly a Japanese and Chinese phenomenon, represents the latter. The main savior figure is Boddhisattva Dharmakara, who, through the rigorous and pure practice of forty-eight vows, reached enlightenment and became Amitabha Buddha, also known as Avalokitesvara. He opened the path of salvation in primordial times by establishing the Western Pure Land and made it possible for all sentient beings reborn in that land to reach enlightenment, "salvation."[131] "The Buddha embodied his virtue in his Name for all beings, enabling them to enter the Pure Land at death. Through their faith in, and meritorious recitation of the Name, they are saved by its power."[132] Boddhisattva Dharmakara's enlightenment in the Pure Land was contingent on the inclusion of others.[133] The Christian reader, however, has to be reminded that behind this salvific outreach of Amitabha there is absolutely no idea of sacrificial suffering and death for the atonement of sins.[134] Different from other forms of Buddhism, Pure Land speaks of faith as "a gift infused in the heart-mind of a person in fulfillment of the Buddha's Vow. The source of the name and Faith is in Amitabha Buddha." As a result, "[g]ratitude for a salvation received characterizes the religious life of a devotee."[135]

Now that we have introduced the broad visions of salvation and libera-

130. For the historical background of Shinran's developments and key ideas, particularly of his teacher Genku Honen, see P. S. Chung, *Martin Luther and Buddhism*, pp. 381-93; a monographic presentation is Bloom, *Shinran's Gospel of Pure Grace*.

131. Boddhisattva is a Buddha-in-the-making aiming at enlightenment. Indeed, there is more than one Pure Land in those traditions. Wherever there is an enlightened Buddha, there is Pure Land. The Western Pure Land created by Boddhisattva Dharmakara is the main Pure Land and combines teachings and features of others.

132. Bloom, "Jesus in the Pure Land," p. 33; see also, p. 32. According to Shinran, the founder of Japanese Pure Land traditions, Amitabha Buddha not only resides in the Pure Land but also is ever-present in the world as a spiritual influence or potential in all beings to become Buddha (p. 33).

133. For the eighteenth vow, see Inagaki, *The Three Pure Land Sutras*, p. 243.

134. See Bloom, "Jesus in the Pure Land," p. 34.

135. Bloom, "Jesus in the Pure Land," p. 34.

tion in four other living traditions, it is time to delve into key Christian soteriological topics. In each case, where relevant in light of the self-understanding of other faiths, a sympathetic and critical dialogue will be attempted.

9. The Divine Favor and Invitation for Eternal Fellowship

The Impasse of Classical Debates on the Doctrine of Election

Historical Debate in Theological Assessment

In light of the importance of the doctrine of election in traditional theology, particularly in the Reformed tradition, it is instructive to recall that in patristic theology until Augustine there was very little specific interest in formulating any theory of election, let alone debating about it.[1] While the Fathers were convinced of divine election, their concerns were different from those of later tradition in which the individual person's salvation (or damnation) became the burning issue. For patristic thinkers, pagan fatalism loomed large. Particularly for the Eastern segment of the church, the fear of fatalism and determinism was urgent. A related factor is the less negative anthropology (because of the lack of a formulated doctrine of original sin in early theology) throughout patristic theology, particularly in the East.[2] Different from later tradition, for the Fathers, "the natural ability of sinners to turn from their sin in response to the preaching mission of the church was simply assumed as beyond question." These observations may also help one better understand the appeal of Pelagianism.[3]

---

1. The Fathers touched on the issue only sporadically; see, e.g., Athanasius, *Defense against the Arians* 2.22.76-77.
2. For details, see chap. 15 in *Creation and Humanity*.
3. Jewett, *Election and Predestination*, p. 5.

The ancient controversy between Pelagius and Augustine is about the nature of the human condition before it is about election,[4] the former rejecting the Augustinian (and later mainline Christian) idea of the serious weakness of the will because of the Fall.[5] Pelagius maintained that men and women are able to choose between good and evil not only concerning this life but also "before God."[6] Although Pelagianism died hard, already as early as the Council of Orange (529) it was ruled that the human person is not free apart from God's grace to believe and that God's salvific response does not come as the rewarding of the uttermost effort of humanity.[7] That said, the defeat of Pelagianism did not constitute in any way an unconditional, let alone unreserved, establishment of the Augustinian view, which "had in many ways gone beyond even the Western theological tradition (not to mention the Eastern tradition) by positing a doctrine of predestination, including predestination to damnation, and of the irresistibility of grace."[8]

Not unaware of criticism by his opponents,[9] Augustine consolidated his view of the sovereignty of God and unconditionality of divine election in eternity[10] (although he also sought to resist pagan fatalism, as had his forebears).[11] The "double predestination" view resulted: people are destined for condemnation unless they will be rescued from it by God's sovereign choice.[12] In Calvinistic theology (particularly as formulated by Calvin's successor T. Beza)[13] and

4. For a succinct description of Pelagianism, see Kelly, *Early Christian Doctrines*, pp. 357-61.

5. For the complicated history of the doctrine of sin and Fall, see chap. 15 in *Creation and Humanity*.

6. A particularly important text is Pelagius's *Commentary on St. Paul's Epistle to the Romans*, which was written before the controversy with Augustine, thus highlighting the original form of his ideas.

7. The canons (twenty-five altogether) of the Council of Orange can be found, e.g., at http://www.fordham.edu/halsall/basis/orange.txt (6/20/2014) and in many standard editions of the creeds and councils.

8. Pelikan, *CT* 1:318. For a detailed and insightful discussion of the ways tradition handled Augustine's legacy and sought to find a middle way, see Pelikan, *CT* 1:307-31 (until the end of the patristic era), and Pelikan, *CT* 3:80-95 (medieval times). In support of the nomenclature of semi-Pelagianism, see Pelikan, *CT* 1:319, and on rejecting it, see McGrath, *Iustitia Dei*, 1:72.

9. He responded to criticism in *On the Predestination of the Saints and On the Gift of Perseverance*.

10. See Kelly, *Early Christian Doctrines*, pp. 366-69.

11. See further, Pelikan, *CT* 1:297.

12. For a succinct statement, see Augustine, *A Treatise on the Soul and Its Origin* 4.16; see also, Pelikan, *CT* 1:297-98.

13. See Muller, "Calvin and the 'Calvinists' [1995]" and "Calvin and the 'Calvinists' [1996]."

in Anglicanism,[14] this idea came to its fullest fruition[15] and, not surprisingly, was vehemently resisted by the Arminian party.[16] While in Luther's own view the human will is unable to take any initiative toward salvation — as evident in his extended fight with the humanist Catholic Erasmus[17] — there is, strictly speaking, no doctrine of double predestination in Lutheranism.[18] Rather than encouraging abstract speculation about the divine mystery, the Lutheran Confessions guide the believers to only search Scripture and Christ therein when it comes to matters of election.[19] A further difference between the Reformed and Lutheran traditions is that the latter do not distinguish between the "external" and "effectual" calling;[20] rather, "they regard this ministry of the Spirit as effectual except in the case of those who willfully resist it."[21]

Between Roman Catholics and Protestants, particularly the Reformed, there is, generally speaking, a marked difference in the approach to election.[22] Notwithstanding Augustine's heritage, the Roman Catholic Church does not endorse the doctrine of divine predestination or reprobation apart from hu-

---

14. In the Methodist tradition, the issue of predestination became a dividing issue as John Wesley advocated strongly Arminian views whereas George Whitefield, gleaning from the ultra-Calvinist American Puritan Jonathan Edwards, advocated strong Calvinism, as visible in his 1754 *Freedom of the Will*.

15. For the classic statement, see Calvin, *Institutes* 3.21.5; for a useful detailed summary of later Calvinistic views with documentation, see Jewett, *Election and Predestination*, pp. 12-13.

16. See Arminius, *Writings*, vol. 1, V.I, "On Predestination" (available at ccel.org; n.p.). The classic texts with critical notes of *Five Points of the Remonstrants* (1610) on the Arminian side and the *Canons of Dort* (1618-1619) on the Calvinist side can be found in Philip Schaff's *Creeds of Christendom*, vol. 3, available at ccel.org. For careful historical discussion, see Pelikan, *CT* 4:217-44.

17. The classic texts for the debate and mutual rejection of the other's views are Luther's *Bondage of Will* (1525) and Erasmus's *Freedom of Will* (1524), found in Rupp and Watson, eds., *Luther and Erasmus*; highly useful discussion can be found in the editors' introduction (pp. 1-32). On the lack of freedom of will *coram Deo*, see Augsburg Confession #18; see also, Formula of Concord #2.

18. See the important rejection of Calvinistic views of limited atonement and predestination for reprobation in *Saxon Visitation Articles* (1592), #4 (available at http://bookofconcord .org/visitation.php); for details, see also, Jewett, *Election and Predestination*, pp. 11-12.

19. The classic statements on election can be found in Formula of Concord #11.

20. See Horton, *The Christian Faith*, pp. 572-75.

21. Horton, *The Christian Faith*, p. 563.

22. It is interesting, however, to note views such as those of the Jansenists, who basically agreed with the Protestant, even Reformed, interpretations of depravity, predestination, and grace; even when condemned harshly by the establishment (see final paragraph in Pope Clement XI, *Unigenitus Dei Filius*), they show the diversity of views within the doctrinally solid system of Rome.

man response.[23] In other words, the continuing "stumbling block in the Augustinian view of grace" throughout history remained the doctrine of reprobation, which was variously negotiated among the medieval masters Anselm, Aquinas, Bonaventure, and others.[24] What can be named "milder predestinarianism"[25] became the mainstream (though not the only) opinion in the Christian West, according to which election to salvation is affirmed, but not reprobation.[26]

Although the Eastern Church is of course not Pelagian,[27] it is totally removed from the Protestant views and debates. Illustrative is the catechism for the currently largest Orthodox Church, the Russian. The question, "How are we to understand the predestination of God, with respect to men in general, and to each man severally?" is answered as follows: "God has predestined to give to all men, and has actually given them preparatory grace, and means sufficient for the attainment of happiness."[28]

Although these historical debates have not lost all their urgency, they also have to be put in perspective. While not only the Western tradition (Roman Catholic and Protestant) but also the Eastern[29] must reject Pelagianism for its too-thin account of human sinfulness and diluted view of the "newness" of salvation brought about by the triune God, neither can constructive theology be content with the Augustinian alternative (and its later Protestant, particularly Calvinist, developments). The problem is: the traditional way of trying to solve the problem of election and calling is formulated in a way that leads to an impasse.[30]

---

23. *Catholic Catechism* ##600, 1037. See also the "Conclusion" to Council of Orange; Council of Trent (1547), Session IV, #13, in Schaff, *The Creeds of Christendom*, 2:103-4. See also, Trent's "Decree on Justification" (Session VI), #12, in Schaff, 2:103.

24. For these medieval debates, see Pelikan, *CT* 3:271-84 (citation on p. 275) and *CT* 4:28-35.

25. So named by Jewett, *Election and Predestination*, p. 7.

26. Jewett, *Election and Predestination*, p. 8.

27. Recall that Luther (*Lectures on Romans*, LW 25:261-62), in his extreme criticism of the Roman Catholic Church, accused his former church of Pelagianism!

28. *The Longer Catechism of the Orthodox, Catholic, Eastern Church*, in Schaff, *The Creeds of Christendom*, 2:465, available at ccel.org; I am indebted to Horton, *The Christian Faith*, p. 562.

29. This is not to deny the historical fact that Pelagianism is in some real sense an Eastern offshoot and variation; Pelikan, *CT* 1:316.

30. Unlike other liberals, Schleiermacher at least discussed the topic while rejecting vehemently reprobation (Schleiermacher, *CF*, pp. 546-51); for liberalism's dismissal, see Jewett, *Election and Predestination*, pp. 17-19. See also, Gockel, *Barth and Schleiermacher on the Doctrine of Election*.

Christ and Election: Barth's Contested Proposal

Moltmann, in his brilliant revision of the treatment of the *ordo salutis* (part 2 in *The Spirit of Life*), dismisses the topic of election, a highly surprising move from a Reformed theologian. While I may understand why he does so — if not for other reasons, then to ground his talk about salvation in "earthly realities" and so avoid abstract speculations — I also think it is not a fair and useful tactic. A better way to reorient the discussion is to try one's hand at it. In that sense, Barth's massive effort to revise the doctrine of election merits commendation, although unfortunately his proposal ends up being highly problematic.[31]

Barth rightly argued that the standard Augustinian-Calvinistic view of election is both "obscure" and "dark" in its one-sided emphasis on divine determinism; Barth is particularly critical of *decretum absolutum*.[32] That idea simply casts a shadow on the freedom of grace, a main concern for Barth.[33] In a radical departure from tradition, Barth famously shifted the focus from the election of human beings to that of Christ, the Mediator who is both the Electing God and the Elected Man,[34] not only "one of the elect" or "alongside the rest of the elect, but before and above them as the One who is originally and properly the Elect." Indeed, Christ is "the organ and instrument of the whole election of God"[35] — from eternity.[36] The traditional "double predestination" is strictly rejected and a radically revised "double predestination" in terms of the dual role of Christ and his "dual treatment" — rejection (crucifixion) and vindication (resurrection) — is put in its place.[37]

Is it justifiable to shift the focus of election to Jesus Christ? Assessments vary.[38] Whereas I fully affirm Barth's general insistence on looking at all works

31. For the importance of election in theology, see the epithet to §32 in Barth, *CD* II/2, p. 3; the discussion in *CD* II/2 alone comprises over 500 pages! For differing assessments, see McCormack, "'Grace and Being,'" p. 92; Berkouwer, *Triumph of Grace*, pp. 89-122; McDonald, "Barth's 'Other' Doctrine of Election."

32. The extended criticism of tradition can be found in §32 of *CD* II/2, pp. 3-93; the citation is on p. 104; on the criticism of *decretum absolutum*, see, e.g., pp. 115, 158.

33. The phrase appears everywhere in Barth's discussion; see, e.g., *CD* II/2, pp. 9, 12, 28, 74, etc.

34. Barth, *CD* II/2, p. 103. A succinct discussion can be found in O'Neill, "Karl Barth's Doctrine of Election," pp. 313-16.

35. All citations from Barth, *CD* II/2, p. 116.

36. See further, McCormack, "'Grace and Being,'" p. 101.

37. See Barth, *CD* II/2, pp. 166-67.

38. An affirmative response is that of McCormack, *Orthodox and Modern*, pp. 183-84; cf. Hunsinger, "Election and the Trinity," pp. 179-98.

of God through the christological lens (rather than attempting to discern the "naked God," which would only lead to speculation),[39] I do not think there is any biblical basis for making Christ the "object" of election. It is routinely noted that exegetically Barth's interpretation cannot be maintained. It seems to me that even theologically it cannot stand scrutiny. Barth's proposal also suffers from the dangers of universalism[40] (a topic to be discussed in eschatology).

The Need to Reorient the Discourse of Election

An important part of the task of reorientation relates to the locating of the doctrine of election in dogmatics. For Augustine, the proper locus of election was in soteriology; election thus focused on the sorting out of those going to be saved and those going to be damned. Aquinas moved election from soteriology to the doctrine of God, more precisely to divine providence.[41] While better than that of Augustine, even Aquinas's choice is far from ideal, as it leads us into abstract speculation concerning the "mind of God." Calvin's way of locating the doctrine is quite surprising. That it belongs to soteriology and hence bears resemblance to Augustine's location is not surprising at all, but that it comes after the discussion of most soteriological topics and just before the long section on the church (*Institutes 4*) merits acknowledgment.[42] Intuitively it points in the right direction (although Calvin seemed not to have grasped it), namely, that rather than abstract speculation into either the destiny of human beings, which has been decided in eternity, or the mind of God (in his providence), election has to do with Christian life and history, and it is linked with the community.

Here comes the brilliance of Pannenberg's radically revised version of the discussion of election. He places it after soteriology and the church,[43] and

39. As correctly observed by Van Til, *Christianity and Barthianism*, p. 34; I am indebted to Scheuers, "An Evaluation of Some Aspects," p. 162.

40. See the harsh assessment in Brunner, *Christian Doctrine of God*, 1:314. Oliver D. Crisp makes the compelling case that Barth's logic of election leads either to universalism or to incoherence: "The Letter and the Spirit of Barth's Doctrine of Election."

41. Aquinas, *ST* 1.23.1; 1.23.3.

42. Calvin, *Institutes* 3.21-24. See Jewett, *Election and Predestination*, p. 22; this paragraph as a whole is indebted to his short addendum, "The Place of the Doctrine in Systematics" (pp. 22-23).

43. Pannenberg, *ST* 3 (chaps. 12 and 13) includes the hefty treatment of ecclesiology, with over 400 pages (in the midst of which soteriology comprises a subsection in chap. 13 [pp. 97-236]), just before sacraments and ministry.

it is ominously titled "Election and History" (vol. 3, chap. 4). Having critiqued harshly the Augustinian-Calvinistic view of election (§1, of which more below), he discusses "the church as the people of God" (§2) and then moves to consider "the election of the people of God and the experience of history," linking election not only to the formation of the peoplehood but also to the "historical constitution of the cultural order"; he even discusses "secular belief in election and nationalism in the history of Christianity." The chapter ends with the widest possible horizons under the rubric "The Goal of Election and God's Government of the World in the Process of History." This multilayered and complex doctrine of election encompasses individual and community experiences, as well as cultural, national, and historical experiences, and so forms the bridge to considering the consummation of God's redemptive work in the eschaton.

A Trinitarian-Pneumatological Account of Divine Election

History, Community, and Election

Rather than abstract speculation, any credible theology of election and calling is both built on and reflects the theology of revelation. While the doctrine of revelation in Christian tradition was often conceived in terms of abstract concepts such as the idealistically oriented modern idea of *self*-revelation, the biblical revelation of the nature of *revelation* is relational, invitational, and historically rooted.[44] In the words of Vatican II's *Dei Verbum*,

> In His goodness and wisdom God chose to reveal Himself and to make known to us the hidden purpose of His will (see Eph. 1:9) by which through Christ, the Word made flesh, man might in the Holy Spirit have access to the Father and come to share in the divine nature (see Eph. 2:18; 2 Peter 1:4). Through this revelation, therefore, the invisible God (see Col. 1:15; 1 Tim. 1:17) out of the abundance of His love speaks to men as friends (see Ex. 33:11; John 15:14-15) and lives among them (see Bar. 3:37), so that He may invite and take them into fellowship with Himself. (#2)

With Augustine, the theology of election lost this personalistic, historically oriented, and invitational nature. Instead, divine election was located

---

44. For details, see my *Trinity and Revelation*, chaps. 2 and 3 particularly.

in eternity, apart from and unrelated to historical happenings and choices of human beings.[45] Illustrative here is the difference between Origen and Augustine. Origen's commentary on Romans 8:29-30 carefully follows the Pauline line of thought, viewing "election as an act of divine foreknowledge. God sees in advance our future conduct and sets us accordingly on the way to salvation or the way to perdition," thus linking human destiny with future free decisions.[46] Augustine, as is well known, referred the decision of divine election into eternity,[47] and appealed instead to Romans 9:15-16.[48]

In summary form, the main challenges of the traditional doctrine of election are as follows:

1. It makes the divine decision timeless, in abstraction from the concrete historicity of the divine acts of elections as the Bible bears witness to them.
2. It detaches individuals as the object of election from all relations to society.
3. It restricts the purpose of election to participation in future salvation in disjunction from any historical function of the elect.[49]

All these lacunae need correction. A different kind of approach to considering election is needed, one that happens "from the perspective of time" (sub specie temporis, as opposed to sub specie aeternitatis) and can also be called "historical."[50] That is the main approach of the biblical narrative,[51] in which persons such as Abraham and David are elected (for the sake of the community and the mission of Yahweh to the nations); similarly in the NT persons are called to salvation for which they have been foreordained.[52] This is not to ignore or deny those biblical passages that indeed trace the

45. See also, Jewett, *Election and Predestination*, p. 6. For critical comments against this in medieval theology, see Anselm of Canterbury, *De Concordia* 1.5, p. 442.

46. Pannenberg, *ST* 3:440; see Origen, *Commentary on the Epistle to the Romans* 7.7-8 (pp. 83-93).

47. Calvin, *Institutes* 3.21.5.

48. See Augustine, *Letter to Simplianus* (Letter 37 in *NPNF*[1]), which focuses on exposition of Rom. 9, and more extensively his *Predestination of the Saints*. For shared liabilities between the two, see Pannenberg, *ST* 3:441.

49. Pannenberg, *ST* 3:442.

50. So named by Jewett, *Election and Predestination*, pp. 67-68.

51. Jewett, *Election and Predestination*, chap. 2, summarizes succinctly some key biblical perspectives on election.

52. See Pannenberg, *ST* 3:442-43.

origins of divine election in eternity (such as Rom. 8:28-30 or Eph. 1:4), but rather to insist on that act's link with and coming to manifestation in the historical realm. Just consider Ephesians 1:4, often used in support of the traditional view. Having mentioned that God "chose us in him [Christ] before the foundation of the world," the text says that its goal is "that we should be holy and blameless before him" and continues highlighting the blessings of grace, redemption, forgiveness of sins, and the gift of the Holy Spirit, which all relate to Christian life on this earth. The historically oriented view seeks to "resolve the problem of election and the reprobation it implies by inferring that since God wills the salvation of all, offers it to all, and holds those to be without excuse who reject it, his predestination must be based on his foreknowledge of who will and who will not accept the grace offered in Christ."[53] There is of course an important biblical support for this: "For those whom he foreknew he also predestined to be conformed to the image of his Son" (Rom. 8:29).[54] Predestination then becomes the correct answer to the catechism question: "Has not that will of God, which man is designed for eternal happiness, its own proper name in theology?" and it is linked with foreknowledge.[55] Along with the earliest patristic theology,[56] this view dominates throughout the Eastern Orthodox tradition and is materially similar to that of Arminianism.[57]

Furthermore, the one-sided focus on the individual's election has to be balanced and corrected with both christological and communitarian orientations. To Barth's credit, he shifted the focus in election from humans to Christ. It is indeed in Christ (Eph. 1:4) that God's elective acts, like all other salvific works, take place — and Christ of course is a "corporate person," so to speak.[58] In the OT the focus of election is in the community: people are chosen with a view toward inclusion among the people of God, which in itself is chosen to bring the knowledge of Yahweh to the nations (Gen. 12:1-3). Even the choice of individuals such as kings and prophets is linked with the community rather

53. Jewett, *Election and Predestination*, p. 68; similarly Pelikan, *CT* 1:326-27, which is cited by Jewett.

54. See Pannenberg, *ST* 3:439.

55. Larger Catechism of the Orthodox, Catholic, Eastern Church, questions 121 and 125, pp. 464-65, cited in Jewett, *Election and Predestination*, pp. 68-69.

56. See Pannenberg, *ST* 3:439.

57. For basing predestination on divine foreknowledge, see Arminius, *Writings*, 1:247-48 (available at ccel.org), cited in Jewett, *Election and Predestination*, p. 69.

58. See Zizioulas, "Human Capacity," p. 438. Similarly, the late Canadian Baptist Grenz, *Theology for the Community of God*, p. 453.

than with their individuality.[59] Only gradually does personal responsibility emerge in the OT.[60] In the NT the meaning of election becomes more complex: while the communal orientation is still dominant, the focus on individual election also comes to the fore. Even though the election of individuals is with a view toward joining the messianic community, by and large the call to join the community is directed to individuals, and unlike in the OT, it cannot be based on birthright but is based on personal choice.[61] Throughout the biblical narrative, the expression "'People of God' is a description that involves election. . . . For election involves sending, which is moving toward the future of the reign of God."[62] And although, as mentioned, in the NT the inclusion in the "people of God" does not happen by birthright, it still is an inclusion in the *people,* that is, community.[63]

The negotiation between eternal election and temporal calling has to consider the result of the discussion on the eternity-time relationship in the doctrine of creation (*Creation and Humanity,* chap. 6). Rather than the opposite of time, God's eternity also embraces and "overcomes" (by bringing to fulfillment) time. "To the thought of an eternal counsel of God there thus corresponds as its temporal realization only the totality of temporal occurrence that the ultimate future alone will complete."[64] Although at present election implies selection, "the number of the elect remains open to all who by Jesus Christ and his gospel are later brought into the fellowship of the Son with the Father. To all these there extends the electing counsel of God before the foundation of the world, even though it does not find actualization in all of them at the same time."[65]

What about the difficult passages of the "hardening of heart" by God (Exod. 7:3; 9:12)? On the one hand, for those included in the membership of the people of God there is no ultimate guarantee that they will never willfully sever the link with eternal life; in some extreme cases that may even apply to most of the people of God, as warned by the prophets (Jer. 7:29; 1 Thess. 2:16), although the election of the fellowship itself remains inviolable (Jer. 31:37; cf. Rom. 11:1-2, 28-29). On the other hand, "[w]e must not confuse temporary

---

59. For a detailed discussion, see Jewett, *Election and Predestination,* chap. 3.

60. Pannenberg, *ST* 3:443; see *1 Enoch* 1:1, 2.

61. See further, Pannenberg, *ST* 3:455-526.

62. Pannenberg, *ST* 3:431-34, 437 (p. 434).

63. See also the extended discussion of individual-communal dialectic in election in Pannenberg, *ST* 3:455-62; for the tight link between election and the people of God, see pp. 463-65 and passim.

64. Pannenberg, *ST* 3:449.

65. Pannenberg, *ST* 3:450.

hardening with eternal rejection" because even the hardened heart may still be converted (Ezek. 18:21-22) as long as the gospel's call continues and God's long-standing patience is waiting for the sinner — even in the last minute! As Pannenberg finely summarizes: "There is no guarantee of an ultimate universal reconciliation, but in a history that is still open, the possibility of forgiveness is promised to those who repent."[66]

The Role of the Spirit in Election

As with any work of God, election and calling are the joint work of the Father, Son, and Spirit. The problem with traditional formulations of the doctrine has been the lack of trinitarian, particularly pneumatological, emphasis.[67] It is counterintuitive that on the basis of the idea of the Spirit as the bond of love, the union between Father and Son, and by extension, between the triune God and world, the Spirit's role as the agent of election and calling — the one who "pulls" humanity into the union with God — was missed.[68] Even though the medieval tradition in a sense gave the Spirit a more robust place in soteriology, the tendency to make the Spirit a "commodity" is not useful; that is, "delivered by or through the Holy Spirit, the grace that comes as predestination became something that is installed in our soul, remaining as a deposit or character stamped into our moral fabric."[69]

Instead of marginalizing the Spirit's role in election, we should see the Holy Spirit, in the words of the Reformed theologian Suzanne McDonald, as the "electing God."[70] If, as another Reformed theologian, the late Colin Gunton, says incisively, the Holy Spirit is "God's eschatological transcendence, his futurity," then it means that the Spirit is also God "present to the world as its liberating other, bringing it to the destiny determined by the Father, made actual, realized, in the Son."[71] Placed in the proper trinitarian framework, we

66. Pannenberg, *ST* 3:462.

67. See further, Pinnock, *Flame of Love*, pp. 33-35.

68. For a historical survey, see Henderson, "Election as Renewal," pp. 24-34.

69. Henderson, "Election as Renewal," pp. 45-46; the nomenclature "commodity" is from the American Benedictine Killian McDonnell, "Communion Ecclesiology and Baptism in the Spirit," p. 691 n. 117.

70. McDonald, *Re-imaging Election*, p. xviii.

71. Gunton, "God the Holy Spirit," p. 122. I am indebted to Henderson, "Election as Renewal," p. 9 (but have corrected the mistaken reference); for some other references in this section I am also indebted to Henderson.

can say that "election" in the theological sense is a general divine call to every human being; the Father calls everyone to salvation because of the work of Christ. The Holy Spirit then makes that calling effective by communicating "electing" grace to everyone. This "electing" grace is efficacious in that it fulfills the Father's will that the Holy Spirit empower each person to make an eschatological choice, either to receive the gift of life by resting in grace or actively to resist the call and the work of the Holy Spirit.[72]

The trinitarian-pneumatological framework helps a theology of election also keep in mind the link between calling, election, and sending.[73] "Christian life is life in movement toward a goal. God not only justifies and sanctifies human life in the power of the Spirit but also gives it a particular vocation and a great hope. When this aspect of God's work of liberation and reconciliation is neglected, a certain narrowness and even narcissism creeps into the life of faith and the work of theology."[74] The Christian theology of election is intertwined with the idea of calling, as can be seen from the beginning of the biblical canon in the case of Abraham (Gen. 12:2-3).[75] Coupled with the vocational orientation is the need to establish the empowering and charismatic nature of electing grace as the "empowering presence of the Holy Spirit."[76] To those called to new life and the mission of God to the world, charismatic gifting is also given with a view to making them fit for the vocation. In this regard we may say that "Grace is not a 'power' but the aid of a Person. Rather than an impersonal power or a kind of substance, we should think of grace as the empowerment and help of the Holy Spirit."[77]

The fact that the Spirit is not an impersonal force but rather a person places the framework for considering all divine works, including election, in a personal and relational context. Hence, we "can understand the grace that comes to [us] as a relational work, a work of love more than power, directed at restoring the relationship of the human person to the divine persons of the Trinity. Such a personal work draws the human person towards salvation, but it is resistible."[78] A hospitable person does not coerce another's will any more than does a loving parent. Even when the mother may be utterly devastated

---

72. Henderson, "Election as Renewal," p. iv.

73. Suggested but not developed by Pannenberg, *ST* 3:438.

74. Migliore, *Faith Seeking Understanding*, p. 246.

75. For Christian life as "costly service," see Bonhoeffer, *The Cost of Discipleship*, p. 48.

76. Heading in Henderson, "Election as Renewal," p. 153.

77. Henderson, "Election as Renewal," p. 155.

78. Henderson, "Election as Renewal," p. 157, with reference to Maddox, *Responsible Grace*, p. 87.

by her child's lack of response, parental love does not translate into a tyrant's blind use of force. Hospitality — or lack thereof — is at stake in the doctrine of election.

Human Responsibility and Election

The question of freedom of will (or lack thereof) and its relation to determinism is one of the oldest philosophical and religious issues. We discussed it in detail elsewhere,[79] so let it suffice here to recount two important options, namely, "compatibilism," which allows determinism along with free will, and "incompatibilism," which demands that (at least in principle) a person would have been able to choose otherwise than the person did.[80]

The traditional (Augustinian-Calvinist) doctrine of election does not fare well in its capacity either to honor the (relative) human freedom graciously granted by the Creator or to defend the hospitality of God. What I have in mind is something similar to what the Canadian Reformed theologian Hans Boersma argues under the nomenclature "preferential hospitality" of God. As opposed to "limited hospitality," it seeks to "present an understanding of predestination as an embodiment of God's hospitality in Jesus Christ . . . [which] stems from an unconditional, eternally absolute hospitality that describes what God is truly like."[81] This desire to affirm robustly preferential hospitality does not stem from a cheap desire to accommodate the Christian gospel to every other human desire; rather, it is a *theo*logical statement, a statement about God.[82] If the doctrine of election reflects God's revelation, as established above, then it also tells us about God. As the late Canadian Baptist Clark Pinnock puts it, "A fundamental point . . . is the conviction that God's redemptive work in Jesus Christ was intended to benefit the whole world. . . . The dimensions are deep and wide. God's grace is not niggardly or partial. . . . For according to the gospel of Christ, the outcome of salvation will be large and generous."[83]

Perhaps this desire to embrace as many as possible can be named the "optimism of salvation." It is based on one's understanding of God as "unbounded

79. Chap. 13 in *Creation and Humanity.*

80. A more sophisticated typology of views is offered in Murphy and Brown, *Did My Neurons Make Me Do It?* pp. 270-72, making a distinction between "hard" and "soft" determinism.

81. Boersma, *Violence, Hospitality, and the Cross,* chap. 3; citation on p. 76.

82. Boersma, *Violence, Hospitality, and the Cross,* p. 49.

83. Pinnock, *Wideness in God's Mercy,* p. 17.

generosity." "The God we love and trust is not One to be satisfied until there is a healing of the nations and an innumerable host of redeemed people around his throne (Rev 7:9; 21:24-26; 22:2-6)." This attitude speaks of hospitality, a "hermeneutic of hopefulness"[84] as opposed to the "fewness doctrine," according to which only a small number of people will be saved.[85] Rightly Pinnock claims that this optimistic hermeneutic was lost early in Christian theology with the introduction of the Augustinian notion of the doctrine of election that focused on individuals and often led to apathy before the sovereign choice of God. This Pinnock calls "a megashift in historical theology."[86]

What the "monergistic" Calvinistic tradition rightly emphasizes are the sovereignty and grace of God in salvation.[87] What it misses and where it has to be corrected is the way it formulates the idea of God's graciousness and power in terms of the human person's total incapacity and passivity. Not only may the goodness and desire to save all (1 Tim. 2:4) on the part of the hospitable God of the Bible be in danger of being marginalized in those Christian traditions that affirm dual predestination and nontemporal, nonhistorical, individually oriented doctrines of election, but also the responsibility and (relative) independence of the creature graciously granted by the same hospitable God.[88] The condition for the existence of the creature is God's decision to "make room" for it. Freedom is granted; it does not have to be won by the creature.[89] Yet, the freedom granted is partial and limited for two simple reasons. First, so much about our lives are simply givens, beginning with the fact that we were not asked, so to speak, if we wished to be born, what gender we would be, which nationality, and so forth. Second, for the world in which we live to be consistent, by and large it has to be deterministic.[90] That said, the freedom granted by the Creator to humanity is real and should be appreciated. Hence, "for us to be formed in the image of God, for which we are destined . . . we need to participate actively."[91] This is not to diminish the glory and graciousness of

---

84. Pinnock, *Wideness in God's Mercy*, pp. 18-24, 99.

85. Pinnock, *Wideness in God's Mercy*, pp. 13-14.

86. Pinnock, *Wideness in God's Mercy*, p. 35.

87. For the necessary importance of monergism to traditional Calvinism, see Warfield, *Calvin and Calvinism*, p. 359.

88. For the failure to see distinctions in differing notions of God's sovereignty in Calvinism, see F. S. Clarke, *The Ground of Election*, p. 168 and passim.

89. For details, see chap. 4 in *Creation and Humanity*.

90. For the discussion of determinism and freedom, see chap. 13 of *Creation and Humanity*.

91. Pannenberg, *ST* 3:436.

God, nor claim an improper degree of autonomy for humans; indeed, "[e]ven our appropriation of grace is a divine work."[92] Different from tradition, the scholastic thinker Peter Aureolus rightly argued that while God does not attribute merit to human response regarding election and calling, God also does not consider meaningless the human response to the offer of grace.[93] Because every human response is "graced," there should be no fear of merit since the good choice is already graced.[94]

Highlighting properly the role of the graced human response has nothing to do with Pelagianism, and one does not have to be an Arminian (or Wesleyan) to do so. What the Methodist Thomas Oden says of the patristic view prior to Augustine accurately describes it: "synergy of grace and freedom."[95] Human freedom (as limited as it is) is no less a result of grace than is the divine offer of grace. In this regard the literal meaning of "prevenient grace," namely, grace that "goes before," should be minded:[96] any human motion toward God, the Hospitable Giver, has graced the human life even before the offer of grace is received. This view can also be called "empowered synergism," which "begins with grace and ascribes the initiative and true power to God [but] is not Pelagian (which ascribes the power to choose to our nature as human beings) and so is not the opposite of monergism." An "empowered synergism" does not assert that we save ourselves, since salvation is by grace alone. It does assert that salvation "requires a free reception" rather than resistance by the person.[97]

"Preferential" Divine Hospitality

While it may sound trivial, the following statement by Alan P. F. Sell is worth mentioning: "the ideas of God's sovereignty and man's responsibility must be held together if the theological basis of Christianity is adequately to be

92. Henderson, "Election as Renewal," pp. 5-6.

93. For details, see Halverson, "Franciscan Theology," pp. 1-26.

94. No doubt, Arminius's view echoed Aureolus's views of election, but independently as far as I know. For Arminius in this respect, see Olson, *Arminian Theology*, pp. 183-85 particularly. Similarly, John Wesley's theology of election reflects the same orientations; see, e.g., John Wesley, "On Working Out Our Own Salvation."

95. T. Oden, *Transforming Power of Grace*, p. 98.

96. So also, Henderson, "Election as Renewal," p. 148.

97. Henderson, "Election as Renewal," p. 143; for a similar description of "synergism" (from an Arminian perspective), see Olson, *Arminian Theology*, p. 165.

set forth, and if Christian living is to flourish."[98] The question posed by Augustine's interlocutor Evodius still begs for a reasonable response: "how God can have foreknowledge of everything in the future, and yet we do not sin by necessity."[99] Eliminating all human choice — on the basis of eternal divine determination done before time and unrelated to the historical happenings[100] — seems a strange and perverted way of appreciating the fatherly love of the Creator God who wishes to have creatures with independence and freedom of choice (as limited as that is). Would a human parent do so? Could we think of the heavenly Father as any "worse" than the earthly counterpart of fatherhood created by the same God (Eph. 3:14-15)?

In defense of preferential hospitality, Boersma takes his point of departure from the election theology of the Deuteronomic literature (which in contemporary understanding embraces not only Deuteronomy but also Joshua, Judges, 1-2 Samuel, and 1-2 Kings). Boersma discerns in it four characteristics:

1. Election is based on sovereign grace (a dear theme to the Augustinian-Calvinistic tradition).
2. Election happens in history.
3. Therefore, it is a corporate act.
4. It is an "instrument," that is, "election is not futuristic in the sense that it determines who in the end will be saved," but rather "election has in view the maintenance of the covenant relationship and is therefore instrumental in character."[101]

Election is never an occasion for pride; it is rather a humbling event. God chooses that which is nothing in itself to make it worthy — as Luther's theology of the cross classically put it[102] and Deuteronomy reminds us (7:7). Election is never in violation of justice: the God who elects is also a righteous God who judges immorality, godlessness, and evil whether among the nations or (particularly) among his people. Election may also include

---

98. Sell, "Augustine versus Pelagius," p. 118, cited in Henderson, "Election as Renewal," p. 6.

99. Augustine, *On the Free Choice of Will* 3.2 (p. 73).

100. For this emphasis in recent "New Calvinism," see Duncan, "Resurgence of Calvinism in America," pp. 227-40; for a theological assessment and critique by a Reformed theologian, see Billings, "Calvin's Comeback?" pp. 22-25; and by an Arminian: Olson, *Against Calvinism*, chap. 1 and passim.

101. Boersma, *Violence, Hospitality, and the Cross*, pp. 75-79 (p. 78).

102. Luther, *Heidelberg Disputation* #28; *LW* 31:57.

discrimination, which is based not on immutable eternal decisions unrelated to history but rather on human choices.[103] Hence, election may include violence if any kind of use of power is considered to be violence. That "violence," however, is not self-serving, capricious, or tyrannical. It stems from holy love, fatherly love. Such is the world in which we live: only in the eschaton may we hope for final resolution of peace and overcoming of all violence and discrimination.[104]

Although surprisingly many liberation theologians of various sorts[105] have missed the potential liability of the Christian (and other Abrahamic faiths') doctrine of election with regard to unconditional divine hospitality, some First Nation (American Indian), feminist, and womanist, as well as postcolonialist, scholars have made it a theological theme. The German feminist Reformed theologian Margit Ernst-Habib lists important reasons for "the trouble with predestination," including particularly the denial of human "agency" and "the implicit or explicit danger of exclusive and hierarchical understanding of the chosen ones."[106] The issue of agency, or "being in control of one's own life[,] . . . is of particular importance for women who have been denied this control over much of history and are, in fact, still denied this control both outside and inside the rich Northern Hemisphere."[107] Divine hospitality and grace, as well as human liberation, should be the aim of the reworked theology of election, Ernst-Habib asserts.[108]

Postcolonial theologians relentlessly remind us, on the one hand, that it is time for theology to acknowledge the power play in its various forms, whether political, financial, educational, cultural, or any other, and on the other hand, that we are "all in a postcolonial situation as both colonized and colonizing persons. We all bear the marks of colonial histories that have formed us."[109] They

103. See Boersma, *Violence, Hospitality, and the Cross*, p. 87.

104. For extended discussions of hospitality and violence, see *Christ and Reconciliation*, chap. 12 (regarding the cross and suffering); *Trinity and Revelation*, chap. 14 (regarding faith in God); and *Creation and Humanity*, chap. 16 (concerning human flourishing).

105. The African American James H. Evans *(We Have Been Believers)* simply ignores the whole topic, as does another black theologian, James Cone, whose celebrated *Black Theology of Liberation* makes only occasional references. The Hispanic (Cuban American) Justo L. Gonzales *(Mañana)* does not even mention the words "election" or "predestination."

106. Ernst-Habib, "'Chosen by Grace,'" p. 77; on pp. 81-89, she offers a critical feminist reading of election tradition from Augustine via Calvin to Barth.

107. Ernst-Habib, "'Chosen by Grace,'" p. 79; she also refers to important comments in K. Tanner, *The Politics of God*, p. 23.

108. See Ernst-Habib, "'Chosen by Grace,'" pp. 89-94.

109. L. Russell, *Just Hospitality*, Kindle location 675-676.

rightly note that the idea of the divine "selection" has been used in Christian tradition as a means of excluding the "Other."[110] The critical reading of the biblical exodus traditions by Robert Allen Warrior of the Osage tribe (First Nation of America) in terms of subjugation of the nations already in the land in favor of the Israelites should concern all constructive theologians, particularly in light of the history of colonialism by the "Christian" nations.[111] Whereas those on the side of the power structures by default identify with the conquerors, the colonized mind-set finds a home with those expelled from their homeland and stripped of their rights.[112]

In light of these legitimate criticisms, constructive theology should acknowledge first that, unlike the various forms of abuses of the idea of election, the biblical teaching gives no legitimation whatsoever for the followers of Christ to exercise a colonialist mind-set. Indeed, they are called to "turn the other cheek" and follow in the path of the cross, to be servants rather than lords to all people. With the postcolonial readers of the Bible, we need to be reminded of the need to adopt various perspectives on texts — and so place the contemporary reader on both sides of the conflict when seen from the human perspective(s).[113] Most importantly, constructive theology should keep in mind that election in the Bible is not based at all on the superiority of the chosen people; rather, election is based on the mercy and wisdom of God and offers hope for the future for all men and women. In that respect, we should listen carefully to the remark of the Jewish feminist Judith Plaskow, that "it is not in the chosenness that cuts off, but in the distinctiveness that opens itself to difference that we find the God of Israel and of each and every people."[114]

Now that we have constructed a contemporary theology of election, it is time to delve into comparative theological work and see whether — and in what ways — two other Abrahamic faiths and two Asiatic traditions know the ideas of divine election and predestination, as well as the relationship between them and human freedom of will (or lack thereof).

---

110. L. Russell, *Just Hospitality*, Kindle location 815-816.

111. Warrior, "A Native American Perspective," pp. 287-95.

112. See L. Russell, *Just Hospitality*, Kindle location 836-855.

113. Tolbert, "When Resistance Becomes Repression," p. 332; I am indebted to L. Russell, *Just Hospitality*, Kindle location 2259-2261.

114. Plaskow, *Standing Again at Sinai*, p. 107, cited in L. Russell, *Just Hospitality*, Kindle location 822-824.

Determinism, Fatalism, and Freedom of Will among Religions

On the one hand, "[t]he essential presupposition of most major religions is that humans are born with freedom of choice."[115] On the other hand, most of the religions at the same time embrace the idea of divine election or divine determinism of some sort. Generally speaking, belief in divine election in some form is part not only of the three Abrahamic faiths[116] but also of all religious traditions that espouse an idea of an almighty and "personal" God. Notwithstanding widely differing versions of the belief in divine election, religions that endorse it share the following kinds of dilemmas and questions:

- First, how can belief in the election of a particular group of people be reconciled with belief in a universal God?
- Second, does the concept of election necessarily imply belief in the superiority of the chosen?
- Third, what is the relationship among election, predestination, and free will?
- And finally, how, in the face of competing claims to election, can one know if one's own claim is true?[117]

Because of the prominence of the themes of election and freedom of will versus determinism in Abrahamic traditions, let us first focus on them and thereafter consider Asiatic faith traditions.

Election and Free Will in Abrahamic Traditions

The "Chosen People" of Israel The most peculiar and formative doctrine of election can be found in Judaism. The idea of "chosen people" defines her identity. It is based on the covenant between Yahweh and his people. The beginning of election theology goes back to the choice of Abram (later: Abraham) as the father of the nation (Gen. 12). Exodus traditions (particularly chap. 19) apply the election to the whole nation, which is made a "priestly" people to spread the name of Yahweh among the nations. Deuteronomy 7:6 summarizes elec-

---

115. Marcoulesco, "Free Will and Determinism," p. 3200.

116. For an accessible recent discussion, see Firestone, *Who Are the Real Chosen People?*

117. Umansky, "Election," pp. 2744; I have added the bullet points to make it a list. This section is deeply indebted to this essay both in outline and in references.

tion succinctly: "For you are a people holy to the LORD your God; the LORD your God has chosen you to be a people for his own possession, out of all the peoples that are on the face of the earth" (see also 14:2).[118]

An important theme in Israelite election theology is the sovereignty of God in making the choice; it is solely based on Yahweh's love and purposes (which also include all other nations through the agency of his own people) and happens despite the unworthiness of the elected one (rather than because of her superiority).[119] Another defining theme is the selection of some for the sake of the people and her mission to other nations rather than for their own benefit.[120] Furthermore, the OT teaching espouses freedom of will to choose between either good or evil, as is evident in passages such as Deuteronomy 30:15-20 and the apocryphal Sirach 15:11-17.[121] Although in the "intertestamental" and NT times, among the three leading Jewish groups — Pharisees, Sadducees, and Essenes — there were understandably differing emphases,[122] none took divine action as overruling human responsibility.

As with everything else in Jewish tradition, catastrophic events helped consolidate and reshape theological views. With regard to election, the exile was the first such formative event. For the first time known as the "Jews," the people came to link suffering and tragedy to the destiny of the elected people, and the prophets (particularly Second Isaiah), tasked with a mission to be "a light to the nations" (Isa. 42:6), spoke more robustly of the universal implications of the election. (This is not to ignore the existence of Jewish voices that were deeply exclusivist, such as those among the sectarian Qumran community.)[123] The destruction of the temple and ensuing Diaspora in 70 C.E. was the next important shift in the consciousness of election: as a result of living "as a minority among people who often sought to oppress them, the concept of election continued to serve as a source of pride, strength, and hope for a better future." The emerging rabbinic tradition that came to guide the Jews from then on placed the emphasis on the close relationship between Yahweh and his people, as well as "on the life of Torah, by which Jews, chosen for holiness by God, were to live."[124] The rab-

---

118. Umansky, "Election," p. 2744.

119. This is in contrast to some later interpretations that highlight the spiritual superiority of the Jews, such as that in Philo, *Life of Moses* 1.278-279. Similarly differing are the later interpretations of *Numbers Rabbah* 14.10. See Umansky, "Election," p. 2745.

120. These include priests (Deut. 18:5; 1 Sam. 2:28) and kings (2 Sam. 6:21).

121. See D. Wallace, "Free Will and Predestination," p. 3203.

122. As accurately defined in Josephus, *Jewish Antiquities* 13.5.9.

123. For details, see Umansky, "Election," p. 2745.

124. Umansky, "Election," p. 2745.

binic emphasis on Yahweh's election also had to do with the strong resistance to Christian theology's implication that Israel was no longer the chosen people.[125]

Medieval theology, particularly as evident in the (even currently) hugely influential work *The Khuzari* by Judah Halevi, presents a highly idealized picture of the creation and superiority of the Jewish race, including Adam's perfect nature.[126] The tendency of "assigning of supernatural uniqueness to the Jewish people finds further expression in Jewish mystical works of the Middle Ages. One finds in qabbalistic literature, for example, the claim that only the souls of Israel are from God while the souls of others are base material."[127] It was not until the eighteenth century, among the European Jews who began to be accepted into society, that the uniqueness of the Jewish election was downplayed. That was made a leading theme in Moses Mendelssohn's *Jerusalem: Or on Religious Power and Judaism,* which also — in the spirit of the Christian Enlightenment thinkers — labored to make Judaism a religion of reason.[128] Some twentieth-century theologians went so far as to virtually deny, or, as in reconstructionist Mordecai Kaplan's case, replace with vocation, the whole idea of divine election.[129] That kind of dismissal of the ancient identity-forming proposal can only invite a response from the other end of the spectrum.[130]

What about freedom of the will vis-à-vis divine determinism? It is safe to say that, differently from Christian and Islamic versions of robust predeterminism, Jewish tradition does not interpret divine action in a way that would frustrate the exercise of human free will, and consequently of personal responsibility. In other words, divine predestination is not understood as undermining freedom of choice and responsibility.[131] Moses Maimonides' oft-cited description serves as a defining example. Having first considered "four different theories concerning Divine Providence," namely, pure chance, partial chance–partial providential, total control (which Maimonides believes is the mainstream Islamic view), and freedom of will (which he attributes to the

---

125. The standard study is Benjamin Helfgott, *The Doctrine of Election in Tannaitic Literature.* A shorter, highly useful discussion can be found in Urbach, *The Sages,* pp. 525-54 particularly.

126. *Judah Hallevi's Kitab al Khazar,* part 1, #95 (p. 64).

127. Umansky, "Election," p. 2746.

128. Highly useful is Gottlieb, "Introduction: Moses Mendelssohn and the Project of Modern Jewish Philosophy."

129. In the introduction to M. Kaplan's acclaimed work *Judaism as a Civilization.*

130. A bold and contested revisionist proposal is M. Wyschogrod, *The Body of Faith;* a moderate Orthodox proposal is that of David Novak, *The Election of Israel.*

131. See further, Gaon, *Book of Beliefs and Opinions,* pp. 181, 186.

Islamic Mu'tazilite tradition), he presents his own view: "According to this principle man does what is in his power to do, by his nature, his choice, and his will; and his action is not due to any faculty created for the purpose. All species of irrational animals likewise move by their own free will. This is the Will of God; that is to say, it is due to the eternal divine will that all living beings should move freely, and that man should have power to act according to his will or choice within the limits of his capacity."[132]

No wonder Maimonides was extremely critical of particularly the Asharite occasionalism. It is safe to say that unlike in its two sister faiths, Judaism has had no important long-term debates about the balancing of divine sovereignty and created human freedom. This standpoint is firmly anchored in Torah, which, as discussed, teaches both the covenant-God Yahweh's election and the covenant people's responsibility to stay faithful. This is not to ignore the incompatibility of the covenant partners, but is rather a persistent effort "to make sense of the intersection of the incompatible — the relative and the absolute, the human imperfection and divine perfection, the brawling chaos of historical experience and God's promise to fulfill a design in history."[133] The Catholic theologian Burrell succinctly summarizes the Jewish ethos: "What stands out in the Jewish tradition . . . is an untrammeled insistence on men and women as freely responding — positively or negatively — to the gift of Torah, for that divine invitation to a response constitutes this tradition."[134]

Divine Determinism and Human Responsibility in Islam Although in Islam the idea of divine election is less well developed than in the other two Abrahamic cousin traditions, "[f]ree will and predestination has been a prominent topic."[135] Regarding election, there is more emphasis in Islam on the election of several key persons such as Noah, Abraham, and several (other) prophets than in the OT, and of Jesus in the NT. The greatest stress understandably is placed on the election of the Prophet, Muhammad, and the community established by him *(ummah).* Somewhat similarly to Judaism, Islam teaches that while other nations might have known God, only Muslims know Allah intimately and are rightly related to God. That is most probably the meaning

132. Maimonides, *Guide for the Perplexed* 3.17; p. 287.

133. Alter, *Art of Biblical Narrative*, p. 154, cited in Burrell, *Freedom and Creation*, p. 84.

134. Burrell, *Freedom and Creation*, p. 85.

135. Watt and Afsaruddin, "Free Will and Predestination," p. 3209; see also, Hourani, "Ibn Sīnā's 'Essay on the Secret of Destiny'"; the essay can be found in Ibn Sina, *Risalah fi sirr al-qadar,* pp. 227-48; Perho, "Man Chooses His Destiny."

of the Qur'anic statements that Muslims, in distinction from others, are "God's sincere servants" (37:40), and "they are of the elect, the excellent" (38:40).[136]

> Not surprisingly, in Sufi movements the mystically oriented grasp of election comes to the fore: They identified the mystical insight, gnosis, as the inward essence of *islam,* or submission to God, an essence that, they maintained, could be penetrated only by the elect. . . . Believing that gnosis led one to attain the highest rank of human perfection, second only to the prophets, Sūfīs laid claim to sainthood. They based this claim not on personal merit but on Allāh's love or grace. To be chosen, then, was to receive the gift of sainthood, a gift that enabled one to penetrate into mysteries that could not be grasped through rational comprehension.[137]

A dominant principle of the Qur'anic teaching has to do with human responsibility, the shorthand for which is obedience (submission) to Allah and the consequences thereof.[138] M. A. Rauf frames the issue succinctly: "Hundreds of [Qur'anic] texts speaking of human responsibility could be quoted. . . . Holding man responsible for his deeds presupposes acknowledging his freedom of choice; and this freedom is clearly indicated or even categorically stated in several . . . passages" (such as 28:18; 25:62; 13:29, among others).[139] That said, as is well known, other important Qur'anic passages seem to deny any notion of human freedom of choice. Consider 35:8: "Indeed God leads astray whomever He will and guides whomever He will" (see also, e.g., 8:17-18).[140] Rauf makes the appealing argument that while the term *qadar* (to determine) for its first audience did not necessarily sound fatalistic, "[t]he political upheavals and the misfortunes they brought about seem to have disposed the psychology of the Muslim public to resignation to some sort of inevitability, and prepared their mentality to unconsciously develop a fatalistic notion of *qadar.*" In other words, those witnessing the catastrophic events beginning with the murder

---

136. Umansky, "Election," p. 2748.

137. Umansky, "Election," pp. 2748-49.

138. Whereas in pre-Islamic Arabic thinking human fate, particularly misfortune, was attributed to "time" *(dahr, zaman),* in the Qur'an it is of course attributed to Allah. This view is reflected in Q 45:24 (Watt and Afsaruddin, "Free Will and Predestination," p. 3209).

139. Rauf, "Qur'ān and the Free Will [I]," p. 206; see also, Rauf, "Qur'ān and the Free Will [II]," pp. 289-99. See also, Gorjian, "Determinism and Free Will in the Qur'an," pp. 47-62.

140. Typical Qur'anic passages that also seem to imply divine determinism over human life (and death) are 6:2; 45:24; 63:11, and with regard to human plans and action, are 3:154; 3:37; 57:22. For details, see Watt and Afsaruddin, "Free Will and Predestination," p. 3209.

of the third caliphate and the rise and aftermath of the Umayyad Caliphate "searched for comfort under the shelter of *qadar* in adverse circumstances, especially where the role of man was not prominent."[141] Be that as it may, similar to the polarity in the biblical canon, which has caused wide and long debates among Jewish and Christian commentators, from early on Muslim scholars found opposite ways of negotiating the hermeneutical standpoint. Not unlike in Abrahamic sister faiths, the dispute had to do with how to best reconcile God's omnipotence and righteousness (fairness).[142] (Although current scholarship is far less insistent on making key Islamic debates on determinism and free will a matter of Christian tradition's influence,[143] there is no denying the possibility of some important influence and exchange of views.)

Already at the end of the first Islamic century, a vigorous protest arose to challenge and refute the prevailing deterministic, often fatalistic, emphasis on divine determinism.[144] One of the most ironic — if not also confusing — nomenclatures in Muslim tradition is the "Qadarites." Obviously from the term *qadar,* it was applied astonishingly to both those who subscribed to divine determinism and those who excluded human free choice from under divine determination![145] The term, however, came to be applied to the latter group (and is used in that sense in this essay).

Generally speaking, the Qadarites (whose heyday was from the seventh to tenth centuries) wished to affirm human free will, which in turn justified God's punishment for intentional wrongdoings. In other words, freedom of will entails responsibility. Whether a full-blown Qadarite or not (a debated issue among Muslim scholars), al-Hasam al-Basri robustly defended free will. An important early formulation of what became the standard Qadarite view can be found in his famous letter to the Umayyad caliph 'Abd al-Malik[146] — a groundbreaking early theological treatise. Refuting the prevailing view of God determining all human actions, it "admitted the validity of a doctrine of *qadar*

---

141. Rauf, "The Qur'ān and the Free Will [II]," p. 290.

142. See further, Ansari, "Taftāzānī's Views on taklīf, gabr and qadar," p. 66. It is widely believed that whereas the Qur'an has two kinds of perspectives on divine determinism, as discussed, Hadith in the mainline has a robust deterministic view. A classic example is *Sahih Bukhari,* vol. 4, book 55, #549; see further, Watt and Afsaruddin, "Free Will and Predestination," p. 3211.

143. See Guillaume, "Some Remarks."

144. See further, Watt and Afsaruddin, "Free Will and Predestination," p. 3210.

145. For historical issues, see W. Watt, *Islamic Philosophy and Theology,* chap. 5; a more detailed discussion of this and related issues relevant to this discussion can be found in W. Watt, *Formative Period of Islamic Thought,* chap. 4.

146. For a detailed analysis, see M. Schwarz, "The Letter of al-Hasan al-Baṣrī."

covering all divine creations but excluding the area of human deeds. Man . . . brings about his own acts by his own free choice." If so, then the main difference from the Sunni position was that the Qadarite position is not willing to include human choice under the *qadar*.[147]

Later the influential Mu'tazilite movement adopted materially the Qadarite view (as part of its five basic tenets of faith) in contrast to the fierce opposition by the dominant Asharite tradition (ratified by the majority Sunni movement).[148] The most famous Asharite is of course the celebrated philosopher al-Ghazali, widely considered the founder of "occasionalism," a theory of causation according to which God is the sole acting agent and created beings are not acting agents.[149] This, however, does not rule out all human freedom. Generally speaking, two versions of the anti-Qadarite predestinarian positions developed in the debates. The more moderate form argued that while what happens is determined by Allah, each person's responses are not necessarily determined. The more extreme position took even the person's reactions as the work of Allah.[150] Rauf summarizes strikingly the end result of the debates: "The Qadarites exaggerated their views in a manner that shocked the Muslim public. The Sunnites, on the other hand, exaggerated their views into a harsh fatalistic interpretation."[151]

Concerning the modern and contemporary views among Muslim thinkers, it is safe to say that modernist Muslim commentators insist that the complexity of the Qur'anic teaching on freedom and determinism be duly acknowledged. A majority of them argue that, read as a whole, the Qur'an endorses the concept of human freedom in choosing one's belief and human responsibility for human actions. God has foreknowledge of human actions, but this divine knowledge does not compel humans to commit sin. Mu'tazili influence is clearly detected here.[152]

---

147. Rauf, "The Qur'ān and the Free Will [II]," pp. 295-96.

148. For the five Mu'tazilite tenets, see Watt, *Islamic Philosophy*, chap. 8, and for Asharites, chap. 10; see further, Burrell, *Freedom and Creation*, pp. 49-56.

149. See the definition and materials provided by the International Society for the Study of Occasionalism: http://occasionalism.org/.

150. The common nicknames for the predestinarians are Mujbirites and Jabrites; W. Watt, *Islamic Philosophy and Theology*, p. 29.

151. Rauf, "The Qur'ān and the Free Will [II]," p. 293.

152. Watt and Afsaruddin, "Free Will and Predestination," p. 3213. See also, Bhat, "Free Will and Determinism," p. 1.

A Brief Christian Engagement of Abrahamic Traditions

The Roman Catholic David B. Burrell places the discussion of election, freedom, and determinism among the Abrahamic faiths in proper perspective: "[H]uman freedom ought to take on a new cast in the light of those religious traditions which believe that the universe was freely created by God, and whose account of creation reserves a special place for free creatures and their response to the creator."[153] Following the intuitions won in the discussion of Christian doctrine of election, several conclusions and suggestions follow.

It seems to me that in keeping with Burrell's insight, all Abrahamic faiths are bound to robustly affirm relative, yet genuine, freedom of will and ensuing moral and religious responsibility. For any theist who believes in a personal Creator, freedom of the creature seems to be a "necessary" conclusion — if not for other reasons, then on the basis of analogy from personal life. Neither the parent-child, spouse-spouse, nor friend-friend relationship can be imagined without freedom of sorts. Jewish tradition reminds us that the incompatibility of the two partners, infinite God and finite human being, in no way does away with either freedom or responsibility. While I understand the reasons for the Augustinian-Calvinist-Edwardsean template of Christian "occasionalism," similar to that of the Asharites, I also consider it a misconstrual[154] for the reasons explained above in the defense of the hospitality of God.

Indeed, it seems to me that all Abrahamic faiths have much at stake in this question: provided that we all worship the same God[155] — God who freely creates a world distinct from himself with creatures with (relative and "graced") independence — we all have the need to seek a robust middle way between total determinism and independence of the creature (the latter viewpoint of which has never been a defining view in these traditions). Notwithstanding the fact that this negotiation can take place in more than one way, as the rich history of debates tells us, the common *intention* should be there. The ultimate reason for this goal is that at stake here is the hospitality of God (as argued above).

How would Asiatic traditions relate to Abrahamic views? That is the theme for the rest of the chapter.

---

153. Burrell, "Freedom and Creation in the Abrahamic Traditions."
154. It seems to me that Burrell, in *Freedom and Creation*, agrees.
155. For a detailed discussion, see my *Trinity and Revelation*, chap. 15.

Determinism, Fatalism, and Free Will in Asiatic Traditions

The Diversity of Hindu Interpretations Given the great diversity between and within the two traditions, the following statement helps us gain perspective:

> The main traditions of Hinduism and Buddhism do not posit a personal deity with an omnipotent will, and thus the polarity of free will and pre-destination in relation to the salvation of souls has not been so prominent as in Judaism, Christianity, and Islam. The doctrine of *karman* can consti-tute a kind of determinism whereby an individual's lot in life is determined by his behavior in past lives, but the doctrine can also imply that a soul is in charge of its future destiny; its modern proponents therefore sometimes consider the doctrine to imply freedom more than fatalism.[156]

Fatalistic or not, the Abrahamic traditions' followers to whom the pan–South Asian concept of karma is foreign need to be reminded that at its core, "*karma* encompasses the unity and interrelatedness of all phenomena, their fundamental contingency" as well as, importantly, "the acts or rituals *(kar-man)* capable of destroying the bonds of transmigration." The critical point to understand about karma is that it reaches beyond incarnations, not only this life — another concept foreign to Abrahamic faiths.[157]

On the one hand, then, karma means that everyone's destiny is prede-termined by the behavior in past lives, but on the other hand, as the quote above indicates, "a soul is in charge of its future."[158] The latter viewpoint comes to the fore particularly in the ancient concept of *svāraj* (self-ruling), which can be found already in Chandogya Upanishad (7.25.2).[159] (As many know, Mahatma Gandhi took this conception as the basis for his social activism and desire to make a real change in life conditions, including political and moral spheres.)[160] Klaus K. Klostermaier's remark expresses pointedly the essence of the karmic dynamic: "*Karma* does not cancel free will and genuinely free decision, nor do free will and one's own decisions neutralize *karma*."[161] In light of the capacity of Hinduism to embrace both "orthodox" and "heretical"

---

156. D. Wallace, "Free Will and Predestination," p. 3204.

157. Marcoulesco, "Free Will and Determinism," p. 3200.

158. D. Wallace, "Free Will and Predestination," p. 3204. For useful comments, see also, Sharma, *Classical Hindu Thought*, pp. 99-100.

159. Marcoulesco, "Free Will and Determinism," p. 3201.

160. See Gandhi, *Hind Swaraj and Indian Home Rule*.

161. Klostermaier, *Survey of Hinduism*, p. 176.

teachings and their applications, this means that the mere following of Vedic authority and caste rules (which regulate both social and religious life) may not be enough for "salvation by Visnu — the person must be elected by Him, an election that must be earned through acts of devotion and service," and "such behavior also is insisted upon by Vaisnava writers." It also means that "the perfect one, the saint, the guru can take liberties with rules and regulations: divine license suspends human law." To make things even more complicated, in a *bhakti* context (that is, devotion to a deity), a person may be considered a saint even if his or her rights are denied based on caste regulations; similarly, in that environment even one who denies Vedic authority (a *nāstika*, that is, "heretic") is given access to "salvation"![162]

Among the diverse Hindu traditions, there is perhaps no other that takes freedom of will as seriously as *Yoga Vasistha*, the famous Purana mentioned above (chap. 7). Named *paurusa*, free will may even gain control over karma; this is astonishing in that, generally speaking, not only all creatures but also deities are under karma! In some real sense, it is possible for the present to overrule the past. Although not limitless, human effort may work out great things if done according to the scriptures and, because of human weakness, in the community of the faithful. Indeed, one's destiny *(daiva)* is not predetermined but can be fashioned according to the powers of *paurusa*.[163] On the other end of the spectrum is the curious teaching of predestination by the Vaishnavite Madhva tradition. Unlike most Hindu traditions, it embraces a fairly rigid doctrine according to which some people are predestined for an eternal blessed state while others are predestined for judgment (without a possibility of changing one's destiny) — and that is not contingent upon their merits.[164]

Unlike the strictly advaitic (Sankara) tradition (to which *Yoga Vasistha* also belongs), there are theistic movements of Hinduism that are personalistically oriented and in which the idea of "election" appears in some form. Particularly influential are various Vaishnavite movements (followers of the Vishnu deity) and its most important theologian, Ramanuja. Although it is clear that these hold no doctrine of divine election and predestination similar to the teachings of Abrahamic faiths, particularly Christian, some common themes and concerns may be found.[165] Generally speaking, "even though the blame for evil is usually cast upon the god who causes human imperfections and thus dooms humanity

---

162. Klostermaier, *Survey of Hinduism*, p. 43.

163. Dasgupta, *History of Indian Philosophy*, 2:252-56.

164. D. Wallace, "Free Will and Predestination," p. 3204; Klostermaier, *Survey of Hinduism*, pp. 239-40.

165. Barua, "Dialectic of Divine 'Grace' and 'Justice,'" p. 46.

to downfall, people are still held morally responsible for their woes, as they are for corrupting other human beings."[166] At first glance, Ramanuja's apparent endorsement of the teaching of the Kaushitaki Upanishad,[167] according to which both good and evil deeds are predetermined by "the lord of the universes," seems to support a view similar to the Christian doctrine of double predestination. His comments on this scriptural text, however, admit that that Upanishadic text "does not agree with the partial independence claimed above for the soul," and therefore it "means that the Lord, wishing to do a favour to those who are resolved on acting so as fully to please the highest Person, engenders in their minds a tendency towards highly virtuous actions, such as are means to attain to him; while on the other hand, in order to punish those who are resolved on lines of action altogether displeasing to him, he engenders in their minds a delight in such actions as have a downward tendency and are obstacles in the way of the attainment of the Lord."[168] This interpretation is in keeping with his general understanding that "some persons were led to repentance by a divine initiative," whereas "the choice of good or evil nonetheless included personal acts performed by means of a God-given freedom."[169]

There is a genuine concept of "grace" visible in Ramanuja's teaching, as he claims — somewhat like Christian tradition stemming from Saint Augustine — that "the self derives its agency not from itself but from the Lord who is the inner Controller of all its actions."[170] In other words, Ramanuja makes every effort to hold in dynamic balance "the Lord's help offered to the devotee in a 'gracious' manner, on the one hand, and the active response to this help of the devotee, on the other."[171] Not surprisingly, his followers came to be divided over this issue. These two main groups are commonly known as "Cat School,"

---

166. Marcoulesco, "Free Will and Determinism," p. 3200; for the dynamic between God's "will" and the existence of suffering in the world, see Radhakrishnan, *Indian Philosophy*, 2:440-41.

167. Kaushitaki Upanishad 3.8; *SBE* 1:299-300.

168. Ramanuja, *Vedanta Sutras* 2.3.41; *SBE* 48:558; I am indebted to Barua, "Dialectic of Divine 'Grace' and 'Justice,'" p. 52.

169. D. Wallace, "Free Will and Predestination," p. 3204. For a highly useful and nuanced discussion of Ramanuja's view, see also, Radhakrishnan, *Indian Philosophy*, 2:693-96, 703 particularly; for Sankara's views, see, p. 635.

170. Barua, "Dialectic of Divine 'Grace' and 'Justice,'" p. 52, with reference to Ramanuja, *Vedanta Sutras* 2.3.40; *SBE* 48:557.

171. Barua, "Dialectic of Divine 'Grace' and 'Justice,'" p. 52. Divine grace and favor — without overruling human response — also come to the fore in Ramanuja, *Vedanta Sutras* 1.1.1 ("The Small Sidhanta"); *SBE* 48:15, which comments on the well-known passage in Katha Upanishad 1.2.23 (*SBE* 15:111); see further, Barua, pp. 51-52.

the Tenkalai, and "Monkey School," the Vatakali. Whereas the former envisions "God's irresistible grace" working similarly to the mother carrying a baby kitten by the nape of the neck, the latter believes in synergism between divine grace and human will, using the analogy of a baby monkey clinging to her mother.[172]

A somewhat similar dynamic to that of Ramanuja is expressed in the Bhagavad Gita, the "bible" of the common folk: the spiritual influence of that delightful scripture on the Indian faithful masses should never be underestimated. The classic locus of discussion is at the end of the Gita (18.14-15), where five factors seem to be enumerated as contributing to human action — not merely free will and fate: (1) the "material" basis, (2) the doer, (3) instruments, (4) efforts, and (5) fate.[173] If this is a correct interpretation, then it simply means that for any human action and choice, "[t]he outcome seems to be the result of both free will as represented by the doer and his efforts, and fate acting in a given environment involving given instruments."[174] This may be the best way to account for the dynamic picture of fate and free will as represented in the narrative of the Gita. Consider the advice by Krishna to Arjuna concerning what to do about the fight (against his own family):

> The Lord abides in the heart of all beings, O Arjuna, causing all beings to act (or work out their Karma) by His power of Maya as if they are (puppets of Karma) mounted on a machine.
>
> Seek refuge in Him alone with all your heart, O Arjuna. By His grace you shall attain supreme peace and the eternal abode. Thus the knowledge that is more secret than the secret has been explained to you by Me. After fully reflecting on this, do as you wish. (18.61-63)[175]

What is also highly interesting for a Christian — and I expect also for the Jewish reader — about the Gita is that there seem to be events that are totally and sovereignly predetermined by Krishna, the Lord, namely, the destruction of the Kauravas family, along with many other nations (11.26-34).[176]

All in all, particularly in those Hindu theistic movements that are per-

---

172. D. Wallace, "Free Will and Predestination," pp. 3204-5.

173. Translation of v. 14 particularly is difficult and has caused wide disagreement among the commentators. See Sharma, "Free Will and Fate," p. 531.

174. Sharma, "Free Will and Fate," p. 532.

175. See also the many preceding verses in which the same dynamic is brought to bear on the topic; cf. Sharma, "Free Will and Fate," pp. 532-33, for a somewhat different outlook on this and some other relevant passages.

176. See further, Sharma, "Free Will and Fate," pp. 534-36.

sonalistically oriented, there appears to be a dynamic between divine determinism and human response similar to that of Christian (and more widely, Abrahamic) traditions. Furthermore, there are also individual traditions that seem to major in either "libertarian" or "Augustinian-Calvinist" orientations, to use Christian nomenclature. What about Buddhist movements?

The Complexity of the Buddhist Interpretations of Freedom and Determinism To Theravadins whose faith is not theistic at all (apart from theistic orientations of folk religiosity), but also to most Mahayana followers, except for Pure Land,[177] talk about divine election is not relevant.[178] This is not to completely deny the possibility of an idea of divine favor or election among some theistically driven Mahayana movements; it is rather a summary statement about Buddhism at large. No wonder current scholarship agrees that the wide question of freedom (of will) and determinism is an utterly complex and complicated theme in Buddhist tradition.[179] Briefly put: the Buddha's own teachings in the scriptures can hardly be reconciled in an agreed-upon manner.[180] Some experts take for granted the lack of freedom of will in Buddhism,[181] and others not only affirm its existence but also claim that the Buddha's teaching endorses an even more robust idea of freedom than that held by Christians![182] The reasons for this dilemma are not hard to find: on the one hand, because Buddhist philosophy seeks to explain the world in terms of causal relations and interdependence, and because of its denial of the existence of "soul,"[183] there seems to be very little room for personal choice, even responsibility.[184] On the other hand, precisely because there is no god to depend on, the human person is left totally on his or her own in the pursuit of "salvation" — particularly in light of the lack of any kind of atonement teaching after Abrahamic faiths.[185]

177. See Nakamura, "Pure Land Buddhism and Western Christianity Compared."

178. See P. Harvey, "'Freedom of the Will' in the Light of Theravada Buddhist Teachings."

179. For a balanced discussion, see Gier and Kjellberg, "Buddhism and the Freedom of the Will."

180. For a careful and accessible scrutiny of some key scriptural texts, see Gómez, "Some Aspects of the Free-Will Question in the Nikāyas."

181. Wallace and Searle, "Consciousness East and West," referenced in Federman, "What Kind of Free Will Did the Buddha Teach?" p. 1 n. 1.

182. Gombrich, "Appreciating the Buddha," cited in Federman, "What Kind of Free Will Did the Buddha Teach?" p. 1 n. 1.

183. For a careful recent discussion, see Sridharan, "The Metaphysics of No-Self."

184. Federman, "What Kind of Free Will Did the Buddha Teach?" p. 1.

185. For differing views, see Federman, "What Kind of Free Will Did the Buddha Teach?" pp. 2-3 and passim.

Absent scholarly consensus, let it suffice to refer to the statement by the Buddhist B. Alan Wallace. Having acknowledged both the general Buddhist view of lack of freedom of will (in any independent sense) and Buddha's well-known reluctance to delve into the metaphysical speculations of those issues, Wallace concludes:

> [T]he Buddha rejected the philosophical extremes of both determinism and indeterminism and discouraged his followers from embracing any view that might undermine their inspiration to devote themselves to an ethical life in the pursuit of liberation. In pragmatic terms, as ordinary sentient beings we do not have free will to achieve what is of value within our range of circumstances in so far as our minds are dominated by ignorance and its derivative mental afflictions. But the Buddha declared that these sources of bondage are not inherent to our very existence, that they may be dispelled through sustained, skilful spiritual practice.[186]

It seems to me this "practical" and at the same time radically middle-way argument is as good as any and helps Christians better understand the distinctive ethical-spiritual pursuit of Buddhists.

In this chapter we have sought to delve in some detail into the complicated set of questions concerning the divine initiative of human salvation in Christian tradition. We have argued for a constructive doctrine of election based on a merciful invitation for fellowship by the hospitable God, a call for true human response, and then placed that proposal in dialogue with the views of freedom, determinism, and fatalism in four living faiths. Out next task will be to look at the human response to such an invitation, which in Christian tradition is related to *ordo salutis* concepts such as conversion, repentance, and forgiveness of sins. Once a Christian theology of "graced human response" to God's favorable invitation is constructed, in keeping with the method of this project, a comparative theological exercise will be attempted as far as it makes sense and honors the distinctive nature of each of the four living faith traditions' soteriological visions.

---

186. B. A. Wallace, "Buddhist View of Free Will."

10. (Re-)Turning to God — and to the Neighbor

Conversion and Repentance

A common term in the Christian thesaurus — although in no way distinctively biblical nor unique in the history of religions[1] — "conversion" elicits a number of debates about its meaning[2] and suitability for the current postmodern[3] and pluralistic context of ours. "Conversion" also has a loaded history, as it has been linked with proselytism, colonialization, and similar suspicious activities. The ambiguity about its meaning is heightened by the long-term philosophical and later interdisciplinary debates (in behavioral, social, neurological, and other science-related fields).[4]

In the traditional theological *ordo salutis*, conversion has an established locus. It was typical to include under conversion "repentance" as the way to turn away from sin with accompanying regret and remorse and turn to Christ in faith.[5] Depending on one's theological tradition, conversion is either followed by regeneration/new birth (Lutheranism) or preceded by it.[6] Similarly

---

1. See, e.g., Finn, *From Death to Rebirth.*

2. Note Kerr and Mulder's title: *Conversions: The Christian Experience.* For the diversity of biblical and theological definitions, see Peace, *Conversion in the New Testament,* pp. 5-7; Gaventa, *From Darkness to Light,* pp. 1-16.

3. See van der Veer, ed., *Conversion to Modernities;* Viswanathan, *Outside the Fold;* Kallenberg, "Conversion Converted."

4. See Darroll and Lamb, eds., *Religious Conversion.*

5. Erickson, *Christian Theology,* pp. 933-42, 942-46, respectively.

6. For details and original sources, see McKim, "Mainline Protestant Understanding of Conversion," pp. 129-30.

to forgiveness, repentance and conversion, as personal acts as they are, are also integrally related to sacraments, particularly to the sacrament of reconciliation (penance) and the Eucharist.[7] Although *Christian* conversion, in line with the teachings of other Abrahamic traditions, always takes return to God as primary, it "implies a reorientation to God and to fellow human beings at the same time."[8]

This section will first construct a theological account of conversion and then place that in sympathetic and critical dialogue with interdisciplinary, intercultural, and interreligious interpretations and issues.

Conversion in a Theological Perspective

Recall that the very first public announcement of Jesus in Mark's Gospel has to do with repentance (1:15).[9] Similarly to the main term denoting conversion in the OT, *shuv*,[10] the NT *epistrephō* means "to turn (around)."[11] The religious usage of these terms entails turning away from evil and disobedience to serving God. Other important NT terms are *metanoeō*, "to repent" (from the literal meaning, "thinking-after"), and *metamelomai*, "to regret." The presence together of the first two in Acts 3:19-20 ("Repent . . . and turn again, that your sins *may* be blotted out") demonstrates the idea of conversion in terms of returning and repentance/regret.[12] Behind the OT term *nacham*, another main OT term for repentance, is the meaning "to pant" or "to groan," out of which the meaning "to lament or to grieve" is derived; interestingly, it is also used many times of Yahweh (as in Gen. 6:6 and Exod. 32:14).[13]

Similar to the reception of forgiveness, the act of repentance and remorse takes a lot of humility, as one has to admit, at times publicly, one's failure to meet the standard. Human self-love and self-righteousness oppose that.[14]

---

7. See further, Lyden, "From Sacrifice to Sacrament," pp. 50-55.

8. DeVries, "What Is Conversion?" p. 28, cited in Langmead, "Transformed Relationships," p. 11.

9. For comments, see Cox, "Repentance and Forgiveness," pp. 21-22.

10. Among the over 1,000 occurrences, the distinctly religious usage occurs about 120 times (Laubach, "Epistrephō").

11. Laubach, "Epistrephō."

12. See Peace, *Conversion in the New Testament*, pp. 346-53. See also, Löffler, "Biblical Concept of Conversion," pp. 24-45.

13. BDB, pp. 636-37.

14. For comments, see H. O. J. Brown, "Godly Sorrow," p. 33.

Yet "godly sorrow" due to one's mistakes and sins not only looks at the past, it is "hopeful sorrow" as it also anticipates restoration.[15]

Unlike common assumptions, in the Bible, particularly in the OT, conversion is rarely linked with the change of religion; it is rather a call for the people of Israel to (re-)turn to God. This is of course not to undermine the possibility of changing religion in our contemporary pluralistic world, but rather to remind us of the central place of the idea of conversion in the life of the people of God.

What was the main target of conversion and repentance in Jesus' message? Did he address mainly individuals or the whole people of God? Building on long tradition, stemming all the way from the beginning of the original quest of the historical Jesus, N. T. Wright and several other contemporary NT theologians have argued that the main target was Israel as a nation. In that understanding, Jesus' call was a unique, onetime eschatological call for the people of God to repent in order to be prepared for the restoration.[16] Consequently, the call for repentance has little to do with the individualistic turn that the church adopted thereafter. Is that correct? Hardly as a main interpretation. On the contrary, it seems clear to me that while in the preaching of the OT prophets, the people of God was the main audience, Jesus seemed to call for repentance primarily of individuals, although "[u]ltimately of course the individual and the national will not be unrelated."[17] That seemed to have been the way the church understood and continued the legacy of Jesus.

In Christian tradition, Saint Paul's conversion experience has drawn wide interest[18] (as narrated in Acts 9:1-19; 22:3-21; 26:1-23 and referred to by Paul in his own writings).[19] Whereas conversion clearly was a process in the lives of the disciples, for Paul it seems to have been an event.[20] While we have to leave to the NT experts the continuing debate about whether Paul's

---

15. See further, H. O. J. Brown, "Godly Sorrow," pp. 39-40.

16. See, e.g., N. T. Wright, *Jesus and the Victory of God*, p. 251.

17. Caird, *New Testament Theology*, p. 359. For a balanced discussion and critique, see Chatraw, "Jesus' Theology of Repentance and Forgiveness" (the previous citation is indebted to it).

18. See Peace, *Conversion in the New Testament*, chaps. 1–4. For a detailed scrutiny of Paul's own references to conversion, see Seyoon Kim, *Origin of Paul's Gospel*, pp. 3-31. For a shorter discussion of "models of conversion in the New Testament," see Smith, *Beginning Well*, chap. 5; Tyson, "John Wesley's Conversion at Aldersgate," pp. 27-42.

19. See also, Talbert, "Conversion in the Acts of the Apostles," pp. 141-53; Méndez-Moratalla, *The Paradigm of Conversion in Luke*.

20. Peace, *Conversion in the New Testament*, p. 106.

was a call (to ministry)[21] more than an initial conversion, systematically we shouldn't keep these two at arm's length from each other. Indeed, as established above in the discussion of election, God's invitation through the Spirit entails also a missionary vocation and call to everyone.[22] It also seems clear that in the NT, unlike in much of later revivalism, conversion is not usually linked with the feeling of a guilty conscience.[23] Related to this is the insight of Moltmann that conversion, the "re-turn," is not so much a "turn back" as a *"turn to the future,"*[24] a dedication and pledge of loyalty to the message and lifestyle of Jesus. Conversion and repentance point to the possibility of a new beginning.

What, then, are the place and meaning of conversion in a systematic theological outlook? Theologically, we may say that conversion is "a work of the Holy Spirit, involving the mystery of divine initiative and human response at the same time. It is a restoration of relationship between us and God which involves a reordering of relationships with others."[25] Conversion needs to be placed in a wider context in the encounter between God and human persons: "Christian conversion can be seen as reconciliation in at least three dimensions: being reconciled to God, ourselves and others."[26] An illustration of this wider perspective is the late Canadian Baptist Stanley J. Grenz's way of making conversion an umbrella concept in the *ordo salutis.* First he discusses "the dynamics of conversion," focusing on individual aspects such as repentance and faith, including what he calls the "divine aspects," namely, the Holy Spirit's role in conviction, call, illumination, and enablement. He further argues that this "process of salvation" can be expressed under various nomenclatures when it comes to individual life such as regeneration, justification, and liberation. The second part of his discussion deals with "the community aspect of conversion," focusing on the community's role in preaching the gospel with the expectation of joining the community; therein he also discusses the rites of initiation, including water baptism.[27] In a similar vein, the American Methodist biblical

---

21. As famously argued by Stendahl, *Paul among Jews and Gentiles,* p. 7.

22. Similarly, Peace (*Conversion in the New Testament,* p. 29) refuses to separate conversion and call.

23. See Stendahl, *Paul among Jews and Gentiles,* pp. 12-13, 17.

24. Moltmann, *Experiences of God,* p. 24, emphasis in original, cited in Ledgerwood, "The Hope of Forgiveness," p. 15.

25. Langmead, "Transformed Relationships," p. 10.

26. Langmead, "Transformed Relationships," p. 10.

27. Grenz, *Theology for the Community of God,* pp. 405-40; see also, McKim, "Mainline Protestant Understanding of Conversion," pp. 130-35.

scholar Joel B. Green speaks importantly of conversion as "a many-sided affair": "It is first the story of God's provenience, God's gracious visitation that precedes and opens the way for human responses of changed hearts and lives. This conversion reaches the whole of life and cannot be reduced to one's inner being."[28] Indeed, one of the emerging themes in contemporary theology of conversion involves its linking with the whole human being, not merely the inner or spiritual. Conversion has to do with the transformation of the whole human being and thus also has much to do with embodiment.[29] Naming it "embodied cognition," Green urges us to get rid of "the fallacy of imagining that intellect and affect are separable, the fallacy of imagining that human life can be understood merely or primarily with respect to individuals," and instead see that "human formation is a process."[30]

Revivalism and "Conversionist Piety": An Affirmation and a Critique

As is well known, conversion has become a main theme in revivalism, whether in Pietism following Reformation times, the Great Awakenings of the nineteenth century on both sides of the Atlantic,[31] evangelicalism,[32] Pentecostalism,[33] or a number of similar phenomena in the twentieth century.[34] Although, understandably, the revivalist conversion tradition is liable to easy criticism, theologians should avoid a premature negative judgment[35] and first consider the positive impulse of that conversionist orientation. If evangelicals, Pentecostals/charismatics, independent Christians, and huge numbers of Christians in the Global South may appear to be overly enthusiastic in winning converts, the same cannot be said of established churches, particularly in the Global North! Among many "liberal" churches the whole idea of evangelization and mission

---

28. J. Green, *Why Salvation?* p. 115.

29. For a passionate call, see Markham, *Rewired,* chap. 1 and passim. Similarly, J. Green, *Body, Soul, and Human Life,* chap. 4.

30. J. Green, *Body, Soul, and Human Life,* p. 122.

31. For the centrality of conversion for Jonathan Edwards, see his "Narrative of Surprising Conversions," p. 40.

32. Bebbington, *Evangelicalism in Modern Britain,* pp. 1-19, lists "conversionism" as one of the four defining features of evangelicalism.

33. In Creemens, "Ecumenical Dialogue with a Non-Institutional Movement," pp. 16-22.

34. For the term "convertive piety," see Dayton, "The Limits of Evangelicalism," p. 48.

35. See a recent example by the Greek Orthodox theologian Christ Yannaras of an unnuanced, harsh judgment of the conversionist element: "Pietism as Ecclesiological Heresy," pp. 120-22.

in terms of invitation for conversion has become not only marginalized but almost taboo. Importantly in the Roman Catholic Church, which speaks much more robustly of conversion and evangelization (usually with the emphasis on reaching out to those Catholics who have grown passive in faith), some theologians are lamenting that "the dominant Scholastic mode of theology effectively lost the experience of conversion in the metaphysical analysis of faith, grace, and justification."[36]

In terms of constructive critique of the revivalist paradigm, noteworthy is the dual view of conversion in the NT. Clearly, in the NT, conversion both as event and process is present. To account for that, R. Peace speaks of "encounter evangelism" and "process evangelism," respectively. The former includes mass evangelism, personal evangelism, and the use of media, among other strategies. Although encounter evangelism is an easy target of critique because of its frequently thin message, its weak follow-up, its tendency to triumphalism, its neglect (or even rejection) of previous religious experiences of the people, and so forth, there is no biblical, pastoral, or theological reason for leaving it behind. At the same time, advocates of the encounter approach should be reminded not to juxtapose it with the process approach, which sees conversion more in gradual terms and relating to the whole of life. The latter also honors the quest itself, values deep commitment, and often displays a more holistic view of what makes Christian life and pilgrimage. That approach also includes spiritual disciplines as part of cultivation of Christian life.[37] The Anabaptist ethicist Erin Dufault-Hunter's expression of "conversion to thick faith [that] envelops all aspects of a person's life, infusing one with new meaning, habits, and goals" captures important aspects of this inclusive paradigm.[38]

In light of the perceived liabilities of the revivalistic traditions' view of conversion, some leading evangelical theologians and missiologists are working toward redefining conversion. In his seminal study on the understanding of conversion in various evangelical traditions, the Canadian Gordon T. Smith exposes its limitations and liabilities:

> Older revivalism assumed that conversion was punctiliar, that the focus of a converted life was religious activities, in anticipation of a life "in heaven"

36. Conn, *Christian Conversion*, p. 6, cited in Hudson, "Catholic View of Conversion," p. 110; see also, pp. 115-16.

37. For a pastorally and theologically important discussion and critique, see Peace, *Conversion in the New Testament*, chaps. 11, 12, 13; for similar reflections from a Wesleyan perspective. see Knight, "Transformation of the Human Heart," pp. 43-55.

38. Dufault-Hunter, *Transformative Power of Faith*, p. x.

that would come after death, and that this "conversion" was essentially an interior, personal, and subjective transaction. Revivalists had little appreciation of the place of the sacraments or the intellect in spiritual life. For the revivalists, the church has only one agenda: to obtain converts; to be successful, congregations should have plenty of growth by conversion.[39]

To that litany can be added the use of fear of death as a motive for conversion, as is evident for example in John Wesley.[40] As a way of correction, in a new paradigm of understanding conversion,

- heart and mind will be integrated;
- body and mind will be integrated;
- individual and communal aspects will be noted;
- human will and divine initiative will be put in a dialectical mutual relationship;
- conversion will be seen as both an "arrival" and a "beginning";
- the sacraments will be incorporated into conversion;
- the transmission of Christian faith from one generation to another will not be dismissed; and
- the hope for the world to come and this-worldly focus will be put in a dialectical relationship.[41]

The maturation of the revivalist tradition, as clearly evident in this revised account of conversion, possesses amazing ecumenical potential. It may also help the more traditional ecclesiastical families to rediscover in their daily practice the importance of conversion.

Theologically significant is also the wide interest in the category of conversion among philosophers and scientists from various disciplines. To that we turn next, to be followed by the location of conversion in the wider cultural and religious plurality.

---

39. Smith, *Transforming Conversion*, p. ix; for details, see pp. 1-16.
40. Collins, "John Wesley and the Fear of Death," pp. 56-68.
41. Smith, *Transforming Conversion*, pp. 17-18.

A Theological Assessment of Philosophical and
Interdisciplinary Study of Conversion

The rise of new religious movements in recent decades has elicited interest among researchers of conversion.[42] Another important reason why many sociologists and other scholars studying the society have become interested in conversion has to do with the widespread concern about "seriously deteriorating social conditions in the industrialized world," which result not only in crime, abuse, and other social problems but also in alienation and marginalization, what the sociologist Francis Fukuyama named "the great disruption."[43] Linked with this is the acknowledgment of the difficulty of current Western societies to deal with the topics of repentance, remorse, and guilt. Indeed, there are no established social processes, for example, for "ex-cons" or fallen politicians to "convert" and gain acceptance in the media and public opinion,[44] particularly now that the religion-based social order has been left behind.[45]

All contemporary philosophical and scientific accounts of the category of conversion take note of the classic definition of the American pragmatist William James. The key to his phenomenologically focused account of the *experience* of conversion was the change "by which a self hitherto divided . . . becomes unified . . . in consequence of its firmer hold upon religious realities."[46] This profound transformation brings about a moral change. While doctrinal and rational content is secondary,[47] "[i]t makes a great difference to a man whether one set of his ideas, or another, be the centre of his energy," because of the fact "that religious ideas, previously peripheral in his consciousness, now take a central place, and that religious aims form the habitual centre of his energy."[48]

Unlike in James, a thoroughgoing dismissal (often even pejorative ridiculing) of the *content*[49] of the experience or influence that stimulates conversion

---

42. Richardson, "Conversion and New Religious Movements."

43. Fukuyama, *The Great Disruption*, p. 4; I am indebted to Dufault-Hunter, *Transformative Power of Faith*, pp. 2-8.

44. See further, "Introduction," in *RCP*, pp. 1-4; Braithwaite, *Crime, Shame, and Reintegration*.

45. See Bellah, *The Good Society*; Etzioni, *The New Golden Rule*.

46. James, *Varieties of Religious Experience*, p. 188.

47. See James, *Varieties of Religious Experience*, pp. 433-34.

48. James, *Varieties of Religious Experience*, pp. 194-95. This section is indebted to Dufault-Hunter, *Transformative Power*, chap. 2.

49. For the grave limitations of a mere empirical approach to the study of conversion, see Jindra, "How Religious Content Matters."

comes through in several forms in contemporary thinking. For those who oppose religion per se, whether because of its alleged irrationality (the new atheism of R. Dawkins and a host of others),[50] or its violence (M. Mark Juergensmeyer, among others),[51] or its reduction to a "neurological basis" (S. Harris),[52] or its pathological nature (F. Nietzsche, S. Freud, K. Marx, all in their own ways),[53] "behind" conversion there is nothing — except falsehood, illusion, or bad imagination.[54] Even when the critique of religion is not the driving force, "the tendency in sociology has been to assume that sincere observance of certain faiths ... must also imply irrationality on the agent's part."[55] Not infrequently, the convert appears not only as an object of proselytizing activity[56] but even as a victim of it. Conversion may be attributed for example to "an emotional upheaval and promises of relief by a new attachment."[57] Part of this tendency is the linkage of religious conversion with social and economic deprivation.[58]

Although no one wishes to deny that in some cases conversion can be explained with the help of these models, many seemingly healthy, rational, and well-to-do people undergo and sustain a conversion experience. Similar critique can be targeted against the neuropsychological and neurocognitive study of conversion that has tended to explain conversion with the help of abnormal experiences such as seizures or epilepsy. Although the relationship between epilepsy and heightened religious activity and mystical experiences can be statistically established,[59] it would be absurd to dismiss the vast majority of conversions in which no extraordinary neuropsychological or neurocognitive activity is present. All these approaches to the study of conversion among various disciplines tend to be reductionist and limited on more than one account. First, they focus solely on phenomenology or experience or alleged sociological reasons such as deprivation. Second, these paradigms have a strong tendency to try to explain conversion using only one model of

50. See *Trinity and Revelation*, pp. 198-201.

51. See *Trinity and Revelation*, pp. 324-31.

52. See chap. 13 in *Creation and Humanity*.

53. See *Trinity and Revelation*, pp. 195-98.

54. Consult Stark and Finke, *Acts of Faith*, pp. 28-31.

55. Dufault-Hunter, *Transformative Power*, pp. 45-46.

56. For the related "social influence" theory in conversion, see Bainbridge, "The Sociology of Conversion," pp. 182-84.

57. Ullman, *The Transformed Self*, p. xvii, cited in Dufault-Hunter, *Transformative Power*, p. 43.

58. Bainbridge, "The Sociology of Conversion," pp. 179-81.

59. Persinger, "People Who Report Religious Experiences"; Brown and Caetano, "Conversion, Cognition, and Neuropsychology," pp. 147-58.

explanation. Third, the main theological lacuna has of course to do with the dismissal of the content of belief.

More conducive to theological intuitions is the emerging study of conversion in "neurotheology" or "spiritual neuroscience," which, on the one hand, takes seriously the neurological basis of all human experiences but, on the other hand, does not necessarily reduce conversion experience to the physical basis.[60] Neural plasticity is a well-known fact nowadays. It allows for the human being to change and transform behavior and attitude even beyond the younger years as "the neuronal systems and pathways responsible for much of what we think, feel, believe, and do are shaped by learning."[61] As a result, the old dilemma between nature and nurture is mistaken since both are necessary. Keeping in mind the insight won above, namely, that deep spiritual experiences such as conversion do not relate to only one aspect of the human person, say, spirituality, but relate to everything, including embodiment, Green puts it succinctly: "Transformation of 'my inner person' can be nothing more or less than transformation of 'me,' understood wholistically."[62]

Similarly, a step in the right direction — although theologically still woefully inadequate — is the holistic model of conversion advocated with great skill by Lewis Rambo. He believes that the phenomenon of conversion is so complex and diverse that various approaches can be seen as complementary. Furthermore, he argues for a stage model (with seven stages), which can accommodate both instant and progressive ways of conversion. Finally, he considers both the changing of denomination within one's own religion and the switch of religion in the context of conversion.[63]

Theologically, the reductionist approaches do not offer much help to theologians, and as such are not interesting.[64] Even Rambo's vastly improved approach only marginally touches on the question of the truth of the religious message, as even it is predominantly phenomenological.[65] In this light, James's approach to conversion, notwithstanding its outdated and still limited nature,

---

60. For a formative essay, see Newberg and Lee, "Neuroscientific Study of Religious and Spiritual Phenomena"; see also, the fascinating discussion in Blevins, "Neuroscience, John Wesley, and Christian Life."

61. Green, *Body, Soul, and Human Life*, p. 115 (this section is indebted to pp. 115-22).

62. Green, *Body, Soul, and Human Life*, p. 115; for a detailed discussion, see Brown and Reimer, "Embodied Cognition, Character Formation, and Virtue."

63. Rambo, *Understanding Religious Conversion*.

64. Rightly noted (with regard to neurocognitive approach) by Brown and Caetano, "Conversion, Cognition, and Neuropsychology," p. 158.

65. So also, Dufault-Hunter, *Transformative Power*, pp. 55-58.

is in some ways more useful to theologians, as it gives some credit to the content of the belief.

Conversion in the Religiously and Culturally Pluralistic World

Whereas the distinctively Jewish, Muslim, Hindu, and Buddhist "theologies" of conversion and repentance will be discussed toward the end of this chapter, this section seeks to offer some theological reflections on the role and meaning of conversion in a culturally, ideologically, and religiously pluralistic world. Conversion continues to be an area of interest to anthropologists;[66] they have undertaken significant research to better understand conversions to Christianity from indigenous cultures[67] and cultures outside the Global North. Furthermore, because of its deeply missionary nature, conversion to Islam has also been widely studied in various global locations.[68]

Not surprisingly, postcolonialist theorists have approached the topic with great suspicion as "[c]onversion to a world religion, such as Islam or Christianity, is interpreted as a part of the 'colonization of the mind and spirits' of the dominated peoples."[69] Similarly, some feminist theorists have also raised not only the obvious question as to whether women and men experience conversion differently but also whether there is a "power play" behind at least some conversions.[70] Particularly in two geographical and cultural areas, Africa and India, discussions of conversions have received a lot of attention.

The main challenge to African Christianity has been the question of how to conceive conversion in a way that would not mean abandoning one's cultural heritage; as is well known, in missionary history there are plenty of examples to the contrary.[71] This question has everything to do with the way the Christian finds and affirms one's identity.[72] Particularly important

---

66. See the seminal work by Buckser and Glazier, eds., *Anthropology of Religious Conversion;* from a Christian perspective, see Tippett, "Cultural Anthropology of Conversion."

67. S. Kaplan, ed., *Indigenous Responses to Western Christianity.*

68. See, among others, Kose, *Conversion to Islam;* Levtzion, ed., *Conversion to Islam;* Robinson and Clarke, eds., *Religious Conversion in India,* section 1 (pp. 23-118).

69. Rambo and Farhadian, "Conversion," p. 1971.

70. See Juster, "'In a Different Voice,'" pp. 34-62; Davidman, *Tradition in a Rootless World.*

71. Togarasei, "Conversion of Paul," pp. 111-14.

72. See Mucherera, *Pastoral Care from a Third World Perspective,* p. 15; I am indebted to Togarasei, "Conversion of Paul," p. 118.

is the presence of the influence of African traditional religions. While in many ways their significance has been marginalized because of rapid cultural transformations and globalization, at least implicitly their importance is still central.[73] A related issue has to do with power and privilege.[74] The Zimbabwean scholar Lovemore Togarasei has recently sought to imagine African conversion with the analogy of Saint Paul's conversion experience as a "prototype."[75] While I sympathize with Togarasei's approach, I also think one has to be mindful of the difference between Judaism and Christianity vis-à-vis Christianity and African traditional religions. Undoubtedly the former two are much closer to each other scripturally and theologically. With that in mind, it is better to conceptualize the relationship between Christianity and African traditional religions in terms of critical mutual reshaping, to use the Nigerian Cyril C. Okorocha's expression: "No people will change from one religion to the other unless they can see in the new vestiges of the old and a possibility of realizing within the new, goals and ideals desired but not gained in the old."[76]

In India, the continuing heated discussions around conversion also have everything to do with proselytism and the question of the legitimacy of evangelization. Similarly, the questions of equality and caste are deeply intertwined in this conversation.[77] Furthermore, in India as well as in Africa and elsewhere, the dynamic among premodern, modern, and late modern cultural shifts shapes and challenges the idea of conversion in any religion.[78] Indeed, one has to speak of "the many meanings of religious conversion on the Indian Subcontinent."[79]

Beginning from the time of independence, Christians and Hindus, including the government representatives, have carried on lively and at times heated conversations about conversion.[80] Why do Hindus convert to Christianity? At the sociological level, different kinds of explanations have been of-

---

73. For important insights, see Togarasei, "Conversion of Paul," pp. 117-18.

74. Ifeka-Moller, "White Power."

75. Togarasei, "Conversion of Paul," pp. 117-19.

76. Okorocha, *Meaning of Religious Conversion in Africa*.

77. See Kooiman, *Conversion and Social Equality in India*; R. Robinson, *Conversion, Continuity, and Change*.

78. See Viswanathan, *Outside the Fold*.

79. Subheading to Robinson and Clarke, introduction to *Religious Conversion in India*, p. 2.

80. A detailed history and theological/missiological assessment can be found in S. C. H. Kim, *In Search of Identity*.

fered. A popular reason has to do with the socioeconomic change provided by Christianity, particularly for those from lower levels of the societal hierarchy.[81] A related factor has to do with enhanced feelings of dignity and self-respect, as well as belonging. In other words, the argument is that "Christian conversion, unlike Sanskritization, was able to facilitate structural change and that conversion movements represent caste mobility or the realization of a communal identity."[82] Whereas this paradigm obviously highlights discontinuity with the past, a competing type of explanation seeks to discern more continuity. In that template, conversion in India has much more to do with "people's assimilation of new ideas and values in the course of their own progress towards modernity."[83] It is not of course possible to arbitrate that complicated debate in this discussion; let it suffice to mention the complexity of the issue(s) of conversion in contexts such as India and the need for theologians to look at conversion through interdisciplinary lenses.

One of the many reasons conversion is such a complicated issue both in India and in Africa has to do with communalism. Missionaries shaped by hyperindividualism stemming from the Enlightenment had a hard time imagining a conversion in which the individual would not have to break off from the community. An added complication in India is the caste system (even after its official eradication by legislation), including its internal dynamics and change processes.[84] Yet another factor adds complexity to the Indian discussion of conversion: the Hindu counterconversion movements. That is also linked to the rising Hindutva movement, that is, to be an Indian is to be a Hindu.[85]

Constructive theology has to take very seriously all these challenges concerning the ideological, power-play-driven, and otherwise destructive potential implications of conversion. The key term here is "potential." There is no justification for the blunt judgment that any experience of conversion by default is harmful and counterproductive — either in a Christian or in a member of any other faith tradition. Each and every human being or group must be guaranteed the freedom to choose any religion (or no religion), including conversion to a new one. Every faith tradition, and also secularism

---

81. Oddie, "India," pp. 228-53.

82. S. C. H. Kim, *In Search of Identity,* p. 2, with reference to Michael, *Anthropology of Conversion in India.*

83. S. C. H. Kim, *In Search of Identity,* p. 3, with reference particularly to the important work by Bayly, *Saints, Goddesses, and Kings.*

84. For literature, see S. C. H. Kim, *In Search of Identity,* pp. 4-5.

85. For details of the highly influential Hindutva ideology of Veer Savarkar, see the page on the Veer Savarkar Web site: http://www.savarkar.org/en/hindutva (7/13/2014).

and atheism, should be given a free opportunity to seek to convince others of its message, including the possibility of conversion. Evangelization belongs not only to the concept of freedom of religion but also to the missionary nature of religions (whether religions wish to promote it or not). The importance of the category of conversion and repentance, as well as forgiveness, is also heightened by the observation that virtually all faith traditions have these concepts, albeit quite differently from each other. That important topic will be discussed at the end of this chapter.

A Trinitarian Theology of Divine Forgiveness

For Orientation: The Place of Forgiveness in the Christian Vision of Salvation

While the topic of forgiveness has been part of the vocabulary of Jews and Christians and members of other faith traditions for thousands of years, only recently has it caught the attention of behavioral and social scientists.[86] In recent decades, massive research projects have gotten under way[87] and new "models" of forgiveness are being constructed.[88] A flood of "self-help" books on forgiveness has also seen daylight.[89] Whereas theological/religious approaches to forgiveness major on the side of the offender (and his or her need to receive forgiveness), psychological ones focus on the victim.[90] While no serious constructive theology can ignore the contributions and insights of the behavioral sciences in the field of forgiveness, a crucial theological task is also to critique and reshape their paradigm. That said, it is promising that while a lot of suspicion remains among behavioral scientists toward the role of religion in relation to forgiveness, there are also a growing number of attempts at collaboration.[91]

---

86. See Worthington, introduction to *Dimensions of Forgiveness,* p. 1. See also, McCullough, Pargament, and Thoresen, eds., *Forgiveness.*

87. Pioneering work is Enright and Fitzgibbons, *Helping Clients Forgive;* for up-to-date information and resources, see http://www.thepowerofforgiveness.com/about/people inthefilm/enright.html (7/31/2014). See also, McCullough, Pargament, and Thoresen, "The Psychology of Forgiveness," pp. 1-14.

88. Walker and Gorsuch, "Dimensions Underlying Sixteen Models of Forgiveness and Reconciliation."

89. See, e.g., Luskin, *Forgive for Good.*

90. Couenhoven, "Forgiveness and Restoration," p. 160.

91. Helmick and Petersen, eds., *Forgiveness and Reconciliation.*

It is one of the ironies of Christian *doctrinal* tradition that the place of forgiveness in the *ordo salutis* presentations is far less established than that of many other concepts such as justification and sanctification, notwithstanding its centrality in the ministry of Jesus of Nazareth[92] and of his followers;[93] forgiveness is also the only soteriological concept mentioned in the ecumenical creeds.[94] For much of Lutheran tradition, forgiveness means divine "favor" *(favor)*, the forensic side of justification (to be completed with *donum,* "gift," the indwelling of Christ).[95] Protestant scholastics continued the limiting of forgiveness merely to a forensic act, and hence ruled out the internal change present in Catholicism.[96] For Calvin, forgiveness encompassed both imputation of righteousness and justification.[97] The Catholic linking of forgiveness with change of heart is to be deemed a more satisfactory view. It points in the same direction as Milbank's demand that mere forgetting of sins (letting them go) is not enough; a gift of reconciliation also belongs to forgiving.[98] Liberationists also rightly remind us that mere forgiveness apart from tackling structural sins behind wrongdoings hardly suffices.[99]

Since, theologically speaking, divine forgiveness is the basis and source of all other levels of forgiveness, we will first delve into its meaning and thereafter seek to clarify the importance of forgiveness among human persons and communities.

92. Just observe key passages in one Gospel: Matt. 6:12, 14-15; 9:2, 5-6; 12:31-32; 18:21-23, 35; 26:28.

93. Luke 24:47; Acts 2:38.

94. In fairness to tradition, though, it has to be said that, as is well known, in Paul the term "forgiveness" almost totally disappears, and he speaks of it materially by using other terms.

95. See Saarinen, "Forgiveness, the Gift, and Ecclesiology," p. 58. For a nuanced and integrated linking of forgiveness and justification, see Tillich, *ST* 3:223-27.

96. For Lutheran statements from Hollaz, *Examen Theologicum Acroamaticum* (1707), see Schmid, *Doctrinal Theology of the Evangelical Lutheran Church,* p. 428; for the Reformed tradition, from Maastricht, *Theoretico-Practica Teologica* (1725), p. 436; I am indebted to Shults and Sandage, *Faces of Forgiveness,* p. 153.

97. Calvin, *Institutes* 3.11.4, 21; see further, Shults and Sandage, *Faces of Forgiveness,* pp. 144-45.

98. Milbank, *Being Reconciled,* pp. 44-60; for a nuanced discussion of "negative" and "positive" (for)giving, see Saarinen, *God and Gift,* chap. 3. For useful reflections on giving and taking in relation to forgiveness, see also, chap. 2 in Volf, *Free of Charge.*

99. See Tamez, *The Amnesty of Grace,* pp. 19-21.

The Evolvement of Biblical Theology of Forgiveness

Although divine forgiveness is at the forefront in the biblical narrative, the First Testament contains a number of narratives about human forgiveness, such as Joseph forgiving his brothers (Gen. 45:1-15; 50:15-20), Moses the people of Israel (Exod. 32:11-14, 30-33; Num. 12:11-13), and David his son Absalom (2 Sam. 14:21, 33).[100] In these and many similar narratives, the horizontal and vertical dimensions are intertwined, in the midst of all the ambiguities of dramatic human stories.

The main Hebrew terms for forgiveness in the OT are *nāsā* (whose primary meaning is "to carry" and "release"; Gen. 18:26; Pss. 25:18; 32:1, 5; Isa. 33:24); *sālah,* used only in reference to God's forgiveness (Lev. 4:20; 5:10; Num. 14:19; Isa. 55:7); and *kipper* ("to make atonement," only used of divine forgiveness, as in Isa. 22:14).[101] Notwithstanding the debates about whether (and when) in the preexilic period Israel knew forgiveness, certainly during and after the exile divine forgiveness became a treasured belief.[102] The formula of Yahweh as the merciful and faithful God who extends forgiveness becomes almost semitechnical and is repeated time after time in changing circumstances.[103] Although as a rule turning to God (repentance) is required (2 Kings 17:13-14; Jer. 3:11-24) — meaning that refusal to do so may lead to withdrawal of forgiveness (Isa. 22:14; Jer. 5:1-9) — in the later prophets it is also emphasized that what really matters is the right attitude rather than mechanical following of cultic practices (Amos 5:21-25; Isa. 1:11-17; Hos. 6:6).[104]

The two main words used for forgiveness in the NT are *aphiemi* ("let go, cancel, remit, leave") and *aphesis* ("release, pardon, cancellation"); however, they are used unevenly and in contexts not always related to religion. Of the almost 150 occurrences of the former, only one-third refer, strictly speaking, to "forgiveness"; the latter, which appears fewer than 20 times, almost always has the meaning of "forgiveness." Furthermore, as is well known, both terms are virtually limited to the Gospels; Paul hardly knows them. Why so? Paul expresses the idea using other words, particularly "justification," "reconciliation," "redemption," and similar ones. Often the *idea*

100. For a number of other examples, see Musekura, "Assessment of Contemporary Models of Forgiveness," pp. 37-38.

101. Morro, "Forgiveness," p. 340.

102. Vorländer, "Forgiveness," pp. 697-700.

103. Exod. 34:6-7; Num. 14:18-19; Pss. 86:15; 103:8-10; 145:8-9. For details, see Shults and Sandage, *Faces of Forgiveness,* pp. 127-30.

104. For details, see Shults and Sandage, *Faces of Forgiveness,* pp. 130-31.

of forgiveness may be present even if the word is missing (as in the parable of the prodigal son).

Two issues strike the reader of the Gospel stories of forgiveness (whether or not that word appears). First, Jesus' teaching on forgiveness is often striking in its generosity. Particularly important is the table fellowship with "sinners," a technical term for those outside the covenant; in that culture, table fellowship not only meant an embrace of the other but also was believed to take place before God.[105] Clearly, these examples point to the unconditionality of compassionate forgiveness. It seems that repentance is often presented in the Gospels as the response to forgiveness rather than the condition for it.[106] As Joseph Liechty brilliantly observes, "forgive" may be read as "fore-give," that is, "give before."[107] But second, even a cursory reading of the Gospels reveals that both John the Baptist (Mark 1:4) and Jesus also link forgiveness with repentance (1:15); the same mandate is given by the risen Lord to the disciples (Luke 24:46-47), and the early church carries on with this tradition (Acts 2:38; 5:31; 8:22; 26:18).

What should we conclude then? Looking at the NT as a whole, we see a trajectory: whereas in the Gospels and Acts, a fairly tight linking of forgiveness with repentance is in the fore, in the rest of the NT, particularly in Paul, "both divine and human forgiveness are about sharing grace *(charis)* with the other in a way that evokes joy *(chara)* and thanksgiving *(eucharistia)*." Hence, Paul's favorite term, *charizomai,* "to manifest grace." In this understanding, "forgiveness has a surplus of meaning that overflows the boundaries of transactional metaphors." While not set aside, often in Paul the juridical, legal, transactional terms of forgiveness (the Gospels' *aphiemi* and *aphesis*) "are subsumed into a larger picture of life 'in Christ.'"[108] Ultimately, the NT perspective at large on forgiveness aims at reconciliation, healing of broken relationships both on the horizontal and vertical planes.[109] Below, in the systematic development of the theology of forgiveness, the question of (un)conditionality is clarified.

All in all, it is evident that the biblical idea of forgiveness evolves and is being clarified throughout the biblical narrative. First, the trajectory in the

---

105. See L. G. Jones, *Embodying Forgiveness,* p. 121.

106. Cf. Tombs, "The Offer of Forgiveness," p. 590.

107. Liechty, "Putting Forgiveness in Its Place," p. 62 n. 6, cited in Tombs, "The Offer of Forgiveness," p. 590.

108. See, e.g., Col. 2:13; 3:13; 2 Cor. 2:10; Eph. 4:32; Shults and Sandage, *Faces of Forgiveness,* pp. 136-37.

109. Clark, "Redemption," pp. 78-81, cited in Musekura, "Assessment of Contemporary Models of Forgiveness," p. 46; so also, Shults and Sandage, *Faces of Forgiveness,* p. 23.

First Testament, slowly and painfully clarifying and highlighting the availability of divine forgiveness, "is taken up and transformed in the New Testament texts as they witness to the manifestation of divine forgiveness in Jesus Christ through the power of the Spirit."[110] There is clearly a trinitarian logic there.

Divine Forgiveness as the Basis and Source

On the basis of the biblical trajectory, the underlying conviction in Christian theology is that "[i]n forgiveness, the grace of God is ultimately at work."[111] All Abrahamic faiths materially affirm that. This theological conviction, however, sounds hollow in the secular culture of the Global North. The British philosopher and novelist Iris Murdoch has often wrestled in her writings with the question, "Is forgiveness possible without God?" Her view is that because "the *desire* to be forgiven is so closely linked with the desire for God . . . we should not give up either of these desires even when we can no longer believe in God."[112] Although Murdoch's explanation points in the right direction, it also says much too little: God is not only the guarantee of human religious feelings. God is the only one who can initiate and execute forgiveness of sins, which leads not only to the cancellation of sin but also to reconciliation.[113] He is "[t]he God who lives in trinitarian relations of peaceable, self-giving communion and thereby [is] willing to bear the cost of forgiveness in order to restore humanity to that communion in God's eschatological Kingdom."[114] There is a profound gift-giving here, indeed nothing less than "divine self-donation for the enemies and their reception into the eternal communion of God."[115]

Christ's righteous life, innocent death on the cross, and glorious resurrection and ascension form the basis for divine forgiveness. At the cross, Christ "paid the price" and took upon himself the judgment of our sinful acts, particularly our turning away from God.[116] Resurrection means the completion of that atoning work, and it is at the same time "the revelation of God's

---

110. Shults and Sandage, *Faces of Forgiveness*, p. 133.

111. L. G. Jones, "Crafting Communities of Forgiveness," p. 122; more widely, chap. 5 in Shults and Sandage, *Faces of Forgiveness*.

112. As interpreted by Pettigrove, "Forgiveness without God," p. 540.

113. L. G. Jones, *Embodying Forgiveness*, p. xii.

114. L. G. Jones, *Embodying Forgiveness*, p. xii.

115. Volf, *Exclusion and Embrace*, p. 23; italics in the original deleted.

116. For an important NT study, see Moule, "Scope of the Death of Christ," pp. 3-18; for theological reflections, see Volf, *Free of Charge*, pp. 138-51; Volf, *The End of Memory*, pp. 207-9.

loving embrace"[117] of the violators. Atonement and forgiveness, hence, belong together. That said, this statement does not necessarily entail a particular kind of theology of sin and fall, neither a "theory of atonement."[118] Diverse theologies of sin and atonement in Christian tradition have successfully worked out theologies of forgiveness.[119]

All of them, however, could affirm that, having suffered a violent death at the hands of sinners, Jesus stops the cycle of violence.[120] Resurrection completes that work: "Jesus' resurrection means, quite simply, two things: (1) there is no evil on earth that we might *suffer* which is beyond the scope of healing and (2) there is no evil on earth that we might *commit* that is beyond God's forgiveness."[121]

No wonder that the church, Christ's body on earth, which continues the reconciling ministry among sinners, carries the work of forgiveness at her center. Recall that the charge to the church by the risen Christ was: "If you forgive the sins of any, they are forgiven; if you retain the sins of any, they are retained." Importantly, that task was given only after Jesus "breathed on them, and said to them, 'Receive the Holy Spirit'" (John 20:22-23). This statement highlights the pneumatological dimension of forgiveness. The Paraclete, who continues Jesus' work on the earth, the Spirit of Truth, testifies to sin and righteousness and thus facilitates the judgment of sin and forgiveness of wrongdoings.[122]

Not everyone, however, is convinced that the Judeo-Christian teaching of divine forgiveness can be maintained with intellectual integrity.[123] The two most important challenges are these: first, it is often wondered if divine forgiveness compromises divine justice. Kant famously established that standpoint.[124] The second one has to do with "whether God has the standing to forgive" in light of the fact that typically it is the offended person to whom the right to forgiveness belongs.[125] The Jewish philosopher Emmanuel Levinas made this

---

117. Crysdale, *Embracing Travail*, p. 10.

118. Contra Terry, "Forgiveness of Sins and the Work of Christ," pp. 9-24.

119. See chap. 5 in McIntyre, *The Shape of Soteriology*.

120. So also, Crysdale, *Embracing Travail*, pp. 32-33.

121. Crysdale, *Embracing Travail*, p. 30, emphasis in original.

122. See further, L. G. Jones, *Embodying Forgiveness*, pp. 129-34; he refers also to R. Williams, *Resurrection*, p. 42.

123. For detailed argumentation of several typical challenges, see Minas, "God and Forgiveness."

124. Kant, "Part II: Moral Philosophy," pp. 113-14. For a detailed discussion with documentation, see North, "Wrongdoing and Forgiveness," pp. 499-508. A strong rebuttal of Kant's view is Talbott, "Punishment, Forgiveness, and Divine Justice," pp. 151-68.

125. Pettigrove, "Dilemma of Divine Forgiveness," p. 457; this objection is argued in

point most vocally.[126] Let me take up the first challenge in what follows and respond briefly to the second one here: according to Judeo-Christian tradition, God is not a "bystander" when it comes to wrongdoings against other human persons (and even more widely, other creatures). Human beings have been created in God's image and, therefore, violating another person also affects God (Gen. 9:6). Consider David's confession after the affair and murder:

> Against thee, thee only, have I sinned,
>   and done that which is evil in thy sight. (Ps. 51:4)

Yet another familiar challenge often faces the theology of divine forgiveness. It has to do with the deep Christian conviction that forgiveness takes humility. Forgiveness is only possible for those who know themselves to be forgiven and also to be standing under God's judgment.[127] Rather than a virtue, for Nietzsche humility was deplorable. He surmised that religion has to make us feel guilty and shamed in order to pour out divine forgiveness.[128] However, long before Nietzsche, in Greece and Rome — whose religions Nietzsche admired over against the Judeo-Christian traditions — forgiveness similarly was definitely not a virtue.[129] In this matter, the Judeo-Christian convictions and secular cultural intuitions simply collide and cannot be reconciled.

Are There Any Conditions for Forgiveness?

Christian tradition does not speak with a unanimous voice about the unconditionality of forgiveness.[130] Historically, from the early centuries repentance came to be linked with the more or less technically defined rite of penitence. Particularly in the Western Church, the influence of a Roman, legally oriented concept

---

Downie, "Forgiveness," pp. 128-34. A robust argument critiquing the views of the "radical evil" camp that in one way or another refuses to give God the standing to forgive is Milbank, *Being Reconciled*; I agree with his main reasoning in this regard.

126. Levinas, *Difficult Freedom*, p. 20; for finding the reference, I am indebted to L. G. Jones, *Embodying Forgiveness*, p. 104.

127. Musekura, "Assessment of Contemporary Models of Forgiveness," pp. 31-32, building on R. Niebuhr's ideas.

128. Nietzsche, *Human, All Too Human*, 3.114 ("Religious Life"); for other such examples from Nietzsche, see S. Williams, "What Christians Believe about Forgiveness," pp. 148-49.

129. See further, Couenhoven, "Forgiveness and Restoration," p. 149.

130. See Nelson, "Exegeting Forgiveness," pp. 33-58.

of justice led to the tight linking of forgiveness with repentance and penitence. Especially important was the Roman demand of satisfaction as the prerequisite for forgiving (an idea Saint Anselm made a leading theme later). A related, important development was the emerging distinction between sins forgiven at baptism and those committed after baptism.[131] By the fifth century an elaborate "Order of Penitents" was put in place, and later the rite of penance became one of the sacraments.[132] At Vatican II, the Roman Catholic Church redefined and clarified the theology of penance, and ruled that reconciliation can be called a sacrament of conversion, penance, confession, forgiveness, and reconciliation, which includes the proper attitude and actions toward the violated neighbor.[133]

According to the NT testimony, it seems clear that repentance should not be made a prerequisite: "God unilaterally makes forgiveness possible by offering forgiveness 'while we were yet sinners' (Rom. 5:8)."[134] This is the first — albeit not the only — thing to be said in light of Christian revelation. This principle, as discussed above, was present everywhere in Jesus' earthly ministry. Recall that the very first words from the cross as narrated by Luke (23:34) were "Father, forgive them; for they know not what they do."[135] Talk about unconditionality![136] Here is, as far as I understand, a difference between Jewish and Christian theologies of forgiveness. Although Judaism of course knows divine forgiveness,[137] it normally entails repentance and restitution as the condition, as well as the forgiving of others.[138] With Jesus comes "judgment of *grace*," which not only condemns sin and wrongdoings but also gives the energy and capability to re-turn to God and others in repentance and acknowl-

131. This was definitely established by Augustine, *On the Merits and Forgiveness of Sins* 1.39 (baptism, including infants); 2.3 (postbaptismal sin). So also, Aquinas, *Summa Contra Gentiles* 4.72.

132. See Shults and Sandage, *Faces of Forgiveness*, pp. 140-43; Favazza, *The Order of Penitents*.

133. *Catholic Catechism* (##1423-24); for a basic definition, see #1422. See Duffy, "Penance." With all his criticism against the abuses of his own church, Luther did not do away with penance, nor do the Lutheran Confessions. *The Defense of the Augsburg Confession*, XI: Of Confession.

134. Couenhoven, "Forgiveness and Restoration," p. 165. I endorse L. G. Jones's (*Embodying Forgiveness*, pp. 150-60) detailed critique of the British philosopher Richard Swinburne's *(Responsibility and Atonement)* demand that repentance be made the necessary precondition for forgiveness.

135. That not all the earliest manuscripts have these words is no reason to consider them "inauthentic." That the church preserved them establishes their theological meaning.

136. See further, Moule, "Preaching the Atonement," p. 24.

137. See Sanders, *Jesus and Judaism*, p. 202 and passim.

138. See further, L. E. Newman, "The Quality of Mercy," pp. 155-72.

edgment of one's faults.[139] The same judgment of grace also makes us willing to receive forgiveness from others.[140] That said, this is the second foundational Christian claim: the affirmation of unconditionality is not an abandonment of repentance[141] or of the need to be reconciled with one's neighbor.

What happens, indeed, is a threefold transformation of the relationship between forgiveness and repentance. First of all, repentance (and restitution) becomes the necessary consequence of the reception of divine forgiveness. Second, now "repentance [is] contextualized within the announcement of God's inbreaking Kingdom."[142] Third, in contrast with Judaism, the focus is shifted from the cult and temple as the place of forgiveness to life and human relationships in the Christian community.[143] Furthermore, there was also a radical shift in the whole idea of repentance in Jesus' message: rather than meant only for some, its audience was everybody, including the "poor" and the marginalized; that is, both the perpetrators and victims were called to repentance. This is because forgiveness always has in view not only reconciliation but also transformation and change.[144]

This principle of unconditional forgiveness should also guide our understanding of forgiveness between human persons. We are called to forgive our enemies and violators simply because God has forgiven us. On the one hand, we should not require repentance or restitution from the violator; only the violator can decide on that. On the other hand, contrary to Derrida's advice, we should expose the sinful act for the sake of the reconciliation and healing of the offender (if he or she is willing to accept that).[145] How these two aspects cohere will be taken up below with the focus on forgiveness among human beings.

Forgiveness with Neighbors — and Enemies

"As We Also Have Forgiven Our Debtors"

Having received divine forgiveness, an unconditional gift, men and women are called to imitate that act of hospitality. In forgiving, humans mediate the gift of

139. See L. G. Jones, *Embodying Forgiveness*, p. 146.

140. The phrase is from L. G. Jones, *Embodying Forgiveness*, pp. 136, 145-50.

141. Contra Sanders, *Jesus and Judaism* (p. 111), who claims that repentance was altogether missing in Jesus' original proclamation.

142. L. G. Jones, *Embodying Forgiveness*, p. 110.

143. L. G. Jones, *Embodying Forgiveness*, p. 121.

144. See Volf, *Exclusion and Embrace*, pp. 111-19 (p. 114; italics in original deleted).

145. See also, Musekura, "Assessment of Contemporary Models of Forgiveness," p. 126.

forgiveness they have received themselves.[146] "Failure to offer forgiveness indicates a devaluation of God's forgiveness."[147] Withholding forgiveness would mean the exclusion of another and would be nothing other than the exclusion of God.[148] This is less a moral requirement; it has everything to do with the core Christian identity. Indeed, in the words of the Roman Catholic Susan K. Wood, "By taking the name *Christian* in baptism and being incorporated into Christ's body, the baptized assume the responsibility to offer forgiveness to one another in imitation of the one into whom they are baptized."[149] That said, we must recall that only God is able to take away sin; we cannot.[150]

Miroslav Volf locates forgiving in the context of two opposing movements, namely, embrace and exclusion. Exclusion may happen in many ways, including elimination (as in ethnic cleansing), assimilation (when acceptance is based on the demand to be like us), domination, and abandonment.[151] Embrace, on the contrary, is based on "the mutuality of the self-giving love in the Trinity," "the outstretched arms of Christ on the cross for the 'godless,'" the welcoming by the father of the prodigal son.[152] This "will to embrace" includes both opening to the other and drawing to intimate touching, making space for the otherness of the Other.[153] Creating space for the other makes it possible for us to grow toward a "catholic personality" in which we do not lose our particularities, our identities, but rather are enriched, shaped, and challenged by other identities. This is anything but natural to human nature and behavior.[154] Here again we depend on the divine aid: it is the Spirit of God who is the source of this kind of constructive and healing "exocentricity," catholicity reflecting "a personal microcosm of the eschatological new creation."[155]

Forgiveness is not done for our own sake; it is a manifestation of love for the neighbor. Forgiveness is a profound act of hospitality. The victims decide "no

---

146. Klassen, *The Forgiving Community*, p. 151.

147. McLellan, "Justice, Forgiveness, and Reconciliation," p. 13, cited in Musekura, "Assessment of Contemporary Models of Forgiveness," p. 73.

148. Volf, "Exclusion and Embrace," p. 241.

149. Wood, "I Acknowledge One Baptism for the Forgiveness of Sins," p. 200.

150. Couenhoven, "Forgiveness and Restoration," p. 167.

151. Volf, *Exclusion and Embrace*, pp. 72-79 (particularly p. 75).

152. Volf, *Exclusion and Embrace*, p. 29.

153. Volf, *Exclusion and Embrace*, pp. 72, 141.

154. In a penetrating analysis, the Indian clinical scholar Sudhir Kakar shows evidence of how partisan, that is, "non-catholic," human nature is beginning from childhood. *The Colors of Violence*, p. 243, cited in Amaladoss, "Identity and Harmony," p. 27.

155. Volf, *Exclusion and Embrace*, p. 51. See also, Pope John Paul II, *Forgiveness*, p. 131.

longer to hold the injury they have suffered against their offender."[156] This gift has the potential to set the violator free from the guilt and grip of the wrongful act.[157] However, the act of gift giving is costly. Indeed, forgiving means willingness to pay the price for the neighbor, even the one who has sinned against us.[158] Particularly costly and painful is the long process of forgiving.[159] Ironically, the victim undergoes suffering in two moments, first in the act of being violated, and then in the willingness to suffer in offering the gift of forgiveness.[160]

Theologically, forgiveness is not done primarily for the sake of one's own well-being but out of the neighborly love to which followers of Christ are called in the imitation of their heavenly Father.[161] This is not to deny the potential benefits to the forgiver; it is rather to make those benefits secondary. This principle goes contrary to the emphasis in much of contemporary popular self-help literature and behavioral sciences concerning the therapeutic value of forgiveness and its benefits to the forgiver.[162] Ultimately, the therapeutic goal may trump the theological goal, at times to the point that "feelings" are made the central criterion for a "successful" act of forgiveness.[163] Theology's task is to critique and reorient that tendency.

If the act of forgiveness has as its ultimate goal the well-being and restoration of the neighbor, it means that it looks not only into the past but also to the future. The orientation to the future is present in God's forgiveness. Its ultimate goal is the eschatological shalom and peace with the coming of God's righteous rule. In anticipation of that final reconciliation, God has reconciled the world to himself (2 Cor. 5:17-20) and empowers humans to spread that reconciling influence at personal, communal, and even cosmic levels. In that sense, forgiveness is not only a gift to help reconcile the effects and guilt of wrongdoing; forgiveness is also a promise for the future, an act of trust on behalf of the other one.

This idea can be linked with what the Jewish philosopher Hannah Arendt, in a profound analysis of the conditions of human action, says when she

156. Terry, "Forgiveness of Sins and the Work of Christ," p. 13.

157. Augsburger, "Justice in Forgiveness," p. 5, cited in Terry, "Forgiveness of Sins and the Work of Christ," p. 13.

158. Brümmer, "Kairos, Reconciliation," p. 48, from Quick, *Essays in Orthodoxy*, pp. 92-93.

159. See further, Tombs, "The Offer of Forgiveness," p. 589.

160. See also, Brümmer, "Kairos, Reconciliation," p. 48.

161. See further, Volf, *The End of Memory*, p. 9.

162. Among a number of such titles, see Luskin, *Forgive for Good*.

163. For a useful critique, see Boersma, *Violence, Hospitality, and the Cross*, p. 211.

connects the power to forgive with the power to promise. The former is needed to reverse "irreversibility," and the latter, to reverse "unpredictability," two key features of human action. She explains that, on the one hand, "[w]ithout being forgiven, released from the consequences of what we have done, our capacity to act would, as it were, be confined to one single deed from which we could never recover; we would remain the victims of its consequences forever." On the other hand, "without being bound to the fulfillment of promises, we would never be able to keep our identities; we would be condemned to wander help-lessly and without direction in the darkness of each man's lonely heart."[164] A forgiven person dares to face the future and its openness. When forgiveness is coupled with promise, at least some of the unpredictability is overcome as one is bound to a certain course of action. These are conditions of human freedom. The South African archbishop Tutu puts it well: "In the act of forgiveness we are declaring our faith in the future of a relationship and in the capacity of the wrongdoer to make a new beginning on a course that will be different from the one that caused us the wrong. We are saying[,] here is a chance to make a new beginning. It is an act of faith that the wrongdoer can change."[165]

Beyond Resentment

A long tradition of philosophical and theological reflection on forgiveness has linked it with resentment.[166] In this view, forgiveness primarily means a process of overcoming resentment, the feeling of anger caused by having been the object of wrongdoing.[167] Building on that tradition, the philosopher Jeffrie Murphy defines forgiveness as "the principled overcoming of feelings of resentment that are naturally (and perhaps properly) directed toward a person who has done one a moral injury."[168] A version of this view is that forgiveness is supposed to free the wronged person from all forms of negative feelings, even disappointment.[169] Yet another version — common also among many

---

164. Arendt, *The Human Condition*, pp. 236-47 (p. 237).

165. Tutu, *No Future without Forgiveness*, p. 220.

166. Formative influence came from the nineteenth-century Bishop Butler's series of sermons. The fifteen sermons preached in 1846 at Rolls Chapel are available at http://anglican history.org/butler/rolls/ (7/28/2014).

167. French et al., "Forgiveness and Resentment," pp. 503-16; McGary, "Forgiveness," pp. 343-50; among others.

168. J. Murphy, "Forgiveness," pp. 561-62, cited in Hughes, "Forgiveness," n.p.

169. Narayan, "Forgiveness, Moral Reassessment, and Reconciliation," pp. 169-78.

self-help works, both secular and Christian — demands that even the critical judgment of the offender be suspended. Behind this theory of forgiveness lies the great appreciation the Greeks and Romans placed on the virtues of self-control and good temper; a morally virtuous and strong person is not affected by wrongdoings of lesser persons.[170]

The resentment theory has to be subjected to theological critique. Jesus' teaching in the NT invites us not only to "turn the other cheek" and embrace the offender in forgiveness but also to expose the wrong act for the sake of justice and for the possibility of the wrongdoer to find reconciliation in accepting guilt and receiving forgiveness.[171] Here Christian tradition may follow Aristotle's oft-cited rule (in opposition to Plato's view) according to which a truly moral person is "angry at the right things and with the right people, and, further, as he ought, when he ought, and as long as he ought."[172] Still worth recalling are the oft-cited words of Dietrich Bonhoeffer: "God does not 'overlook' sin; that would mean not taking human beings seriously as personal beings in their very culpability."[173] Hence, resentment can be regarded as "God's good gift,"[174] rather than something whose removal is the criterion for what makes forgiveness, forgiveness.

Restoration cannot happen without the wrongdoing being exposed and judged. As Moltmann aptly puts it, forgiveness is about "the new life to which [God] desires to awaken the guilty."[175] To that act may also belong a protest, even an emotional protest — unlike pop psychology (often followed by some theologians as well), which seems to say that a truly forgiving person has to be able to contain one's negative emotions.[176]

So far in the discussion of forgiveness among humans the emphasis has been on the importance of forgiving the offender and on forgiveness as a hospitable gift. Now it is time to look at the other side: how to help heal and restore the wronged one and how to pursue justice and fairness.

170. See Plato, *Republic* 4; for details, see Hughes, "Forgiveness," n.p.

171. For important current discussion, see Wolterstorff, "Jesus and Forgiveness," pp. 194-214.

172. Aristotle, *Nicomachean Ethics* 1125b32.

173. Bonhoeffer, *Sanctorum Communio*, p. 155, cited in Couenhoven, "Forgiveness and Restoration," p. 164. So also, Volf, *Free of Charge*, pp. 165-69; Moltmann, *Way of Jesus Christ*, p. 193.

174. McClendon, *Ethics*, pp. 153, 227.

175. Moltmann, *In the End, the Beginning*, p. 75, cited in Ledgerwood, "The Hope of Forgiveness," p. 14.

176. See, e.g., Govier, *Forgiveness and Revenge*. For a thoughtful critique, see Couenhoven, "Forgiveness and Restoration," pp. 154-55.

Forgiveness, Justice, and Memory

The talk about unconditional forgiveness raises questions such as the following: What about justice? Does forgiveness simply trump the demand for fairness? Shouldn't an authentic act of forgiveness be able to erase from the offended person's mind all negative feelings? In much of earlier self-help forgiveness literature, it was taken for granted that an authentic act of forgiveness also helps erase the painful and negative memories of the offender's acts from the victim's mind. Hence, book titles such as *Forgive and Forget*.[177] Is that correct? Hardly. Contrary to that commonsense advice, we should rather insist that for authentic forgiveness and healing to happen it is essential that we remember *rightly*[178] the pain of the wrongdoings against us.

Remembering rightly is absolutely necessary for two important reasons. The first is to establish the truth. Acknowledging and recalling the wrong act is indeed a moral obligation, or else justice and righteousness cannot be established.[179] The second reason is that, without it, the victim cannot be healed and restored. But not only for the victim's sake, it is also required for the offender to be restored. Mere forgetting can be nothing more than a way of repressing negative memories yet leaving the victim with the enmity and hatred.[180]

Furthermore, only right remembering allows the victim to let the offender know the moral wrongdoing and so help that person seek forgiveness and reconciliation. This is what Jesus taught: "If your brother sins against you, go and tell him his fault, between you and him alone. If he listens to you, you have gained your brother" (Matt. 18:15). At times, help from other trusted persons and the Christian community is needed (vv. 16-20).[181] The feminist process theologian Marjorie Hewitt Suchocki makes the case in a most succinct manner. Her definition of forgiveness as "willing the well-being of victim(s) and violator(s) in the context of the fullest possible knowledge of the nature of the violation" makes right remembering a key element. Indeed, she rightly continues: "[w]ithout

177. Smedes, *Forgive and Forget*. More than a decade later, Smedes corrected his view. In a chapter ominously titled "Forgive and Remember," he states that a "healed memory is not a deleted memory"; "Forgive and Remember," p. 171; I am indebted to Musekura, "Assessment of Contemporary Models of Forgiveness," p. 94.

178. See further, Volf, *The End of Memory*, pp. 11-16; for Jewish reflections, see Elie Wiesel, *From the Kingdom of Memory*; for clinical and therapeutic viewpoints, see McNally, *Remembering Trauma*.

179. See further, Volf, *The End of Memory*, pp. 51-62 and chap. 10.

180. McClendon, *Ethics*, p. 228.

181. See further, McClendon, *Ethics*, pp. 227-28.

memory, empathy, and imagination there can be no forgiveness."[182] This does not necessarily mean — against common folk intuitions — that forgiveness requires feelings of love or even acceptance of the violator (although the latter probably should be the end goal). In some extreme cases of violence, forgiveness and reconciliation may even require distance from the perpetrator, such as in a case of sexual assault on a child or another vulnerable person.[183]

In sum: true forgiveness entails the condemnation of sin — lest we be found to advocate "[c]heap grace [which] denies any real need for deliverance from sin since it justifies the sin instead of the sinner."[184] But this condemnation of the wrongful act should not be confused with retribution, and it does not work on the principle of retributive justice.[185] Nor is it based on vengeance.[186] Rather, forgiveness (even in its judgment of the sinful act) is the refusal to press charges against the violator and instead offering the way of reconciliation even if the victim has the right to press charges.[187]

Commensurately, the reception of forgiveness entails the acceptance of condemnation, and this is why the reception may sometimes be too difficult. When confessing wrongdoing, "I recognize myself as the one who needs forgiveness."[188] The person who says *no* to forgiveness offered is in reality saying that he or she has not done anything in need of being forgiven. To the art of remembering rightly also belongs the capacity to make a distinction between violator as *violator* and as a human person. Perhaps apart from some extreme cases of violence and abuse (such as the mass murder of Hitler and other mass murderers), the victim should avoid reducing the violator to the violation. That is the difference between remembering rightly and cultivating vengeance. The "transcendence" of memory helps the victim differentiate "oneself from absorption into the past by allowing the past to be past. This also involves openness to reclaiming a fuller past that contextualizes violence." Ultimately, then, "[f]orgiveness is release of the violation to its place in the past; it is a release into time and the hope of transformation."[189]

---

182. Suchocki, *The Fall to Violence*, p. 144. So also, Volf, *Free of Charge*, p. 129.

183. Suchocki, *The Fall to Violence*, pp. 145-46.

184. L. G. Jones, *Embodying Forgiveness*, p. 13.

185. Rather, as Moule argues on the basis of NT theology, it is a matter of restorative justice. See his "Retribution or Restoration," pp. 41-47.

186. Vengeance and retribution of course lead to further violence — and vengeance; Shriver, *An Ethic for Enemies*, p. 19; Volf, *Exclusion and Embrace*, pp. 121-22.

187. For details, see Volf, *Free of Charge*, pp. 168-71.

188. Volf, *Free of Charge*, p. 153.

189. Suchocki, *The Fall to Violence*, pp. 150-53 (pp. 152, 153 respectively).

Does this mean that forgiveness, after all, means "forgetting"? Yes, in this qualified sense explained here. While it has nothing to do with the commonsense "forgive and forget" attitude because it names and condemns the wrongful act and begins to process it by remembering rightly, the forgiver has as the ultimate goal the imitation of God, who does not remember our sins anymore (Jer. 31:34; Heb. 8:12; 10:17).[190] Only at the eschaton, when all tears have been wiped away and all injustices rectified, will this blessed forgetting be complete.[191]

How can a sinful and finite human being remember — and forget — rightly? It is a capacity beyond even the best of us. Similar to forgiveness as a whole, it is based on and has its source in divine resources. Judeo-Christian tradition lifts up remembering as a sacred act.[192] The exodus and subsequent salvific acts of God form the Jewish identity and shape Jewish memory. How can one even begin to remember in the post-Holocaust era without the memory of the sacred acts and Yahweh's faithfulness? Based on the same sacred Scripture and tradition, Christianity defines its identity on exodus, which we believe came to culmination in the Jewish Messiah: his righteous life, innocent death, and glorious resurrection form the center of Christian memory. On the cross hung the one who pled for forgiveness for the sinners who put him on the cross, and he took upon himself all their sin and wrongdoings. In every sacramental celebration throughout history, this memory is being revived and given as a task for the church.[193] At the foot of the cross, those who remember the experiences and pains of their lives do so as ones who have been forgiven. Only as the forgiven may they become forgivers.[194]

If forgiveness entails the acknowledgment and condemnation of violation, it means that forgiving, rightly understood, puts us, ideally both the victim and the offender, on the path of fighting violence and abuse. The prevalence of violence in our world at both the personal and the collective levels makes this commitment an essential part of the work of reconciliation.

---

190. Volf, *Free of Charge*, p. 175; Volf, *Exclusion and Embrace*, pp. 131-40.

191. Augustine, *City of God* 22.30; I am indebted to Volf, *The End of Memory*, p. 22.

192. Yerushalmi, *Zakhor*, p. 9, cited in Volf, *The End of Memory*, p. 96.

193. For profound reflections from Judeo-Christian perspectives, see Volf, *The End of Memory*, chaps. 5-6.

194. See also, Volf, *Free of Charge*, pp. 202-5.

Stopping Violence and Seeking Reconciliation

Christian tradition sets forth the bold claim that, rather than violence, peace and harmony stand in the "beginning." Even when violence and strife are rampant in the fallen world, it is because it is *fallen*. This Judeo-Christian account is dramatically different from those accounts of origins in which violence in one form or another is ontological, that is, an essential part of the world. As is well known, social Darwinism not only has "the survival of the fittest" as its core principle but, in its more perverse interpretations (particularly among the Nazis and some communists), it has funded cruelty and violence.[195] Well known also are the "global" claims of Nietzsche concerning the presence of power (abuse) and violence not only in the texture of human language but also in the "genealogy of morals."[196] Even René Girard's theory of scapegoating ultimately is based on the ontology of violence rather than on an ontology of hospitality.[197] While it is a more nuanced and complex account, there is no doubt that Derrida's fight against a "metaphysics of presence" (that is, "concept" always represents not only use but also abuse of power) is related to his foundational claim about the presence of violence in human language and life that cannot be avoided.[198]

Christian theology of atonement and forgiveness condemns violence and stops it. Maximus the Confessor put it succinctly: "The death of Christ on the cross is a judgment of judgment."[199] Volf says the same when speaking of "the crucified Messiah" who absorbs aggression, challenges violence by unearthing scapegoating, and struggles actively against it.[200] In this struggle against and condemnation of violence, the Christian account collides with the philosophy of Derrida not only because it denies the priority of violence but also because the two differ in understanding what unconditional forgiveness and hospitality mean. As is well known, according to this late French

195. Just consider the sociobiologist Edward O. Wilson's *On Human Nature*.

196. Milbank (*Theology and Social Theory*, p. 389) insightfully contrasts Nietzsche's *On the Genealogy of Morality*, with its claim of the priority of violence and power, with Augustine's *City of God*, based on the primacy of divine peaceableness and hospitality. I am indebted to L. G. Jones, *Embodying Forgiveness*, p. 79 n. 7.

197. See Boersma, *Violence, Hospitality, and the Cross*, p. 134; and more widely, chap. 12 in my *Christ and Reconciliation*.

198. See particularly, Derrida, "Violence and Metaphysics."

199. Maximus the Confessor, *Questions to Thallasius*, p. 43, cited in Placher, "Christ Takes Our Place," p. 14.

200. Volf, *Exclusion and Embrace*, pp. 290-95.

deconstructionist, forgiveness must be absolutely unconditional, without any anticipation of changed behavior in the perpetrator.[201] Derrida's demand for a totally unconditional forgiveness parallels his call for an absolute hospitality,[202] which in its extreme mode of welcoming should "say yes to who or what turns up, before any determination, before any anticipation, before any *identification*," even if the guest "may be the devil."[203] He wishes to get rid of all notions of an economy of give and take; that is, some conditions are put as preconditions, most often repentance.[204] While noble in its ideal, Derrida's demand of unconditionality has to be qualified in two important senses. First, only God is capable of absolute unconditionality; we humans are not. If absolute unconditionality is made a prerequisite for pronouncing forgiveness, no forgiveness can be available to anyone. Second, the violator has to be identified and the violent act exposed in order for true forgiveness and reconciliation to happen. True hospitality, rather than "welcoming" all forms of violence, should join forces in resistance of the works of the "devil" and join in the pursuit of justice, love, and fairness.[205]

Envisioning Forgiveness as a Communal Act

One of the legacies of post-Enlightenment culture in the Global North is hyperindividualism, which has also left a definite mark on Christian faith. The communal and public implications of violence are often marginal in the Christian theology of forgiveness. Yet we are nowadays well aware that "[g]roup pride, collective evil, and the demonization of races, tribes, nations, and communities have caused more human suffering in the last century than in any other period of human history."[206] Rightly, the Rwandan theologian Celestin Musekura, whose country has experienced colossal massacre and violence, has critiqued the prevailing forgiveness paradigm

---

201. Derrida, *On Cosmopolitanism and Forgiveness*, p. 39.

202. Derrida builds on and radicalizes the lengthy twentieth-century philosophical discussion on "gift" started by Marcel Mauss, *Essay on the Gift*. A useful discussion is Alan D. Schrift, ed., *The Logic of Gift*. I have responded to Derrida and others in *Christ and Reconciliation*, pp. 30-32.

203. Dufourmantelle and Derrida, *Of Hospitality*, p. 77.

204. Derrida, *On Cosmopolitanism and Forgiveness*, p. 34.

205. See further, Boersma, *Violence, Hospitality, and the Cross*, pp. 35-38. For the dangers of uncritical unconditional forgiveness, see Bash, "Forgiveness," pp. 137-38.

206. Musekura, "Assessment of Contemporary Models of Forgiveness," p. 6.

as hopelessly individualistic and urges us to imagine a truly communal way of forgiveness.[207] Musekura reminds us vividly of the stark realities plaguing our world:

> Forgiveness as a virtue is learned not in an isolated, self-excluded life but rather in a community of faith where members of the community experience the reality of sin and brokenness together. Today's stories of genocide, mass murder, racism, tribalism, religious wars, terrorism, and church conflicts indicate not only the fragility of our commitment to life in community of friendship and embrace but also how difficult it is for individuals to unlearn the habits of sin of exclusion by domination, elimination, abandonment, and assimilation, and to the extreme by genocide.[208]

While the practice of forgiveness among Christian individuals is absolutely necessary, we are also in dire need of "communities of forgiveness" that pursue stopping violence and facilitating the work of reconciliation.[209] What McClendon named "the politics of forgiveness" aims at forging a robust link between ethics, theology, and communal life in the church and beyond. Whereas our society seeks to eliminate violence primarily — and at times exclusively — with the help of judicial and penitentiary systems, the church should demonstrate combating violence with a credible pursuit of justice and practice of restorative forgiveness.[210]

Musekura reminds us that both among the earliest Christian communities in the book of Acts and in most current African cultures, individual autonomy,[211] which is a leading motif in the post-Enlightenment Global North, does not rule but rather communalism. What are badly needed in this fractured and divided world are communities that practice forgiveness at all levels.[212] In this kind of world Christians are called to work for forgiveness and reconciliation not only beyond racial and cultural barriers but also with

207. Musekura, "Assessment of Contemporary Models of Forgiveness," chap. 5.

208. Musekura, "Assessment of Contemporary Models of Forgiveness," p. 126.

209. See further, L. G. Jones, "Crafting Communities of Forgiveness," pp. 121-34. The heading to this section is indebted to his title.

210. McClendon, *Ethics*, chap. 8 (p. 224).

211. See the useful description by the Canadian philosopher and cultural analyst Charles Taylor, *Human Agency and Language*, 1:4-5; for a theological critique of individual autonomy, see Kraus, *The Authentic Witness*, p. 109.

212. See further, Volf, *Free of Charge*, p. 214.

a view toward the unity of all humankind. For that to happen, the church has a lot of work to do in ecumenism, helping reconcile its own internal divisions.[213]

The contours and horizons of communal forgiveness, pursuit of justice, and seeking reconciliation will be taken up again in chapter 14 and linked with the work toward healing and restoration of persons and communities. In the meantime, this chapter concludes by connecting with themes of conversion, repentance, and forgiveness in the teachings of four other living faiths.

Conversion, Repentance, and Forgiveness among Religions

What the Muslim scholar Mahmoud Ayoub says of repentance echoes common intuitions among followers of diverse faith traditions: "Repentance may be regarded as the cornerstone of the religious life of both the individual and society. For the pious of any religious community, repentance is an outward manifestation of faith and a link between the divine and the heart and soul of the person of faith."[214] That said, as with many doctrinal topics, the *Christian* theologian should be mindful of the difference (and at times, incompatibility) of categories among religions.[215] Regarding repentance, Guy L. Beck observes that "the negative feeling of remorse for sin, if any, in Eastern religions such as Hinduism, Buddhism, or Jainism seems overshadowed by more visible assortments of self-help measures for positive reparation."[216] Without doubt the category of conversion fits more naturally Christianity, Islam, and (particularly early forms of) Buddhism.[217] An indication of how deeply conversion is linked with Christianity and Islam is the rise of Christianization and Islamization theory.[218] Mindfulness of potential differences, however, should not hinder the attempt to reach out to other traditions and compare notes. In a more general sense, most religions know the category of conversion and repentance.[219]

We will first look at two other Abrahamic traditions in which the theol-

213. Consult Pannenberg, "Christian Morality and Political Issues," p. 38.
214. Ayoub, "Repentance in the Islamic Tradition," p. 96.
215. For the famous distinction between "conversion" in prophetic religions and "adhesion" in others, see Nock, *Conversion*, pp. 7-16; cf. H. F. Fisher, "Conversion Reconsidered."
216. Beck, "Fire in the Ātman," p. 76.
217. Rambo and Farhadian, "Conversion," p. 1969.
218. Rambo and Farhadian, "Conversion," p. 1972.
219. See Hunter, "Forgiveness," p. 30.

ogy of repentance and forgiveness is similar to Christianity,[220] and then more briefly at Asiatic faiths.

Repentance and Forgiveness in Abrahamic Traditions

Jewish Interpretations and Practices The basic scriptural word for repentance is *sub*, which develops into the rabbinic term *teshuvah;* the word comes "from the root for return, and the concept is generally understood to mean returning to God from a situation of estrangement."[221] In Torah it "is constantly and closely connected with eschatological ideas of the Judgment and of the Messianic Age."[222] The Christian message of repentance and forgiveness in John the Baptist and Jesus' ministry builds on these same themes.

Although the idea of forgiving was known by the Israelites since the beginning of their existence, the topic became all the more important as the people of God continued sinning over and over again and yet claimed to be the chosen ones. Particularly after the sixth century B.C.E., in the aftermath of the exile, the importance of repentance became an urgent theme.[223] The availability of God's forgiveness was taken as the confirmation of election and covenant.[224] The petition for the forgiveness of sins in the Amidah (#6), the central prayer for all Jewish services, demonstrates its importance.[225] Even more widely, "[t]he conception could involve the prophetic notion of restoration as well as the conversion of pagans."[226]

Although like other Abrahamic traditions in that only God has the prerogative to forgive sins,[227] a defining feature of the Jewish idea of conversion has to do with obedience and willingness to follow Torah. Even the Spirit's role, often emphasized in Christian theology of conversion as the necessary divine endowment, is "at best an unpredictable emergency measure to remind

220. For a useful comparison, see Destro and Pesce, eds., *Rituals and Ethics.*

221. Neusner, "Repentance in Judaism," p. 61.

222. Montefiore, "Rabbinic Conceptions of Repentance," p. 211. For the high value of repentance in rabbinic literature, see also, Milgrom et al., "Repentance," p. 221.

223. See further, Jacobs, *A Jewish Theology,* chap. 17.

224. For this kind of "biblical optimism" concerning the availability of forgiveness for those who repent, see Milgrom and Unterman, "Forgiveness," pp. 127-28.

225. The Amidah can be found, e.g., at http://www.chabad.org/library/article_cdo/aid/867674/jewish/Translation.htm (7/25/2014); in this section I am indebted to Thoma, "Christian Theology and Judaic Thought."

226. Aune, "Repentance," p. 7755.

227. In support, see Johansson, "'Who Can Forgive Sins?'"

Israel that the best way to draw close to God is to follow the teachings of the Torah."[228]

Both of the two early formative Jewish figures, Philo[229] and Josephus, praised the value of repentance and forgiveness. For Philo, "God's forgiveness is deeply related to sacrifice" and accompanying purification rituals.[230] Reflecting on the disastrous effects of the wars, Josephus was convinced that "when the Jewish people repent, confess their sins, abide by God's law, and place their trust in God, forgiveness will be granted, and the tragic fall of Jerusalem and the Temple will be ended."[231] At the same time, he felt a deep tension between the divine forgiveness and God's righteousness. Not surprisingly, forgiveness is also a theme in the Jewish Apocrypha (Sirach 2:11; 5:6; 17:29; 28:2, among others) and Pseudepigrapha (*1 Enoch* 1:8; 5:6; *Jubilees* 23:31; 31:25; 45:3, among others). A summative observation about Second Temple ("intertestamental") Judaism's theology is that the main characteristics of divine forgiveness "focus on the covenantal faithfulness to God's law. Jewish groups of the Second Temple period were trying to receive God's forgiveness through the covenantal faithfulness to God's law."[232]

Similar to pietistic and revivalistic forms of Christianity and Sufi Islam, the mystically oriented Jewish movements such as Hasidism have focused much on repentance and forgiveness as a way to ensure the genuine nature of spiritual life.[233] The Kabbalistic tradition's emphasis on repentance as the way of rectification *(tikkun)* belongs to the same category.[234]

A defining Mishnah text (*Yoma* 8:8-9) outlines the key principles of Jewish theology of repentance and forgiveness.[235] The sin offering atones for

228. Gertel, "'Holy Ghost' and Judaism," p. 45.

229. For Philo's view of repentance, see his *Special Laws* 1.101-4; 1.187; 1.236-41, among others.

230. Behind many OT metaphors used of divine forgiveness is the idea of purity and cleansing, e.g., Jer. 33:8; Isa. 1:16; 43:25; Ps. 51:4, 9; see Milgrom and Unterman, "Forgiveness," p. 127.

231. Bilde, *Flavius Josephus*, pp. 186-87.

232. This paragraph (including direct citations) is based on Lee, Hughes, and Viljoen, "Forgiveness in the Intertestamental Period."

233. See the important teaching manual *Igeret HaTeshuva* ("On Repentance," p. 1548) in the Tanya collection, the basic resource for Hasidic spirituality; available in English at http://www.chabad.org/library/tanya/tanya_cdo/aid/7877/jewish/Igeret-HaTeshuva.htm (7/25/2014).

234. For an important discussion, see Shokek, *Kabbalah and the Art of Being*, pp. 135-40.

235. Another important traditional text is Nathan, *The Fathers according to Rabbi Nathan*, chap. 29 (pp. 121-22); for exposition, see Neusner, "Repentance in Judaism," pp. 64-65.

all unintentional sins, but intentional sins require repentance and returning to God — even though full atonement may come only at death or through the Day of Atonement, provided that the sinner refrains from further intentional sins. In other words, one cannot expect forgiveness if "one has insinuated repentance into the sinful act itself, declaring at the outset that afterward one will repent."[236] Furthermore, asking for forgiveness without repentance "also humiliates the law of mercy, cheapening and trivializing the superhuman act of forgiveness by treating as compulsive what is an act of human, and divine, grace."[237]

On the basis of the scriptural and traditional teaching, Jacob Neusner concludes that although the "sinner should be, and is punished . . . sin is not indelible. If the sinner repents the sin, atones, and attains reconciliation with God, the sin is wiped off the record, the sinner forgiven, the sinner's successors blameless."[238] Forgiveness entails repentance because without it the rule of justice is violated as repentance "defines the key to the moral life."[239] While the "act of repentance commences with the sinner . . . [it] compels divine response"[240] because Jewish theology believes that the violator's attitude really makes a difference. So essential and fruitful is repentance that it can be said that "repentance overrides negative commandments of the Torah (the more important kind); brings redemption; changes the character of the already-committed sin; lengthens the life of the penitent."[241]

Similar to other Abrahamic faiths, Jewish tradition highlights the importance of forgiveness in relation to the neighbor as well. Divine forgiveness cannot be had if an intentional violation against the neighbor has been committed and there is not yet reconciliation.[242] What about the possibility of repentance for those guilty of grave violations? Could a Nazi leader find a

---

236. Neusner, "Repentance in Judaism," p. 64. In interpreting this Mishnaic teaching, I draw widely from pp. 63-64. For a fine summary of Maimonides' teaching on this topic, see Stern, "Al-Ghazzalī, Maimonides, and Ibn Paquda on Repentance," pp. 593-96.

237. Neusner, "Repentance in Judaism," p. 61.

238. Neusner, "Repentance in Judaism," p. 60. His main reference is to Babylonian Talmud, *Gittin* 57B.

239. Neusner, "Repentance in Judaism," pp. 61-62. See also, Dan-Cohen, *Revising the Past.*

240. Neusner, "Repentance in Judaism," p. 68; the OT contains a number of admonitions about human initiative for repentance: Josh. 24:23; Ezek. 18:31; Jer. 4:4, 14; Hos. 10:12; etc. See further, Milgrom et al., "Repentance," p. 221.

241. Neusner, "Repentance in Judaism," p. 68.

242. For sources, see Milgrom et al., "Repentance," p. 22; Milgrom and Unterman, "Forgiveness," p. 129.

way back to redemption?[243] Neusner reminds us that this depends much on whether the Jewish community follows the scriptural and theological tradition outlined above or whether it follows "secular" nationalistic Judaism. As is well known, in Israel and particularly in the USA, a majority of Jews, at least among the scholarly world, are atheists. For them the possibility of redemption of a mass murderer of their own people is not (necessarily) guided by theological resources; it is dependent on common human intuitions, similar to those of other secularists.[244]

What about conversion for non-Jews who wish to join the community? Is that possible? And if so, what is the way to do it? According to the Talmudic tradition, Abraham successfully converted other men to Jewish monotheism (while his wife Sarah converted women). Tradition also teaches that in the book of Exodus some people "joined the liberated slaves who were to receive the Tablets of the Law and enter the Promised Land to adopt their religious and ethnic identity."[245] Indeed, "Talmud praises converts who in daily prayers are equated to the righteous, the pious and scribes of the Jewish people, asking for mercy for every one of them."[246] For the outsider, the act of conversion requires a three-judge court, circumcision, and immersion in ritual water.[247] Once ratified properly, unlike in other Abrahamic faiths, "Conversion is irreversible in principle. Converts who change their mind about their decision would still be considered Jews according to the religious rules, even if they actively practice another religion. Children conceived after the conversion will be considered Jewish, regardless of the wish of the

---

243. See the fascinating recent essay by leading Jewish philosopher E. Wyschogrod, "Repentance and Forgiveness," pp. 157-68.

244. For a contemporary case study, see Neusner, "Repentance in Judaism," pp. 70-75.

245. *Midrash Rabbah: Genesis* (1:324) comments on Gen. 12:5 ("And Abram took Sarai his wife, and Lot his brother's son, and all their possessions which they had gathered, and the persons that they had gotten in Haran; and they set forth to go to the land of Canaan"), that what is meant is the helping of people to convert to Judaism. For details, see Barylka, "Conversion in Judaism," p. 5.

246. Said Rabbi Eleazar ben Pdat: "'G-d did not redeem Israel among the nations except to take in converts' (Pesachim 87 b). Said Rabbi Shimon ben Lakish, 'Converts are desired by G-d more than those who were at Sinai. Why? If those had not heard the voices, seen the torches and thunder, and the mountains shaking and the sound of trumpets and horns, they would not have received the divine yoke. And he who saw nothing of the sort, comes and approaches the Lord, and receives the heavenly yoke. Is there anything to be loved more than that?' (Tanchuma Lech Lecha 6)." Cited in Barylka, "Conversion in Judaism," p. 5 n. 24.

247. Barylka, "Conversion in Judaism," p. 6, with supporting references in the Talmud and Maimonides.

family and their own. This condition is shared with all the Jews born to a Jewish mother."[248]

Islamic Interpretations Similar to the OT, the earliest Qur'anic passages were not calling people to convert to a new religion. Rather, the Meccans were called to "worship the Lord of this House [Ka'ba]" (Q 106:3). Only later, with the rising opposition from the worshipers of local deities, was a decisive break announced (106:9) and the confession became "There is no god except God" (37:35). Moving to Medina, the Prophet with his companions lived among the Jews and obviously assumed that the new faith was in keeping with theirs as well as Christian faith (2:40-41).[249] Recall that at that time the term *muslim* could also be applied to non-Muslims such as Solomon (27:45) and disciples of Jesus (3:52). Only when the Jews rejected the Prophet was the direction of prayer changed from Jerusalem to Mecca (2:142).

Because the Qur'an teaches that "[t]here is no compulsion in religion" (2:256), conversion should be a matter of one's choice.[250] Herein the Prophet's practice of inviting people to Islam through preaching and issuing spiritual warnings serves as an example.[251] This is not to deny — similar to Christian history — occasions of forced conversions, but those have to be considered anomalies rather than the norm.[252] Importantly, in early Muslim lands the Jews and Christians belonged to the "protected people" who were not put under pressure to convert and who could own property. "Nevertheless, pressure for conversion existed because conversion to Islam meant the right to own land and slaves, lower taxes, and privileges in certain types of trade, as well as polygyny and the attainment of higher social positions."[253] In recent years, massive emigrations have helped spread Islam in all continents.

What, however, is strictly forbidden is conversion to another religion. For many Muslims, the very idea of conversion from Islam is an unknown phenomenon. According to Islamic law, it is apostasy and at least in principle could lead to punishment by death. However, what is not uncommon is con-

---

248. Barylka, "Conversion in Judaism," p. 6.

249. Woodberry, "Conversion in Islam," p. 24.

250. Friedmann, *Tolerance and Coercion in Islam*.

251. For "warning," see Q 74:2. For a gentle and respectful approach in evangelization, see 16:125.

252. See Brinner and Stewart, "Conversion"; Brett, "Spread of Islam in Egypt and North Africa," pp. 1-12.

253. "Conversion," in *The Oxford Dictionary of Islam*.

version from one Muslim movement to another (similar to the change from one Christian denomination to another).[254]

Instead of using the term "conversion," Islam speaks of the corresponding process of transformation in terms of *islam* (submission), *iman* (faith), and *ihtida'* (following guidance). Ultimately, conversion is about "restoration, a returning, and a remembering. . . . The greatest challenge upon this earth is not so much to explore God as to remember that there is one."[255] The "conversion" entails confession of two simple but necessary aspects: that Allah is the only god and that Muhammad is the prophet of God (usually recited in Arabic and followed by "the greater ablution" of the whole body). Part of the conversion process is a continuous mind-set of penitence and contrition, although there are no mandatory formal rites or rituals.[256] The internal process of remorse and repentance is accompanied with ritual prayers and *zakat*, "almsgiving" (Q 9:5, 11); submission *(islam)* to God is part of the act (39:54).[257]

According to Islamic tradition, Muhammad has declared, "I am the Prophet of repentance."[258] In the Qur'an, and particularly in the later Hadith tradition, repentance plays an important role.[259] Among several terms denoting repentance and remorse, the key scriptural term, akin to Hebrew, is *tawbah* (Q 3:90; 4:17, 18, 92, 104; 40:3; 43:25, among others), meaning not only "to return" but also to do so frequently.[260] The Qur'an speaks of the process of

254. See further, Brinner and Stewart, "Conversion." For an important theological discussion, see Afsaruddin, "Celebrating Pluralism and Dialogue," pp. 389-406.

255. Askari, *Inter-Religion*, p. 18, cited in Cragg, *Jesus and the Muslim*, p. 260. Similarly Nasr, *Islam and the Plight of Modern Man*, pp. 4-5, 12.

256. Woodberry, "Conversion in Islam," pp. 22-23; see also, pp. 26-35. For a highly useful historical discussion, see Bulliet, *Conversion to Islam in the Medieval Period.*

257. Woodberry, "Conversion in Islam," pp. 24-26 (this whole section is largely based on it); see also, Aune, "Repentance," p. 7758. W. Watt tells us that almsgiving as an external sign of true repentance is so important that its lack equals apostasy; "Conditions of Membership of the Islamic Community," pp. 5-7; see also, his important essay, "Conversion in Islam at the Time of the Prophet."

258. Quoted in Khalil, "Early Sufi Approaches to *Tawba*," p. 2.

259. For the cultural and religious background, see Abu-Nimer and Nasser, "Forgiveness in the Arab and Islamic Contexts." For Hadith texts, see, e.g., *Fiqh-us Sunnah*, vol. 4, section 65: Supplications; *Sahih Muslim*, book 37: "Repentance and Exhortation of Repentance."

260. *Tawbah* appears almost ninety times in the Qur'an, and most occurrences appear in the Medinan period, that is, during the time of establishing the community. The closely related term *awbah* is used in the wider sense of humbly returning to God with devotion and praise, and yet another, *inābah*, highlights the importance of total submission. For details, see Ayoub, "Repentance in the Islamic Tradition," pp. 96-98; Denny, "The Qur'anic Vocabulary of Repentance."

re-turning in terms of "people entering God's religion in throngs" and asking for forgiveness (Q 110:2, 3). While forgiveness is based on God's grace, clearly human initiative is needed: "Indeed God does not alter the state of a people unless they have altered the state of their souls" (13:11).[261] As in Jewish-Christian Scriptures, feelings of remorse and sorrow over sin and forgetting God and God's commandments are emphasized (Q 21:87-88).[262] According to Hadith teaching, remorse indeed can be said to be repentance itself.[263]

As mentioned above, this (re-)turning to God in repentance is not one isolated act but rather a daily attitude, and indeed should take place "more than seventy times a day."[264] This continuous repentance is particularly important in Sufi mysticism, which is deeply concerned about repentance and conversion in its desire for deepening spiritual life. Repentance is "a life-altering process of 'interior conversion,' and not merely a simple act of turning away from a particular sin."[265] Similarly the Mu'tazilite tradition has paid much attention to the category of conversion and often conceives it in terms of three interrelated aspects: restitution, an effort to avoid repeating the violation, and continuing remorse.[266] In Qur'an 20:82, faith *(iman)* is linked with repentance and forgiveness: "And indeed I am Forgiving toward him who repents, and believes, and acts righteously, and then follows guidance."[267]

The normative medieval theologian al-Ghazali, who also gleans from Sufi mysticism, names repentance as the starting point for followers of the spiritual path, and therefore "it must be put first in the Quarter of Salvation."[268] Sin's "toxic," harmful effects can be cleansed by an authentic act of repentance.[269] It

---

261. According to Muslim commentators, the apparent difference of the order in 9:118 ("Then He turned [relenting] to them that they might also turn [in repentance]") is explained by the larger context and does not conflict with the general demand for humans to take the initiative; see Woodberry, "Conversion in Islam," pp. 27-28.

262. For a detailed comparison (albeit with quite an apologetic tone), see Moucarry, *The Search for Forgiveness.*

263. *Mishkat al-Masabih,* book 10, chap. 3, in vol. 2, p. 501.

264. *Mishkat al-Masabih,* book 10, chap. 3, in vol. 2, p. 493, cited in Woodberry, "Conversion in Islam," p. 26.

265. Khalil, "Early Sufi Approaches to *Tawba,*" p. iii.

266. Aune, "Repentance," p. 7758. For distinctive ways of describing the process of repentance and conversion among Islamic theological traditions, see Woodberry, "Conversion in Islam," pp. 30-31.

267. See further, Woodberry, "Conversion in Islam," pp. 28-29.

268. *Al-Ghazzali on Repentance,* pp. 29-30; available at http://www.ghazali.org/books/gz-repent.pdf (7/29/2014).

269. *Al-Ghazzali on Repentance,* p. 41.

consists of knowledge of the seriousness of the violation, remorse, and change of behavior.[270] As in the other Abrahamic traditions, the key elements of repentance in Islam include, then, "awe in the presence of the Holy, awareness of sin and genuine remorse for it, regret over the lost opportunities, sincere contrition and the resolve to mend one's ways." Although human initiative is necessary, ultimately true repentance is a gift of God, divine grace, as evident in one of the important names of God, "All-Forgiving" (*ghafūr;* Q 5:98; 25:70).[271]

That Islam does not have the Christian tradition's type of doctrine of atonement and redemption does not necessarily make its theology of forgiveness radically different from the Christian view.[272] Even when Muslims and Christians interpret differently the Fall narrative and Adam and Eve's penalty, both traditions, widely speaking, connect divine forgiveness with human sinfulness.[273]

All this is to say that, notwithstanding popular misconceptions to the contrary, the idea of forgiveness is deeply embedded in the Qur'anic and Hadith traditions.[274] What about its conditions? Is divine forgiveness unconditional or conditional in Islam? It is conditional in a sense that it entails a true change of heart. A prideful and arrogant attitude blocks forgiveness.[275] That said, materially similar to Judeo-Christian tradition, "God's mercy takes precedence over God's wrath."[276] Yet — again like other Abrahamic traditions — Islamic theology has to be able to maintain God's justice in all of that.[277]

As in the other Abrahamic traditions, forgiveness in Islam encompasses both divine forgiveness and (asking for and receiving) human forgiveness

270. *Al-Ghazzali on Repentance,* p. 31. See further, Stern, "Notes on the Theology of Ghazzali's Concept of Repentance."

271. Ayoub, "Repentance in Islamic Tradition," pp. 98-99 (p. 98). Of the 99 Beautiful Names, two names explicitly mention forgiveness (both from the radicals gh-f-r), namely, Al Ghaffar (20:82; 38:66; 39:5, among others) and Al-Ghafur (2:173; 8:69, among others). English renderings are usually "Forgiving" and "All-Forgiving."

272. See further, Lazarus-Yafeh, "Is There a Concept of Redemption in Islam?" pp. 48-57; Siddiqi, "The Doctrine of Redemption," pp. 91-102; I am indebted to Khalil, "Early Sufi Approaches to *Tawba,*" p. 3 n. 11.

273. For a detailed exposition and comparison between Islamic and Christian (including also Jewish) interpretations of sin and "fall," see chap. 15 in *Creation and Humanity.* For a thoughtful comparison regarding forgiveness, see LaHurd, "'So That the Sinner Will Repent'"; Davary, "Forgiveness in Islam," p. 132; so also, Abu-Nimer and Nasser, "Forgiveness in the Arab and Islamic Contexts," p. 477.

274. Davary, "Forgiveness in Islam," p. 127.

275. Davary, "Forgiveness in Islam," p. 134.

276. Davary, "Forgiveness in Islam," p. 135.

277. See further, Davary, "Forgiveness in Islam," pp. 138-40.

when the neighbor has been violated.[278] In keeping with Judeo-Christian teaching, before praying to God one must be reconciled with one's neighbor.[279] Similar to what is argued above in this project, forgiveness means going beyond resentment as it seeks to reconcile and heal not only the violated person but also the perpetrator. As such, it calls for a change of heart toward the violator without excluding the need to expose and judge the wrong act. Forgiveness can be regarded as a virtue, as it calls for reconciliation and the extending of grace.[280] The main Qur'anic term for forgiveness, *afw*, "is often used along with a realization of the wrongdoing by those who have committed wrong either to themselves or to others." Accordingly, violating others means acting wrongly against oneself. As a result, "[a]sking forgiveness for a sin . . . is therefore a realization of a wrongdoing against one's self."[281]

Lately, some Islamic ethicists and other scholars have also begun to work toward models of reconciliation in which forgiveness may relate to communal and national conflicts. One such is the "transformative reconciliation model," which may include religious ritual elements as part of a complex process of forgiveness and conflict resolution. It acknowledges an affinity with and indebtedness to work done by Christian theologians.[282] Collaborations between scholars of these two traditions are also emerging in this area.[283]

Conversion, Repentance, and Forgiveness in Asiatic Traditions

Hindu Perspectives Rather than conversion, says S. Radhakrishnan, what counts in Hinduism is a religious experience, spiritual "realization," and conduct.[284] Rather than acceptance of set doctrine, turning to Hinduism is about embracing "a particular meta-theological view of doctrines themselves — in other words, a Hindu worldview." Rather than "deliverance from sin," conversion is "progressive enlightenment in which the ignorance and desire that keep

---

278. Davary, "Forgiveness in Islam," p. 127.

279. For details, with sources in Hadith and other traditions, see Davary, "Forgiveness in Islam," pp. 130-31.

280. Davary, "Forgiveness in Islam," p. 128-29.

281. Davary, "Forgiveness in Islam," p. 129.

282. Abu-Nimer, ed., *Reconciliation, Justice, and Coexistence*; Abu-Nimer, *Nonviolence and Peace Building in Islam*.

283. Abu-Nimer and Augsburger, eds., *Peace-building*.

284. "Intellect is subordinated to intuition, dogma to experience, outward expression to inward realization." Radhakrishnan, *Hindu View of Life*, p. 13; see also, p. 37.

us trapped in our human dilemma are expelled."[285] With this view, Hinduism rejects the Abrahamic traditions' call for conversion.[286] Even when Mahatma Gandhi used the term "conversion," he carefully distinguished it from the Abrahamic faiths' view and spoke of "change of heart."[287]

As mentioned above, a major issue for any Hindu conversion is the caste system, which is based on birth. For those who by their conduct, relocation, or other circumstances fall away from their proper caste, there is a way of returning to orthodoxy by the rite of *shudhi*, literally "purification" or "conversion."[288] It is significant that Vinayak Damodar Savarkar, the founder of the renewal movement Arya Samaj, opposed conversion of Hindus to Islam and Christianity. Yet this movement strongly advocated reconversion of recent converts to Christianity back to Hinduism. Under the slogan "India for Indians," Saraswati also worked enthusiastically for the return to the teachings of the Vedas.[289]

Notwithstanding the hesitancy against conversion, Hinduism knows not only the reconversion of lapsed faithful but also active missionary efforts to convert "pagans." This was certainly the case in the third to fifth centuries during the establishment of Hindu *rajas* in South India to replace Buddhism. Itinerant "evangelists" played a critical role in that enterprise. More recently, Hare Krishna and a number of less well-known revival movements in the West have sought new converts.[290]

What about repentance? Fully cognizant of the danger of "foisting Western theological categories upon" Hinduism, Beck argues that both in classical Vedic religion and in theistic (particularly *bhakti*) traditions, repentance is present; indeed, therein the idea itself predates any other religious traditions. The seriousness of sin is certainly present, although, unlike the classical Christian interpretation, there is not an "original sin" but rather a form of contamination and defilement.[291] In the Rig Veda, a number of hymns are dedicated to the deity Varuna, the highly elevated King of the Universe whose eyes watch

---

285. Hiebert, "Conversion in Hinduism and Buddhism," p. 10; a typo in the quotation was corrected.

286. See Radhakrishnan, *Hindu View of Life*, p. 28; similarly Vivekananda, "Addresses at the Parliament of Religions"; I am indebted to Hiebert, "Conversion in Hinduism and Buddhism," p. 12.

287. Catterjee, *Gandhi's Religious Thought*, p. 49; Hiebert, "Conversion in Hinduism and Buddhism," pp. 13-14.

288. Jordens, "Reconversion to Hinduism," pp. 145-61.

289. Ahluwalia, "Shudhi Movement."

290. Hiebert, "Conversion in Hinduism and Buddhism," pp. 15-16.

291. See further, Beck, "Fire in the Ātman," pp. 82-83.

over all the affairs of the world.[292] Consider this petition: "What, Varuṇa, hath been my chief transgression, that thou wouldst slay the friend who sings thy praises? Tell me, Unconquerable Lord, and quickly sinless will I approach thee with mine homage. Free us from sins committed by our fathers, from those wherein we have ourselves offended."[293] Indeed, virtually all hymns dedicated to Varuna (sometimes joined with either Mitra or Indra) contain petitions for mercy and an attitude of contrition.[294] Here is a similarity with the Judeo-Christian God as the source of forgiveness.[295]

The importance of praying for mercy from Varuna has to do with the key Vedic concept of *rita*, the cosmic and moral order. Whatever else "sin" is in Vedic religion, it has to do with violation of this cosmic order, the guarantee of peace, harmony, and blessings. Vedic religion conceives violation against *rita* as an accumulation of "debt" to be paid to restore balance.[296] Again, somewhat like Christian tradition, some Vedic traditions made a distinction between unintentional and intentional sins: whereas the former can be cleansed with the help of reciting proper Vedic passages, the latter can only be rectified by restitution.[297] Religiously and societally, it is important to note that the Vedic development of ideas of sin and repentance in the highly influential *Laws of Manu* not only helped regulate judicial affairs in general but also laid the foundation for handling issues related to various castes.[298]

The most serious offenses can be "burned off" only in the process of numerous reincarnations, including temporary time spent in various hells. In Hinduism, the reconciliation of the most serious offenses may also entail various kinds of vows, a practice echoing the rationale of merits to be earned in the process of penance (rite of reconciliation) in Roman Catholic tradition.[299]

For ordinary Hindus, the gateway to reflecting on forgiveness comes in the form of the authoritative "secondary" scriptural stories found in *Ma-*

292. For a dramatic account of Varuna, see Basham, *The Wonder That Was India*, pp. 236-37.

293. Rig Veda 7.86.4-5; see also, 1.24.14-15; 7.89.

294. Beck, "Fire in the Ātman," pp. 77, 856; see further, *The Laws of Manu*, 11.228-31; *SBE* 25, n.p.

295. The correlation between Yahweh and Varuna is pointed out by Basham, *The Wonder That Was India*, p. 237, cited in Beck, "Fire in the Ātman," p. 80.

296. See J. Miller, *Vision of Cosmic Order*, p. 142; Beck, "Fire in the Ātman," p. 78.

297. *The Laws of Manu* 11.46; *SBE* 25, n.p.; see further, Beck, "Fire in the Ātman," p. 83.

298. For details, see Beck, "Fire in the Ātman," pp. 81-82. An example of repentance is in *The Laws of Manu* 11.44; *SBE* 25, n.p.

299. For details in Hindu religion, see Beck, "Fire in the Ātman," pp. 83-85; the links with Judeo-Christian tradition are mine.

habharata, particularly the Bhagavad Gita (16.3),[300] which lists forgiveness, along with other noble characteristics such as "splendor . . . fortitude, cleanliness, absence of malice, and absence of pride [as] . . . qualities of those endowed with divine virtues." In the story of the war between two families (the Kauravas and Pandavas), Arjuna of the Pandava family consults his cousin Krishna[301] about the wisdom of fighting against his family, an issue that brings to the surface difficult questions of forgiveness and reconciliation. In these stories of the Great Epic, an ambiguous picture of forgiveness emerges: on the one hand, it looks as though duty (of the soldier Arjuna to follow orders) trumps forgiveness; on the other hand, it is not difficult to find passages in which forgiveness is celebrated as one of the highest virtues, as mentioned.[302]

All forms of theistic Hinduism and *bhakti* devotion include a felt need to cleanse oneself from sins committed. Although atonement by the deity is not an unknown idea in Vedic religion, the emphasis by and large is still on "self-atonement." The situation is different with *bhakti* spirituality: grace and divine forgiveness are in the forefront.[303] Every theistic Hindu knows the famous ending of the Bhagavad Gita (18.66): "Setting aside all noble deeds, just surrender completely to the will of God (with firm faith and loving contemplation). I shall liberate you from all sins (or bonds of Karma). Do not grieve." Various opportunities and ways for forgiveness are offered in these traditions, from pilgrimage to a sacred site, to bathing in the sacred river Ganges, to being tutored by the Guru (who is believed to bear sins as well), and so forth.[304] Particularly important is the recitation of Sanskrit hymns and divine names.[305] Sri Ramakrishna said: "All the sins of the body fly away if one chants the name of God and sings His glories. The birds of sin dwell in the tree of the body. Singing the name of God is like clapping your hands. As, at a clap of the hands, the birds in the tree fly away, so do our sins disappear at the chanting of God's name and glories."[306]

300. I am using the version available at the University of Evansville "Exploring Ancient World Cultures" Web site (copyright 1988 by Dr. Ramanand Prasad, American Gita Society): http://eawc.evansville.edu/anthology/gita.htm (10/8/2014).

301. In later tradition, Krishna becomes one of the main *avataras* of the deity Vishnu, a hugely popular part of *bhakti* spirituality.

302. See the important discussion in *Mahabharata,* book 3 *(Vana Parva),* section 29 (pp. 59-62; http://sacred-texts.com/sbe/index.htm); see also, Hunter, "Forgiveness," pp. 36-37.

303. See further, Beck, "Fire in the Ātman," pp. 86-87, 91.

304. Hunter, "Forgiveness," p. 39.

305. Beck, "Fire in the Ātman," p. 85.

306. M. Gupta, *Gospel of Sri Ramakrishna,* pp. 181-82, quoted in Hunter, "Forgiveness," p. 39. See Klostermaier, *Survey of Hinduism,* p. 171.

Similar to Abrahamic traditions, there are Hindu teachings about the need to extend forgiveness also to fellow humans.[307] Rig Veda (5.85.7) contains the plea to Varuna: "if we have sinned against the man who loves us, have ever wronged a brother, friend, or comrade, The neighbour ever with us, or a stranger, O Varuṇa, remove from us the trespass."

Buddhist Views As in Hinduism, Buddhist traditions display an ambiguity concerning conversion.[308] On the one hand, it looks as though beginning from Gautama's enlightenment experience, a radical break with the past is the norm; on the other hand, it can also be argued that (apart from some exceptions such as conversion by force)[309] the people who joined the movement hardly underwent any radical crisis experience. One way to reconcile this apparent tension is to argue that only when the religious seeker made the decisive decision to break off from the "world" and become a Theravadin (an ascetic or similar devotionalist in a traditional form of Buddhism), the break was a crisis. Merely to be a religious seeker and even to change between various (at the time, Hindu) sects did not have to be a cause of crisis. History tells us that a significant number of disciples who joined Gautama already belonged to religious movements.[310]

The complexity of the issue of forgiveness in Buddhism could also be framed in the following manner when compared with Christian tradition. No doubt, forgiveness is an important Buddhist concept and necessary for the attainment of the final goal of nirvana. That said, in all forms of Buddhism, with perhaps the exception of Pure Land, forgiveness is not linked with divine pardon for ensuring entrance to eternal blessedness.[311] Gods play little (or virtually no) role in conversion, repentance, and forgiveness.[312]

Similar to scriptures of other traditions, Buddhist sacred writings illustrate the themes of conversion, repentance, and forgiveness with the help of key religious figures. Perhaps the most well-known conversion story (after that of Gautama himself)[313] is the legend of the third-century B.C.E. Indian king Asoka. Once a cruel tyrant, Asoka experiences a deep sense of remorse after an extraordinarily bloody conquest and becomes a Buddha devotee and

307. See further, Hunter, "Forgiveness," p. 39.

308. See Tilakaratne, "Buddhist View on Religious Conversion," pp. 58-82.

309. Keyes, "Monks, Guns, and Peace," pp. 145-63.

310. Brekke, "Conversion in Buddhism?" pp. 181-91.

311. See Su, "Forgiveness," p. 229.

312. Eckel, "Buddhist Approach to Repentance," p. 122.

313. See Eckel, "Buddhist Approach to Repentance," pp. 127-29.

advocate.[314] Another well-known Theravada narrative tells about a king, an early follower of the Buddha, Ajatasattu, who was murdered by his son, who wished to replace his father. The murderer son, upon knowing that he was destined to be killed by his own son and sent into the lowest regions of hell, comes to consult the Buddha. Going "to the Blessed One for refuge, to the Dhamma, and to the community of monks," he makes the confession of the "transgression" to the Buddha, who receives it and pronounces: "But because you see your transgression as such and make amends in accordance with the Dhamma, we accept your confession."[315]

These and some other passages that seem to illustrate confession of sin imply that "the early Buddhist doctrine of kamma allows for mitigation, though not eradication, of the consequences of actions under some circumstances";[316] the kind of expiation of sins present in Hindu traditions discussed above is not present, however.[317] What is in the forefront in the Buddhist tradition are the "practices of self-examination, feelings of remorse, the renunciation of unwholesome patterns of life, and the possibility of radical moral change."[318] Similar to other faith traditions, teaching manuals have been devised to help in this process.[319] They are particularly important in monasticism.[320]

Unknown to many, there is even a famous "prodigal son" narrative in the Mahayana's authoritative *Lotus Sutra*. The son is going away from his father's house and loses all his possessions. For fifty years the father misses his son greatly, although he keeps silent about the issue. Finally the wayward son comes to the area where his father's mansion is, but seeing the beauty of the estate, he turns away with shame. The father sends servants to fetch him, which they do, against the fearful son's will. While concealing from others his son's true identity, the father begins to treat him like his son and soon observes how the son turns a new chapter in life. Then, at his deathbed, the father proclaims

---

314. *The Legend of King Aśoka*. For his conversion and remorse, see *Edicts of Asoka*, pp. 27-30 particularly.

315. *Samaññaphala Sutta*.

316. Attwood, "Did King Ajātasattu Confess to the Buddha?" p. 279; for a list of other instances, see pp. 286-90.

317. Attwood, "Did King Ajātasattu Confess to the Buddha?" pp. 290-92.

318. Eckel, "Buddhist Approach to Repentance," p. 122.

319. Noteworthy among them is the Mahayana text *Introduction to the Practice of Enlightenment*, written by the Indian monk Santideva of the seventh century. For a brief discussion, see Eckel, "Buddhist Approach to Repentance," pp. 133-37.

320. See Eckel, "Buddhist Approach to Repentance," pp. 132-35.

publicly that this son is his child. When the father donates all his riches to the son, the son is totally astonished by this gracious gesture. The spiritual lesson is simply this: the rich man is Tathagata (Buddha) and his followers are the prodigal sons.[321] Notwithstanding similarities with the biblical narrative (Luke 15), the Buddhist story is not about once-for-all redemptive forgiveness but rather about the possibility of gradual heightening of insights and spiritual development.[322]

That said, there is no denying the internal diversity of the Buddhist religion. The major difference exists between the oldest Theravada tradition and what currently is the much larger Mahayana tradition: whereas in the former the renunciation of the world ideally means devotion to full-time religious life with a view to personal salvation, including joining the community *(sangha),* the latter accepts the simple fact that for most of the masses this radical call is too much.[323] Hence, Mahayana with its theistic orientation offers the way of "salvation" somewhat similarly to forms of theistic Hinduism, that is, with devotion to the Ultimate Reality ("divinized" Buddha figure), and encourages delaying one's own stepping into nirvana for the sake of helping others. In Pure Land Buddhism, these features are present most robustly: intense contemplation and recitation of the wonderful name of Buddha Avalokitesvara (Amitayus) will cleanse from all wrongdoings.[324] A distinct Mahayana tradition in Tibet, Tantric (or Yogic) Buddhism, like mystic Sufism and forms of popular theistic Hinduism, focuses on mystical, even sexually loaded, devotion to goddesses *(taras).*[325]

In keeping with other faith traditions, Buddhism highlights the importance of forgiving other persons.[326] The Zen master Kinrei Bassis puts it succinctly: "Whether it is anger and criticism of others, anger at groups of people and institutions, or anger and criticism of ourselves, the Buddhist teaching is to always try to offer everything our unconditional forgiveness. Whenever we choose not to forgive, we are closing our hearts to something and rejecting an aspect of reality."[327] Forgiveness will also release the forgiver from harboring anger and resentment. Deciding not to cling to negative feelings toward the

---

321. *Saddharma-Pundarika* (or *Lotus Sutra*), chap. 4; *SBE* 21, n.p.

322. So also, Valea, "Parable of the Prodigal Son," n.p.

323. See O'Leary, "Mahāyāna Buddhism and Forgiveness," pp. 94-110.

324. *The Contemplation Sutra* #18, p. 77.

325. See Hiebert, "Conversion in Hinduism and Buddhism," pp. 16-21.

326. See Dalai Lama, *Freedom in Exile,* p. 261; for comments, see Eckel, "Buddhist Approach to Repentance," pp. 135-36.

327. Bassis, "Forgiveness," n.p.

other (detachment) along with forgiveness "grounds our practice in seeing how the hardness of our heart is the problem, not the mistakes of others"; this is an important lesson in spiritual development.[328]

328. Bassis, "Forgiveness," n.p.

11. One with God: Rightwising, Renewal, and Integrity of Life

For Orientation: The Need to Reframe the Doctrine of Justification

In the Christian West, "justification by faith" has become an umbrella concept that covers virtually all aspects of salvific relationship to God.[1] That usage cannot be established biblically, as in the Bible the concept of justification/righteousness is but one of many metaphors of salvation, nor historically (before the Reformation era); theology may be justified in reshaping the concept and giving it a wider meaning. The problem arises only when the distinction between the "concept" and the "doctrine" of justification is ignored and claims are made to consider that particular phenomenon the (only) "biblical" view.[2] Recall that in the Eastern Church the concept is virtually unknown. The sharp difference between the East and the West goes beyond terminology; whereas in the West the Holy Spirit's work was set under grace, in the East the "stress upon the immediacy of the divine, and the direct encounter of man with the Holy Spirit," led to speaking of salvation in terms of union, deification, participation in divine life. Furthermore, the more positive anthropology of the Greek tradition coupled with a lack of interest in Roman legal and juridical metaphors was highly influential.[3] The way the

---

1. For a classic formulation by Luther, see the Smalcald Articles 2.1.5; for Melanchthon, see the Apology of the Augsburg Confession 4.2; *BC*, p. 107. Similar statements can be found in M. Chemnitz and others (see Vainio, *Justification and Participation*, pp. 2-3).

2. For contemporary statements, see Barth, *CD* IV/1, p. 523; Packer, "Justification in Protestant Theology," p. 84.

3. McGrath, *Iustitia Dei*, 1:3-4. For a useful discussion, see Matts, *Role of Justification in Contemporary Theology*.

Western doctrine of justification emerged — as *the* defining form of soteriology — is related to the late medieval culture of divinely sanctified hierarchical society, prominence of guilt, condemnation, and penitential attitude.[4] "Contemporary existential concerns have changed," however, says the Brazilian liberationist Walter Altmann. "[T]hey are couched less in terms of guilt and condemnation and more in terms of the meaning of life and the prospects for material survival."[5]

Hence, it is about time to get beyond these fairly narrow — albeit theologically very significant — juxtapositions between the Christian West and East, as well as in the West between Catholics and Protestants, in order to seek a common understanding of salvation. Indeed, now for the first time in post-Reformation history this goal is attainable thanks to groundbreaking ecumenical achievements. Let me lay out briefly the main theses of the chapter, each of which will be developed in what follows:

- Justification by faith means both pronouncing (forensic) and making (effective) righteous. As a result, the separation between justification and sanctification should be left behind without lapsing into works righteousness or undermining divine grace as the basis.
- This understanding of justification comes materially close to the Eastern Orthodox concept of deification (*theosis*, "divinization"). Ecumenically this means establishing a common basis between the Christian East and West regarding key issues of soteriology.
- The doctrines of justification, sanctification, and deification not only speak of one's relationship to God and fellow Christians; they also have communal and sociopolitical relevance in our pluralistic world.

The plan of this lengthy chapter is as follows: first, we will study critically the Western churches' Reformation disputes in light of historical developments and the Eastern churches' radically different soteriology. The second task is to inquire into several significant ecumenical achievements that help us work toward a new consensus, including the "new perspective" in NT studies, a reconceptualization of the law-gospel relationship, and results of ecumenical dialogues, as well as a reworking of Luther's own soteriology. These resources help develop a new constructive theology of salvation as deification and justification (including sanctification and renewal of life). The last major task is to

---

4. See also, Pannenberg, *ST* 3:81; Hinlicky, "Theological Anthropology," pp. 44-47.
5. Altmann, *Luther and Liberation*, pp. 4-5.

relate these doctrines to the cultural, sociopolitical, economic, and religious diversity of our pluralistic world.

Before proceeding into detailed discussion, however, a word of warning with regard to a search for a consensual view of salvation is in order. Ecumenical thinking does not mean collecting pieces from here and there and putting them together to make a more appealing mixture. Nor does it mean making compromises (unless they are justified!) or looking for the lowest common denominator.[6] Major Christian doctrines in their specific denominational and/ or ecclesio-cultural forms are connected with deeper underlying orientations. Hence, it is possible that sometimes the result of ecumenical inquiry is a sharpening of differences. Ecumenical theology should be open to both discovering how different the various traditions may be and how much more commonality there may be than was previously believed. Even when a consensual view is on the horizon, differences should not be too quickly hidden. We should mind that an encounter with other traditions challenges any conversation partner.[7] Often, what emerges out of ecumenical exchange is a changed Orthodox, Lutheran, Methodist, Episcopalian, etc., theology. Conversation with another theological tradition helps clarify one's own views and make oneself more critical toward one's own convictions.

The Critique of Reformation Controversies and Solutions in Light of Historical Developments

Justification in Pre-Reformation Traditions

Generally speaking, patristic writers did not choose to express the doctrine of salvation under the concept of justification. That is of course not to say that this biblically based metaphor is absent from the Fathers[8] — and certainly not that it took until the Reformation to discover the "true" doctrine of justification[9] — but that throughout the first Christian millennium and even beyond, the

6. It seems to me that Milbank (*Being Reconciled*, pp. 110-11) is profoundly mistaken in his unnuanced criticism of ecumenism in general and the Catholic-Lutheran conversations on justification in particular.

7. For a recent call for "challenging ecumenism," see Braaten, "Lutherans and Catholics Together," p. 7.

8. For a typical statement from one of the earliest witnesses, see *1 Clement* 32. See the important discussion in Roukema, "Salvation *Sola Fide* and *Sola Gratia*," pp. 27-49.

9. See Jüngel, *Justification*, pp. 70-73.

justification concept was marginal and, when used, did not have the technical meaning adopted later. Even the two-volume *Commentary on the Epistle to the Romans* by Origen neither caused debates nor offered substantially new perspectives.[10] Pauline theology did not play the *central* role that it did later in medieval and Reformation debates. Only with the rise of Pelagian "works righteousness" did the Western Church have to begin to articulate a doctrine that later became highly technically formulated.[11]

As is well known, Augustine's soteriology underwent a radical transformation, including the shift from "free will" to "bound will" (see above, chap. 9).[12] Important in his anti-Pelagian reaction was the distinction between "operative" and "cooperative" modes of grace, later further elaborated by Aquinas. For the human to cooperate with God, there needs to be an initial divine operation on human will, whose positive powers have come to nil because of the Fall.[13] A human person's "justification is therefore an act of divine mercy, in that he does not desire it (because the *liberum arbitrium captivatum* is incapable of desiring good) nor does he deserve it (because of sin and lack of merit)."[14] After the "act" of justification (operative grace), whatever merit accrued in the "process" of justification (cooperative grace) is also on account of divine mercy.[15] Also well known, in Augustine, the working of God's operative grace is linked tightly to the sacrament of baptism, a feature established firmly in Catholic and later sacramental Protestant and Anglican traditions.[16]

The bishop of Hippo considered justification and renewal the work of the Holy Spirit.[17] Related to this is the emphasis on love rather than "faith alone" as the primary aspect of justification. Building on the Pauline rule of "faith working through love" (Gal. 5:6), Augustine established the highly influential *fides caritate formata* principle, which was followed by the Catholic

10. For a careful discussion, see Scheck, *Origen and the History of Justification,* chap. 6; for useful comments, see Beilby, Eddy, and Eenderlein, "Justification in Historical Perspective," pp. 17-19.

11. See McGrath, *Iustitia Dei,* 1:17-23; D. H. Williams, "Justification by Faith," p. 651.

12. See D. H. Williams, "Justification by Faith," p. 651 n. 6. See also, McGrath, *Iustitia Dei,* 1:23-27.

13. E.g., Augustine, *Treatise on Grace and Free Will* 17.

14. McGrath, *Iustitia Dei,* 1:27.

15. Augustine, *Treatise on Grace and Free Will* 15.

16. For a representative statement, see Augustine, *The Enchiridion (A Handbook of Faith, Hope, and Love)* 8.52; more widely in *On the Merits and Forgiveness of Sins and on Infant Baptism.*

17. See Augustine, *Letter* 98.

tradition and strongly opposed by Protestants.[18] It is linked with another Pauline passage, Romans 5:5, according to which, "God's love has been poured into our hearts through the Holy Spirit." The Holy Spirit poured out as love at justification is the key to renewal. Importantly, this love is nothing else but the Spirit himself.[19] The teaching of the supremacy of love has strong biblical support (1 Cor. 13:13), as endorsed also by the Eastern Church.[20] Furthermore, to combat Pelagianism, Augustine also emphasized that both faith and love are divine gifts.[21]

Unlike the later Protestant Reformation's separation of justification from sanctification, Augustine unambiguously taught that justification means "to make righteous,"[22] although of course he believed that the renewal begun in justification had to be finished.[23] Righteousness for him was inherent — although the Thomistic idea of "habitual grace" remains undeveloped. He simply taught that while justifying grace has its origin in God, it "is nevertheless located within man, and can be said to be *his*, part of his being and intrinsic to his person." To sum up: "It is certainly true that Augustine speaks of the real interior renewal of the sinner by the action of the Holy Spirit, which he later expressed in terms of participation in the divine substance itself."[24] Clearly, there is a link with the Eastern Church's *theosis* concept as well.

With the high medieval thinkers, the first millennium's cosmological *(Christus Victor)* and mystical-personal approach to salvation shifts to satisfaction (Anselm) and juridical categories. At the same time, technical accounts of justification emerge and reach their zenith in post-Reformation orthodoxy. Yet, importantly, the Protestant divide between justification (as an initial event) and sanctification (as the process of renewal) is still missing. Justification covers the whole process.[25] Thomas's fourfold description of the "process of justification" is influential: after the infusion of grace, free will is moved toward God and away from sin, leading to forgiveness of sins. Different,

18. For a lucid discussion, see Wilken, *"Fides Caritate Formata,"* pp. 1089-1100.

19. Augustine, *The Spirit and the Letter* 5.

20. "If love is taken from us, how shall we be united to God?" asks Gregory of Nyssa, *On the Soul and Resurrection; NPNF²* 5:442. For details, see Wilken, *"Fides Caritate Formata,"* p. 1092.

21. For details and references, see McGrath, *Iustitia Dei,* 1:29-30.

22. Augustine takes the Latin word *iustificare,* rooted in *facere* (to make), in its literal, obvious meaning.

23. See, e.g., Augustine, *Treatise on Grace and Free Will* 33.

24. McGrath, *Iustitia Dei,* 1:48.

25. For details, see McGrath, *Iustitia Dei,* 1:37-43.

however, from the Protestant Reformers, the last aspect (forgiveness of sins) is not to be equated with a merely forensic act; it also entails an inner change. The new thing in Aquinas is the introduction of habitual grace; that is, the remission of sins elevates the sinner to a "state of justice."[26]

In medieval theology, as also formulated at Trent, preparation of the sinner for justification became an important theme. What was debated was whether such disposition obliged God to grant the gift of justification or not. One extreme was represented by Gabriel Biel, who, on the basis of theology of *pactum* (covenant), formulated the famous slogan *facienti quod in se est Deus non denegat gratiam*, "God does not deny grace to the one who does everything in his or her power."[27] Although Luther endorsed it while young,[28] he later became a vehement critic. In the Dominican school, preparation was believed to be introduced by grace, termed *created* grace (in contrast to the *uncreated*, that is, the Holy Spirit). In the mature theology of Thomas, preparation was definitely a divine work, "so that no preparation is required for man's justification which God himself does not provide."[29] A new development in medieval theology was the rise of the sacrament of penance, which was conceived as the continuation of justification (begun in baptism).[30]

A long-term debate in medieval theology concerns the relationship between the change brought about by justification and the infusion of (supernatural) grace, habitual grace. "Are these habits infused into man in order that he may be regarded as acceptable by God? Or is man regarded as acceptable by God, as a result of which the supernatural habits are infused?" Peter Lombard's well-known identification of *caritas* (love) with the Holy Spirit[31] (rooted in Augustine's pneumatological concept of charity) represented one opinion different from Thomas's argument that there is no way to equate the uncreated (Spirit) with the created (habitual) grace; hence, "created gift."[32]

So far we have looked only at the developments in the Christian West. For the sake of the contemporary global diversity of the Christian church and

---

26. Aquinas, *ST* I-2ae.113; see McGrath, *Iustitia Dei*, 1:43-51.

27. A useful discussion of the *facienti* principle in the wider historical context is McGrath, *Iustitia Dei*, 1:81-93. Still worth consulting is the magisterial study by Oberman, *Harvest of Medieval Theology*.

28. WA 55[1]:70.9-11.

29. Aquinas, *ST* I-2ae.112.2-3; McGrath, *Iustitia Dei*, 1:78-83, 86-87 (p. 82).

30. McGrath, *Iustitia Dei*, 1:91-100.

31. See Saarinen, "Ipsa dilectio Deus est."

32. McGrath, *Iustitia Dei*, 1:145. For the subsequent debates, particularly with Scotus, see pp. 146-54.

the need to work toward a joint Christian witness in the pluralistic world, the important contributions of the soteriologies of the Christian East should be brought to bear on our topic.[33] Only in light of the history of soteriology, both in the West and the East, can the Reformation solutions be properly assessed.[34]

Salvation as Theosis and a Pneumatological Concept of Grace in the Christian East

A number of distinctive terms and metaphors of salvation are used in the Christian East, including transformation, participation, partaking, intermingling, elevation, interpenetration, transmutation, commingling, assimilation, reintegration, and adoption.[35] Common to all of them is the idea of union with God,[36] named deification (divinization, *theosis*).[37] Irenaeus spoke of the "Word of God, our Lord Jesus Christ who because of his limitless love became what we are in order to make us what even he himself is."[38] Athanasius taught that "Christ became human that humans might become divine."[39] Although Christ alone is God by nature, all people are called to become God "by participation." In such participation we become the likeness of Christ and perfect images of God the Father.[40] Even though the comment by Orthodox theologian Vladimir Lossky, that *theosis* is "echoed by the fathers and the theologians of every age,"[41] may be an overstatement, it does reflect the general mind-set of the Fathers.[42]

Eastern theologians do not speak of deification only as a metaphor; they

---

33. See Norris, "Deification," p. 422.

34. See further, Fairbairn, "Patristic Soteriology," pp. 289-310.

35. Ware, *The Orthodox Way*, p. 168.

36. See further, Lossky, *In the Image and Likeness of God*, chap. 5, esp. pp. 97-98; Lossky, *Mystical Theology of the Eastern Church*, chap. 10; Meyendorff, *Byzantine Theology*, pp. 159-65 especially.

37. Mantzaridis, *The Deification of Man*, p. 12. See also, Nellas, *Deification in Christ*.

38. Irenaeus, *Against Heresies* 5, preface.

39. Athanasius, *On the Incarnation* 54 (p. 93).

40. Lossky, *The Vision of God*, p. 98; Clendenin, "Partakers of Divinity," p. 372. See, e.g., Clement of Alexandria, *The Instructor* 1.6.

41. Lossky, *Mystical Theology of the Eastern Church*, p. 134. See also, Mantzaridis, *The Deification of Man*, p. 105.

42. For a profound statement, see Bishop Kallistos of Diokleia, foreword to Mantzaridis, *The Deification of Man*, p. 7.

also stress the reality of the union with God.[43] Sure, it is — and was already in patristic times — a daring way to speak of salvation. Non-Christians employed it to speak of pagan gods deifying creatures. The philosophers had earlier used *theoo* in that way. Christians boldly took up this concept and reoriented it to fit Christian meaning.[44]

Whereas the Bible offers materials for this way of speaking of salvation,[45] perhaps it does not speak about it as much as Eastern Orthodox theologians sometimes lead us to believe. The two cardinal texts are 2 Peter 1:4, which speaks of becoming "partakers of the divine nature," and Psalm 82:6 (quoted by the Johannine Jesus in John 10:34-36a), mentioned above.[46] The Petrine passage accentuates the key idea of release from the corruption and mortality caused by the evil desires of the world. Eastern theology does not focus so much on guilt as on mortality as the main problem of humanity.[47] Unlike what is often done in the West, Eastern theology does not juxtapose divine grace (and initiative) with human freedom (and responsibility).[48]

The fourteenth-century theologian Gregory of Palamas helped conclusively establish the main theological ramifications of the doctrine. The key aspects of his teaching are (1) the creation of the human being "in the image and after the likeness of God," (2) the incarnation of the Logos of God, and (3) the strength of the human being's communion with God in the Holy Spirit.[49] Palamas also helped clarify the most obvious problem of the teaching on *theosis*, namely, the compatibility of two seemingly opposite ideas: the absolute incommunicability of the divine being and a real partaking of humanity in God. The distinction between God's essence and God's "energies" makes it possible to say that deification means participating in divine energies but not in the divine essence as such. Pantheism is thus avoided. God still remains God, and humans remain human, though participating in the divine.[50]

---

43. Lossky, *Mystical Theology of the Eastern Church,* p. 67.

44. Norris, "Deification," p. 415.

45. See the somewhat exaggerated claim in Stavropoulous, *Partakers of Divine Nature,* pp. 17-18.

46. Other texts referred to by Orthodox theologians include Exod. 34:30; 7:1; Matt. 17:4; John 3:8; 14:21-23; 15:4-8; 17:21-23; 2 Cor. 8:9; Heb. 4:15; 1 John 3:2; 4:12; see further, Ware, *The Orthodox Church,* pp. 236-37.

47. See chap. 15 in *Creation and Humanity.*

48. See Tsirpanlis, *Introduction to Eastern Patristic Thought,* pp. 46, 52; Meyendorff, *Byzantine Theology,* p. 139.

49. See further, Mantzaridis, *The Deification of Man,* pp. 15-39.

50. Kamppuri, "Theosis in der Theologie des Gregorios Palamas," pp. 49-60.

Behind the Eastern Christian *theosis* soteriology is a trinitarian pneumatology.[51] Participation in the triune God is made possible by the divine Spirit.[52] While Christ's role as Savior is properly highlighted, the Spirit's constitutive role in salvation is robustly presented.[53] Irenaeus's formulation is classic: in the last days, the Son "was made a man among men . . . in order that man, having embraced the Spirit of God, might pass into the glory of the Father."[54] Whereas in later theology, especially in the Christian West, soteriology came to be linked predominantly with Christology, Eastern theology keeps in place a healthy balance between christological and pneumatological understandings of salvation.[55] Eastern theology even speaks about Christians as "christs," anointed ones.[56]

It is not that pneumatology is missing in the West, however; indeed, the *ordo salutis* usually comes under the doctrine of the Spirit. What is different is that in the West the Spirit's role is secondary, subservient to that of Christ. In particular, justification is almost exclusively christologically loaded (whereas in sanctification the Spirit's role is more pronounced). A related issue has to do with the context of salvation: whereas Latin traditions have been dominated by legal, juridical, and forensic categories, Eastern theology understands the need for salvation in terms of deliverance from mortality and corruption. The idea of divine-human cooperation in salvation is not only accepted but is also enthusiastically championed, although it is not understood as nullifying the role of grace. The Eastern tradition never separates grace and human freedom. Therefore, the charge of Pelagianism does not apply here. It is not a question of merit but of cooperation, a synergy. Grace is a presence of God within us that demands constant effort on our part.[57] In keeping with the apophatic theological approach, a deep mystical coloring is a frequent feature in description of the union.[58] Often

51. A wonderful example is Cyril, *Catechetical Lectures* 4.16-17; for the pneumatological concept of grace, see also, 16.11-12. For a rich discussion of the Spirit's role in Eastern soteriology, see Congar, *I Believe in the Holy Spirit,* especially 1:73-77 and 3:29-36.

52. Meyendorff, *Byzantine Theology,* p. 13. See, e.g., Athanasius, *Letters to Serapion on the Holy Spirit* 1.15-33, esp. 1.22-24, pp. 221-24.

53. See Gregory of Nyssa, *On the Baptism of Christ; NPNF²* 5:518-20; Gregory of Nazianzus, *On the Holy Spirit* 28; *NPNF²* 7:327.

54. Irenaeus, *Against Heresies* 4.20.5; see also, 5.1.1.

55. Fairbairn, "Salvation as *Theosis*," pp. 42-43. Consider these: Irenaeus, *Against Heresies* 5.1.1; *ANF* 1:527; Pseudo-Macarius, *The Great Letter,* in Pseudo-Macarius, "*The Fifty Spiritual Homilies*" and "*The Great Letter,*" pp. 269-70; see also, pp. 274-75.

56. Lossky, *Mystical Theology of the Eastern Church,* p. 174.

57. See, e.g., Lossky, *Mystical Theology of the Eastern Church,* pp. 196-99.

58. See, e.g., Maximus the Confessor, "Four Hundred Chapters on Love," 87, 88, 90, p. 45; Palamas, *The Triads of Gregory Palamas,* p. 33.

the metaphor of (divine) light is used.[59] Similar to the Roman Catholic tradition, Eastern Fathers also believe that there are "grades" or levels of deification and rewards.[60]

In light of the historical developments both in the East and in the West, the radical changes brought about in the mainline Reformation interpretations can now be discerned.

The "Newness" and Diversity of Protestant Reformation Formulations

Although the Protestant Reformation failed to provide a coherent, single understanding of justification,[61] it is fair to say that mainline Protestantism from the 1530s until the heyday of Protestant orthodoxy (mid–eighteenth century) embraced the following tenets, which obviously represent new developments from tradition (and were sharpened because of the Roman Catholic Tridentine condemnations): justification as forensic declaration rather than a process of change in which the status but not the (inner) nature of the sinner is changed; consequently, a categorical distinction between justification as an initial "once-and-for-all" change of state and progressive growth in renewal, named most often sanctification; the imputation of Christ's alien righteousness to the human person;[62] and the vehement rejection of the idea of habitual grace.[63]

That said, the overall picture of a Reformation theology of justification is far more complex and complicated. Most importantly, Martin Luther himself did not by and large endorse what is presented above as the standard view; for him Christ's presence and union are linked not only, or even primarily, with declaration, but also with continuous change of life.[64] It is also clear now that although Philip Melanchthon helped consolidate the standard view, his

59. Symeon the New Theologian, *The Discourses* 15.3, pp. 195-96; Palamas, *The Triads of Gregory Palamas*; Meyendorff, *Byzantine Theology*, pp. 57-60.

60. E.g., Gregory of Sinai, *Texts on Commandments and Dogmas* 56, p. 47.

61. See Braaten, *Justification*, pp. 10-15. There are a number of Protestant ("at least a dozen") and Lutheran doctrines of justification, claims Pannenberg, *Hintergründe des Streites um die Rechtfertigungslehre*, p. 3. A major monograph showing the details of the diversity of interpretations is Vainio, *Justification and Participation*.

62. The doctrine of "imputation" in its widest sense in Protestant orthodoxy includes not only the imputation of Christ's righteousness to us but also the nonimputation of our sin and imputation of our faith *(imputatio fidei)*. See Rolf, *Zum Herzen sprechen*, p. 27.

63. McGrath, *Iustitia Dei*, 1:182-84. See also, Horton, "Traditional Reformed View," pp. 85-91.

64. See further, Vainio, *Justification and Participation*, pp. 42-53.

own theology underwent serious changes throughout his career.[65] No wonder, then, among Reformation specialists, that widely differing assessments have been offered on the primary view and how Luther's (effective) interpretation may be related to later Lutheranism.[66] It is also clear that Calvin's Reformed interpretation, while much closer to the Reformation mainstream than that of Luther, also marks a deviation from it (let alone the interpretation of Zwingli, whose humanist leanings connect him more strongly with the Catholic Erasmus).[67] Furthermore, the English Reformation and Anglican divines developed a doctrine of justification with a focus on renewal, thus emphasizing "making righteous" rather than a forensic interpretation.[68]

Calvin is often depicted as one who took Luther's view of justification and, like Melanchthon, helped make it predominantly forensic and external.[69] A look at the *Institutes,* however, yields another picture: the concept of union with Christ is central to Calvin's soteriology, and under that he includes both sanctification (regeneration) and justification. Curiously, in his order of discussion, sanctification comes first, and only thereafter comes justification. The classic opening passage of the third book of the *Institutes,* a preamble to *ordo salutis,* states "that so long as we are without Christ and separated from him, nothing which he suffered and did for the salvation of the human race is of the least benefit to us. To communicate to us the blessings which he received from the Father, he must become ours and dwell in us."[70] Thereby he links together tightly justification and sanctification in order to refute the charge of "cheap grace" and complaints about a lack of emphasis on good works as the fruit of salvation.[71] Whereas the Reformed experts are likely to continue heated debates about many details concerning Calvin's emphasis on union — such as whether it is "mystical" union[72] or can be linked with *theosis*[73] — for the sake

65. Melanchthon moved from Luther's type of making righteous (*Loci,* 1521), to mere imputation (*Romans,* 1531), to "both imputation and donation of the Spirit," with the caveat that (different from Catholics and perhaps Luther) the "qualitative change caused by the Spirit . . . is not righteousness *coram Deo.*" Vainio, *Justification and Participation,* pp. 63-93 (p. 91).

66. For a detailed review of approaches taken in the history of research, see Vainio, *Justification and Participation,* pp. 6-14.

67. See further, McGrath, *Iustitia Dei,* 2:32-39.

68. For a detailed discussion, see chap. 8 in McGrath, *Iustitia Dei,* vol. 2.

69. Partee, *Theology of John Calvin.*

70. Calvin, *Institutes* 3.1.1; so 3.11.9-10. For the centrality of union in Calvin's theology at large, see Purves and Achtemeier, *Union in Christ.*

71. See the important statements in Calvin, *Institutes* 3.16.1.

72. See, e.g., Tamburello, *Union with Christ.*

73. See, e.g., Billings, "United to God through Christ."

of this constructive proposal, it suffices to acknowledge its ecumenical significance. Similar to Luther's, it points toward a convergence with the Catholic and Orthodox traditions, as well as Holiness-Methodist views.[74]

The most significant deviation from the Reformation forensic orientation came from the Radical Reformers.[75] The legitimate concern among the Anabaptists was the lack of emphasis on good works and neighborly love. Like Saint James of the NT, Balthasar Hubmaier declared: "Mere faith alone is not sufficient for salvation . . . for a true faith can never exist without deeds of love."[76] Similar appeals can be found among these early Reformation dissenters.[77] Later English Puritans echoed strongly similar kinds of concerns with their emphasis on renewed life.[78]

In sum: the Protestant camp stood divided by the time the harsh Roman Catholic rebuttal came in the middle of the sixteenth century, and it has continued this divergence since.

The Catholic Response in Theological Perspective

Concerning the response of the Council of Trent to the Reformation in 1547,[79] one has to remember two important points. First, as a *reaction*, it hardly attempted — let alone achieved — any kind of comprehensive formulation of the doctrine.[80] Second, it still is the binding formulation of the Catholic tradition concerning key aspects of the doctrine of justification.[81] Furthermore, we need to keep in mind that justification by faith, like any other doctrine, is integrally linked with other theological convictions. Here we can only highlight

---

74. Cf. Calvin's harsh criticism of what he saw as Catholic errors in *Institutes* 3.4; 3.5.

75. Beachy, *Concept of Grace in the Radical Reformers*.

76. Cited in McClendon, *Doctrine*, p. 117. For a similar, current Anabaptist statement, see Mennonite Church Canada, "Confession of Faith"; see further, Beilby, Eddy, and Eenderlein, "Justification in Historical Perspective," pp. 39-41.

77. See statements from the Schleitheim statement in 1527, Jacob Kautz (the former Lutheran preacher), and Menno Simons of Holland in McClendon, *Doctrine*, pp. 117-18; see also, Friedman, *The Theology of Anabaptism*, p. 91.

78. See McGrath, *Iustitia Dei*, 2:111-21.

79. For the difficulty of the process, see Pelikan, *CT* 4:281-83 particularly.

80. A particularly important unresolved question at the time was the issue of freedom of the will not only in relation to Protestants but also among Catholic schools; no major contribution was offered by Trent in this regard. See further, O'Collins and Rafferty, "Roman Catholic View," pp. 265-66.

81. Embarrassing is the disparaging comment by Barth, *CD* IV/1, p. 626.

the differing anthropologies: generally speaking, the postmedieval Catholic assessment of the Fall and sin was far less pessimistic than that of Luther and other Reformers.[82]

In keeping with the early established link between sacraments and justification, Trent's discussion of the doctrine follows that of baptism[83] and makes baptism necessary for justification (#7).[84] That is of course not controversial for magisterial Protestants. Where the Lutheran position was confronted had to do with several contested convictions. Although it takes God's gracious preparation of the will for reception of justification (#6), it cannot happen without human consent (##4, 9). Although faith is necessary for justification, without love it does not suffice (##11, 12); on the basis of Hebrews 11:6 ("without faith it is impossible to please [God]"), the Protestant emphasis on justification as a free gift is rejected (#8). Most controversial to Protestants is the formulation on merit. Although, following Augustine, merit means God's crowning of his own work, Trent teaches that on the basis of inherent righteousness Christians may merit eternal life (#16). What is probably a concession to Luther is the statement on justification as "alien," although Trent does not deny its being inherent righteousness as well. It is "alien" in the sense of coming from outside human efforts and resources (#16). Finally, Trent rejects the Protestant claim of assurance of salvation as well as perseverance (##9 and 16, respectively).[85]

Whereas Trent's response, as polemical as it is, is a useful reminder for Protestants to not lose sight of the twofold nature of justification — pronouncing and making righteous — it also speaks past the dearest concerns of the Reformers. Trent seems to totally miss the fact that notwithstanding different terminology and orientation, not only for Catholics but also for Luther (and of course Calvin), "the incorporation into Christ is decisive for their justification." The acknowledgment of this foundational common conviction would have significantly softened and made more constructive the response. On the other hand, the Reformers should have embraced the definite anti-Pelagian teaching of the inability of human persons to restore fellowship with God. Similarly, Protestants missed the best intentions of the complex teaching of the

82. For details, see *Creation and Humanity*, chap. 15.

83. Already the 1520 papal bull *Exsurge Domine* by Pope Leo connected justification to baptism. For comments, see O'Collins and Rafferty, "Roman Catholic View," pp. 278-79.

84. "Decree on Justification: Sixth Session" (January 13, 1547), in Schaff, *The Creeds of Christendom*, 2:89-118. Numbers in parentheses refer to this document.

85. A succinct, dense discussion is in O'Collins and Rafferty, "Roman Catholic View," pp. 280-81; see also, Kärkkäinen, *One with God*, pp. 100-102.

council on the role of grace in preparation for and in the process of justification (as they took it "as statements about a creaturely reality of grace distinct from Jesus Christ and the work of the Spirit"). Finally, the council's highlighting of the role of the freedom of will could have been interpreted as conditioned by grace rather than as an affirmation of human independence.[86] This is not to whitewash the differences between Catholic and Protestant traditions — either then or even now after the signing of the joint declaration — but rather to relativize and put them in perspective.[87] This is what has happened in current ecumenical advancements, to which we turn next.

Resources for Reconceptualization and Revision of the Doctrine of Justification

The "New Perspective" in Biblical Theology

The terms "justice," "justification," "righteous," and "righteousness"[88] have a long history beginning in the OT. One of the most heated debates in biblical scholarship has centered on the precise meaning of the term "righteousness/justification" *(dikaiosynē)*.[89] Ancient times did not hold to the currently standard separation between executive, legislative, and judicial tasks. Israel was a monarchy in which Yahweh, as the highest monarch, and kings, as his appointees, handled all three functions. Hence, tasks such as "acquitting" and "condemning" are related to both divine and earthly rulers in Israel (Job 10:2, 14). The covenant called for right relationships, to which of course belonged acts of righteousness, that is, works in keeping with Yahweh's righteous rule and character. (Hence, I use at times the Old English term "rightwising"[90] — or, as E. P. Sanders prefers it, "righteousing"[91] — to speak of justification in its more inclusive sense, namely, pronouncing and making righteous.) Paul and other early Christians adopted this Hebrew, covenant-based, divinely authorized

---

86. Pannenberg, *ST* 3:220-22 (p. 221).

87. I agree wholeheartedly with Pannenberg (*ST* 3:234) that both parties should robustly acknowledge the limitations of the Reformation approaches.

88. For a most careful linguistic-theological analysis, see McGrath, *Iustitia Dei*, 1:4-16.

89. For a careful recent survey, see Reumann, "Justification and Justice in the New Testament."

90. Similarly, Beker, *The Triumph of God*, p. 129; Helyer, *Witness of Jesus, Paul, and John*, p. 259; Macchia, *Justified in the Spirit*, p. 3.

91. Sanders, *Paul, the Law, and the Jewish People*, p. 6.

terminology of law/justice/righteousness. The church also *"adapted* it to express the radical, eschatological inbreaking of the new, the end of the ages, that disciples were coming to know in the risen Christ." To that template belonged essentially setting relations right, establishing God's covenant faithfulness and righteousness, as well as newness of life in Christ.[92] As the late Baptist systematician James McClendon put it aptly: to the term "'righteousness of God,' belong 'justify,' 'justification [by faith],' and 'justified.'" Separating any one of them leads to distortions and reductionism, which can be seen not only in later history (of Protestant-Catholic debates) but also already in the NT. The Epistle of James (2:14-26) seeks to defeat the corruption in which "'justification by faith' separates *dikaiosynē* from . . . the right human relations James saw were essential." Justification, faith, and right relations for him could not be separated. Similarly, Paul (Rom. 6) combated another distortion, the antinomian belief that "anything goes" now that we have been saved and grace abounds, which ignored the newness of life in Christ, including its social aspects.[93]

This preliminary attempt to reorient the discussion of the doctrine of justification leans strongly toward what in NT studies has come to be known as the "new perspective" (on Paul), heralded by the scriptural scholar E. P. Sanders and his initial publication in 1977 of *Paul and Palestinian Judaism,*[94] and soon thereafter distinctively developed by J. D. G. Dunn[95] and N. T. Wright,[96] among others. In a programmatic essay, Dunn lamented "the loss or neglect of . . . crucial Biblical insights related to the . . . theme of divine justice. . . . Luther's discovery of 'justification by faith' and the theological impetus it gave especially to Lutheran theology has involved a significant misunderstanding of Paul, not least in relation to 'justification by faith' itself." Dunn is not arguing that Protestant doctrine is wrong, but that it needs to be supplemented, corrected, and reoriented in light of Paul's own theology.[97] Different from tradition, the new perspective undermines the importance of Luther's conversion experience and alleged struggle of conscience as the framework for the

92. For a useful, constructive critique of primarily judicial and "external" understandings of the covenant instead of relationality and personalism, see Doctrine Commission of the Church of England, *The Mystery of Salvation,* p. 106. More extensively, see McIlroy, "Towards a Relational and Trinitarian Theology of Atonement," p. 19.

93. This whole paragraph is based on McClendon, *Doctrine,* pp. 111-12.

94. With the subtitle *A Comparison of Patterns of Religion.*

95. See Dunn, *New Perspective on Paul,* rev. ed.

96. A massive recent work is N. T. Wright, *Paul and the Faithfulness of God.*

97. Dunn, "The Justice of God," p. 2; similarly also, N. T. Wright, *What Saint Paul Really Said,* p. 113.

doctrine.[98] The main claims of the new perspective on Paul are well known and can be briefly summarized for the sake of this discussion.[99]

Dunn suggests that among the many justifiable translations of *dikaiosynē*, such as "justification," "righteousness," and "justice," the last one should be preferred. This choice corrects the shift of Protestantism from the "justice of God" to "justification by faith."[100] Recently, N. T. Wright has commented that to understand correctly the term "righteousness of God," its relationship to the covenant has to be established.[101] The major difference, though, is that in the Old Testament the covenant community was defined by external boundary markers, whereas in the New Testament it is governed by faith in Christ.[102]

The nature of Second Temple Judaism as a legalistic and merciless religion has been radically corrected. Jewish scholars have reminded us for years that such a view of Palestinian Judaism in Jesus' time is not the Judaism they knew.[103] It has been the legacy of Sanders and others to paint another picture of the Judaism of that time as a religion of grace, with human obedience always understood as a response to that grace.[104] The covenant was given by divine initiative, and the law provided the framework for life within the covenant, the means of living within the covenant, not a means of acceptance into the covenant in the first place.[105] According to Sanders's key term "covenantal nomism," God's dealings with his people are based on covenant, which, on the one hand, is based on grace and provides atonement,[106] and on the other hand, requires obedience. Obedience, hence, is not about works righteousness.[107] As Dunn aptly notes, the "Judaism of what Sanders christened as 'covenantal nomism' can now be seen to preach good Protestant doctrine: that grace is always prior; that human effort is ever the

98. This was already noted by the Lutheran Krister Stendahl, "Apostle Paul and the Introspective Conscience of the West," pp. 78-96.

99. A highly useful introduction and balanced appraisal is Westerholm, *Perspectives Old and New on Paul;* shorter, succinct introductions particularly geared for justification debates are Beilby, Eddy, and Eenderlein, "Justification in Contemporary Debate," pp. 53-82; Aune, "Recent Readings of Paul Relating to Justification by Faith," pp. 188-245.

100. Dunn, "The Justice of God," p. 21.

101. N. T. Wright, *Climax of the Covenant.*

102. N. T. Wright, *Climax of the Covenant,* pp. 148-51, 255.

103. For examples, see Sanders, *Paul and Palestinian Judaism,* pp. 4-8.

104. For a lucid exposition, see Dunn, "New Perspective View," pp. 177-83.

105. For a differing interpretation of Wright, see *What Saint Paul Really Said,* p. 119.

106. Sanders, *Paul and Palestinian Judaism,* p. 422.

107. Sanders, *Paul and Palestinian Judaism,* pp. 75, 420. 543; so also, N. T. Wright, *What Saint Paul Really Said,* p. 19.

response to divine initiative; that good works are the fruit and not the root of salvation."[108] The reason, then, for Paul's rejection of his own religion was not legalism but rather its stern rejection of Christ as the crucified Messiah of Israel and the pagans.[109] Paul's concern was also that the "boundary markers" of Judaism, such as circumcision and Sabbath, were taken as a means of keeping the nations outside the salvation that belongs to the people of God alone.[110] (Wright's distinctive view among the new perspective advocates is that for Paul justification is merely a forensic declaration rather than a transformation,[111] a claim I find unconvincing.)

The new paradigm laments the almost exclusively individualistic orientation of the traditional doctrine and reminds us that for Paul, particularly in Galatians and Romans, the focus is relational — relationship between the Jews as the elected people and the Gentiles, the outsiders.[112] Paul based his doctrine of justification in the OT covenant theology on the concept of *relation;* people are righteous when they meet the claims that others have on them by virtue of their relationships.[113]

A particularly complex issue has to do with the role of works in final justification, eschatological judgment. The debate has to reckon with Paul's statement that "the doers of the law . . . will be justified" (Rom. 2:13; also 2:26-29). Unless one is willing to consider that Paul is inconsistent on his teaching between faith and works or, as does Protestant tradition, to juxtapose the alleged Pauline gospel of "grace" with Jewish "works righteousness,"[114] one must try one of several tactics. One of them claims that in the main Paul's approach is in keeping with covenantal nomism, in which the entrance to covenant/salvation is by grace but staying within is conditioned on obedience. In other words, the expectation is "that one's outward behavior . . . will correspond to,

---

108. Dunn, "The Justice of God," p. 8.

109. Sanders, *Paul and Palestinian Judaism,* pp. 482-84; see also, p. 552.

110. Dunn's distinctive contribution is to consider the "works of law" solely (or at least primarily) as boundary markers between Israel and the nations, including circumcision. See, e.g., his "New Perspective View," pp. 183-89. For N. T. Wright's somewhat differently formulated idea of the boundary markers, see his *Climax of the Covenant,* p. 240.

111. N. T. Wright, *Justification,* pp. 90-91 particularly. See also, his "New Perspectives on Paul," p. 260.

112. This is again supported by Stendahl, *Paul among Jews and Gentiles,* pp. 1-2.

113. See further, Dunn, "The Justice of God," p. 16.

114. Yet another traditional tactic is to take Paul's statement in Rom. 2:13 as a purely theoretical option: in principle one could be saved by fulfilling the law, but that is absolutely impossible for anyone; for details, see Beilby, Eddy, and Eenderlein, "Justification in Contemporary Debate," p. 70; this paragraph is indebted to pp. 68-73.

and be a visible manifestation of, inward reality." The main difference from Judaism has to do with Paul's replacement of the covenant identity markers with faith in Christ.[115] Wright's initial solution had to do with an eschatological reference: "Present justification declares, on the basis of faith, what future justification will affirm publicly . . . *on the basis* of the entire life."[116] Sensitive to the obvious critique of leaning toward works righteousness, he recently modified his position by speaking of this eschatological "law court verdict" as something "in accordance with the life that the believer has then lived."[117] While I acknowledge the critique of traditionalists to the effect that the works be given merely an evidentiary role,[118] I also wish to endorse the biblical scholar Michael Bird's view (generally in keeping with that of Wright) that "Paul's anthropological pessimism about the human inability to keep the law is matched only by his pneumatological optimism that Spirit-empowered persons will be able to fulfill the requirements of the law when they walk by the Spirit (Rom. 8:4; Gal. 5:25)."[119] This in no way takes away the foundation of salvation in Christ's work,[120] nor does it undermine justification by *faith*, but rather it is consistent with the point emphasized in the beginning of this section: it avoids separating the interrelated meanings of justification/righteousness. It also affirms the teaching of James 2:14-26. Obviously Paul (Romans, Galatians) and James use terms in different senses: whereas for the former, "faith" denotes trusting dependence on Christ for salvation, for the latter it is about (intellectual) affirmation of certain beliefs. Similarly, "works" for Paul mean pressure for noncovenant persons (Gentiles) to adopt Jewish identity markers in order to be included, whereas for James it means authentic fruit of salvation in terms of good deeds and right behavior.[121]

Not surprisingly, responses to the new perspective have been varied: from embrace,[122] to a careful, scholarly critique,[123] to outright negative re-

---

115. Yinger, *Paul, Judaism, and Judgment,* pp. 15-16, 290, cited in Beilby, Eddy, and Eenderlein, "Justification in Contemporary Debate," p. 69.

116. N. T. Wright, *What Saint Paul Really Said,* p. 129.

117. N. T. Wright, *Justification,* p. 251.

118. Recently most vocally argued in criticism of Wright by Piper, *The Future of Justification,* p. 110 and passim.

119. Bird, *Saving Righteousness of God,* p. 173, cited in Beilby, Eddy, and Eenderlein, "Justification in Contemporary Debate," p. 71.

120. Rightly underscored by Bird, *Saving Righteousness of God,* p. 173.

121. See the useful discussion in Bird, "Progressive Reformed View," pp. 152-56.

122. Garlington, *In Defense of the New Perspectives on Paul.*

123. Particularly important is Carson, O'Brien, and Seifrid, eds., *Justification and Variegated Nomism,* vol. 1, *The Complexities of Second Temple Judaism.*

jection.[124] Then there are some who suggest that with all the contributions of the new perspective, there is need to move beyond both the "old" and "new" perspectives.[125] This project endorses the main implications of the new perspective for the doctrine of justification in a modified way as indicated in the critical review of its central claims.

Law and Gospel: A Revision of the Reformation Understanding

Whereas in ancient cultures, including Israel, a close relationship existed between law (including order of the society and government) and religion, as both the political and judicial order (as discussed above) were believed to be divinely authorized,[126] what happened in Israel after the exile can be described as "the legal tradition . . . frozen by traditionalist hardening." As a result, the law "became in the form of the torah a special feature in the national tradition of the people of Israel instead of representing a universal expression of the righteous will of the one God for all people." An endless number of more or less fixed rules and regulations emerged to guard and protect the people of God. The radically new thing in Jesus' understanding of the law was that now law "found fulfillment in terms of the eschatological future of God and its inbreaking with this message." Rather than arguing "from the authority of the legal tradition, . . . he based his statement on the claim of God's future on us and on the inbreaking of this future in his own coming." This helped free the OT law from casuistry and make it universal in content, based on love (an idea deeply rooted in OT theology itself).[127]

The question to Christians now is what, if anything, is the role of the law? Had Christ come to bring the law to an end (Rom. 10:4) or to fulfill it (Matt. 5:17)? Pannenberg boldly argues that (even with all the advancements of the new perspective, whose early results, particularly those of Sanders, he widely utilizes) this question still awaits systematic clarification after two millennia

124. Piper, *The Future of Justification;* a representative listing can be found in "Challenging the New Perspective."

125. Watson, *Paul, Judaism, and the Gentiles;* note the replacement of the original 1986 edition's subtitle, *A Sociological Approach,* in this edition; Byrne, "Interpreting Romans Theologically," pp. 227-42. A materially similar kind of call can be found in Campbell, *The Deliverance of God.*

126. In Asiatic religions, law is also cosmically ordered and justified; hence, the key Hindu concept of *rita.*

127. Pannenberg, *ST* 3:58-60 (p. 59).

of theological reflection. I find his schematization of the main developments highly illuminative, as he discerns three main phases.

First, for Paul, who understood the law in terms of salvation history, law is contrasted not with gospel[128] but rather with faith (Rom. 3:21-31; 4:13-25) or grace (6:14-15) or the Spirit (7:6). Law and faith represent "two realities in salvation history that belong to two different epochs." The coming of Christ brought the era of law to an end (Gal. 3:24-25; Rom. 10:4).[129] The term *te-los* used in Romans 10:4 means "bring to fulfillment," and thus implies that Christ is the goal toward which the law — which in itself is good, having been given by God (7:12) — was given. The reason law found its fulfillment in Christ is that "in his vicarious death for sin (3:25), God demonstrated his covenant righteousness, and we can respond only by faith, not by works of the law (3:22)."[130] Paul supports this interpretation of law and its relation to faith by arguing that already Abraham was justified by faith (3:31; 4:3). Abraham's circumcision (stipulated by law) came later (4:10-25).[131] So, is there any positive role left for law in a Christian's life? Yes, in the sense explained in the previous section, namely, that Christians, "born again" and empowered by the Spirit, who now "are dead to self-seeking in Christ will by the Spirit keep the righteous demands of the law (Rom. 8:4). . . . Love is the fulfilling of the law (Rom. 13:10)."[132]

The second phase of the law-gospel negotiation is the patristic-medieval interpretation of the gospel as "new law" *(lex nova)*. In the analogy of Jesus as a new Moses, the "new law" was given by him,[133] particularly in the Sermon on the Mount and in the commandment of love (John 13:34). A restoration of the law of nature of ancient philosophy (often linked with Paul's teaching in Rom. 2:14-15), it was complemented by Augustine with the principle of love as the divine power that enables us to fulfill the law (on the basis of Rom. 5:5).[134] Linked with love, this view materially (although not conceptually) agrees with Jesus and Paul's emphasis on love as the fulfillment of the righteous will of God as expressed in the law, including the Ten Commandments. Augustine rightly saw that "love as a motivating force differs in nature from a command and its

---

128. Rightly noted already by Harnack, *Constitution and Law of the Church*, pp. 301-2.

129. Pannenberg, *ST* 3:61. An important discussion is Ebeling, "Reflexions on the Doctrine of the Law," pp. 247-81.

130. Pannenberg, *ST* 3:62-63.

131. See Pannenberg, *ST* 3:63.

132. Pannenberg, *ST* 3:68.

133. *The Epistle of Barnabas,* chap. 2, speaks of "the new law of our Lord Jesus Christ."

134. For details and references, see Pannenberg, *ST* 3:70-72.

observance. It is a gift of grace that enables us for the first time to respond in our own conduct to God's kindness as Creator and to his redeeming love, to participate in them."[135]

The third way of negotiating law and gospel, well known to all Protestants and named by Luther the "the supreme art in Christianity,"[136] is the radical juxtaposing of the two. The newness of and difference of this interpretation, which "viewed the law as an expression of God's demand in antithesis to the gospel as promise and pronouncement of the forgiveness of sins,"[137] can now be seen in light of the historical developments. Rather than considering the law as "old" (in the sense of the bygone era), Luther "saw it structurally as law in the absolute," and he found a parallel in the "Christian" use of law in the church with the legalism Paul opposed in the NT — the only difference being that the demand of circumcision and food laws were represented by pilgrimages, penance, and other such requirements.[138] Although Luther's view also takes for granted the continuity of the law with natural law (as expressed particularly in the Decalogue), the difference from the patristic *lex nova* scheme was that in Luther natural law is not linked with the new spiritual law but rather with the law that accuses sinners. In keeping with this is Luther's "structurally defined contrast of law and gospel,"[139] as famously defined in the early work *Lectures on Galatians* (1519): "The Law proclaims what must be done and left undone; or better, it proclaims what deeds have already been committed and omitted, and also what possible things are done and left undone (hence the only thing it provides is the knowledge of sin); the Gospel, however, proclaims that sins have been remitted and that all things have been fulfilled and done. For the Law says: 'Pay what you owe'; but the Gospel says: 'Your sins are forgiven you.'"[140] This interpretation makes sense in the deeply penitential culture of the time and personal inclinations of Luther himself; in examining one's conscience in preparation for the sacrament of penance, Luther found here the law's "theological use."[141] As argued above, Paul's criticism of the law lies not so much in its inability to save those who follow it but in the Jewish insistence that salvation is brought about by virtue

135. Pannenberg, *ST* 3:76-78 (p. 78).
136. WA 36:9.28-30.
137. Pannenberg, *ST* 3:61.
138. Pannenberg, *ST* 3:79.
139. Pannenberg, *ST* 3:80.
140. WA 2:466.3-7 (on Gal. 1:11-12); *LW* 27:183-84.
141. WA 40^1:490-91 (on Gal. 3:19); *LW* 26:309-10 particularly. For comments, see Pannenberg, *ST* 3:81.

of membership in the elected covenant people. Paul insisted, as did Jesus, that it is only by a response of faith rather than the legal righteousness of faith that salvation comes.[142] For Paul, any kind of nationalistic pride of Judaism was anathema; here he was following in the footsteps of earlier Jewish preachers such as Amos (Amos 9:7), John the Baptist (Matt. 3:9), and, of course, Jesus himself (Matt. 8:10-12). For Paul, justification means that God accepts persons without reference to being born into a particular race (Rom. 9:6-8). So the way of justification, the right relationship with God, is open to all people — Gentiles included.[143]

What are we to think of Luther's solution? Its advantage is that it reminds us of the inability of the human person, even the best one, to save oneself. Its problem, however, is twofold: first, it differs remarkably from the view of law and gospel in Paul as explained above. Second, although its "focus on the pronouncing of forgiveness of sins [once the law has done its negative judgment] is understandable in terms of penitential teaching, it does not do justice to the breadth of the biblical concept of the gospel." Particularly missing in Luther's theology of forgiveness is the eschatological orientation of Jesus' proclamation, which "has its basis in the proximity of the divine rule . . . and its acceptance by those who believe his message."[144] In Jesus' announcement, as theologically argued by Paul, participation in this new life, the righteous rule of God, was opened to all regardless of race, religion, and status as long as the message was received (see especially Mark 2:5 and Luke 7:48). In this light, "it is impossible to set the saying about forgiveness in antithesis to God's righteous demand. Against the eschatological background of the message of Jesus the claim of God's lordship on us and the pronouncing of forgiveness of sin belong very closely together, and they do so in this order." The Lutheran Pannenberg boldly concludes: "The isolated stress on forgiveness in opposition to the law as an expression of God's righteous will truncates the message of Jesus and also the Pauline gospel."[145] As a result, Pannenberg argues (and I fully agree) that on the basis of scriptural witness, the Lutheran conception of law and gospel must be revised: "according to Paul's teaching about the gospel the turn from law to grace has taken place once and for all, so that space opens up for the existence and history of the church. . . . This eschatological turn from law to gospel is not something that

142. Sanders, *Paul, the Law, and the Jewish People,* pp. 68-69; *Paul and Palestinian Judaism,* pp. 442-47; Pannenberg, *ST* 3:64.

143. See further, Dunn, "The Justice of God," pp. 14-15.

144. Pannenberg, *ST* 3:82.

145. Pannenberg, *ST* 3:82-83 (p. 82).

takes place again and again in the church in the pronouncing of forgiveness. It has taken place definitely in Jesus Christ" and aims at salvation of all and reconciliation of all things in Christ.[146]

It is not that for the Protestant Reformation all notions of law are merely negative, aiding penitence. Luther saw the use of law also as a positive indication of the righteous will of God. In the antinomian fight in the late 1530s, Luther more robustly acknowledged the role of law (as expression of God's will) as an aid in Christian growth. Particularly important for Luther is the "law of love."[147] On the Lutheran side, Melanchthon, and on the Reformed side, Calvin, made that use of law a theme.[148] However, it might be better to speak of exhortation or guidance rather than law. Naming it "law" may easily lead us to miss the important point that the apostolic *paraclesis* in Pauline letters is not really law, "for it is meant only as exposition of being in Christ."[149] Barth saw this clearly in his stress on free obedience brought about by the Holy Spirit.[150] Only by linking the concept of "new law" *(lex nova)* tightly with the new life brought about by the Spirit and focusing it on the "law of love," are two common mistakes avoided. The first one is the inability of tradition to make a distinction between natural law and the "third" use of law (Luther), that is, *paraclesis* and exhortation. Although there is no need to undermine the importance of natural law per se, its identification with the "new law" obscures the Pauline teaching of the coming to an end (and finding its telos) in Christ. Second, even more importantly, the free, Spirit-driven obedience of the Christian is replaced by a casuistic, legalistic, forced "obedience."[151]

Now that we have clarified the historical and biblical ramifications of the topic of justification, the next crucial step toward a constructive proposal is the investigation of contemporary ecumenical developments.

---

146. Pannenberg, *ST* 3:87.

147. WA 2:580-81 (particularly comments on Matt. 7:12); *LW* 26:353-57. A major study is Raunio, *Summe des christlichen Lebens.*

148. Melanchthon, *Chief Theological Topics,* pp. 120-23; Calvin, *Institutes* 2.7.12 speaks of the "third" use of law. For comments, see Pannenberg, *ST* 3:88.

149. Pannenberg, *ST* 3:80; an important discussion is Schlink, "Gesetz und Paraklese," pp. 323-35.

150. For an important discussion, see Barth, *CD* III/4, pp. 4-31 particularly; for comments, see Pannenberg, *ST* 3:89-90.

151. At times, Luther saw this fairly clearly, as in WA 2:477-79 (on Gal. 2:5); *LW* 27:203-4; for details, see Pannenberg, *ST* 3:90-91.

Contemporary Ecumenical Breakthroughs

The establishment in the aftermath of Vatican II of the influential dialogue between the Vatican and the Lutheran World Federation (LWF) prepared the way for the focused conversation process that finally led to the groundbreaking 1999 *Joint Declaration on the Doctrine of Justification.*[152] Its purpose was "to show that on the basis of their dialogue the subscribing Lutheran churches and the Roman Catholic Church are now able to articulate a common understanding of our justification by God's grace through faith in Christ." Although its scope is limited in that it only focuses on the doctrine of justification and matters directly related to it (rather than on many other dividing issues) and, even when discussing them, does not seek to be comprehensive or to hide some remaining differences,[153] its ecumenical significance is unsurpassed. Following the currently widely used convergence methodology, it both states what the agreements are and makes room for each party to delineate (within this consensus) dearly held distinctive views and emphases.

The agreement lists under seven points the mutual understanding:

- "[A]ll persons depend completely on the saving grace of God for their salvation" (#19).
- "God forgives sin by grace and at the same time frees human beings from sin's enslaving power and imparts the gift of new life in Christ" (#22).
- "[S]inners are justified by faith in the saving action of God in Christ. By the action of the Holy Spirit in baptism, they are granted the gift of salvation, which lays the basis for the whole Christian life" (#25).
- "[I]n baptism the Holy Spirit unites one with Christ, justifies, and truly renews the person. But the justified must all through life constantly look to God's unconditional justifying grace" (#28).
- "[P]ersons are justified by faith in the gospel 'apart from works pre-

---

152. Lutheran World Federation and the Roman Catholic Church, *Joint Declaration on the Doctrine of Justification* (hereafter *JDDJ*). Several important previous documents were released in preparation, including the initial common report, "The Gospel and the Church" (known also as the "Malta Report"), 1972, http://www.prounione.urbe.it/dia-int/l-rc/doc/e_l-rc_malta.html (8/5/2014); followed by "Church and Justification" (1994) by the Lutheran–Roman Catholic Joint Commission; "Justification by Faith" (1983) of the Lutheran–Roman Catholic dialogue in the USA; and "The Condemnations of the Reformation Era — Do They Still Divide?" (1986) by the Ecumenical Working Group of Protestant and Catholic theologians in Germany. For bibliographic details, see *JDDJ* #3.

153. *JDDJ* #5.

scribed by the law' (*Rom* 3:28). Christ has fulfilled the law and by his death and resurrection has overcome it as a way to salvation. We also confess that God's commandments retain their validity for the justified" (#31).

- "[T]he faithful can rely on the mercy and promises of God" (#34).
- "[G]ood works — a Christian life lived in faith, hope and love — follow justification and are its fruits. When the justified live in Christ and act in the grace they receive, they bring forth, in biblical terms, good fruit" (#37).

Even though both Catholic[154] and Lutheran[155] emphases and qualifications are stated regarding each mutual statement, huge, unprecedented ecumenical steps have been taken to overcome the mutual condemnations of the Reformation times. A summary of the main mutual agreement goes something like this: not by works but solely on the basis of God's grace, in union with Christ, through faith sinners are forgiven and made righteous even when the fight with sin and pursuit of renewal are a daily task; renewed persons bring forth good works, and they can be confident that the just and faithful God will see to their final salvation.

Importantly, the World Methodist Council cosigned the joint agreement in 2006 and so expanded the Protestant participation.[156] The Reformed churches, while closely observing and following the process, have decided not to sign the agreement. Other responses to the joint document have been understandably diverse. Among Protestants,[157] both some traditionally minded German Lutheran theologians[158] and (Missouri Synod–related) American Lutherans,[159] as well as conservative American evangelicals,[160] strong opposition

154. On the Catholic side, the main challenges have to do with "(1) the meaning of *simul iustus et peccator;* (2) the question of merit; (3) the doctrine of justification as the sole criterion; (4) whether human beings are passive or whether they cooperate with grace; and (5) the authority of the consensus reached by the Lutheran World Federation." Wood, "Catholic Reception of the Joint Declaration," pp. 43-59 (p. 45).

155. On the Lutheran side, continuing challenges have to do with how to understand concupiscence and the role of human action in justification.

156. "World Methodist Council Statement."

157. I. Taylor, "Without Justification?" pp. 106-18.

158. A leading figure has been Eberhard Jüngel; see his highly polemical work, *Justification;* for other Protestant critiques, see Brandt, "Gemeinsame Erklärung," pp. 63-102.

159. Lutheran Church–Missouri Synod, "Joint Declaration on the Doctrine of Justification."

160. Blocher, "Lutheran-Catholic Declaration on Justification," pp. 197-217; Glomsrud

has arisen, similar to that of conservative Roman Catholics.[161] In contrast, most American Lutherans (affiliated with the Evangelical Lutheran Church in America), a number of leading international Lutheran theologians,[162] and the rest of the LWF communities have supported it. By and large, Orthodox churches have not commented on it.[163]

While Lutheran-Catholic talks on soteriology have received the most attention, the topic has been discussed widely in a number of other bilateral dialogues. Catholics have had official talks with the Reformed, Anglicans, and the Methodists. Cardinal Walter Kasper rightly summarizes that these dialogues have "produced statements on justification which show many similarities with the presentation of JDDJ."[164] Catholics and Reformed agreed not only on "justification by grace, through faith" but also on the importance of good works as the fruit of salvation (##77-79).[165] The Catholic-Anglican dialogue *Salvation and the Church* (1986),[166] having first reminded us of the multiplicity of metaphors for salvation in the NT (#13), helpfully listed the areas of contention, issues closely related to Protestant-Catholic relations as well, namely, the questions of free will, assurance of salvation, the role of good works in relation to faith, and the role of the church (##2-7). It was agreed that while based on faith, salvation is never divorced from good works and love (##9-11, 19). While the believer is "at once just and sinner" (#15), justification means both forgiveness of sins and being made righteous (#18). In other words, "[j]ustification and sanctification are two aspects of the same divine act (1 Cor 6:11)" (#15). Although even in the *JDDJ* there is not necessarily full agreement about the concept of sanctification, the strong agreement about justification as both forgiveness of sins and being made righteous is reflected in three other dialogues.[167]

---

and Horton, eds., *Justified.* Cf. the more positive, although somewhat reserved, response by the British evangelical Anthony N. S. Lane, *Justification by Faith in Catholic-Protestant Dialogue.*

161. Sungenis, "Lutheran/Catholic Joint Declaration on Justification."

162. In addition to his extended discussion in *ST* 2:211-36, see Pannenberg's contribution to a volume that he coedited with the Roman Catholic theologian Bernd Jochen Hilberath: "Die 'Gemeinsame Erklärung zur Rechtfertigungslehre aus evangelischer Sicht.'"

163. Turcescu, "Soteriological Issues in the 1999 Lutheran-Catholic Joint Declaration," p. 67.

164. Kasper, *Harvesting the Fruits,* #21, p. 40.

165. "Towards a Common Understanding of the Church," ##77-79.

166. "Second Anglican/Roman Catholic International Commission" (1986). Numbers in parentheses refer to this document.

167. For discussion and documentation, see Kasper, *Harvesting the Fruits,* #22, pp. 42-44.

Notwithstanding the centrality of the concept of justification as a controlling concept, current ecumenical developments also remind us not to limit soteriological talks to that one metaphor. Other metaphors stemming from the biblical witness and early Christian tradition are equally meaningful. Catholic and Protestant conversations with the Orthodox churches have enabled rediscovery of the concept of *theosis* (deification, divinization). The theological dialogues between various Orthodox and Lutheran churches have also contributed significantly to an emerging ecumenical convergence. Highly significant is the input of the long-standing conversations between the Lutheran Church of Finland and the Orthodox Church.[168] From the beginning of that dialogue in the 1970s, Professor Tuomo Mannermaa and his school at the University of Helsinki have undertaken a groundbreaking investigation into the ecumenical implications of Martin Luther's own theology of justification and found that there is affinity not only with the Roman Catholic interpretation but also, importantly, with the Orthodox notion of *theosis*. The details will be given below.

Another reminder of the importance of embracing a diversity of metaphors of and perspectives on soteriology is the groundbreaking seven-year conversation between Catholics and Pentecostals. The latest phase of the continuing long-term dialogue process started in 1972 — indeed, one of the oldest in the modern ecumenical movement — is known by the title "On Becoming a Christian: Insights from Scripture and the Patristic Writings; With Some Contemporary Reflections."[169] In keeping with other such dialogues, Catholics and Pentecostals agreed that "[c]onversion is related to a variety of biblical themes (including sin, forgiveness, repentance, salvation, justification, baptism, faith)" and that the "root notion of conversion in the Bible is change, that is, turning from sin, death and darkness to grace, new life, and light" (#29; also #39). With reference to Augustine, they spoke of human responsibility, although God's grace is the basis of conversion and salvation: "'He who created you without you does not justify you without you' (*Sermon* 169, 11.13)" (#45).

---

168. The standard reference work is Saarinen, *Faith and Holiness*. For the American scene, see Meyendorff and Tobias, eds., *Salvation in Christ*.

169. "On Becoming a Christian"; numbers in parentheses refer to this document.

Ecumenical Breakthrough in the Interpretation
of Martin Luther's Theology of Justification

Under the leadership of Professor Tuomo Mannermaa, a number of Luther
scholars at the University of Helsinki have not only helped radically revise the
canons of interpretation of the Reformer's own theology but also accomplished
unprecedented ecumenical achievements.[170] It was a great surprise that important commonalities were discerned between Luther's theology of justification and
the Orthodox concept of *theosis* — notwithstanding the largely negative (or dismissive) reception of deification among Protestants.[171] The breakthrough came at
the end of the 1970s, thanks to ecumenical contacts with the Orthodox tradition
(of Russia).[172] Soon it was also discovered that similarly important convergences
could be discerned between the soteriologies of Luther and of Catholics.[173]

The basic theses and claims of the new interpretation can be summarized
as follows:

1. Luther's understanding of salvation can be expressed not only in terms
   of the doctrine of justification, but also as *theosis*. Thus, while there are
   differences between the Eastern and Lutheran understandings of soteriology, over questions such as free will and understandings of the effects
   of the Fall, Luther's own theology should not be set in opposition to the
   ancient Eastern idea of deification.

2. For Luther, the main idea of justification is Christ present in faith *(in
   ipsa fide Christus adest)*. Justification for Luther means a "real-ontic"[174]
   participation in God through the indwelling of Christ in the heart of the
   believer through the Spirit.

3. In contrast to the theology of the Lutheran Confessions, Luther does

---

170. In English, see Braaten and Jenson, eds., *Union with Christ*; Mannermaa, *Christ Present in Faith*; for a succinct introduction, see Mannermaa, "Why Is Luther So Fascinating?"

171. See further, Kretschmar, "Die Rezeption der orthodoxen Vergöttlichungslehre," pp. 61-80.

172. See Kamppuri, *Dialogue between Neighbours*, p. 73 (from the 1977 common state-ment, "Salvation as Justification and Deification").

173. See Wendebourg, *Reformation und Oikonomia*.

174. This somewhat ambiguous and contested term "real-ontic" is used by the Manner-maa School to combat the neo-Protestant, neo-Kantian distinction between God's "essence" and "effects," according to which we have no means of knowing anything about God; we only can know the effects of God in our lives. Similarly, the Mannermaa School rejects the exis-tentially oriented notions of God's presence in the believer in favor of a "real" presence. The methodological basis is offered by Saarinen, *Gottes Wirken auf uns*.

not make a distinction between forensic and effective justification, but rather argues that justification includes both. In other words, in line with Catholic theology, justification means both declaring righteous and making righteous.

4. Therefore, justification means not only sanctification but also good works, since Christ present in faith makes the Christian a "christ" to the neighbor.[175]

Justification in Luther can be described with the help of several closely related concepts such as participation in God, the presence of Christ in the believer through the Holy Spirit, union with God, *perichoresis,* and *theosis.* Regardless of the term used, Luther saw justification as the union between Christ and the believer, as Christ through faith abides in the Christian through the Spirit. In fact, Luther says, Christ is "one with us"[176] and "Christ lives in us through faith."[177] For the Reformer, "[Christ] is the divine and inestimable gift that the Father has given to us to be our Justifier, Lifegiver, and Redeemer. To put on Christ according to the Gospel, therefore, is to put on, not the Law or works but an inestimable gift, namely, the forgiveness of sins, righteousness, peace, comfort, joy in the Holy Spirit, salvation, life, and Christ Himself."[178] For the reception of this wonderful Gift, the Reformer uses the important term "apprehension," rendered in English as "taking hold": "faith itself is a gift of God, a work of God in our hearts, which justifies us because it takes hold of [*apprehendit*] Christ the Savior."[179] The term *apprehendere* (which occurs in his commentary on Galatians [1535] about 300 times!) is a key scholastic philosophical concept denoting not only "intellectual apprehension when seen in terms of understanding and comprehension" but also the idea that "the object of knowledge becomes the property of a knowing subject." For Luther this means "knowing Him as God who gives Himself to and on behalf of all sinners," in other words, participation and union; Christ indeed is the righteousness of the Christian.[180]

---

175. For various aspects of the discussion, see Kärkkäinen, *One with God.* See also, my "Justification as Forgiveness of Sins and Making Righteous," pp. 32-45; "Ecumenical Potential of Theosis," pp. 45-77; "Holy Spirit and Justification," pp. 26-39; "Salvation as Justification and Deification," pp. 59-76.

176. *HDT* 26; *LW* 31:56 (WA 1:364.24).

177. *HDT* 27; *LW* 31:56 (WA 1:364.30); see also, WA 40¹:540.17-19; *LW* 26:352.

178. WA 40¹:541.17-20; *LW* 26:353.

179. WA 40¹:164.18-21; *LW* 26:88.

180. Vainio, *Justification and Participation,* pp. 20-22, 26 (pp. 21, 22). Luther often uses the expression of Christ as the "form of faith" *(forma fidei),* for which see p. 27.

In the same context Luther also wishes to defeat the Augustinian-Thomist principle of *ordo caritatis,* that is, love as a natural capacity may reach out to the highest end, which is God, and therefore (as Trent put it), love is the "form of faith" *(fides caritate formata).*[181] Luther denies any such capacity to fallen human love and instead makes "Christ the form of faith" *(fides Christo formata).*[182] "Therefore faith justifies because it takes hold of [*apprehendit*] and possesses this treasure, the present Christ."[183]

In this understanding, justification for Luther is forensic (imputation) and also signifies renewal (sanctification). This can be expressed briefly in terms of justification as gift *(donum)* and favor *(favor;* the forgiveness of sins).[184] In keeping with Catholic tradition, Luther states it unambiguously: "But 'the grace of God' and the 'gift' are the same thing, namely, the very righteousness which is freely given to us through Christ."[185] One of the criticisms against the Mannermaa School interpretation is that the investigation of Luther's theology has mainly focused on early writings. That is true. Yet it is also true, as the quotations above indicate, that even the final form of the *Commentary on Galatians* (1535), endorsed "officially" by the drafters of the Formula of Concord as a reliable guide to the Lutheran doctrine of salvation,[186] presents justification as participation in Christ and thus goes beyond and amplifies the forensic paradigm.[187]

Importantly, so the Helsinki scholars argue, Luther's view of justification can also be called *theosis.* Justification and deification, then, mean the "participation" of the believer in Christ, which, because Christ is God, is also a participation in God himself. This participation is the result of God's love.[188] Of this participation, Luther says boldly: "[I]t is true that a man helped by grace is more than a man; indeed, the grace of God gives him the form of God and

---

181. WA 40¹:164.15-19; *LW* 26:88.

182. Among many other passages, representative are WA 40¹:228-29; *LW* 26:128-30.

183. WA 40¹:229.22-23; *LW* 26:130; see Vainio, *Justification and Participation*, pp. 27-36.

184. For discussion on the Galatians commentary (1535), see Vainio, *Justification and Participation*, pp. 36-42.

185. WA 56:318.28-29; *LW* 25:306.

186. Formula of Concord 3.67 (other numbering 3.59).

187. For a detailed analysis, see Vainio, *Justification and Participation*, chap. 2.

188. Mannermaa argues that for Luther the structuring principle of theology is not justification as is routinely assumed but rather a creative juxtaposition between the theology of the cross and love. This comes to culmination in the 1518 Heidelberg Disputation, the last thesis of which (#28) contrasts the love of God and human love. See further, Kärkkäinen, "Evil, Love and the Left Hand of God."

deifies him, so that even the Scriptures call him 'God' and 'God's son.'"[189] And: "Just as the Word of God became flesh, so it is certainly also necessary that the flesh become Word. For the Word becomes flesh precisely so that the flesh may become Word. In other words: God becomes man so that man may become God."[190] In contrast to existentialist and modern Luther interpretations, the Helsinki School scholars argue strongly that, for Luther, "[j]ustification is not a change of self-understanding, a new relation to God, or a new ethos of love. God changes the sinner ontologically in the sense that he or she participates in God and in his divine nature, being made righteous and 'a god.'"[191]

Yet another way of considering the idea of justification and *theosis* in Luther is in reference to the concept of giving and gift. For Luther the divinity of the triune God consists in that "God gives" himself. The essence of God, then, is identical with the essential divine properties in which he gives of himself, called the "names" of God: Word, justice, truth, wisdom, love, goodness, eternal life, and so forth. "The *theosis* of the believer is initiated when God bestows on the believer God's essential properties; that is, what God gives of himself to humans is nothing separate from God himself."[192] God is, as Luther says, the whole "beatitude" *(beatitudo)* of his saints: "And so He gives Himself, and He does not give, but is Himself the good and complete blessing of the saints. For as it is said that 'God gives Himself to the saints,' which means that 'God is the good [*beatitudo*] of his saints,' so also His name gives Him to them, that is, it is their good. But the name of God is Christ Himself, the Son of God, the Word by which He verbalizes Himself and the name by which He calls Himself in eternity."[193]

Although the distinction between effective and forensic righteousness does not feature as important to Luther himself, another kind of distinction between two kinds of righteousness is important: the righteousness of Christ and the righteousness of the human being. The first Luther defines as "alien" righteousness that is being infused to us from outside; it is that kind of righteousness that Christ is in himself and is the righteousness of faith. It is this righteousness of Christ that makes the human being just.[194] Furthermore, this type of righteousness is given without our own works, solely on the basis of grace.[195] This is the famous

189. WA 2:247-48; *LW* 51:58.
190. WA 1:28.25-32, quoted in Mannermaa, "Theosis as a Subject," p. 43.
191. Peura, "Christ as Favor and Gift," p. 48.
192. Mannermaa, "Why Is Luther So Fascinating?" p. 10.
193. WA 3:303.20-26; *LW* 10:253; see Peura, "Christ as Favor and Gift," p. 50.
194. WA 2:145.9-14; *LW* 31:297 ("Two Kinds of Righteousness").
195. WA 2:146.29-30; *LW* 31:299.

sola gratia. Human activity is totally excluded in this process. The infusion of this righteousness is more than mere forensic imputation, though; it also means the realization of the righteousness of Christ in the believer. The other kind of righteousness Luther calls "our" righteousness.[196] It is a result of the first kind of righteousness and makes it effective, "perfects" it.[197] Even though it is called "our" righteousness, its origin and source are outside the human being, in the righteousness of Christ.[198] Christ present in faith "absorbs all sin in a moment," since the righteousness of Christ infused into the human heart is "infinite"; at the same time, the power of sin and death is deteriorating day by day but is not fully destroyed until death.[199]

Good deeds follow as a result.[200] Although, in line with *sola gratia,* we can do nothing for our salvation, good works spring from the union, Christ's presence through Spirit in the believer. The Christian becomes a "work of Christ," and even more, a "christ" to the neighbor; the Christian does what Christ does.[201] "[S]ince Christ lives in us through faith . . . he arouses us to do good works through that living faith in his work, for the works which he does are the fulfillment of the commands of God given us through faith."[202]

To no one's surprise, responses to the Mannermaa School's reinterpretation of Luther have been varied. Whereas the Continental, particularly German, Luther scholarship has been deeply critical,[203] a number of leading American Lutherans have enthusiastically endorsed it.[204] Understandably, conservative Lutherans (Missouri Synod), along with many evangelicals, to whom the forensic-imputational template is the only correct interpretation, have expressed deep reservations.[205]

196. WA 2:146.36; *LW* 31:299.

197. WA 2:147.12-13; *LW* 31:300.

198. WA 2:146.16-17; *LW* 31:298.

199. WA 2:146.12-16, 32-35; *LW* 31:298-99.

200. WA 2:146.36-147; *LW* 31:299-300.

201. See further, Kärkkäinen, "Christian as Christ to the Neighbor." For a careful study on the concept of *nihil* in Luther and its relationship to Luther's view of participation, see Juntunen, *Der Begriff des Nichts bei Luther.*

202. *HDT* 27; *LW* 31:56-57 (WA 1:364.30-33).

203. The leading German scholar Bernhard Lohse (*Martin Luther's Theology,* p. 221) virtually dismisses the Mannermaa School's insight altogether.

204. See Braaten and Jensen, eds., *Union with Christ,* among others.

205. See Kolb, "Contemporary Lutheran Understandings of Justification," pp. 153-76; Kolb and Arand (*Genius of Luther's Theology,* p. 48) level the fancy charge of "Osianderism" against this view. (For a careful engagement with Osiander, see Peura, "Gott und Mensch in der Unio," pp. 33-61.)

Having now reassessed the meaning of Reformation disputes and having inquired into several groundbreaking contemporary theological and ecumenical results, we are ready to develop a constructive theology of salvation as deification and justification. It is based on the idea of union with and participation in God, and hence is trinitarian in its form.

Salvation as Union with the Triune God: A Trinitarian Theology of Salutary Participation

The Trinitarian Form of Salvation as Participation in Divine Life

There is a curious trinitarian deficit in most soteriological accounts, particularly in justification. Quite striking is the passive (or almost nonexistent) role of the Spirit in most accounts of justification[206] (as opposed to the Eastern theology of deification).[207] In a typical Protestant conception of justification, the Spirit's role is somewhat external; as the Pentecostal Frank Macchia puts it: "the Spirit function[s] from the outside, inspiring faith in the gospel" without having to do with the "substance of justification," and the Father "seems to be a relatively passive spectator who happily accepts Christ's advocacy" without having an active role to play.[208] Referring to passages such as Titus 3:5-7, which speaks about the "washing of regeneration and renewal in the Holy Spirit, which he poured out upon us richly," Moltmann rightly emphasizes that "'regeneration' as 'renewal' comes about through the Holy Spirit" when the "Spirit is 'poured out.'"[209] By making further reference to John 4:14, the metaphor of the divine "wellspring of life" that begins to flow in a human being, he contends that "through this experience of the Spirit, who comes upon us from the Father through the Son, we become 'justified through grace.'"[210]

Indeed, the Christ event itself, reconciliation, has an integral trinitarian form.[211] The identification with humanity in incarnation and the voluntary

---

206. For a corrective, see Macchia, "Justification through New Creation."

207. Macchia, *Justified in the Spirit*, p. 5.

208. Macchia, *Justified in the Spirit*, p. 5; see also, p. 39.

209. Moltmann, *Spirit of Life*, p. 146. See further, my "'By the Washing of Regeneration and Renewing by the Holy Spirit,'" pp. 303-22.

210. Moltmann, *Spirit of Life*, p. 146. See also, Bakken, "Holy Spirit and Theosis," pp. 410-11.

211. For a trinitarian theology of reconciliation (and atonement), see chap. 13 in *Christ and Reconciliation*.

suffering at the cross through which the Father "justifies" himself (Rom. 3:25) are followed by the raising to new life "for our justification" (Rom. 4:25) of the Son by the Father, and the ascension, which propel the Pentecostal pouring out of the Spirit.[212] Even when forensic/legal aspects of justification are in the forefront, the Spirit's role is not excluded: the Spirit as the Paraclete is both Advocate and Judge according to the Johannine testimony (John 14 and 16). Hence, "[r]ighteousness is not *imputed;* it is *accessed* or *participated in* through faith and by the life of the Spirit."[213] The *Joint Declaration* got it right: "Christ himself is our righteousness, in which we share through the Holy Spirit in accord with the will of the Father" (#15). Set in this wider trinitarian framework of the divine economy, justification gains its proper horizon:

> This gift of righteousness involves God's self-justification as the faithful Creator and covenant partner to creation; but it also involves the participation of the creature, for the kingdom of God is "righteousness, peace, and joy in the Holy Spirit" (Rom. 14:17). Seen from the lens of the Spirit, this right relationship is a *mutual indwelling* that has communion and the "swallowing up" of mortality by life as its substance (2 Cor. 5:4). It is based on the self-giving embrace of the triune God and is manifested in new birth, witness, and, ultimately, resurrection.[214]

Luther's focus on justification as the presence of Christ through the Spirit reminds us of an integral trinitarian-pneumatological reading of the account of justification. In a remarkable comment on Galatians 3:7, he equates righteousness "imputed" to the believer with the gift of the Spirit:

> Now is not the fact that faith is reckoned as righteousness a receiving of the Spirit? So either he proves nothing or the reception of the Spirit and the fact that faith is reckoned as righteousness will be the same thing. And this is true; it is introduced in order that the divine imputation may not be regarded as amounting to nothing outside God, as some think that the apostle's word "grace" means a favorable disposition rather than a gift. For when God is favorable, and when He imputes, the Spirit is really received, both the gift and the grace. Otherwise grace was there from eternity and

---

212. See also, Macchia, *Justified in the Spirit,* pp. 7-8.
213. Macchia, *Justified in the Spirit,* p. 6, emphasis in original.
214. Macchia, *Justified in the Spirit,* p. 3, emphasis in original.

remains within God, if it signifies only a favorable disposition in the way that favor is understood among men.[215]

Reference to the Holy Spirit, the eschatological Spirit, also reminds us of the importance of the reference to future, final consummation. Although not prominent in Luther, neither the eschatological nor the anticipatory dimension is lacking. In his later work "The Disputation concerning Justification" (1536), Luther has this orientation clearly in mind as he speaks of God who "sustains and supports them on account of the first fruit of his creation in us, and he thereupon decrees that they are righteous and sons of the kingdom."[216] That is the anticipatory aspect, and here is the culmination: "For justification is healing for sin, which slays the whole world eternally and brings it to destruction with its infinite evils."[217]

Only a healthy trinitarian theology of salvation may yield an account of deification, justification, and sanctification that is linked with the whole divine economy and is not restricted merely to the salvation of individuals but also includes the salvation of communities, and even the whole of creation. Salvation means participation in the triune life.

Union, the "Ecstatic" Nature of Faith, and Adoption

As has become clear, I take union with the triune God as the leading motif of soteriology and so glean from the theology of the Christian East and Protestant Reformers, Calvin and Luther. Having replaced the Scholastic concept of "infused grace" by the idea of faith as the work of the Holy Spirit,[218] Luther saw the importance of the eccentric (or "ecstatic," as in *ek-stasis*, "to stand outside of oneself") nature of faith. Faith places trust "outside" of itself, in Christ.[219] Luther's profound statement in the pamphlet *The Freedom of a Christian* (1520) puts it succinctly: "We conclude, therefore, that a Christian lives not in himself,

215. Luther, "Lectures on Galatians" (1519), on 3:7; *LW* 27:252; WA 2:511.13-20; for comments, see Macchia, *Justified in the Spirit*, pp. 63-64.

216. Luther, "The Disputation concerning Justification," #22 (Third Disputation), in *LW* 34:152; WA 39^1:83.14-15.

217. *LW* 34:156; WA 39^1:86.10-11.

218. For the classic statement of the Spirit's role in faith from the third article of the Small Catechism (1531), see WA 30^1:367-68; *BC*, p. 345; see further, Pannenberg, *ST* 3:2-3.

219. More generally, all creaturely life is ecstatic in that it finds its origins and maintenance "outside" itself, in the environment (or "field"); see Pannenberg, *ST* 3:33-34, 128-30, and passim.

but in Christ and in his neighbor. Otherwise he is not a Christian. He lives in Christ through faith, in his neighbor through love. By faith he is caught up beyond himself into God [*rapitur supra se in deum*]. By love he descends beneath himself into his neighbor. Yet he always remains in God and in his love."[220] Comments the Lutheran Pannenberg: "This understanding of faith as ecstatic is the reason why the Reformer was able to avoid identifying the uncreated Spirit (and love poured out into our hearts through the Spirit after Romans 5:5) with our creaturely reality. Spirit is Gift who lives in our hearts but remains uncreated."[221]

Building on this key insight, Pannenberg states that through faith in God the Spirit lifts us "up to participation in the sonship of Jesus Christ" and "binds believers together in the fellowship of the body of Christ. This faith lifts us above our particularity inasmuch as God is powerfully present to us as the light of our final future and assures us at the same time of our own eternal salvation." This is because, indeed, "[i]n all their forms of manifestation the works of God's Spirit have an ecstatic character."[222] Faith has this *extra nos* character[223] and at the same time "links believers to Jesus Christ as they rely on him and on the promise of salvation that is given in his message and history"; indeed, this means nothing less than the believer's participation in the filial relation of the Son to the Father.[224]

As a result, Pannenberg selects — surprisingly to his Lutheran readers — "adoption" as the overarching and determining concept of *ordo salutis*. Whereas highlighting the importance of the concept of adoption is of course nothing new in Lutheran (or Reformed tradition),[225] making it an overarching concept that also regulates justification is.[226] The surplus of opting for adoption as the main framework, namely, that "[b]eing God's children is thus of the essence of the Christian life," helps utilize not only the Pauline theology (Rom. 8:16, among others) but also Jesus' teaching (Luke 18:17; Mark 10:15; Matt. 5:9).[227] Adoption in this theological template means that the believer is lifted up by the Spirit through

---

220. WA 7:69.12-16; *LW* 31:371.

221. Pannenberg, *ST* 3:200.

222. Pannenberg, *ST* 3:134-35.

223. Pannenberg, *ST* 3:136-37.

224. Pannenberg, *ST* 3:211.

225. For the importance of adoption as the *result* of justification in Protestant orthodoxy and modern Protestant theology, see Pannenberg, *ST* 3:212 n. 352. Both Schleiermacher (*CF* §109, pp. 496-505) and Barth (*CD* IV/1, p. 599) equated the two, justification and adoption.

226. See the long and detailed section 4, titled "Adoption as God's Children and Justification" (pp. 211-36), in *ST* 3.

227. Pannenberg, *ST* 3:211-12.

faith into the filial relationship with Christ and is united with other believers in the same body. This is an eschatological move, as "by the Spirit the future of Jesus Christ is already present to believers as their personal and common future of salvation" in anticipation of "the eschatological fellowship of a humanity that is renewed in the kingdom of God,"[228] a theme developed in ecclesiology. (As will be argued in the doctrine of the church, this ecstatic lifting-up helps resolve the perennial problem of one-and-many, personal-and-communal. Union and participation of course communicate the same idea.)

The Protestant Reformers' emphasis on faith as trust *(fiducia)*[229] as it looks into the promises of God,[230] thereby also linking faith closely with hope as well,[231] helps us correct the misplaced fear of assurance of salvation at Trent and in later Catholic tradition. Trust in the reliability and faithfulness of the promissory God rather than in one's own resources laid the basis for assurance. Indeed, it "belongs to the nature of God's promise that it implicitly *commands* those who receive it to be sure of the promised salvation no matter what may be the actual condition of these recipients of the promise."[232] Luther reminds us that it is not based on either human accomplishment or feelings but is the work of the Holy Spirit and can be trusted on the basis of promises of God.[233] In Hebrew, "faith" (from *he-'emûn*) comes from the *(qal)* stem that was used in the context of a mother nursing her child. Hence, trust, deep trust, is at the heart of the term; there is a similar connotation with the Greek term *(pistis, pisteuo)*.[234] Similar to faith, hope has its basis outside itself, namely, in Christ. Hope always reaches beyond our own resources and what is seen; herein comes hope's capacity for self-transcendence and its *extra nos* nature.[235]

Justification as Pronouncing and Making Righteous: The Theological Significance of the Forensic Aspect

Although the rediscovery of the centrality of union, participation, and adoption as controlling metaphors has helped contemporary theology to establish

---

228. Pannenberg, *ST* 3:134-35.
229. See Pannenberg, *ST* 3:138.
230. Pannenberg, *ST* 3:136.
231. See Luther, WA 9:9.7-12 (not in *LW*); for comments, see Pannenberg, *ST* 3:139-40.
232. Pannenberg, *ST* 3:162-63 (p. 162); see also, p. 170.
233. See the long comments of Luther on Gal. 4:6 in WA 40¹:571-92; *LW* 26:375-89.
234. McClendon, *Doctrine*, pp. 110-11, with documentation.
235. Pannenberg, *ST* 3:174-75.

a more satisfactory and integral account of justification, the downplaying of the forensic element (particularly by the Mannermaa School)[236] also calls for reconsideration. It does not do — nor is it necessary — to juxtapose union and forensic justification; that was also rightly noted by Trent. I embrace wholeheartedly the *JDDJ*'s affirmation of justification as both forgiveness of sins (forensic) and making righteous (effective) and refuse to consider union as an alternative to forensic declaration. Indeed, both aspects of justification stem from and are anchored in union. In this way the "twofold" justification materially approaches the *theosis* (Orthodox) and Roman Catholic views. I also welcome wholeheartedly the groundbreaking ecumenical achievements detailed above.

Although I disagree with N. T. Wright's limiting of justification to the forensic aspect, I also consider it an important reminder that, differently from the Latin term *iustificatio,* which includes the idea of making righteous (the verb *facere,* "to make"), the Greek term *dikaiōsis* (a rare term in itself in the NT, appearing only in Rom. 4:25 and 5:18) does not have that aspect.[237] Central to the meaning of *dikaiosynē* is the idea of keeping to the norm and standard set by God.[238] But that of course speaks of the need for continuous change!

Those interpreters who advocate the effective understanding of justification (that is, justification includes also the inner change) understandably have undermined the idea of "imputation" (of Christ's righteousness), a key mainstream Protestant idea. The reason is self-evident: in Protestantism at large imputation has been seen as a forensic act (similar to how the contemporary Anglican N. T. Wright sees it).[239] But does it have to be so? Only if justification as imputation is understood *exclusively* as a forensic act that blocks the way for making righteous is the opposition justified. But what if, as the most recent research has allowed us to understand,[240] the concept of imputation of Christ's righteousness does not have to be solely (or even primarily) forensic but could also include the process of change and renewal? Indeed, Luther's own concept of "Christ present in faith" *(in ipsa fide Christus adest)* is just that: the "imputed" Christ's "real" presence in the believer also instantly brings about the lifelong process of change.[241] Even semantically, "imputation" has a number of

---

236. So also, Saarinen, *"De Iustificatione,"* pp. 291-304 (this section is indebted to it).

237. See N. T. Wright, *Justification,* p. 88.

238. Saarinen, *"De Iustificatione,"* pp. 292-93; N. T. Wright, *Justification,* p. 46.

239. N. T. Wright, *Justification,* pp. 46-49 and passim.

240. The key investigation is the massive study by Rolf, *Zum Hertzen sprechen.*

241. This is the brilliant conclusion of Saarinen (*"De Iustificatione,"* pp. 295-97), combining Rolf's and the Mannermaa School's insights.

meanings, from commercial exchange and accounting (the primary meaning in Protestant orthodoxy) to personal (not to count the friend's mistake as a reason for breaking relationship) to hermeneutical (to consider one's own experience as the key to understanding), and so forth.[242] What clearly comes to the fore in Luther's theology is the personal orientation. As Risto Saarinen importantly argues: whereas in Augustine righteousness could be imputed to the believer in a nonpersonal manner (as a liquid is poured into a container), in Luther it is always a matter of personal trust, personal relationship.[243] His catchword *fides facit personam* makes this point most succinctly.[244]

At the same time, the importance of forgiveness of sins — again, undermined by the Mannermaa School because in the context of the doctrine of justification it meant only *favor* (but not *donum*) — should be more robustly highlighted. That justification is more than forgiveness should not hinder us from lifting up its significance, if not for other reasons, then because it is mentioned both in the Lord's Prayer and in the creeds. Importantly, in Jesus' ministry forgiveness was also linked with physical healings — and we can extend the meaning more widely into "healing," as in salvation.[245]

Rightwising and the "Active Reception of the Gift"

Another way of speaking of union and participation is to build on the concept of divine giving and gift. This is in keeping with the Christian vision of the triune God as the supremely hospitable Giver — and Gift![246] An essential feature of the divine love is self-giving.[247] In Luther's theology the meaning of divine Gift serves as a defining feature: God's love seeks that which is worthless in itself and donates not only gifts but oneself.[248] The Holy Spirit particularly is presented as "Gift" in Christian tradition, as discussed above.[249] The basic

242. Saarinen, *"De Iustificatione,"* p. 296, with reference to Rolf, *Zum Hertzen sprechen,* p. 27.

243. Saarinen, *"De Iustificatione,"* p. 296; for details, see Rolf, *Zum Hertzen sprechen,* pp. 33-40.

244. WA 39^1:283.18-19 (not in *LW*).

245. Saarinen, *"De Iustificatione,"* p. 297.

246. See further, Newlands and Smith, *Hospitable God.*

247. See Oord, *Defining Love.*

248. Mannermaa, *Kaksi rakkautta,* pp. 9-13; I have developed in detail the theology of divine giving in chap. 13 of *Trinity and Revelation,* titled "Divine Hospitality."

249. Augustine, *On the Trinity* 5.12.13; 5.15.16.

Greek verb *didōmi* appears over 400 times in the NT alone![250] The Pentecostal systematician Frank D. Macchia rightly reminds us that "'justification' refers fundamentally to the gift of *righteousness* (or 'just relation') that is granted to the sinner."[251]

On the contemporary theological scene, the Radical Orthodox theologian Milbank has made "gift" a determining and guiding principle of theology: "gift is a kind of trancendental [*sic*] category in relation to all the topoi of theology, in a similar fashion to 'word.'"[252] Coupled with Milbank's focus on gift is Radical Orthodoxy's underlying focus on *methexis*, which talks not only about the sharing of all "being" in the Divine (or else it cannot exist because the created finite creature is neither self-generating nor self-sustaining)[253] but also about salvation as "participation" in the triune life; the divine life itself is the most profound form of "participation," that is, communion among the Three.[254]

I also agree with Milbank's insistence (against Derrida and like-minded thinkers) that gift is possible even in a world like ours, notwithstanding the (legitimate) concerns of reciprocity in the human exchange of gifts and that, when speaking of divine giving, the element of mutuality and reciprocity is to be acknowledged rather than resisted.[255] It is in this light that Milbank's theological criticism of the overly "passive" reception of justification in mainstream Protestant tradition is to be welcomed (although, oddly enough, it is resisted by some Reformed thinkers).[256] Rightly he demands that "an account of the arrival of grace must . . . also mean an account of sanctification, and of ethics."[257] Again, it has elicited critical opposition from some conservative Reformed thinkers.[258]

---

250. For a detailed discussion, see Saarinen, *God and Gift*, pp. 36-45.

251. Macchia, *Justified in the Spirit*, p. 3, emphasis in original.

252. Milbank, *Being Reconciled*, p. ix.

253. Milbank, *Being Reconciled*, p. xi.

254. See Milbank, *Being Reconciled*, p. x.

255. My critique of Derrida's one-sided and unnuanced denial of the possibility of gift can be found in *Christ and Reconciliation*, pp. 29-33, and *Trinity and Revelation*, pp. 310-12; for Milbank, see his "Can a Gift Be Given?" pp. 119-61; for brief notes, see *Being Reconciled*, pp. x-xi, 160, 181.

256. See the harsh criticism of Milbank by the Reformed theologian J. T. Billings, *Calvin, Participation, and the Gift*; for a shorter discussion, see Billings, "John Milbank's Theology of the 'Gift' and Calvin's Theology of Grace."

257. Milbank, *Being Reconciled*, p. 138; for endorsement of Sanders's critique of the Protestant view, see p. 103. In this light the connection to Eastern Orthodoxy is interesting: Pabst and Schneider, eds., *Encounter between Eastern Orthodoxy and Radical Orthodoxy*.

258. For a theological response, see Horton, "Participation and Covenant."

Indeed, there is a need for what Milbank labels "active reception" of gift.[259] Although common sense is not always the best guide in matters theological, I believe it is here: it just does not make any sense to think of the recipient of a gift — say, a child at a birthday party or a spouse on an anniversary — as totally passive; a gift can also be "unreceived," as when a spouse who is transgressed against by the partner in adultery wishes to make amends. "After all, the creature is not destined to act without any element of choice involved, and God does not commit violence on creation."[260] Christian tradition at large agrees that all human response is *graced* and that — again, following common sense — no parent (the heavenly Father in this case) would enjoy giving a gift to a "robot" rather than to a child who passionately and "actively" looks forward to a gift (say, for Christmas).

I argue that the paranoid fear of "works righteousness" of much of Protestantism has to be challenged and corrected by the "synergistic" (Eastern Orthodox) and "cooperational" (Roman Catholic) understanding of ("prevenient") grace — while at the same time (in agreement with the whole of Christian tradition) all forms of Pelagianism must be resisted. Here John Wesley's robust theology of grace as "therapeutic" is a needed reminder for other Protestants; the "sanctifying" grace begins to heal and change the person the moment the person is justified, the founder of Methodism taught.[261] Luther's profound theology of the Christian as "christ" to the neighbor is yet another pointer in this direction. This emphasis brings to light the importance not only of good works but also of holiness and renewal of life. In keeping with Eastern Orthodoxy, Roman Catholicism, and Luther's reluctance to make a categorical distinction between justification/deification and sanctification, I integrate the discussion of holiness into the current chapter rather than making it a separate locus. In this effort, the great contribution of Wesleyan-Holiness traditions serves as an ecumenical resource along with key insights from the traditions of both the Christian East and West. To that discussion we turn next.

---

259. Milbank coins the term "active reception" in his essay "Gregory of Nyssa," p. 95.
260. Macchia, *Justified in the Spirit*, p. 25.
261. See further, Runyon, *The New Creation*, pp. 27-30.

Renewal, Holiness, and Integrity of Life

Beyond Justification: The Pursuit of Spiritual Progress

Although Calvin linked tightly together sanctification and justification through the concept of union[262] — even to the point of placing union first (as discussed above)[263] — and expressed grave concerns about the liability of the Protestant doctrine of justification's lapse into complacency (so astutely pointed out by the regular Catholic critique),[264] that was not enough for the post-Reformation Pietist movement and other renewal movements. Regeneration rather than (forensic) declaration became the chief aspect in their soteriology.[265] Regeneration was understood as a dynamic event and — unlike external forensic acquittal — an act that brought about inner change. It pointed to new life, holiness, sanctification. Whereas forensic justification is a onetime event, the same to all, holiness is a matter of growth and progress, and a typical Orthodox and Catholic idea. Not for nothing did A. Ritschl name Pietism "an approach to the Catholic view" of justification.[266]

We note the viewpoint of Anglican John Henry Newman in his lectures on justification before he became Catholic. He clearly seems to assume that what is declared in justification is already a promise or a pledge of what is going to happen: "A *declaration* on the part of God may in itself presuppose, or involve, or attend, or cause, or in any other way imply, the actual communication of the thing declared: still it does not thereby cease to be a declaration, and justification need not cease to be in itself an accounting, though it may involve a making righteous."[267] Indeed, the "declaration for Newman thus functions sacramentally, as 'an external word effecting an inward grace.'"[268]

262. Calvin, *Institutes* 3.11.6.

263. See Garcia, *Life in Christ.*

264. Having explained in detail the doctrine of sanctification and moving to justification, Calvin defends the rationale of the order of discussion in *Institutes* 3.11.1. For comments, see Hunsinger, "Tale of Two Simultaneities."

265. See further, D. W. Brown, *Understanding Pietism*, p. 66; see also, Welch, *Protestant Thought in the Nineteenth Century*, 1:29.

266. Ritschl, *The Christian Doctrine of Justification and Reconciliation*, p. 108; I am indebted to Macchia, *Justified in the Spirit*, p. 68; see pp. 66-69 for details.

267. J. H. Newman, *Lectures on Justification* (Lecture 3, section 4), p. 69, emphasis in original.

268. Macchia, *Justified in the Spirit*, p. 69, with citation from J. H. Newman, *Lectures on Justification*, p. 94.

Here is a definite shift toward the Catholic (and materially, also Orthodox) vision of soteriology. Importantly, modern Protestantism has moved toward that kind of mediating position. An example is the Reformed theologian
Emil Brunner's title of a chapter on soteriology, "Regeneration as a Special
Aspect of Justification," in which justification as a relational event means inner
transformation; thematically Brunner resisted what he saw as the standard
Lutheran idea of extrinsic declaration alone (although he also had deep reservations concerning the Wesleyan vision of sanctification).[269] Tillich similarly
points to the mediating position, although as a Lutheran he more carefully
begins from the premise (which he saw as the Catholic position) in which
justification is based on renewed lives.[270] In the Reformed theologian Moltmann's theology, the pneumatological orientation yields a deeply "synergistic"
renewal-oriented liberationist account of justification (as discussed above) and
sanctification (to be discussed below).[271]

Earlier in modern theology a much more radical turn to the pursuit
of renewal and change of life in the justified person was taken in the former
Anglican John Wesley's theology.[272] Like his Pietist and Puritan forebears, as
well as the Anabaptists (and in keeping with later Holiness movements),[273]
Wesley faced the dilemma of wanting to hold on to the forensic Protestant
understanding of justification, including the distinction between justification
and sanctification,[274] while also, with Pietists, understanding justification as
regeneration,[275] and as such, as an inner change.[276] Or to put it another way:
although justification (which he in this context equates with conversion) is
an instantaneous event, regeneration (which he considers also as justification) allows for degrees.[277] Sanctification marks the "last and highest state"
of this progress.[278] Wesley even used at times the daring word "perfection" to
mark the highest level of progress in spiritual life. Although — against mis-

---

269. Brunner, *Dogmatics*, 3:269-75; I am indebted to Macchia, *Justified in the Spirit*,
p. 70.

270. For details and sources, see Macchia, *Justified in the Spirit*, pp. 69-70.

271. See the pneumatological account of soteriology by the American Methodist student
of Moltmann, Dabney, "Justification by the Spirit."

272. See Abraham, "Christian Perfection."

273. See Dieter, "Holiness Movement," pp. 4082-84.

274. See, e.g., Wesley, "Sermon 5: Justification by Faith," in *WJW* 5:56. For an extensive
forensic explanation of Wesley's view, see Collins, *Theology of John Wesley*, pp. 155-93.

275. Wesley, "The Principles of a Methodist," in *WJW* 8:369.

276. See Wesley, "Sermon 107: On God's Vineyard," in *WJW* 7:206.

277. For details and references, see Macchia, *Justified in the Spirit*, p. 68.

278. Wesley, "The Principles of a Methodist," in *WJW* 8:373.

understandings — perfection for him did not entail perfect sinlessness,[279] it definitely set Wesley's vision of soteriology outside the Protestant mainstream. Holding on tightly to Jesus' admonition to "be perfect, as your heavenly Father is perfect" (Matt. 5:48), Wesley firmly believed that

> [t]here is more to salvation than forgiveness, for salvation principally involves both justification and sanctification; it is mistaken to set limits to what the grace of God can do this side of the grave; Christ is deadly serious in the call to perfection; the Scriptures portray a model of pure religion in which those who are born of God do not commit sin; it really is possible in this life to love God with all our heart, soul, and mind and to love our neighbours as ourselves. By the grace of God, human agents can come to purity and singleness of intention; they can perfectly love God; they can be cleansed and cured of their evil tempers and dispositions; they can have the mind of Christ here and now; they can be pure in heart; they can be delivered from the power as well as the guilt of sin.[280]

As suspicious as the desire for perfectionism may sound to mainstream Protestant and Anglican ears, Wesley's vision aligns itself with deep and wide Christian tradition. The pursuit of perfection is evident everywhere among the Fathers, both in the East and in the West. Just think of the trinitarian order of exposition in the very beginning of Origen's *On First Principles*. Origen states that those who participate in the Spirit are made holy. In fact, Christians may advance in "various stages of progress" both with regard to righteousness (which is Christ's) and in sanctification; in other words, they are being made "purer and holier." Origen doesn't spare words in describing the intense longing for and pursuit of higher and higher levels of attainment in holiness until one reaches the desired state.[281] Similarly, think of the "divine race along the course of virtue," "the perpetual progress" in Gregory of Nyssa's *Life of Moses*[282] or Irenaeus's detailed exposition of a distinctively *Christian* vision of perfection in opposition to the Gnostic view of redemption in which the

279. Collins, *Scripture Way of Salvation*, p. 182.

280. Abraham, "Christian Perfection," p. 2. For representative texts in the Wesleyan corpus, particularly in *A Plain Account of Christian Perfection*, see Kärkkäinen, ed., *Holy Spirit and Salvation*, pp. 219-29.

281. Origen, *On First Principles* 1.3.8.

282. Gregory of Nyssa, *The Life of Moses*, p. 29; for details, see Robb-Dover, "Gregory of Nyssa's 'Perpetual Progress.'"

idea of "perfection" is central.[283] Numerous other examples could be added, particularly from earlier Fathers.[284]

It is not without significance that Wesley read and helped translate some of the key texts of the Eastern Fathers.[285] The Eastern tradition at large preserved this tradition in its *theosis* doctrine, which does not make sanctification a separate topic but rather considers progress in holiness and spirituality as a daily practice, to be completed in the eschaton. Significant similarities have been recently uncovered between Orthodox and Pentecostal pursuits of holiness; recall that Pentecostalism's roots lie partly in Holiness movements of the nineteenth century.[286] In the Christian West, the same pursuit of progress in holiness has been the hallmark of the Catholic tradition. Importantly, a recent investigation has found many similarities between the pursuit of perfect love and holiness in Aquinas's and Wesley's theologies.[287]

Rediscovering Life-Affirming Holiness for Today

The Protestant Reformation's categorical separation between justification and sanctification should be corrected without compromising the underlying legitimate concern about lapsing into "works righteousness" or making the state of progress the basis for salvation. Protestant theology should have listened to the Anabaptist, Orthodox, and Catholic critique of lack of emphasis on change and good works (notwithstanding its exaggerated and somewhat misplaced target, as discussed above). Most ironically, the Lutheran tradition has come to be known as one that supports "bold sinning."[288] Not for nothing whines the Lutheran Hinlicky that in Protestant tradition "justification by faith easily becomes an abstract declaration of divine permissiveness that leaves secularized persons to work out their own spiritual ruin with a foolishly happy conscience."[289] On the contrary, the biblical tradition, both in the Old Testament

---

283. Bounds, "Irenaeus and the Doctrine of Christian Perfection," pp. 161-76.

284. *1 Clement* 1:2; 9:2; 44:2, 5; etc.; Ignatius of Antioch, *To the Ephesians* (short) 14-15; *Didache* 1:4; 6:2; etc.; *Barnabas* 1:5; 4:11; etc.; Bounds, "Irenaeus and the Doctrine of Christian Perfection," p. 161 n. 1.

285. See Christensen, "Theosis and Sanctification."

286. Rybarczyk, *Beyond Salvation.*

287. For a massive recent study, see also, Colon-Emeric, *Wesley, Aquinas, and Christian Perfection.*

288. Gritsch, "Bold Sinning."

289. Hinlicky, "Theological Anthropology," p. 41.

and in the New, approaches the question of salvation from the perspective of the likeness of God's people to God. For this to happen, a change has to take place in the human person. Of course, this may entail a change of status, as if somebody who has committed a crime is being pardoned. This, however, is not the main direction of the biblical data. For a corrective, Protestants should learn from Luther's teaching on Christ present in faith through the Spirit, making the believer a "christ," although perfection can only be had in the eschaton. They would also benefit from Wesley's insight that sanctification, rather than an optional second moment, so to speak, is "the inevitable consequence of justification."[290]

Although the pursuit of holiness and likeness with God should be made a stated theme and daily affair, talk about "perfectionism" has to be qualified (notwithstanding its wide attestation in patristic theology and Methodism). Although perfection in love and holiness is to be set as the ultimate goal, constant *pursuit* toward that goal, inspired and energized by the power of the Spirit, is to be seen as the focus of Christian life with the understanding that perfection is never to be had in this life. Otherwise the term itself has to be qualified to the point that it begins to lose its meaning. Here one may acknowledge the wisdom of the slogan *simul iustus et peccator,* "simultaneously just and sinner" — or *peccator in re et iustus in spe,* "sinner in fact, just in hope."[291]

Now that we have established the importance and urgency of inner change (holiness, sanctification) as an integral part of the Christian doctrine of justification and deification, the constructive task is to imagine what a contemporary, "earth-grounded," life-affirming, and liberationist account of holiness would look like for the sake of our pluralistic world. Christian life is not static; it is not a matter of having once been pronounced righteous — and then letting it be. "Every life that is born wants to grow. . . . The life we say has been 'born again' or 'born anew' from God's eternal Spirit also wants . . . to arrive at its proper form."[292] Although human effort is called forth, ultimately growth — both natural and spiritual — is the matter of the power of life, the divine Spirit. That same divine Spirit as an eschatological Gift also links the present with the future.[293] Sanctification and deification reach their goal once we are fully one with God through Christ in the Spirit. To that end Christians should leave aside everything that hinders and slows down the race.

290. Moltmann, *Spirit of Life,* p. 164.

291. See also, Moltmann, *Spirit of Life,* p. 164.

292. Moltmann, *Spirit of Life,* p. 161; a similar view is presented by Wesley, for which, see Runyon, *The New Creation,* pp. 71-74.

293. So also, Moltmann, *Spirit of Life,* p. 162.

Protestants need to work toward a better balance of two mutually conditioned aspects of sanctification, *mortificatio sui* and *vivificatio in Spiritu*, classical terms denoting the dying to oneself and its worldly propensities, on the one hand, and being made alive in the Spirit, on the other. The former has tended to dominate Western traditions, which have been deeply influenced by the penitential culture of the medieval and Reformation period and its overly negative anthropology. For the Eastern Church and Wesleyan movements, the finding of balance is easier because of a more robust pneumatological orientation and an idea of sin not so much as a transgression to be atoned as a sickness to be healed.[294]

There is profound truth in the assumption that holiness is "something 'contagious,' that is, humans and things become holy from contact with the holy God."[295] Like in justification, for which divine righteousness is the source, for sanctification, God's holiness is the basis.[296] Although not a biblical term, the philosophical concept of "infinity" is an appropriate way to highlight the nature of holiness as divine perfection. Following Descartes and Hegel, divine holiness can be defined as both a characteristic that separates God from everything else and that which makes it possible to embrace everything. Were "infinity" to mean only separation from but not inclusion of its opposites, it would lead to the negation of the concept altogether, because then the infinite would be limited by the finite.[297] This means that the holiness of God "enters the profane world, penetrates it, and makes it holy."[298]

A trinitarian-driven account of holiness may best avoid the common liabilities of the traditional doctrine of sanctification, particularly the withdrawal-from-the-world mentality and related "elitist 'privatizing' of spiritual experience" that lead to "detachment from the community of faith and the service to the world." That kind of escapist holiness is only "attained at the expense of the more pressing task of serving Christ in the world."[299] Liberationists and others have rightly critiqued this perversion.[300] The anchoring of the Christian's progress in holiness and integrity of life in infinite divine holiness that both separates from and penetrates the world helps avoid this danger. Indeed, as Moltmann insightfully reminds us, sanctification means "rediscovering *the sanctity of life*

---

294. For comments, see Moltmann, *Spirit of Life*, p. 164.
295. S. Chan, "Sanctification," p. 789.
296. For comments, see Moltmann, *Spirit of Life*, pp. 174-75.
297. Pannenberg, *ST* 1:399; for details, see my *Trinity and Revelation*, pp. 295-96.
298. Pannenberg, *ST* 1:400.
299. Fergusson, "Reclaiming the Doctrine of Sanctification," p. 380.
300. Gutiérrez, *We Drink from Our Wells*, p. 13.

and *the divine mystery of creation,* and defending them from life's manipulation, the secularization of nature, and the destruction of the world through human violence." Why so? Because all "life comes from God and belongs to God, so it has to be sanctified through the people who believe God."[301] Recall the etymology of the term "holy" in various Western languages: "entire, healthy, unhurt, complete, and 'belonging especially' to someone."[302] Holy life is a "whole" life. Wesley's deeply socially oriented holiness spirituality offers a positive example of the deep link with earthly realities.[303] It is no wonder that Methodist Christians founded trade unions for workers, and many early founders of the labor movement at the turn of the twentieth century came from the same background.[304]

A cure against individualism and elitism is the NT observation that it is not an individual "saint" — in exclusion from the community — but rather every Christian, even one in the beginning states (or even temporarily backslidden), who is called holy. "Saints" is a plural in the biblical testimonies![305] Even when — following ancient tradition — the church pays special homage to some individuals who have excelled in holiness and service, it is the holiness of the whole church that is meant.

Taking up this God-modeling pursuit of holiness — integrity of life — is of course a highly practical, "earth-grounded" daily exercise rather than an abstract tenet of faith. One way to understand this is to link holiness with virtues and virtue ethics. This puts into a different language the Pauline teaching of the indwelling of the Holy Spirit actualizing the fruit of the Spirit, the virtues (in contradistinction to the "works of the flesh" [Gal. 5:19-23]).

> The sanctified life as a life of virtues has much in common with virtues in other faith communities and nonreligious communities. What distinguishes Christian virtues from those of other communities is the Christian story, which provides the basic motive for these virtues and gives them their distinct Christian configuration. Thus for Christians love is the cardinal and defining virtue because the ultimate reality is the triune God who is eternally Persons-in-loving-communion, whereas for Buddhists, whose vision is dominated by a suffering world, the chief virtue is compassion.[306]

301. Moltmann, *Spirit of Life,* p. 171, emphasis in original.

302. Moltmann, *Spirit of Life,* p. 175.

303. For a fine detailed discussion, see Runyon, *The New Creation,* chap. 6.

304. See Jennings, *Good News to the Poor;* for comments, see Moltmann, *Spirit of Life,* pp. 165-66.

305. Fergusson, "Reclaiming the Doctrine of Sanctification," p. 381.

306. S. Chan, "Sanctification," pp. 790-91.

This citation from the Chinese theologian Simon Chan of Singapore reminds us of the need to link the Christian vision of justification/sanctification and deification with the wider framework of the pluralistic world in which we find ourselves today. What do these doctrines say to cultural, sociopolitical, and economic diversity?[307] What about interfaith issues? How would they be reshaped in those kinds of environments?

Justification, Deification, and Holiness in the Pluralistic World

Soteriology and Liberation

One of the most pertinent aspects calling for revision in the systematic theological discussions of salvation has to do with its "fit" in our pluralistic world. Deification, justification, and sanctification have to be linked with the cultural and religious diversity of the pluralistic world. This allows "theology to 'speak' from the different contexts and to define it in a different, contextually related way."[308] Luther's theology represents a contextual theology par excellence in that it attempted a new interpretation of salvation and Christian vision in sixteenth-century Europe by challenging and reformulating both ecclesiastical and social norms and practices.[309] On the other hand, "[i]t is amazing that Protestant theology has failed to note the analogy between God's righteousness which 'justifies' and God's justice which 'executes justice.'"[310]

Liberationists from various contexts have sought to highlight the liberationist impulses behind traditional soteriological concepts.[311] The Brazilian W. Altmann surmises that "justification by grace and faith implies a radical principle of equality among human beings and of the valuing of each one of them before God."[312] With some justification, liberationists in Latin America, Africa, and beyond have lamented the severing of liberation and justification at the personal level from that at the socioeconomic and political levels.[313] It

307. Consult Maddox, ed., *Rethinking Wesley's Theology.*

308. Greive, "The Significance of Justification," p. 11. See also, Kirst, ed., *Rethinking Luther's Theology.*

309. See further, G. Robinson, "Justification in a Multireligious Context," pp. 141-42; Moyo, "Time for an African Lutheran Theology," p. 96.

310. Moltmann, "Justice for Victims and Perpetrators."

311. See Shaull, *The Reformation and Liberation Theology,* p. 25.

312. Altmann, *Luther and Liberation,* p. 5.

313. See P. S. Chung, *Martin Luther and Buddhism,* p. 117.

has to be said, though, that while focusing on the individual's own salvation, Luther never lost sight of neighborly love and one's duties in society, including social, economic, and at times even political duties; just think of treatises such as *Brief Sermon on Usury* (1519) and *The Sermon on the Magnificat* (1521). However, he was hardly able to tie the spiritual liberation (justification) into the sociopolitical liberation (justice) in any programmatic manner.[314] In contemporary Lutheran theology such a search, and its resulting debate, is under way.[315]

Issues of justice, inclusion, and liberation are as deeply contextual — or "local" — as the need in itself is universal. As discussed above (chap. 10), for example, in some Asian contexts, shame (and the attempt to "save face") rather than guilt and judgment is in the forefront of culture.[316] In the African context, liberation from evil powers is a leading theme, and the doctrine of justification and deification should have something important to say to it.[317] Similarly, it is common on that continent to imagine the good life in terms of "celebrating life and harmony."[318] How is this all related to our current interpretations of the meaning of salvation? Or how would sanctification and liberation link with each other in various global settings?[319] "Contextual" issues are also pertinent in the Global North: How would the theology of justification speak to the issues of economic justice?[320]

Deification in the World's Context

A particularly exciting and fruitful task for ecumenical theology would be to collaborate in investigating and unleashing the rich potential of the Eastern doctrine of deification with regard to burning issues in ecology, creation, and society. In fact, the cosmic orientation of Eastern anthropology and the communitarian emphasis of much of Eastern theology could provide unprec-

---

314. P. S. Chung, *Martin Luther and Buddhism*, p. 115.

315. Thomsen, "On Relating Justification and Justice," p. 7. For important, similar contributions and processes among world Lutherans, see Greive, ed., *Justification in the World's Context*; Kirst, ed., *Rethinking Luther's Theology*; Bieler and Gutmann, *Embodying Grace*.

316. See the discussion by the Mennonite C. Norman Kraus, *Jesus Christ Our Lord*, pp. 205-17.

317. See Ngah, "Liberation from Evil Powers," p. 133.

318. Pöntinen, *African Theology as Liberating Wisdom*.

319. See Runyon, ed., *Sanctification and Liberation*.

320. See chap. 5 in Chung, Duchrow, and Nessan, *Liberating Lutheran Theology*.

edented theological resources for a revived theology of creation and social concern. Due to the more conservative and isolationist mentality of many of those cultures where the Eastern Church exercises its influence, so little work in this direction has been presented to the ecumenical world.

Recently it has been suggested that in the African context the traditional Eastern Orthodox idea of *theosis* may provide a challenging encounter with the African concept that has been called "vital participation."[321] The noted Methodist ecumenist M. M. Thomas of India has remarked that "there is no question about the tremendous potentiality of a positive relation between orthodox spirituality and modernity."[322] The words of Protestant theologian F. W. Norris are both challenging and daring: "Conforming to the world is not our goal. Yet by allowing our minds to be transformed, we may be prepared to contextualize the Gospel for this new wave of spirituality. To do that while still being true to Christian Tradition, we must recapture one great spiritual vision of Christian salvation which twentieth-century Protestants have largely ignored. *Koinonia,* fellowship with God, is actually deification, participation in God."[323]

Interestingly, the Anglican physicist-priest J. Polkinghorne notes that in the midst of such discussions on the relationship between modern science and theology, the claim of Orthodox theologians may be correct: deification is "the destiny of creation."[324] Similarly, another scientist-priest, Arthur Peacocke, in his seminal work *Theology for a Scientific Age,* suggests that deification is probably "more congenial to an evolutionary perspective than the traditional, often Western, language of redemption, salvation, sanctification, etc."[325]

The issues of justice, equality, and inclusivity also call for focused reflection. Here the expansion of the doctrine of justification toward a liberative force provides great potential.

---

321. Mulago, "Vital Participation," p. 157; Schönherr, "Concepts of Salvation in Christianity," p. 160.

322. M. M. Thomas's report delivered to the Central Committee in Berlin, August 1974, quoted in Schönherr, "Concepts of Salvation in Christianity," p. 162.

323. Norris, "Deification," p. 413.

324. Polkinghorne, *Reason and Reality,* p. 103.

325. Peacocke, *Theology for a Scientific Age,* p. 430 n. 22; see also, Norris, "Deification," pp. 425-28.

Justification, Justice, and Inclusivity:
The Rediscovery of Communal and Liberationist Impulses

The Anglican–Roman Catholic conversations on justification help place the traditional doctrine in a wider sociopolitical context.

> Those who are justified by grace, and who are sustained in the life of Christ through Word and Sacrament, are liberated from self-centeredness and thus empowered to act freely and live at peace with God and with one another. . . . Thus the message of the Church is not a private pietism irrelevant to contemporary society, nor can it be reduced to a political or social programme. Only a reconciled and reconciling community, faithful to its Lord, in which human divisions are being overcome, can speak with full integrity to an alienated, divided world, and so be a credible witness to God's saving action in Christ and a foretaste of God's Kingdom.[326]

Similar to Anabaptists of old and contemporary times, liberation theologians from various global contexts remind us that "God's righteousness is manifested in liberative deeds,"[327] and that, therefore, justification is about justice.[328] We see that clearly in the biblical testimonies in which "justice is grounded in God's divine nature and this conception has far-reaching implications for righteous living, righteous judging and righteous reigning. The works expected of the *tsadiq,* one who practices justice and righteousness, stem from obedience to covenant regulations and result in justice or living a good or upright life, thus preserving peace and ensuring the prosperity of the community as a whole."[329] Taking a lesson from advances in biblical studies, the Anglican feminist Kathryn Tanner seeks to establish a robust link with justification and justice "in the context of covenant relations" and faithfulness to God and fellow human beings: "[d]oing justice in this sense is how covenant faithfulness is expressed in human social relations."[330] To that task belongs the attempt to "remove the individualistic focus from justification and apply it also to systems and structures."[331]

326. "Second Anglican/Roman Catholic International Commission" (1986), #30.
327. Boesak, *Black and Reformed,* p. 8; Boff, *Liberating Grace,* pp. 151-52. I am indebted to Beilby, Eddy, and Eenderlein, "Justification in Historical Perspective," pp. 41-42.
328. See Mortensen, *Justification and Justice.*
329. Dolamo, "Justification," p. 125.
330. K. Tanner, "Justification and Justice," p. 517.
331. Deifelt, "Relevance of the Doctrine of Justification," pp. 38-39 (p. 39).

Luther's 1520 pamphlet on Christian freedom[332] has served as an inspiration for the current struggle of "rediscovering the liberating power of the central message of justification with regard to the life of the poor" and other marginalized and oppressed persons.[333] The African American civil rights leader Dr. Martin Luther King Jr.'s call for freedom famously served as a great incentive.[334] Human justice, which in itself is an expression of God's justice, must take some concrete form in the world of suffering and injustice.[335] According to Moltmann, we should affirm the principle of "the justification of life," a fitting title in his *ordo salutis*,[336] which speaks of the justifying faith as the catalyst for making the Christian support life by acting justly.

As mentioned above, the pursuit of justice, peace, and integrity of life is a deeply contextual affair. The Mexican–Puerto Rican theologian Elsa Tamez admits that her advocacy of justification does not come from an "objective" point of view but rather comes "from the reality of poverty, oppression, repression, discrimination, and struggles that large sectors of our peoples are experiencing, and from their experiences of God in that situation." From this vantage point she wonders "whether the doctrine of justification is good news for the poor and for those discriminated against on the basis of color or sex."[337] She notes that the theological debates of the past, say between "faith" and "works," sound quite meaningless and hollow in the context of killings of the innocent, poverty, injustice, and violence. No wonder she wishes "to take on that doctrine as a concrete affirmation of the life of all human beings."[338] Tamez is after the doctrine in which "God 'justifies' (makes and declares just) the human being in order to transform the unjust world that excludes, kills, and dehumanizes that same human being."[339] Even societal, corporate, and other transpersonal sins should be exposed under the standard of divine justice and integrity lest the understanding of justification by faith solely in relation to God "has principally an individual and abstract meaning." Can we speak similarly of the reconciliation among human communities, tribes, and nations?[340]

Consider also the "contextual" challenges in diverse North American

332. Luther, *The Freedom of a Christian*, in *LW* 31:343-77; *WA* 7:49-73.

333. Greive, "The Significance of Justification," p. 13.

334. King, *Why We Can't Wait*, p. 92.

335. Moltmann, *Spirit of Life*, pp. 115-16; so also, Altmann, *Luther and Liberation*, p. 37.

336. Chap. 6 in Moltmann, *The Spirit of Life*.

337. Tamez, *The Amnesty of Grace*, p. 13.

338. Tamez, *The Amnesty of Grace*, p. 14.

339. Tamez, *The Amnesty of Grace*, p. 14.

340. Tamez, *The Amnesty of Grace*, pp. 19-25 (p. 24).

contexts: while deeply indebted to African heritage, salvation in African *American* Christianity is quite differently intuited in the context of the racism and marginalization of the United States.[341] Similarly, the experiences of liberation in various Asian *American* communities are unique, unlike those of diverse Asian ones. The Japanese American Sang Hyun Lee speaks of "justification of the marginalized," which has to do with people stuck between two (or more) cultures. While he appreciates the traditional doctrine of justification, he also believes it must be linked with experiences of liminality. "In the marginalized Asian Americans' context, justification means acceptance, belonging, recognition, and inclusion."[342] It is noteworthy that in *Mañana: Christian Theology from a Hispanic Perspective,* by the *Cuban* American Justo L. Gonzáles, the term "justification by faith" does not even appear once![343]

Justification, Deification, and Holiness among Religions

The final element in our discussion of the Christian doctrine of justification, deification, and sanctification is the teachings and insights of other religions. As with all other topics in this constructive project, Christian soteriology has to be constantly tested against and put in relation to living faith traditions.

In presenting in outline form the broad "salvific" visions of Judaism, Islam, Buddhism, and Hinduism (chap. 8), we have also related to those teachings all the main *ordo salutis* topics. The current chapter's topics do not easily yield to interfaith comparisons. Justification/deification/holiness *sola fide* and *sola gratia,* based on the trinitarian work of reconciliation in Jesus Christ, is the distinctively Christian vision of salvation and liberation. Of course, this is not to say that no parallels whatsoever exist — the most obvious one (as exceptional as it may be in itself) is the importance of "faith" (trust) and "grace" in Pure Land Buddhism or forms of piety in (deeply) theistic *bhakti* traditions of Hinduism, as discussed above. Instead, what is argued here is that these kinds of "exceptional" (or at least not mainstream) orientations should be put in perspective against the wider "theological" framework of each living faith. Where parallels exist among religions on topics such as conversion, forgiveness, and healing, they have to be acknowledged and carefully compared.

341. See Evans, *We Have Been Believers,* pp. 16-18.

342. S. H. Lee, *From a Liminal Place,* pp. 101-4 (p. 101). The *Korean* American Andrew Sung Park is more critical of the traditional formulation and calls for a radical revision of the meaning of justification: *From Hurt to Healing,* pp. 4-7, 105-6.

343. The index includes a few occurrences of "justification" used with another meaning.

Where alleged parallels are only superficial or not representative of the whole faith tradition, they should not be given undue attention. As curious as it may sound, in a project called "Explorations in Lutheran Perspectives on People of Other Faiths,"[344] worked on by globally representative teams of Lutheran theologians, the term "justification by faith" (unless used to describe generally Lutheran soteriology) is virtually absent in all comparative exercises (whereas other significant parallels, similar to this project, were discerned). Let me be more specific and develop this claim — that the topic of this chapter is the uniquely Christian take on salvation — in more detail with regard to each of the four dialogue partners.

Although the Jewish scriptural tradition knows the idea of justification by faith, its meaning differs vastly from Christian teaching because Christian theology claims that even the salvation of Abraham (Gen. 15:6), the father of faith, is by virtue of the Messiah having come, Jesus the Christ. Israel's faith categorically rejects all those claims (as discussed in detail in *Christ and Reconciliation*, chaps. 10 and 15). Instead, the Jewish vision of redemption and deliverance is focused on the following of Torah; unlike the Christian vision, its eschatological dimension is marginal, with its focus on this-worldly renewal with the coming of the yet-awaited Messiah of Israel. No need to mention that to Jewish intuitions, the idea of salvation by faith being contingent on the sacrificial death of the innocent Messiah borders on blasphemy.

Salvation in Islam is about submission to Allah and has little to do with the Christian idea of justification by faith; the only role of "faith" in Islam has to do with the knowledge of the Qur'anic (and later, the Prophet's traditional) teachings and confidence in the truth of Islam. Furthermore, a significant difference between Christian and Islamic traditions is that whereas in the former, forgiveness "costs" God (and hence, requires a sacrifice or satisfaction or similar), in Islam God just forgives, without any sacrifice.[345] While "salvation" in Islam is ultimately dependent on Allah, the idea of an "undeserved" gracious gift is foreign to that sister tradition. Behind the radical difference from Christian soteriology of both Abrahamic faiths is also the vastly different view of the human condition.

Compared to Asiatic traditions, the Christian claim of salvation by faith in Jesus Christ seems even stranger and more meaningless. Given the significant differences both between the Buddhist and Hindu religions and among

---

344. Martinson, "Explorations in Lutheran Perspectives on People of Other Faiths."

345. For this insight, I am indebted to the British Islamicist David Marshall of Duke University.

various "denominations" within each, this much can be said in broad terms: neither the Hindu nor the Buddhist diagnosis of the human condition based on "ignorance" due to the karmic cycle of endless births has any real use for the Christian diagnosis of "inherited" sinfulness and lostness because of accountability to God. Hence, the means of "salvation" differ greatly from the gospel of grace and are ultimately a matter of human effort, as much as "grace" and divine favor may be of help in theistic, particularly devotionally oriented (folk), expressions of both traditions.[346]

In sum: a truthful and authentic interfaith engagement is not helped but rather obscured by artificially worked-out convergences and alleged similarities. In contrast, genuine hospitality calls for a discernment of differences as much as similarities and the honoring of the other.

What about deification? Wouldn't that conception of salvation fare better among religions, particularly those of Asiatic origin? Perhaps — and some tentative comments have been made to that effect above. Certainly, the generic idea of union with the Divine is not foreign to any Asiatic theistic faith tradition, whereas it easily becomes a stumbling block to both Abrahamic partners' strict monotheistic insistence. Although, again, the wider religious framework in Christianity puts deification (and union) in a radically different framework from Asiatic visions of oneness, a significant task for ecumenical and interfaith communities would be to pursue further the potential of convergences.

Although holiness and sanctity are common themes among religions, the commonality with the Christian theology of sanctification in general and particularly as developed in this project, that is, as an integral part of justification/*theosis,* is merely formal and materially not very useful for comparison. While human effort is acknowledged in Christianity (and other theistic faiths also acknowledge the divine influence), at its root the Christian notion of sanctification is totally God-driven and part of the larger "package" of salvation, without which it only stays as a generic religious ideal. The next chapter, on the two interrelated topics of healing/restoration and empowerment/gifting — themes that ironically have been almost totally ignored in Christian presentations of *ordo salutis* — provides more commonalities with the four other living faith traditions.

346. See further, Sumithra, "Justification by Faith," p. 216.

12. Healing, Restoration, and Empowerment

Introduction: The Neglect of Theologies of Healing and Empowerment in Soteriology

The Omission of the Categories of Healing and Empowerment in Systematic Theology

More than with any other theological topic, a deep irony and profound omission come to the surface when we speak of healing, restoration, and empowerment. The dilemma is simply this: although no major Christian tradition at any historical period has denied the healing and empowering capacity of the Creator God, no major doctrinal/systematic presentation has cared to include the topic of healing in the *ordo salutis*. With the exception of an important discussion of healings, exorcisms, and charismatic effects in the revisionist *ordo salutis* of Moltmann's *Spirit of Life* (chap. 9), one looks in vain for that category in any noteworthy doctrinal manuals, even the most recent ones.[1]

This state of affairs is even more ironic and deplorable because Jesus of Nazareth was an itinerant healer and exorcist, and Christian soteriologies claim to present a "full gospel" of the salvific gifts wrought by Jesus the Savior. But what justification is there to pick and choose which aspects of salvation to accept and which to reject? Why are the categories of faith, forgiveness of sins, sanctification, and, say, justification (of which Jesus spoke precious little) es-

---

1. For a distinctively Pentecostal discussion, see Yong, *The Spirit Poured Out on All Flesh*, chap. 2.

sential aspects of Jesus' work of salvation but healings, exorcisms, charismatic endowments, and, say, social criticism, love for the poor and marginalized, and rejection of human-made religious establishments (topics on which Jesus did speak much!) do not belong to doctrinal theology? Rightly, N. T. Wright argues that the miraculous acts are such an integral part of the story and ministry of Jesus that there "is no dividing line, enabling us to bracket off different aspects, isolating the mighty works" from the rest of his ministry.[2]

The Centrality of Healing and Empowerment in Christian Life — and Beyond

It is also quite ironic that whereas current systematic theology displays a wide rediscovery of the NT and patristic contributions to the theology of salvation, the earliest theologians' pronounced interest in healings and exorcisms is routinely set aside! Particularly in the book of Acts, the practice of exorcism and casting out devils continued along with healings and other miraculous actions as an integral part of the church's regular activity of prayer, liturgy, sacraments, and missionary outreach (5:16; 8:7; 13:6-12; 16:18, among others).[3]

One indication of the centrality of the theme of healing for the church is the great diversity in ways it has been approached. The Canadian Pentecostal church historian Ronald Kydd's outline of various complementary "models" of healing through the centuries illustrates this pluriformity. Among the various models are the following:

- In the "confrontational" model, the emphasis is on liberty and defeat of powers of evil, as represented by Irenaeus, Tertullian, Origen, and others. In later times, the Reformed theologian J. C. Blumhardt's healing ministry in nineteenth-century Germany and the ministry of the charismatic American John Wimber echo this approach.
- The "intercessory" model calls upon the saints to intervene on behalf of the sick and suffering. This approach is less evident in Protestantism but widespread throughout Orthodox and Catholic traditions. Its roots also go deep into the apocryphal literature of the NT times.
- Closely related is the "reliquarial" model in which relics, whether corporeal (remains of bodies), real (objects the saints used during their lives), or representative (such as tombs or covers of tombs), are believed

---

2. N. T. Wright, *Jesus and the Victory of God*, p. 189.
3. Porterfield, *Healing in the History of Christianity*, p. 3; so also, M. Kelsey, *Healing and Christianity*.

to have curative powers. A few references in the NT to healing handker-chiefs and aprons touched by the apostles belong to this category. The Cappadocians and other Greek Fathers of the Christian East have been more favorable to this model. The miracles at Saint Medard attributed to the remains of the eighteenth-century Frenchman François de Paris represent the Western version.

- The "incubational" model is related to the long history of establishing sanitariums, hospitals, and other "healing rooms" for patients for a longer period of restoration.[4]

With all the emphasis on various types of divine healing, beginning from early Christianity, medical sciences and hospitals have been dear to Christian tradition. Indeed, the origins of the hospital institution as we have it today are greatly indebted to the Christian church.[5]

Focusing on the contemporary scene, the Czech Reformed theologian Pavel Hejzler has discerned "two paradigms for divine healing." The "healing evangelists" expect an instantaneous recovery to normally take place, and often the charismatically endowed healer is the instrument. The "pastoral healers" equally believe in a rapid restoration of health, but they are open to both the gradual and the instantaneous work of God; the healer's role is less pronounced and may also include a group of Christians over a period of time.[6]

In some Christian traditions, a predominantly sacramentally oriented approach to healing is in the forefront, particularly in Eastern Orthodoxy, Roman Catholicism, and Anglicanism;[7] in others the charismatic gifts and hope for instantaneous healing are more typical, as in Pentecostal/charismatic movements.[8] With the global expansion of Christianity beginning in the early twentieth century to the Global South, healing practices, approaches, and theological interpretations are intensifying.[9]

---

4. Kydd, *Healing through the Centuries.*

5. Porterfield, *Healing in the History of Christianity,* pp. 51-53; for a fuller discussion, see T. Miller, *Birth of the Hospital;* Avalos, *Health Care and the Rise of Christianity.*

6. The first category is represented by the Pentecostals/charismatics Fred F. Bosworth and Kenneth E. Hagin; the latter by the Episcopalian Agnes Sanford and the Roman Catholic Francis MacNutt. Hejzlar, *Two Paradigms for Divine Healing.*

7. For the importance of sacraments to healing, see the Orthodox theologian George Mathew Nalunnakkal, "Come Holy Spirit, Heal and Reconcile," p. 18.

8. Alexander, *Pentecostal Healing.*

9. See further, Porterfield, *Healing in the History of Christianity,* chap. 5; Jenkins, *New Faces of Christianity,* chap. 5 (including also exorcisms).

The importance of healing and restoration to theology — as well as to religion[10] — is attested not only by their centrality in the life of the church, but also by the wide interest in the topics in secular interdisciplinary studies in psychology, sociology, and various health sciences,[11] as well as in the media and popular press — let alone in new religious movements.

Before moving into a systematic theological construction of a contemporary theology of healing, we must address the most pertinent challenge from the naturalistic epistemology of the contemporary scientific worldview that was also adopted by much of post-Enlightenment theology, namely, the rejection of the category of the miraculous (or "supernatural"). Somewhat ironically, there is also a related, though substantially very different, challenge to the discussion of healings and exorcisms coming from theological tradition. It is often called cessationism, a claim by some Christian traditions that miracles have come to an end in the postbiblical church and therefore any talk about, and thus the actuality of, healings, exorcisms, and charismatic gifts is deeply suspicious, if not outright forbidden.

The Category of the Miracles and the Claims to Cessationism

Whereas pre-Enlightenment theology took miraculous acts as proof of the divinity of Jesus of Nazareth, the Enlightenment epistemology rejected their factual and historical nature. At its best, classical liberalism took the miracles as "myths" elicited by the powerful encounter with Jesus; even if the miracles never happened, they were still meaningful in pointing to the influence of Jesus on his followers. Both of these paradigms fail. Unlike the precritical interpretation, the key NT passages that speak of incarnation and divinity do not refer to miracles. And unlike the reductionistic modernist rejection of the miraculous, a contemporary epistemology and worldview allow us to accept the possibility of the miraculous.

Behind the modern rejection of miracles is a specific understanding of what makes the miracle a "violation" of nature's laws.[12] This calls for clarification: because of the link of the term "miracle" with the "supernatural," we need to be reminded of the radical changes in the understanding of that term. The

---

10. See Swinton, "From Health to Shalom," pp. 219-41.

11. Koenig, *Is Religion Good for Your Health?*

12. For the classic definition of David Hume, see *An Enquiry concerning Human Understanding*, p. 58.

term "miracle" is foreign to the worldview of the NT. Instead, the terms used in the NT include "*paradoxa,* things one would not normally expect; *dunameis,* displays of power or authority; and *terata* or *semeia,* signs or portents." The only word used in the Gospels that comes close to the Western term "miracle" is *thaumasia,* "marvels." The critical difference between the biblical worldview and our term "miracle" is that in the Bible there is no overtone of invasion from another world; rather, the mighty deeds happen "*within* what we could call the 'natural' world."[13] The same mind-set still prevailed in early theology, in which the supernatural-natural distinction did not yet exist in any modern sense as denoting two distinct realms of reality, that of God and that of sciences; rather, all of reality was governed by God.[14]

Only in the thirteenth century did the category of "supernatural" emerge as something "going beyond" *(super)* nature.[15] But even then, it did not mean going *against* nature.[16] What makes a miracle miraculous is not that it is against nature, but that "it surpasses the faculty of nature"[17] and hence is God's work. Only in later tradition was the Thomistic distinction between the natural and the supernatural rendered in a way familiar to modern people — even though, ironically, it was done first to defend the supremacy of God (in medieval Scholasticism).[18] Diametrically opposed to that view, modernity's epistemology divorced the supernatural from God and thus blocked the way for miraculous interventions altogether. In that "new world," science explained world processes.[19]

Since in part 1 (chap. 3) the prevailing naturalist paradigm of contemporary natural sciences was subjected to critique, there is no need to repeat that discussion here.[20] It suffices to be reminded of the final conclusion there: the plural paradigm of pneumatology allows for the Non-Interventionist Objective Divine Action (NIODA) based on the "openness" of the cosmos permeated through and through by the Creator God through the divine Spirit. As a result, there are no compelling scientific, philosophical, or theological reasons to write off the possibility of miracles, whether healings or exorcisms or similar. More challenging and interesting than the blunt naturalist rejection

---

13. N. T. Wright, *Jesus and the Victory of God,* p. 188, emphasis in original.

14. Augustine, *Literal Meaning of Genesis* 6.13.24; *City of God* 21.8; Aquinas, *ST* 1.105.6.

15. See Aquinas, *ST* 3a.13.2.

16. H. Schwarz, *Creation,* p. 215, with reference to Aquinas, *ST* 1.105.5.

17. Aquinas, *ST* 1.105.7.

18. God alone is capable of doing miracles strictly speaking; Aquinas, *ST* 1.110.4.

19. H. Schwarz, *Creation,* pp. 215-16.

20. For a detailed discussion, see chaps. 2 and 7 of *Creation and Humanity.*

of all miracles is the highly nuanced naturalistic paradigm in a deeply theistic and theological form as represented by the late British chemist-priest Arthur Peacocke. Because his proposal was also engaged and corrected earlier, there is no need to repeat that discussion either, but only to remember the supreme importance of Christ's resurrection as a "new work" of God that points to "a transformation of the present nature *beyond* what emergence refers to."[21] Rather than going against nature, it transcends and lifts up the natural. It points to the eschatological consummation when, according to the biblical promises, creation "will be set free from its bondage to decay" (Rom. 8:21). In resurrection, even death will be defeated (1 Cor. 15:55). Healings and restoration anticipate that fulfillment.[22]

In this light, the so-called cessationist rejection of miracles has to be deemed a profoundly mistaken idea. Cessationism is deeply embedded in some Christian traditions, particularly traditional Protestantism and current conservative Reformed churches; its roots, however, go back to patristic theology, particularly Augustine (although before the Reformation, cessationism rarely was a formulated, strict doctrinal standpoint).[23] Unlike the post-Enlightenment "naturalist" rejection of miracles[24] (which standpoint was adopted quite naively by modern biblical scholarship),[25] theological cessationism affirms the presence and reality of miracles in the biblical world and until the time of the closing of the Christian canon by the end of the fourth century; after that, the argument goes, they came to an end. The reason is simply this: once the written Word of God (the Bible) came to function as the norming norm, no spiritual experiences, even the charismatic ones that before that were often taken as divine confirmations, were needed. There are two forms of theological cessationism, which I have named the "soft" and the "hard-core" views. Whereas the former does not categorically reject the possibility of miraculous events now, they are made nonexistent, practically

---

21. R. Russell, *Cosmology*, p. 37, emphasis in original.

22. See further, Ward, "Divine Action in an Emergent Cosmos," p. 297; Polkinghorne, *Quarks, Chaos, and Christianity*, chap. 6.

23. Ruthven, *On the Cessation of the Charismata*, pp. 24-40; see also, Hejzlar, *Two Paradigms for Divine Healing*, pp. 48-51. For the reasons why Catholic tradition has been less prone to cessationism, see MacNutt, *Healing*, chap. 1. For the "natural" place of healings and other miracles in Eastern Orthodox (and Pentecostal/charismatic) traditions, see Nalunnakkal, "Come Holy Spirit, Heal and Reconcile," p. 18 particularly.

24. Cf. Mullin, *Miracles and the Modern Religious Imagination*.

25. Classically the modernist rejection of miracles was formulated by Bultmann, *New Testament and Mythology*, p. 4.

speaking, not only because they are not needed but also because they seem not to take place anymore. The "hard-core" version categorically denies the existence of all miraculous events after the apostolic era and judges all claims to their existence as counterfeits, as argued in the fundamentalist Reformed theologian B. B. Warfield's classic *The Counterfeit Miracles* (1918).[26] What is highly ironic about cessationism is that it boasts no biblical reasons to support it, yet its advocates are fundamentalist scriptural "inerrantists." Clearly, the NT data speaks against any idea of a certain historical time bringing to an end charismatic gifts; only at the eschaton will a new "world order" be ushered in.[27]

That said, we also have to resist the call by some Christians to return to the idyllic pre-Enlightenment mind-set and so, allegedly, be more receptive to healings, exorcisms, and other miracles. That would be a profoundly mistaken tactic, as it would make a certain cultural epoch (pre-Enlightenment times) a precondition for experiencing fullness of salvation. It would also cut off bridges with the rest of the modern world. A related common claim is that Christians in certain global locations, particularly in Africa, are by default more open to the miraculous. This template is the target of the fierce criticism of David Tonghou Ngong of Cameroon of what he names an African "endorsement pneumatological soteriology." In that view, African traditional religions as the backdrop of African indigenous Christianity, in the form of a spiritualized cosmology, are set over against the Western culture, particularly its rationality and use of critical reasoning; furthermore, emphasis is laid one-sidedly on materialistic and health concerns.[28] While I agree with the general content of Ngong's critique, I need to balance and reorient it. He is too harsh and quite one-sided toward the whole tradition of the African indigenous theological paradigm. He also elevates post-Enlightenment Western critical rationality to a higher level than do many late modern people in the Global North! Finally, his description of the Pentecostal/charismatic tradition's view of healings, exorcisms, and other miraculous events is hopelessly unnuanced, almost a caricature.[29]

Now that we have defeated both naturalist and theological forms of ces-

---

26. Warfield, *The Counterfeit Miracles*. The most recent highly aggressive fundamentalist-Reformed cessationist campaign in the USA is the "Strange Fire" movement; see http://www.monergism.com/thethreshold/sdg/warfield/warfield_counterfeit.html (8/20/2014).

27. See Blue, *Authority to Heal*, p. 99; Hejzlar, *Two Paradigms for Divine Healing*, chap. 2.

28. Ngong, *The Holy Spirit and Salvation;* chap. 2 contains the critique, and chap. 5, his own constructive proposal.

29. See Attanasi, "Introduction," pp. 1-5; Yong, "Typology of Prosperity Theology," pp. 15-34.

sationism, let us attempt a constructive theology of restoration, healing, and charismatic endowment for the sake of our pluralistic world.

Toward a Constructive Theology of Healing and Restoration — and Suffering

The Theological Meaning of Jesus' Healings and Exorcisms

Healings feature prominently in the OT. This is in keeping with the general mind-set of the ancient world, which linked closely healing and religion. God, active in all affairs of the world, was naturally looked upon as the agent of healing.[30] Furthermore, because of Israel's uncompromising monotheism, she received both healing and suffering from Yahweh.[31] In that respect, Jesus' prominent healing and exorcism ministry — as well as willingness to suffer himself — is in keeping with the Jewish faith.[32]

All four Gospels narrate numerous healings and miraculous cures,[33] and the Synoptic Gospels add to the picture acts of deliverance and exorcisms.[34] Indeed, "[a]mong all the activities ascribed to Jesus in the New Testament gospels, exorcism and healing are among the most prominent."[35] Among the churches of the Global South, the connection between healings and exorcisms continues.[36]

Why, then, does later doctrinal tradition almost totally miss the theological significance of healings, exorcisms, and empowerment? As discussed in *Christ and Reconciliation* (chap. 2), a glaring omission of traditional systematic theologies and Christologies is the theological significance of Jesus' earthly ministry and life. Totally unlike the Gospel writers of the NT, to whom the earthly ministry of Jesus, in all its aspects, was the focus, theological tradition

30. Gaiser, *Healing in the Bible,* pp. 9-10; for a fine exegetical-theological study of healing in the OT, see chaps. 2–10.

31. Gaiser, *Healing in the Bible,* p. 26; M. L. Brown, *Israel's Divine Healer.*

32. See further, Feldman, *Health and Medicine in the Jewish Tradition,* pp. 15-21.

33. A reliable nontechnical discussion is Remus, *Jesus as Healer.* For the historical reliability of the miracle tradition of the NT, the earliest strata, see Dunn, *Jesus and the Spirit,* p. 70; N. T. Wright, *Jesus and the Victory of God,* p. 188.

34. See S. L. Davies, *Jesus the Healer.* Jesus' ministry as exorcist "belongs to the base-rock historicity of the gospels"; Dunn, *Jesus and the Spirit,* p. 44.

35. Porterfield, *Healing in the History of Christianity,* p. 21. See also, Grundmann, "Inviting the Spirit to Fight the Spirits?" pp. 51-73.

36. See further, Asamoah-Gyadu, "Mission to 'Set the Captives Free.'"

focused its energies merely on the suffering, cross, and resurrection.[37] With the neglect of Jesus' earthly ministry, the "therapeutic relevance of Christology" was lost.[38]

Another limitation of traditional Christologies that has direct bearing on the lack of interest in healing, exorcism, and empowerment has to do with the eclipse of Spirit Christologies at the expense of Logos Christologies.[39] In NT-based Spirit Christologies, Jesus' earthly life with cures, exorcisms, and other forms of liberation plays a prominent role.[40] Intuitively, Pentecostal theology, with its focus on different roles of Jesus as Savior, Sanctifier, Healer, Baptizer-with-the-Spirit, and the Soon-Coming Eschatological King in the power of the Spirit, has also helped highlight the then and current ministry of Jesus.[41]

According to the NT testimonies, Jesus used various "methods," from touch,[42] to laying on of hands,[43] to healing from a distance, to curious things such as use of saliva (Mark 7:33; 8:23; John 9:6). No doubt, there are similarities to shamanic healing techniques, widely known in ancient cultures — and in those of today's Global South. What are we to think of them? On the one hand, the use of then-common techniques is a given; what else would one expect in a culture of the times? On the other hand, "God's willingness to use first-century methods in the healing ministry of Jesus hardly prescribes these forever as the sole signs of divine healing."[44]

The healing ministry of Jesus is a robust statement about the all-inclusive nature of God's salvation; it includes the physical and emotional as well as the spiritual.[45] Whatever other ends the healings and exorcisms served in Jesus' ministry, they were signs of profound sympathy, cosuffering (Matt. 14:14). At the same time, other miracles, particularly feeding multitudes and stilling a storm, besides being tangible ways of meeting human needs, also carry overtones of covenant renewal and exodus.[46]

---

37. Moltmann, *Way of Jesus Christ,* p. 150. For an extended discussion of the theological significance of Jesus' earthly ministry, see *Christ and Reconciliation,* chap. 2; for healings and exorcisms, see pp. 63-66 particularly.

38. Moltmann, *Way of Jesus Christ,* p. 44.

39. For a detailed discussion of Spirit Christology, see chap. 8 in *Christ and Reconciliation.*

40. Moltmann, *Way of Jesus Christ,* p. 73.

41. See further, Alfaro, *Divino Compañero,* pp. 29-46.

42. On the theological meaning of touch in healings, see Gaiser, *Healing in the Bible,* pp. 166-71.

43. On the laying on of hands, see Gaiser, *Healing in the Bible,* pp. 173-75.

44. Gaiser, *Healing in the Bible,* pp. 152-55 (p. 154).

45. See further, Moltmann, *Way of Jesus Christ,* p. 104.

46. N. T. Wright, *Jesus and the Victory of God,* p. 193.

Salvation as Healing: A Vision of a Holistic Soteriology

There is a marked difference between the content of preaching in the early church and in later Christian church life. The gospel message in the book of Acts, based on Christ's life, cross, resurrection, ascension, and subsequent Pentecostal pouring out of the Spirit, integrally linked forgiveness of sin ("salvation") with healing and deliverance (Acts 3:12-16; 4:8-12, among others). As the late Scottish Reformed theologian T. F. Torrance put it, for the early church the forgiveness and healing[47] meant nothing less than the manifestation of the "full reality in the healing and creative work of God upon the whole man," effected as a result of resurrection.[48]

Importantly, the Eastern Orthodox bishop George M. Nalunnakkal of India says that not only is "the theme of healing . . . central to the theology, and particularly the soteriology, of almost all churches," but it is so central that "[i]n Orthodox theology, 'healing' is almost a synonym for 'salvation.'"[49] With the spread of Christianity to the Global South, the significance of a holistic view of salvation in Christian theology has been rediscovered. For masses of Christians in the Global South, salvation and healing belong integrally together. Among the several titles appropriate for Jesus Christ in the African culture is Healer.[50] A parallel can be found between the figure of Jesus of the Gospels as the itinerant healer and the traditional African medicine man. Both practice a holistic form of healing on the physical, mental, and social levels, even on the environmental level.[51] Pentecostalism and later charismatic movements similarly focus on Jesus Christ as the healer. This is manifested particularly in what is named the "Pentecostalization" of African Christianity, with healing and exorcisms as integral ministries of various churches' lives.[52]

A biblically based way of expressing the vision of a holistic, all-encompassing salvation is the OT term "shalom." In its range of uses, "shalom" includes reconciliation and well-being in all its aspects, including physical health and prosperity.[53] Similarly in the Global South, particularly in Africa,

---

47. For the integral relationship between the two, see McNeill, *History of the Cure of Souls*.

48. T. Torrance, *Space, Time, and Resurrection*, p. 62.

49. Nalunnakkal, "Come Holy Spirit, Heal and Reconcile," pp. 17-18.

50. See Tennent, *Theology in the Context of World Christianity*, pp. 109-22.

51. See further, Kole, "Jesus as Healer?" pp. 128-50; Bujo, *African Theology in Its Social Context*, p. 79.

52. See further, Anderson, "The Gospel and Culture," pp. 220-30.

53. P. Yoder, *Shalom*, p. 11; for details, see Westermann, "Peace (Shalom) in the Old Testament," pp. 16-48.

health means not only lack of sickness but also well-being in a holistic sense. Sickness is not primarily a result of physical symptoms but is the result of deeply spiritual causes. As was widely argued in part 2 of *Christ and Reconciliation*, Christian theology of atonement and reconciliation not only has to do with "spiritual" salvation of individuals but also encompasses holistic healing in personal and communal dimensions and sociopolitical issues such as equality, peace, and ecological balance.

In the biblical understanding, shalom brings "not only physical health but [also] renewed membership in the people of YHWH."[54] Jesus' healing bodily contact with people considered "untouchable," such as the woman with bleeding (Mark 5:24-34), meant that "Jesus challenged the ideology that women's bodies were polluted by refusing to consider that he became unclean by touching her."[55] Thereby Jesus fought dehumanization by placing human need above sacred traditions such as Sabbath purity (Mark 2:23–3:6). Blind Bartimaeus, whom the crowds silenced, was given voice and healed by Jesus (Mark 10:46-52). A woman with a flow of blood and no financial resources touched Jesus and subsequently "told him the whole truth" (Mark 5:33).[56]

Ultimately, healing and deliverance have an eschatological perspective, as they point to the coming of the kingdom of God: "But if it is by the Spirit of God that I cast out demons, then the kingdom of God has come upon you" (Matt. 12:28). As eschatological signs, the restoration and renewal taking place in healings, deliverances, and other mighty works refer to the expectation of the eventual fulfillment of divine promises of shalom.[57] Raising people from the dead was a profound sign of the victory over death. At the same time, these "signs" pointed to the final defeat of death and decay.

Atonement, Faith, and Healing:
A Need for Clarification and Theological Critique

Christian theology affirms the close link between the atonement and healing based on OT testimonies (Isa. 53:4-5) and their creative use in the NT (Matt. 8:17; 1 Pet. 2:24). The connection between healing and atonement is further accentuated by the close link both in the OT and in the NT between healing and

---

54. N. T. Wright, *Jesus and the Victory of God*, p. 192.

55. Levison and Pope-Levison, "Christology," p. 178.

56. Pope-Levison and Levison, *Jesus in Global Contexts*, p. 35. For the Korean *minjung* perspective, see Ahn, "Jesus and the People (Minjung)," pp. 163-72.

57. See also Pannenberg, *ST* 2:333-34.

salvation/forgiveness of sins (Pss. 30:3-6; 41:3-4; 2 Chron. 7:14). With the rise of the modern Wesleyan Holiness and Higher Christian Life (Keswick) healing movements, including the Christian and Missionary Alliance, the doctrine of "healing in atonement" was established.[58] It was picked up and radicalized among some twentieth-century "healing evangelists." They argue vocally that as surely as there is atonement for sin, there is also healing by virtue of the cross. In other words, there is a universal provision of healing for all. On the other end of the spectrum are traditional theologies that spiritualize the link between atonement (forgiveness) and healing.[59]

But how exactly are the two — atonement and healing — linked theologically?[60] It is instructive to see how Matthew (8:17) applies Isaiah 53:4-5 to Jesus' healing ministry: "He took our infirmities and bore our diseases." There is no reference to the cross here. And even if later Christian theology makes the connection to the cross, there is no justification to do so in the manner that the technical contemporary phrase "healing in the atonement" claims.[61] Even less can that formula be supported in the context of 1 Peter's use of Isaiah's passage. Both in the context of the epistle as a whole and in the immediate context, it appears that Jesus' suffering provides encouragement for Christians to follow Jesus in suffering. Whereas in Matthew the link to (physical) healings is clearly presented, in Peter that connection is missing altogether. Thus, the first conclusion is that the link between healing and atonement can be affirmed only at a general level, that is, in light of Christian salvation stemming from the atoning and reconciling work of Christ. But there is nothing "causal" or automatic there.

Second, like salvation in general, healing "now" is a foretaste of the coming eschatological fulfillment based on the reconciling work of the triune God. Living as we are now between the "already" of the coming of the kingdom and the "not yet" of its consummation, healings serve as signs affirming for us the final victory. The raising of Lazarus makes the point succinctly: having been resuscitated, he died again because the defeating of death and decay was not yet finalized.

58. See, e.g., Simpson, *The Gospel of Healing*, p. 300; for details, see Hejzlar, *Two Paradigms for Divine Healing*, pp. 80-81.

59. For representative passages in Calvin's comments on Isa. 53 and Matt. 8:16-17, see Hejzlar, *Two Paradigms for Divine Healing*, pp. 81-85.

60. Highly useful discussions can be found in Bokovay, "Relationship of Physical Healing to the Atonement"; Reichenbach, "Healing View" (which includes informative responses by three other contributors).

61. A useful discussion is in Gaiser, *Healing in the Bible,* chap. 17.

Third, I find useful Moltmann's observation that the reference to Isaiah's prophecy of suffering can be interpreted to mean that Jesus' "power to heal is the power of his suffering," and that is its "atoning representation."[62] That is to say that in healings and deliverances, Jesus participated in our suffering. He showed compassion and stooped to our level. This points to the final conclusion: it is not only one aspect of Jesus' life, the cross, but the whole history of Jesus Christ that saves, heals, and gives hope.

What about healing and faith? There are healing evangelists and others who not only make faith the necessary condition for the healing to take place but have also devised a "faith formula" — that is, a certain type of faith automatically, without exception, leads to healing and deliverance.[63] They speak of faith in terms of "claiming" God's promises and assign to "positive confession" almost a magical power. Faith in that case is like a signed check to be redeemed![64] Rightly, the Catholic "pastoral healer" MacNutt disagrees with this "absolutist theory."[65] The faith formula leads to preoccupation with one's own faith rather than recognition of divine power and mercy. It also brings about anxiety and "turns grace into law as people struggle to produce the requisite."[66] This criticism is not to undermine the importance Jesus placed on faith but rather to put it in a proper perspective.[67] While the faith formula must be rejected as a theologically mistaken idea and pastorally disastrous technique,[68] systematic reflection is needed for a proper understanding of the relation between faith and healing — another task unfortunately ignored by mainstream theologians.

The Gospels show an integral link between faith and healing. Jesus seemed to attribute some healings to faith (Mark 1:40-44; 5:25-34; 10:46-52; Matt. 8:2-4; 9:20-22; 20:29-34; Luke 17:11-19). At times Jesus rebuked people for lack of faith, with the obvious implication that a stronger faith would have made a difference (Matt. 14:31; 17:20; 21:21). A closer look at the Gospels' data

---

62. Moltmann, *The Source of Life*, pp. 64-65, cited in Gaiser, *Healing in the Bible*, p. 228.

63. For a detailed exposition of the faith teaching of Bosworth, Hagin, and Sanford, see Hejzlar, *Two Paradigms for Divine Healing*, pp. 97-107.

64. See further, Blue, *Authority to Heal*, p. 47 (who does not endorse this view); see chap. 3 for a thoughtful critique of the "faith formula."

65. MacNutt, *Healing*, p. 93.

66. As paraphrased by Hejzlar, *Two Paradigms for Divine Healing*, p. 107; the quotation from MacNutt, *Healing*, p. 112.

67. For details of MacNutt's seasoned view, see Hejzlar, *Two Paradigms for Divine Healing*, pp. 107-8.

68. So also, Perriman, ed., *Faith, Health, and Prosperity*; McConnell, *A Different Gospel*; Fee, *Disease of the Health and Wealth Gospels*.

(alone), however, yields a more complex and elusive link between the two. A number of healing incidents make no mention of faith (Mark 3:1-5; 7:32-35; Matt. 8:5-13; 15:21-28; Luke 4:38-39; 7:12-15; 22:50-51; John 9:1-7). While in many instances the healed person's faith plays a role, there are also incidents in which the faith of other involved persons is commended; a prime example is the paralyzed man brought to Jesus by his friends (Mark 2:1-12; Matt. 9:1-8; Luke 5:17-26; for other examples, see Mark 5:35-43; Matt. 8:5-13; John 4:46-53). Furthermore, at times faith seemed to precede healing (Mark 2:4; 5:36; Matt. 8:10; 14:31; Luke 7:50), and at other times, faith emerged as a result of healing (Matt. 11:4; Luke 24:13-35; John 12:37).[69]

Several theological conclusions follow from this discussion.[70] First, there is no "causal" relationship between the work of God and human response (faith). God's works are based on grace and compassion. Hence, while faith and healing are related in some way, the most that can be said is that the relationship is ambiguous and cannot be made into a formula. Second, when speaking of faith in relation to healing, we also have to insist on hope (for God's continuing care amidst sickness and suffering) and love (for those who were not healed — and those who were and will in the future face other kinds of calamities).[71] We have to remember that "God's power is as near to us in sickness and in death as it is in healing."[72] Third, although there is no direct link between faith and healing, prayer for healing matters. Christians who hope for the divine touch of healing pray for divine "intervention." Again, while healing may also happen without prayer, the biblical testimonies clearly encourage praying. As the American Lutheran OT scholar Frederick J. Gaiser succinctly puts it: "God does not become a God of love and healing because of our prayer. But our prayer opens us to the God of love, who desires our healing."[73]

Fourth, healing can be experienced at personal and communal levels in a variety of ways.[74] Healing can be focused on a "healing evangelist" or "pastoral healer" paradigm; it can be instantaneous or gradual; it may be attributed mainly to prayer and spirituality or to medical expertise; it may be had in a healing meeting or at a sacramental encounter.[75] Some room should also be

---

69. For the last point, see Blue, *Authority to Heal,* pp. 49-51.

70. A highly insightful and balanced account can be found in Hejzlar, *Two Paradigms for Divine Healing,* pp. 109-52; also important is Macchia, "Call for Careful Discernment."

71. For the importance of hope, see Smail, *The Forgotten Father,* p. 142.

72. Blue, *Authority to Heal,* p. 49.

73. Gaiser, *Healing in the Bible,* p. 55.

74. Gaiser, *Healing in the Bible,* p. 3.

75. See Gusmer, *And You Visited Me.* For the rediscovery of the sacrament of the

left for different types of church traditions to employ their distinctive "models," as the brief survey of church history above indicates. Fifth, although sickness and healing are personal matters, the role of the faith community is not unimportant. James (5:13-16) recommends that a sick person contact the elders of the church for prayer and anointing with oil (a common OT practice).[76] After all, healing ministry is an integral part of the church's daily life and ministry. Finally, as established above, ultimately healings and deliverances point to the eschatological consummation. Healings are "signs" pointing toward fullness. On the way there, we live between the "now" (of the kingdom's arrival in Jesus' ministry) and the "not yet" (of its final appearance in the eschaton).

What about suffering in relation to healing? While some well-meaning but profoundly mistaken Pentecostal/charismatic and other Christian healers claim total health and well-being already in this life,[77] it is clear from the biblical teaching that both the pain of suffering and hope for healing coexist until the eschaton.[78] While the acknowledgment of the presence of suffering is not to be made a pretext for not praying for divine healing,[79] theological reflection on suffering, pain, and disability is an important part of a theology of restoration.

Human Flourishing, Sickness, and Disability

While the desire to flourish seems to be universal,[80] and until modernity even the Western cultures intuited a close relation between human flourishing and religion,[81] in the aftermath of the Enlightenment deeply divergent visions of

---

"anointing of the sick" (which used to be the "extreme unction" offered for the dying) in Roman Catholic theology, see *Sacrosanctum Concilium* (Constitution on Sacred Liturgy), ##73-75; *Catholic Catechism*, §§1499-1525.

76. For a careful study, see Warrington, "James 5:14-18."

77. For discussion of such belief in Bosworth, Hagin, and Sanford, see Hejzlar, *Two Paradigms for Divine Healing*, pp. 52-57.

78. For details, see Hejzlar, *Two Paradigms for Divine Healing*, pp. 62-72. For the important statement by the Assemblies of God (USA), the most well-known American Pentecostal body, see "Divine Healing: An Integral Part of the Gospel" at http://ag.org/top/Beliefs/Position _Papers/pp_downloads/PP_Divine_Healing.pdf (8/15/2014).

79. For a detailed discussion of MacNutt's view, see Hejzlar, *Two Paradigms for Divine Healing*, pp. 60-62; see also the critique of "sanctification through sickness" ideology by the charismatic Ken Blue, *Authority to Heal*, pp. 21-31.

80. For an important statement, see Charles Taylor, *A Secular Age*, p. 16.

81. See Volf, "Human Flourishing," p. 10.

what makes flourishing possible have emerged. For many, any reference to religion seemed to block the way to human flourishing (and freedom).[82] On the contrary, the Christian vision of flourishing is deeply embedded in the goodness and value of creation and life "in the now." It is unabashedly anchored in the triune God, the source and goal of all human life.[83] Saint Augustine put it well: "God is the only source to be found of any good things, but especially of those which make a man good and those which will make him happy; only from him do they come into a man and attach themselves to a man."[84] This *theologically* funded Christian vision is also capable of acknowledging death as an inescapable part of finite creaturely life.[85] But rather than advocating a culture of death, the Christian eschatological vision anticipates the triumph of life, of which Christ's resurrection is a pledge and foretaste. Empowered by such a vision, the Christian may experience day by day "flourishing as dying life."[86]

Furthermore, because it is finite life, a Christian theology of health and flourishing also acknowledges sickness and woundedness as a "natural," although not hoped-for, part of creaturely experience. Indeed, ordinary human life in the quotidian is always ambiguous, imperfect, and vulnerable. It belongs to the nature of finite existence that there are hurdles, riddles, unresolved problems, potential for growth, "fallings down," and so forth. "Creaturely being is limited being. This is an ontological claim."[87] What a powerful critique of the "values" of the consumer society with ideals of lasting fitness and beauty, economic security, and everlasting health.[88] Moltmann incisively remarks that "the more unreservedly and passionately he loves life, the more intensely he also experiences the pains of life. . . . [T]he more a person loves, the more intensely he experiences both life and death."[89]

In this light the definitions of health[90] that are unrealistic or hopelessly "perfectionist" have to be subjected to critique.[91] "Health" should not be made

---

82. See Charles Taylor, *A Secular Age*, pp. 16-17; Ford, "God's Power and Human Flourishing," pp. 1-28.

83. See D. Kelsey, "On Human Flourishing." pp. 3-4.

84. Augustine, *The Trinity* 13.10, cited in Volf, "Human Flourishing," p. 4.

85. See Schloss, "From Evolution to Eschatology," pp. 65-85.

86. Subheading in D. Kelsey, *Eccentric Existence*, 1:314.

87. D. Kelsey, *Eccentric Existence*, 1:201.

88. D. Kelsey, *Eccentric Existence*, 1:205.

89. Moltmann, *God in Creation*, p. 268.

90. For the rich and complex discussion in philosophy and public life of health and well-being, see Messer, *Flourishing*, chap. 1.

91. Oft-cited is the World Health Organization's definition: "Health is a state of complete physical, mental and social well-being and not merely the absence of disease or infirmity,"

an idol. "Only what can stand up to both health *and* sickness, and ultimately to living *and* dying, can count as a valid definition of what it means to be human."[92] Hence, the secular definition as an index of human flourishing in terms of functionality — meaning that opposite to healthy is "dysfunctional" — is highly problematic.[93] This is not to deny that healthy life is preferred over sickness; of course it is. Rather, "Love for life says 'yes' to life in spite of its sicknesses, handicaps and infirmities, and opens the door to a 'life against death.'"[94]

What about disability?[95] It may come as a surprise to many that "people with disabilities [make up] the largest and most diverse minority group in the United States" and, roughly speaking, in the rest of the world as well.[96] Theologically speaking, even a most seriously disabled person, similar to the sick, is no less human.[97] Having been created in God's image, human personhood does not admit degrees. One cannot be more or less of a human person.[98] Defining the image of God in terms of being related to God saves theology from anchoring human dignity in the possession of a quality or commodity such as intelligence or health. One's relation to the Creator is not affected in the least by one's disabilities, not even intellectual ones.

Hence, the Christian vision allows us to expect healing, whether instantaneous or gradual, as the sign of the coming of God's kingdom,[99] and simultaneously allows the celebration of the "charisma of the handicapped life." This statement is not an attempt to glorify — let alone stigmatize[100] — the disabled, but rather is to resist the cultural intoxication with success, health, and youth.[101]

---

available at http://www.who.int/about/definition/en/print.html (8/17/2014); for a theological critique, see Messer, *Flourishing*, pp. 3-6.

92. Moltmann, *God in Creation*, p. 273, emphasis in original.

93. See D. Kelsey, *Eccentric Existence*, 1:317.

94. Moltmann, *Spirit of Life*, p. 86.

95. For an important recent discussion, see Messer, *Flourishing*, chap. 2.

96. Schumm and Stoltzfus, "Editors' Introduction," p. xiii.

97. A pioneering theological study was Eiesland, *The Disabled God*; for more recent studies, see Creamer, *Disability and Christian Theology*; Reynolds, *Vulnerable Communion*; and Yong, *Theology and Down Syndrome*.

98. D. Kelsey, *Eccentric Existence*, 1:204.

99. See Moltmann, *Way of Jesus Christ*, pp. 104-16; Moltmann, *Spirit of Life*, pp. 188-92.

100. See Iozzio, "Thinking about Disabilities." Ironically, antidisability attitudes can be found among some female theologians; see Betcher, "Becoming Flesh of My Flesh"; for a Jewish perspective, see Belser, "Returning to Flesh."

101. For comments, see Soulen, "Cruising toward Bethlehem," p. 105.

To human flourishing and well-being also belongs the capacity to handle constructive feelings such as guilt and shame, which in the popular mind-set are often made casualties of religions and therefore considered detrimental by default. To defeat that naive, mistaken opinion, we need to take a careful theological and interdisciplinary look at these topics.

Guilt, Shame, and Forgiveness: Healing of the Mind

Shame and Guilt

According to psychologists (in the Global North), shame[102] is often juxtaposed with pride: "Pride is a positive feeling about the self, and shame is a negative feeling about the self."[103] Shame may block forgiveness,[104] including forgiveness of oneself.[105] Although people seem to differ in how prone they might be to a shame or guilt orientation,[106] all of us have to come to terms with both. Shame makes us liable to the feeling of worthlessness and often elicits defensive mechanisms such as anger, shifting blame, aggression, and self-contempt.

Understandably, shame orientation makes it hard to forgive both others and oneself. In contrast, guilt proneness[107] allows one "to focus on specific wrong actions one has committed (i.e., 'I did a bad thing') rather than the global negative self-evaluation (i.e., 'I am a bad person). . . . [G]uilt proneness is positively correlated with empathy, apology, forgiving others, seeking forgiveness, and other reparative actions in relationships." In sum, research suggests that "guilt-proneness represents certain qualities of humility, while shame-proneness represents a proclivity toward humiliation."[108]

---

102. For a psychological and psychiatric analysis of shame, see S. Fisher, "Identity of Two."

103. Shults and Sandage, *Faces of Forgiveness*, pp. 54-55 (p. 55); this section is indebted to their work, including finding many sources herein.

104. See further, Wharton, "Hidden Face of Shame," pp. 279-99; Halling, "Shame and Forgiveness," pp. 74-87.

105. Fisher and Exline, "Moving toward Self-Forgiveness," pp. 548-58.

106. Tagney, "Shame and Guilt in Interpersonal Relationships."

107. For a psychological definition, see Kugler and Jones, "On Conceptualizing and Assessing Guilt," p. 318; for unhealthy and destructive guilt feelings, see Faiver, O'Brien, and Ingersoll, "Religion, Guilt, and Mental Health," pp. 155-61; Räikkä, "Irrational Guilt," pp. 473-85.

108. Shults and Sandage, *Faces of Forgiveness*, pp. 54-55 (including references). For an important current essay, see Kim, Thibodeau, and Jorgensen, "Shame, Guilt, and Depressive Symptoms," pp. 68-96.

Guilt is both a central religious/theological concept and a psychological/psychiatric phenomenon. Many critics of religions, including not only psychologists but also philosophers and cultural critics such as Nietzsche and Freud,[109] have a hard time in acknowledging the health-building value of any concept of guilt, particularly religion-driven guilt. In response, theologians should follow some secular scholars in making a useful distinction between "local guilt," that is, feeling of remorse for a specific wrong action the person knew was wrong, and "existential guilt," which means "a persistent feeling of imperfection"[110] (approaching the feeling of shame). Some critics of Christianity,[111] particularly Nietzsche,[112] have virtually ignored the first dimension and focused on the latter, and so debunked all notions of guilt. While this kind of naive religious critique (of both Freud and Nietzsche) can be easily defeated by the mere appeal to the constructive function of guilt even in a psychological point of view, theologians are often faced with a more serious challenger to guilt: What about the fact that undeniably the feelings of guilt seem to be conditioned at least to some extent on geographical, cultural, religious contexts?[113] One theological response says, "Of course, guilt, similar to all other human experiences and conceptions, including religiosity itself,[114] is evolving and liable to contextual factors."

What about the most persistent challenge to religious talk about guilt, namely, effects on the conscience? The sick conscience and its many harmful effects on mental well-being are well documented.[115] But evolutionary biology is telling us that the "capacity for guilt is innate — we are born with it hardwired into our brain in evolution."[116] Furthermore, it seems that, in the perspective of evolutionary biology, guilt is also societally and culturally beneficial, related to "necessary social emotions" such as shame, embarrassment, regret, and pride. These are also called "moral emotions," as they allow one to make social judgments that are needed for the welfare of the society and culture.[117]

109. See Westerink, *A Dark Trace;* Speziale-Bagliacca, *Guilt.*

110. Risse, "On God and Guilt," p. 46.

111. See further, Murray and Ciarrochi, "Dark Side of Religion."

112. See particularly Nietzsche, *On the Genealogy of Morality.*

113. Albertsen, O'Connor, and Berry, "Religion and Interpersonal Guilt"; Asano, "Cultural Values, Ethnic Identity, Interpersonal Guilt and Shame."

114. For the complex relationship between evolution and the rise of religion (including the theme of evolutionary epistemology), see chap. 10 in my *Creation and Humanity.*

115. An up-to-date interdisciplinary study on conscience from evolutionary, behavioral, sociological, cultural, and religious sciences' viewpoints is Karchadourian, *Guilt.*

116. Karchadourian, *Guilt,* p. xiii.

117. Karchadourian, *Guilt,* chap. 1 (p. 7).

Furthermore, guilt and a corresponding concept of "conscience" are universally present among all religions, both Abrahamic[118] and Asiatic.[119] The conclusion, then, is that neither Christian tradition nor other (theistic) traditions should leave behind the concept of guilt but rather should seek to cultivate a healthy, life-affirming, and morality-enhancing sense of guilt and shame.

Shame and "Face-Work"

Along with guilt and judgment, the twin concepts of shame and honor are present everywhere in the biblical testimonies, as well as in many contemporary cultures of the Global South.[120] Although the old, unnuanced categorization of two kinds of cultures — shame cultures (ancient cultures and many cultures in the Global South) and guilt cultures (European-American postmedieval cultures)[121] — is in need of revision, there is some justification for the categories.[122]

A related concept has to do with "face"(-work). Face and facing (as well as their opposite, defacing)[123] seem to be a universal phenomenon across cultures and religions, including all ages of human life.[124] Quite insightfully, physiognomy of old contended that much of human personality can be gleaned from facial expressions.[125] Face (and face-work) is a lively interdisciplinary topic in anthropology,[126] psychology, primatology,[127] philosophy,[128] theol-

---

118. See chap. 8 in Karchadourian, *Guilt.*

119. See chap. 9 in Karchadourian, *Guilt.*

120. See DeSilva, "Turning Shame into Honour," pp. 159-86.

121. Rightly critiqued in Piers and Singer, *Shame and Guilt.*

122. Albers, *Shame.*

123. What many Asian and some African cultures call "losing face" is named by some contemporary behavioral scientists "defacement"; for a highly useful and richly documented current discussion, see chap. 3 in Pattison, *Saving Face.*

124. For the importance of face to the child and its relation to divine Presence, see Loder, *The Transforming Moment,* p. 163.

125. The classic modern work by Swiss pastor Lavater is *Essays on Physiognomy;* for a brief description, see Pattison, *Saving Face,* pp. 16-17.

126. For basic guidance to the key insights and vast literature concerning various dimensions of face in contemporary research (with a view to theologians, particularly practical theologians), see Pattison, *Saving Face,* pp. 19-24 and chap. 2 particularly.

127. Primatologists raise questions on whether higher animals such as mammals (chimpanzees) may be able to discern facial expressions; see Hauser, *Wild Minds,* pp. 96-103.

128. As is well known, for the Jewish theologian Emmanuel Levinas, the "Other" is a

ogy,[129] as well as missiology and intercultural studies.[130] What is its value for constructive theology?

"Face" is a familiar theme in the Bible (Num. 6:24-26). The face of God denotes divine presence and is highly sought (Gen. 32:30; 33:10; Pss. 31:16; 67:1-2; 2 Chron. 30:9). In the "face" of Jesus Christ, God has come to be fully revealed to us, and therefore Christians look for the day when they see him face-to-face (1 Cor. 13:12; 2 Cor. 3:18; 4:6).[131] The Cambridge theologian David Ford states insightfully: "Christianity is characterized by the simplicity and complexity of facing: being faced by God, embodied in the face of Christ; turning to face Jesus Christ in faith; being members of the community of face; seeing the face of God reflected in creation and especially in each human face, with all the faces in our heart related to the presence of the face of Christ."[132] Yet, curiously enough, "both human and divine faces seem to have been almost wholly absent in recent Christian theology and practice."[133]

Because the face of God is narrated in the OT, it is no wonder that some Jewish theologians have also tapped into those resources. Melissa Raphael's *The Female Face of God in Auschwitz* is "a Jewish feminist theology of the Holocaust," to quote her subtitle. It is a profound post-Holocaust theology delving into the mystery of the hiddenness of Yahweh's face in the midst of the horrendous suffering of Yahweh's people. Drawing from the Kabbalistic theology of *Shekinah,* Raphael reconceives divine presence in female terms and so helps balance the patriarchal post-Holocaust tradition. Whereas Yahweh's face was hidden, the steady and courageous women stand up against the enemy; many female heroes helped keep alive hope.[134]

To widen the interfaith dimension, let us continue looking at the topics of this chapter in relation to other faiths.

---

key concept; face plays an important role in the reciprocal encounter between I and the Other; see his *Totality and Infinity,* pp. 50-51.

129. Marion, "The Face," pp. 9-10.

130. Flander, "About Face"; R. Lienhard, "Restoring Relationships"; T. R. Song, "Shame and Guilt in the Japanese Culture."

131. A fine study on the face of God in the Bible is Pattison, *Saving Face,* chap. 5; historical and contemporary developments are discussed in chaps. 6 and 7 (this paragraph is indebted to Pattison's work). Also useful is Shults and Sandage, *Faces of Forgiveness,* pp. 105-24.

132. Ford, *Self and Salvation,* pp. 24-25.

133. Pattison, *Saving Face,* p. 2. The English philosopher Richard Scruton's *The Face of God* issues a bold diagnosis of the turning away from the presence and reality of God by the atheistic and secular cultures of the Global North.

134. Raphael, *Female Face of God in Auschwitz.* For an insightful Christian appropriation, see Pattison, *Saving Face,* pp. 141-43.

Healing and Sickness among Religions

Health and sickness feature prominently in religions.[135] Healing occupies a prominent place in religious experience throughout the world. The existence of personal suffering in the world may serve as a springboard for theological and mythological exploration and explanation.[136] All scriptural traditions deal with the problem of sickness and the possibility of restoration. That said, all religious traditions also have a mixed record in handling the issues of sickness and disability.[137] There is need for correction in light of deep underlying theological convictions and current knowledge of disability.[138] At the same time, most religious traditions have at least allowed for accommodations for sick, disabled persons.[139]

Abrahamic Traditions

The views of healing and sickness among the three Abrahamic traditions share a wide common basis. They speak of healing and well-being as a promise of God. Well known are the OT promises of Yahweh as healer. Indeed, in the Israelite faith both calamity and healing come from one and the same Lord:

> "I kill and I make alive;
>   I wound and I heal." (Deut. 32:39)

So deeply is healing instilled in Jewish scriptural tradition that a petition from Jeremiah (17:14) is recited in daily Jewish liturgy: "Heal us, O Lord, and we shall be healed." A seriously ill person may also do private recitations from the Psalms, praying for "healing, courage, and faith." Judaism contains a number of different kinds of healing petitions;[140] offering petitions is a common

---

135. For a useful discussion of the role of healing across cultures and religions, see Kinsley, *Health, Healing, and Religion.*

136. For a standard resource, see L. Sullivan, ed., *Healing and Restoring.*

137. Yong, *Theology and Down Syndrome,* chaps. 2, 5. For specialized recent studies among Abrahamic faiths, see Abrams, *Judaism and Disability;* Creamer, *Disability and Christian Theology;* Galy, *Islam and Disability.*

138. See Belser, "Reading Talmudic Bodies"; for a Christian perspective, see Yong, "Disability and the Love of Wisdom."

139. See, e.g., Dokumaci, "Performance of Muslim Daily Prayer."

140. Freeman, "Healing and Medicine," p. 3828; other highly useful resources are Cutter, ed., *Midrash and Medicine;* Meier, ed., *Jewish Values in Health and Medicine.*

technique of healing in all traditions. Judaism also has a long history of folk healing, which is already present in the biblical narratives.[141]

Although healing in Jewish faith is a deeply spiritual matter, deriving from the whole of human being having been made in the divine image, it is also a thoroughly physical and this-worldly matter.[142] Unlike common instances in Christian tradition, the mainline Jewish tradition does not relegate healing and happiness primarily to the afterlife. God's blessings, including prosperity, posterity, and shalom, are meant first and foremost for this age.[143]

According to the Qur'anic promise in 41:44, the divine word is "guidance and a healing" for believers but brings about deafness to the disobedient.[144] Similar to Judeo-Christian tradition, ultimately it is God who is the healer (26:80).[145] The Hadith tradition continues and deepens this idea. According to the Prophet, "God has not sent down a disease without sending down a remedy for it."[146] Not surprisingly, all Islamic traditions also invite the faithful to pray for healing; it is particularly important in the mystical Sufi tradition.[147] Folk healing tradition is long and wide in Islam.[148]

Asiatic Traditions

If there is a common denominator between widely divergent Asiatic faith traditions concerning insights into wellness, it has to do with harmony and balance.[149] The human being's health is part of a larger cosmic network. Al-

---

141. Isa. 38:21 tells about Isaiah using figs to treat the king's intestinal ailment; for later tradition, see, e.g., Josephus, *Jewish Antiquities* 8.2; Freeman, "Healing and Medicine," p. 3829.

142. Freeman, "Healing and Medicine," p. 3831. Among several current sources, unique is the anthology of texts by Freeman and Abrams, eds., *Illness and Health in the Jewish Tradition*. See also, Person, ed., *The Mitzvah of Healing*.

143. As in all other topics, the most important Jewish theologian, Maimonides, also is known for writings on sickness and health; see M. Reich, "Some Insights into Maimonides' Approach," pp. 167-72.

144. Similarly, Q 10:57.

145. For details, see N. Gallagher, "Healing and Medicine," p. 3831.

146. *Mishkat al-Masabih* 3:945; for other such references, see N. Gallagher, "Healing and Medicine," p. 3831. A reliable philosophical-theological account of healing in Islam is Rahman, *Health and Medicine in the Islamic Tradition*.

147. N. Gallagher, "Healing and Medicine," p. 3832.

148. See, e.g., "Islamic Folk Healing" at http://islamichealingsystems.wordpress.com/islamic-folk-healing/ (8/27/2014).

149. Note the title of Vargas-O'Bryan, "Keeping It All in Balance: Teaching Asian Religions through Illness and Healing."

though all faith traditions locate sickness and health in a matrix of influences and factors, from religious to secular, in Hinduism the network of effects is unusually wide. It includes not only karma, the spiritual "cause-effect" chain, and other foundational theological themes such as "ignorance," as well as complicated rules and rites regarding ritual pollution and purity, but also caste and class, gender, and other such issues related to the sociocultural hierarchy. As is true of scientific work even in the current fairly secularized India,[150] the medical and religious are deeply intertwined.[151] Some diseases are conceived to be the result of the anger of a god. Similarly, some major deities are closely linked with healing, particularly Vishnu, Shiva, and Shakti. These deities are known in local temples as divine physicians.[152] Commensurately with other faith traditions (and as discussed in part 1 above), Hinduism also provides for deliverance from possession and demonic influence.[153]

In Hindu traditions, the all-encompassing term for well-being, happiness, integrity of life is *vastu* (or *svasti*). Materially similar to the Hebrew concept of shalom, it is "dependent on a harmonious relationship with the earth, the planets, and the stars; appropriate balances between the various elements within the body, family, and society; and a good relationship with the natural world, ancestors, and deities."[154] Astrology plays a particularly important role in religiously driven medical thinking.[155]

Part of the Vedic scriptural tradition is Ayurveda, which aims at the knowledge of true happiness and well-being in life, and is sometimes called "Science of Life."[156] In this scripturally based tradition, "[h]ealth is not only a goal in itself, but, perhaps more importantly, the means by which to achieve longevity."[157] A special role is played by one of the incarnations of Vishnu, Dhanvantari, "[c]ommonly worshipped as the Hindu God of Medicine, the Master of Universal Knowledge, Physician of Gods and the

---

150. See chaps. 2 and 4 in *Creation and Humanity*.

151. See Desai, *Health and Medicine in the Hindu Tradition*.

152. Narayanan, "Shanti," pp. 61-65. This section is indebted to this article, including some references.

153. Bharathi, "Spirit Possession and Healing Practices," pp. 343-52.

154. Narayanan, "Shanti," p. 61; for an accessible account, see the Vasstu Living Web site: http://www.vastuliving.com/about-vastu-living.php (8/27/2014).

155. See further, Narayanan, "Shanti," pp. 70-72.

156. Academically the most respectful account can be found in Wujastyk, *The Roots of Ayurveda*. A shorter reliable account is *"Āyurveda."* For other ancient Indian healing concepts, see Benner, "Healing and Medicine," p. 3853.

157. Benner, "Healing and Medicine," p. 3855.

Guardian Deity of Hospitals."[158] It is not uncommon at all for Hindus to pray to the deities for their well-being; their ritual may include making vows and pacts.[159]

Given that in India religion and medicine are mutually conditioned, it is no surprise that as recently as 1970 the Indian parliament organized an official council for the indigenous medical systems of Ayurveda (and two less well-known ones, Siddha and Unani).[160] This gesture is totally unknown in the contemporary secular Global North. Differences of opinions and splits in the influential Ayurveda political coalition have also stirred up quite a bit of debate and controversy.[161]

The question of the place of suffering and sickness in all diverse Buddhist traditions is linked with the concept of *dukkha,* which is best left untranslated because "suffering" is only one rendering. Since that concept has been exhaustively explained in several places in this constructive theology project,[162] let it suffice here to say this: *dukkha* is related to other key concepts in Buddhism, particularly impermanence and "no-self." Hence, the main goal of the Buddhist pursuit is to be freed from craving, clinging to something that is only a fleeting reality. Furthermore, the principle of interrelatedness implies that "[s]uffering is not unique to those who struggle with chronic disability or illness. The point is that even those who are physically healthy and materially wealthy nonetheless experience a chaotic, continually festering dissatisfaction."[163] So far so good, but I have to disagree with the next step of the reasoning: because suffering and pain are a universal human condition, it means that "[f]or example, when the chronically ill or disabled crave and become attached to the idea of individual care, so central to both medical and religious restitution narratives, they may find that such craving increases their suffering and sense of chaos while doing little to decrease their pain."[164] While I understand that in Buddhist teaching "suffering decreases and healing increases when we let go of wanting things to be different from how they are and instead move toward an acceptance of what is available in the present moment,"[165] it also sounds

158. Priya, "Dhanvantari the Hindu God of Medicine." For other important local healer gods, see Narayanan, "Shanti," pp. 65-66.

159. Narayanan, "Shanti," p. 68.

160. See Carl Taylor, "Place of Indigenous Medical Practitioners," pp. 285-99.

161. Benner, "Healing and Medicine," pp. 3857-58.

162. See, e.g., *Creation and Humanity,* chap. 15.

163. Schumm and Stoltzfus, "Chronic Illness and Disability," p. 164.

164. Schumm and Stoltzfus, "Chronic Illness and Disability," p. 165.

165. Schumm and Stoltzfus, "Chronic Illness and Disability," p. 165.

to me quite merciless to discourage the suffering person from seeking more immediate release.[166]

If the original Theravada tradition has focused much more energy on "healing" in terms of spiritual healing, following Gautama's profound analysis of the foundational "illness" among us, namely, craving and clinging to something that after all is impermanent, the theistically oriented Mahayana traditions imagine healing as both spiritual and physical. Not unlike other theistic traditions, Mahayana can link healing directly to Buddha.[167] Indeed, one of the most interesting developments in this regard is the emergence of the "Medicine Buddha," a hugely important object of worship and prayer in devotional movements throughout East Asia.[168] Tibetan, Chinese, Japanese, and other forms of Mahayana have developed their own distinctive rites and rituals for healing. The authoritative, widely used manual is *The Sutra of Medicine Buddha,* which recounts the twelve vows, represented by as many deities around the Buddha. The vows represent a holistic view of healing from ignorance, immorality, various kinds of physical illnesses, demonic oppression, suffering from imprisonment, lack of clothing, and so forth.[169] What does it take to receive these healing gifts? They "need only to hear my [Buddha's] name to be freed from all these afflictions, thanks to the awesome power of my merits and virtues."[170] No doubt this theistic version of healing in Buddhism echoes important themes not only in Abrahamic but also in other theistic traditions.

Empowerment, Charismatic Gifting, and Spirit Baptism

If possible, doctrinal theology's omission of the category of empowerment is even more striking than its omission of healing. The themes of Spirit baptism, charismatic empowerment, and gifting are simply missing altogether in any *ordo salutis* presentations (with the exception of Pentecostal/charismatic ones). Why should we be concerned about this category? Three reasons come to mind. The first has to do with early Christian tradition. Both in the biblical

166. A useful discussion can be found in Skorupski, "Health and Suffering in Buddhism," pp. 139-65.

167. Birnbaum, *The Healing Buddha,* pp. 3-26.

168. For an accessible, widely used primer, see Chopra, *Journey into Healing.*

169. As with other scriptural traditions, there are embarrassing items herein: the ninth vow promises the opportunity for females who detest their own body and female nature to be born as males (*Sutra of Medicine Buddha,* p. 22).

170. Tenth vow in *Sutra of Medicine Buddha,* p. 22.

and early Christian tradition the charismatic element, at times named Spirit baptism, was integral to the process of Christian initiation. Second, with the rise of Pentecostal/charismatic Christianity, Spirit baptism may be "as important today as justification by faith (alone) in the time of Luther."[171] Third, theologically it can be argued that a holistic view of salvation properly includes the dynamic element of gifting, inspiration, and empowerment.[172]

This discussion will first clarify the meaning of the widely contested concept of Spirit baptism and thereafter will attempt to construct a fresh and dynamic theology of empowerment and gifting. The section ends with a brief theological look at the category of the charismatic.

The Baptism in the Holy Spirit as an Ecumenical Problem

Several paradigms seek to explain the theological meaning of the experience of the Spirit baptism in the context of Christian initiation.[173] I divide the interpretations into four broad categories,[174] the first of which I call the "traditional soteriological view." Its main idea is that Spirit baptism is another name for everything that the Holy Spirit is doing in salvation.[175] Calvin's identification of baptism in the Holy Spirit with the work of regeneration[176] and Roman Catholic theologian Yves Congar's identification of Spirit baptism with water baptism[177] represent this mainstream conception. Barth's view also belongs to this tradition: in distinction from water baptism, which represents the human response, Spirit baptism is "the power of the divine change in which the event of the foundation of the Christian life of specific men takes place,"[178] "the divine preparation of man for the Christian life in its totality."[179] The way the

171. Bradford, *Releasing the Power of the Holy Spirit*, p. 5, cited in Lederle, *Treasures Old and New*, p. 1.

172. See my *Spiritus ubi vult spirat*, p. 198.

173. The heading for this section comes from McDonnell and Bittlinger, eds., *The Baptism in the Holy Spirit as an Ecumenical Problem*.

174. For others, not included in this typology, see Lederle, *Treasures Old and New*, chap. 4.

175. This view can also be called "the unified pattern of Christian experience," as described by Lederle, *Treasures Old and New*, pp. 2-5.

176. Calvin, *Institutes* 3.1.4.

177. Congar, *I Believe in the Holy Spirit*, 3:218, 222-24.

178. Barth, *CD* IV/4, p. 30.

179. Barth, *CD* IV/4, p. 31. For a detailed discussion of Barth's elusive theology of Spirit baptism, see Yun, *Baptism in the Holy Spirit*, pp. 109-24.

Orthodox thinker John of Damascus explains the meaning of "twofold puri-fication, of water and of the Spirit," similarly illustrates this paradigm.[180] The implication of the traditional soteriological view is that if the term were not used, nothing would be lost, because it is *another* way to speak of the Spirit's work in Christian initiation and life.[181]

The most novel interpretation is provided by the Pentecostal movement. Therein Spirit baptism is a necessary and distinct category in the *ordo salutis* and cannot be removed or replaced by something else. Notwithstanding in-ternal differences, most Pentecostal movements "agree that Spirit baptism is distinct from and generally subsequent to regeneration or initial conversion and that speaking in tongues provides the initial evidence of the reception of Spirit baptism."[182] The distinctive features of this template are the follow-ing.[183] Rather than being a Christian-making event as in the traditional view or being integrally linked with initiation as in a charismatic-sacramental view, Spirit baptism happens "after" one has become a Christian.[184] Whereas Spirit baptism happens only once in life, it is supposed to be followed by daily fill-ings with the Spirit. The experience belongs to every Christian, and its main purpose is empowerment for witness and service (Acts 1:8 is the Pentecostal paragon). The most distinctive feature of the Pentecostal interpretation is the expectation that every believer experiences *glossolalia* (speaking in tongues) as an "initial physical evidence." Whereas this is a normative experience for all, many may also receive the continuing gift of speaking in tongues through-out their Christian life. In other words, there is a distinction between the onetime "evidential" glossolalia patterned after several instances in the book of Acts (2:4-6; 10:46; 19:6) and a regular "prayer language" as mentioned in 1 Corinthians (12:28-30). This last item is not universally affirmed by all Pen-tecostals,[185] although a majority of world Pentecostals own the belief in some form or another.

---

180. John of Damascus, *Exposition of the Orthodox Faith* 4.9.

181. In Luther the term "Spirit baptism" is virtually absent; the closest he comes to using it is in his exposition *Lectures on Titus, Philemon, Hebrews* (on Titus 3:5); *LW* 29:81-84.

182. Yun, *Baptism in the Holy Spirit*, pp. 24-25.

183. For a detailed discussion of all these items with reference to Pentecostal literature and doctrinal statements, see Yun, *Baptism in the Holy Spirit*, pp. 33-34; J. R. Williams, "Baptism in the Holy Spirit," pp. 354-63; Macchia, *Baptized in the Spirit*, chap. 2.

184. See also, Dunn, *Baptism in the Holy Spirit*, pp. 21-22, 54.

185. The largest African American Pentecostal body in the USA, Church of God in Christ, does not mention glossolalia in its statement of faith; see its Web site, http://www.cogic.org/our-foundation/our-statement-of-faith/ (4/3/2014).

The third view, which I name "charismatic-sacramental," represents a radical middle way between the first two views. It forges an integral link between the sacramental water baptism in which the Holy Spirit is given to the baptized and the later experience of Spirit baptism as an occasion for the actualization and surfacing of the Spirit through a conscious charismatic experience.[186] The Benedictine Kilian McDonnell defines it as "a bringing to awareness and a new actuality the graces of initiation already received."[187] Similar to the Pentecostal interpretation, this charismatic-sacramental view expects the release of a charismatic gift, but unlike Pentecostals, it leaves open what kind of gift that might be. This general template is followed by the majority of theologians in the Roman Catholic charismatic movement[188] and is also influential among some leading Anglican[189] and Lutheran renewals.[190]

The final category among the four interpretations I name the "nonsacramental-charismatic view." In this outlook, represented by the influential Roman Catholic theologian Francis Sullivan, Spirit baptism is seen "as a special grace, a new imparting of the Spirit unrelated to any immediate sacramental context."[191] The idea of more than one imparting of the Spirit is not novel even in the sacramental Catholic tradition. It seeks to oppose the tendency to limit the conferring of charisms merely to the sacramental context.[192]

In the constructive ecumenical proposal, I will take up these four categories under a sympathetic-critical scrutiny and incorporate their valid insights into my own theology.

---

186. A concise, well-documented discussion can be found in Lederle, *Treasures Old and New*, chap. 3.

187. McDonnell and Montague, *Christian Initiation*, p. 84.

188. The formative Roman Catholic "Malines Document 1: Theological and Pastoral Orientations on the Catholic Charismatic Renewal" (1974) can be found at http://www.stucom .nl/document/0236uk.pdf (8/29/2012); for comments, see Yun, *Baptism in the Holy Spirit*, pp. 46-52. For a number of other Catholic documents and theologians embracing this view, see McDonnell and Montague, *Christian Initiation*, p. 86.

189. Gunstone, *Greater Things Than These*, p. 31.

190. Bittlinger, "Baptism in Water and in Spirit," p. 11.

191. As paraphrased by McDonnell and Montague, *Christian Initiation*, p. 83; basic exposition can be found in F. Sullivan, "Baptism in the Spirit," pp. 59-75.

192. See F. Sullivan, "Baptism in the Spirit," pp. 69-70. His fellow Catholic McDonnell acknowledges this fear but also states that there is no such desire even in the sacramental-charismatic view. McDonnell and Montague, *Christian Initiation*, p. 84 n. 4.

Spirit Baptism: A Constructive Ecumenical Proposal

The expression "baptism with the Holy Spirit" does not appear as a noun in the NT; only "baptize," the verb, appears. The earliest version in Mark (Q) associates baptism with power as the Baptist presents Jesus, the Baptizer with the Spirit, as the "mightier" (or more powerful) one (Mark 1:7). Hence, healings, exorcisms, and authoritative teaching "function as confirming signs of Jesus' identity as revealed in the baptism: he is the Son of God (1:1; 3:11; 5:7) upon whom the Spirit rests." Mark assumes the continuation by disciples (and by implication, the church) of this ministry (see 3:14-15, among other passages).[193]

Older NT theology tended to juxtapose Lukan and Pauline pneumatologies, the idea being that whereas Luke is charismatic, Paul is soteriological in the conception of the Spirit's work. This interpretation, however, cannot be sustained in light of the NT materials. It is clear that Paul is also deeply charismatic, although "Spirit baptism is more intimately connected to faith, confession, and sealing through water baptism."[194] Furthermore, there is no reason not to assume that Luke also knows the soteriological dimension, although his interests clearly are more in the empowering, gifting, and prophetic dimensions.

Luke's presentation of the Spirit's work is highly unique.[195] First, in Luke 7:18-23, in response to the question by the Baptist's disciples whether he was the one John meant, Jesus referred to miraculous deeds and compassionate ministry as the confirmation; that is understandable because, in his inaugural sermon, Jesus had placed all his ministry under the Spirit (4:18-19). These two programmatic passages remind us of the manifold dimensions of Jesus' ministry as the "Man of the Spirit," in terms of mighty deeds and compassionate ministry to the poor, marginalized, and suffering people. Second, in Acts 1:5 Luke has the promise of Spirit baptism on the lips of Jesus himself. Third, Luke is the only one to report the event of the Pentecost along with extraordinary phenomena, including the tongues. Astonishingly, the description of "fire" of Luke 3:16 in Acts 2:3 is linked with "tongues as of fire, distributed and resting on each one of them."[196] The Jesuit NT scholar George Montague draws this theologically important conclusion from the Lukan evidence: "it is clear from

193. McDonnell and Montague, *Christian Initiation*, pp. 4-11; Congar, *I Believe in the Holy Spirit*, 2:189-201.

194. Macchia, *Baptized in the Spirit*.

195. Stronstad, *Charismatic Theology of St. Luke*.

196. This paragraph is based largely on McDonnell and Montague, *Christian Initiation*, pp. 23-26.

the paradigmatic nature of Acts 2:1-38, 10:44-48, and 19:5 not only that the gift of the Spirit belongs essentially to Christian initiation, but that some external expression of its reception is normal. Among these expressions, tongues and prophecy have a privileged place." He continues: "If I may phrase Luke's view another way: the Spirit cannot be known to have been poured *in* unless it somehow pours *out*."[197] This principle applies well to the NT situation, in which the baptized were adults. What about infant baptism? Montague argues that "subsequent prayer for the outpouring of the Spirit (such as the contemporary 'baptism in the Holy Spirit') is wholly appropriate. In this way the baptized may effectively claim their patrimony"[198] (the gift of the Father). Finally, he reminds us that on the basis of passages such as Luke 11:13, it can be concluded that the prayer for the Spirit is not tied merely to baptism or Christian initiation.[199]

The same template seemed to have been at work during the first centuries of the Christian church, although after the patristic era and with the rise of infant baptism, the charismatic element was by and large lost. This is the main conclusion of a massive historical study by McDonnell, which he based on extensive research into Latin, Greek, and Syrian traditions all around the Mediterranean region during the first eight centuries of the church. The basic elements present at Christian baptism at the end of a lengthy catechumenate were "(1) a sign of the prayer for the descent of the Spirit, usually the imposition of hands, but also anointing, (2) praying for the descent of the Spirit, (3) an expectation that the charisms will be manifested, and/or the actual manifestation. The baptism in the Spirit is the whole rite of initiation."[200] McDonnell further argues that "[i]f the baptism in the Holy Spirit is integral to Christian initiation, to the constitutive sacraments, then it belongs not to private piety but to public liturgy, to the official worship of the church. Therefore the baptism in the Spirit is not special grace for some but common grace for all."[201] And similarly, in Luke's presentation of Jesus, Spirit baptism "is also integral to the paradigm for social transformation. Initiation equips one to do what Jesus did: to preach the good news to the poor, to proclaim liberty to the captives, to restore sight to the blind, to let the oppressed go free (Luke 4:18)."[202]

---

197. McDonnell and Montague, *Christian Initiation*, p. 40, emphasis in original. Dunn rightly notes that in the NT the reception of the Spirit is "often dramatic experience." *Baptism in the Holy Spirit*, p. 4.

198. McDonnell and Montague, *Christian Initiation*, p. 41.

199. McDonnell and Montague, *Christian Initiation*, p. 41.

200. McDonnell and Montague, *Christian Initiation*, p. 315.

201. McDonnell and Montague, *Christian Initiation*, p. 334.

202. McDonnell and Montague, *Christian Initiation*, p. 335.

In light of this NT and patristic evidence, the traditional soteriological view is to be deemed failing because it simply says too little about empowerment. Indeed, it does not say anything at all, as Spirit baptism is made to be just another way of naming the works of Spirit salvation, which can also be otherwise captured. This is of course not to undermine — and certainly not to debunk — the authenticity of Christian initiation that lacks the charismatic and "experiential" element, but it is to say that a more holistic and integral vision of salvation is needed. The other three Spirit baptism interpretations are clearly superior on this count. They all in their distinctive manner incorporate the charismatic element in a holistic vision of *ordo salutis*.

The Pentecostal interpretation does it most robustly. Ironically, its separation of Spirit baptism from water baptism is both its strength and its liability. The benefit of the separation lies in the legitimate reminder to us that there are no necessary biblical nor theological (any more than pastoral) reasons to limit the charismatic breakthrough, even in its first occurrence, to water baptism. "The Spirit blows where it wills" (John 3:8). On the other hand, so categorically separating it from the wider framework of Christian initiation is also a liability because in the NT, particularly in the book of Acts, water baptism and Spirit baptism are clearly related.[203] In that respect, more coherent theologies of Spirit baptism are offered by the sacramental and nonsacramental charismatic views.

Which of the two — sacramental- or nonsacramental-charismatic — is to be preferred? Ecumenically I think it is best to be open to both. As McDonnell rightly notices, the nonsacramental is appealing to those Protestant traditions whose theology is not sacramental.[204] Personally I find the nonsacramental-charismatic stronger for the simple reason that it can be embraced by both (deeply) sacramental theologies and those that are not sacramental. Apart from the sacramental apparatus, all three views, in a qualified yet real sense, establish a link between initiation and Spirit baptism; even for Pentecostals, the Holy Spirit indwells their hearts at the moment they become Christians, followed by water baptism (if not immediately, then soon thereafter). On the other hand, in the nonsacramental-charismatic interpretation, the new imparting of the Spirit is just that — *new* — and hence it assumes that there was an "old" imparting at initiation. In the final analysis, this means that the way the Pentecostal view and the two sacramental interpretations negotiate the relation of Spirit baptism to water baptism has little to do with pneumatology and everything to do with the divide between sacramental and nonsacramental traditions.

203. See also, the Pentecostal theologian Macchia, *Baptized in the Spirit*, p. 62.
204. See further, McDonnell and Montague, *Christian Initiation*, p. 84.

Another important common denominator among the three interpretations has to do with the desire to be continually filled with the Holy Spirit after the initial breakthrough experience. In other words, whether at water baptism (or confirmation) or outside of Christian initiation, the charismatic experience one has is not an event to be left behind but rather a call for daily renewal.

What about the external manifestations of Spirit baptism? All three interpretations have to be commended for expecting, as normal, an experiential dimension to Spirit baptism (to be followed by subsequent fillings). That consensus should not be lost when differences of opinion about its exact nature are being negotiated. It seems clear that the Pentecostal insistence on one definite and exclusive "initial physical evidence" as glossolalia cannot be found convincing. While there is some biblical precedent in Acts for the link between speaking in tongues and Spirit baptism, one can hardly make a strong exegetical case for such a rule.[205] Even more impossible is the novel and artificial (albeit necessary in a Pentecostal template) distinction between the tongues of the Day of Pentecost and those mentioned by Paul in 1 Corinthians.[206] Furthermore — highly ironically for Pentecostals who everywhere issue calls for other churches to open up for the freedom of the Spirit — that rule implicitly imprisons the Spirit "who blows where it wills" (John 3:8). Finally, it seems to me that this kind of talk about "evidence" smacks more of modernist epistemology than of a lively, dynamic spirituality![207]

In no way undermining the importance of charismatic experience and accompanying signs, we also have to keep clearly in mind that Spirit baptism is meant for empowerment and gifting, that is, for vocation and ministry. We also know on the basis of Romans 5:5 that "[t]hrough Christ as the Spirit Baptizer, God imparts his divine self as all-embracing love and not just something about God."[208] Rather than self-glorification or spiritual enjoyment, Spirit baptism brings about a loving heart and serving hands in the service of the kingdom of

---

205. This is well argued by the Pentecostal exegete Gordon Fee, "Baptism in the Holy Spirit," pp. 87-99.

206. There is of course another kind of difference between them: Acts 2 clearly refers to understandable languages *(xenolalia)* whereas 1 Cor. 12 and 14 describe the tongues as mysterious prayer language whose meaning is not known even to the speaker but only to God. That distinction, however, has nothing in common with the modern Pentecostal hermeneutical distinction.

207. Somewhat disturbingly, empirical sociological studies indicate that fewer than half of U.S. Assemblies of God members (one of the most ardent defenders of the initial evidence doctrine) ever speak in tongues; see Poloma, *Assemblies of God at the Crossroads,* chap. 3.

208. Macchia, *Baptized in the Spirit,* p. 261.

God. As such, while a deeply personal experience, Spirit baptism has profound communal and ecclesiological implications, as will be discussed in *Church and Hope.*[209]

Following the biblical precedent, particularly the Lukan Jesus' inauguration speech, the empowerment by the Spirit also has social and political implications. Those who are sent out to share testimony to Christ (Acts 1:8) are also mandated to care for the poor, support the marginalized, heal the sick, and free prisoners.

Let me now briefly summarize key ideas of a constructive theology of the Spirit. First, with a holistic Christian vision of salvation belong empowerment and charismatic gifting, along with restorative and other soteriological dimensions. Christian traditions that have omitted the charismatic category should work toward rediscovering it in a manner that is in keeping with their own sources and teachings. Second, it is clear that rather than a commodity of any particular tradition (in this case, Pentecostalism), Spirit baptism, as evinced by the NT and early Christian experience, is a normal expectation and normative for Christian initiation and life. Third, Spirit baptism can take place either in connection with water baptism or apart from it, and ecumenically we should be open to embracing both sacramental and nonsacramental interpretations. Fourth, as a profound experience, normally Spirit baptism is expected to be accompanied by charismatic manifestations. While there are no normative or exclusive manifestations, the NT evidence seems to consider speaking in tongues and prophetic speech as typical. Fifth, the purpose of Spirit baptism is to empower and equip each Christian for service and ministry. Finally, it is useful to call subsequent fillings with the Holy Spirit just that — *fillings* — as a dynamic and fresh charismatic dimension is a characteristic of normal Christian life. Recall that for Paul every Christian is charismatic (Rom. 12:6). The discussion of ecclesiology takes up a deeper investigation and constructive theology of the category of charisms.

This chapter has argued that healing, restoration, empowerment, and charismatic gifting are not alternatives or optional but belong to the Christian vision of salvation, to the *ordo salutis.* It is about time to let systematic/constructive theology widen its horizons to include these. The communal aspects of salvation also need to be included in the *ordo salutis.* Reconciliation with God is not only a matter of personal salvation. It also includes the reconciliation of communities, the last major topic in soteriology.

209. See further, Macchia, *Baptized in the Spirit,* p. 63.

13. Reconciliation, Liberation, and Peacebuilding

At the end of part 1, the Spirit's liberative work in a number of areas of culture and public life was developed. It is appropriate and necessary to continue that theological work in the context of the *ordo salutis,* particularly with a view to reminding us that while personal, salvation is never individualistic; it encompasses also communities at various levels. Furthermore, while spiritual at its core, the Christian view of salvation does not separate spirituality and the rest of life; rather, these two belong together. Furthermore, while the ultimate aim of Christian salvation is transcendent, eternal communion with God and God's people, it is not escapist, as there is a dynamic continuity-in-discontinuity between the "now" and the "then." Hence, this section seeks to widen the role of the Spirit in Christian soteriology toward the topics of sociopolitical and economic liberation and reconciliation.

The Work of the Spirit in Liberation and Reconciliation of Communities

Rather than abstract and generic, the works of the Spirit are historically anchored, specific, and particular. The Spirit works in the midst of particular earthly realities, social conflicts, and personal problems.[1] Already in the OT narratives, the Spirit's advocacy and liberative work in the midst of chaos, anarchy, and confusion can be discerned. Take, for example, the book of Judges. Cycles of chaos, defeat by the enemies, and loss of hope follow one after an-

---

1. Moltmann, *Spirit of Life,* pp. 110-12.

other. Yet the Spirit of God is mightily at work. God facilitates liberation by forging the bond of unity and unanimity. As M. Welker puts it, the Spirit "causes the people of Israel *to come out of a situation of insecurity, fear, paralysis, and mere complaint.*"[2] The desire for mutual support and the sharing of common vision emerge as a result.[3]

The same formative presence of the Spirit is at work in the midst of the early church as narrated in the book of Acts, so much so that the newly established communities of Christ, in the midst of opposition from both religious and secular authorities, were empowered to live out *koinonia* both at the spiritual and at the socioeconomic levels: "And all who believed were together and had all things in common; and they sold their possessions and goods and distributed them to all, as any had need" (2:44-45).

The Spirit of liberation is at work not only in the pages of the Bible. An increasing number of theological reports are confirming that the rediscovery of the liberative work of the Spirit is under way in international and ecumenical theologies, in the *minjung* and other liberative movements in Korea,[4] in India,[5] in Latin America,[6] in Africa,[7] and beyond. Probably no other figure has spoken as deeply and widely of the Holy Spirit and liberation as José Comblin, a Belgian Catholic theologian, pastor, and social critic who resides in Latin America. His basic thesis is that "the experience of God found in the new Christian communities of Latin America can properly be called experience of the Holy Spirit" in its liberative aspects, although, somewhat ironically, "most of the Christians who make up these communities do not know that this is their experience; because of their religious upbringing, this Holy Spirit is still the Great Unknown for them."[8] Working among the Catholic base communities, he discerns various liberative dimensions to the experience of the Spirit, including the experience of action: rather than being acted upon, now the poor take initiative; rather than being passive, Amerindians, black slaves, slum dwellers, the unemployed, and peasants are now being energized by the Spirit.[9] The Spirit works for the freedom of those under oppression, whatever form

---

2. Welker, *God the Spirit,* p. 56, emphasis in original.

3. See Welker, *God the Spirit,* pp. 52-65.

4. For a report and careful theological reflection, see K. Kim, *Holy Spirit in the World,* chap. 6.

5. Rayan, *The Holy Spirit;* K. Kim, *Holy Spirit in the World,* chap. 5.

6. D. Petersen, *Not by Might Nor by Power.*

7. Daneel, "African Independent Church Pneumatology," pp. 143-66.

8. Comblin, *Holy Spirit and Liberation,* p. xi.

9. Comblin, *Holy Spirit and Liberation,* p. 21.

that may take. After more than five hundred years of slavery, masses of people in Latin America know economic, cultural, social, and ideological slavery as a daily experience.[10] Speechless and silent ones are being empowered by the Spirit to raise up their voice against injustice and oppression. This "earthly" liberation is not exclusive of "spiritual" transformation; the two belong together.[11] Rather than juxtaposing the divine and human dimensions, both are part of the Spirit's domain. Theology and praxis, doctrine and practicing virtues belong together. The public role of the Spirit in liberation reminds us of the tight link between belief and action, doctrine and praxis — too often ignored in the post-Enlightenment dualistic epistemology.[12]

God's Spirit is also graciously inviting the followers of Christ to collaborate in the work of liberation and justice. In this respect (provided I have correctly understood his intentions), the view of the prominent German Reformed pneumatologist M. Welker comes under critical scrutiny. Having spoken vocally about the role of God's Spirit in liberation (see chap. 6 above), Welker also seems to consider all political engagement by Christians a futile effort, whether sociopolitical, environmental, or similar.[13] Even though I agree with him that the Messiah, the Suffering Servant, "does not make himself and his action prevail by means of a public campaign," it is not true that "the bearer of the Spirit does not . . . make use of a public proclamation of law or of judgment," or that his voice could not be heard in the public spaces.[14] Even more importantly, Welker's "resistance to all attempts to assert the power of 'making it happen'" and his overly sensitive fear of "managing" the Spirit[15] if too actively involved in the actual work of liberation seem to cut off the legs from all human efforts. While I agree with him that a naive equation of any human effort with the work of God the Spirit is to be rejected, I also do not wish to juxtapose the divine and human initiative the way Welker does.[16] Even when fallible and imperfect, human effort is called forth and incorporated into the Spirit's mission in the world, similar to work toward peacebuilding, po-

---

10. Comblin, *Holy Spirit and Liberation*, p. 24.

11. Comblin, *Holy Spirit and Liberation*, p. 31.

12. See Hütter, *Suffering the Divine Things*.

13. Welker, *God the Spirit*, pp. 303-7 particularly.

14. Welker, *God the Spirit*, p. 125.

15. Welker, *God the Spirit*, p. 319.

16. For his suspicion toward all human initiatives for liberation, see, e.g., Welker, *God the Spirit*, pp. 125-28, and on the categorical distinction between the work of God the Spirit and ours, see, e.g., pp. 46-48, 321. For a similar critique of Welker, see Min, *Solidarity of Others*, pp. 214-15.

litical forgiveness, and reconciliation at various levels, to which we turn next. Doing so, we assume the insights won in earlier discussions on forgiveness and related themes (particularly in chap. 10) and seek to further develop them.

"Truth and Reconciliation": Forgiveness and Peacebuilding

One of the lasting contributions of liberation theologies is their critique of the church's lack of a public role in the world's conflicts and places of injustice.[17] While the church has been quick to condemn Jesus' crucifiers, it has been far slower to recognize that many people in the margins discover "themselves in Jesus as the *crucified*," and for them forgiveness is a deeply sociopolitical and economic reality as well.[18] In his passionate book *The Principle of Mercy*, Jon Sobrino argues that a true "spirituality of forgiveness" cannot merely pronounce pardon; it also has the mandate of "destroying the person oppressing, in his formal capacity as oppressor."[19] While I do not wish to take literally the latter part of the sentence (as it fosters further violence), Sobrino's passionate call for a sociopolitically responsible spirituality is to be welcomed. In recent years a number of other theologians,[20] Christian leaders,[21] and ecclesiastical bodies[22] from diverse backgrounds have begun to reflect carefully on the conditions and meaning of forgiveness in the public realm, whether among ethnic groups or within a nation or even in international relations.[23] Forgiveness also comes to bear on interfaith relations.[24] One important form of political forgiveness is the establishment of processes that aim at reaching reconciliation and forgiveness after conflicts have been resolved. The most well known is of course the truth and reconciliation process in South Africa, which, unlike most others, also had a determined Christian orientation in its matrix. It also

17. See, e.g., Gutiérrez, *A Theology of Liberation*, p. 108.

18. Crysdale, *Embracing Travail*, pp. 10-11, emphasis in original.

19. Sobrino, *The Principle of Mercy*, p. 65; I am indebted to Boersma, *Violence, Hospitality, and the Cross*, p. 253.

20. A. Torrance, "Forgiveness"; Shriver, *An Ethic for Enemies*; de Gruchy, *Reconciliation*; Wolterstorff, "Place of Forgiveness in the Actions of the State," pp. 87-111; see also, the many writings of Volf engaged in this chapter.

21. Tutu, *No Future without Forgiveness*.

22. United States Conference of Catholic Bishops, *Forgiveness in International Politics*.

23. For important symposium proceedings, see Helmick and Petersen, eds., *Forgiveness and Reconciliation*. A highly useful, recent critical review of the state of the art in political forgiveness is L. P. Barnes, "Talking Politics, Talking Forgiveness"; this section is indebted to it.

24. R. Petersen, "A Theology of Forgiveness."

employed robustly the African form of communalism expressed with the term *ubuntu*.[25]

What are we to think *theologically* of attempts for political forgiveness? L. Philip Barnes has pointed to some potential liabilities such as their often thin theological basis, particularly with regard to the wider atonement and reconciliation narrative of Christian faith, and that these attempts tend to operate at a too-general level. He also notes that there is often an unspoken assumption of nonviolence regardless of the conditions of the situation, and that there is lack of critical reflection on what "unconditional" forgiveness may or may not mean.[26] These are challenges to be taken seriously, and until more theological clarity is cast on them, we have to patiently wait for the clarification of a distinctively *Christian* theology of political forgiveness. On the positive side, we can refer to the seasoned note by Mark R. Amstutz, a leading authority in the field. Having studied the process of twenty or so truth commissions of sorts in various global locations, he concludes that the significance of a truth commission is "not that it de-emphasizes punishment but that it focuses on the reformation of communal bonds by encouraging moral reflection based on truth telling, confession, forgiveness, and reconciliation."[27] Theologically speaking, we have to insist that the ultimate goal of any reconciliation process has to do with "wounds as well as sins, healing as well as forgiveness."[28]

Reconciliation as the Ultimate Aim of Salvation

While the jury is still out on assessing the ways and forms of a specifically political forgiveness, it is safe to say that all Christians and Christian communities should be deeply involved in the continuing work of reconciliation.[29] Peacebuilding and seeking to help end conflicts[30] are a particularly urgent task in our pluralistic and globalizing world.[31] Not for nothing did the recent

25. See Graybill, *Truth and Reconciliation in South Africa*; Battle, *Reconciliation*. For a fine theological reflection, see Shaw, "Suffering, Hope and Forgiveness," pp. 477-89.

26. L. P. Barnes, "Talking Politics, Talking Forgiveness," pp. 72-78.

27. Amstutz, *The Healing of Nations*, p. 188, cited in Musekura, "Assessment of Contemporary Models of Forgiveness," p. 156.

28. Crysdale, *Embracing Travail*, p. 25.

29. See Schwöbel, "Reconciliation," pp. 26-35.

30. See further, Schreiter, Appleby, and Powers, eds., *Peacebuilding*; Kim, Kollontai, and Hoyland, eds., *Peace and Reconciliation*.

31. See Schreiter, "Globalization and Reconciliation."

WCC International Ecumenical Peace Convention make this programmatic statement: "We understand peace and peacemaking as an indispensable part of our common faith. Peace is inextricably related to the love, justice and freedom that God has granted to all human beings through Christ and the work of the Holy Spirit as a gift and vocation. It constitutes a pattern of life that reflects human participation in God's love for the world."[32] This call for churches is also heightened by the sad observation that so far "Christianity has not been distinguished by its nonviolence for most of Christian history. Indeed, so-called Christian nations have gone to war readily over the centuries, more often than not with the blessing of their chaplains and archbishops."[33] Yes, there have been blessed exceptions, and in this regard the work and testimony of the Mennonites[34] (Anabaptists) and Quakers should be acknowledged.

Theologically I take reconciliation as the most inclusive soteriological concept, including "cosmic reconciliation, the Hebrew notion of *shalom,* the meaning of the cross, the psychological effects of conversion, the work of the Holy Spirit, the overcoming of barriers between Christians, the work of the church in the world, peacemaking, movements towards ethnic reconciliation and the renewal of ecological balances between humanity and its natural environment."[35] In many contexts such as Australia and North America, an integral, continuing part of reconciliation has to do with relationship between the First Nations and "latecomers."[36] Originally a secular concept, used particularly in international diplomacy in antiquity, "reconciliation" was adopted by Christians and reoriented to Christ.[37] Enthusiastically, reconciliation has been adopted as a model of Christian mission.[38]

Such a comprehensive, multifaceted view of reconciliation comes to the fore in Pauline theology. In the first chapter of Colossians, Christ, the agent of

32. "Glory to God and Peace on Earth."

33. Langmead, "Transformed Relationships," p. 12.

34. See, e.g., the U.S. Mennonites' Peace and Justice Web site: http://www.pjsn.org/Pages/default.aspx (8/25/2014).

35. Similarly, Langmead, "Transformed Relationships," pp. 5-20.

36. See, e.g., Habel, *Reconciliation.*

37. See Aletti, "God Made Christ to Be Sin," p. 104. For its importance to the church's continuing work of reconciliation between social, political, and religious factions, see "Final Document 1," Second European Ecumenical Assembly (EEA2), Graz, Austria, June 23 to 29, 1997.

38. For the important statement from WCC's Athens 2005 World Conference on Evangelism and Mission, see Preparatory Paper no. 10: Mission as Ministry of Reconciliation (May 10, 2005). For important theological and missiological developments of the paradigm, see Schreiter, "Reconciliation and Healing"; Baum and Wells, eds., *The Reconciliation of Peoples.*

creation and head of the church, is the actor and locus of universal reconciliation without any borders: "For in him all the fulness of God was pleased to dwell, and through him to reconcile to himself all things, whether on earth or in heaven, making peace by the blood of his cross. And you, who once were estranged and hostile in mind, doing evil deeds, he has now reconciled in his body of flesh by his death" (Col. 1:19-22a). This kind of extraordinary breadth and width of the vision of reconciliation is echoed similarly in the second chapter of Ephesians: Christ, "our peace," has made peace between and reconciled Jews and Gentiles (the two blocks of humanity from the perspective of Israel's election theology), "thereby bringing the hostility to an end" (Eph. 2:14-16). Other passages could be added from Paul such as Galatians 3:28, in which racial (Jews and Gentiles), societal (free and slaves), and sexual (female and male) boundaries have been transcended because all are "one in Christ."[39] "In Christ Jesus you who once were far off have been brought near in the blood of Christ" (Eph. 2:13). A particularly important passage is 2 Corinthians 5:17-20, which is placed in the context of new creation: "God, who through Christ reconciled us to himself," has entrusted to us "the ministry of reconciliation," making us ambassadors of his eternal plan to overcome and reconcile enmities and strife.[40]

These and other biblical teachings declare that the divine initiative of reconciliation, based on the work of the cross,[41] forms the foundation of reconciliation and forgiveness.[42] This is not to make us passive and complacent but rather to make us active and enthusiastic in joining the divine movement of shalom (2 Cor. 5:19-20). While spirituality and faith support the task, it is deeply embedded in the complexities of the violent and hostile world.[43]

When God begins the work of reconciliation on earth, the starting point is with the victim. As Robert J. Schreiter explains it: "This 'victim first' approach finds experiential corroboration in the fact that, after a time of conflict and oppression or violation of human rights, the perpetrators of wrongdoing seldom or ever apologize or take responsibility for their actions." This does not definitely mean forgoing the pursuit of justice.[44] As argued above (chap. 10),

---

39. See also, Eph. 1:10.

40. Botman, "Truth and Reconciliation"; Müller-Fahrenholz, *The Art of Forgiveness.*

41. Cf. C.-S. Song, "Christian Mission," pp. 130-48.

42. This is the repeated emphasis of the leading theologian of reconciliation, the Roman Catholic Schreiter, "Practical Theology of Healing, Forgiveness, and Reconciliation," pp. 368-71. Among his many seminal contributions, see *Reconciliation* and *The Ministry of Reconciliation.*

43. See further, Phan, "Peacebuilding and Reconciliation."

44. Schreiter, "Practical Theology of Healing," pp. 371-72, 385-90.

forgiveness has everything to do with restoring broken relationships, establishing justice, and working toward healing in a most comprehensive sense.[45] Beginning with the victim means taking the side of the weak and the vulnerable; it seeks to reestablish her or his humanity. A distinctively Christian work of reconciliation also seeks to help the victim turn to God, although that should not be made a precondition for the work of reconciliation concerning current earthly realities. Divine love and forgiveness are unconditional. But there also is the need to help the perpetrator find repentance, remorse, and forgiveness through which his or her humanity can be reestablished. Both the victim and the perpetrator have an urgent need for healing to happen. What helps here immensely is the opportunity to "lodge their suffering in the story of the suffering and death of Christ." If restoration can take place, ideally on both sides of the violation, nothing less than "new creation" takes place, anticipating the eschatological consummation of the new creation (2 Cor. 5:17). This is when finally God will be all in all (1 Cor. 15:28). Hence, Christian reconciliation is not only return (to what was before the wrongdoing) but also re-turn, as in changing the course and looking toward future possibilities.[46]

Even though all healing and restoration processes take time both at the personal and the communal level, the complexity of psychological, psychiatric, emotional, physical, and spiritual woundedness after conflicts, particularly ethnic cleansings and mass murders, calls for much patience and support. Even when wounds are beginning to heal, human dignity may be at stake. Particularly painful and long is the process of healing memories. Typically both personal and social healing are deeply intertwined in this therapeutic process.[47]

---

45. For comments, see Fiddes, *Past Event and Present Salvation*, p. 15.
46. Schreiter, "Practical Theology of Healing," pp. 372-76; here p. 373.
47. For details, see Schreiter, "Practical Theology of Healing," pp. 376-82.

14. Epilogue: The Faithfulness of God and the End of Human Yearning

Confidence in God's Faithfulness until the End

The motive behind the Reformed doctrine of "the perseverance of the saints to the end" *(perseverantia sanctorum usque ad finem)* had to do not only with the theological reasoning of the Calvinist system but also with a wider existential question. For "Christians living in a minority situation or under persecution," this concern arose: Can the experience of the Holy Spirit in the rebirth to new life and to a living hope ever be lost or not? On all sides of the Reformed movement, from Huguenots to the Dutch and others, it was a deeply felt concern testing the reliability of the faithfulness of God.[1] The Lutheran version of perseverance is ecclesiologically founded. According to the Augsburg Confession, "one holy Christian church will be and remain forever."[2] Notwithstanding differences in nuancing the doctrine of perseverance,[3] the Reformation theologians agreed on the basis of the confidence:

> 1. God the Father is faithful; he cannot deny himself (II Tim. 2.13). He never lets go of the person he has chosen. 2. God the Son prayed for those who are his "that your faith might not fail" (Luke 22.32). 3. As advance payment and beginning of eternal life, the Holy Spirit remains with the

---

1. Moltmann, *Spirit of Life*, p. 156.
2. Augsburg Confession VII, in *BC*, p. 32.
3. For a standard, historically oriented discussion, see chap. 11 in L. Berkhof, *Systematic Theology.*

people who are his to the end *(usque ad finem)*. The Holy Spirit "seals" God's children for the day of redemption.[4]

The Catholic rebuttal of the Reformation doctrine of assurance of salvation and perseverance at Trent *(Decree on Justification,* chapters 9 and 16) mistook it for self-assurance and overly optimistic trust in human steadfastness. Trent was unwilling to acknowledge that the Reformation doctrine of perseverance indeed highlighted the same principle of divine faithfulness that the Catholic doctrine also underlined. Interestingly, in the Arminian-Calvinist exchange about election (as discussed above in chap. 9), the Arminian critique of the technically formulated Calvinist doctrine of perseverance of saints wanted to shift the focus onto the faithfulness of God rather than a "cold" philosophico-theological reasoning. The conclusion, hence, is that as long as the locus of the doctrine of perseverance — whether it be formulated by Protestants or Catholics — is placed in God's faithfulness, it provides confident assurance to the believer. It does not mean that a Christian could not fall away from grace (defined in a semi-automatic way) but that even in their darkest moments of life men and women, as well as the whole church of Christ, may confidently rest in the assurance of God's fatherly love and care.

After discussing perseverance, typical Protestant *ordo salutis* presentations culminate in the doctrine of glorification.[5] The classical biblical support was found in Romans 8:29-30, the most comprehensive Pauline presentation of the order: "For those whom he foreknew he also predestined to be conformed to the image of his Son, in order that he might be the first-born among many brethren. And those whom he predestined he also called; and those whom he called he also justified; and those whom he justified he also glorified."

For the Hebrew Saint Paul, the term "glory" resonated with the key OT word *kabod*, which functions as a semitechnical term denoting God's presence (along with expressions such as the "name"). Even the Reformed tradition with its emphasis on the union with God (Calvin), however, failed to make the connection between glorification and union a theological theme. Although the Eastern tradition does not subscribe to the doctrine of glorification in the same sense as the Christian West, its intuition of salvation as deification materially makes that connection. Even though the divine uncreated glory

---

4. Moltmann, *Spirit of Life,* p. 156.

5. One of the few monograph-long presentations is Ramm, *Them He Glorified.* A useful, mainly biblically oriented discussion can be found in Erickson, *Christian Theology.* pp. 997-1002.

always remains that, namely, *uncreated* and distinct from all that is created, the ultimate goal of salvation is participation in the glorious life of the triune God. In the doctrine of glorification, hence, the themes of soteriology and eschatology are linked together. Glorification is a matter of eschatological hope and consummation.

Christian tradition believes that the insatiable human yearning for fulfillment and happiness can be met only by the ultimate encounter with God that "glorification" seeks to conceptualize. As Moltmann pointedly says, "men and women are erotic beings, driven by hungry hearts which can find fulfilment only in God."[6] In mystical experiences, there is "an anticipation of the eschatological, immediate and direct seeing of God 'face to face.'"[7] Although it is not a biblical term, the Roman Catholic tradition speaks of the consummation of salvation in terms of the beatific vision,[8] a dream of ultimate fulfillment of all human yearnings expressed in the Eastern traditions as the completion of deification.[9] Having first concluded that no created good may bring ultimate and final happiness,[10] Saint Thomas teaches that, indeed, human yearning meets fulfillment in the vision of God, indeed, in the "essence" of God as based on the scriptural promise in 1 John 3:2 ("we shall see him as he is").[11] However, this vision cannot be had with physical eyes, and even in the beatific vision itself, after resurrection the glorified humans' knowledge of God is not exhaustive.[12] That said, the beatific vision goes beyond reason and faith and, hence, can be considered, not "strictly speaking, a doctrine, but . . . the consummation of all doctrine" in that the vision of God really is "the content of eternal bliss."[13]

6. Moltmann, *Spirit of Life*, p. 199.

7. Moltmann, *Spirit of Life*, p. 205.

8. For the classic Roman Catholic statement, see the encyclical in 1336 by Pope Benedict XII, *Benedictus Dei (On the Beatific Vision of God)*, at http://www.papalencyclicals.net/Ben12/B12bdeus.html (5/9/2014). Although less technically defined, even Protestant tradition has materially the same kind of vision. Said Melanchthon: "Eternal life will be perpetual adoration"; cited in Jenson, *Systematic Theology*, 2:340.

9. Although the Eastern Church does not use the same terminology, materially it affirms the vision of God. See Lossky, *The Vision of God*.

10. Aquinas, *ST* 2a.2.

11. Here lies the difference between Aquinas and Eastern tradition: according to the essence-energy distinction, Gregory of Palamas and the whole tradition speaks of inability to see the essence of God. See further, Jenson, *Systematic Theology*, 2:342-43.

12. Aquinas, *ST* 3 suppl. 92.1-3.

13. Pelikan, *CT* 3:303. For the importance of mystical experiences in this regard, see Moltmann, *Spirit of Life*, pp. 198-99.

The Wideness of Soteriological Vision:
From Creation to Redemption to Eschatological Consummation

The hope for personal salvation is to be set within the widest horizons of Christian soteriological vision and the providential world governance of the loving Creator. Barth rightly saw that the idea of world governance speaks of God's faithfulness to his creation.[14] According to the biblical testimonies, it first comes to manifestation in Yahweh's dealings with his people[15] and culminates in the pronouncement of the dawning of the righteous rule of the Father as announced by Jesus, the Son. It is faithfulness rather than immutability that secures the preservation, cooperation, and loving guidance of world affairs toward the divinely desired goal. As are all God's dealings with the world, faithfulness is funded by trinitarian logic: "God's faithfulness, which proceeds from the mutual faithfulness of the Son to the Father and the Father to the Son, is the basis of the identity and continuation of his creatures."[16]

What is the final goal of providential world governance? For Aquinas it was God himself,[17] and for the Protestant scholastics, the glory of God.[18] We can follow tradition in that from the perspective of the creatures giving glory to God, that is indeed the highest calling. From God's perspective, however, "the creature was not created in order that God should receive glory from it. God does not need this, for he is already God in himself from all eternity." This notion combats the common atheistic and even religious suspicion that is ultimately guided by a form of self-seeking and self-love. Rather, God's love and faithfulness to his creation will become evident in cooperation and governance, the goal of which is the redemption and fulfillment of creation.[19]

Creation, redemption, and consummation are intertwined in the divine economy of salvation. But how are they to be linked with each other systematically? And to complicate the question: How does the Fall relate to this issue? The late Scottish theologian Colin Gunton helpfully juxtaposed two systematic alternatives. The first one he named "restorationist," in which the perfectly completed creation in the beginning was destroyed by the Fall and left to wait for "a return to the condition of perfection." The other one he named

---

14. E.g., Barth, *CD* III/3, pp. 40-41.

15. Throughout *CD* III/3, §§48 and 49, Barth discusses the OT, particularly the Abrahamic narrative, to illustrate providence and guidance.

16. Pannenberg, *ST* 2:53.

17. Aquinas, *Summa contra Gentiles* 3.17, 18.

18. For Reformed examples, see Heppe, *Reformed Dogmatics*, p. 136.

19. Pannenberg, *ST* 2:56-57 (earlier quotation from p. 56).

an "evolutionary" view, in which creation is not perfect in the beginning and is thus waiting for the final perfection; this view is typical of "those modern theologies which are shaped by Hegelian and Darwinian influences." If the former one builds on the problematic idea of the return to Paradise rather than the expectation of God's new creation in the eschatological future, the latter is marred by its undermining of the seriousness of evil and the newness of Christ's redemption. To correct these weaknesses but also to learn from these views, Gunton recommends as an alternative the vision of creation as a "*project* — that is to say, it is made to go somewhere — but by virtue of the fall can reach that end only by a redemption which involves a radical redirection from the movement it takes backwards whenever sin and evil shape its direction." Gunton believes that Irenaeus supports this third option, although often he is linked with basic intuitions of the second one.[20] The current project supports this third basic vision as well.

A critical step in this divine "project" is the resurrection from the dead of the One in whom everything was created and is being upheld together. While resurrection, as discussed in *Christ and Reconciliation* (chaps. 6 and 13), has blessed salvific effects on humanity, from creation's perspective it means nothing less than the *"redemption of space and time."*[21] Space and time as creational acts of God will neither be suspended nor abrogated but healed and, in anticipation of the coming of God's eternity into time, taken up by God. The Johannine Jesus' resurrection appearances (John 21), as much as exegetical disputes should be noted, may be pointers to this healing of space and time.[22] The eschatological dimension of the resurrection also reminds us of the integral link between creation and new creation: the redemption of space and time also bespeaks the healing and renewal of nature. The same God who in the first place created the heavens and earth is going to show his faithfulness in renewing creation.[23]

Christ's resurrection as a "miraculous" event belongs to this world, time, and space in order to secure not only the redemption of human life on this earth,[24] but also all created life, as well as space and time. It is not a matter of violating the laws of nature but rather of pointing to the eschatological reality in which "new kinds of laws" will be put in place by the almighty God. Resurrection represents a "new" kind of happening, anticipating the coming to

---

20. Gunton, *The Triune Creator*, pp. 11-12, emphasis added.
21. T. Torrance, *Space, Time, and Resurrection*, p. 90, emphasis in original.
22. See further, T. Torrance, *Space, Time, and Resurrection*, pp. 90-91.
23. For a robust discussion of this theme, see Moltmann, *Way of Jesus Christ*, pp. 246-73.
24. See further, T. Torrance, *Space, Time, and Resurrection*, pp. 86-87.

fulfillment of the creational project, as it were. On the basis of the hypostatic union principle, Christian theology affirms that "in the risen Christ . . . there is involved an hypostatic union between eternity and time, eternity and redeemed and sanctified time, and therefore between eternity and new time."[25] The ascension of the resurrected Christ takes this development even further and completes the process of the "taking up of *human time* into God." Similarly, in the risen and ascended Christ, "the life of human beings is wedded to eternal life."[26]

In sum: the hope of salvation for humanity is deeply embedded in the wider context of cosmic renewal. God, the Creator, will show himself to be loving and faithful in redeeming the promises of Holy Scriptures for the establishment of the new heaven and new earth. That is the topic for the fifth and final volume of this project.

---

25. T. Torrance, *Space, Time, and Resurrection*, p. 98.
26. T. Torrance, *Space, Time, and Resurrection*, p. 98, emphasis in original.

Bibliography

Abe, Masao. "Beyond Buddhism and Christianity: 'Dazzling Darkness.'" In *DEHF*, pp. 224-43.

———. "Kenotic God and Dynamic Sunyata." In *DEHF*, pp. 25-90.

Abelson, Joshua. *The Immanence of God in Rabbinical Literature*. London: Macmillan, 1912.

Abraham, William J. "Christian Perfection." In *The Oxford Handbook of Methodist Studies*, edited by James E. Kirby and William J. Abraham, chap. 34, pp. 587-601. Oxford: Oxford University Press, 2014.

Abrahams, Israel, Jacob Haberman, and Charles Manekin. "Belief." In *EJ* 3:290-94.

Abram, David. *Becoming Animal: An Earthly Cosmology*. New York: Vintage, 2010.

Abrams, J. Z. *Judaism and Disability: Portrayals in Ancient Texts from the Tanach through the Bavli*. Washington, D.C.: Gallaudet University Press, 1998.

Abu-Nimer, Mohammed. *Nonviolence and Peace Building in Islam*. Gainesville: University Press of Florida, 2003.

———, ed. *Reconciliation, Justice, and Coexistence: Theory and Practice*. Lanham, Md.: Lexington Books, 2001.

Abu-Nimer, Mohammed, and David Augsburger, eds. *Peace-building by, between, and beyond Muslims and Evangelical Christians*. Lanham, Md.: Lexington Books, 2009.

Abu-Nimer, Mohammed, and Ilham Nasser. "Forgiveness in the Arab and Islamic Contexts: Between Theology and Practice." *Journal of Religious Ethics* 41, no. 3 (2013): 474-94.

Adeyemo, Tokunboh. "Unapproachable God: The High God of African Traditional Religion." In *The Global God: Multicultural Evangelical Views of God,* edited by Aida Besancon Spencer and William David Spencer, pp. 127-45. Grand Rapids: Baker, 1998.

Adiprasetya, Joas. *An Imaginative Glimpse: The Trinity and Multiple Religious Participation*. Eugene, Ore.: Pickwick, 2013.

Afsaruddin, Asma. "Celebrating Pluralism and Dialogue: Qur'anic Perspectives." *Journal of Ecumenical Studies* 42, no. 3 (2007): 389-406.

Ahlstrand, Kajsa. *Fundamental Openness: An Enquiry into Raimundo Panikkar's Theological Vision and Its Presuppositions.* Studia Missionalia Upsaliensia 57. Uppsala: Swedish Institute for Missionary Research, 1993.

Ahluwalia, Kewal. "Shudhi Movement: 85th Shardhanand Shudhi Divas — December 23rd." http://www.aryasamaj.com/enews/2012/jan/4.htm (2/27/2014).

Ahn, Byung Mu. "Jesus and the People (Minjung)." In *Asian Faces of Jesus,* edited by R. S. Sugirtharajah, pp. 163-72. Maryknoll, N.Y.: Orbis, 1995.

Albers, Robert H. *Shame: A Faith Perspective.* New York: Haworth, 1995.

Albertsen, Elisabeth J., Lynn E. O'Connor, and Jack W. Berry. "Religion and Interpersonal Guilt: Variations across Ethnicity and Spirituality." *Mental Health, Religion and Culture* 9, no. 1 (March 2006): 67-84.

Albertz, Rainer. "Monotheism and Violence: How to Handle a Dangerous Biblical Tradition." In *The Land of Israel in Bible, History, and Theology: Studies in Honour of Ed Noort,* edited by Jacques van Ruiten and J. C. de Vos, pp. 373-87. Boston: Brill, 2009.

Aletti, Jean-Noël, S.J. "God Made Christ to Be Sin (2 Corinthians 5:21): Reflections on a Pauline Paradox." In *The Redemption: An Interdisciplinary Symposium on Christ as Redeemer,* edited by Stephen T. Davis, Daniel Kendall, S.J., and Gerald O'Collins, S.J. Oxford: Oxford University Press, 2004.

Alexander, Kimberly Ervin. *Pentecostal Healing: Models in Theology and Practice.* Dorset, U.K.: Deo Publishing, 2006.

Alfaro, Sammy. *Divino Compañero: Toward a Hispanic Pentecostal Christology.* Princeton Theological Monograph Series. Eugene, Ore.: Pickwick, 2010.

Alon, Nahi, and Haim Omer. *The Psychology of Demonization: Promoting Acceptance and Reducing Conflict.* Mahwah, N.J.: Erlbaum, 2006.

Alter, Robert. *The Art of Biblical Narrative.* New York: Basic Books, 1981.

Altmann, Walter. *Luther and Liberation: A Latin American Perspective.* Translated by Mary M. Solberg. Minneapolis: Fortress, 1992.

Amaladoss, Michael, S.J. "Identity and Harmony: Challenges to Mission in South Asia." In *Mission in the Third Millennium,* edited by Robert J. Schreiter, pp. 25-39. Maryknoll, N.Y.: Orbis, 2002.

Amstutz, Mark R. *The Healing of Nations: The Promise and Limits of Political Forgiveness.* Lanham, Md.: Rowman and Littlefield, 2005.

Anatolios, Khaled. *Athanasius.* Early Church Fathers. London and New York: Routledge, 2004.

Anderson, Allan. "Demons and Deliverance in African Pentecostalism." In *A&D,* chap. 2, pp. 42-62.

———. "The Gospel and Culture in Pentecostal Mission in the Third World." *Missionalia* 27, no. 2 (1999): 220-30.

———. *Zion and Pentecost: The Spirituality and Experience of Pentecostal and Zionist/Apostolic Churches in South Africa.* Pretoria: University of South Africa Press, 2000.

Anees, Munawar A. "Salvation and Suicide: What Does Islamic Theology Say?" *Dialog* 45, no. 3 (Fall 2006): 275-76.

Ansari, Zafar Ishaq. "Taftāzānī's Views on taklīf, gabr and qadar: A Note of the Development of Islamic Theological Doctrines." *Arabica* 16, no. 1 (1969): 65-78.

Anselm of Canterbury. *De Concordia* 1.5. In *Anselm of Canterbury: The Major Works*, edited by G. R. Evans and Brian Davies. Oxford: Oxford University Press, 1998.

The Apostolic Tradition of Hippolytus. Edited and translated by Burton Scott Easton. Cambridge: Cambridge University Press, 1934.

Appasamy, A. J. [Aiyadurai Jesudasan]. *An Indian Interpretation of Christianity*. Madras: Christian Literature Society, 1924.

———. *The Use of Yoga in Prayer*. Madras: Christian Literature Society, 1926.

Aquinas, Thomas. *Summa contra Gentiles*. Edited, with English, especially scriptural references, updated by Joseph Kenny, O.P. New York: Hanover House, 1955-1957. http://www.dhspriory.org/thomas/ContraGentiles.htm.

Arendt, Hannah. *The Human Condition*. Chicago: University of Chicago Press, 1958. http://yaleunion.org/wp-content/uploads/2013/12/HannahArendthumancondition .pdf (2/11/2014).

Arnold, Clinton E. *Ephesians: Power and Magic — the Concept of Power in Ephesians in Light of Its Historical Setting*. Cambridge: Cambridge University Press, 1989.

———. *Powers of Darkness: Principalities and Powers in Paul's Letters*. Downers Grove, Ill.: InterVarsity, 1992.

Artson, Bradley Shavit. "Vibrating over the Face of the Deep: God's Creating and Ours." *CCAR Journal: The Reform Jewish Quarterly* 57, no. 1 (2010): 40-47.

Asad, Muhammad. "The Spirit in Islam." In *Islam — Its Meaning and Message*, edited by Khursid Ahmad. Leicester: Islamic Foundation, 1993.

Asamoah-Gyadu, J. Kwabena. "Mission to 'Set the Captives Free': Healing, Deliverance, and Generational Curses in Ghanaian Pentecostalism." *IRM* 93, no. 370 (July/October 2004): 389-406.

———. "Spirit and Spirits in African Religious Traditions." In *IRDSW*, chap. 3, pp. 41-54.

Asano, S. E. "Cultural Values, Ethnic Identity, Interpersonal Guilt and Shame: A Comparison of Japanese Americans and European Americans." Ph.D. diss., Wright Institute, Berkeley, Calif., 1998.

Askari, Hasan. *Inter-Religion: A Collection of Essays*. Aligarh, India: Printwell Publications, 1977.

Asvaghosa. *Açvaghosa's Discourse on the Awakening of Faith in the Mahâyâna*. Translated by Teitaro Suzuki (1900). www.sacred-texts.com.

Athanasius. *Letters to Serapion on the Holy Spirit*. In *Athanasius*, translated and edited by Khaled Anatolios, pp. 221-24. London: Routledge, 2004.

Attanasi, Katherine. "Introduction: The Plurality of Prosperity Theologies and Pentecostalisms." In *Pentecostalism and Prosperity: The Socioeconomics of the Global Charismatic Movement*, edited by Katherine Attanasi and Amos Yong, pp. 1-12. New York: Palgrave Macmillan, 2012.

Attwood, Jayarava Michael. "Did King Ajātasattu Confess to the Buddha, and Did the Buddha Forgive Him?" *Journal of Buddhist Ethics* (no issue, no year), pp. 279-307. http://blogs.dickinson.edu/buddhistethics/files/2010/05/attwood-article.pdf (3/12/2014).

Augsburger, Myron S. "Justice in Forgiveness." *Living Pulpit,* April-June 2007, p. 5.

Augustine. *On the Free Choice of Will.* Translated by Thomas Williams. Indianapolis: Hackett, 1993.

Aune, David E. "Recent Readings of Paul Relating to Justification by Faith." In *Rereading Paul Together: Protestant and Catholic Perspectives on Justification,* edited by David E. Aune, pp. 188-245. Grand Rapids: Baker Academic, 2006.

―――. "Repentance." In *ER* 11:7755-60.

Aurobindo (Ghose), Sri. *The Life Divine.* Complete Works of Sri Aurobindo, vols. 21, 22. Pondicherry, India: Sri Aurobindo Ashram Press, 2005. http://www.aurobindo.ru/workings/sa/18-19/the_life_divine_21-22_e.pdf.

Avalos, Hector. *Health Care and the Rise of Christianity.* Peabody, Mass.: Hendrickson, 1999.

Averbeck, Richard E. "Breath, Wind, Spirit and the Holy Spirit in the Old Testament." In *Presence, Power, and Promise,* edited by David G. Firth and Paul D. Wegner, pp. 25-37. Downers Grove, Ill.: InterVarsity, 2011.

Ayoub, Mahmoud M. "Repentance in the Islamic Tradition." In *RCP,* pp. 96-121.

―――. "Trinity Day Lectures." *Trinity Seminary Review* 32 (Winter-Spring 2011): 7-18.

"Āyurveda." In *Medicine across Cultures: History and Practice of Medicine in Non-Western Cultures,* edited by Helaine Selin, pp. 75-83. Norwell, Mass.: Kluwer Academic Publishers, 2003.

Baer, Yitzhak. *A History of the Jews in Christian Spain.* Translated by Louis Schjoffman. Vol. 1. Philadelphia: Jewish Publication Society, 1993.

Baier, Karl. "Ultimate Reality in Buddhism and Christianity." In *Buddhism and Christianity in Dialogue,* edited by Perry Schmidt-Leukel, pp. 87-116. London: SCM, 2005.

Bainbridge, William Sims. "The Sociology of Conversion." In *HRC,* pp. 178-91.

Baker, Carolyn Denise. "Created Spirit Beings: Angels." In *Systematic Theology,* edited by Stanley Horton, pp. 179-94. Rev. ed. Springfield, Mo.: Gospel Publishing House, 1995.

Baker-Fletcher, Karen. *Dancing with God: The Trinity from a Womanist Perspective.* St. Louis: Chalice, 2006.

Bakhtin, Mikhail. "Author and Hero in Aesthetic Activity." In *Art and Answerability: Early Philosophical Essays,* translated by Kenneth Brostrom. Austin: University of Texas Press, 1990.

―――. *Toward a Philosophy of the Act.* Translated by Vadim Liapunov. Austin: University of Texas Press, 1993.

Bakken, Kenneth L. "Holy Spirit and Theosis: Toward a Lutheran Theology of Healing." *St. Vladimir's Theological Quarterly* 38, no. 4 (1994): 410-11.

Balthasar, Hans Urs von. *Theo-Logic.* Vol. 3, *The Spirit of Truth.* Translated by Adrian J. Walker. San Francisco: Ignatius, 2005.

Bannister, Andrew G. "Angels in Islamic Oral Tradition from the Qur'an to Tha'labi." In *A&D,* chap. 9.

Barna, George. *Revolution.* Wheaton, Ill.: Tyndale House, 2005.

Barnes, L. Philip. "Talking Politics, Talking Forgiveness." *Scottish Journal of Theology* 64 (2011): 64-79.

Barnes, Michel René. "The Beginning and End of Early Christian Pneumatology." *Augustinian Studies* 39, no. 2 (2008): 169-86.

———. "Demythologization in the Theology of Karl Rahner." *Theological Studies* 55, no. 1 (1994): 24-45.

———. "Rereading Augustine's Theology of the Trinity." In *The Trinity: An Interdisciplinary Symposium on Trinity,* edited by Stephen T. Davis, Daniel Kendall, S.J., and Gerald O'Collins, S.J. Oxford: Oxford University Press, 1999.

Barr, Stephen M. "Theology after Newton." *First Things* 187 (November 2008): 31-33.

Barth, Karl. *Dogmatics in Outline.* Translated by G. T. Thomson. London: SCM, 1949.

———. "The Holy Spirit and Christian Life." Translated by Michael Raburn. 2002. http://people.duke.edu/~mr33/Barth%20Holy%20Spirit.pdf (1/28/2014).

Barth, Karl, and Heinrich Barth. "Der Heilige Geist und das christiliche Leben." In *Zur Lehre vom Heiligen Geist,* Beihefte 1, *Zwischen den Zeiten,* pp. 39-105. Munich, 1930.

Barua, Ankur. "The Dialectic of Divine 'Grace' and 'Justice' in St. Augustine and Sri-Vaisnavism." *Religions of South Asia* 4, no. 1 (2010): 45-65.

Barylka, Yerahmiel. "Conversion in Judaism." On the JDC International Centre for Community Development Web site, November 3, 2011. http://www.jdc-iccd.org/en/article/38/conversion-in-judaism.

Bash, Antony. "Forgiveness: A Re-appraisal." *Studies in Christian Ethics* 24 (2011): 133-46.

Basham, A. L. *The Wonder That Was India.* New York: Grove Press, 1954; London: Sigwick and Jackson, 1988.

Bassis, Kinrei. "Forgiveness." n.p. http://www.berkeleybuddhistpriory.org/pages/articles/online_articles/forgiveness.html (3/14/2014).

Battle, Michael. *Reconciliation: The Ubuntu Theology of Desmond Tutu.* Cleveland: Pilgrim Press, 1997.

Baum, Gregory, and Harold Wells, eds. *The Reconciliation of Peoples: Challenge to the Churches.* Geneva: WCC Publications, 1997.

Baur, F. C. *Paul the Apostle of Jesus Christ, His Life and Work, His Epistles and His Doctrine.* Translated by A. Menzies. Vol. 2. London: Williams and Norgate, 1875. http://books.google.com/books?id=xxJKAAAAMAAJ&printsec=frontcover&source=gbs_ge_summary_r&cad=0#v=onepage&q&f=false (1/28/2014).

Bayly, Susan. *Saints, Goddesses, and Kings: Muslims and Christians in South Indian Society, 1700-1900.* Cambridge: Cambridge University Press, 1990.

Beachy, A. J. *The Concept of Grace in the Radical Reformers.* Nieuwkoop: De Graaf, 1977.

Beaton, Richard. "New Testament Metaphors and the Christian Mission." *Evangelical Missions Quarterly* 37 (January 2001): 60-64.

Bebbington, D. W. *Evangelicalism in Modern Britain: A History from the 1730s to the 1980s.* London: Routledge, 1988.

Beck, Guy L. "Fire in the Ātman: Repentance in Hinduism." In *RCP,* pp. 76-95.

Bede. *The Venerable Bede: Commentary on the Acts of the Apostles.* Translated by Lawrence T. Martin. Kalamazoo, Mich.: Cistercian Publications, 1989.

Bediako, Kwame. *Christianity in Africa: The Renewal of a Non-Western Religion.* Edinburgh: University Press; Maryknoll, N.Y.: Orbis, 1995.

Beilby, James K., Paul Rhodes Eddy, and Steven E. Eenderlein. "Justification in Contemporary Debate." In *Justification: Five Views,* edited by James K. Beilby and Paul Rhodes Eddy, pp. 53-82. Downers Grove, Ill.: IVP Academic, 2011.

―――. "Justification in Historical Perspective." In *Justification: Five Views,* edited by James K. Beilby and Paul Rhodes Eddy, pp. 13-52. Downers Grove, Ill.: IVP Academic, 2011.

Beker, Christiaan. *The Triumph of God: The Essence of Paul's Thought.* Translated by Loren T. Stuckenbruck. Minneapolis: Fortress, 1990.

Bellah, Robert. *The Good Society.* New York: Knopf, 1991.

Belser, Julia Watts. "Reading Talmudic Bodies: Disability, Narrative, and the Gaze in Rabbinic Judaism." In *Disability in Judaism, Christianity, and Islam: Sacred Texts, Historical Traditions, and Social Analysis,* edited by Darla Schumm and Michael Stoltzfus, chap. 1. New York: Palgrave Macmillan, 2011.

―――. "Returning to Flesh: A Jewish Reflection on Feminist Disability Theology." *Journal of Feminist Studies in Religion* 26, no. 2 (Fall 2010): 127-32.

Benner, Dagmar. "Healing and Medicine: Healing and Medicine in Āyurveda and South Asia." In *ER,* pp. 3852-58.

Bergen, Jeremy M. "The Holy Spirit in the World." *Vision: A Journal for Church and Theology* 13, no. 1 (Spring 2012): 84-92.

Berger, Peter L. *A Rumor of Angels: Modern Society and the Rediscovery of the Supernatural.* Garden City, N.Y.: Doubleday, 1969.

Berkhof, Hendrikus. *Christ and Powers.* Translated by John H. Yoder. Scottdale, Pa.: Herald, 1962.

―――. *The Doctrine of the Holy Spirit.* Atlanta: John Knox, 1964, 1976.

Berkhof, Louis. *Systematic Theology.* Grand Rapids: Eerdmans, 1996.

Berkouwer, G. C. *Faith and Justification.* Translated by Lewis B. Smedes. Grand Rapids: Eerdmans, 1954.

―――. *The Triumph of Grace in the Theology of Karl Barth.* Grand Rapids: Eerdmans, 1956.

Berkson, William. *Fields of Force: The Development of a World View from Faraday to Einstein.* London: Routledge and Kegan Paul, 1974.

Betcher, Sharon V. "Becoming Flesh of My Flesh: Feminist and Disability Theologies on the Edge of Posthumanist Discourse." *Journal of Feminist Studies in Religion* 26, no. 2 (Fall 2010): 107-18.

Betty, Stafford. "The Growing Evidence for 'Demonic Possession': What Should Psychiatry's Response Be?" *Journal of Religion and Health* 44, no. 1 (Spring 2005): 13-30.

Bevans, Stephen B. "God Inside Out: Toward a Missionary Theology of the Holy Spirit." *International Bulletin of Missionary Research* 22, no. 3 (1998): 102-5.

Bhagavadgita. Translated by Ramanand Prasad. EAWC Anthology, 1988. http://eawc .evansville.edu/anthology/gita.htm.

Bharathi, B. S. "Spirit Possession and Healing Practices in a South Indian Fishing Community." *Man in India* 73, no. 4 (1968): 343-52.

Bhat, Abdur Rashid. "Free Will and Determinism: An Overview of Muslim Scholars' Perspective." *Journal of Islamic Philosophy* 2, no. 1 (2006): 1-24.

Bhattacharyya, N. N. *Indian Demonology: The Inverted Pantheon.* Delhi: Monahar, 2000.

Bieler, Andrea, and Hans-Martin Gutmann. *Embodying Grace: Proclaiming Justification in the Real World.* Translated by Linda M. Maloney. Minneapolis: Fortress, 2010.

Bilde, Per. *Flavius Josephus between Jerusalem and Rome: His Life, His Works, and Their Importance.* Sheffield: Sheffield Academic Press, 1988.

Billings, J. Todd. *Calvin, Participation, and the Gift.* Oxford: Oxford University Press, 2007.

————. "Calvin's Comeback? The Irresistible Redeemer." *Christian Century* 126, no. 24 (December 1, 2009): 22-25.

————. "John Milbank's Theology of the 'Gift' and Calvin's Theology of Grace: A Critical Comparison." *Modern Theology* 21, no. 1 (2005): 87-105.

————. "United to God through Christ: Assessing Calvin on the Question of Deification." *Harvard Theological Review* 98, no. 3 (2005): 315-34.

Bird, Michael F. "Progressive Reformed View." In *Justification: Five Views,* edited by James K. Beilby and Paul Rhodes Eddy, pp. 131-57. Downers Grove, Ill.: IVP Academic, 2011.

————. *The Saving Righteousness of God: Studies on Paul, Justification, and the New Perspective.* Colorado Springs: Paternoster, 2007.

Birnbaum, Raoul. *The Healing Buddha.* Boulder, Colo.: Shambhala, 1989.

Bittlinger, Arnold. "Baptism in Water and in Spirit: Aspects of Christian Initiation." In *The Baptism in the Holy Spirit as an Ecumenical Problem,* edited by Kilian McDonnell and Arnold Bittlinger. Notre Dame: Catholic Renewal Service, 1972.

Blevins, Dean G. "Neuroscience, John Wesley, and Christian Life." *Wesleyan Theological Journal* 44, no. 1 (Spring 2009): 219-47.

Blocher, Henri A. "The Lutheran-Catholic Declaration on Justification." In *Justification in Perspective: Historical Developments and Contemporary Challenges,* edited by Bruce L. McCormack, pp. 197-217. Grand Rapids: Baker Academic, 2006.

Bloom, Alfred. "Jesus in the Pure Land." In *JWF,* chap. 3.

————. *Shinran's Gospel of Pure Grace.* Association for Asian Studies Monographs 20. Tucson: University of Arizona Press, 1965.

Blue, Ken. *Authority to Heal.* Downers Grove, Ill.: InterVarsity, 1987.

Bobrinskoy, Boris. *The Mystery of the Trinity: Trinitarian Experience and Vision in the Biblical and Patristic Tradition.* Translated by Anthony P. Gythiel. Crestwood, N.Y.: St. Vladimir's Seminary Press, 1999.

Boersma, Hans. *Violence, Hospitality, and the Cross: Reappropriating the Atonement Tradition.* Grand Rapids: Baker Academic, 2006.

Boesak, Allan A. *Black and Reformed: Apartheid, Liberation, and the Calvinist Tradition.* Maryknoll, N.Y.: Orbis, 1984; reprint, Eugene, Ore.: Wipf and Stock, 2015.

Boff, Leonardo. *Holy Trinity, Perfect Community.* Maryknoll, N.Y.: Orbis, 2000.

————. *Liberating Grace.* Translated by John Drury. Maryknoll, N.Y.: Orbis, 1979.

————. *Trinity and Society.* Translated by Paul Burns. Maryknoll, N.Y.: Orbis, 1988.

Bokovay, W. Kelly. "The Relationship of Physical Healing to the Atonement." *Didaskalia* 3, no. 1 (October 1991): 24-39.

Bolt, Peter G. "Jesus, the Daimons and the Dead." In *UW,* chap. 5.

Bonhoeffer, Dietrich. *The Cost of Discipleship.* London: SCM, 1959.

————. *Sanctorum Communio: A Theological Study of the Sociology of the Church.* Edited by Clifford Green. Translated by Reinhard Krauss and Nancy Lukens. Minneapolis: Augsburg Fortress, 1998.

Boonyakiat, Satanun. "A Christian Theology of Suffering in the Context of Theravada Buddhism in Thailand." Ph.D. diss., School of Theology, Fuller Theological Seminary, 2009.

Botman, Russell. "Truth and Reconciliation: The South African Case." In *Religion and Peace*, edited by Howard Coward and Gordon S. Smith, pp. 243-60. New York: State University Press, 2004.

Bounds, Christopher T. "Irenaeus and the Doctrine of Christian Perfection." *Wesleyan Theological Journal* 45, no. 2 (Fall 2010): 161-76.

Boyd, Gregory. *God at War: The Bible and Spiritual Conflict.* Downers Grove, Ill.: InterVarsity, 1997.

————. "The Ground-Level Deliverance Model." In *USW*, pp. 129-72.

————. "Response to C. Peter Wagner and Rebecca Greenwood." In *USW*, pp. 210-15.

————. *Satan and the Problem of Evil: Constructing a Trinitarian Warfare Theodicy.* Downers Grove, Ill.: InterVarsity, 2001.

Boyd, Robin H. S. *An Introduction to Indian Christian Theology.* Madras: Christian Literature Society, 1969.

Boyd, W. *Satan and Mara: Christian and Buddhist Symbols of Evil.* Leiden: Brill, 1975.

Bozack, Michael J. "The Thermodynamical Triple Point: Implications for the Trinity." *Perspectives on Science and Christian Faith* 39, no. 1 (1987): 39-41.

Braaten, Carl E. *Justification: The Article by Which the Church Stands or Falls.* Minneapolis: Fortress, 1990.

————. "Lutherans and Catholics Together — What's Next?" *Pro Ecclesia* 7, no. 1 (1998): 5-9.

————. *Principles of Lutheran Theology.* Philadelphia: Fortress, 1983.

————. *That All May Believe: A Theology of the Gospel and the Mission of the Church.* Grand Rapids: Eerdmans, 2008.

Braaten, Carl E., and Robert W. Jenson, eds. *Union with Christ: The New Finnish Interpretation of Luther.* Grand Rapids: Eerdmans, 1998.

Bracken, Joseph. *The Divine Matrix.* Maryknoll, N.Y.: Orbis, 1995.

Bradby, Ruth. "Coping with the Non-Existent: A *Course in Miracles* and Evil." In *A&D*, chap. 11.

Bradford, Brick. *Releasing the Power of the Holy Spirit.* Oklahoma City: Presbyterian Charismatic Communion, 1983.

Brahma-Sūtra-Bhāsya. In *Brahma-Sūtra-Bhāsya of Sri Sankarācārya*, translated by Swami Gambhirananda. 4th ed. Calcutta: Advaita Ashrama, 1983.

Braithwaite, John. *Crime, Shame, and Reintegration.* New York: Cambridge University Press, 1989.

Brandt, Reinhardt. "Gemeinsame Erklärung — Kritische Fragen. Die 'Gemeinsame Erklärung zur Rechtfertigungslehre' und Fragen zu ihrer Rezeption in den Deutschen Lutherischen Kirchen." *Zeitschrift für Theologie und Kirche* 95 (1998): 63-102.

Bray, Gerald. "The *Filioque* Clause in History and Theology." *Tyndale Bulletin* 34 (1983): 91-143.

Brekke, Torkel. "Conversion in Buddhism?" In *Religious Conversion in India,* edited by Rowena Robinson and Sathianathan Clarke, pp. 181-91. New York: Oxford University Press, 2007.

Brett, Michael. "The Spread of Islam in Egypt and North Africa." In *Northern Africa: Islam and Modernization,* edited by Michael Brett, pp. 1-12. London: Frank Cass and Co., 1973.

Brinner, William M., and Devin J. Stewart. "Conversion." In *The Oxford Encyclopedia of the Islamic World,* edited by John L. Esposito. Oxford: Oxford University Press, 2009; Oxford Islamic Studies Online. http://www.oxfordislamicstudies.com/article/opr/t236/e0165.

Brown, Dale W. *Understanding Pietism.* Grand Rapids: Eerdmans, 1978.

Brown, Francis, S. R. Driver, and Charles A. Briggs. *Hebrew and English Lexicon of the Old Testament.* Oxford: Clarendon, 1952.

Brown, Harold O. J. "Godly Sorrow, Sorrow of the Word: Some Christian Thoughts on Repentance." In *RCP,* pp. 31-42.

Brown, Michael L. *Israel's Divine Healer.* Grand Rapids: Zondervan, 1995.

Brown, Robert E. "On the Necessary Imperfection of Creation." *Scottish Journal of Theology* 28 no. 1 (1975): 17-25.

Brown, Warren S., and Carla Caetano. "Conversion, Cognition, and Neuropsychology." In *HRC,* pp. 147-58.

Brown, Warren S., and Kevin S. Reimer. "Embodied Cognition, Character Formation, and Virtue." *Zygon* 48 (2013): 832-45.

Brümmer, Vincent. "Kairos, Reconciliation and the Doctrine of Atonement." *Journal of Theology for Southern Africa* 88 (Summer 1994): 42-60.

Brunner, Emil. *The Christian Doctrine of God: Dogmatics.* Translated by O. Wyon. Vol. 1. London: Lutterworth, 1949.

―――. *Dogmatics.* Vol. 3, *The Christian Doctrine of the Church, Faith, and the Consummation.* Translated by David Cairns. Philadelphia: Westminster, 1962.

Buber, Martin. *Der Jude und Sein Judentum: Gesammelte Aufsätze und Reden.* Cologne: n.p., 1963.

Buckser, Andrew, and Stephen D. Glazier, eds. *The Anthropology of Religious Conversion.* Lanham, Md.: Rowman and Littlefield, 2003.

Bujo, Bénézet. *African Theology in Its Social Context.* Maryknoll, N.Y.: Orbis, 1992.

Bulgakov, Sergius. *The Comforter.* Translated by Boris Jakim. Grand Rapids: Eerdmans, 2004.

Bulliet, Richard W. *Conversion to Islam in the Medieval Period.* Cambridge: Harvard University Press, 1979.

Bultmann, Rudolf. *New Testament and Mythology, and Other Basic Writings.* Edited and translated by Schubert M. Ogden. Philadelphia: Fortress, 1984.

Burgess, Stanley M. *The Holy Spirit: Ancient Christian Traditions.* Peabody, Mass.: Hendrickson, 1984.

―――. *The Holy Spirit: Eastern Christian Traditions.* Peabody, Mass.: Hendrickson, 1989.

————. *The Holy Spirit: Medieval Roman Catholic and Reformation Traditions.* Peabody: Hendrickson, 1997.

Burns, Charlene. "'Soul-Less' Christianity and the Buddhist Empirical Self: Buddhist-Christian Convergence?" *Buddhist-Christian Studies* 23 (2003): 87-100.

Burrell, David B. "Freedom and Creation in the Abrahamic Traditions." Occasional Papers Series of Center for Christian-Muslim Understanding, Georgetown University, 1995.

————. *Freedom and Creation in Three Traditions.* Notre Dame: University of Notre Dame Press, 1993.

Byrne, B. "Interpreting Romans Theologically in a Post-'New Perspective' Perspective." *Harvard Theological Review* 94 (2001): 227-41.

Cage, Gary T. *The Holy Spirit: A Sourcebook with Commentary.* Reno, Nev.: Charlotte House Publishers, 1995.

Caird, G. B. *New Testament Theology.* Edited by L. D. Hurst. Oxford: Oxford University Press, 1995.

————. *Principalities and Powers: A Study in Pauline Theology.* Oxford: Clarendon, 1956.

Calvin, John. *Commentary on Psalms 93–119.* Translated by James Anderson. Grand Rapids: Christian Classics Ethereal Library, n.d. http://www.ccel.org.

Campbell, Douglas A. *The Deliverance of God: An Apocalyptic Rereading of Justification in Paul.* Grand Rapids: Eerdmans, 2009.

Carman, John B. *Majesty and Meekness: A Comparative Study of Contrast and Harmony in the Concept of God.* Grand Rapids: Eerdmans, 1994.

Carr, Wesley. *Angels and Principalities: The Background, Meaning, and Development of the Pauline Phrase hai archai kai hai exousia.* New York: Cambridge University Press, 1981.

Carson, D. A., Peter T. O'Brien, and Mark A. Seifrid, eds. *Justification and Variegated Nomism.* Vol. 1, *The Complexities of Second Temple Judaism.* Tübingen: Mohr Siebeck; Grand Rapids: Baker, 2001.

Carter, John Ross. "The Path Is Not My Way." In *Of Human Bondage and Divine Grace: A Global Testimony,* edited by John Ross Carter, chap. 8. La Salle, Ill.: Open Court, 1992.

Cary, Phillip. "Historical Perspectives on Trinitarian Doctrine." *Religious and Theological Studies Fellowship Bulletin* (November-December 1995).

Case, Shirley Jackson. *The Origins of Christian Supernaturalism.* Chicago: University of Chicago Press, 1946.

Catherine of Siena. *The Dialogue.* Translation and introduction by Suzanne Noffke, O.P. New York: Paulist, 1980.

————. *The Letters of St. Catherine of Siena.* Edited by Suzanne Noffke, O.P. Vol. 1. New York: Binghamton, 1988.

————. *The Prayers of Catherine of Siena.* Edited by Suzanne Noffke, O.P. New York: Paulist, 1983.

Catterjee, Margaret. *Gandhi's Religious Thought.* Notre Dame: University of Notre Dame Press, 1983.

"Challenging the New Perspective." *The Paul Page* at http://www.thepaulpage.com/

new-perspective/around-the-web/articles-challenging-the-new-perspective/ (4/17/2014).

Chan, Michael Jay. "Reflecting on Roots: Robert Jenson's Theology of Judaism in a Pentecostal Key." *Journal of Pentecostal Theology* 20 (2011): 27-37.

Chan, Simon K. H. "'An Asian Review,' Review of Jürgen Moltmann's *The Spirit of Life: A Universal Affirmation*." *Journal of Pentecostal Theology* 4 (1994): 35-40.

————. "Sanctification." In *GDT*, pp. 789-91.

Chandngarm, Saeng. *Arriyasatsee [The Four Noble Truths]*. Bangkok: Sangsan Books, 2001.

Charlesworth, James, ed. "Hellenistic Synagogal Prayers." In *The Old Testament Pseudepigrapha*, 2:686-88. Garden City, N.Y.: Doubleday, 1983.

Chatraw, Joshua D. "Jesus' Theology of Repentance and Forgiveness as Both Individual and Corporate: A Response to N. T. Wright." Ph.D. diss., Southeastern Baptist Theological Seminary, 2013.

Chopra, Deepak. *Journey into Healing: Awakening the Wisdom within You*. London: Ebury Publishing, 2010.

Christensen, M. "Theosis and Sanctification: John Wesley's Reformulation of a Patristic Doctrine." *Wesleyan Theological Journal* 31, no. 2 (Fall 1996): 71-94.

Chung, Hyun Kyung. "'Han-pu-ri': Doing Theology from a Korean Women's Perspective." *Ecumenical Review* 40 (January 1988): 27-36.

Chung, Paul S. *Martin Luther and Buddhism: Aesthetics of Suffering*. 2nd ed. Portland, Ore.: Pickwick, 2008.

Chung, Paul S., Ulrich Duchrow, and Craig L. Nessan. *Liberating Lutheran Theology: Freedom for Justice and Solidarity with Others in the Global Context*. Minneapolis: Fortress, 2011.

Clark, M. Wayne. "Redemption: Becoming More Human." *Expository Times* 115, no. 3 (2003): 76-81.

Clarke, Clifton. "The Wide Reach of the Spirit: A Renewal Theology of Mission and Interreligious Encounter in Dialogue with Yves Congar." In *Global Renewal, Religious Pluralism, and the Great Commission: Towards a Renewal Theology of Mission and Interreligious Encounter*, edited by Clifton Clarke and Amos Young, chap. 2. Lexington, Ky.: Emeth Press, 2011.

Clarke, F. Stuart. *The Ground of Election: Jacobus Arminius' Doctrine of the Work and Person of Christ*. Bletchley, U.K.: Paternoster, 2006.

Clayton, Philip C. "Conceptual Foundations of Emergence Theory." In *Re-emergence of Emergence*, edited by Philip Clayton and Paul Davis, pp. 1-31. Oxford: Oxford University Press, 2006.

————. "The Impossible Possibility: Divine Causes in the World of Nature." In *GLC*, pp. 249-80.

————. *Mind and Emergence: From Quantum to Consciousness*. Oxford: Oxford University Press, 2004.

————. "The Spirit in Evolution and in Nature." In *IRDSW*, chap. 13, pp. 187-96.

————. "Toward a Theory of Divine Action That Has Traction." In *SPDA*, pp. 85-110.

Cleary, J. C. "Trikaya and Trinity: The Mediation of the Absolute." *Buddhist-Christian Studies* 6 (1986): 63-78.

Clendenin, Daniel B. "Partakers of Divinity: The Orthodox Doctrine of Theosis." *Journal of the Evangelical Theological Society* 37, no. 3 (1994): 365-79.

Cleve, Fredrik. "Samtalen mellan Finlands och Rysslands kyrka." In *Nordisk Ekumenisk Årsbok 1978-1979*. Helsinki: Kirkkohallitus, 1980.

Clifford, Anne M. "Creation." In *Systematic Theology: Roman Catholic Perspective*, vol. 1, edited by Francis Schüssler Fiorenza and John P. Galvin, pp. 193-248. Minneapolis: Fortress, 1991.

Clifford, Richard J. "The Hebrew Scriptures and the Theology of Creation." *Theological Studies* 46 (1985): 508-12.

Clooney, Francis X., S.J. "Trinity and Hinduism." In *Cambridge Companion to the Trinity*, edited by Peter C. Phan, pp. 309-24. Cambridge: Cambridge University Press, 2011.

Cobble, James F., Jr. *The Church and the Powers: A Theology of Church Structure*. Peabody, Mass.: Hendrickson, 1988.

Cohen, Hermann. *Religion of Reason out of the Sources of Judaism* (1919). Translation and introduction by Simon Kaplan. 2nd rev. ed. New York: Frederick Ungar, 1972.

Cohen, Stuart A. *The Three Crowns: Structures of Communal Politics in Early Rabbinic Jewry*. Cambridge: Cambridge University Press, 1990.

Cohon, Samuel S. *Essays in Jewish Theology*. Cincinnati: Hebrew Union College Press, 1987.

———. *Jewish Theology: A Historical and Systematic Interpretation of Judaism and Its Foundations*. Assen, Netherlands: Van Gorcum, 1971.

Cole, Philip. *The Myth of Evil: Demonizing the Enemy*. Westport, Conn.: Praeger, 2006.

Collins, Kenneth J. "John Wesley and the Fear of Death as a Standard of Conversion." In *Conversion in the Wesleyan Tradition*, edited by Kenneth J. Collins and John H. Tyson, pp. 56-68. Nashville: Abingdon, 2001.

———. *The Scripture Way of Salvation: The Heart of John Wesley's Theology*. Nashville: Abingdon, 1997.

———. *The Theology of John Wesley: Holy Love and the Shape of Grace*. Nashville: Abingdon, 2007.

Colon-Emeric, Edgardo A. *Wesley, Aquinas, and Christian Perfection: An Ecumenical Challenge*. Waco: Baylor University Press, 2009.

Comblin, José. *The Holy Spirit and Liberation*. Translated by Paul Burns. Maryknoll, N.Y.: Orbis, 1989.

Cone, James H. *A Black Theology of Liberation*. 2nd ed. Twentieth anniversary ed. Maryknoll, N.Y.: Orbis, 1986.

———. *God of the Oppressed*. Rev. ed. Maryknoll, N.Y.: Orbis, 1997.

Congar, Yves. *I Believe in the Holy Spirit*. Translated by David Smith. New York: Seabury Press, 1983. 3 vols. in 1, New York: Herder, 1997.

Conn, Walter. *Christian Conversion: A Developmental Interpretation of Autonomy and Surrender*. Mahwah, N.J.: Paulist, 1986.

The Contemplation Sutra (Sutra on the Visualization of the Buddha of Infinite Life Delivered by Śākyamuni Buddha). #18 in *Three Pure Land Sutras*, translated by Hisao

Inagaki and Harold Stewart. 2nd rev. ed. Berkeley, Calif.: Numata Center for Buddhist Translation and Research, 2003.

"Conversion." In *The Oxford Dictionary of Islam*, edited by John L. Esposito. Oxford Islamic Studies Online. http://www.oxfordislamicstudies.com/article/opr/t125/e456 (1/30/2014).

Coomaraswamy, Ananda K. "Angel and Titan: An Essay in Vedic Ontology." *Journal of the American Oriental Society* 55 (1935): 373-419.

Cormie, Lee. "Movements of the Spirit in History." In *Talitha Cum! The Grace of Solidarity in a Globalized World*, edited by Mario DeGiglio Bellemare and Gabriela Miranda Garcia. Geneva: WSCF Publications, 2004.

Couenhoven, Jesse. "Forgiveness and Restoration: A Theological Exploration." *Journal of Religion* 90, no. 2 (2010): 148-70.

Cousins, Emily. "Mountains Made Alive: Native American Relationship with Sacred Land." *Cross Currents* 46 (Winter 1996/1997): 497-509.

Cousins, Ewert H. "Panikkar's Advaitic Trinitarianism." In *The Intercultural Challenge of Raimon Panikkar*, edited by Josef Prabhu, pp. 119-30. Maryknoll, N.Y.: Orbis, 1996.

Coward, Harold. *Sin and Salvation in the World Religions: A Short Introduction*. Oxford: Oneworld, 2003.

Cox, Harvey. *Fire from Heaven: The Rise of Pentecostal Spirituality and the Reshaping of Religion in the Twenty-First Century*. Reading, Mass.: Addison-Wesley, 1995.

————. "Repentance and Forgiveness: A Christian Perspective." In *RCP*, pp. 21-30.

Cragg, Kenneth. "God and Salvation (an Islamic Study)." *Studia Missionalia* 29 (1980): 154-66.

————. *Jesus and the Muslim: An Exploration*. London: George Allen and Unwin, 1985.

Creamer, Deborah. *Disability and Christian Theology: Embodied Limits and Constructive Possibilities*. New York: Oxford University Press, 2009.

Creemens, Jelle. "Ecumenical Dialogue with a Non-Institutional Movement: A Systematic-Historical Analysis of the International Roman Catholic–Classical Pentecostal Dialogue (1972-2007)." Ph.D. diss., Evangelische Theologische Faculteit of Heverlee, Leuven, Belgium, 2014.

Crisp, Oliver D. "The Letter and the Spirit of Barth's Doctrine of Election: A Response to Michael O'Neil." *Evangelical Quarterly* 79 (2007): 53-67.

Crollius, Arya Roest. "Salvation in the Qur'an." *Studia Missionalia* 29 (1980): 125-39.

Crysdale, Cynthia S. W. *Embracing Travail: Retrieving the Cross Today*. New York: Continuum, 1999.

Cutter, William, ed. *Midrash and Medicine: Healing Body and Soul in the Jewish Interpretive Tradition*. Woodstock, Vt.: Jewish Lights, 2011.

Dabney, D. Lyle. "Justification by the Spirit: Soteriological Reflections on the Resurrection." *International Journal of Systematic Theology* 3, no. 1 (2001): 46-68.

Dalai Lama [Tenzin Gyatso]. *Freedom in Exile: The Autobiography of the Dalai Lama*. New York: HarperCollins, 1990.

Dammapitaka, Ven. Para [P. A. Payette]. *Dictionary of Buddhism*. Bangkok: Mahachulalongkornrajavidyala University, 2003.

Danan, Julie Hilton. "The Divine Voice in Scripture: *Ruah ha-Kodesh* in Rabbinic Litera-

ture." Ph.D. diss., University of Texas at Austin, 2009. http://repositories.lib.utexas
.edu/bitstream/handle/2152/17297/dananj31973.pdf?sequence=2 (3/22/2014).

Dan-Cohen, Meir. *Revising the Past: On the Metaphysics of Repentance, Forgiveness, and Pardon.* Toronto: University of Toronto Press, 2006.

Daneel, M. L. "African Independent Church Pneumatology and the Salvation of All Creation." *IRM* 82, no. 326 (April 1993): 143-66.

Daniélou, Alan. *The Myths and Gods of India: The Classic Work on Hindu Polytheism.* Bollingen Series, no. 73. Rochester, Vt.: Inner Traditions International, 1991.

Darroll, Bryant M., and Christopher Lamb, eds. *Religious Conversion: Contemporary Practices and Controversies.* New York: Casell, 1999.

Dasgupta, Surendranath. *A History of Indian Philosophy.* Cambridge: Cambridge University Press, 1922. The five-volume set in one volume is available at https://archive .org/details/AHistoryOfIndianPhilosophyBySurendranathDasgupta-5Volumes.

Davary, Bahar. "Forgiveness in Islam: Is It an Ultimate Reality?" *Ultimate Reality and Meaning: Interdisciplinary Studies in the Philosophy of Understanding* 27, no. 2 (2004): 127-41.

Davidman, Lyn. *Tradition in a Rootless World: Women Turn to Orthodox Judaism.* Berkeley: University of California Press, 1991.

Davies, P. C. W. *Other Worlds: A Portrait of Nature in Rebellion — Space, Superspace, and the Quantum Universe.* New York: Simon and Schuster, 1980.

Davies, Steven L. *Jesus the Healer: Possession, Trance, and the Origins of Christianity.* New York: Continuum, 1995.

Davies, W. D. "Reflections on the Spirit in the Mekilta: A Suggestion." *Journal of the Ancient Near Eastern Society of Columbia University* 5 (1973): 95-105.

Davis, John R. *Poles Apart: Contextualizing the Gospel in Asia.* Bangalore: Theological Book Trust, 1998.

Davis, Stephen T. "Karma or Grace." In *The Redemption: An Interdisciplinary Symposium on Christ as Redeemer,* edited by Stephen T. David, Daniel Kendall, S.J., and Gerald O'Collins, S.J., pp. 237-38. Oxford: Oxford University Press, 2004.

Dayal, Har. *The Bodhisattva Doctrine in Buddhist Sanskrit Literature.* Delhi: Motilal Banar-Sidass, 1972.

Dayton, Donald W. "The Limits of Evangelicalism." In *The Variety of Evangelicalism,* edited by Donald W. Dayton and Robert K. Johnston. Downers Grove, Ill.: InterVarsity, 1991.

D'Costa, Gavin. "The Holy Spirit and the World Religions." *Louvain Studies* 34, no. 4 (2010): 279-311.

―――. *The Meeting of Religions and the Trinity.* Maryknoll, N.Y.: Orbis, 2000.

Deane-Drummond, Celia. "Jürgen Moltmann on Heaven." In *UW,* chap. 3, pp. 49-64.

"Decree on Justification: Sixth Session" (January 13, 1547). In *The Creeds of Christendom,* edited by Philip Schaff, vol. 2 (1887). http://www.ccel.org/ccel/schaff/creeds2.v.i.i .iv.html.

Decrees of the Ecumenical Council. Vol. 1. Edited and translated by Norman P. Tanner, S.J. London and Washington, D.C.: Sheed and Ward and Georgetown University Press, 1990.

De Gruchy, John. *Reconciliation: Restoring Justice.* Minneapolis: Fortress, 2002.

Deifelt, Wanda. "The Relevance of the Doctrine of Justification." In *Justification in the World's Context,* edited by Wolfgang Greive, pp. 33-42. Geneva: Lutheran World Federation, 2000.

Demarest, Victoria B. *Sex and Spirit: God, Woman, and Ministry.* St. Petersburg: Sacred Arts Int'l, 1977.

Denny, Fredrick M. "The Qur'anic Vocabulary of Repentance: Orientations and Attitudes." *Journal of the American Academy of Religion* 47, no. 4 (1979): 649-64.

————. "Salvation in the Qur'an." In *In Quest of an Islamic Humanism,* edited by A. H. Green. Cairo: American University in Cairo Press, 1984.

Derrida, Jacques. *On Cosmopolitanism and Forgiveness.* London: Routledge, 2001.

————. "Violence and Metaphysics: A Thought on Emmanuel Levinas." In *Writing and Difference,* translated by A. Bass, chap. 4. Chicago: University of Chicago Press, 1978.

Desai, Prakash N. *Health and Medicine in the Hindu Tradition: Continuity and Cohesion.* New York: Crossroad, 1989.

Descartes, René. *Meditations on the First Philosophy* (1641). In *The Method, Meditations and Philosophy of Descartes, translated from the Original Texts, with a new introductory Essay, Historical and Critical by John Veitch and a Special Introduction by Frank Sewall.* Washington, D.C.: M. Walter Dunne, 1901. http://oll.libertyfund .org/titles/1698 (7/9/2014).

DeSilva, David. "Turning Shame into Honour: The Pastoral Strategy of 1 Peter." In *The Shame Factor: How Shame Shapes Society,* edited by Robert Jewett, Wayne Alloway Jr., and John G. Lacey, pp. 159-86. Eugene, Ore.: Cascade Books, 2011.

Destro, Adriana, and Mauro Pesce, eds. *Rituals and Ethics: Patterns of Repentance in Judaism, Christianity, Islam.* Paris and Louvain: Peeters, 2004.

DeVries, Dawn. "What Is Conversion?" In *How Shall We Witness? Faithful Evangelism in a Reformed Tradition,* edited by Milton J. Coalter and Virgil Cruz, pp. 27-46. Louisville: Westminster John Knox, 1995.

Dharmaraj, Jacob S. "Sin and Salvation: Christianity and Islam." *Bangalore Theological Forum* 30 (1998): 45-67.

Dialogue between Neighbours: The Theological Conversations between the Evangelical-Lutheran Church of Finland and the Russian Orthodox Church, 1970-1986. Edited by Hannu Kamppuri. Helsinki: Luther-Agricola Society, 1986.

Dieter, Melvin E. "Holiness Movement." In *ER,* pp. 4082-84.

Dionysius the Areopagite. *Works.* Translated by John Parker (1899). http://www.tertullian .org/fathers/index.htm#Dionysius_the_Areopagite (7/9/2014).

Doctrine Commission of the Church of England. *The Mystery of Salvation: The Story of God's Gift.* London: Church House Publishing, 1995.

Dokumaci, Arseli. "Performance of Muslim Daily Prayer by Physically Disabled Practitioners." In *Disability in Judaism, Christianity, and Islam: Sacred Texts, Historical Traditions, and Social Analysis,* edited by Darla Schumm and Michael Stoltzfus, chap. 7. New York: Palgrave Macmillan, 2011.

Dolamo, Ramathate T. H. "Justification — a Human Rights Issue: Reconciliation and

Economic Justice in South Africa and the Role of the Church and Theology." In *Justification in the World's Context,* edited by Wolfgang Greive, pp. 125-31. Geneva: Lutheran World Federation, 2000.

Donahoe, Daniel Joseph. *Early Christian Hymns.* Ser. 2. Middletown, Conn.: Donahoe, 1911.

Downie, R. S. "Forgiveness." *Philosophical Quarterly* 15 (1965): 128-34.

Dreyer, Elizabeth A. "An Advent of the Spirit: Medieval Mystics and Saints." In *Advents of the Spirit: An Introduction to the Current Study of Pneumatology,* edited by Bradford E. Hinze and D. Lyle Dabney. Milwaukee: Marquette University Press, 2001.

Dufault-Hunter, Erin. *The Transformative Power of Faith: A Narrative Approach to Conversion.* Lanham, Md.: Lexington Books, 2012.

Duffy, Regis A. "Penance." In *Systematic Theology: Roman Catholic Perspectives,* edited by Francis Schüssler Fiorenza and John P. Galvin, 2:233-49. Minneapolis: Fortress, 1991.

Dufourmantelle, Anne, and Jacques Derrida. *Of Hospitality.* Translated by Rachel Bowlby. Stanford: Stanford University Press, 2000.

Duncan, Ligon. "The Resurgence of Calvinism in America." In *Calvin Today,* pp. 227-40. Grand Rapids: Reformation Heritage, 2009.

Dunn, James D. G. *The Baptism in the Holy Spirit: A Re-examination of the New Testament Teaching on the Gift of the Spirit in Relation to Pentecostalism Today.* London: SCM, 1970.

—————. *The Christ and the Spirit: Collected Essays.* Vol. 2, *Pneumatology.* Edinburgh: T. & T. Clark, 1998.

—————. *Jesus and the Spirit: A Study of the Religious and Charismatic Experience of Jesus and the First Christians as Reflected in the New Testament.* Grand Rapids: Eerdmans, 1997.

—————. "The Justice of God: A Renewed Perspective on Justification by Faith." *Journal of Theological Studies,* n.s., 43 (1992): 1-22.

—————. *The New Perspective on Paul.* Rev. ed. Grand Rapids: Eerdmans, 2005.

—————. "New Perspective View." In *Justification: Five Views,* edited by James K. Beilby and Paul Rhodes Eddy, pp. 176-201. Downers Grove, Ill.: IVP Academic, 2011.

Dupuis, Jacques. *Toward a Christian Theology of Religious Pluralism.* Maryknoll, N.Y.: Orbis, 1997.

Durst, David M. "Fighting the Good Fight: Missional Use of Militant Language." Ph.D. diss., Asbury Theological Seminary, 2010.

Dussel, Enrique. *Philosophy of Liberation.* Maryknoll, N.Y.: Orbis, 1985.

Dwivedi, O. P. "Classical India." In *A Companion to Environmental Philosophy,* edited by Dale Jamieson, pp. 37-51. Oxford: Blackwell, 2001.

Dwyer, Graham. *The Divine and the Demonic: Supernatural Affliction and Its Treatment in North India.* London and New York: Routledge Curzon, 2003.

Dyer, Anne E. "Angels and Pentecostals: An Empirical Investigation into Grassroots Opinions on Angels among the Assemblies of God, UK Members." In *IRDSW,* chap. 8, pp. 111-22.

Ebeling, Gerhard. "Reflexions on the Doctrine of the Law." In *Word and Faith,* translated by James W. Leitch, pp. 247-81. Philadelphia: Fortress, 1963.

Ebhomielen, Paul Omieka. "Gustaf Aulen's *Christus Victor* View of Atonement as It Relates to the Demonic in Africa." Ph.D. diss., Department of Religion, Baylor University, Waco, Tex., 1982.

Eck, Diana L. *Encountering God: A Spiritual Journey from Bozeman to Banaras.* New Delhi and New York: Penguin Books, 1995.

Eckel, Malcolm David. "A Buddhist Approach to Repentance." In *RCP,* pp. 122-42.

Eckel, Malcolm David, with John J. Thatamanil. "Beginningless Ignorance: A Buddhist View of the Human Condition." In *The Human Condition: A Volume in the Comparative Ideas Project,* edited by Robert Cummings Neville, pp. 49-72. Albany: State University of New York Press, 2001.

Eddy, Paul Rhodes. "Remembering Jesus' Self-Understanding: James D. G. Dunn on Jesus' Sense of Role and Identity." In *Memories of Jesus: A Critical Appraisal of James D. G. Dunn's* Jesus Remembered, edited by R. B. Stewart and G. R. Habermas. Nashville: B&H Academic, 2010.

Eddy, Paul Rhodes, and James K. Beilby. "Introduction: Introducing Spiritual Warfare; A Survey of Key Issues and Debates." In *USW,* pp. 1-45.

———, eds. *Understanding Spiritual Warfare: Four Views.* Grand Rapids: Baker Academic, 2012.

The Edicts of Asoka. Edited and translated by N. A. Nikam and Richard McKeon. Chicago: University of Chicago Press, 1959.

Edwards, Denis. "The Discovery of Chaos and the Retrieval of the Trinity." In *C&C,* pp. 157-75.

———. *Ecology at the Heart of Faith: The Change of Heart That Leads to a New Way of Living on Earth.* Maryknoll, N.Y.: Orbis, 2007.

Edwards, Jonathan. *Freedom of the Will* (1754). Vol. 1 of *The Works of Jonathan Edwards,* edited by Paul Ramsey. New Haven, Conn.: Yale University Press, 2009.

———. "A Narrative of Surprising Conversions." In *The Select Works of Jonathan Edwards: With an Account of His Life,* vol. 1. London: Banner of Truth Trust, 1965.

———. *Works* (1834). Vol. 2. ccel.org.

Eenderlein, Steven E. "Justification in Historical Perspective." In *Justification: Five Views,* edited by James K. Beilby and Paul Rhodes Eddy, pp. 13-52. Downers Grove, Ill.: IVP Academic, 2011.

Eiesland, N. L. *The Disabled God: Toward a Liberatory Theology of Disability.* Nashville: Abingdon, 1994.

Einstein, Albert. *Autobiographical Notes: A Centennial Edition.* Translated and edited by Paul Arthur Schilpp. Chicago: Open Court, 1979.

Ekelund, Robert B., Robert F. Hébert, Robert D. Tollison, Gary M. Anderson, and Audry B. Davidson. *Sacred Trust: The Medieval Church as an Economic Firm.* New York: Oxford University Press, 1996.

Eller, Vernard, ed. *Thy Kingdom Come: A Blumhardt Reader.* Grand Rapids: Eerdmans, 1980.

Ellul, Jacques. *Ethics of Freedom.* Translated by Geoffrey W. Bromiley. Grand Rapids: Eerdmans, 1976.

—————. *The Subversion of Christianity.* Translated by Geoffrey W. Bromiley. Grand Rapids: Eerdmans, 1986.

Emeghara, Nkem L. "The Igbo Concept of Chi: The Destiny Spirit." *Journal of Dharma* 33, no. 3 (1998): 399-405.

Enright, R. D., and R. P. Fitzgibbons. *Helping Clients Forgive: An Empirical Guide for Resolving Anger and Restoring Hope.* Washington, D.C.: American Psychological Association, 2000.

Ephrem, Saint. "Eighty Rhythms upon the Faith against the Disputers." In *Select Works of Saint Ephrem the Syrian,* edited and translated by J. B. Morris. London: Oxford University Press, 1897.

Epste, Isidore. *Judaism.* New York: Penguin Books, 1987.

Erickson, Millard J. *Christian Theology.* 3 vols. in 1. Grand Rapids: Baker, 1984.

Ernst-Habib, Margit. "'Chosen by Grace': Reconsidering the Doctrine of Predestination." In *Feminist and Womanist Essays in Reformed Dogmatics,* edited by Amy Plantinga Pauw and Serene Jones, pp. 75-94. Louisville: Westminster John Knox, 2006.

Ess, Josef van. "Islam and the Other Religions: Jesus in the Qur'an — Islamic Perspectives." In *Christianity and World Religions: Paths to Dialogue with Islam, Hinduism, and Buddhism,* edited by Hans Küng et al., pp. 97-132. New York: Doubleday, 1986.

Etzioni, Amitai. *The New Golden Rule.* New York: Basic Books, 1997.

Etzioni, Amitai, and David E. Carney. "Introduction." In *RCP,* pp. 1-20.

Evans, James H., Jr. *We Have Been Believers: An African-American Systematic Theology.* Minneapolis: Fortress, 1992.

Fairbairn, Donald. "Patristic Soteriology: Three Trajectories." *Journal of the Evangelical Theological Society* 50, no. 2 (June 2007): 289-310.

—————. "Salvation as *Theosis:* The Teaching of Eastern Orthodoxy." *Themelios* 23, no. 3 (1998): 42-54.

Faiver, Christopher M., Eugene M. O'Brien, and R. Elliott Ingersoll. "Religion, Guilt, and Mental Health." *Journal of Counseling and Development* 78 (Spring 2008): 155-61.

Farrow, Douglas. "St. Irenaeus of Lyons: The Church and the World." *Pro Ecclesia* 4 (1995): 333-55.

Fatula, Ann, O.P. *The Holy Spirit: Unbounded Gift of Joy.* Collegeville, Minn.: Liturgical Press, 1998.

Favazza, Joseph A. *The Order of Penitents: Historical Roots and Pastoral Future.* Collegeville, Minn.: Liturgical Press, 1989.

Federman, Asaf. "What Kind of Free Will Did the Buddha Teach?" *Philosophy East and West* 60, no. 1 (2010): 1-19.

Fee, Gordon D. "Baptism in the Holy Spirit: The Issue of Separability and Subsequence." *Pneuma* 7, no. 2 (1985): 87-99.

—————. *The Disease of the Health and Wealth Gospels.* Vancouver, B.C.: Regent College Publishing, 2006 (1985).

Feldman, David M. *Health and Medicine in the Jewish Tradition.* New York: Crossroad, 1986.

Ferdinando, Keith. "Screwtape Revisited: Demonology Western, African, and Biblical." In *UW*, pp. 103-32.

————. "The Spiritual Realm in Traditional African Religion." In *A&D*, chap. 1, pp. 21-41.

Fergusson, David. "Reclaiming the Doctrine of Sanctification." *Interpretation* 53, no. 4 (1999): 380-90.

Fiddes, Paul S. *Past Event and Present Salvation: The Christian Idea of Atonement*. Louisville: Westminster John Knox, 1989.

"Final Document 1." Second European Ecumenical Assembly (EEA2). Graz, Austria, June 23 to 29, 1997. http://www.cec-kek.org/English/Graz1.htm.

Finger, Thomas N. *A Contemporary Anabaptist Theology: Biblical, Historical, Constructive*. Downers Grove, Ill.: InterVarsity, 2004.

Finn, Thomas M. *From Death to Rebirth: Ritual and Conversion in Antiquity*. New York: Paulist, 1997.

Firestone, Reuven. *Who Are the Real Chosen People? The Meaning of Chosenness in Judaism, Christianity, and Islam*. Woodstock, Vt.: Skylight Paths Publishing, 2008.

Fisher, H. F. "Conversion Reconsidered: Some Historical Aspects of Religious Conversion in Black Africa." *Africa* 43, no. 1 (1973): 21-40.

Fisher, Mickie L., and Julie J. Exline. "Moving toward Self-Forgiveness: Removing Barriers Related to Shame, Guilt, and Regret." *Social and Personality Psychology Compass* 4, no. 8 (August 2010): 548-58.

Fisher, Sebern F. "Identity of Two: The Phenomenology of Shame in Borderline Development and Treatment." *Psychotherapy* 22 (1985): 101-9.

Flander, Christopher L. "About Face: Reorienting Thai Face for Soteriology and Mission." Ph.D. diss., Fuller Theological Seminary, 2005.

Ford, David F. "God's Power and Human Flourishing: A Biblical Inquiry after Charles Taylor's *A Secular Age*." Yale Center for Faith and Culture Resources, n.d., pp. 1-28. http://www.yale.edu/faith/downloads/David%20Ford%20-%20God%27s %20Power%20and%20Human%20Flourishing%202008.pdf (5/23/2012).

————. *Self and Salvation: Being Transformed*. Cambridge: Cambridge University Press, 1999.

Forde, G. O. "Christian Life." In *Christian Dogmatics*, edited by Carl E. Braaten and Robert W. Jenson, 2:395-469. Philadelphia: Fortress, 1984.

Fourth Lateran Council of 1215 (canon 1). Available in *Internet Medieval Sourcebook*. http://www.fordham.edu/halsall/basis/lateran4.asp (8/7/2013).

Franck, Frederick. "A Buddhist Trinity." *Parabola* 14, no. 4 (Winter 1989): 49-54.

Fredericksen, Linwood. "Angel and Demon." *Encyclopaedia Britannica. Encyclopaedia Britannica Online Academic Edition*. Encyclopædia Britannica Inc., 2014. http://www.britannica.com/EBchecked/topic/24463/angel (7/1/2014).

Freeman, David L. "Healing and Medicine: Healing and Medicine in Judaism." In *ER*, pp. 3828-31.

Freeman, David L., and Judith Z. Abrams, eds. *Illness and Health in the Jewish Tradition: Writings from the Bible to Today*. Philadelphia: Jewish Publication Society, 1999.

French, Peter A., et al. "Forgiveness and Resentment." *Midwest Studies in Philosophy* 7 (1982): 503-16.

Friedman, Robert. *The Theology of Anabaptism.* Scottdale, Pa.: Herald, 1973.

Friedmann, Yohanan. *Tolerance and Coercion in Islam: Interfaith Relations in the Muslim Tradition.* New York: Cambridge University Press, 2003.

Fritsch-Oppermann, Sybille. "Trikaya and Trinity: Reflecting Some Aspects of Christian-Buddhist Dialogue." *Journal of Ecumenical Studies* 30 (Spring 1993): 245-61.

Fukuda, Mitsuo. *Developing a Contextualized Church.* Translated by Mitsuo Fukuda. Shizioka, Japan: Harvest Time Ministries, 1993.

Fukuyama, Francis. *The Great Disruption: Human Nature and the Reconstitution of the Social Order.* New York: Free Press, 1999.

"Furqan, al-." In *The Oxford Dictionary of Islam,* edited by John L. Esposito. Oxford Islamic Studies Online, April 7, 2014. http://www.oxfordislamicstudies.com/article/opr/t125/e684.

Gabriel, Theodore. "The Sura-Asura Theme in Hinduism." In *A&D,* chap. 6.

Gadamer, Hans-Georg. *Truth and Method.* Translated by Joel Weinsheimer and Donald G. Marshall. 2nd rev. ed. New York: Continuum, 2006 (1960).

Gaiser, Frederick J. *Healing in the Bible: Theological Insights for Christian Ministry.* Grand Rapids: Baker Academic, 2010.

Gallagher, Nancy. "Healing and Medicine: Healing and Medicine in Islamic Texts and Traditions." In *ER,* pp. 3831-33.

Gallagher, Richard E. "A Case of Demonic Possession." *New Oxford Review* 75 (March 2008): 22-32.

Galy, M. M. I. *Islam and Disability: Perspectives in Theology and Jurisprudence.* London: Routledge, 2010.

Gandhi, Mohandas K. *The Bhagavad Gita according to Gandhi.* Blacksburg, Va.: Wilder Publications, 2011.

———. *Hind Swaraj and Indian Home Rule.* Online version available at http://www.mkgandhi.org/swarajya/coverpage.htm (1/27/2014).

Gaon, Saadia. *The Book of Beliefs and Opinions.* Translated by Samuel Rosenblatt. New Haven: Yale University Press, 1967.

Garcia, Mark A. *Life in Christ: Union with Christ and Twofold Grace in Calvin's Theology.* Milton Keynes, U.K., and Colorado Springs: Paternoster, 2008.

Garlington, Don. *In Defense of the New Perspectives on Paul: Essays and Reviews.* Eugene, Ore.: Wipf and Stock, 2005.

Gatumu, Kabiro wa. *The Pauline Concept of Supernatural Powers: A Reading from the African Worldview.* Colorado Springs: Paternoster, 2008.

Gaventa, Beverly Roberts. *From Darkness to Light: Aspects of Conversion in the New Testament.* Philadelphia: Fortress, 1986.

Gertel, Elliot B. "The 'Holy Ghost' and Judaism." *Conservative Judaism* 49, no. 2 (New York, Rabbinic Assembly, 1997): 34-55.

———. "The Holy Spirit in the Zohar." *CCAR Journal: A Reform Jewish Quarterly* 56, no. 4 (2009): 80-102.

Geschiere, Peter. *The Modernity of Witchcraft: Politics and the Occult in Postcolonial Africa.* Charlottesville: University Press of Virginia, 1997.

Ghazali [Ghazzali], Abu Hamid Muhammad al-. *The Alchemy of Happiness.* Translated by Claud Field. London: M. E. Sharpe Inc., 1991. sacred-texts.com.

―――. *Al-Ghazzali on Repentance.* Translated by M. S. Stern. New Delhi: Sterling Publishers, 1990. http://www.ghazali.org/books/gz-repent.pdf (3/9/2014).

―――. *Inner Dimensions of Islamic Worship.* Translated by Muhtar Holland. Leicestershire: Islamic Foundation, 1983.

Gier, Nicholas F., and Paul Kjellberg. "Buddhism and the Freedom of the Will: Pali and Mahayanist Responses." In *Freedom and Determinism,* edited by Joseph Keim Campbell, Michael O'Rourke, and David Shier. Cambridge: MIT Press, 2004.

Gingerich, Raby, and Ted Grimsrud, eds. *Transforming the Powers: Peace, Justice, and the Domination System.* Minneapolis: Fortress, 2006.

Ginzberg, Louis. *Legends of the Jews.* Vol. 1. Philadelphia: Jewish Publication Society of America, 1968.

Glomsrud, Ryan, and Michael Horton, eds. *Justified: Modern Reformation Essays on the Doctrine of Justification.* N.p.: CreateSpace, 2010.

"Glory to God and Peace on Earth: The Message of the International Ecumenical Peace Convocation." May 17-25, 2011, Kingston, Jamaica.

Gnanakan, Chris. "The Manthiravadi: A South Indian Wounded Warrior-Healer." In *A&D,* chap. 7, pp. 140-57.

Gockel, Matthias. *Barth and Schleiermacher on the Doctrine of Election: A Systematic-Theological Comparison.* Oxford: Oxford University Press, 2007.

Goldberg, Carl. *Speaking with the Devil: A Dialogue with Evil.* New York: Viking, 1996.

Gombrich, Richard. "Appreciating the Buddha as a Pivotal Figure in World History." Bukkyo Dendo Kyokai Lectures. London, 2006.

Gómez, Luis O. "Some Aspects of the Free-Will Question in the Nikāyas." *Philosophy East and West* 25, no. 1 (1975): 81-90.

González, Justo L. *Mañana: Christian Theology from a Hispanic Perspective.* Nashville: Abingdon, 1990.

Goodman, Felicitas D. *How about Demons? Possession and Exorcism in the Modern World.* Bloomington: Indiana University Press, 1988.

Gorder, A. Christian van. *No God but God: A Path to Muslim-Christian Dialogue on God's Nature.* Maryknoll, N.Y.: Orbis, 2003.

Gorjian, Mohammad Mihdi. "Determinism and Free Will in the Qur'an." *Message of Thaqalayn* 11, no. 3 (Autumn 2010): 47-62.

Gottlieb, Michah. "Introduction: Moses Mendelssohn and the Project of Modern Jewish Philosophy." In *Moses Mendelssohn: Writings on Judaism, Christianity, and the Bible,* edited by Michah Gottlieb, pp. xi-xxvii. Lebanon, N.H.: Brandeis University Press, 2011.

Govier, Trudy. *Forgiveness and Revenge.* New York: Routledge, 2002.

Grant, Sara, R.S.C.J. *Towards an Alternative Theology: Confessions of a Non-Dualist Christian.* Introduction by Bradley J. Malkovsky. Notre Dame: University of Notre Dame Press, 2002.

Graybill, Lyn S. *Truth and Reconciliation in South Africa: Miracle or Model?* Boulder, Colo., and London: Lynne Rienner Publishers, 2002.

Greear, J. D. "*Theosis* and Muslim Evangelism: How the Recovery of a Patristic Understanding of Salvation Can Aid Evangelical Missionaries in the Evangelization of Islamic Peoples." Ph.D. diss., Southeastern Baptist Theological Seminary, 2003.

Green, Arthur. "*Shekinah,* the Virgin Mary, and the Song of Songs: Reflections on a Kabbalistic Symbol in Its Historical Context." *Association for Jewish Studies Review* 26 (April 2002): 1-52.

Green, Joel B. *Body, Soul, and Human Life: The Nature of Humanity in the Bible.* Grand Rapids: Baker Academic, 2008.

———. *Why Salvation?* Nashville: Abingdon, 2013.

Gregersen, Niels Henrik. "Emergence: What Is at Stake for Religious Reflection?" In *Re-emergence of Emergence,* edited by Philip Clayton and Paul Davis, pp. 279-300. Oxford: Oxford University Press, 2006.

———. "Special Divine Action and the Quilt of Laws: Why the Distinction between Special and General Divine Action Cannot Be Maintained." In *SPDA,* pp. 179-99.

Gregorios, Paulos M. *Religion and Dialogue.* Kottayam, India: ISPCK, 2000.

Gregory of Nyssa. *The Life of Moses.* Edited by Abraham J. Malherbe and Everett Ferguson. New York: Paulist, 1978.

———. "On What It Means to Call Oneself a Christian." In *Ascetical Writings,* translated by Virginia Woods Callahan. Fathers of the Church 58. Washington, D.C.: Catholic University of America Press, 1967.

Gregory of Sinai. *Texts on Commandments and Dogmas.* In *Writings from the Philokalia on Prayer of the Heart,* translated by E. Kadloubovsky and G. E. H. Palmer. New York: Faber and Faber, 1951.

Greive, Wolfgang, ed. *Justification in the World's Context.* Documentation 45. Geneva: Lutheran World Federation, 2000.

———. "The Significance of Justification in the World's Context: Towards a New Interpretation of the Doctrine of Justification." In *Justification in the World's Context,* edited by Wolfgang Greive, pp. 11-21. Geneva: Lutheran World Federation, 2000.

Grenz, Stanley J. *Reason for Hope: The Systematic Theology of Wolfhart Pannenberg.* New York: Oxford University Press, 1990.

———. *Rediscovering the Triune God: The Trinity in Contemporary Theology.* Minneapolis: Fortress, 2004.

———. *The Social God and Relational Self: A Trinitarian Theology of the Imago Dei.* Louisville: Westminster John Knox, 2001.

———. *Theology for the Community of God.* Grand Rapids: Eerdmans, 1994.

Griffin, David Ray. *Reenchantment without Supernaturalism: A Process Philosophy of Religion.* Ithaca, N.Y.: Cornell University Press, 2001.

———. "Why Demonic Power Exists: Understanding the Church's Enemy." *Lexington Theological Quarterly* 28, no. 3 (1993): 223-39.

Gritsch, Eric W. "Bold Sinning: The Lutheran Ethical Option." *Dialog* 14 (1975): 26-32.

Grundmann, Christoffer H. "Inviting the Spirit to Fight the Spirits? Pneumatological Challenges for Missions in Healing and Exorcism." *IRM* 94, no. 371 (2005): 51-73.

Guillaume, Alfred. *The Life of Muhammad: A Translation of Ibn Ishaq's Sirat Rasul Allah.* Oxford: Oxford University Press, 1955; Karachi: Oxford University Press, 1967.

————. "Some Remarks on Free Will and Predestination in Islam, Together with a Translation of the Kitabu-l Qadar from the Sahih of al-Bukhari." *Journal of the Royal Asiatic Society of Great Britain and Ireland* 56, no. 1 (1924): 43-63.

Gunkel, Hermann. *The Influence of the Holy Spirit: The Popular View of the Apostolic Age and the Teaching of the Apostle Paul.* Translated by R. A. Harrisville and P. A. Quanbeck II. Philadelphia: Fortress, 1979; original 1888.

Gunstone, J. *Greater Things Than These: A Personal Account of the Charismatic Movement.* New York: Morehouse, 1974.

Gunton, Colin E. "Augustine, the Trinity, and the Theological Crisis of the West." *Scottish Journal of Theology* 43, no. 1 (1990): 33-58.

————. "God the Holy Spirit: Augustine and His Successors." In *Theology through the Theologians: Selected Essays, 1972-1995,* pp. 105-28. 1996. Reprint, London: T. & T. Clark, 2003.

————. *The Promise of Trinitarian Theology.* 2nd ed. Edinburgh: T. & T. Clark, 1997.

————. *The Triune Creator: A Historical and Systematic Study.* Edinburgh Studies in Constructive Theology. Grand Rapids: Eerdmans, 1998.

Gupta, Mahendranath. *The Gospel of Sri Ramakrishna.* Translated by Swami Nikhilananda. Indian ed. Madras: Sri Ramakrishna Math, 1996.

Gupta, Sanjukta. "Jivanmukti." In *ER,* pp. 4925-26.

Guruge, Ananda W. P. "The Buddha's Encounters with Mara the Tempter: Their Representation in Literature and Art." *Access to Insight* 23, July 2013. http://www.access toinsight.org/lib/authors/guruge/wheel419.html.

Gusmer, Charles W. *And You Visited Me: Sacramental Ministry to the Sick and the Dying.* Rev. ed. Collegeville, Minn.: Liturgical Press, 1990.

Guthrie, A., and E. F. F. Bishop. "The Paraclete, Almunhamanna and Ahmad." *Muslim World* 41, no. 4 (October 1951): 251-56.

Gutiérrez, Gustavo. *A Theology of Liberation: History, Politics, and Salvation.* Translated and edited by Sister Caridad Inda and John Eagleson. Maryknoll, N.Y.: Orbis, 1986 (1973); rev. ed. with a new introduction, 1988.

————. *We Drink from Our Wells: The Spiritual Journey of a People.* Translated by Matthew J. O'Connell. Maryknoll, N.Y.: Orbis, 1984.

Habel, Norman C. *Reconciliation: Searching for Australia's Soul.* Sydney: HarperCollins, 1999.

Habito, Ruben L. F. "On Dharmakaya as Ultimate Reality: Prolegomenon for a Buddhist-Christian Dialogue." *Japanese Journal of Religious Studies* 12, nos. 2-3 (June 1975): 233-52.

————. "The Trikaya Doctrine in Buddhism." *Buddhist-Christian Studies* 6 (1986): 53-62.

Haight, Roger J., S.J. "The Case for Spirit Christology." *Theological Studies* 53, no. 2 (1992): 257-87.

Hakim, Souad. "The Spirit and the Son of the Spirit: A Reading of Jesus (īsa) according to Ibn Arabīm." *Journal of the Muhyiddin Ibn Arabi Society* 31 (2002): 1-28.

Halamish, Moshe. *An Introduction to the Kabbalah.* Translated by Ruth Bar-Ilan and Ora Wiskind-Elper. Albany: State University of New York Press, 1999.

Halevi, Judah. *Judah Hallevi's Kitab al Khazar.* Translated by Hartwig Hirscheld. New York: George Routledge and Sons, 1906.

Halling, S. "Shame and Forgiveness." *Humanistic Psychologist* 22 (1994): 74-87.

Halverson, James. "Franciscan Theology and Predestinarian Pluralism in Late-Medieval Thought." *Speculum* 70, no. 1 (January 1995): 1-25.

Hanh, Thich Nhat. *Living Buddha, Living Christ.* New York: Riverhead Books, 1994.

Happel, Stephen. "Metaphors and Time Asymmetry: Cosmologies in Physics and Christian Meanings." In *QCLN*, pp. 103-34.

Harnack, A. von. *The Constitution and Law of the Church in the First Three Centuries.* London: Williams and Norgate, 1910.

Harvey, Peter. "'Freedom of the Will' in the Light of Theravada Buddhist Teachings." *Journal of Buddhist Ethics* 14 (2007): 35-98. http://blogs.dickinson.edu/buddhist ethics/2010/05/10/theravada-sources-on-free-will/ (1/30/2014).

Harvey, Susan Ashbrook. "Feminine Imagery for the Divine: The Holy Spirit, the Odes of Solomon, and Early Syriac Tradition." *St. Vladimir's Theological Quarterly* 37 (1993): 111-39.

Haugh, Richard. *Photius and the Carolingians: The Trinitarian Controversy.* Belmont, Mass.: Norland, 1975.

Hauser, Marc D. *Wild Minds: What Animals Really Think.* New York: Holt, 2000.

Hay, David. *Something There.* West Conshohocken, Pa.: Templeton Foundation Press, 2006.

Hegel, Georg Wilhelm Friedrich. *Philosophy of Mind.* Translated by W. Wallace and A. V. Miller. Oxford: Oxford University Press, 1971.

———. *Reason in History: A General Introduction to the Philosophy of History.* Translated by Robert S. Hartman. New York: Liberal Arts Press, 1953.

Hejzlar, Pavel. *Two Paradigms for Divine Healing: Fred F. Bosworth, Kenneth E. Hagin, Agnes Sanford, and Francis MacNutt in Dialogue.* Leiden and Boston: Brill, 2010.

Helfgott, Benjamin. *The Doctrine of Election in Tannaitic Literature.* New York: Columbia University, King's Crown Press, 1954.

Heller, Michael. "Adventures of the Concept of Mass and Matter." *Philosophy in Science* 3 (1988): 15-35.

Helmick, Raymond G., and Rodney L. Petersen, eds. *Forgiveness and Reconciliation: Religion, Public Policy, and Conflict Transformation.* Philadelphia: Templeton Foundation Press, 2001.

Helyer, Larry R. *The Witness of Jesus, Paul, and John: An Exploration in Biblical Theology.* Downers Grove, Ill.: InterVarsity, 2008.

Henderson, James M. "Election as Renewal: The Work of the Holy Spirit in Divine Election." Ph.D. diss., Regent University, School of Divinity, 2012.

Hendry, George S. *The Holy Spirit in Christian Theology.* Rev. and enlarged ed. London: SCM, 1965.

Henzel, Jan. "Perseverance within an Ordo Salutis." *Tyndale Bulletin* 60 (2009): 129-56.

Heppe, Heinrich. *Reformed Dogmatics: Set Out and Illustrated from the Sources.* Revised and edited by Ernst Bizer. Translated by G. T. Thomson. London: Allen and Unwin, 1950.

Heredero, J. M., S.J. *The Dead Rescue the Living: Spirit Possession in a Gujarati Christian Community*. Anand, India: Gujarat Shitya Prakash, 2001.

Hiebert, Paul G. "Conversion in Hinduism and Buddhism." In *HRC*, pp. 9-21.

————. "Discerning the Work of God." In *Charismatic Experiences in History*, edited by Cecil M. Robeck, pp. 147-63. Peabody, Mass.: Hendrickson, 1985.

————. "The Flaw of the Excluded Middle." *Missiology: An International Review* 10, no. 1 (1982): 35-47. http://www.nextworldwide.org/atf/cf/%7B9F65686B-1641-4838-9D00-E1F0768CAF6B%7D/FlawofExcludedMiddle.pdf (3/19/2014).

Hilberath, Bernd Jochen. "Pneumatologie." In *Handbuch der Dogmatik*, edited by Theodor Schneider et al., vol. 1. Düsseldorf: Patmos, 1992.

Hinlicky, Paul R. "Theological Anthropology: Toward Integrating *Theosis* and Justification by Faith." *Journal of Ecumenical Studies* 34, no. 1 (Winter 1997): 38-73.

Hinze, Bradford E. "Ecclesial Impasse: What Can We Learn from Our Laments?" *Theological Studies* 72 (September 2011): 470-95.

————. "Talking Back, Acting Up: Wrestling with Spirits in Social Bodies." In *IRDSW*, chap. 11, pp. 155-70.

Hiriyanna, M. *Essentials of Indian Philosophy*. Delhi: Motilal Banarsidass Publishers, 2000.

Hobbes, Thomas. *Leviathan* (1651). (1909 ed.). http://oll.libertyfund.org/title/869.

Hollaz, D. *Examen Theologicum Acroamaticum* (1707). Holmiae et Lipsiae: G. Kiesewetter, 1750.

Horsley, Richard A. *Jesus and the Powers: Conflict, Covenant, and the Hope for the Poor*. Minneapolis: Fortress, 2011.

Horton, Michael S. *The Christian Faith: A Systematic Theology for Pilgrims on the Way*. Grand Rapids: Zondervan, 2011.

————. "Participation and Covenant." In *Radical Orthodoxy and the Reformed Tradition: Creation, Covenant, and Participation*, edited by James K. A. Smith and James H. Olthuis. Grand Rapids: Baker Academic, 2005.

————. "Traditional Reformed View." In *Justification: Five Views*, edited by James K. Beilby and Paul Rhodes Eddy, pp. 85-91. Downers Grove, Ill.: IVP Academic, 2011.

Hourani, George F. "Ibn Sīnā's 'Essay on the Secret of Destiny.'" *Bulletin of the School of Oriental and African Studies* 29, no. 1 (1966): 25-48.

Hubbard, Robert L., Jr. "The Spirit and Creation." In *Presence, Power, and Promise*, edited by David G. Firth and Paul D. Wegner, pp. 71-90. Downers Grove, Ill.: InterVarsity, 2011.

Hudson, Deal W. "The Catholic View of Conversion." In *HRC*, pp. 108-22.

Hughes, Paul M. "Forgiveness." In *The Stanford Encyclopedia of Philosophy*, Winter 2011 edition, edited by Edward N. Zalta. http://plato.stanford.edu/archives/win2011/entries/forgiveness/.

Hume, David. *An Enquiry concerning Human Understanding* (1748). Translated by Jonathan Bennett and available at http://www.earlymoderntexts.com/pdfs/hume1748.pdf. Copyright 2010-2015. Last amended January 2008.

Hunsinger, George. "Election and the Trinity: Twenty-Five Theses on the Theology of Karl Barth." *Modern Theology* 24, no. 2 (2008): 179-98.

————. "A Tale of Two Simultaneities: Justification and Sanctification in Calvin and Barth." *Zeitschrift für dialektische Theologie* 18 (2002): 316-38.

Hunt, Anne. *Trinity: Nexus of the Mysteries of Christian Faith.* Maryknoll, N.Y.: Orbis, 2005.

Hunter, Alan. "Forgiveness: Hindu and Western Perspectives." *Journal of Hindu-Christian Studies* 20 (2007): 30-42.

Hütter, Reinhard. *Suffering the Divine Things: Theology as Church Practice.* Translated by Doug Scott. Grand Rapids and Cambridge, U.K.: Eerdmans, 2000.

Ibn Sina. *Risalah fi sirr al-qadar* (Essay on the secret of destiny). Translated by G. Hourani. In *Reason and Tradition in Islamic Ethics,* pp. 227-48. Cambridge: Cambridge University Press, 1985.

Idowu, Bolaji. "The Spirit of God in the Natural World." In *The Holy Spirit,* edited by Dow Kirkpatrick. Nashville: Tidings, 1974.

Ifeka-Moller, Caroline. "White Power: Social Structural Factor in Conversion to Christianity, Eastern Nigeria, 1921-1966." *Canadian Journal of African Studies* 8, no. 1 (1974): 55-72.

Imasogie, Osadolor. *Guidelines for Christian Theology in Africa.* Achimota, Ghana: Africa Christian Press, 1993.

Inagaki, Hisao. *The Three Pure Land Sutras.* Kyoto: Nagata Bunshodo, 1994.

Inoue, Naoki. "Spirit and Spirits in Pantheistic Shintoism: A Critical Dialogue with Christian Panentheism." In *IRDSW,* chap. 4, pp. 55-68.

Iozzio, Mary Jo. "Thinking about Disabilities with Justice, Liberation, and Mercy." *Horizons* 36, no. 1 (Spring 2009): 32-49.

Iqbal, Muhammad. *Reconstruction of Religious Thought in Islam.* Lahore: Kashimiri Bazar, 1960.

Irigaray, Luce. *I Love to You: Sketch of a Possible Felicity in History.* Translated by Alison Martin. New York and London: Routledge, 1996.

Jacobs, Louis. *A Jewish Theology.* London: Darton, Longman and Todd, 1973.

James, William. "Report on Mrs. Piper's Hodgson-Control." *Proceedings of the English Society for Psychical Research* 23 (1909).

————. *The Varieties of Religious Experience: A Study in Human Nature* (1902). An Electronic Classics Series Publication. http://www2.hn.psu.edu/faculty/jmanis/wjames/varieties-rel-exp.pdf (2/24/2014).

Jathanna, Vasantha. *The Decisiveness of the Christ Event and the Universality of Christianity in a World of Religious Plurality.* Berne: Peter Lang, 1981.

Jenkins, Philip. *The New Faces of Christianity: Believing the Bible in the Global South.* New York: Oxford University Press, 2006.

————. *The Next Christendom: The Coming of Global Christianity.* Oxford: Oxford University Press, 2011.

Jennings, Theodore W., Jr. *Good News to the Poor: John Wesley's Evangelical Economics.* Nashville: Abingdon, 1990.

Jenson, Robert W. "Aspects of a Doctrine of Creation." In *The Doctrine of Creation: Essays in Dogmatics, History, and Philosophy.* Edinburgh: T. & T. Clark, 1997.

————. *Systematic Theology.* 2 vols. New York: Oxford University Press, 1997, 1999.

Jewett, Paul K. *Election and Predestination.* Grand Rapids: Eerdmans, 1985.

Jindra, Ines W. "How Religious Content Matters in Conversion Narratives to Various Religious Groups." *Sociology of Religion* 72, no. 3 (2011): 275-302.

"Jinn." In *The Oxford Dictionary of Islam,* edited by John L. Esposito. Oxford Islamic Studies Online. http://www.oxfordislamicstudies.com/article/opr/t125/e1204 (6/3/2013).

Johansson, Daniel. "'Who Can Forgive Sins but God Alone?' Human and Angelic Agents, and Divine Forgiveness in Early Judaism." *Journal for the Study of the New Testament* 33, no. 4 (2011): 351-74.

John, Mary. "The Complementary Dimensions of the Concepts of *Agni* and the Spirit in the Indian and Christian Traditions." *Journal of Dharma* 33, no. 3 (1998): 327-40.

John Paul II. *Forgiveness: Thoughts for the New Millennium.* Kansas City, Mo.: Andrews McMeel Publishing, 1999.

Johnson, Elizabeth. *She Who Is: The Mystery of God in Feminist Theological Discourse.* New York: Crossroad, 1993.

————. *Women, Earth, and Creator Spirit.* Mahwah, N.J.: Paulist, 1993.

Johnston, Robert K. "Art and the Spiritual." In *IRDSW,* chap. 6, pp. 85-96.

————. *Reel Spirituality: Theology and Film in Dialogue.* 2nd ed. Grand Rapids: Baker Academic, 2000.

Jones, Charles B. "Emptiness, Kenōsis, History, and Dialogue: The Christian Response to Masao Abe's Notion of 'Dynamic Sünyatä' in the Early Years of the Abe-Cobb Buddhist-Christian Dialogue." *Buddhist-Christian Studies* 24 (2004): 117-33.

Jones, L. Gregory. "Crafting Communities of Forgiveness." *Interpretation* 54, no. 2 (2000): 121-34.

————. *Embodying Forgiveness: A Theological Analysis.* Grand Rapids: Eerdmans, 1995.

Jordens, J. T. F. "Reconversion to Hinduism, the Shudhi of the Arya Samaj." In *Religion in South Asia: Religious Conversion and Revival Movements in South Asia in Medieval and Modern Times,* edited by Geoffrey A. Oddie, pp. 145-61. London: Curzon, 1977.

Jørgensen, Jonas Adelin. "'Word of God' and 'Spirit of God' in Christian and Islamic Christologies: A Starting Point for Interreligious Dialogue?" *Islam and Christian-Muslim Relations* 20, no. 4 (2009): 389-407.

Joseph, Jojo. "Trinitarian Experience of a Christian and Advaitic Experience of a Hindu." *Journal of Dharma* 27, no. 2 (2002): 207-31.

Joseph, P. V. *Indian Interpretation of the Holy Spirit.* Delhi: ISPCK, 2007.

Jung, Leo. *Fallen Angels in Jewish, Christian, and Mohammedan Literature.* New York: Ktav Publishing House, 1974 (1926).

Jüngel, Eberhard. *Justification: The Heart of the Christian Faith; A Theological Study with an Ecumenical Purpose.* Translated by J. F. Cayzer. Edinburgh: T. & T. Clark, 2001.

Juntunen, Sammeli. *Der Begriff des Nichts bei Luther in den Jahren von 1510 bis 1523.* Schriften der Luther-Agricola-Gesellschaft 36. Helsinki: Luther-Agricola Society, 1996.

Juster, Susan. "'In a Different Voice': Male and Female Narratives of Religious Conversion in Post-Evolutionary America." *American Quarterly* 41 (March 1989): 34-62.

Kakar, Sudhir. *The Colors of Violence: Cultural Identities, Religion, and Conflict.* Chicago: University of Chicago Press, 1996.

Kallenberg, Brad. "Conversion Converted: A Postmodern Formulation of the Doctrine of Conversion." *Evangelical Quarterly* 67 (1995): 335-64. http://www.biblicalstudies .org.uk/pdf/eq/1995-4_335bk.pdf.

Kalluveettil, Paul. "Towards the New Age of the Spirit: The Old Testament Vision of Society as a Spirit-Energized Movement." *Journal of Dharma* 23, no. 3 (1998): 360-79.

Kalu, Ogbu. *African Pentecostalism: An Introduction.* Oxford: Oxford University Press, 2008.

———. "*Sankofa*: Pentecostalism and African Cultural Heritage." In *The Spirit in the World: Emerging Pentecostal Theologies in Global Contexts,* edited by Veli-Matti Kärkkäinen, pp. 135-52. Grand Rapids: Eerdmans, 2009.

Kamppuri, Hannu T. "Theosis in der Theologie des Gregorios Palamas." In *Luther und Theosis: Vergöttlichung als Thema der abendländischen Theologie,* edited by Simo Peura and Antti Raunio, pp. 49-60. Helsinki and Erlangen: Martin-Luther Verlag, 1990.

Kant, Immanuel. "Part II: Moral Philosophy; Collins' Lecture Notes." In *Lectures on Ethics,* edited by Peter Heath and J. B. Schneewind, translated by Peter Heath, pp. 113-14. Cambridge: Cambridge University Press, 1997.

Kaplan, Mordecai M. *Judaism as a Civilization: Toward a Reconstruction of American-Jewish Life.* New York: Thomas Yoseloff, 1934.

Kaplan, Steven, ed. *Indigenous Responses to Western Christianity.* New York: New York University Press, 1995.

Kapolyo, Joe M. *The Human Condition: Christian Perspectives through African Eyes.* Downers Grove, Ill.: InterVarsity, 2005.

Karchadourian, Herant. *Guilt: The Bite of Conscience.* Stanford: Stanford University Press, 2010.

Karingadayil, Santhosh Thomas. *From Darkness to Light: The Concept of Salvation in the Perspectives of Thomas Aquinas and Sankara.* Frankfurt am Main: Peter Lang, 2011.

Kärkkäinen, Veli-Matti. "'By the Washing of Regeneration and Renewing by the Holy Spirit': Toward a Pneumatological Account of Justification in Christ." In *Spirit and Christ: Essays in Honour of Max Turner,* edited by Howard Marshall, Cornelis Bennema, and Volker Rabens, pp. 303-22. Grand Rapids: Eerdmans, 2012.

———. *Christ and Reconciliation.* A Constructive Christian Theology for the Pluralistic World, vol. 1. Grand Rapids: Eerdmans, 2013.

———. "Christian as Christ to the Neighbor." *International Journal of Systematic Theology* 6, no. 2 (April 2004): 101-17.

———. *Creation and Humanity.* A Constructive Christian Theology for the Pluralistic World, vol. 3. Grand Rapids: Eerdmans, 2015.

———. "The Ecumenical Potential of Theosis: Emerging Convergences between Eastern Orthodox, Protestant, and Pentecostal Soteriologies." *Sobornost/Eastern Churches Review* 23, no. 2 (2002): 45-77.

———. "'Evil, Love and the Left Hand of God': The Contribution of Luther's Theology of the Cross to Evangelical Theology of Evil." *Evangelical Quarterly* 79, no. 4 (2002): 215-34.

———. "The Holy Spirit and Justification: The Ecumenical Significance of Luther's Doctrine of Justification." *Pneuma: The Journal of the Society for Pentecostal Studies* 24, no. 1 (2002): 26-39.

————. "'How to Speak of the Spirit among Religions': Trinitarian Prolegomena for a Pneumatological Theology of Religions." In *The Work of the Spirit: Pneumatology and Pentecostalism,* edited by Michael Welker, pp. 47-70. Grand Rapids: Eerdmans, 2006.

————. "'How to Speak of the Spirit among Religions': Trinitarian 'Rules' for a Pneumatological Theology of Religions." *International Bulletin of Missionary Research* 30, no. 3 (July 2006): 121-27.

————. "Introduction: Pentecostalism and Pentecostal Theology in the Third Millennium; Taking Stock of the Contemporary Global Situation." In *The Spirit in the World: Emerging Pentecostal Theologies in Global Contexts,* edited by Veli-Matti Kärkkäinen, pp. xiii-xviii. Grand Rapids: Eerdmans, 2009.

————. "Is the Spirit Still the Dividing Line between the Christian East and West? Revisiting an Ancient Problem of Filioque with a Hope for an Ecumenical Rapprochement." *Perichoresis: The Theological Journal of Emanuel University of Oradea* 9, no. 2 (2011): 125-42. http://www.emanuel.ro/eng/files/Perichoresis/Perichoresis%209_2%20web.pdf (2/11/2014).

————. "Justification as Forgiveness of Sins and Making Righteous: The Ecumenical Promise of a New Interpretation of Luther." *One in Christ* 37, no. 2 (April 2002): 32-45.

————. *One with God: Salvation as Deification and Justification.* Collegeville, Minn.: Liturgical Press, 2004.

————. "Ordo salutis." In *GDT,* pp. 622-23.

————. *Pneumatology: The Holy Spirit in Ecumenical, International, and Contextual Perspectives.* Grand Rapids: Baker Academic, 2002.

————. "Salvation as Justification and Deification: The Ecumenical Potential of a New Perspective on Luther." In *Theology between West and East: Honoring the Radical Legacy of Professor Dr. Jan M. Lochman,* edited by Frank Macchia and Paul Chung, pp. 59-76. Lanham, Md.: University Press of America, 2002.

————. *Spiritus ubi vult spirat: Pneumatology in Roman Catholic–Pentecostal Dialogue (1972-1989).* Schriften der Luther-Agricola-Gesellschaft 42. Helsinki: Luther-Agricola Society, 1998.

————. *The Trinity: Global Perspectives.* Louisville: Westminster John Knox, 2008.

————. *The Trinity and Religious Pluralism: The Doctrine of the Trinity in Christian Theology of Religions.* Aldershot: Ashgate, 2004.

————. *Trinity and Revelation.* A Constructive Christian Theology for the Pluralistic World, vol. 2. Grand Rapids: Eerdmans, 2014.

————, ed. *Holy Spirit and Salvation: The Sources of Christian Theology.* Louisville: Westminster John Knox, 2010.

Kasper, Walter. *The God of Jesus Christ.* Translated by Matthew J. O'Connell. New York: Crossroad, 1983.

————. *Harvesting the Fruits: Basic Aspects of Christian Faith in Ecumenical Dialogue.* London and New York: Continuum, 2009.

————. *Jesus the Christ.* Translated by V. Green. London: Burns and Oates; New York: Paulist, 1976.

Kay, William K. "Pentecostals and Angels." In *A&D,* chap. 3.

Keck, David. *Angels and Angelology in the Middle Ages.* Oxford: Oxford University Press, 1998.

Keener, Craig. *Miracles: The Credibility of the New Testament Accounts.* Grand Rapids: Baker Academic, 2011.

————. "Spirit Possession as a Cross-Cultural Experience." *Bulletin for Biblical Research* 20, no. 2 (2010): 215-36.

Keller, Catherine, and Laurel C. Schneider, eds. *Polydoxy: Theology of Multiplicity and Relation.* New York: Routledge, 2011.

Kelly, J. N. D. *Early Christian Creeds.* 3rd ed. London: Longman, 1972.

————. *Early Christian Doctrines.* Rev. ed. New York: Harper and Row, 1978 (1960).

Kelsey, David H. *Eccentric Existence: A Theological Anthropology.* 2 vols. Louisville: Westminster John Knox, 2009.

————. "On Human Flourishing: A Theocentric Perspective." Yale Center for Faith and Culture Resources, n.d. http://www.yale.edu/faith/downloads/David%20Kelsey%20%20-%20God%27s%20Power%20and%20Human%20Flourishing%202008.pdf (1/5/2012).

Kelsey, Morton. *Healing and Christianity.* New York: Harper and Row, 1973.

Kepnes, Steven. "'Turn Us to You and We Shall Return': Original Sin, Atonement, and Redemption in Jewish Terms." In *Christianity in Jewish Terms,* edited by Tikva Frymer-Kensky et al., pp. 293-319. Boulder, Colo.: Westview Press, 2000.

Kerr, Hugh T., and John M. Mulder, eds. *Conversions: The Christian Experience.* Grand Rapids: Eerdmans, 1983.

Keyes, Charles F. "Monks, Guns, and Peace." In *Belief and Bloodshed: Religion and Violence across Time and Tradition,* edited by James K. Wellman Jr., pp. 145-63. Lanham, Md.: Rowman and Littlefield, 2007.

Khalil, Atif. "Early Sufi Approaches to *Tawba:* From the Qur'ān to Abū Ṭālib al-Makkī." Ph.D. diss., University of Toronto, 2009.

Khan, Benjamin. *The Concept of Dharma in Valmiki Ramayana.* 2nd ed. New Delhi: Munshiram Mannoharlal Publishers, 1983.

Khodr, G. "Christianity in a Pluralistic World." In *Living Faiths and the Ecumenical Movement,* edited by S. J. Samartha. Geneva: WCC, 1971.

Kim, Grace Ji-Sun. *The Holy Spirit, Chi, and the Other: A Model of Global and Intercultural Pneumatology.* New York: Palgrave Macmillan, 2011.

Kim, Jaegwon. *Physicalism, or Something Near Enough.* Princeton: Princeton University Press, 2005.

Kim, Joon-Gon. "Korea's Total Evangelization Movement." In *Korean Church Growth Explosion,* edited by Bong Rin To and Marlin L. Nelson, pp. 45-73. Rev. ed. Seoul: Word of Life Press, 1975.

Kim, Kirsteen. "The Holy Spirit in Mission in India: Indian Contribution to Contemporary Mission Pneumatology." Presentation at Overseas Christian Missionary

Society, April 6, 2004. http://www.ocms.ac.uk/docs/TUESDAY%20LECTURES
_Kirsteen.pdf (7/10/2014).

———. *The Holy Spirit in the World: A Global Conversation*. Maryknoll, N.Y.: Orbis, 2007.

———. "How Will We Know When the Holy Spirit Comes? The Question of Discernment." *Evangelical Review of Theology* 33, no. 1 (2009): 93-96.

———. *Mission in the Spirit: The Holy Spirit in Indian Christian Theologies*. Delhi: ISPCK, 2003.

———. "The Potential of Pneumatology for Mission in Contemporary Europe." *IRM* 95, nos. 378-379 (2006).

———. "Spirit and 'Spirits' at the Canberra Assembly of the World Council of Churches, 1991." *Missiology: An International Review* 32, no. 3 (2004): 349-65.

Kim, Sam-Hwan, and Yoon-Su Kim. "Church Growth through Early Dawn Prayer Meetings." In *Korean Church Growth Explosion*, edited by Bong Rin To and Marlin L. Nelson, pp. 83-116. Rev. ed. Seoul: Word of Life Press, 1975.

Kim, Sangmoon, Ryan Thibodeau, and Randall S. Jorgensen. "Shame, Guilt, and Depressive Symptoms: A Meta-analytic Review." *Psychological Bulletin* 137, no. 1 (2011): 68-96.

Kim, Sebastian C. H. *In Search of Identity: Debates on Religious Conversion in India*. Oxford: Oxford University Press, 2003.

———. "Spirits of the Political: Theological Engagement in the Public Sphere." In *IRDSW*, chap. 9, pp. 125-40.

Kim, Sebastian C. H., Pauline Kollontai, and Greg Hoyland, eds. *Peace and Reconciliation: In Search of Shared Identity*. Aldershot: Ashgate, 2008.

Kim, Seyoon. *The Origin of Paul's Gospel*. Grand Rapids: Eerdmans, 1981.

King, Martin Luther, Jr. *Why We Can't Wait*. New York: Harper and Row, 1964.

Kinsley, David. *Health, Healing, and Religion: A Cross-Cultural Perspective*. Upper Saddle River, N.J.: Prentice-Hall, 1996.

Kirst, Nelson, ed. *Rethinking Luther's Theology in the Context of the Third World*. Geneva: Lutheran World Federation, 1990.

Klassen, William. *The Forgiving Community*. Philadelphia: Westminster, 1966.

Klostermaier, Klaus K. *A Survey of Hinduism*. Albany: State University of New York Press, 1964.

Knight, Henry H., III. "The Transformation of the Human Heart: The Place of Conversion in Wesley's Theology." In *Conversion in the Wesleyan Tradition*, edited by Kenneth J. Collins and John H. Tyson, pp. 43-55. Nashville: Abingdon, 2001.

Knitter, Paul F. "A New Pentecost? A Pneumatological Theology of Religions." *Current Dialogue* 19 (1991): 32-41.

———. *Without Buddha I Could Not Be a Christian*. Oxford: Oneworld, 2009.

Koenig, Harold G. *Is Religion Good for Your Health? The Effects of Religion on Physical and Mental Health*. New York: Haworth Pastoral Press, 1997.

Kogan, Michael S. *Opening the Covenant: A Jewish Theology of Christianity*. Oxford: Oxford University Press, 2008.

Kolb, Robert. "Contemporary Lutheran Understandings of Justification: A Select

Glimpse." In *Justification: What's at Stake in the Current Debates*, edited by Mark Husbands and Daniel J. Treier, pp. 153-76. Downers Grove, Ill.: InterVarsity, 2004.

Kolb, Robert, and Charles P. Arand. *The Genius of Luther's Theology: A Wittenberg Way of Thinking for the Contemporary Church*. Grand Rapids: Baker Academic, 2008.

Kole, Cece. "Jesus as Healer?" In *Faces of Jesus in Africa*, edited by R. J. Schreiter. Maryknoll, N.Y.: Orbis, 1991.

Kooiman, Dick. *Conversion and Social Equality in India*. Delhi: Manohar Publications, 1989.

Kose, Ali. *Conversion to Islam: A Study of Native British Converts*. London: Routledge, 1996.

Kraus, C. Norman. *The Authentic Witness: Credibility and Authority*. Grand Rapids: Eerdmans, 1979.

———. *Jesus Christ Our Lord: Christology from a Disciple's Perspective*. Scottdale, Pa.: Herald, 1987.

Kretschmar, Georg. "Die Rezeption der orthodoxen Vergöttlichungslehre in der protestantischen Theologie." In *Luther und Theosis: Vergöttlichung als Thema der abendländischen Theologie*, edited by Simo Peura and Antti Raunio, pp. 61-80. Helsinki and Erlangen: Martin-Luther-Verlag, 1990.

Kritzeck, James. "Holy Spirit in Islam." In *Perspectives on Charismatic Renewal*, edited by Edward D. O'Connor, pp. 101-11. Notre Dame: University of Notre Dame Press, 1975.

Kritzeck, James, and William H. Lewis, eds. *Islam in Africa*. New York: Van Nostrand, 1969.

Kugler, Karen, and Warren H. Jones. "On Conceptualizing and Assessing Guilt." *Journal of Personality and Social Psychology* 62, no. 2 (1992): 318-27.

Kumar, B. J. Christie. "An Indian Appreciation of the Doctrine of the Holy Spirit: A Search into the Religious Heritage of the Indian Christian." *Indian Journal of Theology* 30 (1981): 29-35.

Küng, Hans. "God's Self-Renunciation and Buddhist Self-Emptiness: A Christian Response to Masao Abe." In *DEHF*, pp. 207-23.

———. *On Being a Christian*. Garden City, N.Y.: Doubleday, 1976.

———. "What Is True Religion? Toward an Ecumenical Criteriology." In *Toward a Universal Theology of Religion*, edited by Leonard Swidler, pp. 231-50. Maryknoll, N.Y.: Orbis, 1987.

Kuyper, Abraham. "Common Grace." In *Abraham Kuyper: A Centennial Reader*, edited by James D. Bratt. Grand Rapids: Eerdmans, 1998.

———. *The Work of the Holy Spirit*. Translated by Henri De Vries. Grand Rapids: Eerdmans, 1946. www.ccel.org.

Kydd, Ronald A. N. *Healing through the Centuries: Models for Understanding*. Peabody, Mass.: Hendrickson, 1998.

LaCugna, Catherine Mowry. *God for Us: The Trinity and Christian Life*. San Francisco: HarperSanFrancisco, 1991, 1993.

LaHurd, Carol Schersten. "'So That the Sinner Will Repent': Forgiveness in Islam and Christianity." *Dialog* 35, no. 4 (1996): 287-92.

Lai, Pan-chiu. *Towards a Trinitarian Theology of Religions: A Study of Paul Tillich's Thought.* Kampen: Kok Pharos, 1994.

Lai, Pan-chiu, and Yuen-tai So. "Zhang Chunyi's Chinese Buddhist-Christian Pneumatology." *Jing Feng* 4, no. 1 (2003): 51-77.

Lak, Yeow Choo. Preface to *Doing Theology with the Spirit's Movement in Asia,* edited by John C. England and Alan J. Torrance. Singapore: ATESEA, 1991.

Lane, Anthony N. S. *Justification by Faith in Catholic-Protestant Dialogue: An Evangelical Assessment.* London: T. & T. Clark, 2006.

Langmead, Ross. "Transformed Relationships: Reconciliation as the Central Model for Mission." *Mission Studies* 25, no. 1 (2008): 5-20.

Largen, Kristin Johnston. *Baby Krishna, Infant Christ: A Comparative Theology of Salvation.* Maryknoll, N.Y.: Orbis, 2011.

———. *What Christians Can Learn from Buddhism: Rethinking Salvation.* Minneapolis: Fortress, 2009.

Laubach, F. "*Epistrephō.*" In *The New International Dictionary of New Testament Theology,* edited by Colin Brown, 1:354. Grand Rapids: Zondervan, 1975.

Lavater, John Caspar. *Essays on Physiognomy: For the Promotion of the Knowledge and the Love of Mankind.* Translated by Thomas Holcroft. London: G. G. J. and J. Robinson, Paternoster-Row, 1878. http://books.google.com/books?id=cIUAAAAMAAJ& printsec=frontcover&source=gbs_ge_summary_r&cad=0#v=onepage&q&f=false (12/2/2013).

Law, Bimala Churn. *The Buddhist Conception of Spirits.* 2nd ed. 1936. Reprint, Sonarpur Varanasi, India: Bhartiya, 1974.

Lazarus-Yafeh, Hava. "Is There a Concept of Redemption in Islam?" In *Some Religious Aspects of Islam,* pp. 48-57. Leiden: Brill, 1981.

Lederle, Henry I. *Treasures Old and New: Interpretations of "Spirit-Baptism" in the Charismatic Renewal Movement.* Peabody, Mass.: Hendrickson, 1988.

Ledgerwood, Elaine C. "The Hope of Forgiveness." *Compass* 47, no. 1 (2013): 14-20.

Lee, Jung Young. *An Emerging Theology in World Perspective: Commentary of Korean Minjung Theology.* New London, Conn.: Twenty-Third Publications, 1988.

———. *The Trinity in Asian Perspective.* Nashville: Abingdon, 1996.

Lee, Sang Hyun. *From a Liminal Place: An Asian American Theology.* Minneapolis: Fortress, 2010.

Lee, Sang-Mong, Gerald T. Hughes, and Francois P. Viljoen. "Forgiveness in the Intertestamental Period." *Verbum et Ecclesia* (online) 33, no. 1 (2012), n.p. http://www .ve.org.za/index.php/VE/article/view/484/950 (2/5/2014).

The Legend of King Aśoka: A Study and Translation of the Aśokāvadāna. Translated by John S. Strong. Princeton: Princeton University Press, 1983.

Le Saux, Henri [Swami Abhishiktananda]. *Saccidananda: A Christian Approach to Advaitic Experience.* Delhi: ISPCK, 1974.

Leslie, Donald Daniel, David Flusser, Alvin J. Reines, Gershom Scholem, and Michael J. Graetz. "Redemption." In *EJ* 17:151-55.

Letham, Robert. *The Holy Trinity: In Scripture, History, Theology, and Worship.* Phillipsburg, N.J.: P&R Publishing, 2004.

Levinas, Emmanuel. *Difficult Freedom: Essays on Judaism.* Translated by Sean Hand. Baltimore: Johns Hopkins University Press, 1990.

————. *Totality and Infinity: An Essay on Exteriority.* Translated by Alphonso Lingis. Pittsburgh: Duquesne University Press, 1969.

————. "The Trace of the Other." In *Deconstruction in Context: Literature and Philosophy,* edited by Mark C. Taylor. Chicago: University of Chicago Press, 1986.

Levison, John R. *Filled with the Spirit.* Grand Rapids: Eerdmans, 2009.

————. *The Spirit in First-Century Judaism.* Boston: Brill, 2002.

————. "A Stubborn Missionary, a Slave Girl, and a Scholar: The Ambiguity of Inspiration in the Book of Acts." In *IRDSW,* chap. 1, pp. 15-28.

Levison, John R., and P. Pope-Levison. "Christology: 4. The New Contextual Christologies; Liberation and Inculturation." In *Global Dictionary of Theology,* edited by Veli-Matti Kärkkäinen and William Dyrness. Downers Grove, Ill.: InterVarsity, 2008.

Levtzion, Nehamia, ed. *Conversion to Islam.* New York: Holmes and Meier, 1979.

Lewis, Paul W. "A Pneumatological Approach to Virtue Ethics." *Asian Journal of Pentecostal Theology* 1 (1998): 42-61.

Lichtenbarger, Hermann. "Spirits and Demons in the Dead Sea Scrolls." In *The Holy Spirit and Christian Origins: Essays in Honor of James D. G. Dunn,* edited by Graham N. Stanton, Bruce W. Longenecker, and Stephen C. Barton. Grand Rapids: Eerdmans, 2004.

Liechty, Joseph. "Putting Forgiveness in Its Place." In *Explorations in Reconciliation: New Directions for Theology,* edited by David Tombs and Joseph Liechty, pp. 59-68. Aldershot: Ashgate, 2006.

Lienhard, Joseph T. "On 'Discernments of Spirits' in the Early Church." *Theological Studies* 4 (1980): 505-29.

Lienhard, Ruth. "Restoring Relationships: Theological Reflections on Shame and Honor among the Daba and Bana of Cameroon." Ph.D. diss., Fuller Theological Seminary, 2000.

Lints, Richard. "Soteriology." In *Mapping Modern Theology: A Thematic and Historical Introduction,* edited by Kelly M. Kapic and Bruce L. McCormack, pp. 259-91. Grand Rapids: Baker Academic, 2012.

Lipner, Julius L. *Hindus: Their Religious Beliefs and Practices.* London and New York: Routledge, 1994.

Lodahl, Michael E. *Shekhinah/Spirit: Divine Presence in Jewish and Christian Religion.* New York: Paulist, 1992.

Loder, James E. *The Transforming Moment.* 2nd ed. Colorado Springs: Helmers and Howard, 1989.

Löffler, Paul. "The Biblical Concept of Conversion." In *Mission Trends No. 2: Evangelization,* edited by Gerald H. Anderson and Thomas F. Stransky, pp. 24-45. New York: Paulist, 1975.

Lohse, Bernhard. *Martin Luther's Theology: Its Historical and Systematic Development.* Minneapolis: Fortress, 1999.

The Longer Catechism of the Orthodox, Catholic, Eastern Church. In Philip Schaff, *The Creeds of Christendom*, vol. 2, *The Greek and Latin Creeds* (1889). ccel.org.

Longman, Tremper, III. "Spirit and Wisdom." In *Presence, Power, and Promise*, edited by David G. Firth and Paul D. Wegner, pp. 95-110. Downers Grove, Ill.: InterVarsity, 2011.

Lossky, Vladimir. *In the Image and Likeness of God*. Crestwood, N.Y.: St. Vladimir's Seminary Press, 1985.

———. *The Mystical Theology of the Eastern Church*. Crestwood, N.Y.: St. Vladimir's Seminary Press, 1976.

———. "The Procession of the Holy Spirit in Orthodox Trinitarian Doctrine." In *In the Image and Likeness of God*, edited by John H. Erickson and Thomas E. Bird, chap. 4. Crestwood, N.Y.: St. Vladimir's Seminary Press, 1985.

———. *The Vision of God*. Translated by Asheleigh Morehouse. Leighton Buzzard, Bedfordshire: Faith Press, 1973.

Love, Rick. "Muslims and Military Metaphors." *Evangelical Missions Quarterly* 37 (January 2001): 65-81.

Luhmann, Niklas. *Ecological Communication*. Translated by John Bednarz. Chicago: University of Chicago Press, 1989.

Luskin, Frederic. *Forgive for Good: A Proven Prescription for Health and Happiness*. San Francisco: HarperCollins, 2002.

Lutheran Church–Missouri Synod. "The Joint Declaration on the Doctrine of Justification in Confessional Lutheran Perspective." An Evaluation of the Lutheran-Roman Catholic "Joint Declaration on the Doctrine of Justification" by the Departments of Systematic Theology, Concordia Theological Seminary, Fort Wayne, and Concordia Seminary, Saint Louis. Commission on Theology and Church Relations. The Lutheran Church–Missouri Synod, 1999. http://www.google.com/url?sa=t &rct=j&q=&esrc=s&source=web&cd=5&ved=0CEcQFjAE&url=http%3A%2F %2Fwww.lcms.org%2FDocument.fdoc%3Fsrc%3Dlcm%26id%3D339&ei=kMl OU8OfAeOMygHV70Fo&usg=AFQjCNG2hMn5J5qL6shJgOyOhJsikWZmwQ &sig2=V5ejPxviCHpG7pxUYchRVA (8/10/2014).

Lutheran World Federation and the Roman Catholic Church. *Joint Declaration on the Doctrine of Justification*. Grand Rapids: Eerdmans, 2000. http://www.vatican .va/roman_curia/pontifical_councils/chrstuni/documents/rc_pc_chrstuni_doc _31101999_cath-luth-joint-declaration_en.html.

Lyden, John. "Atonement in Judaism and Christianity: Towards a Rapprochement." *Journal of Ecumenical Studies* 29, no. 1 (Winter 1992): 47-54.

——— "From Sacrifice to Sacrament: Repentance in a Christian Context." In *RCP*, pp. 43-59.

Ma, Julie C. *When the Spirit Meets the Spirits: Pentecostal Ministry among the Kankan-ey Tribe in the Philippines*. Frankfurt am Main: Peter Lang, 2000.

Maastricht, P. van. *Theoretico-Practica Teologica* (1725). In H. Heppe, *Reformed Dogmatics: Set Out and Illustrated from the Sources*. London: Allen, 1950.

Macarius, Pseudo-. *"The Fifty Spiritual Homilies" and "The Great Letter."* Translated, edited, and with an introduction by George A. Maloney. New York: Paulist, 1992.

———. *The Great Letter.* In Pseudo-Macarius, *"The Fifty Spiritual Homilies" and "The Great Letter,"* translated, edited, and with an introduction by George A. Maloney. New York: Paulist, 1992.

Macchia, Frank D. *Baptized in the Spirit: A Global Pentecostal Theology.* Grand Rapids: Zondervan, 2006.

———. "A Call for Careful Discernment: A Theological Response to Prosperity Preaching." In *Pentecostalism and Prosperity: The Socioeconomics of the Global Charismatic Movement,* edited by Katherine Attanasi and Amos Yong, chap. 11. New York: Palgrave Macmillan, 2012.

———. "Justification through New Creation: The Holy Spirit and the Doctrine by Which the Church Stands or Falls." *Theology Today* 58, no. 2 (July 2001): 202-17.

———. *Justified in the Spirit: Creation, Redemption, and the Triune God.* Grand Rapids: Eerdmans, 2010.

———. "The Spirit of Life and the Spirit of Immortality: An Appreciative Review of Levison's *Filled with the Spirit.*" *Pneuma: Journal of Pentecostal Theology* 33 (2011): 69-78.

Macdonald, Duncan B. "The Development of the Idea of Spirit in Islam: I." *Moslem World* 22, no. 1 (1932): 25-42.

———. "The Development of the Idea of Spirit in Islam: II." *Moslem World* 22, no. 2 (1932): 153-68.

MacDonald, John. "The Creation of Man and Angels in the Eschatological Literature." *Islamic Studies* 3 (1964): 285-308.

Machida, Soho. "The Holy Spirit through a Buddhist Lens." *Buddhist-Christian Studies* 16 (1996): 87-98.

MacNutt, Francis. *Healing: Revised and Expanded.* Notre Dame: Ave Maria Press, 1999.

Maddox, Randy L. *Responsible Grace: John Wesley's Practical Theology.* Nashville: Abingdon, Kingswood Books, 1994.

———, ed. *Rethinking Wesley's Theology for Contemporary Methodism.* Nashville: Kingswood Books, 1998.

Maimonides, Moses. *The Guide for the Perplexed.* Translated by M. Friedländer. sacred-texts.com (1903), http://www.sacred-texts.com/jud/gfp/index.htm#contents.

Majumdar, A. K. *Bhakti Renaissance.* Bombay: Bharatiya Vidya Bhavan, 1965.

Makransky, John J. "Buddhist Analogues of Sin and Grace: A Dialogue with Augustine." Presentation at 2001 Thagaste Symposium, Merrimack College, 2001. http://www.johnmakransky.org/article_12.html (4/5/2013).

Malek, Sobhi. "Islam Encountering Spiritual Power." In *Called and Empowered: Global Mission in Pentecostal Perspective,* edited by Murray W. Dempster, Byron D. Klaus, and Douglas Petersen, pp. 180-97. Peabody, Mass.: Hendrickson, 1991.

Malkovsky, Bradley J. *The Role of Divine Grace in the Soteriology of Śaṃkarācārya.* Leiden: Brill, 2001.

Mannermaa, Tuomo. *Christ Present in Faith: Luther's View of Justification.* Edited by Kirsi Stjerna. Minneapolis: Augsburg Fortress, 2005 (1979).

———. *Kaksi rakkautta: Johdatus Lutherin uskonmaailmaan.* Suomalaisen Teologisen Kirjallisuusseuran julkaisuja 194, 2. painos. Helsinki: STKJ, 1995 (1983).

———. "Theosis as a Subject of Finnish Luther Research." *Pro Ecclesia* 4, no. 1 (1995): 37-48.

———. "Why Is Luther So Fascinating? Modern Finnish Luther Research." In *Union with Christ: The New Finnish Interpretation of Luther,* edited by Carl E. Braaten and Robert W. Jenson, pp. 1-20. Grand Rapids: Eerdmans, 1998.

Mantzaridis, Georgios. *The Deification of Man: St. Gregory Palamas and the Orthodox Traditions.* Translated by Liadain Sherrar. Crestwood, N.Y.: St. Vladimir's Seminary Press, 1984.

Marcoulesco, Ileana. "Free Will and Determinism." In *ER,* pp. 3199-3202.

Margerie, Bertrand de. *The Christian Trinity in History.* Translated by Edmund J. Fordman. Petersham, Mass.: St. Bede's Publications, 1982.

Marion, Jean-Luc. "The Face: An Endless Hermeneutics." *Harvard Divinity Bulletin* 28, no. 2 (1999): 9-10.

Markham, Paul N. *Rewired: Exploring Religious Conversion.* Eugene, Ore.: Pickwick, 2007.

Martin, F. "Discernment of Spirits, Gift of." In *The New International Dictionary of Pentecostal and Charismatic Movements,* edited by Stanley M. Burgess and Eduard M. van der Maas, pp. 582-84. Revised and expanded ed. Grand Rapids: Zondervan, 2002.

Martindale, Paul. "A Muslim-Christian Dialogue on Salvation: The Role of Works." *Evangelical Missions Quarterly* 46, no. 1 (2010): 69-71.

Martinson, Paul. "Explorations in Lutheran Perspectives on People of Other Faiths: Toward a Christian Theology of Religions." In *Theological Perspectives on Other Faiths: Toward a Christian Theology of Religions,* edited by Hance A. O. Mwakabana. LWF Documentation 41. Geneva: Lutheran World Federation, 1997.

Mascall, Eric L. *The Christian Universe.* New York: Morehouse-Barlow, 1965.

Matts, Mark C. *The Role of Justification in Contemporary Theology.* Grand Rapids and Cambridge, U.K.: Eerdmans, 2004.

Mauss, Marcel. *Essay on the Gift.* London: Routledge, 1990 (1924).

Maximus the Confessor. *Commentary on the Our Father* 1-2. In *Maximus Confessor: Selected Writings,* translation and notes by George C. Berthold. Classics of Western Spirituality. New York: Paulist, 1985.

———. "Four Hundred Chapters on Love." In *Maximus Confessor: Selected Writings,* translation and notes by George C. Berthold. Classics of Western Spirituality. New York: Paulist, 1985.

May, Peter. "The Trinity and Saccidananda." *Indian Journal of Theology* 7, no. 3 (1958): 92-98.

Mbiti, John S. *African Religions and Philosophy.* New York: Praeger, 1969.

———. *Concepts of God in Africa.* 2nd ed. Nairobi: Acton Publishers, 2012.

———. *Introduction to African Religion.* London: Heinemann Educational, 1975.

McClendon, James Wm., Jr. *Doctrine.* Vol. 2 of *Systematic Theology.* Nashville: Abingdon, 1994.

———. *Ethics.* Vol. 1 of *Systematic Theology.* Nashville: Abingdon, 1986.

McClymond, Michael J., and Gerald R. McDermott. *The Theology of Jonathan Edwards.* New York: Oxford University Press, 2012.

McConnell, D. R. *A Different Gospel.* Updated ed. Peabody, Mass.: Hendrickson, 1995.

McCormack, Bruce L. "'Grace and Being': The Role of God's Gracious Election in Karl Barth's Theological Ontology." In *The Cambridge Companion to Karl Barth,* edited by John Webster, pp. 92-110. Cambridge: Cambridge University Press, 2000.

————. *Orthodox and Modern: Studies in the Theology of Karl Barth.* Grand Rapids: Baker Academic, 2008.

McCullough, Michael E., Kenneth I. Pargament, and Carl E. Thoresen. "The Psychology of Forgiveness: History, Conceptual Issues, and Overview." In *Forgiveness: Theory, Research, and Practice,* edited by Michael E. McCullough, Kenneth I. Pargament, and Carl E. Thoresen, pp. 1-14. New York: Guilford Press, 2001.

————, eds. *Forgiveness: Theory, Research, and Practice.* New York: Guilford Press, 2002.

McDaniel, Jay. "Where Is the Holy Spirit Anyway? Response to a Skeptic Environmentalist." *Ecumenical Review* 42, no. 2 (1990): 162-74.

McDonald, Suzanne. "Barth's 'Other' Doctrine of Election in the Church Dogmatics." *International Journal of Systematic Theology* 9, no. 2 (2007): 134-47.

————. *Re-imaging Election: Divine Election as Representing God to Others and Others to God.* Grand Rapids: Eerdmans, 2010.

McDonnell, A. A. *Hymns of the Rig Veda.* Delhi: Motilal Benarsidas, 1898.

McDonnell, Kilian, O.S.B. "Communion Ecclesiology and Baptism in the Spirit: Tertullian and the Early Church." *Theological Studies* 49 (1988): 671-93.

————. "The Determinative Doctrine of the Holy Spirit." *Theology Today* 39, no. 2 (1982): 142-62.

————. *The Other Hand of God: The Holy Spirit as the Universal Touch and Goal.* Collegeville, Minn.: Michael Glazier Books, 2003.

McDonnell, Kilian, O.S.B., and Arnold Bittlinger, eds. *The Baptism in the Holy Spirit as an Ecumenical Problem.* Notre Dame: Catholic Renewal Service, 1972.

McDonnell, Kilian, O.S.B., and George T. Montague. *Christian Initiation and Baptism in the Holy Spirit: Evidence from the First Eight Centuries.* Collegeville, Minn.: Liturgical Press, 1991.

McFague, Sallie. "Models of God for an Ecological, Evolutionary Era: God as Mother of the Universe." In *Physics, Philosophy, and Theology: A Common Quest for Understanding,* edited by R. J. Russell, W. R. Stoeger, S.J., and G. V. Coyne, S.J., pp. 249-71. Vatican City: Vatican Observatory Publications, 1988.

McGary, Howard. "Forgiveness." *American Philosophical Quarterly* 26 (1989): 343-50.

McGrath, Alister E. *Iustitia Dei: A History of the Christian Doctrine of Justification.* Vol. 1, *From the Beginnings to 1500.* Vol. 2, *From 1500 to the Present Day.* Cambridge: Cambridge University Press, 1986.

————. *The Re-enchantment of Nature: Science, Religion, and the Human Sense of Wonder.* London: Hodder and Stoughton, 2002.

McIlroy, David H. "Towards a Relational and Trinitarian Theology of Atonement." *Evangelical Quarterly* 80 (2008): 13-32.

McIntyre, John. *The Shape of Soteriology.* Edinburgh: T. & T. Clark, 1992.

McKim, Donald K. "The Mainline Protestant Understanding of Conversion." In *HRC,* pp. 123-36.

McLellan, Don. "Justice, Forgiveness, and Reconciliation: Essential Elements in Atonement Theology." *Evangelical Review of Theology* 29 (2005): 4-15.

McNally, Richard J. *Remembering Trauma*. Cambridge: Harvard University Press, 2003.

McNeill, John T. *A History of the Cure of Souls*. New York: Harper and Bros., 1977 (1951).

Meier, Levi, ed. *Jewish Values in Health and Medicine*. Lanham, Md.: University Press of America, 1991.

Melanchthon, Philip. *Chief Theological Topics (Loci Praecipui Theologici 1559)*. Translated by J. A. O. Preuss. 2nd English ed. St. Louis: Concordia, 2011.

Méndez-Moratalla, Fernando. *The Paradigm of Conversion in Luke*. London: T. & T. Clark, 2004.

Mennonite Church Canada. "Confession of Faith." Archived commentary on Article 8, "Salvation." http://www.mennonitechurch.ca/about/cof/art.8.htm (August 15, 2014).

Menon, Sangeetha. "Hinduism and Science." In *OHRS*, pp. 7-24.

Menzies, Robert P. *The Development of Early Christian Pneumatology: With Special Reference to Luke-Acts*. Sheffield: JSOT, 1991.

Messer, Neil. *Flourishing: Health, Disease, and Bioethics in Theological Perspective*. Grand Rapids: Eerdmans, 2013.

Meyendorff, John. *Byzantine Theology: Historical Trends and Doctrinal Themes*. New York: Fordham University Press, 1974.

Meyendorff, John, and Robert Tobias, eds. *Salvation in Christ: A Lutheran-Orthodox Dialogue*. Minneapolis: Augsburg, 1992.

Meyer, Brigit. "Commodities and the Power of Prayer: Pentecostalist Attitudes towards Consumption in Contemporary Ghana." In *Globalization and Identity: Dialectics of Flow and Closure*, edited by Brigit Meyer and Peter Geschiere. Oxford: Blackwell, 1999.

―――. *Translating the Devil: Religion and Modernity among the Ewe in Ghana*. Edinburgh: Edinburgh University Press, 1999.

Michael, S. M. *Anthropology of Conversion in India*. Mumbai: Institute of Indian Culture, 1998.

Michel, Thomas. "Criteria for Discerning the Movement of Holy Spirit in Islam." In *Credo in Spiritum Sanctum*, 2:1411-26. Vatican City: Liberai Editrice Vaticana, 1983.

Middleton, Paul. *Radical Martyrdom and Cosmic Conflict in Early Christianity*. New York: T. & T. Clark, 2006.

Midrash Rabbah: Genesis. Translated by H. Freedman and Maurice Simon. Vols. 1-2. London: Soncino Press, 1939.

Migliore, Daniel L. *Faith Seeking Understanding: An Introduction to Christian Theology*. 2nd ed. Grand Rapids: Eerdmans, 1991.

Milbank, John. *Being Reconciled: Ontology and Pardon*. London and New York: Routledge, 2003.

―――. "Can a Gift Be Given? Prolegomena to a Future Trinitarian Metaphysic." *Modern Theology* 11, no. 1 (1995): 119-61.

―――. "Gregory of Nyssa: The Force of Identity." In *Christian Origins: Theology, Rheto-*

ric, and Community, edited by Lewis Ayres and Gareth Jones, pp. 94-116. London: Routledge, 1998.

―――. *Theology and Social Theory.* Oxford: Basil Blackwell, 1990.

Milgrom, Jacob, and Alan Unterman. "Forgiveness." In *EJ* 7:127-29.

Milgrom, Jacob, Louis Jacobs, Samuel Rosenblatt, and Alan Unterman. "Repentance." In *EJ* 17:221-24.

Miller, Jeanine. *The Vision of Cosmic Order in the Vedas.* London: Routledge and Kegan Paul, 1985.

Miller, Roland. "The Muslim Doctrine of Salvation." *Bulletin of Christian Institutes of Islamic Studies* 3, nos. 1-4 (1980): 142-96.

Miller, Timothy S. *The Birth of the Hospital in the Byzantine Empire.* Rev. ed. Baltimore: Johns Hopkins University Press, 1997.

Min, Anselm Kyongsuk. *The Solidarity of Others in a Divided World.* New York: T. & T. Clark, 2004.

Minas, Anne. "God and Forgiveness." *Philosophical Quarterly* 25 (1975): 138-50.

Mishkat al-Masabih. Edited by Al-Baghawi. Translated by James Robinson. 4 vols. Lahore: Sh. Muhammad Ashraft, 1965-1966.

Moltmann, Jürgen. *Experiences in Theology: Ways and Forms of Christian Theology.* Translated by Margaret Kohl. Minneapolis: Fortress, 2000.

―――. *Experiences of God.* Translated by Margaret Kohl. Minneapolis: Fortress, 1980.

―――. *God in Creation: A New Theology of Creation and the Spirit of God.* Translated by Margaret Kohl. Minneapolis: Fortress, 1993.

―――. *In the End, the Beginning: The Life of Hope.* Translated by Margaret Kohl. Minneapolis: Fortress, 2004.

―――. "Justice for Victims and Perpetrators." *Reformed World* 44, no. 1 (March 1994): n.p. http://warc.ch/pc/rw941/01.html (9/25/09).

―――. *The Source of Life: The Holy Spirit and the Theology of Life.* Translated by Margaret Kohl. Minneapolis: Fortress, 1978.

―――. *The Spirit of Life: A Universal Affirmation.* Translated by Margaret Kohl. Minneapolis: Fortress, 2001.

―――. *The Trinity and the Kingdom of God: The Doctrine of God.* London: SCM, 1981.

―――. *The Way of Jesus Christ: Christology in Messianic Dimensions.* Translated by Margaret Kohl. Minneapolis: Fortress, 1993 (1989).

Montague, George T. S. M. "The Fire in the Word: The Holy Spirit in Scripture." In *Advents of the Spirit: An Introduction to the Current Study of Pneumatology,* edited by Bradford E. Hinze and D. Lyle Dabney, pp. 35-65. Milwaukee: Marquette University Press, 2001.

Montefiore, C. G. "Rabbinic Conceptions of Repentance." *Jewish Quarterly Review* 16, no. 2 (January 1904): 209-57.

Morales, Erwin T. "Vector Fields as the Empirical Correlate of the Spirit(s): A Meta-Pannenbergian Approach to Pneumatological Pluralism." In *IRDSW,* chap. 16, pp. 227-42.

Morro, William Charles. "Forgiveness." In *The International Standard Bible Encyclopedia,* vol. 2, edited by Geoffrey W. Bromiley. Grand Rapids: Eerdmans, 1982.

Mortensen, Viggo, ed. *Justification and Justice.* Geneva: Lutheran World Federation, 1992.

Moser, Matt. "Cataclysmic Fall or a Fumbling Slip? A Christian Engagement with Islamic Hamartiology." *Dialog* 48, no. 3 (2009): 231-38.

Moucarry, Chawkat. *The Search for Forgiveness: Pardon and Punishment in Islam and Christianity.* Leicester: Inter-Varsity Press, 2004.

Moule, C. F. D. "Preaching the Atonement." In *Forgiveness and Reconciliation, and Other New Testament Themes,* pp. 19-29. London: SPCK, 1998.

————. "Retribution or Restoration." In *Forgiveness and Reconciliation, and Other New Testament Themes,* pp. 41-47. London: SPCK, 1998.

————. "The Scope of the Death of Christ." In *Forgiveness and Reconciliation, and Other New Testament Themes,* pp. 3-18. London: SPCK, 1998.

Moyo, Ambrose M. "A Time for an African Lutheran Theology." In *Theology and the Black Experience: The Lutheran Heritage Interpreted by African and African-American Theologians,* edited by Albert Pero and Ambrose M. Moyo, pp. 76-96. Minneapolis: Augsburg, 1988.

Mucherera, T. N. *Pastoral Care from a Third World Perspective: A Pastoral Theology of Care for the Urban Contemporary Shona in Zimbabwe.* New York: Peter Lang, 2001.

Muhammad, Sayyid. *A Compendium of Muslim Theology and Jurisprudence.* Translated by Saifuddin Annif-Doray. Sri Lanka: A. S. Nordeen, 1963.

Mühlen, Heribert. *Der heilige Geist als Person: Beitrag zur Frage nach der dem heiligen Geiste eigentümlichen Funktion in der Trinität, bei der Inkarnation und im Gnadenbund.* 2nd ed. Münster: Verlag Aschendorff, 1963.

Mulago, V. "Vital Participation." In *Biblical Revelation and African Beliefs,* edited by Kwesi A. Diuckson and Paul Ellingworth. New York: Orbis, 1969.

Muller, Richard A. "Calvin and the 'Calvinists' [1995]: Assessing the Continuities and Discontinuities between the Reformation and Orthodoxy." *Calvin Theological Journal* 30 (1995): 345-75.

————. "Calvin and the 'Calvinists' [1996]: Assessing the Continuities and Discontinuities between the Reformation and Orthodoxy." *Calvin Theological Journal* 31 (1996): 125-60.

————. *Christ and the Decree: Christology and Predestination in Reformed Theology from Calvin to Perkins.* Durham, N.C.: Labyrinth, 1986.

Müller-Fahrenholz, Geiko. *The Art of Forgiveness: Theological Reflections on Healing and Reconciliation.* Geneva: WCC, 1999.

————. *God's Spirit: Transforming a World in Crisis.* New York: Continuum; Geneva: WCC Publications, 1995.

Mullin, Robert Bruce. *Miracles and the Modern Religious Imagination.* New Haven: Yale University Press, 1996.

Munro, Howard. "Are Demons Real?" *St. Mark's Review* 145 (Autumn 1991).

Murphree, Wallace A. "Can Theism Survive without the Devil?" *Religious Studies* 21, no. 2 (1985): 231-44.

Murphy, Jeffrie. "Forgiveness." In *Encyclopedia of Ethics,* edited by Lawrence C. Becker and Charlotte B. Becker, pp. 561-62. New York: Routledge, 2001.

Murphy, Nancey. "Reductionism: How Did We Fall into It and Can We Emerge from It?" In *E&E*, pp. 19-39.

Murphy, Nancey, and Warren S. Brown. *Did My Neurons Make Me Do It? Philosophical and Neurobiological Perspectives on Moral Responsibility and Free Will.* Oxford: Clarendon, 2007.

Murray, Kelly, and Joseph W. Ciarrochi. "The Dark Side of Religion, Spirituality, and Moral Emotions: Shame, Guilt, and Negative Religiosity as Markers for Life Dissatisfaction." *Mental Health, Religion and Culture* 1, no. 2 (1998): 165-84.

Murray, Robert. "The Holy Spirit as Mother." In *Symbols of Church and Kingdom: A Study in Early Syriac Tradition,* pp. 312-20. New York: T. & T. Clark, 2006.

Musekura, Celestin. "An Assessment of Contemporary Models of Forgiveness." Ph.D. diss., Dallas Theological Seminary, 2007.

Musk, Bill A. "Angels and Demons in Folk Islam." In *A&D,* chap. 10.

Muzorewa, Gwinyai H. *The Origins and Development of African Theology.* Maryknoll, N.Y.: Orbis, 1985.

Myers, Ched. *Binding the Strong Man: A Political Reading of Mark's Story of Jesus.* Maryknoll, N.Y.: Orbis, 1988.

Mylrea, C. G., and Shaikh Iskandur 'Abdul-Masih. *The Holy Spirit in Qur'an and Bible.* London: Christian Literature Society for India, n.d.

Nakamura, Hajime. "Pure Land Buddhism and Western Christianity Compared: A Quest for Common Roots of Their Universality." *International Journal for Philosophy of Religion* 1, no. 2 (1970): 77-96.

Nalunnakkal, George Mathew. "Come Holy Spirit, Heal and Reconcile: Called in Christ to Be Reconciling and Healing Communities." *IRM* 94, no. 372 (2005): 7-19.

Nambara, Minoru. "Ultimate Reality in Buddhism and Christianity: A Buddhist Perspective." In *Buddhism and Christianity in Dialogue,* edited by Perry Schmidt-Leukel, pp. 117-37. London: SCM, 2005.

Narayan, Uma. "Forgiveness, Moral Reassessment, and Reconciliation." In *Explorations of Value,* edited by Thomas Magnell, pp. 169-78. Amsterdam: Rodopi Press, 1997.

Narayanan, Vasudha. "Karma, Bhaktiyoga and Grace in the Srivaisnava Tradition: Ramaniya and Karattabvan." In *Of Human Bondage and Divine Grace: A Global Testimony,* edited by John Ross Carter, pp. 57-94. La Salle, Ill.: Open Court, 1992.

―――. "Shanti: Peace for the Mind, Body, and Soul." In *Teaching Religion and Healing,* edited by Linda L. Barnes and Inés Talamantez, pp. 61-82. New York: Oxford University Press, 2006.

Nasr, Seyeed Hosain. *Islam and the Plight of Modern Man.* Revised and enlarged ed. Chicago: ABC International Group, 2001.

―――. "The Prayer of the Heart in Hesychasm and Sufism." *Greek Orthodox Theological Review* 31 (1986): 195-203.

―――, ed. *Islamic Spirituality: Manifestations.* New York: Crossroad, 1997.

Nathan, Rabbi. *The Fathers according to Rabbi Nathan.* Translated by Judah Goldin. New Haven: Yale University Press, 1955.

Needham, Nick. "The Filioque Clause: East or West?" *Scottish Bulletin of Evangelical Theology* 15 (August 1997): 142-62.

Nellas, Panayiotis. *Deification in Christ: Orthodox Perspectives on the Nature of the Human Person.* Translated by Norman Russell. Crestwood, N.Y.: St. Vladimir's Seminary Press, 1987.

Nelson, Randy. "Exegeting Forgiveness." *American Theological Inquiry* 5, no. 2 (July 2012): 33-58.

Neusner, Jacob. *Introduction to Rabbinic Literature.* New York: Doubleday, 1994.

————. "Repentance in Judaism." In *RCP,* pp. 60-75.

————. *The Way of Torah: Introduction to Judaism.* Encino, Calif.: Dickenson Publishing, 1970.

Newberg, Andrew B., and Bruce Y. Lee. "The Neuroscientific Study of Religious and Spiritual Phenomena: Or Why God Doesn't Use Biostatistics." *Zygon* 40 (2005): 469-89.

Newbigin, Lesslie. *The Light Has Come: An Exposition of the Fourth Gospel.* Edinburgh: Handsel Press, 1982.

Newby, Gordon D. "Angels." In *The Oxford Encyclopedia of the Modern Islamic World,* edited by John L. Esposito. Oxford Islamic Studies Online. http://www.oxfordislamic studies.com/article/opr/t236MIW/e0061 (3/22/2013).

Newlands, George, and Allen Smith. *Hospitable God: The Transformative Dream.* Surrey, U.K.: Ashgate, 2010.

Newman, John Henry. *Lectures on Justification.* Lecture 3, section 4. http://www.newman reader.org/Works/justification/index.html (5/8/2014).

Newman, Louis E. "The Quality of Mercy: On the Duty to Forgive in the Judaic Tradition." *Journal of Religious Ethics* 15, no. 2 (Fall 1987): 155-72.

Ngah, Joseph. "Liberation from Evil Powers — Africa." In *Justification in the World's Context,* edited by Wolfgang Greive, pp. 133-38. Geneva: Lutheran World Federation, 2000.

Ngong, David Tonghou. *The Holy Spirit and Salvation in African Christian Theology: Imagining a More Hopeful Future for Africa.* New York: Peter Lang, 2010.

Nickel, Gordon. "Islam and Salvation: Some On-Site Observations." *Direction* 23, no. 1 (Spring 1994): 3-16.

Nietzsche, Friedrich Wilhelm. *Beyond Good and Evil.* Translated by Marianne Cowan. Chicago: Gateway/Regnery, 1955.

————. *Human, All Too Human: A Book for Free Spirits.* Translated by R. J. Hollingdale. Cambridge: Cambridge University Press, 1996. http://www.gutenberg.org/ files/38145/38145-h/38145-h.htm#THE_RELIGIOUS_LIFE (2/11/2014).

————. *On the Genealogy of Morality.* Edited by Keith Ansell-Pearson. Translated by Carol Diethe. Cambridge: Cambridge University Press, 2006.

Nissiotis, Nikos A. "The Main Ecclesiological Problem of the Second Vatican Council and Position of the Non-Roman Churches Facing It." *Journal of Ecumenical Studies* 2, no 1 (1965): 31-62.

————. "Pneumatological Christology as a Presupposition of Ecclesiology." In *Oecumenica: An Annual Symposium of Ecumenical Research, 1967,* edited by Friedrich Wilhelm Kantzenbach and Vilmos Vajta. Minneapolis: Augsburg, 1967.

Noble, Thomas A. "The Spirit World: A Theological Approach." In *UW,* pp. 185-223.

Nock, Arthur D. *Conversion.* Oxford: Oxford University Press, 1961.

Noll, Stephen F. "Thinking about Angels." In *UW*, pp. 1-27.

Norris, Frederick W. "Deification: Consensual and Cogent." *Scottish Journal of Theology* 49, no. 4 (1996): 411-28.

North, Joanna. "Wrongdoing and Forgiveness." *Philosophy* 62, no. 242 (October 1987): 499-508.

Novak, David. *The Election of Israel: The Idea of the Chosen People.* Cambridge and New York: Cambridge University Press, 1995.

Nyamiti, Charles. *African Tradition and Christian God.* Eldoret, Kenya: Gaba Publications, 1972.

Oberman, Heiko Augustinus. *The Harvest of Medieval Theology: Gabriel Biel and Late Medieval Nominalism.* Cambridge: Harvard University Press, 1963.

Ochs, Peter. "Genesis 1-2: Creation as Evolution." *Living Pulpit* 9, no. 2 (April-June 2000): 8-10.

O'Collins, Gerald, S.J. *The Tripersonal God: Understanding and Interpreting the Trinity.* New York and Mahwah, N.J.: Paulist, 1999.

O'Collins, Gerald, S.J., and Oliver P. Rafferty, S.J. "Roman Catholic View." In *Justification: Five Views,* edited by James K. Beilby and Paul Rhodes Eddy, pp. 265-66. Downers Grove, Ill.: IVP Academic, 2011.

O'Connor, David. *God and Inscrutable Evil: In Defense of Theism and Atheism.* Lanham, Md.: Rowman and Littlefield, 1998.

Oddie, Geoffrey A. "India: Missionaries, Conversion, and Change." In *The Church Mission Society and World Christianity, 1799-1999,* edited by Kevin Ward and Brian Stanley, pp. 228-53. Grand Rapids: Eerdmans, 2000.

Oden, Patrick. "Chaos or Completion: The Work of Spirits in History." In *IRDSW,* chap. 5, pp. 71-84.

Oden, Thomas. *The Transforming Power of Grace.* Nashville: Abingdon, 1993.

Okorocha, Cyril C. *The Meaning of Religious Conversion in Africa.* Aldershot: Avebury, 1987.

Oladipo, Caleb Oluremi. *The Development of the Doctrine of the Holy Spirit in the Yoruba (African) Indigenous Christian Movement.* American University Studies, series II, Theology and Religion 185. Frankfurt: Peter Lang, 1996.

O'Leary, Joseph S. "Emptiness and Dogma." *Buddhist-Christian Studies* 22 (2002): 163-79.

————. "Mahāyāna Buddhism and Forgiveness." *Dialogue* (Colombo, Sri Lanka) 29 (2002): 94-110.

Olson, Roger E. *Against Calvinism.* Grand Rapids: Zondervan, 2011.

————. *Arminian Theology: Myths and Realities.* Downers Grove, Ill.: IVP Academic, 2006.

Olujide, M. A., and D. A. Olujide. *Quran Testifies to the Existence of the Holy Spirit.* Lagos, Ghana: Loyal Printers Industries, n.d.

O'Murchu, Diamuid. *In the Beginning Was the Spirit: Science, Religion, and Indigenous Spirituality.* Maryknoll, N.Y.: Orbis, 2012.

"On Becoming a Christian: Insights from Scripture and the Patristic Writings; With Some Contemporary Reflections." Report of the Fifth Phase of the International Dialogue between Some Classical Pentecostal Churches and Leaders and the Catholic Church (1998-2006).

One God, One Lord, One Spirit: On the Explication of the Apostolic Faith Today. Edited by H.-G. Link. Geneva: WCC, 1988.

O'Neill, Michael. "Karl Barth's Doctrine of Election." *Evangelical Quarterly* 76 (2004): 311-26.

Onyinah, Opoku. "Akan Witchcraft and the Concept of Exorcism in the Church of Pentecost." Ph.D. diss., University of Birmingham, U.K., 2002. http://etheses.bham.ac .uk/1694/1/Onyinaho2PhD.pdf.

————. "Deliverance as a Way of Confronting Witchcraft in Contemporary Africa." In *The Spirit in the World: Emerging Pentecostal Theologies in Global Contexts,* edited by Veli-Matti Kärkkäinen, pp. 181-202. Grand Rapids: Eerdmans, 2009.

Oord, Thomas Jay. *Defining Love: A Philosophical, Scientific, and Theological Engagement.* Grand Rapids: Brazos, 2010.

Opler, Morris E. "Spirit Possession in a Rural Area of Northern India." In *Reader in Comparative Religion: An Anthropological Approach,* edited by William A. Lessa and Evon Z. Vogt, pp. 553-66. Evanston, Ill., and White Plains, N.Y.: Row, Peterson and Co., 1958.

Organ, Troy W. *The Hindu Quest for the Perfection of Man.* Athens: Ohio University Press, 1970.

Origen. *Commentary on the Epistle to the Romans.* Books 6-10. Translated by Thomas P. Scheck. Fathers of the Church 104. Washington, D.C.: Catholic University of America Press, 2002.

O'Shaughnessy, Thomas. *The Development of the Meaning of Spirit in the Koran.* Rome: Pont. Institutum Orientalium Studiorum, 1953.

Ott, Heinrich. "The Convergence: Sunyata as a Dynamic Event." In *DEHF,* pp. 127-35.

Pabst, Adrian, and Christoph Schneider, eds. *Encounter between Eastern Orthodoxy and Radical Orthodoxy: Transfiguring the World through the Word.* Surrey, U.K.: Ashgate, 2009.

Packer, J. I. "Justification in Protestant Theology." In *Here We Stand: Justification by Faith Today,* edited by J. I. Packer et al. London: Hodder and Stoughton, 1986.

Pagels, Elaine. *The Origins of Satan.* New York: Random House, 1995.

Painadath, Sebastian. "The Integrated Spirituality of the Bhagavad Gita — an Insight for Christians: A Contribution to the Hindu-Christian Dialogue." *Journal of Ecumenical Studies* 39, no. 3-4 (2002): 305-24.

Palamas, Gregory. *The Triads of Gregory Palamas.* Edited and with an introduction by John Meyendorff. Translated by Nicholas Gendle. New York: Paulist, 1983.

Panikkar, Raimundo. *The Cosmotheandric Experience: Emerging Religious Consciousness.* Edited with introduction by Scott Eastham. Maryknoll, N.Y.: Orbis, 1993.

————. *Myth, Faith, and Hermeneutics.* New York: Paulist, 1979.

————. *The Rhythm of Being: The Gifford Lectures.* Reprint, Maryknoll, N.Y.: Orbis, 2013.

————. *The Trinity and the Religious Experience of Man.* Maryknoll, N.Y.: Orbis; London: Darton, Longman and Todd, 1973; also titled *The Trinity and the World Religions.*

————. *The Unknown Christ of Hinduism: Towards an Ecumenical Christophany.* Rev. ed. Maryknoll, N.Y.: Orbis, 1991.

Pannenberg, Wolfhart. "Christian Morality and Political Issues." In *Faith and Reality,* translated by John Maxwell. Philadelphia: Westminster, 1977.

————. "The Doctrine of the Spirit and the Task of a Theology of Nature." *Theology* 75 (January 1972): 8-21.

————. "Die 'Gemeinsame Erklärung zur Rechtfertigungslehre aus evangelischer Sicht.'" In *Zur Zukunft der Ökumene: Die "Gemeinsame Erklärung zur Rechtfertigungslehre,"* edited by Wolfhart Pannenberg and Bernd Jochen Hilberath, pp. 70-78. Regensburg: Pustet, 1999.

————. "God as Spirit — and Natural Science." *Zygon* 36, no. 4 (2001): 783-94.

————. "God's Love and the Kenosis of the Son: A Response to Masao Abe." In *DEHF,* pp. 246-47.

————. *Hintergründe des Streites um die Rechtfertigungslehre in der evangelischen Theologie.* Munich: Verlag der Bayerischen Akademie der Wissenschaften, 2000.

————. *Introduction to Systematic Theology.* Grand Rapids: Eerdmans, 1991.

————. "Spirit and Energy: The Phenomenology of Teilhard de Chardin." In *Beginning with the End: God, Science, and Wolfhart Pannenberg,* edited by Carol Rausch Albright and Joel Haugen. Peru, Ill.: Open Court, 1997.

Park, Andrew Sung. *From Hurt to Healing: A Theology of the Wounded.* Nashville: Abingdon, 2004.

Parratt, John. "Introduction." In *An Introduction to Third World Theologies,* edited by John Parratt. Cambridge: Cambridge University Press, 2004.

Parrinder, Geoffrey. "Triads." In *The Encyclopedia of Religion,* edited by Lindsay Jones, 14:9345-50. 2nd ed. Detroit: Macmillan Reference USA, 2005.

————. *Witchcraft: A Critical Study of the Belief in Witchcraft from the Records of Witch Hunting in Europe Yesterday and Africa Today.* Harmondsworth: Penguin Books, 1958.

Parsons, Martin. "Binding the Strong Man: The Flaw of the Excluded Middle." In *A&D,* chap. 5.

Partee, Charles. *The Theology of John Calvin.* Louisville: Westminster John Knox, 2008.

Partridge, Christopher. "Satanism and the Heavy-Metal Subculture." In *A&D,* chap. 12.

Patanjali. *Yoga Sutras.* Translated by Rama Prasada. New Delhi: Oriental Books, 1978.

Pathrapankal, Joseph. "Editorial." *Journal of Dharma* 33, no. 3 (1998): 299-302.

Pattison, Stephen. *Saving Face: Enfacement, Shame, Theology.* Surrey, U.K.: Ashgate, 2013.

Pauw, Amy Plantinga. "Where Theologians Fear to Tread." *Modern Theology* 16 (2000): 39-59.

Peace, Richard V. *Conversion in the New Testament: Paul and the Twelve.* Grand Rapids: Eerdmans, 1999.

Peacocke, Arthur. *Theology for a Scientific Age: Being and Becoming — Natural, Divine, and Human.* Theology and the Sciences. Enlarged ed. Minneapolis: Fortress, 1993.

Peel, John D. Y. *Religious Encounter and the Making of the Yoruba.* Bloomington: Indiana University Press, 2000.

Pelagius' Commentary on St. Paul's Epistle to the Romans. Translated by Theodore De-Bruyn. Oxford: Oxford University Press, 1998.

Pelikan, Jaroslav. *The Christian Tradition: A History of the Development of Doctrine.* Vol. 1, *The Emergence of the Catholic Tradition (100-600).* Vol. 2, *The Spirit of Eastern Christendom (600-1700).* Vol. 3, *The Growth of Medieval Theology (600-1300).* Vol. 4, *Reformation of Church and Dogma (1300-1700).* Chicago: University of Chicago Press, 1971, 1974, 1978, 1984.

Perho, Irmeli. "Man Chooses His Destiny: Ibn Qayyim al-Jawziyya's Views on Predestination." *Islam and Christian-Muslim Relations* 12 (2001): 61-70.

Perriman, Andrew, ed. *Faith, Health, and Prosperity: A Report on 'Word of Faith' and 'Positive Confession' Theologies.* Waynesboro, Ga.: Paternoster, 2003.

Persinger, A. "People Who Report Religious Experiences May Also Display Enhanced Temporal Lobe Signs." *Perceptual and Motor Skills* 58, no. 3 (1984): 963-75.

Person, Hara E., ed. *The Mitzvah of Healing: An Anthology of Jewish Texts, Meditations, Essays, Personal Stories, and Rituals.* New York: UAHC Press/Women of Reform Judaism, 2003.

Pesch, Otto Hermann. "Kernpunkte der Kontroverse. Die antireformatorischen Lehrentscheidungen des Konzils von Trient (1545-1563) — und die Folgen." In *Zur Zukunft der Ökumene: Die "Gemeinsame Erklärung zur Rechtfertigungslehre,"* edited by Wolfhart Pannenberg and Bernd Jochen Hilberath. Regensburg: Pustet, 1999.

Peters, Ted. *God as Trinity: Relationality and Temporality in Divine Life.* Louisville: Westminster John Knox, 1993.

Petersen, Douglas. *Not by Might Nor by Power: A Pentecostal Theology of Social Concern in Latin America.* Carlisle, U.K.: Paternoster, 1996.

Petersen, Rodney L. "A Theology of Forgiveness: Terminology, Rhetoric, and the Dialectic of Interfaith Relationships." In *Forgiveness and Reconciliation: Religion, Public Policy, and Conflict Transformation,* edited by R. G. Helmick and R. L. Petersen, pp. 3-25. Philadelphia: Templeton Foundation Press, 2001.

Pettigrove, Glen. "The Dilemma of Divine Forgiveness." *Religious Studies* 44, no. 4 (2008): 457-64.

———. "Forgiveness without God." *Journal of Religious Ethics* 40 (2012): 518-44.

Peura, Simo. "Christ as Favor and Gift." In *Union with Christ: The New Finnish Interpretation of Luther,* edited by Carl E. Braaten and Robert W. Jenson. Grand Rapids: Eerdmans, 1998.

———. "Gott und Mensch in der Unio: Die Unterschiede im Rechtfertigungsverständnis bei Osiander und Luther." In *Unio: Gott und Mensch in der nachreformatorischen Theologie,* edited by Matti Repo and Rainer Vinke, pp. 33-61. Helsinki: Luther-Agricola-Gesellschaft 35, 1996.

Pew Research Center. "Summary of Key Findings." *Pew Forum on Religion & Public Life/U.S. Religious Landscape Survey* (2008), pp. 3-20. http://religions.pewforum.org/pdf/report2religious-landscape-study-key-findings.pdf.

Phan, Peter C. "Peacebuilding and Reconciliation: Interreligious Dialogue and Catholic Spirituality." In *Peacebuilding: Catholic Theology, Ethics, and Praxis,* edited by

Robert J. Schreiter, R. Scott Appleby, and Gerard F. Powers, chap. 12. Maryknoll, N.Y.: Orbis, 2010.

Photius, Patriarch of Constantinople. *On the Mystagogy of the Holy Spirit.* Astoria, N.Y.: Studion Publishers, 1983.

Pieris, Aloysius, S.J. "The Holy Spirit and Asia's Religiousness." *Spiritus* 7, no. 2 (Fall 2007): 126-42.

Piers, Gerhart, and Milton B. Singer. *Shame and Guilt.* New York: Norton, 1971 (1953).

Pinnock, Clark H. "Evangelism and Other Living Faiths: An Evangelical Charismatic Perspective." In *All Together in One Place: Theological Papers from the Brighton Conference on World Evangelization,* edited by Peter Hocken and Harold D. Hunter, pp. 208-18. Sheffield: Sheffield Academic Press, 1993.

—————. *Flame of Love: A Theology of the Holy Spirit.* Downers Grove, Ill.: InterVarsity, 1996.

—————. *A Wideness in God's Mercy: The Finality of Jesus Christ in a World of Religions.* Grand Rapids: Zondervan, 1992.

Piper, John. *The Future of Justification: A Response to N. T. Wright.* Wheaton, Ill.: Crossway, 2007.

Piras, Andrea. "Angels." In *ER* 1:343-49.

Placher, William C. "Christ Takes Our Place: Rethinking Atonement." *Interpretation* 53 (1999): 5-20.

Plaskow, Judith. *Standing Again at Sinai: Judaism from a Feminist Perspective.* San Francisco: Harper and Row, 1990.

Polanyi, Michael, and Harry Prosch. *Meaning.* Chicago: University of Chicago Press, 1975.

Polkinghorne, John. "Fields and Theology: A Response to Wolfhart Pannenberg." *Zygon* 36 (2001): 795-97.

—————. "The Hidden Spirit and the Cosmos." In *The Work of the Spirit: Pneumatology and Pentecostalism,* edited by Michael Welker, pp. 169-82. Grand Rapids: Eerdmans, 2006.

—————. *Quarks, Chaos, and Christianity: Questions to Science and Religion.* New York: Crossroad, 2005.

—————. *Reason and Reality: The Relationship between Science and Theology.* Philadelphia: Trinity, 1991.

—————. "The Universe in a Trinitarian Perspective: A Theology of Nature." In *Science and Trinity: The Christian Encounter with Reality.* New Haven and London: Yale University Press, 2004.

—————. "Wolfhart Pannenberg's Engagement with the Natural Sciences." *Zygon* 34, no. 1 (March 1999): 151-58.

Poloma, Margaret M. *The Assemblies of God at the Crossroads: Charisma and Institutional Dilemmas.* Knoxville: University of Tennessee Press, 1989.

Pöntinen, Mari-Anna. *African Theology as Liberating Wisdom: Celebrating Life and Harmony in the Evangelical Lutheran Church in Botswana.* Leiden: Brill, 2013.

Pope-Levison, Priscilla, and John R. Levison. *Jesus in Global Contexts.* Louisville: Westminster John Knox, 1992.

Porterfield, Amanda. *Healing in the History of Christianity*. New York: Oxford University Press, 2005.

Prenter, Regin. *Spiritus Creator: Luther's Concept of the Holy Spirit*. Philadelphia: Muhlenberg, 1953.

Prestige, George L. *God in Patristic Thought*. London and Toronto: W. Heinemann, 1936.

Prichard, Rebecca Button. *Sensing the Spirit: The Holy Spirit in Feminist Perspective*. St. Louis: Chalice, 1999.

Priya, Sri Nrisimha. "Dhanvantari the Hindu God of Medicine." *Srivaisnava News Portal*, April 1, 2014. http://anudinam.org/2012/01/31/dhanvantari-the-hindu-god-of-medicine/ (29/8/2014).

Purves, Andrew, and Mark Achtemeier. *Union in Christ: A Declaration of the Church*. Louisville: Witherspoon Press, 1999.

Quick, O. C. *Essays in Orthodoxy*. London: Macmillan, 1916.

Rad, Gerhard von. *Genesis: A Commentary*. Translated by John H. Marks. Rev. ed. Philadelphia: Westminster, 1972.

Radhakrishnan, Sarvepalli. *The Hindu View of Life*. London: Unwin, 1961.

——. *Indian Philosophy*. Vol. 2. New York: Macmillan; London: George Allen and Unwin, 1958 (1927).

——, ed. *The Principal Upanisads*. London: George Allen and Unwin, 1953.

Rahman, Fazlur. *Health and Medicine in the Islamic Tradition*. New York: Kazi Publications, 1998.

Rahner, Karl. "Devil." In *Sacramentum Mundi,* edited by Karl Rahner et al., 2:73-75. New York: Herder and Herder, 1968-1970.

——. *Foundations of Christian Faith: An Introduction to the Idea of Christianity*. Translated by William W. Dych. New York: Crossroad, 1982, 1984, 2004.

——. "On Angels." In *Theological Investigations* 19, translated by Edward Quinn, edited by Paul Imhof, S.J., pp. 252-74. New York: Crossroad, 1983.

——. "The One Christ and the Universality of Salvation." In *Theological Investigations* 16, translated by David Morland, O.S.B. New York: Crossroad, 1979.

Rahula, Walpola. *What the Buddha Taught*. Rev. ed. New York: Grove Press, 1974.

Räikkä, Juha. "Irrational Guilt." *Ethical Theory and Moral Practice* 7 (2004): 473-85.

Raiser, Konrad. "The Holy Spirit in Modern Ecumenical Thought." *Ecumenical Review* 41, no. 3 (1989): 375-87.

Ramachandra, Vinoth. *The Recovery of Mission: Beyond the Pluralist Paradigm*. Grand Rapids: Eerdmans, 1996.

Ramanuja. *The Gitabhasya of Ramanuja*. Translated by M. R. Sampatkumaran. Madras: Ramacharya Memorial Trust, 1969.

Rambo, Lewis R. *Understanding Religious Conversion*. New Haven: Yale University Press, 1993.

Rambo, Lewis R., and Charles F. Farhadian. "Conversion." In *ER*, pp. 1969-74.

Ramm, Bernard. *Them He Glorified: A Systematic Study of the Doctrine of Glorification*. Grand Rapids: Eerdmans, 1963.

Raphael, Melissa. *The Female Face of God in Auschwitz: A Jewish Feminist Theology of the Holocaust*. London and New York: Routledge, 2003.

Ratzinger, Joseph. "The Holy Spirit as *Communio:* Concerning the Relationship of Pneumatology and Spirituality in Augustine." *Communio* 25 (1998): 324-27.

Rauf, M. A. "The Qur'ān and the Free Will [I]." *Muslim World* 60, no. 3 (1970): 205-17.

———. "The Qur'ān and the Free Will [II]." *Muslim World* 60, no. 4 (1970): 289-99.

Raunio, Antti. *Summe des christlichen Lebens: Die "Goldene Regel" als Gesetz in der Theologie Martin Luthers von 1510-1527.* Göttingen: Vandenhoeck & Ruprecht, 2001.

Rayan, Samuel. *The Holy Spirit: Heart of the Gospel and Christian Hope.* Maryknoll, N.Y.: Orbis, 1978.

Reich, K. Helmut. "The Doctrine of the Trinity as a Model for Structuring the Relations between Science and Theology." *Zygon* 30 (1995): 383-405.

Reich, Mordechai. "Some Insights into Maimonides' Approach to Mental Health Issues." In *Moses Maimonides: Physician, Scientist, and Philosopher,* edited by Fred Rosner and Samuel S. Kottek, pp. 167-72. Northvale, N.J.: Jason Aronson, 1993.

Reichenbach, Bruce R. "Healing View." In *The Nature of the Atonement: Four Views,* edited by James Beilby and Paul R. Eddy. Downers Grove, Ill.: InterVarsity, 2009.

Reiterer, F. V., T. Nicklas, and K. Schöpflin, eds. *Angels: The Concept of Celestial Beings — Origins, Development, and Reception.* New York: De Gruyter, 2007.

Remus, Harold. *Jesus as Healer.* Cambridge: Cambridge University Press, 1997.

Reumann, John. "Justification and Justice in the New Testament." *Horizons in Biblical Theology* 21, no. 1 (1999): 26-45.

Reynolds, T. E. *Vulnerable Communion: A Theology of Disability and Hospitality.* Grand Rapids: Brazos, 2008.

Richardson, James T. "Conversion and New Religious Movements." In *Encyclopedia of Social and Political Movements,* edited by D. Snow, D. della Porta, B. Klandermans, and D. McAdam. Oxford: Blackwell, 2013.

Richie, Tony. *Speaking by the Spirit: A Pentecostal Model for Interreligious Dialogue.* Lexington, Ky.: Emeth Press, 2011.

Riddell, Peter G. "How Allah Communicates: Islamic Angels, Devils and the 2004 Tsunami." In *A&D,* chap. 8.

Risse, Matthias. "On God and Guilt: A Reply to Aaron Ridley." *Journal of Nietzsche Studies* 29 (2005): 46-53. http://www.hks.harvard.edu/fs/mrisse/Papers/Nietzsche/OnGodandGuilt.pdf.

Ritschl, Albrecht. *The Christian Doctrine of Justification and Reconciliation: The Positive Development of the Doctrine.* Translated by H. R. Mackintosh and A. B. Macaulay. Eugene, Ore.: Wipf and Stock, 2004.

Rivera, Mayra. *The Touch of Transcendence: A Postcolonial Theology of God.* Louisville: Westminster John Knox, 2007.

Robb-Dover, Kristina. "Gregory of Nyssa's 'Perpetual Progress.'" *Theology Today* 65 (2008): 213-25.

Robeck, Cecil M. *Azusa Street Mission and Revival: The Birth of the Global Pentecostal Movement.* Nashville: Thomas Nelson, 2006.

Robinson, Gnana. "Justification in a Multireligious Context — Asia." In *Justification in the World's Context,* edited by Wolfgang Greive, pp. 139-53. Geneva: Lutheran World Federation, 2000.

Robinson, Rowena. *Conversion, Continuity, and Change: Lived Christianity in Southern Goa*. Delhi: Sage Publications, 1998.

Robinson, Rowena, and Sathianathan Clarke. Introduction to *Religious Conversion in India: Modes, Motivations, and Meanings*, edited by Rowena Robinson and Sathianathan Clarke. New York: Oxford University Press, 2007.

———, eds. *Religious Conversion in India: Modes, Motivations, and Meanings*. New York: Oxford University Press, 2007.

Robson, James. "Aspects of the Qur'anic Doctrine of Salvation." In *Man and His Salvation: Studies in Memory of S. G. F. Brandon*, edited by Eric F. Shape and John R. Hinnels, pp. 205-19. Oxford: Manchester University Press, 1973.

Rogers, Eugene F., Jr. *After the Spirit: A Constructive Pneumatology from Resources Outside the Modern West*. Grand Rapids and Cambridge: Eerdmans, 2005.

Rolf, Sibylle. *Zum Herzen sprechen: Eine Studie zum imputativen Aspekt in Martin Luthers Rechtfertigungslehre und zu seinen Konsequenzen für die Predigt des Evangeliums*. Leipzig: Evangelische Verlagsanstalt, 2008.

Rosato, Philip J. "Spirit Christology: Ambiguity and Promise." *Theological Studies* 38, no. 2 (1977): 423-49.

Roukema, Riemer. "Salvation *Sola Fide* and *Sola Gratia* in Early Christianity." In *Passion of Protestants*, edited by P. N. Holtrop et al., pp. 27-49. Kampen: Kok, 2004.

Runyon, Theodore. *The New Creation: John Wesley's Theology Today*. Nashville: Abingdon, 1998.

———, ed. *Sanctification and Liberation: Liberation Theologies in Light of the Wesleyan Tradition*. Nashville: Abingdon, 1981.

Rupp, Gordon, and Philip S. Watson, eds. *Luther and Erasmus: Free Will and Salvation*. Philadelphia: Westminster, 1969.

Russell, Jeffrey Burton. *The Devil: Perceptions of Evil from Antiquity to Primitive Christianity*. Ithaca, N.Y.: Cornell University Press, 1977.

———. *Lucifer: The Devil in the Middle Ages*. Ithaca, N.Y.: Cornell University Press, 1984.

———. *Mephistopheles: The Devil in the Modern World*. Ithaca, N.Y.: Cornell University Press, 1986.

———. *Satan: The Early Christian Tradition*. Ithaca, N.Y.: Cornell University Press, 1981.

Russell, Letty M. *Just Hospitality: God's Welcome in the World of Difference*. Edited by J. Shannon Clarkson and Kate M. Ott. Kindle ed. Louisville: Westminster John Knox, 2009.

Russell, Robert J. "Challenges and Progress in 'Theology and Science': An Overview of the VO/CTNS Series." In *SPDA*, pp. 3-56.

———. *Cosmology: From Alpha to Omega; The Creative Mutual Interaction of Theology and Science*. Minneapolis: Fortress, 2008.

Ruthven, Jon. *On the Cessation of the Charismata: The Protestant Polemic on Postbiblical Miracles*. Sheffield: Sheffield Academic Press, 1993.

Rybarczyk, Edmund J. *Beyond Salvation: Eastern Orthodoxy and Classical Pentecostalism on Becoming Like Christ*. Carlisle, U.K.: Paternoster, 2004.

Saarinen, Risto. "De iustificatione." *Teologinen aikakauskirja* 118, no. 4 (2013): 291-304.

————. *Faith and Holiness: Lutheran-Orthodox Dialogue, 1959-1994.* Göttingen: Vanden-hoeck & Ruprecht, 1997.

————. "Forgiveness, the Gift, and Ecclesiology." *Dialog* 45, no. 1 (Spring 2006): 55-62.

————. *God and Gift: An Ecumenical Theology of Giving.* Unitas Books. Collegeville, Minn.: Liturgical Press, 2005.

————. *Gottes Wirken auf uns: Die transzendentale Deutung des Gegenwart-Christi-Motivs in der Lutherforschung.* Stuttgart: Franz Steiner, 1989.

————. "Ipsa dilectio Deus est: Zur Wirkungsgeschichte von. 1. Sent. Dist. 17 des Petrus Lombardus bei Martin Luther." In *Thesaurus Lutheri,* edited by Tuomo Manner-maa, Anja Ghiselli, and Simo Peura, pp. 185-204. Helsinki: Suomalainen Teolog-inen Kirjallisuusseura, 1987.

Sabatino, Charles J. "No-God: Reflections on Masao Abe's Symbol of God as Self-Emptying." *Horizons* 29, no. 1 (2002): 64-79.

Samaññaphala Sutta: The Fruits of the Contemplative Life (of *Digha Nikaya* 2). http://www .accesstoinsight.org/tipitaka/dn/dn.02.0.than.html.

Samartha, Stanley J. *Between Two Cultures: Ecumenical Ministry in a Pluralist World.* Geneva: WCC Publications, 1996.

————. *Courage for Dialogue: Ecumenical Issues in Inter-Religious Relationships.* Geneva: WCC Publications, 1981.

————. "The Holy Spirit and People of Other Faiths." *Ecumenical Review* 42, nos. 3-4 (July 1990): 250-63.

————. *Living Faiths and Ultimate Goals: A Continuing Dialogue.* Geneva: WCC, 1974.

Sanders, E. P. *Jesus and Judaism.* Philadelphia: Fortress, 1985.

————. *Paul and Palestinian Judaism: A Comparison of Patterns of Religion.* Philadelphia: Fortress, 1977.

————. *Paul, the Law, and the Jewish People.* Philadelphia: Fortress, 1983.

Sankara. *Atmabodha.* Hyderabad: Sankhyāyana Vidyā Parishat, 1999.

————. *The Crest Jewel of Wisdom.* London: Shanti Sadan, 1997. http://www.sacred-texts .com/hin/cjw/cjw05.htm.

Santideva. *The Introduction to the Practice of Enlightenment.* Available as *Engaging in Bodhisattva Behavior (sPyod-'jug, Bodhisattvacharya-avatara)* by Shantideva, translated by Alexander Berzin (2005). http://www.buddhistische-gesellschaft -berlin.de/downloads/bca.pdf (10/8/2014).

Satyavrata, Ivan. "The Holy Spirit and Advaitic Hindu Spirituality." *Crux* 27, no. 4 (1991): 34-43.

Schacht, Joseph. "Ahmad." In *Encyclopaedia of Islam,* 1:267. 2nd ed. Leiden: Brill, 1960.

Schaff, Philip. *The Creeds of Christendom.* 3 vols. Grand Rapids: Baker, 1984; original 1877. ccel.org.

Scheck, Thomas P. *Origen and the History of Justification: The Legacy of Origen's Commen-tary on Romans.* Notre Dame: University of Notre Dame Press, 2008.

Scheuers, Timothy. "An Evaluation of Some Aspects of Karl Barth's Doctrine of Election." *Mid-America Journal of Theology* 22 (2011): 161-73.

Schlink, Edmund. "Gesetz und Paraklese." In *Antwort: Karl Barth zum siebzigsten*

Geburtstag am 10 Mai 1956, edited by Ernst Wolf, pp. 323-35. Zollikon-Zürich: Evangelischer-Verlag, 1956.

Schloss, Jeffrey P. "From Evolution to Eschatology." In *Resurrection: Theological and Scientific Assessments,* edited by Ted Peters, Robert J. Russell, and Michael Welker, pp. 65-85. Grand Rapids: Eerdmans, 2002.

Schmid, H. *The Doctrinal Theology of the Evangelical Lutheran Church.* Translated by Charles A. Hay and Henry E. Jacobs. 3rd ed. Minneapolis: Augsburg, n.d. www .ccel.org.

Schmidt-Leukel, Perry. "Buddha and Christ as Mediators of the Transcendent: A Christian Perspective." In *Buddhism and Christianity in Dialogue,* edited by Perry Schmidt-Leukel, pp. 151-75. London: SCM, 2005.

Scholem, G. "Zum Verständnis der messianischen Idee." *Judaica* 1. Frankfurt: n.p., 1963.

Schönherr, Hartmut. "Concepts of Salvation in Christianity." *Africa Theological Journal* 12, no. 3 (1983): 159-65.

Schreiter, Robert J. "Globalization and Reconciliation." In *Mission in the Third Millennium,* edited by R. J. Schreiter, chap. 6. Maryknoll, N.Y.: Orbis, 2002.

———. *The Ministry of Reconciliation: Spirituality and Strategies.* Maryknoll, N.Y.: Orbis, 1998.

———. "A Practical Theology of Healing, Forgiveness, and Reconciliation." In *Peacebuilding: Catholic Theology, Ethics, and Praxis,* edited by Robert J. Schreiter, R. Scott Appleby, and Gerard F. Powers, pp. 366-97. Maryknoll, N.Y.: Orbis, 2010.

———. *Reconciliation: Mission and Ministry in a Changing Social Order.* Maryknoll, N.Y.: Orbis, 1992.

———. "Reconciliation and Healing as a Paradigm for Mission." *IRM* 94, no. 372 (January 2005): 74-83.

Schreiter, Robert J., R. Scott Appleby, and Gerard F. Powers, eds. *Peacebuilding: Catholic Theology, Ethics, and Praxis.* Maryknoll, N.Y.: Orbis, 2010.

Schrift, Alan D., ed. *The Logic of Gift.* New York: Routledge, 1997.

Schumm, Darla, and Michael Stoltzfus. "Chronic Illness and Disability: Narratives of Suffering and Healing in Buddhism and Christianity." In *Disability and Religious Diversity: Cross-Cultural and Interreligious Perspectives,* edited by Darla Schumm and Michael Stoltzfus, pp. 159-75. New York: Palgrave Macmillan, 2011.

———. "Editors' Introduction." In *Disability and Religious Diversity: Cross-Cultural and Interreligious Perspectives,* edited by Darla Schumm and Michael Stoltzfus, pp. xi-xx. New York: Palgrave Macmillan, 2011.

Schwarz, Hans. *Creation.* Grand Rapids: Eerdmans, 2002.

Schwarz, Michael. "The Letter of al-Hasan al-Baṣrī." *Oriens* 20 (1967): 15-30.

Schweizer, Eduard. "On Distinguishing between Spirits." *Ecumenical Review* 41 (July 1989): 406-15.

———. "Pneuma." In *TDNT* 6:396.

———. "The Spirit of Power: The Uniformity and Diversity of the Concept of the Holy Spirit in the New Testament." *Interpretation* 6, no. 3 (1952): 259-78.

Schwöbel, Christoph. "Reconciliation: From Biblical Observations to Dogmatic Reconstruction." In *The Theology of Reconciliation,* edited by Colin E. Gunton, pp. 13-38. London and New York: T. & T. Clark, 2003.

Scotland, Nigel. "The Charismatic Devil: Demonology in Charismatic Christianity." In *A&D,* chap. 4.

Scruton, Richard. *The Face of God.* Gifford Lectures. London: Continuum, 2012.

Scudder, Lewis. "The Qur'an's Evaluation of Human Nature: An Inquiry with a View toward Christian-Muslim Dialogue." *Reformed Review: A Journal of the Seminaries of the Reformed Church in America* 61, no. 2 (2008): 71-80. http://www.westernsem .edu/resources/publications/reformed-review/.

"Second Anglican/Roman Catholic International Commission: Salvation and the Church; An Agreed Statement" (1986). http://www.vatican.va/roman_curia/pontifical _councils/chrstuni/angl-comm-docs/rc_pc_chrstuni_doc_19860903_salvation -church_en.html.

Seiple, D., and Frederick W. Weidmann, eds. *Enigmas and Powers: Engaging the Work of Walter Wink for Classroom, Church, and World.* Eugene, Ore.: Wipf and Stock, 2008.

Sekki, Arthur Everett. *The Meaning of Ruah at Qumran.* Atlanta: Scholars Press, 1989.

Sell, Alan P. F. "Augustine versus Pelagius: A Cautionary Tale of Perennial Importance." *Calvin Theological Journal* 12, no. 2 (November 1977): 117-43.

Sen, Keshub Chunder. *Keshub Chunder Sen.* Edited by David C. Scott. Bangalore: Christian Literature Society, 1979.

Seo, Bo-Myung. *A Critique of Western Theological Anthropology: Understanding Human Beings in a Third World Context.* Lewiston, N.Y.: Edwin Mellen Press, 2005.

Sharma, Arvind. *Classical Hindu Thought: An Introduction.* Oxford: Oxford University Press, 2000.

———. "Free Will and Fate in Gita." *Religious Studies* 15, no. 4 (1979): 531-53.

Shaull, Richard. *The Reformation and Liberation Theology: Insights for the Challenges of Today.* Louisville: Westminster John Knox, 1991.

Shaw, Charles G. "Suffering, Hope and Forgiveness: The *Ubuntu* Theology of Desmond Tutu." *Scottish Journal of Theology* 62, no. 4 (2009): 477-89.

Shellabear, W. G. "The Meaning of the Word 'Spirit' as Used in the Koran." *Muslim World* 22, no. 4 (1932): 356-60.

Shokek, Simon. *Kabbalah and the Art of Being: The Smithsonian Lectures.* London: Routledge, 2001.

Shriver, Donald W., Jr. *An Ethic for Enemies: Forgiveness in Politics.* New York: Oxford University Press, 1995.

Shults, F. LeRon. *The Post Foundationalist Task of Theology: Wolfhart Pannenberg and the New Theological Rationality.* Grand Rapids: Eerdmans, 1999.

———. "Theological Responses to Postmodernities or Tending to the Other in Late Modern Missions and Ecumenism." Presentation for Nordic Institute for Missiological and Ecumenical Research Annual Meeting at the University of Abo, Turku, Finland, August 19-22, 2007.

Shults, F. LeRon, and Steven J. Sandage. *Faces of Forgiveness: Searching for Wholeness and Salvation.* Grand Rapids: Baker Academic, 2003.

Siddiqi, Muzammil Husain. "The Doctrine of Redemption: A Critical Study." In *Islamic Perspectives: Studies in Honor of Mawlānā Sayyid Abul A'lā Mawdūdī,* edited by Khurshid Ahmad and Zafar Ansari, pp. 91-102. United Kingdom: Islamic Foundation, 1979.

Siddiqui, Mona. "Being Human in Islam." In *Humanity: Texts and Context; Christian and Muslim Perspectives,* edited by Michael Ipgrave and David Marshall, pp. 15-21. Washington, D.C.: Georgetown University Press, 2011.

Sikkema, Arnold E. "A Physicist's Reformed Critique of Nonreductive Physicalism and Emergence." *Pro Rege,* June 2005, pp. 20-32. http://www.dordt.edu/publications/pro_rege/crcpi/119717.pdf (3/18/2014).

Simmer-Brown, Judith. "Suffering and Social Justice: A Buddhist Response to the Gospel of Luke." *Buddhist-Christian Studies* 16 (1996): 99-112.

Simpson, A. B. *The Gospel of Healing.* In *The Three Great Classics on Divine Healing,* edited by Jonathan L. Graf. Camp Hill, Pa.: Christian Publications, 1992.

Sivaraman, K. "The Meaning of *Moksha* in Contemporary Hindu Thought and Life." In *Living Faiths and Ultimate Goals: Salvation and World Religions,* edited by S. J. Samartha, pp. 2-11. Maryknoll, N.Y.: Orbis, 1974.

Skorupski, Tadeusz. "Health and Suffering in Buddhism: Doctrinal and Existential Considerations." In *Religion, Health, and Suffering,* edited by John Hinnells, pp. 139-65. London: Kegan Paul, 1999.

Slesinski, Robert. "Bulgakov's Angelology." *St. Vladimir's Theological Quarterly* 49, nos. 1-2 (2005): 183-202.

Smail, Thomas A. *The Forgotten Father.* Grand Rapids: Eerdmans, 1980.

Smart, Ninian, and Steve Konstantine. *Christian Systematic Theology in a World Context.* Minneapolis: Fortress, 1991.

Smedes, Lewis B. *Forgive and Forget: Healing the Hurts We Don't Deserve.* New York: Harper and Row, 1984.

———. "Forgive and Remember." In *The Art of Forgiving: When You Need to Forgive and Don't Know How.* Nashville: Moorings, 1996.

Smith, Gordon T. *Beginning Well: Christian Conversion and Authentic Transformation.* Downers Grove, Ill.: InterVarsity, 2001.

———. *Transforming Conversion: Rethinking the Language and Contours of Christian Initiation.* Grand Rapids: Baker Academic, 2010.

Sobrino, Jon. *The Principle of Mercy: Taking the Crucified People from the Cross.* Maryknoll, N.Y.: Orbis, 1994.

———. *Spirituality of Liberation: Toward Political Holiness.* Maryknoll, N.Y.: Orbis, 1988.

Song, Choan-Seng. "Christian Mission toward Abolition of the Cross." In *The Scandal of a Crucified World,* edited by Yacob Tesfai, pp. 130-48. Maryknoll, N.Y.: Orbis, 1994.

———. *Third Eye Theology: Theology in Asian Settings.* Rev. ed. Maryknoll, N.Y.: Orbis, 1991.

Song, Taesuk Raymond. "Shame and Guilt in the Japanese Culture: A Study of Lived Experiences of Moral Failures of Japanese Emerging Generation and Its Relation to the Church Missions in Japan." Ph.D. diss., Trinity International University, 2009.

Sorensen, Eric. *Possession and Exorcism in the New Testament and Early Christianity.* Tübingen: J. C. B. Mohr [Paul Siebeck], 2002.

Soskice, Janet M. *Metaphor and Religious Language.* Oxford: Clarendon, 1985.

Soulen, R. Kendall. "Cruising toward Bethlehem: Human Dignity and the New Eugenics." In *God and Human Dignity,* edited by R. Kendall Soulen and Linda Woodhead, pp. 104-20. Grand Rapids: Eerdmans, 2006.

Southwold, Martin. "Buddhism and Evil." In *The Anthropology of Evil,* edited by David Parkin, pp. 128-41. Oxford and New York: Basil Blackwell, 1985.

Spencer, H. *Islam and the Gospel of God.* Delhi: SPCK, 1956.

Speziale-Bagliacca, Roberto. *Guilt: Revenge, Remorse, and Responsibility after Freud.* Hove, U.K., and New York: Brunner-Routledge, 2004.

"The Spirit at Work in Asia Today: A Document of the Office of Theological Concerns of the Federation of the Asian Bishops' Conferences." FABC Papers no. 81 (1998).

Sridharan, Vishnu. "The Metaphysics of No-Self: A Determinist Deflation of the Free Will Problem." *Journal of Buddhist Ethics* 20 (2013): 287-305. http://blogs.dickinson .edu/buddhistethics/2013/08/12/a-determinist-deflation-of-the-free-will-problem/ comment-page-1/ (1/29/2014).

Staggs, D. Walter, Jr. "*Pneumakinesis* and Stephen King: 'Rebooting' the Discussion on Paranormal Fear." In *IRDSW,* chap. 7, pp. 97-110.

Staniloae, Dumitru. *The Experience of God: Orthodox Dogmatic Theology.* Vol. 2, *The World: Creation and Deification.* Translated and edited by Ioan Ionita and Robert Barringer. Brookline, Mass.: Holy Cross Orthodox Press, 2000.

Stapp, Henry P. *Mind, Matter, and Quantum Mechanics.* Berlin and New York: Springer-Verlag, 1993.

Stark, Rodney, and Roger Finke. *Acts of Faith: The Human Side of Religion.* Berkeley: University of California Press, 2000.

Stavropoulous, C. *Partakers of Divine Nature.* Minneapolis: Light and Life, 1976.

Steenbrink, K. A. "Jesus and the Holy Spirit in the Writings of Nūr al-Dīn al-Ranīrī." *Islam and Christian-Muslim Relations* 1, no. 2 (December 1990): 192-207.

Steiner, George. *Real Presences.* Chicago: University of Chicago Press, 1989.

Stendahl, Krister. "The Apostle Paul and the Introspective Conscience of the West." In *Paul among Jews and Gentiles,* pp. 78-96. Philadelphia: Fortress, 1976; London: SCM, 1977.

———. *Paul among Jews and Gentiles and Other Essays.* Philadelphia: Fortress, 1976; London: SCM, 1977.

Stephens, Walter. "Demons: An Overview." In *ER* 4:2275-82.

Stern, Martin S. "Al-Ghazzalī, Maimonides, and Ibn Paquda on Repentance: A Comparative Model." *Journal of the American Academy of Religion* 47, no. 4 (1979): 589-607.

———. "Notes on the Theology of Ghazzali's Concept of Repentance." *Islamic Quarterly* 23, no. 2 (1979): 82-98.

Stibbe, Mark W. G. "'A British Appraisal': Review of Jürgen Moltmann's *The Spirit of Life: A Universal Affirmation.*" *Journal of Pentecostal Theology* 4 (1994): 5-16.

Stoeger, William R., S.J. "The Mind-Brain Problem, the Laws of Nature, and Constitutive Relationships." In *NP,* pp. 129-46.

Stronstad, Roger. *The Charismatic Theology of St. Luke.* Peabody, Mass.: Hendrickson, 1984.

Studer, Basil. *Trinity and Incarnation: The Faith of the Early Church.* Edited by Andrew Louth. Translated by Matthias Westerhoff. Collegeville, Minn.: Liturgical Press, 1993.

Stylianopoulos, Theodore. "The Biblical Background of the Article on the Holy Spirit in the Constantinopolitan Creed." *Études Théologiques: Le IIe Concile Oecuménique.* Chambésy-Genève: Centre Orthodoxe du Patriarcat Œcuménique, 1982.

Stylianopoulos, Theodore, and S. Mark Heim, eds. *Spirit of Truth: Ecumenical Perspectives on the Holy Spirit.* Brookline, Mass.: Holy Cross Orthodox Press, 1986.

Su, Christine. "Forgiveness." In *Encyclopedia of Love in World Religions,* edited by Yudit Kornberg, 1:229-30. Santa Barbara, Calif.: ABC-CLIO, 2008.

Suchocki, Marjorie Hewitt. *The Fall to Violence.* New York: Continuum, 1995.

———. "Sunyata, Trinity, and Community." In *DEHF,* pp. 136-49.

Sullivan, Francis A. "Baptism in the Spirit." In *Charisms and Charismatic Renewal,* pp. 59-75. Ann Arbor, Mich.: Servant, 1982.

Sullivan, Lawrence E., ed. *Healing and Restoring: Healing and Medicine in the World's Religious Traditions.* New York: Macmillan, 1989.

Sumithra, Sunand. "Justification by Faith: Its Relevance in Hindu Context." In *Right with God: Justification in the Bible and the World,* edited by D. A. Carson. London: Paternoster; Grand Rapids: Baker, 1992.

Summers-Minette, Amy. "Not Just Halos and Horns: Angels and Demons in Western Pop Culture." In *A&D,* chap. 13.

Sungenis, Robert. "The Lutheran/Catholic Joint Declaration on Justification." http://www .christiantruth.com/articles/sungenisjointdeclaration.html (5/7/2014).

Sutherland, Gail Hinich. *The Disguises of the Demon: The Development of the Yaksa in Hinduism and Buddhism.* Albany: State University of New York Press, 1991.

The Sutra of Medicine Buddha. Translated and annotated (under the guidance of Dharma Master Hsuan Jung) by Minh Thanh and P. D. Leigh. North Hills, Calif.: International Buddhist Monastic Institute, 2001. http://www.buddhanet.net/pdf_file/ medbudsutra.pdf (3/31/2014).

Sutton, Kristin Johnston. "Salvation after Nagarjuna: A Reevaluation of Wolfhart Pannenberg's Soteriology in Light of a Buddhist Cosmology." Ph.D. diss., Graduate Theological Union, 2002.

Swinburne, Richard. *Responsibility and Atonement.* Oxford: Clarendon, 1989.

Swinton, John. "From Health to Shalom, Why the Religion and Health Debate Needs Jesus." In *Healing to All Their Flesh: Jewish and Christian Perspectives on Spirituality, Theology, and Health,* edited by Jeff Levin and Keith G. Meador, pp. 219-41. West Conshohocken, Pa.: Templeton Press, 2012.

Symeon the New Theologian. *The Discourses.* In *Symeon the New Theologian,* translated by C. J. deCatanzaro. New York: Paulist, 1980.

Tabbernee, William. "'Will the Real Paraclete Please Speak Forth!': The Catholic-Montanist Conflict over Pneumatology." In *Advents of the Spirit: An Introduction to the Current Study of Pneumatology*, edited by Bradford E. Hinze and D. Lyle Dabney. Milwaukee: Marquette University Press, 2001.

Tagney, J. P. "Shame and Guilt in Interpersonal Relationships." In *Self-Conscious Emotions: Shame, Guilt, Embarrassment, and Pride*, edited by J. P. Tagney and K. W. Fischer, pp. 114-39. New York: Guilford Press, 1995.

Talbert, Charles H. "Conversion in the Acts of the Apostles: Ancient Auditors' Perceptions." In *Literary Studies in Luke-Acts: Essays in Honor of Joseph H. Tyson*, edited by Richard O. Thompson and Thomas E. Phillips, pp. 141-53. Macon, Ga.: Mercer University Press, 1998.

Talbott, Thomas. "Punishment, Forgiveness, and Divine Justice." *Religious Studies* 29 (1993): 151-68.

Tamburello, Dennes E. *Union with Christ: John Calvin and the Mysticism of St. Bernard.* Louisville: Westminster John Knox, 1994.

Tamez, Elsa. *The Amnesty of Grace: Justification by Faith from a Latin American Perspective.* Translated by Sharon H. Ringe. Nashville: Abingdon, 1993.

Tanner, Kathryn E. *God and Creation in Christian Theology.* Minneapolis: Augsburg Fortress, 2004.

———. "Justification and Justice in a Theology of Grace." *Theology Today* 55 (January 1999): 510-23.

———. *The Politics of God: Christian Theologies and Social Justice.* Minneapolis: Fortress, 1992.

Tanner, Norman P., ed. and trans. *Decrees of the Ecumenical Council.* London: Sheed and Ward, 1990.

Taylor, Carl E. "The Place of Indigenous Medical Practitioners in the Modernization of Health Services." In *Asian Medical Systems: A Comparative Study*, edited by Charles Leslie, pp. 285-99. 2nd ed. Berkeley, London, and Los Angeles: University of California Press, 1976.

Taylor, Charles. *Human Agency and Language.* Vol. 1. Cambridge: Cambridge University Press, 1985.

———. *A Secular Age.* Cambridge, Mass., and London: Harvard University Press, Belknap Press, 2007.

Taylor, Iain. "Without Justification? The Catholic-Lutheran Joint Declaration and Its Protestant Critics." *The Way* 43, no. 3 (2004): 106-18. http://www.theway.org.uk/Back/433Taylor.pdf.

Taylor, John V. *The Go-Between God.* London: SCM, 1972.

Tennent, Timothy C. *Theology in the Context of World Christianity: How the Global Church Is Influencing the Way We Think about and Discuss Theology.* Grand Rapids: Zondervan, 2007.

Terry, Justyn. "The Forgiveness of Sins and the Work of Christ: A Case for Substitutionary Atonement." *Anglican Theological Review* 95 (Winter 2013): 9-24.

Thatamanil, John J. *The Immanent Divine: God, Creation, and the Human Predicament; An East-West Conversation.* Minneapolis: Fortress, 2006.

Thoma, Clemens. "Christian Theology and Judaic Thought: Similarities and Dissimilar-

ities." *CTSA Proceedings* 48, no. 61 (1993): 53-64. http://ejournals.bc.edu/ojs/index
.php/ctsa/article/view/3837/3404 (3/4/2014).

Thomas, Günther. "Resurrection to New Life: Pneumatological Implications of the Eschatological Transition." In *Resurrection: Theological and Scientific Assessments,*
edited by Ted Peters, John Robert Russell, and Michael Welker, pp. 255-76. Grand
Rapids and Cambridge: Eerdmans, 2002.

Thomas, M. M. "The Holy Spirit and the Spirituality for Political Struggles." *Ecumenical
Review* 42, nos. 3-4 (1990): 216-24.

Thompson, John. *The Holy Spirit in the Theology of Karl Barth.* Princeton Theological
Monograph Series. Kent, U.K.: Pickwick, 1991.

Thomsen, Mark. "On Relating Justification and Justice." *Word and World* 7, no. 1 (1987):
6-11.

Thorsen, Donald. *Explorations in Christian Theology.* Grand Rapids: Baker Academic,
2010.

Tilakaratne, Asanga. "The Buddhist View on Religious Conversion." *Dialogue* (Colombo,
Sri Lanka) 32-33 (2005-2006): 58-82.

Tillich, Paul. *The Interpretation of History.* Translated by N. A. Rasetzki and Elsa L.
Talmey. New York: Charles Scribner's Sons, 1936.

———. "The Kingdom of God and History." In *The Kingdom of God and History,* edited
by H. G. Wood et al., pp. 105-41. New York and Chicago: Willet, Clark and Co.,
1938.

Timoner, Rachel. *Breath of Life: God as Spirit in Judaism.* Brewster, Mass.: Paraclete Press,
2011.

Tippett, Alan R. "The Cultural Anthropology of Conversion." In *HRC,* chap. 13.

Todorov, Tzvetan. *The Conquest of America: The Question of the Other.* New York: HarperCollins, 1992.

———. *Mikhail Bakhtin: The Dialogical Principle.* Translated by Wlad Godrich. Minneapolis: University of Minnesota Press, 1984.

Togarasei, Lovemore. "The Conversion of Paul as a Proto-type of Conversion in African
Christianity." *Swedish Missiological Themes* 95, no. 2 (2007): 111-22.

Tolbert, Mary Ann. "When Resistance Becomes Repression: Mark 13:9-27 and the Poetics
of Location." In *Reading from This Place: Social Location and Biblical Interpretation in Global Perspective,* edited by Fernando F. Segovia and Mary Ann Tolbert.
Minneapolis: Fortress, 1995.

Tombs, David. "The Offer of Forgiveness." *Journal of Religious Ethics* 36, no. 4 (2008):
587-93.

Torrance, Alan. "Forgiveness: The Essential Socio-Political Structure of Personal Being."
Journal of Theology for Southern Africa 56 (Summer 1986): 47-59.

Torrance, Thomas F. *The Christian Doctrine of God: One Being Three Persons.* London:
T. & T. Clark, 1996.

———. *Space, Time, and Resurrection.* Grand Rapids: Eerdmans, 1998.

———. *Trinitarian Perspectives: Toward Doctrinal Agreement.* Edinburgh: T. & T. Clark,
1994.

————, ed. *Theological Dialogue between Orthodox and Reformed Churches.* Vol. 2. Edinburgh: Scottish Academic Press, 1993.

"Towards a Common Understanding of the Church: Reformed/Roman Catholic International Dialogue: Second Phase (1984-1990)." http://www.prounione.urbe.it/dia -int/r-rc/doc/e_r-rc_2-2.html#a23.

Tracy, Thomas F. "Particular Providence and the God of the Gaps." In *C&C,* pp. 289-324.

Tsirpanlis, Constantine N. *Introduction to Eastern Patristic Thought and Orthodox Theology.* Theology and Life 30. Collegeville, Minn.: Liturgical Press, 1991.

Turcescu, Lucian. "Soteriological Issues in the 1999 Lutheran-Catholic Joint Declaration on Justification: An Orthodox Perspective." *Journal of Ecumenical Studies* 38, no. 1 (2001): 64-72.

Turner, Max. "Levison's *Filled with the Spirit:* A Brief Appreciation and Response." *Journal of Pentecostal Theology* 20, no. 2 (2011): 193-200.

Tutu, Desmond Mpilo. *No Future without Forgiveness.* New York: Doubleday, 1999.

Twelftree, Graham H. *Jesus the Exorcist: A Contribution to the Study of the Historical Jesus.* Tübingen: Mohr-Siebeck, 1993.

Tyson, John H. "John Wesley's Conversion at Aldersgate." In *Conversion in the Wesleyan Tradition,* edited by Kenneth J. Collins and John H. Tyson, pp. 27-42. Nashville: Abingdon, 2001.

Ukpong, Justin S. "Pluralism and the Problem of the Discernment of Spirits." *Ecumenical Review* 41 (1989): 416-25.

Ullman, Chana. *The Transformed Self: The Psychology of Religious Conversion.* New York and London: Plenum, 1989.

Umansky, Ellen M. "Election." In *ER,* pp. 2744-49.

United States Conference of Catholic Bishops. *Forgiveness in International Politics.* Washington, D.C.: USCCB, 2004.

Unno, Taitesu. "When Broken Tiles Become Gold." In *Of Human Bondage and Divine Grace: A Global Testimony,* edited by John Ross Carter, chap. 10. La Salle, Ill.: Open Court, 1992.

Unterman, Alan, Howard Kreisel, and Rivka G. Horwitz. "Ru'ah Ha-Kodesh." In *EJ* 17:506-9.

Upadhyay, Brahmabandhab. *The Writings of Brahmabandhab Upadhyay.* Edited by Julius Lipner and George Gispert-Sauch. 2 vols. Bangalore: United Theological College, 1991, 2002.

Urbach, Ephraim E. *The Sages: Their Concepts and Beliefs.* Translated by Israel Abrahams. Jerusalem: Magnes, 1975; Cambridge: Harvard University Press, 1987.

Vainio, Olli-Pekka. *Justification and Participation in Christ: The Development of the Lutheran Doctrine of Justification from Luther to the Formula of Concord (1580).* Leiden and Boston: Brill, 2008.

Valea, Ernest. "The Parable of the Prodigal Son in Christianity and Buddhism." n.p. http:// www.comparativereligion.com/prodigal.html (3/14/2014).

Van der Veer, Peter, ed. *Conversion to Modernities: The Globalization of Christianity.* London: Routledge, 1996.

Van Til, Cornelius. *Christianity and Barthianism.* Philadelphia: P&R Publishing, 1962.

Vargas-O'Bryan, Ivette. "Keeping It All in Balance: Teaching Asian Religions through Illness and Healing." In *Teaching Religion and Healing,* edited by Linda L. Barnes and Inés Talamantez, chap. 4. New York: Oxford University Press, 2006.

Vedantasara of Sadananda. Translated and edited by Swami Nihilananda. Mayamati, Himalayas: Advaita Ashmara, 1931. http://www.estudantedavedanta.net/Vedantasara-Nikhilananda.pdf.

Villafañe, Eldin. *The Liberating Spirit: Toward an Hispanic American Pentecostal Social Ethic.* Grand Rapids: Eerdmans, 1993.

Vischer, Lukas, ed. *Spirit of God, Spirit of Christ: Ecumenical Reflections on the Filioque Controversy.* London: SPCK, 1981.

Viswanathan, Gauri. *Outside the Fold: Conversion, Modernity, and Belief.* Princeton: Princeton University Press, 1998.

Vivekananda, Swami. "Addresses at the Parliament of Religions." In *Complete Works of Swami Vivekananda,* vol. 1. N.p. http://www.ramakrishnavivekananda.info/vivekananda/complete_works.htm.

———. "Is Vedanta the Future Religion?" In *Complete Works of Swami Vivekananda,* vol. 8. N.p. http://www.ramakrishnavivekananda.info/vivekananda/complete_works.htm.

———. "Steps of Hindu Philosophic Thought." In "Lectures and Discourses," in *Complete Works of Swami Vivekananda,* vol. 1. http://www.ramakrishnavivekananda.info/vivekananda/complete_works.htm.

Volf, Miroslav. *The End of Memory: Remembering Rightly in a Violent World.* Grand Rapids: Eerdmans, 2006.

———. *Exclusion and Embrace: A Theological Exploration of Identity, Otherness, and Reconciliation.* Nashville: Abingdon, 1996.

———. "Exclusion and Embrace: Theological Reflections in the Wake of 'Ethnic Cleansing.'" *Journal of Ecumenical Studies* 29, no. (1992): 230-48.

———. *Free of Charge: Giving and Forgiving in a Culture Stripped of Grace.* Grand Rapids: Zondervan, 2005.

———. "Human Flourishing." Presentation at the Institute for Theological Inquiry, n.d. http://huwhumphreys.files.wordpress.com/2012/10/miroslav_volf-human-flourishing.pdf.

———. *Work in the Spirit: Toward a Theology of Work.* Eugene, Ore.: Wipf and Stock, 2001.

Vondey, Wolfgang. *Heribert Mühlen: His Theology and Praxis; A New Profile of the Church.* Lanham, Md.: University Press of America, 2004.

———. "The Holy Spirit and the Physical Universe: The Impact of Scientific Paradigm Shifts on Contemporary Pneumatology." *Theological Studies* 70 (2009): 3-36.

———. "The Holy Spirit and Time in Contemporary Catholic and Protestant Theology." *Scottish Journal of Theology* 58, no. 4 (2005): 393-409.

Vorländer, H. "Forgiveness." In *New International Dictionary of New Testament Theology,* edited by Colin Brown, 1:697-703. Grand Rapids: Zondervan, 1986.

Wagner, C. Peter [and Rebecca Greenwood]. "The Strategic-Level Deliverance Model." In *USW,* pp. 173-98.

476

Walker, Donald F., and Richard L. Gorsuch. "Dimensions Underlying Sixteen Models of Forgiveness and Reconciliation." *Journal of Psychology and Theology* 32, no. 1 (2004): 12-25.

Wallace, B. Alan. "A Buddhist View of Free Will: Beyond Determinism and Indeterminism." *Journal of Consciousness Studies* 18 (2011): 217-33. http://www.alanwallace.org/buddhistviewoffreewill.pdf (1/31/2014).

Wallace, B. Alan, and John Searle. "Consciousness East and West." Northwestern University, Cognitive Science Program (2005). Internet video broadcast, available at http://faculty.wcas.northwestern.edu/~paller/dialogue/ (1/30/2014).

Wallace, Dewey D. "Free Will and Predestination: Christian Concepts." In *ER*, pp. 3202-6.

Wallace, Mark I. "Christian Animism, Green Spirit Theology, and the Global Crisis Today." In *IRDSW*, pp. 197-212.

————. *Finding God in the Singing River*. Minneapolis: Augsburg Fortress, 2005.

————. *Fragments of the Spirit: Nature, Violence, and the Renewal of Creation*. New York: Continuum, 1996.

————. *Green Christianity: Five Ways to a Sustainable Future*. Minneapolis: Fortress, 2010.

————. "The Green Face of God: Recovering the Spirit in an Ecocidal Era." In *Advents of the Spirit: An Introduction to the Current Study of Pneumatology*, edited by Bradford E. Hinze and D. Lyle Dabney, pp. 444-64. Milwaukee: Marquette University Press, 2001.

Walter, Eugen. *First Epistle to the Corinthians*. Translated by Simon Young and Erika Young. New Testament for Spiritual Reading. London: Sheed and Ward, 1971.

Ward, Keith. "Divine Action in an Emergent Cosmos." In *SPDA*, pp. 285-98.

————. *God, Faith, and the New Millennium: Christian Belief in an Age of Science*. Oxford: Oneworld, 1998.

————. *Images of Eternity: Concepts of God in Five Religious Traditions*. London: Darton, Longman and Todd, 1987. Reissued as *Concepts of God: Images of the Divine in Five Religious Traditions*. Oxford: Oneworld, 1998.

————. *More Than Matter: Is Matter All We Really Are?* Grand Rapids: Eerdmans, 2011.

————. *Religion and Creation*. Oxford: Clarendon, 1996.

————. *Religion and Human Nature*. Oxford: Clarendon, 1998.

————. *Religion and Revelation: A Theology of Revelation in the World's Religions*. Oxford: Clarendon, 1994.

Ware, Timothy. Foreword to *The Deification of Man*, by Georgios I. Matzazridis. Crestwood, N.Y.: St. Vladimir's Seminary Press, 1984.

————. *The Orthodox Church*. New York: Penguin Books, 1993.

————. *The Orthodox Way*. Crestwood, N.Y.: St. Vladimir's Seminary Press, 1995.

Warfield, Benjamin Breckinridge. *Calvin and Calvinism*. In *The Works of Benjamin B. Warfield*, vol. 5. New York: Oxford University Press, 1931; reprint, Grand Rapids: Baker, 2000.

————. *The Counterfeit Miracles*. New York: Charles Scribner's Sons, 1918. http://www.monergism.com/thethreshold/sdg/warfield/warfield_counterfeit.html (3/25/2014).

Wariboko, Nimi. "Spirits and Economics." In *IRDSW,* chap. 10, pp. 141-54.

Warren, Mark R., and Richard L. Wood. *Faith-Based Community Organizing: The State of the Field.* Jericho, N.Y.: Interfaith Funders, 2001. Presented on COMM-ORG: The On-Line Conference on Community Organizing and Development. http://comm-org.wisc.edu/papers2001/faith/faith.htm.

Warrington, Keith. "James 5:14-18: Healing Then and Now." *IRM* 93, no. 370/371 (July/October 2004): 346-67.

Warrior, Robert Allen. "A Native American Perspective: Canaanites, Cowboys, and Indians." In *Voices from the Margin: Interpreting the Bible in the Third World,* edited by R. S. Sugirtharajah, pp. 287-95. Maryknoll, N.Y.: Orbis, 1991.

Watson, Francis. *Paul, Judaism, and the Gentiles: Beyond the New Perspective.* 2nd ed. Grand Rapids: Eerdmans, 2007.

Watt, Jan van der, ed. *Salvation in the New Testament: Perspectives on Soteriology.* Leiden: Brill, 2005.

Watt, William Montgomery. "Conditions of Membership of the Islamic Community." *Studia Islamica* 21 (1964): 5-7.

―――. "Conversion in Islam at the Time of the Prophet." *Journal of the American Academy of Religion* 47, no. 4 (1980): 721-31.

―――. *The Formative Period of Islamic Thought.* Edinburgh: Edinburgh University Press, 1973.

―――. "His Name Is Ahmad." *Muslim World* 43, no. 2 (1953): 110-17.

―――. *Islamic Philosophy and Theology: An Extended Survey.* Edinburgh: Edinburgh University Press, 1962.

Watt, William Montgomery, and Asma Afsaruddin. "Free Will and Predestination: Islamic Concepts." In *ER,* pp. 3209-13.

Welch, Claude. *Protestant Thought in the Nineteenth Century, 1799-1870.* Vol. 1. New Haven: Yale University Press, 1972.

Welker, Michael. "Angels in the Biblical Traditions: An Impressive Logic and the Imposing Problem of Their Hypercomplex Reality." *Theology Today* 51, no. 3 (October 1994): 367-80.

―――. *God the Spirit: A Problem of Experience in Today's World.* Translated by John F. Hoffmeyer. Minneapolis: Fortress, 1994.

Wendebourg, D. *Reformation und Oikonomia: Der ökumenische Briefwechsel zwischen der Leitung der Württembergischen Kirche und Patriarch Jeremias II. Von Konstantinopel in den Jahren 1573-1581.* Göttingen: Vandenhoeck & Ruprecht, 1986.

Wenham, Gordon. "Christ's Healing Ministry and His Attitude to the Law." In *Christ the Lord: Studies in Christology Presented to Donald Guthrie,* edited by Harold H. Rowdon, pp. 115-26. Leicester: Inter-Varsity Press, 1982.

Wesley, John. "On Working Out Our Own Salvation." Sermon 85 in *Sermons III 71-114,* edited by Albert C. Outler, vol. 3 in *The Works of John Wesley.* Nashville: Abingdon, 1986.

Westerholm, Stephen. *Perspectives Old and New on Paul: The "Lutheran" Paul and His Critics.* Grand Rapids: Eerdmans, 2004.

Westerink, Herman. *A Dark Trace: Sigmund Freud on the Sense of Guilt.* Leuven: Leuven University Press, 2009.

Westermann, Claus. "Peace (Shalom) in the Old Testament." In *The Meaning of Peace: Biblical Studies,* ed. Perry B. Yoder and Willard M. Swartley, pp. 16-48. Louisville: Westminster John Knox, 1992.

Wharton, H. "The Hidden Face of Shame: The Shadow, Shame, and Separation." *Journal of Analytical Psychology* 35 (1990): 279-99.

Wheeler, Brannon. "Arab Prophets of the Qur'an and Bible." *Journal of Qur'anic Studies* 8, no. 2 (2006): 24-57.

Wiebe, Phillip H. *God and Other Spirits: Intimations of Transcendence in Christian Experience.* Oxford: Oxford University Press, 2004.

Wiegele, Katherine L. *Investing in Miracles: El Shaddai and the Transformation of Popular Catholicism in the Philippines.* Honolulu: University of Hawai'i Press, 2005.

Wiesel, Elie. *From the Kingdom of Memory: Reminiscences.* New York: Summit, 1990.

Wikramagamage, Chandra. "Mara as Evil in Buddhism." In *Evil and the Response of World Religions,* edited by William Cenkner, pp. 109-15. St. Paul: Paragon House, 1997.

Wilfred, Felix. "Towards a Better Understanding of Asian Theology: Some Basic Issues." *Vidyajyoti: Journal of Theological Reflection* 62, no. 12 (1998): 890-915.

Wilken, Robert Louis. "*Fides Caritate Formata:* Faith Formed by Love." *Nova et Vetera,* English ed., 9, no. 4 (2011): 1089-1100.

Wilkinson, Michael, and Steven Studebaker, eds. *A Liberating Spirit: Pentecostals and Social Action in North America.* Eugene, Ore.: Pickwick, 2010.

Williams, D. H. "Justification by Faith: The Patristic Doctrine." *Journal of Ecclesiastical History* 57, no. 4 (October 2006): 649-67.

Williams, J. R. "Baptism in the Holy Spirit." In *The New International Dictionary of Pentecostal and Charismatic Movements,* pp. 354-63. Revised and expanded ed. Grand Rapids: Zondervan, 2002.

Williams, Rowan. *Resurrection.* New York: Pilgrim Press, 1982.

Williams, Stephen N. "What Christians Believe about Forgiveness." *Studies in Christian Ethics* 24, no. 2 (2011): 147-56.

Wilson, Edward O. *On Human Nature.* Cambridge: Harvard University Press, 1978.

Wink, Walter. *Engaging the Powers: Discernment and Resistance in a World of Domination.* Minneapolis: Fortress, 1992.

———. *Naming the Powers: The Language of Power in the New Testament.* Philadelphia: Fortress, 1984.

———. *The Powers That Be: Theology for a New Millennium.* New York: Doubleday, 1998.

———. *Unmasking the Powers: The Invisible Forces That Determine Human Existence.* Philadelphia: Fortress, 1986.

Wink, Walter, and Michael Hardin. "Response to C. Peter Wagner and Rebecca Greenwood." In *USW,* pp. 199-203.

Witherington, Ben, III. *The Acts of the Apostles: A Socio-Rhetorical Commentary.* Grand Rapids and Cambridge: Eerdmans, 1998.

Witsz, Klaus G. "Vedānta, Nature, and Science." *Religious Studies and Theology* 15, nos. 2-3 (1996): 30-39.

Witzel, Michael. "Vedas and Upanisads." In *The Blackwell Companion to Hinduism,* edited by Gavin Flood, pp. 68-98. Oxford: Blackwell, 2003.

Wolterstorff, Nicholas. "Jesus and Forgiveness." In *Jesus and Philosophy: New Essays,* edited by Paul K. Moser, pp. 194-214. Cambridge: Cambridge University Press, 2009.

———. "The Place of Forgiveness in the Actions of the State." In *The Politics of Past Evil: Religion, Reconciliation, and the Dilemmas of Transitional Justice,* edited by D. Philpott, pp. 87-111. Notre Dame: University of Notre Dame Press, 2006.

Wood, Susan K. "Catholic Reception of the Joint Declaration on the Doctrine of Justification." In *Rereading Paul Together: Protestant and Catholic Perspectives on Justification,* edited by David E. Aune, pp. 43-59. Grand Rapids: Baker Academic, 2006.

———. "I Acknowledge One Baptism for the Forgiveness of Sins." In *Nicene Christianity: The Future for a New Ecumenism,* edited by Christopher R. Seitz, pp. 189-201. Grand Rapids: Brazos, 2001.

Woodberry, J. Dudley. "Conversion in Islam." In *HRC,* pp. 22-40.

———. "Sufism." In *Zondervan Dictionary of Christian Spirituality,* edited by Glen G. Scorgie, Simon Chan, Gordon T. Smith, and James D. Smith III. Grand Rapids: Zondervan, 2011.

World Council of Churches. "Religious Plurality and Christian Self-Understanding." *Current Dialogue* 45 (July 2005). http://www.wcc-coe.org/wcc/what/interreligious/cd45-02.html (3/28/2014).

"The World Methodist Council Statement of Association with the Joint Declaration on the Doctrine of Justification" (2006). http://worldmethodistcouncil.org/wp-content/uploads/2012/02/justificationworld_methodist_council_and_the_jddj.pdf (6/2/2014).

Worthing, Mark William. *God, Creation, and Contemporary Physics.* Theology and the Sciences. Minneapolis: Fortress, 1996.

Worthington, Everett L., Jr. Introduction to *Dimensions of Forgiveness: Psychological Research and Theological Perspectives,* edited by E. L. Worthington Jr., pp. 1-5. Philadelphia and London: Templeton Foundation Press, 1998.

Wright, Christopher J. H. *Salvation Belongs to Our God: Celebrating the Bible's Central Story.* Christian Doctrine in Global Perspective. Downers Grove, Ill.: IVP Academic, 2007.

Wright, Nigel G. "Charismatic Interpretations of the Demonic." In *UW,* pp. 149-63.

Wright, N. T. *The Climax of the Covenant: Christ and the Law in Pauline Theology.* Minneapolis: Fortress, 1993.

———. *Jesus and the Victory of God.* Vol. 2 of *Christian Origins and the Question of God.* Minneapolis: Fortress, 1996.

———. *Justification: God's Plan and Paul's Plan.* Downers Grove, Ill.: IVP Academic, 2009.

———. "New Perspectives on Paul." In *Justification in Perspective: Historical Developments and Contemporary Challenges,* edited by Bruce L. McCormack. Grand Rapids: Baker Academic, 2006.

———. *Paul and the Faithfulness of God.* Minneapolis: Fortress, 2013.

———. *What Saint Paul Really Said: Was Paul of Tarsus the Real Founder of Christianity?* Grand Rapids: Eerdmans, 1997.

Wujastyk, Dominik. *The Roots of Ayurveda.* London: Penguin Books, 2003 (1988).

Wuthnow, Robert. *All in Sync: How Music and Art Are Revitalizing American Religion.* Berkeley: University of California Press, 2003.

Wynne, Jeremy. "The Livingness of God; or, the Place of Substance and Dynamism in a Theology of the Divine Perfections." *International Journal of Systematic Theology* 13, no. 2 (April 2011): 190-203.

Wyschogrod, Edith. "Repentance and Forgiveness: The Undoing of Time." *International Journal for Philosophy of Religion* 60, no. 1 (2006): 157-68.

Wyschogrod, Michael. *The Body of Faith: Judaism as Corporeal Election.* New York: Seabury Press, 1983.

Yannaras, Christ. "Pietism as Ecclesiological Heresy." In *The Freedom of Morality,* pp. 120-22. Crestwood, N.Y.: St. Vladimir's Seminary Press, 1984.

Yerushalmi, Josef Hayim. *Zakhor: Jewish History and Jewish Memory.* Seattle: University of Washington Press, 1982.

Yinger, Kent L. *Paul, Judaism, and Judgment according to Deeds.* New York: Cambridge University Press, 1999.

Yoder, John Howard. *The Politics of Jesus.* Grand Rapids: Eerdmans, 1972.

Yoder, Perry. *Shalom: The Bible's Word for Salvation, Justice, and Peace.* Newton, Kans.: Faith and Life Press, 1987.

Yogananda, Paramahansa. *The Second Coming of Christ: The Resurrection of the Christ within You; A Revelatory Commentary on the Original Teachings of Jesus.* 2 vols. Los Angeles: Self-Realization Fellowship, 2004.

Yong, Amos. *Beyond the Impasse: Towards a Pneumatological Theology of Religions.* Grand Rapids: Baker Academic, 2013.

———. "Christian and Buddhist Perspectives on Neuropsychology and the Human Person: *Pneuma* and *Pratityasamutpada.*" *Zygon* 40 (March 2005): 143-65.

———. *The Cosmic Breath: Spirit and Nature in the Christianity-Buddhism-Science Trialogue.* Leiden and Boston: Brill, 2012.

———. "Disability and the Love of Wisdom: De-forming, Re-forming, and Per-forming Philosophy of Religion." In *Disability in Judaism, Christianity, and Islam: Sacred Texts, Historical Traditions, and Social Analysis,* edited by Darla Schumm and Michael Stoltzfus, chap. 11. New York: Palgrave Macmillan, 2011.

———. *Discerning the Spirit(s): A Pentecostal-Charismatic Contribution to Christian Theology of Religions.* Sheffield: Sheffield Academic Press, 2000.

———. "Discerning the Spirit(s) in the Natural World: Toward a Typology of 'Spirit' in the Theology and Science Conversation." *Theology and Science* 3, no. 3 (2005): 315-29.

———. "Discernment; Discerning the Spirits." In *GDT,* pp. 232-35.

———. *Does the Wind Blow the Middle Way? Pneumatology and the Buddhist-Christian Dialogue.* Unpublished manuscript, 2004.

———. "From Azusa Street to the Bo Tree and Back: Strange Babblings and Interreligious Interpretations in the Pentecostal Encounter with Buddhism." In *The Spirit in the World: Emerging Pentecostal Theologies in Global Contexts,* edited by Veli-Matti Kärkkäinen, pp. 203-26. Grand Rapids: Eerdmans, 2009.

———. "The Holy Spirit and the World Religions: On the Christian Discernment of Spirit(s) 'after' Buddhism." *Buddhist-Christian Studies* 24 (2004): 191-207.

———. *Hospitality and the Other: Pentecost, Christian Practices, and the Neighbor.* Maryknoll, N.Y.: Orbis, 2008.

———. *In the Days of Caesar: Pentecostalism and Political Theology.* Grand Rapids: Eerdmans, 2010.

———. "On Binding, and Loosing, the Spirits: Navigating and Engaging a Spirit-Filled World." In *IRDSW,* pp. 1-12.

———. *Pneumatology and the Christian-Buddhist Dialogue: Does the Spirit Blow through the Middle Way?* Leiden: Brill Academic, 2012.

———. "A Spirit-Filled Creation? Toward a Pneumatological Cosmology." In *The Spirit of Creation: Modern Science and Divine Action in the Pentecostal-Charismatic Imagination,* chap. 6, pp. 173-225. Grand Rapids: Eerdmans, 2011.

———. *The Spirit of Creation: Modern Science and Divine Action in the Pentecostal-Charismatic Imagination.* Grand Rapids: Eerdmans, 2011.

———. *The Spirit Poured Out on All Flesh: Pentecostalism and the Possibility of Global Theology.* Grand Rapids: Baker Academic, 2005.

———. *Theology and Down Syndrome: Reimagining Disability in Late Modernity.* Waco: Baylor University Press, 2007.

———. "A Typology of Prosperity Theology: A Religious Economy of Global Renewal or a Renewal Economics?" In *Pentecostalism and Prosperity: The Socioeconomics of the Global Charismatic Movement,* edited by Katherine Attanasi and Amos Yong, pp. 15-34. New York: Palgrave Macmillan, 2012.

Yun, Koo Dong. *Baptism in the Holy Spirit.* Lanham, Md.: University Press of America, 2003.

———. *The Holy Spirit and Ch'i (Qi): A Chiological Approach to Pneumatology.* Princeton Theological Monograph Series. Eugene, Ore.: Pickwick, 2011.

Zahl, Simeon. "Rethinking 'Enthusiasm': Christoph Blumhardt on the Discernment of the Spirits." *International Journal of Systematic Theology* 12, no. 3 (2010): 341-63.

Zebiri, Kare. *Muslims and Christians Face to Face.* Oxford: Oneworld, 1997.

Zhixu, Ouyi. [No title provided.] In *JBC,* pp. 229-30.

Zimmermann, Jens. *Incarnational Humanism: A Philosophy of Culture for the Church in the World.* Downers Grove, Ill.: InterVarsity, 2012.

Zizioulas, John D. *Being as Communion: Studies in Personhood and the Church.* Crestwood, N.Y.: St. Vladimir's Seminary Press, 1985.

———. "Human Capacity and Human Incapacity: A Theological Exploration of Personhood." *Scottish Journal of Theology* 28, no. 5 (1975): 401-47.

———. "The Teaching of the 2nd Ecumenical Council on the Holy Spirit in Historical and Ecumenical Perspective." In *Credo in Spiritum Sanctum: Atti del congresso teologico internazionale di pneumatologia.* Vatican City: Liberia Editrice Vaticana, 1983.

Index of Authors

Index of Subjects

Abortion, 117
Adoption, 318, 347-48
African American Christianity, 365
African folk religions, 12, 274
Afterlife, 214, 390
Allah, 216, 255, 301; names of, 137; as spirit, 133-34, 137
Anabaptist tradition, 202, 323, 354, 356, 363, 407
Ananda, 143. *See also* Soteriology in Asiatic religions: in Hinduism
Anattā, 160. *See also* Buddhism
Angelology, 22, 88; in ancient Near Eastern religions, 77, 84; in biblical canon, 76, 83, 89; in Christian creedal tradition, 76, 77; in classical liberalism, 78; in Islam, 85; in Jewish apocalyptic, 91; in Jewish Kabbalah, 84; in medieval Christian theology, 77; in modern philosophy, 77, 79; in patristic theology, 85; in postmodern philosophy, 79; in Protestant missions, 78
Angels, 80-83, 93-94, 102, 107-8; in Asiatic religions, 85, 86; fallen nature of, 90; hierarchy of, 86; in Old Testament, 84; ontology of, 80, 88; origin of, 91; personal nature of, 92; in Qur'an, 85; among secular Jews, 84

Anglican tradition, 232-33, 315, 337, 355, 370
Anthropology, 387; Christian theological, 11, 26, 62, 100-101, 324, 361; in Judaism, 251; of religion, 105, 273
Antinomianism, 326, 334. *See also* Law: and gospel
Apocalypticism: Christian, 12, 77; Jewish, 111
Arahant, 163. *See also* Buddhism
Arianism, 29-30, 40
Aristotelianism, Christian, 67
Arminian tradition, 202, 245
Asian American Christianity, 365
Atheism, 159, 276, 299; new, 271
Atman, 121, 141-43, 145, 148, 151, 160-61. *See also* Spirit(s): in Hinduism
Atonement, 280-81, 292, 378; in Christianity, 406; *Christus Victor* theory of, 110, 115, 316; and healing, 378-80; in Hinduism, 307; in Islam, 215-16, 303; satisfaction theory of, 115, 283, 316; vicarious, 214
Attributes of God: omnipotence, 58, 70; omnipresence, 56, 58, 67, 70; omniscience, 58. *See also* Infinity, divine
Augsburg Confession, 410
Ayurveda, 391-92